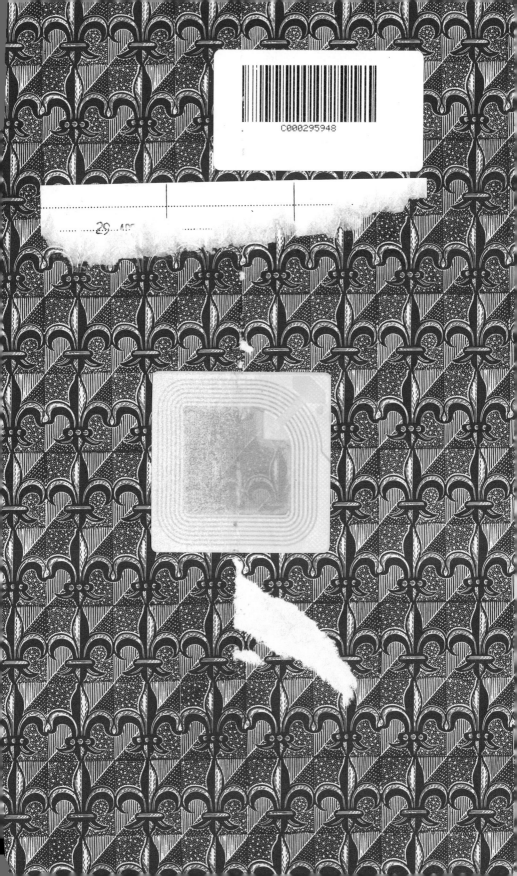

ARTS AND CULTURES

Also by Andrew Sinclair

FICTION
The Breaking of Bumbo
My Friend Judas
The Project
The Hallelujah Bum
The Raker
A Patriot for Hire
The Facts in the Case of E. A. Poe
Beau Bumbo
Gog
Magog
King Ludd

NON-FICTION
Prohibition: the Era of Excess
The Better Half: the Emancipation of the American Woman
The Available Man: Warren Gamaliel Harding
The Concise History of the United States
Che Guevara
The Last of the Best
The Naked Savage
Dylan: Poet of His People
Jack London
John Ford
Corsair: the Life of J. P. Morgan
The Other Victoria
Sir Walter Raleigh and the Age of Discovery
The Red and the Blue
Spiegel: the Man Behind the Pictures
War like a Wasp: the Lost Decade and the Forties
The Need to Give: the Patron and the Arts
The Sword and the Grail
In Love and Anger: A View of the 'Sixties
Francis Bacon: His Life and Violent Times

DRAMA
Adventures in the Skin Trade (play)
Under Milk Wood (screenplay)

TRANSLATION
The Greek Anthology

Andrew Sinclair

ARTS AND CULTURES

The History
of the 50 Years of the
Arts Council of Great Britain

SINCLAIR-STEVENSON

TO SONIA

without whose love and knowledge of the
ways we work, this book could never have
been written

First published in Great Britain in 1995
by Sinclair-Stevenson
an imprint of Reed Consumer Books Limited
Michelin House, 81 Fulham Road, London SW3 6RB
and Auckland, Melbourne, Singapore and Toronto

A CIP catalogue record for this book
is available at the British Library
ISBN 1 85619 342 X

Typeset by Deltatype Ltd, Ellesmere Port, Wirral
Printed and bound in Great Britain
by Mackays of Chatham PLC

CONTENTS

List of Illustrations   vii

Acknowledgements   viii

Foreword by Lord Gowrie   ix

Prologue   1

  1   The Arts and The War   25

  2   The Best and The Most   50

  3   Few, but Roses   77

  4   The Struggle for Survival   103

  5   More Money, More Opportunities   128

  6   The Furnishings of a Capital City   148

  7   Ye Best Things in Ye Worst Times   177

  8   Devolution and Defence   204

  9   Arts Abroad   231

10   Cuts and the Changing of The Guard   247

11   Culture, Cost and City Need   278

12   Holding On   311

13   Foreign Examples   334

14   Art Is Political   351

15   Historically Correct   372

Envoi: Arts and Cultures   395

Appendices   401

Notes   467

Index   487

LIST OF ILLUSTRATIONS

Except where otherwise acknowledged, the photographs listed below are reproduced courtesy of the Arts Council.

John Maynard Keynes (*Ramsay and Muspralt*)
Queen Elizabeth, Queen Mary, the Queen Mother and Princess Elizabeth (*Lynn News and Advertiser*)
Sadler's Wells Ballet at Covent Garden: *Job*
Sadler's Wells Ballet at Covent Garden: *The Sleeping Beauty*
Dr Vaughan Williams, OM: sculpture by Jacob Epstein
Sir William Emrys Williams
Arts Council poster
Lord Goodman: drawing by Nicholas Bentley
Arts Council triennial poetry awards, 1959–62
Arts Council meeting, 1967
Headquarters of the Arts Council, 105 Piccadilly: photograph by A.C. Cooper
Corporate Seal of the Arts Council
Brian Rix and Kenneth Robinson (*AM/Keystone Press Agency Ltd*)
Lord Gowrie and Lord Rees-Mogg (*Images Photography*)
Sir Roy Shaw: photograph by Sophie Baker
Anthony Field (*Keystone Press Agency Ltd*)
James Callaghan and Henry Moore
Luke Rittner and Lord Palumbo: photograph by Chris Taylor (*Chris Taylor*)
Anthony Everitt: photograph by Justin Pumfrey
Margaret Thatcher and Lord Palumbo

ACKNOWLEDGEMENTS

The author and publishers would like to thank all the writers, photographers, publishers, literary representatives and picture libraries, who have given permission for reprinting quoted and illustrative material. In some instances it has been difficult to track down copyright holders and the publishers will be glad to make good any omissions in future editions. Writers whose work has been quoted are listed in order of first appearance below.

T. S. Eliot: extracts from *Notes Towards the Definition of Culture*, Faber and Faber Ltd. Mary Glasgow: extracts from *The Nineteen Hundreds: A Diary in Retrospect*, Oxford University Press. Roy Harrod: Extract from *The Life of John Maynard Keynes*, Macmillan. Charles Landstone: extract from *I Gate-Crashed*, Stainer & Bell. Kenneth Clark: extracts from *The Other Half: A Self Portrait*, John Murray (Publisher) Ltd. V. S. Pritchett: extract from *Midnight Oil*, Chatto & Windus. Eric W. White: extracts from *The Arts Council of Great Britain*, Davis-Poynter. Evelyn Waugh: extract from *Unconditional Surrender*, Chapman & Hall, by permission of Peters, Fraser & Dunlop. Christopher Fry: extract from *A Sleep of Prisoners*, Oxford University Press. Arnold Goodman: extracts from *Tell Them I'm On My Way*, Chapmans. Hugh Jenkins: extracts from *The Culture Gap*, Marion Boyars Publishers Ltd. Roy Shaw: extracts from *The Arts and the People*, Jonathan Cape. John Allen: extract from 'The European Perspective' in *The State and the Arts*, ed. John Pick, John Offord Publications. Norman St John-Stevas: extract from *The Two Cities*, Faber and Faber Ltd. William Rees-Mogg: extract from *An Humbler Heaven*, Hamish Hamilton, by permission of Peters, Fraser & Dunlop. Philip Larkin: extract from *Selected Letters of Philip Larkin: 1940–1985*, ed. Anthony Thwaite, Faber and Faber Ltd. John Pick: extract from *The Art of the State*, Adam Smith Institute. John Pick: extract from *The Arts in a State*, Bristol Classical Press. Raymond Williams: extract from *What I Came To Say*, Hutchinson. Geoff Mulgan and Ken Worpole: extract from *Saturday Night or Sunday Morning?: From Arts to Industry: New Forms of Cultural Policy*, Comedia.

I am deeply indebted to the Chairmen and Officers of the Arts Council of Great Britain for permission to quote from their papers and reports, 1946–1994, and reproduce illustrative material from their archives.

FOREWORD

The publication of a history of public arts funding in Great Britain is
well timed. Andrew Sinclair's survey comes out as the state's role in
support of the arts is changing – the most fundamental change since the
days of William Emrys Williams and John Maynard Keynes more than
fifty years ago. I am writing this, too, shortly before the memorial
service to Arnold Goodman, who with his minister, the late Jennie Lee,
launched the period now coming to an end.

For we now have a new and much bigger sponsoring ministry, the
Department of National Heritage and its Secretary of State, as distinct
from a minister in charge of the old Office of Arts and Libraries. The
Arts Council of Great Britain, the subject of this book, has been
devolved into separate Councils for England, Scotland and Wales.
There has been further devolution of influence and responsibility into
the hands of Regional Arts Boards. While the Arts Council remains at
the accountable centre of their funding and strategy, the recognition
that artistic activity has a strong local and regional character is right
and overdue. It is also an acknowledgement of the significant funding
role of local government. In England alone, towns and cities and
counties distribute the same amount of money annually as the Council
itself. That they do so is a measure of the value and achievement of the
Regional Arts Boards, five of whose ten chairmen sit on the Council by
invitation of the Secretary of State. Devolution does not mean distance.
The chairman of the Arts Councils of Wales, Scotland and Northern
Ireland meet regularly and the new Arts Council of England holds
meetings accompanied by an open forum, outside London.

By far the most significant change has been the arrival of the

National Lottery, instituted by John Major's administration with all-party support. It is little less than a revolution and is in the process of transforming the cultural landscape of the kingdom.

Continual squeezing of subsidy has caused a crisis of investment in the arts as organisations struggle to keep the show on the road today even if the roof is likely to fall upon their heads tomorrow. Current funding remains needlessly tight. From a macro-economic point of view this is unnecessary, as the percentage of public spending is so tiny: you would need hundreds of our mickles to make any kind of a muckle. Nevertheless, the Lottery funds are starting to make a huge dent on investment in projects large and small over the island. In an age of increasingly sophisticated, electronically packaged home entertainment, the living arts need attractive and affordable venues, with good facilities for all, if attendances and revenues and ancillary spending are to make their contribution to current costs. The Government has shown some flexibility in the capital versus current funding debate. We may well press for more. But we must remember that the distinction was asked for by arts organisations as it is an article of faith that lottery money can only supplement, not replace, our core subsidy.

Perhaps the best news of all is that the arts in Britain, threadbare in terms of public support by comparison with our continental neighbours, are in rude and inspiring health. This country is, to borrow an old foreign office phrase, boxing beyond its weight in music, dance, film and the visual arts. Literature and drama are as strong as ever. Those who govern us must recognise that far from being another well-orchestrated lobby pleading and bullying for increased public spending, the arts are among the top five of revenue earners for the exchequer. They need seedcorn investment and the wherewithal to spread pleasure and enlightenment about the land. They are peopled by dedicated and self-reliant individuals who follow the most competitive calling of all.

I welcome Andrew Sinclair's study of the last fifty years. I suspect that the next dozen or so may well be even more fascinating.

Lord Gowrie
Chairman, The Arts Council of England
May 1995

PROLOGUE

Culture is one thing that we cannot deliberately aim at. It
is the product of a variety of more or less harmonious
activities, each pursued for its own sake: the artist must
concentrate upon his canvas, the poet upon his type-
writer, the civil servant upon the just settlement of
particular problems as they present themselves upon his
desk ...

T. S. Eliot in *Notes towards the
Definition of Culture*, 1948

The arts are what we say they are, and play and patronize. So it was
at the beginning of human history, the cave paintings on the rock
walls of gods and animals, the ritual dancing and the body painting,
the construction of observatories and of tombs in stone circles and
pyramids and barrows, and the ceremonies of shamans and kings.
Society began in the service of the divine and the leaders. The tribe
and the barbaric state commanded craftsmen to honour the gods
through the priests and the warlords. By their patronage, sacred
warrior rulers commissioned the pictures and carvings and metal-
work that we now call primitive art, which celebrated the cosmos
and the state as understood in those far times. Enslaved to the
overlord, a theocratic and embryo Arts Council advised Gilgamesh
how to build the Sumerian city of Uruk, also Nebuchadnezzar how
to set up the first art museum in the open courts of his palace beside
the Hanging Gardens of Babylon. Without such royal giving, there
would be hardly any record of bygone ages.

Art in the service of the city state was the beginning of modern
civilization. It was centralized and anonymous. In ancient Egypt,

however, dozens of artists signed their works in the service of the divine Pharaoh and his ministers. Some artists became officials and patrons themselves: one was even raised to heaven. Imhotep, the architect and designer of the pyramid complex at Saqqara, put his name on a statue at his place of creation; he then reached the rank of chief minister of the arts and was later deified. Senenmut, the builder of the tomb and temple of Queen Hatshepsut, was also promoted to act as chief minister in a society that valued architects more than those modern democracies which prefer economists in high office (although they appear to know only how to spend rather than to build). In the third of the great ancient civilizations, Shang and Chou bronzes and tripods and jade carvings proved the aesthetic power of the Chinese state. What the central court gave, the arts took and created.

In western societies, as the Victorian critic John Ruskin has stated, war was the foundation of the arts. Minoan and Mycenean work in pictures and sculptures and pottery and precious metals was contained within the mammoth stone blocks of fortresses: victories and conquests were celebrated, as Homer did in the *Iliad*. A heavenly pantheon above directed the battles of mythical founder heroes below on earth. The creativity of a citadel society became the encouragement of the literature of conflict and discovery. *Mythos* in Greek meant only speech or narrative, whether about the gods or mankind – both shared so many of the same characteristics. The origins and legitimacy of Greek dynasties and aristocracies, citizens and peoples were sought in Homeric epic and there confirmed, as they were in the dramas of Aeschylus and Sophocles and Euripedes. Greek society looked back to the statue and the spoken and written word in order to justify its antecedents and to understand the nature of the divine and its commandments. The wisest Athenian of them all, Socrates, was condemned to death for questioning those verities.

The Greek city state developed the appreciation of the artist and the arts. There was a belief that the rich and powerful citizen should embellish the city which sheltered him and allowed him wealth. Pericles used the war funds of allies and subjects to beautify Athens and erect the Parthenon and the Propylaea and the Odeon for musical contests in the annual festivals. When his city accepted war against Sparta, he declared that patronage of the arts was the duty of the powerful. It contributed to the greatness of the city. 'Our love of what is beautiful does not lead to extravagance; our love of things of the mind does not weaken us. We regard wealth as something to be properly used rather than something to boast about.' All citizens should give to the glory of Athens and fight for the city in its time of need. Their survival depended on it. The rich might pay for a trireme and must stand as hoplites in the battle by the side of poor citizens; even Socrates fought by the privileged Alcibiades. If the temple treasures had to be melted down to replace a lost fleet, later free Athenians would commission goldsmiths to make vessels in celebration of the gods who had saved the city. Not only to commemorate themselves but to be thought worthy of being Athenians – these were the reasons that those who benefited from living in their city endowed it for future generations.

The Greeks invented politics. The Greek word *politikos* means how to live in a city. Aristotle in his *Politics* stated that a man could not live without his city unless he were a beast or a god. While every human being should move towards what is desired, the development of the city state led to the greatest good. The wish and duty of a person should be to contribute to the city, not to the family or oneself, already the beneficiaries of the city. The first exemplar of modern history, Thucydides, believed that Athens made Athenians, although it took them from nature and used them. And when Pericles was in power, he made Athens peerless in its time and its artists renowned forever, particularly Praxitiles the sculptor and Phidias, who was the surveyor-general of all the works of art. They were recognized as individual masters, although their statues served religion. The state Greek temples, which displayed the works of art donated by patrons as gifts to the gods, were the first exhibitions open to the public: their sacred enclosures were gardens for the display of sculpture. The Hellenic world also founded the first museum; the term was derived from a Greek word meaning the sanctuary of all the Muses. A Ptolemy founded a museum and university in Alexandria in Egypt in 280 BC with a modern library, a botanical garden, a zoo and research institutes for many studies including anatomy and astronomy. There, Euclid was to work on theoretical geometry, Eratosthenes of Cyrene to create scientific geography, and Aristarchus of Samos to use trigonometry to speculate that the earth passed round the sun.

3

In the same century in Athens, the Pinakotheke was founded, a building that housed paintings such as those of Alexander's court painter Apelles who painted his master with a thunderbolt in his hand; the gallery in present Munich still bears that name. And the contemporary King Attalus the First of Pergamon in Anatolia collected fine arts more assiduously than Nebuchadnezzar had. He endowed libraries and employed architects and sculptors, who made the *Dying Gaul* for his victory monument. His heirs continued his policy and liberality until they lost their works of art to the conquering Romans, who removed most of them back home. King Attalus had himself looted statues and bronzes from the Greek islands: his plunder served to enrich and embellish Italy.

'When in Rome, do as the Greeks do.' And so the Romans did. Masterpieces and slave artists were brought back by the legions from their campaigns. Emperors and senators, patricians and plutocrats filled their palaces and the galleries in their villas with Greek artefacts and brought Greek craftsmen to embellish their houses. By plunder and patronage, the Romans adorned their city and made it worthy of being the imperial capital of the Mediterranean world. When Marcellus took Syracuse and Mummius sacked Corinth, they dedicated most of their looted treasures to the temples of Rome. All the pictures from the art gallery of Sicyon were sold and carried to Rome to pay off a public debt. An early Lord Duveen called Damasippus hawked Greek masterpieces to the wealthy in Italy and even appeared in a satire by Horace. Art collecting became a Roman activity, although great hoards such as those of Gaius Verres were made by extortion and misgovernment. Yet his greed for fine art proved the death warrant of Verres, who refused to surrender his Corinthian bronzes to Mark Anthony and was struck down for his obsession over his possessions. Agrippa, the chief minister of the Emperor Augustus, declared that classic pictures and statues should become public property and not be sold to the rich for their private viewing in their villas. He built huge baths for the use of the people and adorned them with statues by Lysippus and others; when the Emperor Tiberius later removed Lysippus's statue of a beautiful youth into his bedroom, popular clamour made him restore it to the baths. Yet such concepts that art treasures should be available to all did not deter the Roman collector. Cicero, the arbiter of the Latin language, was always pestering Atticus in Athens to send him statues and reliefs for his town and country places. 'The more the merrier and as soon as possible,' he begged. 'For I am so carried away by my enthusiasm in this that I almost expose myself to ridicule.'

The public and private commissioners and collectors of the arts needed their advisers, who were often their Greek slaves bought in a market. These were the minor arts councils of the day, wholly dependent on the purchasing power and whim of the patron or *patronus*, derived from *pater* or father. The Roman emperor was naturally the primary patron and the imperial cult extinguished the Greek fashion of the individual artist. As in Mesopotamia and usually in Egypt, Roman artists rarely signed their names on the monuments which they built. The Parthenon was known as the work of Phidias and Callicrates as well as of Pericles; but the imperial constructions were anonymous and called the Altar of Augustan Peace, the Baths of Caracalla, the Column of Trajan with its curling curved band of his Dacian campaigns, the Wall and Pantheon of Hadrian, and the Arches of Titus and Constantine. The enduring legacy of the Roman state was the unsigned monument, often a piece of military engineering as well as of imperial glorification – the viaduct and the tower and the gate and the chessboard town-plan invented by Hippodamus at Miletus and used to build the port of Ostia at the mouth of the Tiber.

Above all, architecture was made secular. The Roman circus may have been based on the Greek theatre and stadium, but it ended by presenting gladiatorial shows rather than religious dramas. A similar degeneration took place at Olympia, where the games had been divine festivals and now served to celebrate sportsmen and fawn on the emperor. The arts and sports council of judges at Olympia, drawn from the old Hellenic city states, became imperial tools. There was no arm's length principle, merely a lickspittle practice. The Emperor Nero fell out of his chariot in a race at the Olympics, yet was awarded the first place although he had not completed the course. As an athlete, actor, singer and lyre player, he won more than eighteen hundred prizes at festivals and competitions in Greece, where he was compared to Phoebus Apollo. He believed that this was the praise and reward due to his genius, not to his position. Shortly before his fall, he was distressed by a note in

Greek tied on one of the statues of him in Rome. It read: 'This is a real contest for once, and you are going to lose.' Eventually condemned by the Senate to be flogged to death by rods, his last words before committing suicide were 'What a loss I am to the arts.'

The Augustan age produced the model of the private patron. Maecenas was a wealthy Etruscan noble and ran a literary forum which included Horace and Virgil. He even influenced the writing of the imperial epic poem, the *Aeneid*. Since the days of Plautus, when writers were mainly foreign slaves or clients, authors had depended on patrons whose taste often dictated the way the lines went. In his bucolic *Georgics*, Virgil confessed that he was writing the words demanded by Maecenas: the poems were written in a library at Naples, not on a farm. As Homer had lauded his royal patrons in the lists in the *Iliad*, so Virgil honoured the ancestors of Augustus in the *Aeneid*, making the founder of Rome a Trojan prince rather than the wolf-suckled Romulus. From Hades, among the antique Greek and Roman heroes, Virgil told his countrymen that their arts were conquest and ruling. His art of hexameters was the apogee of Latin poetry, directed by Maecenas towards the glory of the new Caesar, although at his death Virgil asked for his epic poem on the Roman state to be destroyed.

The distinguished council of advisers of Maecenas found an expanding role in Roman society, for the increasing wealth of the empire broadened the scope of patronage. Quantities of portraits and busts were commissioned by tradesmen and merchants, until an army of competent craftsmen depended on them. Thousands of copies of original Greek masterpieces ornamented colonnades and niches in walks and gardens, while paintings and mosaics shone in innumerable villas. One such was the battle scene featuring Alexander and King Darius at the Issus, which covered a wall of the House of the Faun at Pompeii. The popular architect Vitruvius even recommended that art galleries should face north because of the constancy of the light, while libraries should face east because of the brightness of morning. A secular Graeco-Roman art was created with an emphasis on realism and landscape. If wealth, like muck, should be well spread, the spreading of wealth in the later Roman empire led to the diffusion of the patronage of the arts and the creation of a domestic style in decoration and pottery, arts for the people and the home, not for the gods and the country that was the protector of the people.

The rise of Christianity with its figure of the Creator, God the Father, led to a final flowering of art in the late Roman empire. Constantine the Great commissioned churches and paintings to celebrate the new imperial faith. Yet he also removed the surviving treasures of Greece to stand in his new capital at Constantinople – the bronze serpent tripod commemorating the Persian defeat at Plataea and the Athena of Phidias with her gleaming spear point that had signalled ships into the Piraeus for eight hundred years. Even with fresh religious art, Greek masterpieces still set the seal on the greatness of cities. As the Roman empire crumbled before the barbarians of the West, Christian art beautified Constantinople under the first Justinian, whose architects built the basilica and cathedral Sancta Sophia with a dome greater than the Pantheon. The ornamentation was within the house of God, and mosaics showed the Almighty ruling the heavens and the earth that He had created.

All important art was now state art. But if there is a prototype for an arts council in Europe, it must lie in the religious advisers of the Emperor Charlemagne, many of them from Britain. The Carolingian renaissance which ended the Dark Ages in Europe was a derivative of the reform of the church. The clerics employed by the Frankish emperor were his civil servants, intellectuals and instructors. The chief of them, Alcuin, came from the cathedral school of York, which he used as a model for Charlemagne's palace school: he ended as the abbot of St Martin of Tours. He hoped to make Charlemagne's court into a new Athens, where the seven liberal arts would now be blessed with the seven gifts of the Holy Ghost. He oversaw the handiwork on the series of vast and splendid manuscripts of the School of Charlemagne and relied on late Roman paintings as models. Collections of books and documents provided the basis of a royal library, which preserved the texts of the major Latin authors. And church singing was developed from the Gregorian chant into the medieval liturgies that are still sung. The Byzantine simplification of the fifteen classical modes into eight modes and a system of minimal notation became the basis of

7

plainsong and melody. The sung word was the great gift of Charlemagne's arts council.

Notably, the nine Muses of the Greek arts and sciences were feminine, while the seven liberal arts of Rome were masculine. For the Greeks, the liberal arts were music and poetry, where Sappho excelled, and dance and tragedy. To this quartet, the Romans and the medievalists added painting and sculpture and architecture, to make up the 'fine arts', whatever that term was held to mean. This classification was endorsed by the Church of Rome, which joined the new kings of the European nations as the arbiter of the arts. There was not so much a conclave of cardinals about the state of human creation, but a mutual understanding of how Christian art should serve the glory of God and religion. This consensus produced Gothic and perpendicular architecture in the cathedrals of the major European nations. In particular, the Bishop's Chapel at Hereford, modelled on Charlemagne's chapel at Aachen, can be attributed to Bishop Robert of Lorraine, a rare cosmopolitan and savant of the eleventh century, who was a travelling master 'most skilled in all the liberal arts', in the words of William of Malmesbury, 'researching principally into the abacus, into lunar computation and into the course of the heavenly constellations'. In the next century, Abbot Suger of Saint-Denis was the great patron of Gothic architecture and set the style of European church construction for centuries to come. At the time, ecclesiastical patronage of the arts was more important than royal flamboyance, for the kings depended on the clerics to be literate and numerate, their holy civil servants in the name of God.

In the Middle Ages, court patronage could debase and fritter away talent as well as inspire it. Artists were required to work on pageants and objects of conspicuous waste. The court *fêtes* of Burgundy were unbridled in their luxury – twenty-eight-piece orchestras contained in pies, ornamental mock whales and gilded giants. The artists were overemployed on exaggerated display. When Froissart described a decorated fleet, he said that the painters were in such short supply that they received whatever they wanted. The masts of the ships were covered with gold leaf, the sails studded with artificial daisies. The rich costumes of princes and knights exceeded magnificence and beggared utility – the points on the men's shoes were too long to allow walking, their hoods became

8

vast cockscombs, while thousands of gems glittered on trailing and laced court dresses. As Huizinga pointed out in *The Waning of the Middle Ages*, the measure and harmony of pure art were lost in splendour and adornment.

So was the position of the artist. At the Burgundian court, the great painter Jan van Eyck and the supreme sculptor Claus Sluter were known as *valets de chambre*, grooms of the chamber, whose jobs were to repair and restore games and furniture as much as to create masterpieces. In Venice, painters belonged to the guild of harness-makers, case-makers and gilders. Only music was considered one of the seven liberal arts of the *trivium* and the *quadrivium*: painting and sculpture and architecture were held to be mechanical arts on a level with manual labour, although other *artes* included the art of love and the art of war. Leonardo da Vinci, along with Ghiberti and Alberti, protested against such a definition. As he complained, 'Since you have put music among the Liberal Arts, you must either put painting there as well, or else withdraw music.' Painting and sculpture were held to be manual activities, but so was literature. And, if painting was mechanical because it was done for a price, so was writing. Yet, despite his affirmations, Leonardo was used by the Sforza court at Milan to make stage machinery for festivals, inventing mountains that moved, heavens that spun, gods and signs of the zodiac in orbit, stage machinery for festivals, and even statuettes in marzipan which were eaten. This was, indeed, conspicuous consumption and waste of the artist's time and genius. The princely patron could represent Mammon as well as divine majesty.

The elevation of the artist during the Renaissance, however, because of ecclesiastical and princely giving, changed the role of the patron and his advisers. The courts of Italy and France competed for the services of the leading artists. The supreme donor to Florence was a banker, Cosimo de' Medici. Through international finance, he endowed and influenced the arts on a scale that surpassed even Maecenas. He was the first magnate in business to sponsor the arts and, although his collections were mainly of classical antiques, he commissioned works from the leading artists of his time. After the death of his friend Niccolò Niccoli, he acquired the best private library in Florence, also a major collection of Roman and Greek sculpture and jewellery. He bought paintings by Masaccio, Fra Angelico, Uccello, Donatello and Giotto. He gave generously to the family church of the Medici, Brunelleschi's San Lorenzo. He supported libraries and monasteries and convents and foundling hospitals. In acquiring power in his native city from the *Signoria*, he always showed a modesty and a respect for art. He rode a mule in an effort to hide his wealth. Only his successors such as Lorenzo the Magnificent displayed the luxury and conspicuous waste of the medieval courts.

The enduring vision of Medici generosity is of a golden age in which duke and scholar and creator met together for the embellishment of learning and the city state. The Renaissance saw itself as a revolution of the arts, rejecting the relationships of the Dark and Middle Ages and returning to classical values. The medieval patron had directed the work to be made; within a prescribed Annunciation or Crucifixion or royal spectacle, the painter had to impress his individual stamp. The Renaissance patron, however, only guided him in a mutual pursuit of beauty. Vasari in his *Lives* of the Renaissance artists praised Lorenzo de' Medici (the Magnificent) for discovering the genius of Michelangelo as a youth, for recommending him to other wealthy patrons, and for supporting him and his family for life. He also persuaded the Medici to found in 1563 the first Academy of Arts. This freed artists from being thought to be mechanical craftsmen. Michelangelo was its director; thirty-six painters and sculptors were its members, now escaped from the control of the city guilds. They taught pupils, who no longer had to serve from seven to fourteen years as apprentices, worked directly for the Medici court and acquired security and prestige. In a sense, they formed the first arts college and council.

With the increase of international finance and the rise of a merchant class, private patronage became more widespread, particularly in northern Europe. The early Flemish artists were commissioned to paint the likenesses of bankers and guilds and fraternities and university scholars. Domestic and rural subjects became more in demand from lay patrons. The arrival of printing and the availability of cheaper books, however, diffused the appreciation of the works of the leading northern artists across Europe. France still relied on court and aristocratic endowment, particularly when King

Louis the Fourteenth followed the example of the Medici and set up a Royal Academy of Painting and Sculpture to be the arbiter of national taste. In England, too, King Charles the First, perhaps the most discerning art collector ever to grace the throne, surrounded himself with the great and the good of the time, the 'Whitehall group' of noble connoisseurs of art, particularly the Earls of Arundel and Pembroke and Somerset. Yet a civil war destroyed this nucleus of state patronage, and the King lost his head and his treasures.

It was no coincidence that the industrial revolution, which made Britain into a great power in the eighteenth century, linked commerce with the arts. Sir John Soane, the architect and collector, noted the connection between artists and factory-owners. The simple and elegant taste of Robert and James Adam in furniture and fittings lent itself to mechanical reproduction. 'Manufacturers of every kind felt, as it were,' Soane wrote, 'the electric power of this Revolution in Art.' When the Royal Society of Arts (RSA) was founded in 1754, its full title was The Royal Society for the Encouragement of Arts, Manufactures and Commerce, and it gave prizes for new machines. Matthew Boulton of the Soho Mint replaced craftsmen with working men. He may have used Robert Adam and John Flaxman the painter as his designers, but his medallions were struck off by machines operated by semi-skilled labour. As he told King George the Third, 'I sell, Sire, what all the world desires – power'. At his ceramic works at Etruria, Stafford-shire, Josiah Wedgwood sold what all the world desired – quantities of pottery in the Greek classical style. Because of this, he commissioned good artists such as George Stubbs and Joseph Wright of Derby to create models and designs for his wares and particularly to work on statuettes and busts and cameos for his portrait gallery of Worthies, the ancient and modern heroes of Reason and Enlightenment. If his mass-produced ceramics again replaced personal choice with public consumption, he did spread his ideas of classical taste across the civilized world and also set up the first museum attached to an industrial plant. As the Victorian John Pye noted in his *Patronage of British Art*, Wedgwood 'adapted ancient forms of celebrated elegance and beauty ... and thus created from our own earth articles of vast traffic'.

Wedgwood and his group of friends thought that industry and

science and art and liberalism went hand in hand. Although he had reduced potters to factory workers and changed their craft to an industrial process, he saw no contradiction in supporting the abolition of the slave trade and issuing a yellow and black cameo representing an African in chains with the inscription 'Am I not a man and a brother?' He himself performed more than five thousand experiments to produce the jasper body that was the basis of his famous unglazed blue and white pottery ware. He belonged to the Lunar Society of Birmingham with other manufacturers and scientists and artists. Among their members were Erasmus Darwin and James Priestley as well as Matthew Boulton and James Watt of the steam engine. Another member was Joseph Wright of Derby, from whom Wedgwood and his circle commissioned the first pictures that celebrated the industrial revolution. Wright had studied in Italy and was attracted to romantic literature and allegorical subjects; but his pictures of *A Philosopher giving a Lecture on the Orrery* and *An Experiment on a Bird in the Air Pump* along with *An Iron Forge* and *Arkwright's Mill* bred a genre in keeping with changing methods of production and scientific research. His was the antithesis of the romantic revolutionary imagination of William Blake, whose reaction on being shown the first number of *Mechanics' Magazine* was 'Ah, sir, these things we artists HATE!' Yet Blake himself had to work on the Wedgwood catalogue to make ends meet.

The eighteenth century was split in its commissions and its patronage between the old order and the new. The traditional autocratic rulers could command original capitals such as St Petersburg or refurbish previous ones. Major architecture was usually dependent on royal or aristocratic wishes, and music wholly so. The careers of Beethoven and Mozart were dependent upon court patronage. Handel was paid lavishly by King George the First; only at the end of his career did his novelty, the English oratorio, give him a middle-class public, which took to an operatic style with biblical subjects, a happy combination of pleasure with worship. The accession of the young King George the Third promised another renaissance of the arts in England. Initially this was true. Within a decade of his accession, he had founded the Royal Academy as an independent body of leading artists, uniquely free of royal control.

He also bought the works of the chief painters of his country, including Ramsay and Reynolds, Gainsborough and Zoffany, Hoppner and Lawrence, as well as appointing Benjamin West as Court Painter. Only increasing insanity impaired his early zest.

Reynolds became the first president of the Royal Academy and delivered discourses at its prize-givings. He advised the study of the great masters and classical sculptors: 'it is by being conversant with the invention of others that we learn to invent.' Other institutions in England were eclectic in their growth. The first museum, the Ashmolean at Oxford, derived from a natural history collection, while the second, the British Museum, was based on the catholic taste of Sir Hans Sloane, whose interests were scientific rather than artistic, inclining more to fossils than to paintings. Sloane's bequest to the nation stated that his collection tended 'to the manifestation of the glory of God, the confutation of atheism and its consequences, the use and improvement of physic, and other arts and sciences, and the benefit of mankind'. The objects were meant to be a reflection of the whole of divine creation and, when the library of King George the Second was added to what Sloane had amassed, a minor Library of Alexandria was established in Montague House in Bloomsbury, where natural sciences could be pursued as well as pictures be appreciated. The temper of the times did not distinguish between the various disciplines and branches of knowledge in the quest for wisdom.

Although the British Museum was a product of the enlightenment and the urge towards universal knowledge – as were the contemporary encyclopedias – access was restricted to the few, preferably to artists and men of letters. Seeing the diverse treasures was a privilege and a difficulty. One visitor in 1784 found himself rushed round the whole collection with a group of ten strangers by a rude young man, who refused to explain what they were seeing. 'I considered myself in the midst of a rich entertainment, consisting of ten thousand rarities,' the visitor lamented, 'but, like Tantalus, I could not taste one.' He was only allowed thirty minutes to see everything and he could have taken thirty days. Instead, he was 'hackneyed through the rooms with violence ... and came away completely disappointed'.

Access to education was still severely limited, as was appreciation of the arts. The gathering pace of the scientific and industrial revolution would eventually spread knowledge and wealth, but it would take decades to create an educated middle class. It would also alter the relationship of the patron to the artist, as would the material philosophy of 'Economic Man'. Equally, the reaction from a mechanical society and materialism was to change the relationship of the artist to the patron. The swamping of the handmade article by the machine product led to the protests of the craftsmen, who even smashed the machines and were called Luddites. The philosophy of utility and gain provoked a retreat into the romantic imagination. And the spreading might of the bourgeois patron and the industrialist employer and the imperial merchant inspired a change in taste and a fierce counter-attack from those who felt most threatened by alien values and goods.

The link in the Victorian imagination between industry and invention and the arts was to transform the metropolis of London from one of wood and brick and stone into one of metal and glass and smoke. The iron bridges, the huge conservatory of the Crystal Palace, the soaring halls of the railway termini in London were monuments to the age of metal and steam as well as the finer architectural expressions of their time. There were throwbacks in taste: the follies commissioned by the Prince Regent, later King George the Fourth, the crenellated Houses of Parliament, and the Victorian gothic of St Pancras Station – all destined to become reactionary and revered landmarks. Such split patronage, such diversity of style, showed a bustling city supporting innovation and clinging on to tradition, putting its new wine into old and new bottles without distinction.

In response to the spreading of taste and wealth, parliament took a few more steps towards the patronage of the arts. Lord Melbourne might fulminate 'God help the government that meddles with art,' and William Cobbett might question the use of public money to acquire objects for a limited audience, asking, 'Of what use, in the wide world, is this British Museum, and to whom, to what class of persons, is it useful?'. It was, in John Hobhouse's opinion, 'a piece of patchwork'. But local opportunity and international competition prodded parliament into action. In spite of intervention by John Wilkes, Sir Robert Walpole's lavish collection of art at Houghton had not been acquired for the nation, but had been sold to Catherine the Great of Russia, one of the prime collectors of her century. But marbles and bronzes and terracottas from Charles Townley's collection, the Phigalian Marbles from Arcadia, and then the Elgin Marbles, were all bought for the people of Britain by special grant. The select committee, which recommended the purchase of the Elgin treasures, was careful to stress 'how highly the cultivation of the Fine Arts has contributed to the reputation, character, and dignity of every Government by which they have been encouraged, and how intimately they are connected with the advancement of every thing valuable in science, literature and philosophy'.

The first important public gallery in London, however, was founded by a private bequest, that of the wealthy painter Sir Francis Bourgeois, who left his art collection to Dulwich College; the gallery to house it was designed by Sir John Soane. His example was followed by the seventh Viscount Fitzwilliam, whose endowment funded and furnished the Fitzwilliam Museum at Cambridge. Not until the authorization of work on a new building for the British Museum in 1823 in Bloomsbury, after King George the Fourth had presented his father's library to the institution, were plans revived to build a national gallery. The splendid paintings assembled by Sir John Julius Angerstein, the father of the modern insurance giant, Lloyd's, might otherwise have been sold to leave the country, as Sir Robert Walpole's had been; Catherine the Great of Russia had then acquired thirteen paintings by Rubens, twelve by van Dyck and four Murillos. The garnering of the Angerstein collection was an opportunity not to be missed, or so the banker and Member of Parliament Alexander Baring said. It would be a national reproach if such a rich society as England did not keep the pictures and house them well. 'Vast quantities of valuable works had been thrown into the hands of individuals by the French Revolution, which must in the nature of things return again to the great cabinets and collections.'

The sum of £57,000 was authorized for the buying of the Angerstein paintings as the foundation for a national gallery. These were poorly housed for fourteen years, before money for a new building in Trafalgar Square was allocated. Britain was behind Europe in this gesture. A hundred years before, the last of the Medici had presented the profuse art galleries in the Uffizi Palace in Florence to the State of Tuscany – the greatest act of public benefaction in modern Europe at that time. A national gallery in Vienna had opened eleven years before the Louvre, while others in Amsterdam and Madrid and Berlin preceded the one in London. Royal, aristocratic or republican gifts on the other side of the English Channel encouraged the late British parliamentary grant of a picture house for the nation.

It was one thing to provide a British Museum and a National Gallery for the public; it was another to educate the public to appreciate the arts. The industrial workers, degraded by the factory system and scientific innovation, could hardly be expected to enjoy art. They had to be taught and given the leisure. There was neither the will nor the commitment of funds to do this. 'In this country there is no general reverence for the fine arts,' Samuel Taylor Coleridge observed in 1831, 'and the sordid spirit of a money-amassing philosophy would meet any proposition for the fostering of art, in a genial and extended sense, with the commercial maxim – *Laissez faire.*'

Thus far, royal, religious, corporate and private patronage had founded and supported the schools of the country. Edward Bulwer-Lytton, a popular author and Member of Parliament, called for a system of national schools established by state paternalism. The government should educate its children, encourage science and the arts, and help the condition of the poor. These would be Public Blessings. The only measure which came from his initiative was London's first School of Design in Somerset House, an explicit application of the arts to business: schools of design already existed in France and in Germany. It was complementary to the rise of the private Society for the Diffusion of Useful Knowledge, the name of which signified the chief intellectual preoccupation of the age. Unfortunately, the high fees at the School of Design of ten guineas a year and its daytime teaching hours prevented any of the factory workers from using it.

Yet the effort to spread useful learning did spawn seventeen more provincial schools of design and inspire the creation of the Victoria and Albert Museum along with the Royal College of Art. These institutions were to grow on land in South Kensington purchased by government money; there the first artistic, scientific and industrial museum was set up in a series of galleries called the 'Brompton Broilers'. In 1843, the Museums Act also permitted local authorities to provide cultural facilities outside London. A decade later, a Department of Practical Art began to give state aid to art schools; it then joined the Department of Science and Art, which had been heralded in the Queen's Speech to parliament of 1852 with the words, 'The advancement of the Fine Arts and of Practical Science will be readily recognized by you as worthy of the Attention of a great and enlightened Nation'. Furthermore, the passage of the Public Libraries Act of 1855 allowed local rates to be levied to set up schools of arts and sciences as well as public libraries. By the end of the century, however, there would still be fewer than three hundred and fifty public libraries in all Britain, far less in proportion than there had been in Cordoba some thousand years before.

The chief public expenditure on music was on brass bands to play in the ornamental stands being erected in the parks. By 1902, the London County Council was subsidising some twelve hundred concerts a year, including those given by its own orchestra of more than a hundred players; the audience was reckoned at over a million. Although a National Training School for Music was founded at South Kensington, it closed after six years and was reborn because of private initiatives led by the Prince of Wales. Now called the Royal College of Music, it offered fifty permanent scholarships which were funded by individual contributions; then a leading biscuit manufacturer, Lord Palmer, endowed a patron's fund, which enlarged the facilities and opportunities at the Royal College. The government had more to do with supporting a central academy of science at South Kensington, which eventually grew into the Royal College of Science and Imperial College. That was because the teaching of science and art in elementary schools had become a state responsibility after the passing of the Education Act. Teaching music was not yet a national priority.

The hodge-podge growth of South Kensington with its mixture of purposes and buildings devoted to the various sciences and fine arts came to an end with the century and with the organization of a Board of Education to take over many of its teaching functions. This allowed for the construction of separate institutions for music and the natural sciences and for the different branches of the arts, these to be housed in a redesigned Victoria and Albert Museum. There was keen interest in the proposed plans, for museums as teaching mechanisms had been evolving across Europe and America. It was generally agreed that museums should be useful, stimulating efficiency or general knowledge or patriotism. Luckily, the British architect of the Victoria and Albert Museum ignored the wish of the government for a plain and utilitarian structure. He produced an apt monument to Victorian stability and grandeur, which employed the technology of iron and glass to protect and light some of the courts and corridors and galleries. The arrangement of the innumerable objects taken from the British empire and the ancient civilizations of the world posed problems that were not solved. To a German critic, the Victoria and Albert Museum looked like a palace on the outside, but still a warehouse on the inside. And King Edward the Seventh himself, when he opened the edifice named after his mother and father, called it 'a storehouse of masterpieces worthy of the study of designers and manufacturers'.

A spreading use of an old word, 'culture', provided an escape from the concept of the state only aiding the utilitarian arts. In the late Middle Ages, culture meant worship as well as cultivation of the soil. But by Tudor times, it usually signified the improvement of the individual by education or training, and rarely the setting of boundaries. The great Jacobean philosopher Hobbes named the education of children 'a Culture of their mindes'. He suggested images of parents or schools or the state acting as gardeners and growing the green shoots of learning from the earth of young people. With the influence of Goethe on the British Romantics, the idea of an organic 'culture' expressing the best of a national spirit reached the consciousness of Europe's offshore islands. And the Victorian critic Matthew Arnold made it the subject of a study, *Culture and Anarchy*, defining its meaning in words that derived from Aristotle: 'Culture is then properly described not as having its origin in curiosity, but as having its origin in the love of perfection: *it is a study of perfection.*' It should be an individual quest for fulfilment as well as a general growth into knowledge encouraged by the community and state, which should provide the opportunity for that self-realisation. 'The men of culture are the true apostles of equality.' And culture itself was 'to know the best that has been said and thought in the world'. As Carlyle had also written, the great law of culture was to 'let each become all that he was created capable of being'.

The concept of culture through general education put onto the state the responsibility of providing the means for that training in appreciation. Museums and art galleries and public libraries were all very well, but what if the people were not taught to savour the visual arts and literature and drama and music? And when they might be trained, what if they were unable to see or hear the best in their culture because of where they lived, because of what they could afford? Access to the superior was as important as appreciation. Judged by this new concept of a national culture, Cobbett was wrong that only an elite could enjoy the British Museum. The object of culture was to take the many to the best in the country. It was for the benefit of all, and therefore a duty of a good government.

As T. S. Eliot would point out in his *Notes towards the Definition of Culture* in 1948, there was a diversity of local cultures within a nation. Each region might have a distinct culture within the general one of the nation. And culture meant far more than the best in the sciences and liberal arts: it was the way of life of a particular people living together in one place. It included the crafts and folk art, what would be called the community arts, and also cooking and sport. Extremely conscious of the differences of class within a common Christian culture, Eliot stressed the apartness and the common-wealth of the British. 'The culture of an artist or a philosopher is distinct from that of a mine worker or field labourer; the culture of a poet will be somewhat different from that of a politician; but in a healthy society these are all parts of the same culture; and the artist, the poet, the politician and the labourer will have a culture in common, which they do not share with other people of the same occupations in other countries.' In a famous and idiosyncratic attempt to detail what was special about modern Britishness, Eliot stated that culture embraced 'all the characteristic activities and interests of a people: Derby Day, Henley Regatta, Cowes, the twelfth of August, a cup final, the dog races, the pin table, the dart board, Wensleydale cheese, boiled cabbage cut into sections, beetroot in vinegar, nineteenth-century Gothic churches and the music of Elgar'.

Such an inclusive definition of culture meant that it could not be planned or even affected very much by government. And yet two world wars, allied with the advancement of technology and a prolonged depression would lead reluctant British administrations to intrude more directly in the national culture and in the regions. After the First World War, local authorities were empowered to give to museums and often proved more enlightened than central government. The Liverpool Council made annual grants to the Walker Art Gallery to acquire paintings, as did the Lincoln City Corporation to the upkeep and collection of the Usher Art Gallery. By the outbreak of the Second World War, there were more than four hundred museums funded and run by local authorities. The greatest contribution to national culture by parliament during the period was to export it overseas. The British Council was established in 1934 to promote appreciation of British civilization abroad. It was supported by grants attached to the annual budgets of the Foreign and Colonial and Commonwealth Offices. The British empire was given more state subsidy for the arts than the mother country.

The national heritage was to be preserved by private means and small legislative concessions. In 1937, the National Trust Act permitted the Trust to hold land and estates when their owners were no longer able to continue the upkeep. By donating their houses and grounds to the Trust, the owners and their heirs could go on living in part of the house on condition that the residence and its surroundings were opened to visitors on a regular basis. In that way, the particular flowering of British genius in country house and landscaped park slowly became available to the people. Private privilege was changing into public access. It was a gradual and democratic solution without radical change; it suited the English spirit of compromise without government intervention.

The patronage of the National Gallery was left to wealthy citizens, except for a remarkable special grant for the purchase of works by Ingres and Delacroix and Manet from the sale in 1918 of the Degas collection. They complemented the French Impressionist masterpieces bequeathed by Sir Hugh Lane in 1917 after his death by drowning when the *Lusitania* was sunk. The largest donation of the post-war years came from the fortune of the founder of Imperial Chemical Industries: the Mond bequest to the National Gallery included works by Raphael and Botticelli, Giovanni Bellini and Titian. As had happened with Sir Henry Tate, the sugar magnate who gave his collection to the nation, the donor had to pay for a home in which to hang his gifts.

Moreover, the textile manufacturer Samuel Courtauld created a fund for the National Gallery to purchase Impressionist and post-Impressionist French paintings; the pictures were hung in the Tate Gallery, although some were intended for the National Gallery, which could not find the space to show them until after the end of the Second World War. The younger Lord Duveen followed his father's example by paying for a new great room to house the Elgin Marbles – his own fortune had come from dealing in treasures ripped from their countries of origin. He also gave additional painting and sculpture galleries to the Tate, which was now empowered to display foreign pictures, particularly the thirty-nine French master-pieces from the Lane legacy. The Tate, still an appendage of the National Gallery, became a leading European museum of modern art between the wars because of private patronage and lack of hanging space in its parent body.

No progress was made in fully funding a national theatre, except for the purchase of a site in South Kensington. Lilian Baylis and the Old Vic bought the dilapidated Sadler's Wells Theatre and created an unofficial national ballet company without state support except for the lifting of the entertainments duty. Emigré Russian dancers brought the art to England and taught it to the natives. As for opera, even the manufacturing family fortune of Sir Thomas Beecham could not sustain seasons at Covent Garden. His company went bankrupt and its successor, the British National Opera Company, also ended in liquidation. Although its heir, the Covent Garden Opera Syndicate, actually received a subsidy from the state through the Post Office and the British Broadcasting Corporation (BBC), some parliamentarians thought it a public scandal to give tax money to the arts during a depression. One Labour Member wanted the funds transferred to the Ministry of Agriculture to provide allot-ments for the unemployed.

Helping an art for an elite audience in London seemed intolerable at a time of mass unemployment and hunger and so the subsidy was withdrawn. But a precedent had been set. It did not escape the notice of the eminent economist and doyen of the Bloomsbury group, John Maynard Keynes, who was to secure state backing for a national opera at Covent Garden after the end of the next war. However, his pleas for government patronage in peacetime fell on deaf ears. 'Anything would be better than the present system,' he lamented in 1936. 'The position today of artists of all sorts is disastrous.'

The response of the British government to the technological revolution of the times with its new art forms was contradictory. It failed to control or aid the cinema, only to censor it, while it made the wireless industry a monopoly financed by licence fees. In the film industry, a quota was imposed so that one-fifth of films shown in the country had to be made in Britain. As for state funding, the honourable exceptions to the rule were the Post Office Film Units which developed into the Crown Film Unit. These commissioned documentaries from leading directors and writers. Their purpose was public information, and the genius of John Grierson and Humphrey Jennings, Basil Wright and Cavalcanti and even W. H. Auden was to found a national school of realistic cinema. Although the British Film Institute was created in 1933 as a semi-autonomous agency, it was inadequately funded by a tax on cinema owners and never had the resources to educate the nation about the potential of the new medium. While Russia and Germany used the cinema as a powerful means of mass manipulation, the British cinema muddled along from one financial crisis to another.

The government's refusal, however, fully to control wireless technology was its outstanding success. The creation of the British Broadcasting Corporation as a monopoly, subsidized by a tax collected by the Post Office, became a global model for a democratic public body, which maintained high standards and a certain independence, known as 'the arm's length principle'. Its managing director, John Reith, was Victorian in his values; he believed in the moral education of the British people, who should hear 'everything that was best in every department of human knowledge, endeavour and achievement'. The wireless became the medium for the mass teaching of children and adults about the arts, especially in classical music, which was played by the BBC's own symphony orchestra. The Corporation even backed Sir Henry Wood and the Promenade Concerts at the Queen's Hall as well as subsidizing opera at Sadler's Wells. Furthermore, it gave the first performances of original compositions by Ralph Vaughan Williams and William Walton. Instead of spreading political propaganda, the BBC broadcast British culture and reason across the nation and the world. It proved a triumph for the new communications system, rightly used. Keynes himself asserted that the BBC was the greatest and most successful institution which had grown after the First World War – and its patron was the state. Yet direct government funding for all the arts and museums in the year of the outbreak of the Second World War was still less than a million pounds.

There were other bodies interested in adult education in the arts in the nineteen-thirties. The Carnegie United Kingdom Trust was supporting amateur music and drama. There were also the Rural Music Schools, the British Drama League, the National Federation of Music Societies, the National Council of Social Service, the Women's Institutes, the Townswomen's Guilds, and the English Folk Dance and Song Society. The most significant change had been in established movements of adult education. The Worker's Educational Association and the University Extra Mural Departments had been occupied for three decades with the social sciences 'and had assumed that working-class adult students had little time or concern for the arts'. But that attitude was modified and 'music and drama and literature began to hold their own in the curriculum with economics and social history'. It was the same thing in the Evening Institutes of the London County Council and of other Local Education Authorities. 'These were no longer exclusively centres of vocational training for commerce or industry, but places where a clerk or a telephonist could study or practise music and painting and play-production.'

In a curious sense, the rise of Communism and Fascism in Europe gave most people a sense of what their culture really was. While Stalinist and Nazi domination of the media and relentless use of propaganda suggested strong ideological states, the freedom of expression and diversity of opinions in the democracies seemed worth fighting for. The burning of the books in Germany and the famous phrase of Hans Johst, often attributed to Goering, 'When I hear the word Culture, I release the safety-catch on my Browning pistol!', led to an appreciation of democratic values against such barbarism. The sense of what might be lost under a blitzkrieg of totalitarianism encouraged a holding onto what was already there, even though the Fascist success in the Spanish Civil War, followed by the inglorious Munich Agreement by Chamberlain and the infamous Nazi–Soviet pact, made the democracies seem feeble and ready to go under the approaching onslaught. Rather like King Charles the Second, they were apologizing for being an unconscionable time a-dying. This was no climate for the patronage of threatened cultures that might not last for a decade, let alone another thousand years – the period that Hitler sought for his Third Reich, that threatened oblivion for past ages.

John Ruskin proved correct. War was the foundation of the arts. Under menace, people in their places draw together to defend what they have. The imminence of death is known to clear the mind wonderfully. It drives many towards religion and the better qualities of life. It is also a great leveller, for the highbrow and the lowbrow share the same basic preoccupations and dust. At the end of the decade when television was barely begun, the whole nation was listening with foreboding to the news and the wireless was left turned on to hear the popular and chamber and orchestral music, played by the BBC to entertain and elevate the country – the first mass educational programme accessible to nearly all Britons. When war was finally declared at the beginning of September in 1939 with the Nazi and Communist attack on Poland, a synthesis of sympathy began to deny Eliot's apartness of the classes, and a common cause looked for every way to preserve a national culture, whether it were Derby Day or the music of Elgar. The perils of conflict wonderfully enhance the recollected pleasures of peace. In that sense, war encourages the arts for it forges a general desire for them – what Matthew Arnold wanted, a study of and quest for perfection. The struggle was that of Shelley's *West Wind*:

> Wild Spirit, which art moving everywhere;
> Destroyer and preserver; hear, oh hear!

ONE

THE ARTS
AND THE WAR

Culture can never be wholly conscious – there is always more to it than we are conscious of; and it cannot be planned because it is also the unconscious background of all our planning.

T. S. Eliot in *Notes towards the Definition of Culture*, 1948

When the Second World War began, most people in Britain expected an instant obliteration by German bombs. They had seen the newsreels of the strafing of Guernica, the subject of Picasso's most political painting, along with the extravagant film of H. G. Wells's book *The Shape of Things to Come*, and they thought that they would soon be bombed or gassed or live in holes in the ground. Nearly one and a half million women and children were evacuated from the cities by the government in the two days before the declaration of hostilities and another two million people left of their own accord. The British Museum and the Victoria and Albert Museum sent their treasures to a quarry near Bath, while the National Gallery hid three thousand of its best pictures in caverns in North Wales. This clearance of space opened the way for remarkable experiments in musical appreciation and popular art. Improvisation had so long been the inspiration of particular performances. Six weeks after the war broke out, Myra Hess began a series of piano recitals at lunchtime in the octagonal room of the empty National Gallery, soon packed with listeners shouldering their gas masks. The Queen herself often went to hear the music among the thumps and bangs of the air raids, as yet intermittent before the blitz to come.

The quiet desperation which affected Britain on the outbreak of the conflict threw nearly all the performers and artists out of work. The theatres closed in the black-out, the orchestras had no bookings. Outside the BBC and the Ministry of Information, efforts failed to employ writers as war artists or to exempt them from conscription. An informal committee was set up by Lord Esher aided by John Lehmann, but it could not even preserve fifty leading artists from the call-up. An official Authors' Planning Committee had A. P. Herbert and Dorothy L. Sayers serving on it in order to produce plans for harnessing authors to the war effort. It was attacked by many: John Strachey wrote in *The Author*, 'The best thing that the government can do for authors in wartime is to leave them alone. The business of an author is to write.' Osbert Sitwell agreed: 'The writer can do more for his country by writing than by fighting.' So the Authors' Planning Committee was dissolved. All the arts seemed to be marking time. *Mass-Observation* wrote of a suffering culture in 1940 with publishers seeing no future, the closure of art galleries and museums, the cancellation of concerts, no boom in poetry reading as in the First World War, and the refusal of creative artists to do much more than linger and watch. The opening editorial of *Horizon*, written by Cyril Connolly, was quoted: 'At the moment civilization is on the operating table and we sit in the waiting-room.'

The hiatus was ended by an unusual intervention by the government in cultural matters. Certainly, the morale of the beleaguered and bombed citizens on the Home Front was important. The war would not be won without raising the spirits of the armed forces and the Land Army and the drafted workers in the factories and the mines. There would be no victory without uplift as well as entertainment – and that was being dealt with by the Entertainments National Service Association (ENSA), which had also fulfilled that role in the First World War. The need for a more serious organization was stated in a memorandum to an informal conference at the Board of Education on 18 December 1939, which was to result in the founding of the prototype for the post-war Arts Council of Great Britain. 'This country is supposed to be fighting for civilization and democracy and if these things mean anything they mean a way of life where people have liberty and opportunity to pursue the things of peace. It should be part of a national war policy to show that the Government is actively interested in these things. Such an assurance needs to be given equally for the sake of our own people and for the sake of British pride abroad.'

The creation of the Council for the Encouragement of Music and the Arts (CEMA) after that informal conference was due to Welsh inspiration and English administration. The secretary of the Pilgrim Trust, which administered a bequest of two million pounds left by the Anglophile American railway financier Edward J. Harkness, was Dr Thomas Jones. He reminded the first secretary of CEMA, Mary Glasgow, of Samuel Whiskers, 'a self-effacing yet formidable little pyramid of a figure, with a small head and long, pointed nose'. He had been Secretary to the Cabinet for David Lloyd George and knew how government worked, 'a man behind the scenes, famous among those who knew for doing his best to avoid fame'. He also had his hand on a trust fund, the object of which was to sustain and preserve the heritage and social culture of Great Britain. Furthermore, he had been concerned with the Commission for the Special Areas, which had used government funds during the nineteen-thirties to send experts in music and drama and the visual arts and various crafts to provide something for the unemployed miners to do in South Wales and County Durham. With the outbreak of the war and full mobilization, unemployment vanished, as did the need for such pioneer arts and crafts centres. Dr Jones perceived that what the war had ended might be revived to help to win the war.

He took his idea to the Chairman of the Pilgrim Trust, the lawyer Lord Macmillan, who was also the Minister of Information at the time, and Macmillan arranged a meeting with Lord De La Warr, the president of the Board of Education, who was to claim that the funding of the CEMA was his conception. And indeed, Dr Jones supported that claim in his written account of the meeting, on the principle of a later American President, Ronald Reagan, that he could get anything he wanted done as long as he gave the credit to somebody else. Dr Jones maintained that De La Warr telephoned him to propose an idea and get a grant from the Pilgrim Trust. He came to see Lord Macmillan and Dr Jones at the Senate House of the University of London:

> Lord De La Warr was enthusiastic. He had Venetian visions of a post-war Lord Mayor's Show on the Thames in which the Board of Education led the Arts in triumph from Whitehall to Greenwich in magnificent barges and gorgeous gondolas; orchestras, madrigal singers, Shakespeare from the Old Vic, ballet from Sadler's Wells, shining canvases from the Royal Academy, folk dancers from village greens – in fact, Merrie England. Lord Macmillan's grave judicial calm collapsed suddenly and completely. At the moment he was responsible for the national morale, and in the President's dream he saw employment for actors, singers and painters, and refreshment for the multitude of war workers for the duration. Supply and Demand kissed. Would £25,000 be any use? The Secretary blushed and fell off his stool.

The secretary of the Pilgrim Trust should have blushed at writing such an account. In Mary Glasgow's opinion, it was a cover-up for the role of *eminence grise*, which Dr Jones liked to assume, 'and a joke in the best Celtic tradition'. As he was also writing in the CEMA bulletin and working for that organization, he was perhaps wise to credit the Board of Education for the inspiration, and not himself. Certainly, that same afternoon Lord Macmillan told the Trustees of the American fund about the proposal 'for the encouragement in wartime of amateur music and drama, combined with the assistance of unemployed musicians and producers'. He said that Lord De La Warr had expressed the hope that *after the war* the Board of Education 'might continue to interest itself in and assist the activities thus promoted as a part of its normal policy'. He believed that there might also be a matching grant from the Treasury for a project that would be 'a useful contribution to the social life of the rural districts and smaller provincial towns, as well as to the maintenance of public morale at the present time'.

Four days after the Trustees had approved the grant of £25,000, Lord Macmillan and Dr Jones visited the Board of Education with the Director of the National Gallery, Kenneth Clark, who had already organized there the successful lunchtime concerts played by Myra Hess and had launched the War Artists' Advisory Committee to employ painters to record the conflict. With them were two other Welshmen of charisma and influence, Sir Henry Walford Davies,

the Master of the King's Musick, and William Emrys Williams, the
secretary of the British Institute of Adult Education, who had also
been involved in the arts centres in the Special Areas and had
organized the travelling 'Art for the People' exhibitions of paintings
in the nineteen-thirties, impressing Kenneth Clark by his enthusiasm
and intelligence. De La Warr had already written to Jones that the
National Gallery concerts had revealed 'an almost pathetic hunger
for such provision'. He was less concerned with providing music in
the larger towns than with 'those who are making music and acting
plays for themselves, because I realize all that this means to their
own morale'. But he wanted the Pilgrim Trust grant to aid voluntary
organizations in the emergency through 'the next three or four
months of long, dark evenings'. Writing about it later in his booklet
on the first ten years of the future Arts Council, William Emrys
Williams saw different motives in the inception of the new
organization. 'Lord Macmillan saw it primarily as a scheme which
would fortify national morale in the grievous trials of war,
especially among those communities which, evacuated from the
cities, would find themselves without occupation for their enforced
leisure. Dr. Thomas Jones, the vigilant opportunist, discerned in it
fresh opportunities for spreading the arts,' while other advisers saw
it as doing something 'to provide employment for artists whose
useful outlets and opportunities were being diminished by the
effects of war'.

   In this improvised and tentative way, the state lurched into the
funding of the performing and visual arts. On 19 January 1940, a
Committee for the Encouragement of Music and the Arts was set up
with a board consisting of the five visitors to the Board of Education
in the previous December. They were supplemented by Dr Lawrence du Garde Peach, an expert on amateur dramatics, Dr Reginald
Jacques, a disciple of Sir Walford Davies who shared his love of
wandering and teaching minstrels and musicians and by Mary
Glasgow, who had been made redundant in her post as Assistant
Inspector of Schools and now became the secretary of the new
organization. The majority of the board – the three Welshmen and
the three recruits, Peach and Jacques and the secretary Glasgow –
was populist by persuasion and believed in adult education. Only
the Chairman, Lord Macmillan, who was almost to retire to his

Scottish estate, and Kenneth Clark, stood for maintaining professional standards of excellence in the major cities rather than sending on tour teachers of the arts and aiding amateur organizations in the county towns and villages. But with the Vice-Chairman of the later Council and Dr Jones, the initiator of the Committee, effectively running the show, the first of the four objectives of the new organization was subordinated to the other three. These were seen as:

a) the preservation in wartime of the highest standards in the arts of music, drama and painting;
b) the widespread provision of opportunities for hearing good music and the enjoyment of the arts generally for people, who, on account of wartime conditions, have been cut off from these things;
c) the encouragement of music-making and play-acting by the people themselves;
d) through the above activities, the rendering of indirect assistance to professional singers and players who may be suffering from a wartime lack of demand for their work.

After three months, the Committee was changed to a formal Council, because the Treasury had decided to increase its matching grant to £50,000: eventually, grants from the Pilgrim Trust would equal that sum. As Vice-Chairman, Dr Thomas Jones remained the driving force. Although the Board was filled with more peers and Members of Parliament to join Sir Walford Davies and Sir Kenneth Clark, Honorary Directors were appointed to do the real work – Dr Dyson followed by Dr Jacques for music; Lewis Casson, then married to Dame Sybil Thorndike, for professional drama; Dr Peach for amateur drama and William Emrys Williams for art. They were joined by the drama critic of the *Observer*, Ivor Brown, who also organized theatrical events and concerts and publicity and edited the CEMA bulletin, coining its slogan, 'The Best for the Most'. This neatly fudged the conflict between helping the professional or the amateur, sending out the urban expert or aiding the local performer. But while Dr Jones was in control, as he was for two years, the population at large was seen as more important than the recognized artist.

Music travellers were appointed, known as 'Walford's Holy Women', as were drama organizers to raise the standards of amateur dramatics. Featuring two singers and a pianist, concerts were given in works canteens and factories with great success. 'Music-making' was the term that Mary Glasgow most frequently heard round the London office, and when she accompanied Dr Jones to a recital by a full orchestra in a Midlands factory, she heard him exclaim, 'But when are we going to *sing*?'. Participation was the watchword. As one of the music travellers wrote, 'The feeling that one may be singing while England is burning' was sometimes difficult to withstand, but she was overwhelmed by the deep sincerity of the unanimous thanks for her work. In the words of one concert handbill, 'C.E.M.A. wants art to be a vigorous element everywhere enjoyed in public life, not just something set apart for the benefit of privileged people.' Even when professional groups such as the London Philharmonic and London Symphony Orchestras were given grants, they were sent to the industrial areas. 'I am making it a condition that they play and sing in the dreary Dagenhams of the country,' Dr Jones insisted, 'and not in London and centres where amenities are abundant.'

With Lewis Casson as an Honorary Director, professional theatre would not always bow to village dramatics. Small travelling companies, the Pilgrim Players and the Market Theatre, had already been sent on the road to barnstorm in village halls and workplaces. Then Casson and Emlyn Williams, another actor friend of the dominant Welshmen in the organization, were given £2,500 to arrange a large repertory company for a ten-week tour of industrial areas. A further guarantee against loss of £6,000 was given to the Old Vic to tour with two groups in Lancashire and South Wales, where Casson himself performed *Macbeth* in the colliery villages with his wife Dame Sybil Thorndike and minimal sets or costumes. 'We've never played to such audiences,' the actress wrote to her son. 'None of them move a muscle while we're playing, but at the end they go wild and lift the roof with their clapping. This is the theatre that we like best – getting right in amongst people.'

Because the blitz in London became so hellish and the London base of the Old Vic was bombed, it transferred its headquarters to Burnley, where it presented an eight-week season of opera and drama and ballet. The programme note, signed by the director of the company, Tyrone Guthrie, said exactly what CEMA wanted to hear. Spread was all. Burnley was suddenly 'the most important creative centre in the English theatre. The event is symptomatic of the times. For too long London and the great metropolitan cities have owned altogether too much of the cultural life of the country. One of the most important and encouraging symptoms of the turmoil which we are now enduring, is the dispersal of the treasures of art and culture throughout a wider area of the land, and a wider range of people.' To Ivor Brown, the people who filled the theatre in Burnley to see *Macbeth* 'were the counterparts of Shakespeare's own audience'. And Constance Cummings, touring with Robert Donat because she was afraid of London and the bombs, found herself mobbed at the stage door by a new audience which could see film stars on the stage and said, 'We never knew theatre could be like this.'

Ninette de Valois had the same feeling when the Sadler's Wells Ballet went to Birmingham. It was so exciting and a pointer towards resident provincial ballet companies. The war had created the popularity of the dance. 'People couldn't buy clothes or food or drink, so they spent their money in the theatre.' It was difficult to secure young male dancers: even Russia had not called up its ballet stars. But young dancers would rush up to her and explain: 'Madame, it's all right – my eyes are rotten.' They became used to the bombing, wherever they went. 'When the curtains came down, the crusades started of little girls tripping home to the suburbs through the dark. When the sirens went at first, we used to stop the show and put out the lights, but people got jumpy in the dark. And nobody budged, so we kept the lights on and went on and had a huge reception.' This carrying on gave the Sadler's Wells Ballet a wide reputation internationally, and it would become Britain's prime cultural ambassador immediately after the war.

If many of the major companies fled with CEMA's blessing to the north, the Council itself stayed in London and took the arts to air raid victims and centres for the homeless. To the crypt of St Martin's-in-the-Fields and the basements of department stores and the improvised underground shelters, fifty professional musicians were sent to sing folk songs and play their instruments. They revived morale, they passed the dreary hours until the next 'All Clear' sounded on the sirens. Their success was such that they incurred the wrath of the Minister for Home Security, Herbert Morrison, who wanted people to scatter during air raids, not to bunch together as an audience under the bombs and so increase the risk of greater casualties. But then Morrison was hardly a devotee of art for arts sake, saying in the House of Commons, 'The Government's wartime policy with regard to entertainments has been to permit them to continue on a restricted basis in the belief that, within reason, popular establishments act as a lubricant rather than a brake to the war machine.'

Yet CEMA's triumph with its serious music programmes, particularly in the munitions factories, aroused the jealousy of ENSA, with its light entertainment organized by Basil Dean and its directive to uplift and divert all troops and war workers. Thus the Council was steered to arranging performances chiefly in village halls. It was a wrong bureaucratic decision, because CEMA was proving what its founders believed, that most of the population could appreciate the best of the arts. The strange conditions of war had provided a stimulus for the appreciation of a national culture that now seemed so precarious. What had been taken for granted was under threat. Even a poet once opposed to war, Stephen Spender, wrote of that time, that the arts revived with fresh significance. 'This arose spontaneously and simply, because people felt that music, the ballet, poetry and painting were concerned with a seriousness of living and dying with which they themselves had suddenly been confronted ... A little island of civilization surrounded by burning churches – that was how the arts seemed in England during the war.'

In these times of education through television, it is difficult to imagine how much the CEMA companies raised the consciousness of the arts as well as civilian morale. They were regular visitors to the hostels built by the Ministry of Supply for the drafted workers in the royal Ordnance Factories. These gatherings provided 'ready-made audiences of an entirely unsophisticated kind', as Ifor Evans and Mary Glasgow noted. 'It is a startling fact that, at the beginning, only about two per cent of these hostel audiences had ever seen a stage play before. In the early days many of them did not know how to behave before live players. They hardly seemed to realize that the peopled stage before them was not an inanimate cinematographic screen. Gradually they acquired a theatre etiquette and ceased to talk, walk about and drink tea during the performances.'

'Art for the People', with its travelling exhibitions of paintings, organized by William Emrys Williams, had already in the nineteen-thirties accustomed audiences who had never learned to appreciate oils and drawings and prints to listen to informed guides and weekly lectures by experts on the artists represented in the mobile shows. By the summer of 1941, nine collections were criss-crossing the nation, one of them an exhibition of the War Artists being shown in the National Gallery, which had evacuated most of its old masterpieces. Lithographs and reproductions by modern British artists were also supplied to innumerable clubs and canteens and subsidized British restaurants – a hundred and thirty of these were decorated with murals designed by Henry Moore and Graham Sutherland and John Piper, then executed by art students. Music and drama and painting were being taken to the country at war.

Such populism, however, engendered criticism. John Christie, the founder of the private Glyndebourne Opera, was trying to set up his own National Council of Music and could not bear CEMA's support of amateur singing and playing. As far as he was concerned, Sir Walford Davies and Dr Jones were wasting money with nothing to show for it, while standards were 'lagging far behind in a sea of mediocrity'. The death of Davies in the March of 1941 presaged a change of his policy, called by Dr Jones 'the vision of the Music Travellers, a dream of fair women singing their way through the villages of England until all the birds and all the shires joined the choir and filled the land with melody'. Although his successor was another Welshman, the composer Ralph Vaughan Williams, who was also committed in principle to amateur music, the writing was on the keyboard.

More ominously, John Maynard Keynes joined in the attack, when Donald Wolfit's company failed to receive a grant for a provincial tour after a successful season at the Arts Theatre in Cambridge, Keynes's own foundation. Lewis Casson claimed that, except for amateur dramatics, there were only funds enough to subsidize one organization of a national character, the Old Vic.

Keynes found it unfortunate that funds were being given to a monopoly organized by Casson himself. 'If that is to be the policy it would save everyone a lot of trouble if an announcement were made that no outsiders need apply.' The shamed Council did then guarantee Wolfit's tour, but Keynes summoned Mary Glasgow to his government office and continued his assault, which left her battered but exhilarated. He condemned the waste of resources on amateur dramatic companies. Only professional theatre with high standards was important. 'He made mince-meat of me,' she wrote later, 'when I tried (as I had to) to justify my masters on the Council. I reeled out into the night, bloody but I hope unbowed, feeling I had been in the presence of a very great man.'

Glasgow herself now began to suggest that it would be wise to close down the scheme of travelling drama advisers. The Carnegie Trust was already committed to supporting amateur music and play-acting through the National Council of Social Service and other voluntary bodies, while the Pilgrim Trust was withdrawing from support of CEMA because its experimental stage was over. 'In two years its art exhibitions have attracted more than half a million visitors, the plays given under its auspices a million and a half, the number of its concerts in all parts of England, Wales and Scotland almost reached eight thousand.' Such a catalogue of success could now be fully supported by the Treasury through the Board of Education.

Yet the support of the Treasury and the withdrawal of Lord Macmillan and Dr Jones as Chairman and Vice-Chairman of CEMA because they represented the Pilgrim Trust led to fresh blood and an inevitable change of direction. The new president of the Board of Education, R. A. Butler, wanted the wartime arts organization to move from acting on emergencies to planning for a permanent role. Dr Jones had gone for adult education and social pioneering. 'Find out what needs doing,' he told Mary Glasgow, 'make sure no one else is doing it, then move in at once.' Prompted by his subordinate, Lord Macmillan had formerly turned down a grant from the Carnegie Trust because it demanded reports on the needs of artists and audiences. 'Committees and subcommittees,' he said, 'have been the death of democracy in this country. We are entering a dark tunnel of which we cannot see the end. If anything wants doing, it must be *now*.'

Butler did want to do something now and to change the vision of the early Welsh pioneers. He asked Keynes himself to take over and shape the future policy of the state towards a national culture. Already fully occupied with work at the wartime Treasury, Keynes was worried that he would not have enough time to do a thorough job. He also disapproved of the previous concentration of the arts organization on social welfare and education rather than on high standards. Reassured by Butler and Mary Glasgow, who claimed to be the only one not surprised when Keynes jumped at the invitation to be the new CEMA Chairman, he took office, received a peerage and altered the organization according to the imperatives of his imagination, directed by the long arm and influence of his Bloomsbury and Cambridge friends.

Two characters, Dr Jones and Lord Keynes, would bequeath to the embryo Arts Council of Great Britain their emphases and contradictions, which were never to be resolved. Jones probably initiated and certainly directed the Council for the Encouragement of Music and the Arts for its first two experimental years of social welfare. Keynes shaped the wartime organization into an arbiter of artistic excellence until the peace came, then he lit the fire that allowed the Arts Council to rise as a phoenix from the ashes of rationing and the bombs. He appreciated what Jones had done, writing to him that he had done a splendid job in getting the organization going: 'without private enterprise to start the ball rolling, no balls get rolled'. But Keynes had long had a different ambition. His desire was to form a policy for a national culture. He had cut his teeth on his work for the London Artist's Association and the Camargo Ballet Society and the Cambridge Arts Theatre. As his biographer Roy Harrod wrote of Keynes's thoughts in those days:

> In the time to come the mass of people should be able to enjoy the delights of fine art which in the past had been reserved for the favoured few. At the moment economic prospects were black, but there was always running in his mind the theme of 'Economic Possibilities for our Grandchildren'. In the long run, after this set-

back, the economic problem would be 'solved'. It was not too soon to prepare the ground. He saw in C.E.M.A. the germ of a great idea.

Keynes would never engage in anything which he could not dominate or control. In a revealing letter of 1940 to John Christie, his neighbour in Sussex, he refused to join the proposed National Council of Music: Christie later accused him of stealing all its ideas. 'After all, as you well know, I am not a musician,' Keynes wrote to Christie, 'I must not pretend to be, or get into a new field of that kind. I suffer from the congenital disability that, if I do join anything, I have the greatest difficulty in not getting mixed up and cannot manage to remain in a merely sleeping capacity ...' When Keynes did get mixed up in CEMA and later in the Arts Council, Christie fell out with him, accusing him of making a copy of the National Council of Music, 'and, being a copy, perhaps a bad copy'. The two contemporaries at Eton and neighbours in the country ended by studiously taking different compartments on the same morning train up to the metropolis.

The organization of the war itself commandeered a strategy of devolution from a Chairman who wanted centralization. Yet by putting out some power to the regions, he could solve the problem of the Jones' legacy, the strolling minstrels and teaching players. The existing arrangements for civil defence could provide the new creative areas for the arts. The ten early warning regions for England, with London and Middlesex counting as one, and for Scotland and for Wales on their own, became the staging posts for local concerts and plays and arts exhibitions as well as for sounding sirens when there was an air raid. Most of the music travellers and amateur dramatic advisers were absorbed into twelve Regional Offices, which were usually triads, an officer with two assistants, each of the three an amateur or expert in drama or music or the visual arts. Although these bodies in the counties were given little autonomy outside England and Wales, they were 'the germ of a great idea' of future devolution, which was far from the current thinking of Lord Keynes.

He wanted all decisions to be controlled from London. He even attacked the original concept of 'Art for the People' with its guide lecturers: William Emrys Williams was less able to defend his child born in the Depression, because he had now joined the War Office as the Director of the Army Bureau of Current Affairs. Keynes believed that visitors to travelling exhibitions of painting could and should do their own interpretation without commentators. 'There was, alas,' Williams later commented, 'in this great scholar and art connoisseur a streak of donnish superiority and a singular ignorance of ordinary people.' There were two missions – to enlighten people about art as well as to provide shows on the road. Keynes halved the grant for the touring exhibitions, then restored a quarter of it. The guides were diminished. But he did agree to pay hiring fees for artists and to buy contemporary works for a permanent collection. These innovations corresponded with his idea of being a patron of the arts rather than a teacher of the masses.

In his quest for metropolitan control, Keynes appointed paid directors for drama, music and the visual arts, supplemented by three advisory panels under Vice-Chairmen, who could preside in the absence of Keynes himself. But in point of fact, Keynes wished to remain the supremo and set a precedent for the long manoeuvres in the future Arts Council, between the Chairman and the Secretary-General, between the paid directors of the arts and their advisory panels. In his day as the initiator and overlord, Keynes controlled all. As he informed R. A. Butler, his drama and music panels were falling to pieces, 'not competent to give executive decisions'. Absenteeism and squabbling and self-promotion destroyed their effectiveness, while Keynes himself did not like consulting the panels 'since one always gets conflicting views'. Even the Art Panel under Kenneth Clark with its distinguished board – the great patron Samuel Courtauld, William Emrys Williams, Duncan Grant from the Bloomsbury Group, the sculptor Henry Moore, and the Director of the Tate Gallery John Rothenstein – even they induced jealousy from the excluded Royal Academicians. But Keynes refused to appoint any of the old guard to his new body in search of a national culture. As he wrote to Butler, it was unwise 'to start so early in our life on the vicious practice of filling up with respectable deadheads'.

In spite of the demands on his time and his health of manipulating the finances of his country during a world war, Keynes dominated his arts organization and showed an obsessive concern for detail. He believed in a small subsidy for a national culture. He wanted the state only to pay for the costs of administration. He did not favour total grants, but a complicated mixture between grants and loans and guarantees, and only for professional companies or artists themselves. Yet extended as he was, Mary Glasgow noted:

> At a time when he was probably busier than at any other period of his life, often engaged on financial conferences in America and Canada, he wrote to me, the secretary, practically every day, sometimes several times a day, as dictated missives flew into our headquarters in Belgrave Square from the Treasury or across the Atlantic. And they *were* missives, long discourses, lists of questions, detailed comments on all that was happening in the theatre, concert halls and picture galleries. They were full of colourful, indiscreet talk about individuals and organizations which would have made the hair of those concerned stand on end if they had read them. It may well have been that he found relief in this way from the demands of his financial responsibilities. He said he gave about a twentieth of his time to us at the Council and once complained that in order to run things properly a chairman ought to be devoting at least a quarter. What he did give was clearly important to him – to us it seemed the equivalent of any normal person's full time.

As an economist, Keynes prefixed the policy of the future Arts Council by insisting on financial accountability with his clients and by assigning higher proportions of the budget to those arts he favoured in particular. The purse followed his taste, with strings. A Civil Service financial manager was appointed, who proved a disaster; he was superseded by an accountant. During 1943 to 1944, the Treasury allocation to CEMA rose to £115,000: in the following year to £175,000. Keynes knew how to tweak more funds from the state paymasters. Of this sum, over half went to music, a quarter to drama, a tenth to art, and a fifth to the administration of the central office and the twelve Regional Offices.

The music budget was steered more and more towards professional ensembles, such as the Hallé and major symphony orchestras, although the lion's share of the money went on providing concerts in factories and hostels. Keynes's true love, the ballet, danced into subsidy through the back door. In the words of Charles Landstone, the new Assistant Director of Drama:

> Early in 1943, three pretty little girls came to see Lewis Casson and myself at the C.E.M.A. offices. One of these was Sally Gilmour, who

needs no introduction to any balletomane. I remember that it was a bitterly cold January day, with snow upon the ground; we sat grouped round the coal fire in my office while we talked. The Ballet Rambert, of which they had been the leading dancers, was (after its lunch-time performances at the Arts Theatre during the *blitz*), quiescent. They wanted us to reorganize it and to use it on the hostel tours, of which they had heard. We jumped at the chance, and I became personally responsible for the company. It was entirely financed by C.E.M.A. and the Arts Council, and was under my direct management for four years ...

Landstone also admired Marie Rambert, who had 'shared with Ninette de Valois the honour of creating the English Ballet' over the past thirty years. She was small, darting, vitally alive, 'a tyrant to her dancers, relentless in her own efforts and expecting the same relentlessness from them, a tigress on discipline ... quicker than Rommel on the move'. Her wants were few. All that she desired was perfection. Give her that, and she was satisfied. Under Keynes's prodding, the Ballets Jooss was also brought back from South America.

Yet in his pursuit of a national culture after the war, Keynes sought to snare bigger game. He wanted the whole of the Old Vic and the Sadler's Wells with their various companies for drama and opera and ballet brought within the grasp of his Council. Although a repertory group went to the Liverpool Playhouse, both organizations returned to London, where they shared the New Theatre and put on productions 'in close association with C.E.M.A.' Keynes's vision of the future impressed both Landstone and Mary Glasgow. He saw a Chairman whose 'love of the arts was not only a large part of his life, but ... welded into his whole philosophy of the economic structure of Society'. Meanwhile, she saw Keynes as someone who 'did believe in "The Most", not only with lip service; but his aim was "The Best", centres of excellence rather than village halls'.

In another way, Keynes's new policy was to presage one of the more significant actions of the future Arts Council, its programme for Housing the Arts in order to save provincial drama. Keynes intervened to take over the lease of the Georgian Theatre Royal, Bristol; although this action exceeded the powers granted to CEMA, it created the first nationally subsidized theatre in Britain. He was not apologetic about his quick and high-handed behaviour, writing in *The Times*:

> In these latter days, with its beauties undimmed, the oldest theatre we have was, like St Paul's, preserved by extraordinary chance from bombs and fire amidst surrounding desolation. But in this peculiar country so much luck was not enough in itself to save a national monument – even when it was of rare beauty, when it echoed the voices of Siddons, Kemble, Kean, Macready, Irving and Ellen Terry, and when it was still competent and useful to provide fresh delight to new multitudes ... [C.E.M.A.] has, I am thankful to say, an undefined independence, an anomalous constitution and no fixed rules, and is, therefore, able to do by inadvertence or indiscretion what obviously no one in his official senses would do on purpose ... Thus in an undisciplined moment we accidentally slipped into getting mixed up with a theatre building. Making the best of a bad job, we shall come clean tonight, without shirking publicity, in hope of public absolution. And, the precedent having been once created, it will, I hope, be officially improper not to repeat it ...

Keynes was prevented from creating a whole string of subsidized local theatres by opposition from the other members of the Council, chiefly Vaughan Williams, who 'did not want to see money diverted from the provision of concerts in places starved of music to the acquisition of buildings'. The Chairman's plan to lease theatres in Luton and Bedford was shelved, although the Lyric Theatre, Hammersmith, was directly managed for the summer season of 1944, putting on six productions including *Macbeth* and the Ballet Rambert. Keynes did also establish a relationship with the leading management in the West End of London, H. M. Tennent Limited, through which John Gielgud's *Macbeth* and other plays from the classic repertory were sponsored in order that Entertainments Duty could be avoided on tickets sold for the productions. This backing of a commercial rival angered Tyrone Guthrie at the Old Vic, who disliked Keynes, calling him a 'complete amateur' and a 'sucker for glamour'. Guthrie prevented Keynes from involving the Old Vic so closely with CEMA that it might become the nucleus of a future national theatre – a role which it seemed to assume through the marvellous Shakespearean productions in the last year of the war, acted and directed by Ralph Richardson and Laurence Olivier as well as by Guthrie himself.

Keynes was not alone in planning an organization which could influence a national culture after the war was over. One of the very few trained administrators in the general arts in a country of dedicated amateur efforts, Christopher Martin, ran the Arts Department at the experimental college at Dartington in Devon. He was working on the Nuffield College Social Reconstruction Survey and had the idea of setting up an enquiry into the part which the arts might play in Political and Economic Planning in peacetime. Supported by CEMA along with the Ministry of Reconstruction and of Education, three surveys were commissioned on the visual arts and music and drama. Later and significantly, a report on the educational and documentary film became part of the enquiry, while industrial design was included within the scope of the visual arts. Important social planners joined the surveys, chiefly Kenneth Clark and Dr Julian Huxley. But their intervention alarmed Mary Glasgow, who foresaw that the recommendations of this national arts enquiry might involve the future of CEMA and its post-war successor. 'She did everything she could to prejudice the Enquiry's work in the eyes of those to whom it was likely to be of interest in official circles,' an eye-witness and founder member of the future regional South-West Arts Association noted. 'Among the people that she tried to influence was Lord Keynes, her Chairman.'

Unfortunately, Christopher Martin died, not all the surveys were completed, and the delays in printing the various reports meant that their recommendations were often already a matter of history, certainly in the cases of the creation of the Arts Council of Great Britain and the Council of Industrial Design. Many of the papers submitted had already been passed on by Kenneth Clark to R. A. Butler and Lord Keynes, so that, as had happened with John Christie and his proposed National Council of Music, the ideas of others were adopted as well as discarded by Keynes. But there is no copyright on concepts. The worst rejection was the report of the documentary film makers, led by Paul Rotha, Basil Wright and Harry Watt. Their art, along with English literature, was considered at the time to be pre-eminent among all the nations of the world, and the fledgling British Film Institute did not have the funds to subsidize it. Their proposal that the government should sponsor large numbers of films through the Ministry of Information, which would also provide free distribution, led them into disaster and the end of their dominance over their field, once state sponsorship was to be savagely reduced in the late nineteen-forties.

Keynes was not interested in films or prose literature as two of the arts needing subsidy any more than he wanted competition in his vision of what the national culture should become. 'He felt the things he enjoyed everybody should enjoy,' said a later Chairman of the Scottish Arts Council, Sir Alan Peacock. 'He was almost obsessional about that as well as being very tetchy about the Scots. Give them their own money and let them stew in their own feeble juice was his opinion.' There Keynes was to initiate a policy of effective decentralization and much independence first to Scotland and then to Wales in the organization of their arts for their countries. While Scotland had already run its own affairs during the war, Welshmen had initially run and largely staffed CEMA itself. And for them, while they could manage and influence the arts of the nation, there was little reason to demand autonomy in their own back garden.

Keynes felt that he was absolutely necessary. Even at his weakest, he never had the strength to declare himself superfluous. He might wonder to Mary Glasgow whether he could go on or tell Samuel Courtauld that there was nothing he should like better than to escape, but he finally affirmed to R. A. Butler that he did not wish to retire as there was 'really no one else at the moment'. In his own mind, he was the single possible arbiter of British culture. It was the presumption of one of the great intellects of his age. Yet he did what he said. And probably he alone could have done it as well and unobtrusively as it was done. Previously, he had taken over the Theatre Royal at Bristol by a use of opportunity and a sleight of hand. Now he was to have the Arts Council created, as he was to say on the BBC, 'in a very English, informal, unostentatious way'. That was how state patronage of the arts would creep in. He loved to declare his secret stratagems once they had succeeded, so that everybody should know just how clever he was.

If Keynes was to create the machine of the Arts Council, Kenneth Clark was its grease. Even worse than thinking oneself essential as Keynes did was to be thought essential as Clark was – the primal committee man of the war. It was he who translated the practices and retrieved the opinions of one committee for another, both a catalyst and a gun dog. He admitted that he had filled in his war service chiefly by sitting on committees – the Mint Committee, the Post Office Advisory Committee, CEMA, the National Art Collection Fund, the Council of Industrial Design (for which he helped to draw up the charter), the National Gallery Concerts and his only 'worthwhile activity', the War Artists Committee. 'I suppose,' he wrote, 'I was a good committee member for the number of my committees continued to swell, so that for twenty years they took up more than half of my time. Committees often seem to be a complete waste of time; but the convention has grown up that decisions must have the backing of a committee.' And these decisions were most often influenced by Kenneth Clark.

He supported Keynes in what he was creating at the future Arts Council. He also wanted 'music-makers roaming the country' turned into national orchestras. He saw Keynes change CEMA within four years from a social service

> into a universal provider of the arts known by the title, which I am said to have invented, of the Arts Council. Keynes was every bit as clever and charming as he is reported to have been, but although I was on good terms with him, we never became friends. One reason may have been that by this time he was too tired and busy to make new friends. Another that, although I admired his brilliance, I thought he displayed it too unsparingly. I would not like to define the word arrogant, but at least I can say, in a well-worn phrase, that he never dimmed his headlights. Although a kind man, I have seen him humiliate people in a cruel way. However we owe him the Arts Council.

The chance to create a home for a national opera and ballet also concentrated the mind of Keynes wonderfully. The sublease of Mecca Cafés on the Royal Opera House in Drury Lane ended in December 1944 and the indefatigable Keynes set up a Covent Garden Committee with members who aided his work at CEMA: two of his Vice-Chairmen were Sir Kenneth Clark, who had been knighted, and Sir Stanley Marchant, along with Samuel Courtauld and Steuart Wilson and William Walton. A five-year lease was taken on the Opera House by the music publishing firm of Boosey & Hawkes, whose founders were also on the Covent Garden Committee. The Sadler's Wells Ballet Company was asked to become the resident ballet company in Drury Lane, while a new opera company would have to be built from scratch. As Keynes was the Chairman of the new Committee as well as of CEMA and as so many members of the board served on both organizations, it was understood that CEMA and its successor in peacetime would support Keynes's dream of creating a national ballet and opera, the fine arts closest to his heart.

Once again he fell foul of John Christie of Glyndebourne, who was trying to buy the freehold of the Royal Opera House, and also intended to create a national opera, supported by funds from the BBC, the film industry and the City of London. He felt that Keynes through Boosey & Hawkes had again snatched away his ideas for making England the postwar centre of WORLD/MUSIC/DRAMA/ARCHITECTURE/CULTURE/IDEALISM. He thought gargantuanly in terms of further opera houses in Manchester and Glasgow with a million pounds a year to be spent by the state on music alone. 'We are thwarted by the Treasury, by Keynes, and by CEMA', he wrote in a drafted letter to the new Chancellor of the Exchequer, Sir John Anderson. 'Keynes refuses to see me, and I believe that he is there, with the satisfaction of the Treasury, in order to keep me out.' Actually, when Keynes did create the Arts Council, Christie extended to him 'a very amiable, leafy and well-grown olive branch', asking for the four opera groups, Covent Garden, the Carl Rosa, Sadler's Wells and Glyndebourne, to collaborate mutually and be responsible to the new arts body.

What Christie could dream, Keynes could achieve. He knew that cultural politics was the art of the possible and the pragmatic, not of the visionary. Alone, he had the position and the bureaucratic skills to hone the various plans for reconstruction into a small sharp instrument that could unlock minimal funds from a government beggared by the world war. He proposed to set up a Royal Council of the Arts, but finding some disapproval on the CEMA board at such a monarchic title, he settled for 'The Arts Council of Great Britain', to be established by Royal Charter. He wanted a fixed annual grant of half a million pounds for five years. He saw the purposes of the new organization as:

a) to increase and widen the distribution of the audiences of the arts;

b) to improve the standard of execution in the arts;

c) to encourage and aid an adequate system of professional training.

He predicted that the direct management of theatres and the music tours of the wartime years would evolve into co-operation with local and educational authorities and with voluntary bodies. 'He foresaw the need to work with town planning authorities to acquire and adapt buildings for the arts as well as to erect new ones. In addition, the Council would foster the development of national opera, ballet, theatre and orchestras, raise standards of taste, and supervise the training and the way of life of professional artists. His proposals were a curious amalgam of Bloomsbury elitism and state provision on the Soviet model.' When Keynes was to broadcast after the creation of the Arts Council, he would plead for resources to repair and construct homes for the arts, pointing out that 'in Russia theatres and concert-halls are given a very high priority for building'.

Shortly after the war ended in Europe, Sir John Anderson announced on 12 June 1945 that the success of CEMA in creating a national audience had shown there would be a lasting need in peacetime for a body to encourage the knowledge, understanding and practice of the arts. This new body, the Arts Council of Great Britain, would be financed by and responsible to the Treasury, not to the Minister of Education, although R. A. Butler fought to keep it under the wing of his department. At a press conference on that same day and later in a national broadcast, Keynes paid tribute to CEMA for discovering an 'enormous public for serious and fine entertainment'. He even waxed lyrical over the devolution of the arts as well as the freedom of the individual creator from any state interference.

> We look forward to a time when the theatre and the concert-hall and the gallery will be a living element in everyone's upbringing, and regular attendance at the theatre and at concerts a part of organized education ... How satisfactory it would be if different parts of this country would again walk their several ways as they once did and learn to develop something different from their neighbours and characteristic of themselves. Nothing can be more damaging than the excessive prestige of metropolitan standards and fashions. Let every

part of Merry England be merry in its own way. Death to Hollywood! ... The artist walks where the breath of the spirit blows him. He cannot be told his direction; he does not know it himself. But he leads the rest of us into fresh pastures and teaches us to love and to enjoy what we often begin by rejecting, enlarging our sensibility and purifying our instincts. The task of an official body is not to teach or to censor, but to give courage, confidence and opportunity.

Criticized for his flag-waving cry, 'Death to Hollywood!', Keynes explained that he meant Hollywood was for Hollywood, while the British artist must feel free to be different. That was the special nature of the new arts body, which would not be a Ministry of Culture, but a very British nearly-autonomous institution, a compromise between private initiative and state support. And he took the credit for creating this hybrid himself through the secret corridors of power, while extolling a mighty purpose:

I do not believe it is yet realized what an important thing has happened. State patronage of the arts has crept in. It has happened in a very English, informal, unostentatious way – half baked if you like. A semi-independent body is provided with modest funds to stimulate, comfort and support any societies or bodies brought together on private or local initiative which are striving with serious purpose and a reasonable prospect of success to present for public enjoyment the arts of drama, music and painting. At last the public exchequer has recognized the support and encouragement of the civilizing arts of life as a part of their duty ... No one can yet say where the tides of the times will carry our new-found ship. The purpose of the Arts Council of Great Britain is to create an environment, to breed a spirit, to cultivate an opinion, to offer a stimulus to such purpose that the artist and the public can each sustain and live on the other in that union which has occasionally existed in the past at the great ages of a communal civilized life.

Keynes did not live to guide his brainchild born from the womb of war. He spent four months negotiating an American loan to rescue the British economy; he returned to suffer a tremor of the heart at a production by the Sadler's Wells Ballet Company of Tchaikovsky's *The Sleeping Beauty* at the Royal Opera House – his wife Lydia Lopokova had danced the leading role for Diaghilev's Russian Ballet. He died in his country house on Easter Sunday, 1946, after another exhausting trip to North America. He would have been the first Chairman of the Arts Council of Great Britain, which had not yet been instituted by Royal Charter, as he had wished. His legacy was extraordinary, for it contained not only his wishes, but his differences with Dr Thomas Jones, the principal founder of the embryo Arts Council in the war. Few legacies are without ambiguities. In a sense, the achievements of the mother body, CEMA, in the wise words of William Emrys Williams, 'substituted a demonstration for a discussion'. It had worked well by responding to emergencies by practical and immediate decisions. Those who laboured for it had learned on the job, the first group of amateurs trained by experience in war to run the first peacetime state organization for the arts.

The problems posed by the administration of CEMA and by the switch from the control of Jones to that of Keynes, these were not resolved – and they never would be in the future history of the Arts Council. Who led – the Treasury or the Council? Who controlled within the organization – the Chairman of the Council or the Secretary-General, the Chairmen of the Panels or the paid artistic Directors? What was the emphasis in policy – to maintain centres of excellence or to educate the people? Should only the professional arts be supported or should there be provision for community arts, for amateurs and folk artists and craftsmen? Should not the housing of the arts be a priority with the creation of a national grid of theatres and dance and opera houses? And should London rule? Or should the regions, particularly Scotland and Wales, be independent?

The war had created a British state organization for the arts in an 'informal, unostentatious way'. It worked well because it responded to a national need. The bequest of Jones and Keynes to the new Arts Council was not their disagreement about the Most rather than the Best. It was their practical demonstration that government could aid those arts created by voluntary bodies without turning these into instruments of propaganda, even in wartime. That is how state patronage of the arts crept into a national consciousness that was deeply suspicious of the very word 'culture' and doubted whether Britain had one at all. Under attack, however, the thought was that there might be a national culture worth defending. And although that culture might remain various and undefined, it was held to exist. Thus it could be supported and manipulated by common consent.

TWO

THE BEST AND THE MOST

The fact that culture has become, in some sense, a department of politics, should not obscure in our memory the fact that at other periods politics has been an activity pursued within a culture, and between representatives of different cultures.

T. S. Eliot in *Notes towards a Definition of Culture*, 1948

GEORGE THE SIXTH, by the Grace of God of Great Britain, Ireland and the British Dominions beyond the Seas King, Defender of the Faith, Emperor of India:

To all to whom these Presents shall come, Greeting:

WHEREAS it has been represented to Us by Our Chancellor of the Exchequer that for the purpose of developing a greater knowledge, understanding and practice of the fine arts exclusively, and in particular to increase the accessibility of the fine arts to the public throughout Our Realm, to improve the standard of execution of the fine arts and to advise and co-operate with Our Government Departments, local authorities and other bodies on any matters concerned directly or indirectly with those objects, and with a view to facilitating the holding of and dealing with any money provided by Parliament and any other property, real or personal, otherwise available for those objects, it is expedient that the unincorporated Institution formerly known as the Council for the Encouragement of Music and the Arts and now known as the Arts Council of Great Britain should be created a Body Corporate under the name of the Arts Council of Great Britain ...

So began the Royal Charter of the new Arts Council, drafted by

Lord Keynes. He had not been able to resolve his differences with Dr Thomas Jones, the pursuit of the best or the service of the most. Thus the preamble led with his preference, that the primary purpose of the Arts Council was 'developing a greater knowledge, understanding and practice of the fine arts exclusively'. Its secondary purpose in particular was 'to increase the accessibility of the fine arts to the public throughout Our Realm'; thirdly, 'to improve the standard of execution of the fine arts'; fourthly, 'to advise and co-operate with Our Government Departments, local authorities and other bodies on any matters concerned directly or indirectly with those objects'. So Keynes banished folk culture or community arts from the Council's range, which was restricted to the fine arts exclusively. The knowledge and understanding and *practice* of those fine arts was placed above their accessibility to the British public, although this preceded the improvement of the standard of execution of those fine arts. The final requirement of the new Council was co-operation with the Treasury and the Board of Education and the local authorities, for the body was to be autonomous, the first arbiter of a narrow band of cultural excellence, which should be available to the masses.

This ambivalent Royal Charter set a precedent. Keynes's priorities in the fine arts exclusively, especially in opera and ballet to the exclusion of prose literature and film and the community arts, would bias the practice of state giving until a revision of the charter nineteen years later. The deadhead of Bloomsbury values ruled the awards to living artists, and some of those original priorities would remain as part of the policy of the Arts Council for all the first fifty years of its existence: while it was true that some of the performing arts needed subsidy more than other arts, because they cost more to put on, the preferences were expressed. If the Council owed its founding to Keynes, it also felt compelled to execute his legacy.

Of course, Keynes was correct to limit the scope of the Council at first. There were few resources to be had for anyone or anything in the country, let alone for the fine arts. He had warned the new Labour government that it was badly in debt and overstretched because of the 'gay and successful fashion' of slopping out money to anyone who asked. Britain was overplaying its hand as a great power. A financial Dunkirk loomed unless the armies were quickly demobilized, the policing of the empire was reduced, exports rose and the United States continued to loan billions of dollars to pay for reconstruction. Keynes did secure an American loan to replace Lend-Lease, although it was denounced by a Conservative Member of Parliament as selling the British empire for a packet of cigarettes. And far more important than any of the arts was the institution of the welfare state with a national health service, social insurance and family allowances, and policies for full education and employment. There was also the problem of relocating more than five million people in the armed forces, let alone the reconstruction of a New Jerusalem. How much could be spared for the arts with all that to be done? And should the state interfere in them at all?

In fact, the term 'welfare state' at first had a pejorative use. It was held to mean a society in which people depended on the government for nearly everything from cradle to dole to grave. It implied an intrusive and dictatorial administration and the end of private initiative and freedom. It was not so. The measures taken by the Labour government to carry out the plans of the Beveridge Report were admirable in creating a more just and equitable society in Britain with fairer shares for all. But the methods by which the welfare state was created, with repressive controls and prying officials called 'snoopers', damned good intentions by pettifogging means. Most people were not prepared to put up with the authority of wartime in the presumed relaxation of the peace.

'It was a period of reconstruction – social, architectural, emotional,' the poet and editor Alan Ross wrote. 'A time when ex-officers looked for jobs and nobody wanted them. When houses needed rebuilding and licences to build were unobtainable. A time of shortages and the Black Market and soldiers who had learnt the technique of underground morality in Germany exploiting it in London. There were no homes for heroes, but a living wage, social security and a National Health Service. Public ambition took the place of private enterprise.' For another poet G. S. Fraser, 'people of all classes dressed and ate much alike, class barriers seemed blurred, life had a certain improvised, camping-out quality. But it lacked colour. There were no settled tendencies or leading reputations. People did not discuss politics or religion but personal relationships and the books they hoped to write.'

Writers and artists were split throughout the post-war years about the new Utopia which was promised and never came. The severe winter of 1947 was followed by a year of crises and became the nadir of those who still believed in a socialist future. Three months of Arctic weather led to electric power failures: the black-out returned to London's streets and the escalators no longer ran down to the tubes. Cold breakfasts had to be eaten by the light of candles, typists and children suffered from chilblains in unheated offices and schools. Two million people were made unemployed because factories closed, and even the renascent television system was shut down by the BBC to save power – the same action had been taken on the declaration of war. Floods followed the thaw of ice and the snow in the spring, so that the Wash spread over most of the reclaimed Fens. The conspiracy of the bad weather could make the unfortunate Labour government say, *Avec nous le déluge*.

For the writers who feared government control of the arts more than state benefits, post-war privations fulfilled their worst expectations. To the old guard who had been asked their views on reconstruction, such as John Cowper Powys and Gilbert Frankau, tyranny was suppressing free thought and free expression. 'People are putting up with regimentation at the present time,' Frankau had said in 1944, 'because they appreciate the necessity for it, but as soon as the war is over compulsion and restriction will have to go. Hang it all, we're fighting this war for freedom, and we're not going to be dictated to by a bunch of civil servants – or social dreamers – when the dictators of Germany and Italy have been eliminated.' At the opposite end of opinion stood the novelist and playwright J. B. Priestley, who hoped that the peace would achieve the society he had preached during the war. He did not want 'the survival of the slickest', but fair shares for all the people. Interestingly enough, he had opposed the idea of classes during the war, saying that the people were not masses and had superseded the class system. Those who thought themselves members of a class did not belong to the people. 'Go to the nearest A.R.P. post and you find there people, not members of classes. The bombs kill people, not classes. Nevertheless, they may blow classes clean away.'

Priestley foresaw that Britain would be living in crises for years after the war was over. Democratic industrial Britain had fought and won the war, and its reconstruction would act like the blowing-up of a dam, releasing untold energies and opportunities. And he absolutely approved of the creation of the Arts Council, although he wanted more funds for it and a change in its policy on drama, which was still more a social touring service rather than the encouragement of excellence.

Between high expectation and post-war disillusion, the Arts Council was given a hard and spare birth. Its budget was perhaps all that the beggarly times could afford, but it was lean to the point of emaciation. In 1945, the grant for the completed financial year was £175,000; over a half of this sum was spent on music, and a third on the theatre. The budget rose to £235,000 in the Council's first full year of operation. In that same period, as a critic of the new arts body noted, the British public spent nearly one hundred million pounds on dog racing and football pools, and half that sum on going to the cinema. Obviously, state expenditure on the arts was a drop in the ocean of popular expenditure on recreation. Yet it was there and its volume would increase, trickle by trickle.

In order to ensure Treasury funding from a Labour government, Keynes had emphasised that the phoenix Arts Council would grow out of the ashes of CEMA. This was emphasised in the first annual report of the new body:

> When Lord Keynes met the Press, on the day that the future was announced, he told them that no big changes would take place and that the Council's established purpose held good: to encourage the best British national arts, everywhere, and to do it as far as possible by supporting others rather than by setting up state-run enterprises. 'Co-operation with all, competition with none.' He added a remark which comes cheerfully from a Government-sponsored organization. 'The arts,' he said, 'owe no vow of obedience.' ... He spoke of art as something incalculable, not to be confined or measured by planning, but cherished and made available for all who wanted it. Above all, it was something to be enjoyed and 'the Arts Council was no schoolmaster'.

Yet because of Keynes and the need of immediate transfusion, the Arts Council became the major donor to a national opera and ballet. This was not a lesson, it was lifeblood. Covent Garden, the new home of the Sadler's Wells Ballet and future Opera Company engineered by Keynes, received £25,000, over a tenth of the national state budget for the arts. From his grave, without turning in it, he had chosen that priority. 'Other countries have had state opera houses for two hundred years,' Dame Ninette de Valois has said recently. 'Here it is naive. We owe all to Keynes, and still it was a half-hearted venture.' But with some subsidy better than none, the Sadler's Wells Ballet migrated *en masse* with Ninette de Valois, the choreographer and dancer Frederick Ashton, and the composer and conductor Constant Lambert to Covent Garden. There in February 1946, Margot Fonteyn and Robert Helpmann danced *The Sleeping Beauty* in the presence of the King and Queen. Ashton became such a friend of the Queen that he used to take tea with her weekly in Buckingham Palace: ten years later, the ballet company was designated the Royal Ballet and became a jewel in England's crown.

In Ninette de Valois' opinion, Lord Keynes and the Arts Council did everything for dance in Britain. There was no early government recognition and the Ballet was always the poor sister of the Opera at Covent Garden, although it had opened the Opera House there. She wanted a separate ballet company, as was usual in the European capitals, where Sadler's Wells toured at the end of the war. The dancers were sent out in khaki uniforms, officially to entertain troops, but they sneaked in civilians to their performances when they were fellow artists, particularly the Paris Opera Ballet. 'I was staggered by the conditions in the cities,' she remembered. 'Yet the state theatres had never closed down, even during the worst of our bombing raids.' The tour of the United States in 1946 actually earned hundreds of thousands of dollars as well as great acclaim and helped to subsidize the opera productions of that year. The poor sister brought home the bacon.

For if the war stimulated ballet in England by forcing it to use native talent, it diminished opera. With the one shining exception of Benjamin Britten's *Peter Grimes*, followed by *The Rape of Lucretia* with sets by John Piper, English opera seemed stagnant. Bereft of the foreign *divas* who had excelled before the war, no comparable voices had been trained to fill the gap. 'We are suffering from six years of isolation,' a leading critic complained: 'we have no standards, no models, not even a school of opera; our singers drift on to the stage with the minimum of general culture and musical taste.' Yet the opera did return to Covent Garden in December 1949 with a masque, Purcell's *The Fairy Queen*, conducted and arranged by Constant Lambert with superlative sets by Michael Ayrton, who based them on designs by Inigo Jones. Although it was a bold and insular statement of the worth of the British musical tradition, it showed a lack of confidence in available ability, relying as it did too heavily on Ashton's choreography for Fonteyn and Helpmann. The singing was not yet good enough.

If such efforts to encourage a national opera were still tentative, the new Arts Council was more certain in its sponsorship of classical music, with half its budget still committed to guarantees for orchestras and directly provided concerts. For the war had bred the largest and keenest audiences yet known for these. 'In their breeding,' one contemporary critic wrote, 'Sir Henry Wood's "Proms" had the greatest and most influential effect, if not the most refining one. Things went well for orchestral concerts even during the most harrowing period of aerial attacks on London and the large provincial cities. They continued well enough for a period after the war. But then a freezing depression set in.' Although orchestral musicians made good money playing film scores, their salvation became more and more dependent on state and provincial and festival patronage. The Local Government Act of 1948 would permit local authorities to spend money on the arts, and most of this tax money would be used to support orchestras such as the Hallé and the Liverpool Philharmonic and also music festivals. The Edinburgh and the Aldeburgh Festivals were founded; the new musical audiences of the war were now subsidized and encouraged by the Arts Council. And the biggest patron of them all, the BBC, used its Third Programme to provide good music for the ears of the nation, even contributing towards public performances by other orchestras than its own. Enlightened enough to aid all major orchestras from the London Philharmonic to the Hallé, the BBC added to its war reputation in the peace and continued as the great instructor of the nation in musical appreciation.

The new Arts Council recognized in its report the necessary change-over from war to peace, particularly in its Music Department. A large part of its work had been the bulk provision of factory and hostel concerts, and also those for the forces. As the annual reports recognized:

The war-time canteen concert, always a make-shift, is finding its natural conclusion – and showing its results. In many factories concerts will go on, but they will be full-length ones, held in proper conditions at times when they can be listened to at leisure, by choice and for an ordinary entrance charge. Already, numbers of factory music clubs have started with the purpose of running their own concerts, linking them with amateur activities and becoming self-supporting.

Keynes's wish to shift from the improvised and the amateur to the planned performances of the professionals was coming to pass.

The appointment on Keynes's death of Sir Ernest Pooley KCVO as Chairman of the Arts Council was a holding act rather than foresight. Pooley was a businessman and Warden of the Drapers' Company, although also Vice-Chairman of the Old Vic and Sadler's Wells. Sir Kenneth Clark had expected the job and was disappointed for a while in being supplanted by this 'man of bottom'. He saw, however, the reason for the appointment: there were few government resources to give. 'Having no interest in the arts, he [Pooley] could be relied on not to press their claims too strongly.' Clark himself soon resigned from being Chairman of the Art Panel and waited for his turn in office, rather relieved at not having on his hands 'the tricky juggling with human relationships' which he saw would be inevitable. And indeed, Pooley set about the slow undermining of the Secretary-General, Mary Glasgow, who was running the Arts Council still in the manner of a parade ground. And preparing to take her place was a new member of the Council and an old hand at the politics of the arts, William Emrys Williams, who had gone to the Army Bureau of Current Affairs. 'The Council owes a great deal to his original inspiration,' the annual report noted, 'and he is very welcome back again.' Little did Clark know that when he was to become Chairman of the Arts Council at last, Williams would already have the organization fully in his grasp.

The composition of the Council and of its three Panels was a list of the great and the good. Under the Chairman, Pooley, sat Lords Esher and Harlech, also Chairman of the Welsh Committee; Sir Kenneth Clark and Sir Stanley Marchant, also Chairman of the Music Panel; Sir Lewis Casson, Dr R. Vaughan Williams and Dr B. Ifor Evans, also Chairman of the Drama Panel; Mrs Cazalet Keir, Mrs Ayrton Gould, Ivor Brown and Dr O. H. Mavor (James Bridie), also Chairman of the Scottish Committee. The Music Panel, which included specialists in opera and dance, was graced among others by Myra Hess, Ninette de Valois, Benjamin Britten and Michael Tippett; the Drama Panel had the likes of Bronson Albery, Alec Clunes, Alistair Sim, Hugh Beaumont, Val Gielgud, Miles Malleson, Tyrone Guthrie, Beatrix Lehmann and Athene Seyler; while the Art Panel displayed the names of Samuel Courtauld and John Rothenstein along with Duncan Grant and Henry Moore. With such distinction on the board and on the panels, few would dare to question any decision in doling out the various bowls of gruel to the arts in the workhouse.

The change-over from war to peace affected the staff in the new Arts Council. Mary Endacott arrived as a secretary in 1946, ending as an executive officer forty years on. 'When I got there,' she said, 'there was a feeling that the best days were over. During the war, they were really at the coal-face. The change to a charter and government subsidy made them feel they had become a cash-box and had been cut off from the fun.' Although Mary Glasgow remained from the CEMA days, many of those who had been doing the hands-on work and organizing touring had left. This led for Mary Endacott 'to a *fin-de-siècle* feeling'.

The old wartime tradition continued, however, particularly under Michael MacOwan and his successor Llewellyn Rees, the Directors of Drama, with their Deputy and Associate Director Charles Landstone, and also under Steuart Wilson, the ineffable Director of Music, who had been to King's College at Cambridge with Keynes and sported the elegant and ribald manner of an Edwardian gentleman. In Mary Glasgow's opinion, he was a great man:

> A thing impossible to define but consisting in his case of immense vitality, a capacity to enjoy everything one hundred per cent, a full and generous heart, and the kind of individual personality that made him literally unique. He was also that rare thing, a very intelligent, and intellectual, artist ... He loved a fight and attracted disputes, and when he was at the Arts Council he went out of his way to express his opinions publicly and, if he thought necessary, with venom. The one thing he resented was having to hide behind the Council, which as a public servant he was expected to. He was a kind of St Sebastian,

standing up to receive all the arrows personally, and I remember him being rebuked by the Chairman for so doing.

His most notorious quarrel was with John Christie of Glyndebourne, who was 'so determined to be angry with the Arts Council that not much can be hoped for'. This was the opinion of Rudi Bing, the General Manager of the Sussex opera company, whom Christie wanted to serve in the same capacity with Sadler's Wells, if the two companies were to amalgamate at Covent Garden. In fact, Steuart Wilson was opposed to any such conjunction, in view of the old hostility between Christie and Lord Keynes. He flew into a passion at a musical lunch, when Christie told him to get his facts right. He wrote that, if he was called a liar, Christie was a fool. 'In a society of good manners it is considered "rude" to call a man a liar. The remedy was a duel which is now out of fashion; do you wish to revive it? Would that be "dignified enough for both of us"?' Christie never received a grant from the Arts Council, because both Keynes and Wilson believed – as Mary Glasgow wrote – 'that Glyndebourne was a rich man's pleasure, not eligible for support from public funds'. But he did get a guarantee of £3,000 for a Britten tour, after Glyndebourne had reopened: this was used against a box office disaster in the provinces.

Of such difficult and dedicated characters as Wilson, the servants of state funding for the arts were then made. They had developed their skills in a world war, and they had learnt on the job. In the theatre, these skills were particularly important in the peace. As the annual report recognized, the most striking and original feature of the war work was the touring,

> which was started to serve the factory hostels and finally spread to the small towns, some of which had been theatreless for twenty years ... Broadly speaking, the aim has been gradually to replace nationwide touring organized from headquarters by the provision of companies at self-contained centres. It has been necessary to plan this activity on different levels, according to the size of each town to be served, and to choose centres and a method of organizing them.

This work in small towns presented two very serious problems. The first was the lack of adequate halls or theatres. This implied a future where the Arts Council with increased funding would have to concern itself with housing or theatre management: Keynes had already bequeathed it the Theatre Royal at Bristol. The second difficulty was the lack of leading actors and actresses prepared to undertake such arduous work in peacetime. These wanted to work for Laurence Olivier and the Old Vic Company and H. M. Tennent Limited (Tennent Productions), which effectively controlled most of the leading London and some provincial venues. One in five of the theatres in the West End had been badly damaged or destroyed by the air raids, while a similar number were run down or closed. Entertainment tax at ten per cent of gross receipts made a profitable run difficult to achieve. The impresario Prince Littler had picked up for a song and a few pence many of the chief theatres and control over Tennent Productions ('The Group'), which owned three out of seven of the West End theatres still in business and oversaw seven out of ten of the main provincial touring theatres. This empire of drama might be well advised by Hugh 'Binkie' Beaumont, who was also on the Drama Panel of the Arts Council; but it held an undue power that bred resentment, particularly because of the dearth of exciting new British plays after the war and about it. There was nothing to compete against Anouilh's *Antigone* or the *Caligula* of Camus or the *Huis Clos* of Sartre. 'We are too close to the war,' a survey of British drama declared in 1947, 'and too fatigued by it to want to talk about it just now.'

The Old Vic at the New Theatre, however, with Laurence Olivier and Ralph Richardson put on another triumphant repertory season of revivals of classic plays, Shakespeare, Sophocles and Sheridan. Olivier showed his extraordinary mastery and versatility by playing the dashing Hotspur in *Henry IV, Part One* and the ancient Justice Shallow in *Part Two*, then contrasting the tragic Oedipus with the comic Puff in *The Critic*. Except in *Peer Gynt*, Richardson was content to play second fiddle to Olivier, although he was the first of the two to be knighted, beating Olivier to the honour by six months. The Old Vic finally linked with the National Theatre Committee, ensuring that it would eventually enshrine that long mirage; but it was too ambitious for its own good, expanding into two companies (one on tour and one in London), a repertory centre, an experimental studio, a drama school and a children's theatre. Despite some backing from the Arts Council, the organization was underfunded and overstretched, and nearly collapsed when the two stars left for long periods to make films and tour abroad. Although Olivier played King Lear with Alec Guinness as the Fool and Richardson played Cyrano de Bergerac with Margaret Leighton as Roxanne in another splendid season during the terrible winter of 1947, they were summarily dismissed as directors of the Old Vic two years later in a boardroom plot worthy of the Restoration drama of Webster and Ford. The coup was said to be necessary to provide for changes which would establish a National Theatre – an enabling act had passed in parliament. Divine or poetic justice saw that the plotters failed; Olivier would be recalled to set up the National Theatre in the rebuilt Old Vic in Waterloo Road, which would rise from its bombed debris to fulfil its destiny.

The replaying of classical verse drama encouraged the revival of modern verse drama. During the war, the Pilgrim Players had toured the country with three religious verse plays: Norman Nicholson's *The Old Man of the Mountains*, which retold the biblical story of Elijah in contemporary Cumbria; Ronald Duncan's *This Way to the Tomb* in the form of a masque and its antithesis with music by Benjamin Britten and dedicated to the Elizabethan Ben Jonson and to the Director of Television; and Anne Ridler's *The Shadow Factory*, which used the roar of drills as well as the chant of verses and canteen backchat to present a nativity play. After the war, the plays were restaged at the small Mercury Theatre, along with T. S. Eliot's pre-war flop *The Family Reunion*, which now proved a success. Backed by the Arts Council, Christopher Fry's *A Phoenix Too Frequent* was also mounted in a poet's workshop. Fry followed it with *The Lady's Not For Burning* with John Gielgud in the leading role. Its success and that of T. S. Eliot's *The Cocktail Party* seemed to herald the renaissance of British drama in modern verse with religious overtones: Olivier even commissioned Fry's *Venus Observed* for the St James's Theatre, where he was actor-manager in 1950. But all proved a false dawn, rated more highly than its worth by contemporary critics, who should have listened to Lavinia in *The Cocktail Party*: 'To say I always look my best can only mean the worst.' During the few years of their fashion, however, verse plays seemed the phoenix risen from the ashes of the war. As Christopher Hassall wrote in *The Masque*, both stage and broadcasting were reviving the original tradition of British drama, descended from the

Miracle Plays. 'The Third Programme is providing the poet with a sort of Mercury Theatre of the air ... Radio drama can affect the theatre. It has the power to convince its wide audience that poets can still write the *spoken* word, and what is worth hearing is probably worth seeing as well, whenever opportunity serves, and that the verse drama, on stage or air, is part of contemporary life.'

The sum allocated to drama would rise to more than £100,000 by the end of the decade, but it would remain not much more than a sixth of the Arts Council budget. It was enough, however, to provide grants and guarantees to some twenty-five theatre companies 'associated' with the Council, which signed agreements with them. Their objectives were similar, 'to spread the knowledge and appreciation of all that is best in the theatre, and thus to bring into being permanent educated audiences all over the country.' This policy led to the diminution of support to touring and educational groups of actors, although a few of these were to survive into the nineteen-fifties, including the Mercury Theatre. What happened was the rebirth of the provincial repertory theatres with the aim of providing the best for some of the most. In 1948 at the St James's Theatre and the following year at the Embassy Theatre, eight provincial repertory companies were brought to the metropolis by the Arts Council in order to present plays for a fortnight each. So the regions were pulled into the centre in a reverse flow of talent and instruction. And as Charles Landstone wrote, 'There can be no more stimulating experience for provincial repertory than to have a London shop window.'

Also at the end of the decade, a curious struggle for power and purpose was declared and won. Tennent Productions had formed a relationship with CEMA and Lord Keynes, an early commercial and state-funded partnership, by which classic productions were brought mainly to the metropolitan audience. Charles Landstone particularly disagreed. He had fought a nine-year battle over his wish to spend whatever money there was on enhancing repertory theatres. 'Lord Keynes firmly believed that, in its beginnings, the Arts Council needed the publicity of association with resplendent theatrical productions. Though his was a great and towering brain,' Landstone wrote, 'I put against his judgment the knowledge bred of theatrical experience. I say that he was wrong.' And so did Sir Ernest

Pooley at the end of 1950, at an expensive luncheon followed by a meeting at the new headquarters of the Arts Council in St James's Square, where Tennent Productions were solemnly cast out 'with bell, book and candle. Miss Glasgow, though not a member of the Executive, asked permission to say her piece. She went down fighting gamely for Lord Keynes and for his policy. She is an honest and courageous woman; she never swerved from what she believed to be her mission.'

This was the beginning of the end for Mary Glasgow and some of the inherited Keynesian policies. She was too resistant and combative by nature: as Kenneth Clark said of her, 'I have just seen Mary off to box someone's ears.' Pooley's favourite phrase was, 'I'm not such a fool as I look, you know.' Although he was in his seventies, Charles Landstone noted that when Pooley made up his mind, he had 'a way of bulldozing it through, against all apparent obstacles'. When Tennent Productions came back for a final meeting in the silk hands of Hugh 'Binkie' Beaumont, great concessions were offered, but none were accepted. Although the decision was said to be deferred, it was an irrevocable negative. And William Emrys Williams, knowing that Mary Glasgow was in the other camp, and yet coveting her position, declared that he had never felt so ashamed of any action in his life as his vote for the resolution to disassociate from Tennent Productions. 'Dear W. E.!' Landstone noted. 'Like all Welshmen, he allows his note of calculation to be influenced by his Celtic strain of sentimentalism.' The real question was, simply, whether the work Tennent Productions was performing was in line with the fundamental job of the Arts Council. It appeared not, in the last analysis.

In the future ousting of Mary Glasgow, a second issue came to the foreground. That was regionalism, which was anathema to Keynes with his wish for centralism. He was tetchy about the Arts Council in Scotland and reserved about the influence of the Welsh. He was equally opposed to what T. S. Eliot so strongly supported, diverse and regional cultures. He certainly did not believe in what Eliot believed by 1948, that culture in Britain was doomed:

We can assert with some confidence that our own period is one of decline; that the standards of culture are lower than they were fifty years ago; and that the evidences of this decline are visible in every department of human activity. I see no reason why the decay of culture should not proceed much further, and why we may not even anticipate a period, of some duration, of which it possible to say that it will have *no* culture.

Although *no* culture was predicted by Eliot, London was still the centrifuge of any national culture which might remain. If members of the metropolitan establishment mourned the demise of civilization through their own lack of will-power, the provinces seemed to offer a rebirth of various cultures. On his deathbed, George Orwell changed his mind about preserving languages like Welsh and Gaelic; he thought them worth supporting. The word 'regionalism' rose in importance as a literary label almost as meaningless as 'modernism'. It was said to mean that a conscious artistic tradition could be forged outside the metropolis in areas that were grouped together by history or language – Wales, Scotland, Ulster, the North, Celtic Cornwall. Keidrych Rhys had put the ideology strongly as editor of the briefly revived magazine *Wales*: 'The war has made the Welsh realize that they are a nation with a country, a people, a culture and a tradition *different* from England's to fight for. There is a new wave of national feeling among our people.' Although the resurgent *Welsh Review* pointed out the obvious fact that Wales was a divided country with a cleavage of language, tradition, outlook and wealth, the disparate could be united in 'regionalism'. *Scottish Art and Letters* agreed. A region's art had to be locally directed, not from London. 'Most of the world's best artistic work proves on examination to be, not cosmopolitan, however international its appeal, but racial and national in the most uncompromising way.' The revival of Gaelic poetry and the hybrid poetry of the 'Lallans Makars', Hugh MacDiarmid and William Soutar, seemed to herald a distinct language in an historical country.

'Regionalism', as critics pointed out, should have involved the use of the actual *living language* of a region, just as war poetry in its narrowest sense meant using the slang and experience of the armed forces. But if Gaelic or even Lallans were used, the audience became confined to that part of the region which spoke the rare language, ever diminishing under the influence of the universal language of English spread by the wireless and the schools. Better words for local cultural influence were 'provincialism' or 'parochialism'. For the Irish poet and critic Patrick Kavanagh, the provincial was still under the sway of the metropolis, while the parochial mentality was 'never in any doubt about the social and artistic validity of his parish'. All great civilizations were based on parochialism. The poet Norman Nicholson used 'provincial' as Kavanagh used 'parochial' in a talk on being provincial. Living in the place where he was born gave the artist the strength of sharing from childhood in 'the culture of his native region' – in Nicholson's case, Cumbria and the north of England. But he was not sanguine that the rising influence of 'provincialism' would last. 'Civilization is becoming more and more centred on the metropolis,' he wrote in the broadcasting magazine *The Listener* in 1954. 'We must expect that literature and art will continue to be mainly metropolitan.'

The provincials, indeed, could best take their revenge on the metropolis by improving its standards when they came there. The quality of the theatre company at Stratford-upon-Avon under Barry Jackson and then Anthony Quayle and Glen Byam Shaw was to develop into the Royal Shakespeare Company, which would be backed by the Arts Council and transfer its productions to London and set new standards of excellence. And from Cambridge, the exact and stimulating magazine, *Scrutiny*, edited by F. R. Leavis and his wife, would finally dethrone the post-war London editors with university graduate students trained in provincial puritanism and rigorous analysis. Leavis unceasingly attacked 'the currency values of Metropolitan literary tradition', Stephen Spender as a member of 'the Auden Gang', and the Arts and British Councils as mere expressions of 'the coterie spirit' of their founder, John Maynard Keynes. His analyses, applied by his disciples, would subject the old establishment to a new treatment.

Scrutiny itself was to die in 1953 soon after Cyril Connolly's *Horizon* and John Lehmann's *New Writing* which represented the effete and urban values despised by Leavis. But the message of the magazine had been passed on to its acolytes. Leavis did not despair of his achievements or of his generation as Connolly did. His young men would replace the older men, tired by the war and falling silent in the peace. The reasons for that silence were manifold. There was a sense of deflation, a disappointment that the millennium had not come, even if there was more social justice. Evil had not been destroyed by the war, but was still present in the individual. Alan Ross saw a premature literary middle age, V. S. Pritchett a post-war mental and physical exhaustion leading to a retreat into privacy:

> There is nothing as dead as a dead war and, as the pace quickens, the latest war kills the one before it quickly. One is ridiculous to be still alive and the best thing is to keep one's mouth shut. Looking at the war egotistically from a writer's point of view, it was a feverish dispersal and waste of one's life. It is often said that this was a good time when all private defences gave way, especially the defence of class differences, and that we all came together for once; and one hears regrets that after the war this revolution spent itself and that we went back to our traditional privacy. We did; though not to the old kind. I am not sure that to be so drowned in the mass was good for the act of writing ... The unconscious benefits may be deep; the anarchy of war is a release for a time: the ultimate effects are indirect.

Such pessimism was not the belief of the twelve Regional Offices, modelled on civil defence. They retained the qualities of improvisation and dash of war service. One of their members in the south-west, Peter Cox, considered himself as almost the first trained arts administrator in Britain when he succeeded Christopher Martin at the experimental Dartington Hall Arts Centre in South Devon. 'We had a very good regional office,' he said, supported by an extraordinary draper and Territorial Army Colonel called Morgan, who was a lover of music, while the Regional Office Director Cyril Wood had played God in *Outward Bound* – 'a role which suited him totally. He would blow-up things like a balloon ... extend things.' He brought together the little arts centres in places such as Plymouth into triennial co-operative conferences and performances and auctions. Although the Local Government Act of 1948 provided legal sanction to local support of the arts, the initial results were modest and disappointing. London still ruled, except in Wales and Scotland where exceptional personalities and provisions emerged.

Sir Wynn Wheldon already sat on the Arts Council and was friendly with two of its Welsh powers, Dr Jones and W. E. Williams. By the middle of February 1946, the headquarters in London wanted to appoint a high-powered officer for Wales. The choice fell on Wynn Wheldon's son, Huw, who was cynical and excited about the prospect, writing, 'Selling Battle Drill and Political Theory & so on is always pretty easy for me. Sermons and sales talk are pretty much the same thing, and I'd feel no hypocrisy in selling what I take the Council to supply.' His father resigned from the Welsh Committee to avoid any conflict of interest and Huw sought to apply the bifurcated policy of the Arts Council with minimal resources in Wales with its strong appetite for home-made arts. He had both to encourage the music and drama and poetry which flourished in the amateur societies scattered through the Welsh communities and also to produce works of major quality from industrial and Anglicized South Wales. As he told his father, his resources were about enough for the Isle of Anglesey, while the question of a metropolitan culture hardly surfaced, whatever Cardiff claimed as yet.

Huw Wheldon wanted the Welsh Council to think small and back many local activities but not too many choirs. His file on them was labelled BTBHO: 'Bawl Their Bloody Heads Off'. And he was instrumental in refusing the first major grant offered to the Celtic nation – £20,000 to set up a Welsh National Symphony Orchestra. In this he was supported by the Chairman, Wyn Griffith, who declared at a meeting in London in March 1947, in front of Mary Glasgow and Steuart Wilson, 'A full-scale orchestra in Wales would be so consistently expensive as to make the Council's policy top-heavy'. There was a hidden agenda, which was to establish a Welsh National Opera Company – this received the princely grant of £100 the following year. And by 1949, Wyn Griffith could assert that the Opera Company 'was possibly the most important music venture existing in Wales at the moment. The standard of the singers was good, but that of the orchestra was not equal to it'. And Huw Wheldon took the metropolitan and Keynesian line in stating that the Arts Council had imposed limits on itself, namely that it should concentrate on the professional side of the fine arts, the amateur field being provided for by other bodies. The only exception was the support given to the touring of Welsh-speaking plays, which had to rely on the best possible choice of local amateur actors, organized by the Council of Social Service.

With the Welsh influence at the London headquarters still predominant, Huw Wheldon was chosen for the plum job of all, to act as the Council's representative on the executive committee that would run the nationwide Festival of Britain, announced by the government to take place in 1951, a century after the Great Exhibition in Queen Victoria's reign. The new festival, indeed, was meant to be as utilitarian as a Victorian display with its concern for Industrial Design, Science and Technology along with the Arts. One of the first successes of the new Arts Council had been its backing of local festivals, particularly the one at Edinburgh, which did something to re-establish the capital of Scotland as the Athens of the North. In these dark days in the whole of Europe, the first Edinburgh International Festival of Music and Dance was a beacon and brought innumerable visitors from the continent to the Firth of Forth.

The annual report declared:

> The Edinburgh Festival is perhaps the supreme example of the Arts Council's support for the highest possible standards of performance as well as of works performed. At the other end of the scale are the extensive concert tours by maybe two or three musicians and the small touring theatre companies, ballet companies, and puppeteers which the Scottish Committee sends out each season to every part of Scotland. From the earliest days of its autonomy the Committee realized the necessity for spending a large proportion of its funds on the direct provision of the arts in the many small towns and villages which would be culturally starved without this material help. The emphasis here is on diffusion, but at the same time great care is taken to see that a high standard is maintained.

This was, indeed, the perfect marriage of the best and the most.

The success of the festival of Edinburgh was aggregated with the support of the established Festivals of Music and Drama at Canterbury and of Contemporary Music at Cheltenham, as well as aiding Benjamin Britten's operatic festival at Aldeburgh. These local and regional triumphs were a tonic for the planning of the nationwide festivals in Britain in 1951. They also provided an opportunity for Mary Glasgow to point out all that the Local Authorities could do under the new Local Government Act. Its most obvious effect was:

> to make it possible for theatrical enterprise to be subsidized from the rates. But there is more to it than that. The Entertainments Clause simplifies the whole complicated picture and gives to local authorities powers to do for drama and music what they have done during a century for painting and sculpture.

The old limitations were to the provision of concerts only in corporation buildings or parks; to the maintenance of bands only for out-of-door performances and of orchestras only by 'spas and public resorts', and to entertainments which involve no costumes or scenery, no performances 'in the nature of a variety entertainment'; and no films 'other than those illustrative of questions relating to health or disease.'

All these disappear and instead, quite simply, 'a local authority may do, or arrange for the doing of, or contribute towards the expenses of the doing of, anything necessary or expedient for any of the following purposes, that is to say:–

(a) the provision of an entertainment of any nature or of facilities for dancing;

(b) the provision of a theatre, concert hall, dance hall or other premises suitable for the giving of entertainments or the holding of dances;

(c) the maintenance of a band or orchestra;

(d) any purpose incidental to the matters aforesaid, including the provision, in connection with the giving of any entertainment or the holding of any dance, of refreshments or programmes and the advertising of any entertainment or dance.'

The authority may also spend up to the product of a sixpenny rate in doing these things.

The Act, however, did not mean that the Arts Council abrogated its responsibilities or wished to give up central planning. 'It is no failure of courtesy to Local Authorities in general,' Mary Glasgow wrote sternly in the *Municipal Review*, 'to say that few of them have yet had the experience necessary for the successful presentation of music and theatre. This is, after all, a highly specialized, professional affair.' The Arts Council was already working in a different way with a number of local authorities for the furtherance of the arts, as at the Edinburgh Festival and at the Netherton Arts Centre at Dudley in Worcestershire. A whole prefabricated arts centre was designed for instant use anywhere. The Council had a wide knowledge of the whole of this field, welcomed the co-operation of local authorities, and was 'only too ready to make the advice of its experts available to anyone who seeks to explore new territory'.

This eagerness of the centre to advise the regions was reciprocated by a certain local reserve and stinginess. Few local councils would add a half-penny to the rate for the arts, let alone a whole sixpence, and even if they did, they did not particularly want the big brother of the metropolis to tell them how to spend their money. So the prodding forward continued to come from London, and the Festival of Britain created a wonderful opportunity; its executive was Welsh, but the dynamo was focused on the Arts Council headquarters at 4 St James's Square in London. The image of this splendid building was enough to overwhelm the Directors of the Regional Offices scurrying up to town for approval of their major choices. The reserved and shy James McRobert, the Deputy Secretary-General and Finance Officer of the Council for its first twenty-six years, wrote a proud and proprietorial pamphlet about the building. It was started by the first Earl of St Albans in Jacobean times and completed in Georgian days with the great Louis Quinze room on the first floor remodelled on the advice of Lord Burlington. During the war, the house had been requisitioned by the Ministry of Works until it became in 1943 the headquarters of General de Gaulle's Free French Forces in London. To McRobert, the tenancy of such a superb town mansion by the Arts Council was a justification of its purpose in its Royal Charter:

> It is probably inevitable under modern conditions that the private patron should disappear. Few private persons at this time can rise to the Aristotelian virtue of magnificence, but in the hands of its new owners and tenants it may be hoped that No 4 St James's Square will not only be preserved as an example of 18th-century architecture, but will continue to be a centre for the enlightened patronage and encouragement of the arts.

These were still the years, as McRobert noted, when something of the original pioneering spirit of wartime still survived. 'Where no suitable outside body existed, officers of the Council were prepared to go out into the field and do it themselves.' This happened particularly in the field of visual arts because of the abiding influence of William Emrys Williams. He secured the transfer to the Art Department of the travelling 'Art for the People' exhibitions from the British Institute of Adult Education. He also arranged for some of the mansion in St James's Square to be used for art exhibitions and for the Council to acquire works of contemporary British art directly from the artists, the nucleus of what would prove a significant and illuminating collection. There were lesser efforts to go out into the field of music and theatre, McRobert also noticed, and then added with telling indirection, 'Literature had not yet emerged as an Arts Council subject.'

Ironically, the British Council had to encourage literature and criticism for the export of national culture overseas, while the state did next to nothing for its leading art at home. Public libraries and commercial publishers were meant to support authors. There were still paper shortages dating from the war while living conditions for writers were dreadful. England's books, as Osbert Sitwell pointed out, had done more to make it loved in the world than all its politicians or military victories. Books were food. 'You cannot live by bread alone: equally a man cannot live without books. If he does, he is a brute, not a man.' Slow strangulation by short supplies of material, the leading wartime novelist Henry Green wrote, was killing off the English author. 'And in fifty years' time, if all creative work is not stopped meanwhile by the increasing shortage of paper, it will be realized that men and women are writing as well now as they have ever done in this country.'

As for the young demobilized author, his position was nearly hopeless. If he wrote his war novel, he would find no publisher to accept it, because of the paper shortage. There was no way for him to earn a living by his pen except in writing catalogues or technical articles, or radio versions of the classics for the BBC, or pieces for American magazine editors, whose bounty was part of their general aid to the arts. The state would not and did not answer this pressing need because of Lord Keynes's restriction in the scope of the activities of the Arts Council. But the tours and the pamphlets organized by the British Council, not so constricted in its largesse, were a lifeline to many of the literary luminaries of the day. Even T. S. Eliot, so suspicious of state intervention in the arts, called the work of the British Council invaluable, 'but we must not come to accept as permanent or normal or healthy the conditions which make such direction necessary'.

The critical pamphlets, however, on the novel, poetry, prose literature and drama, on ballet, films, music and painting, entitled *Since 1939* and commissioned by the British Council, were arguably the definitive statements on the contemporary state of the arts of the nation and commemorated their survival in the most straitened of circumstances.

The wartime documentary and film had been the other significant British contributions to the arts of the world. These achievements were followed by a loss of concentration in the peace. Hollywood could again influence and entice. As the best of the producers and film-makers had noticed, the war had restored their faith in the national cinema. 'I have seen the British film industry at its best,' the leading producer Michael Balcon wrote in *Soho Centenary*, '– playing a useful role and playing it well – spreading the gospel of Britain and the British way of life throughout the free world – instructing our soldiers, sailors, airmen, war workers and civilians – educating our children.' What had been discovered was that films were really important, a power for good. Although British film production doubled in 1948, when 170 feature films were made, these were usually poor in resources although high in talent. The problem lay in the film strategy of the Labour government, which lurched from the inept to the inexpedient, and ended with the incompetent in pursuit of the ineffable.

The British cinema saw the failure of state aid for the arts. To staunch the outflow of seventy million dollars a year in rentals to America, the Chancellor of the Exchequer imposed a seventy-five per cent duty on imported films. Expecting this, Hollywood stopped sending films to Britain and relied on its stockpile of unreleased features already in the country to keep the dollars flowing back from British cinema circuits. J. Arthur Rank was then encouraged by the Board of Trade to fill the gaps on the screen with features made at home: he announced a new programme of forty-seven films, including Laurence Olivier's *Hamlet*. But the distribution of British films in the United States was imperilled and national audiences still wanted to see American movies. The government lifted the crippling duty, as long as the Americans exported only twenty-five per cent of their earnings in Britain and left the remainder here. This policy pulled the wooden horse inside the besieged walls of London. To spend their blocked currency, the American studios and distributors began to make co-productions in England, thus diluting and almost destroying the indigenous cinema created in the war. Direct state funding of films through five million pounds given to the new

National Film Finance Corporation and through the Eady Levy on box-office receipts was too little and too late, although some major British films were subsidized, including *The Third Man*, *The Wooden Horse* and *The Happiest Days of Your Life*. Within six years and with the best of intentions, the Labour government wrecked the renascent British film industry, forged in the war. Meddle and muddle, delayed action and quick reneging, indecisive measures and inadequate funding, made the socialist dream of a people's cinema in Britain as tawdry as tinsel when the fair has moved on. Lenin had said, 'For us, the most important of all the arts is the cinema.' Harold Wilson, the President of the Board of Trade, reduced the wartime art of the British cinema to unimportance.

The British Film Institute rather than the Arts Council had been charged with looking after that national art – a division that interfered with any possible strategy for the whole culture. Denis Forman, for ten years the Director of the Institute, had learned his trade through Keynes's Arts Theatre in Cambridge before the war. The Chairman of the Arts Council, Sir Ernest Pooley, was a family friend, 'a precise, old-fashioned City man who wanted to rule', very much the appointee as administrator of the more precise and puritanical Chancellor of the Exchequer, Sir Stafford Cripps. Pooley recognized that the art of the film was excluded from the Keynesian brief of the Arts Council and wanted Forman to pick it up and run with it as he could by statute at the British Film Institute. But Forman saw that the great documentary movement of John Grierson and Humphrey Jennings had shot its bolt with its socialist propaganda, now compromised by the start of the Cold War. 'The war had used their talents and they found it difficult to change gear.' The Film Institute was not given the means to support the last state-funded documentary group, the Crown Film Unit, when the government withdrew its funding at the beginning of the nineteen-fifties. So by definition and the withdrawal of finance, Britain's supreme wartime cinema was left to the tender mercies of the rising popular arts of broadcasting and television.

Another significant return to Keynesian imperatives occurred in 1948 when an Opera and Ballet Panel was split from the main Music Panel within the administration of the Arts Council, allowing for peace between the Council and Glyndebourne, and the return of

John Christie to advise on this new panel. A series of operas was commissioned for the Festival of Britain and, most significantly, pressure was put on the government so that the Ministry of Works acquired the lease of the Opera House at Covent Garden to form the basis of a national opera and ballet company. This progress was matched in the budgetary provisions; Pooley himself was happiest at the opera, as were the Secretaries of the Cabinet, who began a long tradition of serving both the government and the Covent Garden Opera Company. The Labour administration increased the grant to the Arts Council to nearly £600,000 for that year, more than three times the sum received at the inception of the council three years before. Of that figure, thirty per cent was given to opera and ballet and twenty-five per cent to music; more than half the total of the state grant was dispensed in those fields of the performing arts. Drama only received some fifteen per cent, and the visual arts six per cent; except for minor grants in Scotland and Wales, literature outside poetry and film received nothing. Lord Keynes's choices still seemed to rule the manger.

Reflecting on the initial organization of the Council twenty-five years later, its Deputy Secretary-General, Eric Walter White, considered that the place of the private patron was being taken over by the public body inevitably, despite the survival of Glyndebourne in particular as an individual opera house. The machinery, which owed so much to the prescience and wisdom of Lord Keynes, had proved on the whole very workable.

> On the one hand, it has the necessary degree of control to which any body expending public funds should be subjected. On the other hand, it has flexibility, for the day to day business can be executed without undue delays. Contact with the professional artists through the specialist Panels is not formal but based on close and genuine co-operation. Further, the Council has always had it in mind that its full-time professional Directors must be permitted a high degree of initiative and that in every possible way the hard definitions of bureaucratic policy should be avoided. As in the early days, the aim has been swift and positive action whenever possible, not to be afraid of inconsistency and to realise that in the arts a certain liveliness is preferable to a cold and egalitarian symmetry. It has been part of the faith of the Arts Council that these ends can only be achieved by considering each project as a separate venture and not by creating a

series of regulations which will have a routine application throughout the country.

As an inheritor of the old tradition, White insisted that the Arts
Council had always been anxious to avoid uniformity or to pay too
much attention to the metropolis. Keynes himself had embodied
these concepts in the Royal Charter, although low in his order of
preferences. State aid for the arts had come about without the
creation of a Ministry for the Heritage or of Culture. The staff of the
Council were not civil servants, but practical people paid from tax
money. The distinction between the civil service and the Council's
employees was important and significant. 'A body which is not part
of the formal machinery of government need not conform to official
regulations and is in practice free to distribute the money allocated
to it as it may decide, according to the particular needs of the time
and the emergencies that may arise and not according to rules
established by law and precedent.'

The sharp rise in state expenditure, particularly in the performing
arts, and the prospect of a large increase in the grant for the Festival
of Britain in 1951 were a fillip to the new state organization.
Although the funding of professional centres of excellence was
growing, and although the Chairman was diminishing the expenditure on the legacy of wartime – the support of amateur groups and
touring companies – the planning of the Festival of Britain allowed
Sir Ernest Pooley to redress the balance between the best and the
most, between superior performance and access to it. At a special
meeting at the Central Hall in Westminster in 1949, Pooley
addressed the representatives of most of the local authorities in
Britain. Within the couple of years before the Festival of Britain, the
work of the Arts Council would be intensified – and it was to be
given a special grant of £400,000 to activate matters, although the
government would spend eight million pounds in total. As always,
the Regional Officers were only too willing to help in that brilliant
summer to be. And here Pooley injected his normal note of
prudence. It would be a mistake to think that the arts must
necessarily be subsidized; a great number of concerts, plays and
exhibitions should be self-supporting. 'Financial support is frequently both unnecessary and undesirable. What is nearly always
necessary is professional guidance.' The wisest policy for 1951 was

to concentrate on what each particular town did best, to bring local and special capacities or traditions to the highest pitch of excellence. There was also a need to provide permanent housing for the arts. 'And do let us be gay,' Pooley entreated the municipal officers. 'Let us have entertainment.' He did not know quite what 'highbrow' exactly meant, but 'in so far as it is a term of reproach, let us not be highbrow. You can have high standards of performance without being highbrow. The arts can provide for those who appreciate them a fuller life and greater happiness. But don't submit to that depressing sense of superiority, and that "preciousness," too often affected by arts clubs and arts circles. Don't let us be afraid of being amused.'

In the first four years of its existence, the Arts Council developed from an embryo into a force within the arts. Although its mission was always a matter of discussion, so much of the limited resources for the best or the most, its practice was usually admirable. It was staffed by low-paid and dedicated people, who often had a practical knowledge of the arts which they were aiding. It had a discipline left over from the war years and also an incorruptibility that was the envy of similar fledgling European organizations. It did not intervene much; it aided the best that had already developed in the metropolis and the regions. Its members had their preferences and their differences, but their distinction gave their choices for funding an acceptable authority. The Arts Council did recognize that within the national culture, there were dozens of separate cultures at different levels within a common society. Because of the experience of the war, it was trying to help the best of these small cultures with the least of resources – imperfectly, perhaps, and with too little, but within Matthew Arnold's Aristotelian concept of culture:

> Not a having and a resting, but a growing and a becoming, is the character of perfection as culture conceives it.

THREE

FEW, BUT ROSES

Always take bribes, so long as you don't act on them.

John Maynard Keynes to Mary Glasgow,
when John Christie invited her to the
private box at Glyndebourne.

The Festival of Britain was the last child of wartime culture. It was dutiful and didactic with the eighteen million people who eventually visited the two thousand local events expecting to be educated as well as entertained. Both utilitarian and uplifting, it was a celebration of British achievements in science and technology and design as well as in the arts. Its saving grace was its sense of humour and widespread use of limited resources. 'One mistake we should *not* make,' wrote the Festival Director Gerald Barry, 'we should not fall into the error of supposing we were going to produce anything conclusive. In this sceptical age, the glorious assurance of the mid-Victorians would find no echo.'

This answer to the centenary of the Great Exhibition was not an expression of empire and might, but of experiment and gaiety. That was what Harold Nicolson discovered when he visited the festival on the South Bank, dominated by the largest hat in the world, the scalloped Dome of Discovery, and by the suspense of the elongated lozenge of the Skylon, which looked like Edward Lear's drawing of the Quangle-Wangle. Nicolson had expected the South Bank Exhibition to provide beauty and power, but not to be 'the very soul of wit ... conceived in a mood of high spirits'. It was full of brave laughter, which might be gallows-humour. Yet it was not a memorial chapel or a monument to past greatness, but a testament to present resilience, 'a clamorous assertion of our infinite gifts of adaptability and resource ... resonant with the cries and gurgles of the world to be. I returned to the drab outside encouraged and entranced.'

The festival was the tribute of the old guard to the new planners of post-war Britain. It heralded the renaissance of British architecture and design and provided official confirmation of the state patronage of the arts. Some fifty architects and a hundred designers were commissioned to fabricate something for the festival: their energies were released from adapting Nissen huts, hangars, pillboxes and prefabs into making buildings bare and strange. If their gods were Gropius and Le Corbusier, if their nineteen-thirties student realism would lead to the mistaken concrete towers and 'new brutalism' of the nineteen-fifties, their festival work showed a sense of play as well as function. 'It was a second rush of discovery,' the Georgian architectural expert John Summerson noted, 'and, as it seems now, the one which was to carry English architecture out of one age into another.' Evelyn Waugh may have ended his autobiographical war trilogy of novels by damning the festival, but *Unconditional Surrender* did recognize the fact that the event was a watershed between two periods:

> In 1951, to celebrate the opening of a happier decade, the government decreed a Festival. Monstrous constructions appeared on the south bank of the Thames, the foundation stone was solemnly laid for a National Theatre, but there was little popular exuberance among the straitened people and dollar-bearing tourists curtailed their visits and sped to the countries of the Continent where, however precarious their condition, they ordered things better.

As the playwright Michael Frayn declared, 'The Festival was a rainbow – a brilliant sign riding the tail of the storm and promising fairer weather. It marked the ending of the hungry 'forties, and the beginning of an altogether easier decade.' Restrictions were being lifted with the last gasp of the Labour government, ousted by Winston Churchill and the Conservatives in the election of 1951. As the agent of the playwright Joe Orton was made to say in Alan Bennett's *Prick Up Your Ears*, the festival was 'when it all came off the ration ... food, sex, life, everything'. So it seemed for the young.

At last, austerity was ending, coupons could be jettisoned, even if there was not much to buy nor much money to spend. Stephen Spender thought that the festival symbolized the disappointment of the Labour Party's social revolution 'with its look of cut-rate cheerfulness cast in concrete and beflagged'. Yet at the half-cock apotheosis of the Festival of Britain, a cheap celebration that cost only eight million pounds and built the Royal Festival Hall to replace the bombed Queen's Hall as a concert centre, there was cause for a joyful requiem on the burial of the war decade. Orchestras and poetry readings, dramatic performances and art exhibitions, fireworks and sports days, radio shows and the first lengthy television programme on an artist, Henry Moore, broadcast the festivities to two thousand cities, towns and villages in Britain. The festival was, as its originator Herbert Morrison declared, 'the people giving themselves a pat on the back'.

One architect at the festival, Basil Spence, who designed the Sea and Ships Pavilion, was to carry with him the style of the event into the new cathedral at Coventry, which was to rise from the rubble of the old blitzed place of worship. Other festival architects, particularly Maxwell Fry and Jane Drew, would translate their construction of the New Schools Pavilion into the things themselves. But sculptors and artists proved the more apt designers of the festival, particularly John Piper and the cartoonist Osbert Lancaster. Their bamboo Grand Vistas and Arcades and Rotundas and Tea Houses and other fantastical creations at upriver Battersea in the Festival Gardens were based on memories of the old London pleasure gardens of Cremorne, Ranelagh and Vauxhall – a style which Rayner Banham has called 'the English Picturesque'. In its role as patron and co-ordinator through Huw Wheldon, the Arts Council commissioned nearly fifty painters and half as many sculptors to grace the festival. Keith Vaughan did a nude Theseus mural for the Dome of Discovery, Michael Ayrton produced an exegesis on *The Elements as the Sources of Power*, Victor Pasmore wrought a ceramic mural for the Regatta Restaurant, and Feliks Topolski decorated a railway arch near the Transport Pavilion with a *Cavalcade of Commonwealth*. So short of funding was the Arts Council, and so short of material were the artists, that the Council presented large canvases to sixty artists for their free festival contributions to an art competition: five winners were awarded £500 apiece, including Lucian Freud for his *Interior near Paddington*. Ayrton, Minton, Vaughan, Colquhoun and MacBryde all failed to win a prize for their pictures. Colquhoun was bitter about his exclusion from the festival, which seemed to mark his decline. And Francis Bacon never appeared there at all.

The sculptors were better represented, with Lynn Chadwick creating an abstract bronze for the courtyard of the Regatta Restaurant and a hanging mobile at the summit of the viewing tower, Reg Butler a wrought-iron birdcage, Barbara Hepworth both an abstract sculpture and the monumental group on the podium of the Dome of Discovery, Frank Dobson his *London Pride* near the main entrance of the Royal Festival Hall, Jacob Epstein a gilded bronze by the Homes and Gardens Pavilion, while Henry Moore executed a bronze *Reclining Figure* for the South Bank Festival itself and a *Standing Figure* for the gardens at Battersea. The Arts Council chose to celebrate Moore as Britain's premier artist, opening London's first retrospective exhibition of his work at the Tate Gallery across the river on the north bank of the Thames. As the biographer of the sculptor wrote, 'The Festival of Britain was in its way a Festival of Moore.'

The contribution of the British cinema to the festival was an accurate prediction of its own suicide. Although it had reached its apogee during the war decade, its achievement was hardly represented. One whole exhibition was devoted to the British invention of television, still unseen in most homes at the time, while the Telecinema was specially designed for the showing of films and television and the latest innovations of the trade, stereophonic sound called 'the borderless screen', cable television, three-dimensional stereoscopic films, and a tribute to the documentary tradition of the island. Television would erode the cinema industry and stereophonics and stereoscopics would not save it. The documentary would desert the big screen in the picture palace for the small box by the fireside; and so it would diminish a great tradition into a common denominator. A film to commemorate the architect of the movie camera, William Friese-Greene, *The Magix Box* was made, but it failed dismally. Already television was inheriting the invention of the moving pictures.

The Arts Council did do something for literature at the festival, sponsoring eight touring exhibitions and one London show of books by a hundred contemporary authors. A few writers and poets lectured beside a rare book display at the Victoria and Albert Museum. One of them was Dylan Thomas, who packed the building for a reading of his verse. As well as the small subsidies to the poetry readers, the Arts Council announced an epic verse competition for poems of over three hundred lines in length and a Panel for Poetry, starring Richard Church, Christopher Hassall and C. Day Lewis, was created to furnish good advice. The list of judges was doughty and worthy of the old establishment – Sir Kenneth Clark, Lord David Cecil, Professor C. M. Bowra, T. S. Eliot's companion John Hayward, George 'Dadie' Rylands and Basil Willey. Fiercely attacked by *Scrutiny*, the judges, indeed, awarded the wrong prizes to the wrong poets. Of the eight who received awards, only Robert Conquest and one minor poet, the Cornishman Jack Clemo, ever achieved a later reputation. It was a swansong of the old literary guard, but a marker of the creation of state patronage for poetry. As John Hayward pointed out when he deplored the standard of the two thousand entries, this was practically the first public support for the art since the post of Poet Laureate had been created, and it coincided with the nadir of the publication of poetry by commercial firms. In principle, the festival competition set a precedent for subsidizing the Muse, although only Laurie Lee was asked to contribute directly to the exhibition, writing all the captions for the enigmatic *Pavilion of the Lion and Unicorn* including the wry statement, 'Democracy begins at home but doesn't stay there'.

For the drama, the festival provided promises without many performances, although the Arts Council did support most of the leading productions. An Old Vic season with seven classic plays in repertory, and the husband-and-wife double act of Laurence Olivier and Vivien Leigh alternating *Antony and Cleopatra* with *Caesar and Cleopatra* at the St James's Theatre, were the major London attractions, while Salisbury commissioned Ronald Duncan to write *Our Lady's Tumbler* for performance in the cathedral there, and Christopher Fry's religious drama, *A Sleep of Prisoners*, progressed from one country church to another, turning crypts into internment camps, and signalling the end of modern poetic drama as well as showing a play about prisoners of war.

PETER   Where are you going?

DAVID   If necessary
              To break our hearts. It's as well for the world.

PETER   There's enough breaking, God knows. We die,
              And the great cities come down like avalanches.

The Arts Council report deplored the fact that so few plays of contemporary merit had emerged for the festival, but it gave the drama prize in its competition to John Whiting for his *Saint's Day* as a new play of contemporary significance. And so it proved to be, although the only step towards the establishment of the long-awaited National Theatre was the laying of a foundation stone on the South Bank site. It was a stone that was to be moved so often before the National Theatre was to be built that the future Queen later suggested it should have been mounted on a trolley.

Music, opera and ballet were the chief beneficiaries of the festival. Orchestral and choral works were commissioned from Sir Arnold Bax and Sir Arthur Bliss and many other composers, the opera of *Billy Budd* from Benjamin Britten, and a new ballet from the ailing Constant Lambert for the Sadler's Wells at Covent Garden. Concerts and festivals of music were encouraged and subsidized across the nation. Alicia Markova and Anton Dolin's small ballet company was successful enough to establish itself as the Festival Ballet, providing another major company for dance. The Arts Council also supported a Wagner season at Covent Garden and set the precedent for the lion's share of state funding to go to the opera, the ballet and the symphony orchestras. To the most expensive arts would it be given, even if their audiences were sometimes small.

The importance of the Festival of Britain was that it happened at all, with its cut-rate cheerfulness. Correctly it celebrated a state of the arts that had flourished in the nineteen-forties in spite of the conditions of war and the austerity of peace. It was also the signal of the end of the dreams of the planners of reconstruction as well as a last fanfare for an original age. King George the Sixth should have been present at the closing ceremony of the festival when its flag was hauled down and the crowd sang 'Abide With Me' and 'Auld Lang Syne' and 'God Save the King', but he was already beginning a descent into dying. The new Conservative Minister of Works showed an indecent haste in having the Pavilions of the Festival dismantled, including the Dome of Discovery and the Skylon. Only the Festival Hall, the Telecinema, a café below Waterloo Bridge and few high verandas survived the demolition. A huge site of twenty-seven acres was cleared. It was to be the most enduring legacy of the festival, which had reclaimed the area from swampland and blitzed buildings. It would become in time, in a long time, the home of the South Bank complex, where at last various disciplines would be housed and subsidized and commingled, a *mélange* of concert halls and galleries, theatres and film auditoria and museums, a conglomeration of the arts that had huddled together with such stimulation and cross-pollination in central London during the previous decade.

The Arts Council was well pleased by the role it had played in organizing the Festival of Britain. For once, the retiring Chairman, Sir Ernest Pooley, blew the trumpet for himself and his organization. He had visited many of the large and small art festivals promoted by partnerships between local bodies and the Council, and he had found the experience an exhilarating one. In the Annual Report at the time of the Korean War he wrote:

> Dangers and anxieties continue to beset Great Britain, yet in this year of so many shadows, there has been more good art and music to be seen and heard in this country than ever before. The public has shown, in its hundreds of thousands, that it has a keen and growing appetite for the serious pleasures, and we must hope for an increasing recognition of that fact by Parliament and Local Authorities, in whom is now invested the major responsibility for the patronage of the arts.

The job of the Council had been to promote a London Season of the Arts in May and June of 1951: to foster arts festivals in twenty-two centres in England, Scotland and Wales, ranging from Bournemouth to Caerwys to Inverness; and to stimulate wherever possible the local effort and the special occasion in artistic endeavour. Nearly two hundred orchestral and choral works by British composers were performed during the London Season. Although the separate Opera and Ballet Panel was now absorbed again by the Music Panel, the opera programmes, arranged in consultation with the Council, at Covent Garden, Sadler's Wells and Glyndebourne, showed the three opera houses at their best, even if the Benjamin Britten season at the Lyric Theatre, Hammersmith, was not a financial success. Yet the national ballet and the Old Vic continued in their popularity and recognition. 'It can truly be claimed for the London Season of the Arts that the high reputation of our producers, actors and actresses was enhanced; that the galleries and the national collections were seen in their glory; and that London's bid to be recognized as the musical centre of the world was made more confidently than ever before.'

Yet the new festivals were the true triumphs. There was no doubt that they not only played a vital part in the Festival of Britain but were significant in their own right.

> York, for example, became for a fortnight a centre of intense brilliance which cannot be without a continuing effect on the cultural life of Yorkshire and the North generally. The magnificent clamour of Northern choirs singing with the great orchestras in the Minster, the performance of the York Mystery Plays, the exhibition of paintings from Yorkshire Houses, the beautifully refurbished Assembly Rooms, the concerts of chamber music, all took place in a city swept and garnished for a momentous occasion. Working to somewhat different ends, and drawing upon different sources, the same was true of Norwich and of Liverpool.

About a quarter of the extra Treasury grant to the Council of £400,000 for 1951 had gone to the provincial arts festivals by way of guarantees, and the whole operation was a notable illustration of the Council's preference for working with established independent organizations wherever possible. The wise administration of the festival societies released the forces of local effort and initiative. And even more important, following the permanent gift to the arts of the Royal Festival Hall in London, 'several other cities, notably York, Liverpool, Norwich, King's Lynn, Inverness and Stratford, showed much imagination in seizing the opportunity offered in 1951 to renovate and put to new uses buildings of great beauty. Many provincial museums and galleries were cleaned and painted, some were refurbished, but there was little sign of any resolute decision to remove the trash that has accumulated over the ages in so many of them.'

These strong words about provincial taste compared with central choice and direction were echoed in what the Arts Council thought that the Festival of Britain had done for its guiding body. There were two notable by-products. The first was the invaluable experience and information about the artistic resources of the country as a whole.

> The Council's Festival files now include much of the raw material for compiling a Domesday Book of British artistic endeavour, and consequently, if its funds increase, the Council may be able to aid the further development of local initiative. Secondly, the press and public alike vigorously supported the Festivals and the London Season; the amount of space and comment devoted to music, drama and the fine arts in the national and foreign press was very gratifying. The Festival of Britain as a whole was largely based on the proposition that the artist plays an important part in the life of the country ... If the Festival has roused great expectations it should be somebody's business to press for their realization, especially as most of the claimants for further aid have shown such readiness to bear their own share of the cost of disseminating the arts among the people of Britain.

This panegyric on the success and the national role of the Arts Council flowed from the sinuous pen of William Emrys Williams. For he had superseded Mary Glasgow as Secretary-General: her five years' contract was not renewed, to her surprise and disappointment. 'I did not leave the Arts Council willingly,' she wrote.

> Just why I was never told. I had adversaries, and supporters who wanted to stir things up on my behalf. There may have been a bit of intrigue – someone who wanted my job, a Chairman [Keynes's successor, Sir Ernest Pooley] who didn't like me, a number of people who were against anything to do with the Keynes era on principle, possibly the fact that I was a woman, although I must say I have never consciously suffered from this disability. Rightly or wrongly (I know I played my cards badly) I did not press for an explanation. I know no more now than I did then, and prefer to think I was simply not up to the demands of the developing responsibilities. That is what I tell people who ask. All I wish is that someone had had the courage to say so. I think I could have taken it, because it was true.

What was true was that William Emrys Williams did want her job and arranged to take it. Indeed, he appeared to stand for the opposition to Keynes, the principle of public education formulated in his 'Art for the People' touring shows of the nineteen-thirties and the wartime efforts of his mentor, Dr Thomas Jones, in CEMA. His long spell directing the Army Bureau of Current Affairs had made him into what Denis Forman called him, a crypto-socialist propaganda expert at committees, who was to become the effective boss at the Arts Council, 'a curt, big, bluff organizer like a football manager in the field of culture, socially oriented rather than arts oriented'. He was also a founding director and editor to Allen Lane and his cheap Penguin and Pelican series of educational books that brought paperback lessons to the nation, as well as being Radio Critic of the *Observer*. To one young Penguin editor, he seemed 'the very powerful *eminence rouge*' of the nineteen-fifties, as much an arbiter of social culture as he could be. And certainly his coming to office in 4 St James's Square transformed policy in an unexpected direction.

For Williams had been formed in wartime office politics, and he, like Keynes, believed in central control. As Michael Frayn had noticed of the Festival of Britain, it was 'the Britain of the radical middle classes – the do-gooders; the readers of the *New Statesman*, the *Guardian*, and the *Observer*; the signers of petitions; the backbone of the BBC'. The working classes were little more than 'the lovable human but essentially inert objects of benevolent administration'. Williams believed in providing that benevolent administration from London, not from the regions other than with lipservice, and he also espoused the Keynesian policy of supporting the best rather than the most. The annual report of the Arts Council, which praised its own importance and its contribution to the Festival of Britain, was drafted by Williams also to contain a declaration of future policy, particularly in the matter of direct management. The connection with Tennent Productions had been severed over a matter of avoiding entertainments tax on a production of a play by Tennessee Williams. The Secretary-General of the Council only wanted to retain a 'hands-on' role in his old favourite Art Department 'for the plain reason that no other body exists, or has ever existed, in this country to disseminate the visual arts on a national scale'. The Music Department still did a modest 'and, happily, declining business in direct provision'. In drama, experiments in direct management were continuing, but 'most of these ventures, even when they have won an artistic success, have proved unable to stand on their own two feet'. Failure in towns as diverse in size as Salisbury and Swansea had shown that they could not sustain a serious theatre of their own.

> These major experiments in direct management have been reinforced by a number of regional tours, for which the Council has been similarly responsible, but despite the popularity of these tours in some Regions, the writing on the wall proclaims decisively the conclusion that the Arts Council cannot afford to participate in further theatrical ventures of direct management unless there is a substantial local contribution in terms of both enthusiasm and finance.
>
> Except in the Art Department, 'direct management' is a declining motive in the Council's work, the bulk of which will continue to be devoted to maintaining, guiding and encouraging the activities of existing bodies and thus acting as an independent instrument of State patronage of the arts.

The Council gave little to numerous local arts centres, clubs and music societies, but then its cupboard was barely furnished. It was aware of the importance in its work of further education, but the training of cadres of volunteers in the proper management of 'such important – but perilous – ventures' would serve a better purpose than direct grants. The tradition of CEMA was over, 'that celebrated war-time improvisation which gaily embodied so many worthy if not wholly reconcilable motives'. That old and dissolved body had not been able to insist that high standards should be maintained during a world war. The present Arts Council was enjoined by its charter to elevate artistic performances and endeavour to spread the appreciation of the arts. But with little money and many claimants, was it not wiser to consolidate standards rather than pursue a policy of greater dispersal? Out of such slender means, how could the Arts Council do anything about 'theatreless towns', when even the most progressive Local Authorities did so little to help?

Williams recorded his opinions in the Annual Report of the Arts Council:

Might it not be better to accept the realistic fact that the living theatre of good quality cannot be widely accessible and to concentrate our resources upon establishing a few more shrines like Stratford and the Bristol Old Vic? Is it good policy to encourage small, ill-equipped expeditions to set out into the wilderness and present meagre productions in village fit-ups? These are the questions to which the Council must address itself earnestly and dispassionately in the immediate future. In reconsidering the exhortation of its Charter to 'Raise and Spread' the Council may decide for the time being, to emphasize the first more than the second word, and to devote itself to the support of two or three exemplary theatres which might re-affirm the supremacy of standards in our national theatre. As the Governors of the Old Vic have recently expressed a similar motive in their policy, the Council may well count upon experienced allies in its further projects.

High standards can be built only on a limited scale. The motto which Meleager wrote to be carved over the door of a patrician nursery might be one for the Arts Council to follow in deciding what to support during the next few straitened years – 'Few, but roses' – including, of course, regional roses.

This was a conversion in the road to Megalopolis. If power does not corrupt, it has its subtle persuasions. For Williams to compare the Arts Council to a patrician nursery was to accept his own role as the aristocratic nanny of the people, while throwing out a few sops to the regions. He was aided, however, in his policies by the arrival of his old confrère on the war committees, Sir Kenneth Clark, to become the new Chairman of the Council. Mary Glasgow always thought that posterity would not say the right things about Clark, because he was two people, each fighting the other:

He is intellectually a giant, with a well-stocked mind and administrative powers to match. He ought to have taken a leading part in the affairs of the country at large, let alone the cultural ones. Yet whenever he has approached the centre of things, as when, early in the war, he went to the Ministry of Information, he has shied away, saying to himself something like, 'All this is dust and ashes; I must devote myself to the things of the mind.' Then he would retire, to think, write and contemplate; until the pendulum swung back and he would say: 'What am I doing in a vacuum? I must go back into the arena.' I think he has suffered all his life from not being himself a creative artist, knowing so much, while never producing original work of painting or sculpture.

It was an accurate and devastating picture. When Sir Kenneth Clark arrived as Chairman of the Arts Council, he found that he was completely run by William Emrys Williams, who had already inspired his staff with his vision and his presence. Mary Glasgow had already been eliminated by Sir Ernest Pooley for ruling him with her rod of iron, but Clark could not rid himself of Williams and his velvet whip. The Secretary-General reigned, while Clark presided. As Williams once informed his Chairman: 'I am the Captain of this ship. You are the Admiral. I pipe you aboard with full honours. But I run the ship, you see.'

Although he may have become wiser after the event, Clark confessed as much in his memoirs, writing:

> I cannot say that the Arts Council prospered under my chairman-ship, or that I enjoyed my spell of office. I sat at an empty desk in a large, dignified room (formerly Lord Astor's library), and once or twice a week had a short interview with the Secretary-General. Almost every day the directors of the departments burst into my room with grievances, and I gave them glasses of sherry. I was not allowed a secretary; the Secretary-General said that his own secretary would bring me in such letters as it was appropriate for me to see, together with his answers. I had not realized that a chairman's duties were so restricted, and apparently said so, as Sir William Haley was asked to invite me to luncheon in order to explain my duties. He said that the best chairman the BBC ever had, J. I. Whitley, had looked in on only two afternoons a week. In other words, a chairman's duty was to whitewash the decisions of his administrative officials when they were discussed by the Board. This is the bureaucrat's dream ... It did not suit me at all.

As the supreme committeeman of his generation, however, Clark did enjoy the Council meetings, as arts in themselves:

> If one must sit on a committee it is preferable to sit in the Chair, because one can not only expedite business but can observe the characteristics of members of one's Board and try to draw them into the discussions, sometimes all too successfully. The Board of the Arts Council was well chosen, and some of its members, especially the Welsh members, left over from the old Tom Jones days, were very helpful to me. But our activities were hindered by a chronic shortage of money.

The main claimants, Covent Garden and Sadler's Wells and the leading orchestras used up the lion's share of the grant. 'As a result our meetings often had that negative and despondent character which has now spread to every branch of a bankrupt country.' Yet even if there had been more money, Clark found state patronage of the arts a baffling problem:

> From the consumer's point of view it is moderately easy. Stage companies and orchestras can be subsidized, and a good many local efforts, especially in the theatre, deserve support. It is easy to run exhibitions, and arguable that the Arts Council should have its own Collection as a supplement to that of the Tate. It can also support young singers or musicians, arranging for them to travel and to train. This is probably the part of its work which is least in dispute. But when one passes from the executant to the creator I doubt very much if there is anything the state can do. We know that certain writers, composers and artists go through bad times, but an Arts Council must not become a charitable organization.

Sidelined by his Secretary-General and crippled by such urbane and antique views on state patronage, Sir Kenneth Clark was hardly the right man in the right place as Chairman of the Arts Council. He once confessed to his admirable learning and elegiac pessimism in the statement, 'The incomprehensibility of our new cosmos seems to me, ultimately, to be the reason for the chaos of modern art. I know next to nothing about science, but I've spent my life in trying to learn about art, and I am completely baffled by what is taking place today.' He was saved from what he called 'the dismal obstructions of the Arts Council' by being given the extraordinary appointment of Chairman of the new Independent Television Authority, although he was booed in the Atheneum for accepting the job. Yet he took to it as a duck to water rather than to the Arts Council, which he had largely left to William Emrys Williams to run for him. Engagingly, he recorded in his memoirs that he could not remember a single thing he did in the Council, while he remembered every event at the Independent Television Authority so clearly that there was enough material for a short book. He was reminded of the famous passage in Pater's *Renaissance*, in which he wrote of hundreds of trivial impressions and tiny incidents, and then he claimed that 'when we have apprehended them we have achieved success in life'. Clark apprehended the details of the Independent Television Authority and forgot the strategy of the Arts Council, which proceeded correctly without his memory. It was perhaps appropriate for the future author and presenter of the superior television series, *Civilization*.

Yet Clark was liked by the staff at the Council, who knew that he was being put on the shelf during his seven years as Chairman, for he had already accepted that the Conservative government was hardly aware of the Council's existence and all work there was on a low key. Joanna Drew, then a junior member of the Art Department, was impressed that Clark always appeared promptly each day. He did not like the Secretary-General's assiduous paring down of his duties, saying, 'I like to be bothered'. When exhibitions were hung in St James's Square, he would wander through them giving impromptu lectures on art to a surprised and passing audience. He was fulfilling exactly what William Emrys Williams wanted from the original teaching 'Art for the People' exhibitions, but in the 'patrician nursery' that the Secretary-General had elected and now managed.

The Arts Council which was directed by William Emrys Williams in the nineteen-fifties was remade in his assiduous image. In a sense, he was to be the Welsh Pericles of a Spartan Athens. In the annual reports of the Arts Council for the early nineteen-fifties, he blew the first clarion blast for enhanced governmental giving in the realm. 'The Arts Council of Great Britain is the instrument of State patronage,' he declared. He thought it appropriate to consider some of the principles upon which that patronage was founded.

> Until relatively recent times the arts were largely nourished by private benefactors: by men of wealth who gained aesthetic and social satisfaction from supporting painters, sculptors, poets and musicians. In the USA, where the redistribution of wealth has not been so drastically carried out as it has here, the arts are still largely sustained by the munificence of private patronage. But in Britain, where the redistribution of wealth has become an axiom of government, the wealthy patrons are dying out ... They are fewer and poorer every year; and if the arts are to survive in the egalitarian State, some form or forms of collective patronage must assume the obligations formerly sustained by the private benefactor. Those who are inclined to fancy that collective patronage is a revolutionary principle should be reminded that the role of the State or City as benefactor of the arts was familiar enough in every ancient civilization, and it is right that

the contemporary successors of those institutions should maintain the tradition of collective patronage.

The question was whether the arts needed any subsidy at all. Grand Opera had to have a huge grant, otherwise it could never make ends meet; 'utility opera' was simply not good enough. Great collections of masterpieces of art could never pay their way, even when the public was charged for admission. A grant for a national theatre was also a must:

> A National Theatre too, even in embryo, is another kind of art which requires patronage. Such an establishment deliberately accepts risks beyond those of the commercial theatre. It must provide, for example, a repertory of the classics in which some plays are bound to draw the public more than others. Unlike the commercial theatre, again, it must try to make 'stars' rather than exploit the made ones; and it should, moreover, apply some of its resources to providing an apprenticeship for the playwrights and producers of tomorrow. A National Theatre must preserve the heritage of traditional drama and, at the same time, provide the opportunity for experiment ... No permanent Symphony Orchestra can exist on the takings at the door, even when the halls in which it plays are consistently full, and even if it accepts dates dangerously close to that maximum at which its playing begins to deteriorate through the sheer fatigue of rehearsal, travel and performance.

The cost of spreading the arts was becoming increasingly uneconomic and subsidies from the state were not more generous. The largest concentration of the arts must inevitably be built up at the big centres of population and the proper place for the best national assemblies of the arts was the capital city of the country. The Arts Council annual report declared:

> The diffusion of the arts must be limited by many factors – by the high cost of mobile operations, by the dearth of proper theatres, galleries and concert halls, and by the availability of good pictures, good orchestras, and good actors. Moreover, there exists in the B.B.C. a most potent agency of diffusion which brings many of the arts in their highest forms to the fireside of every cottage. Yet taking all these considerations into account, the citizen of the Welfare State is entitled to expect the arts to be distributed as widely as is reasonably possible.

Of course, most people in Britain thought that those who wanted a local orchestra should pay for it. Why tax all Britain for

Aldeburgh? That type of rugged individual, however, was increasingly confuted in social legislation and habits:

> We accept, for instance, a collective financial responsibility for that minority of the citizens which enjoys higher education. The minorities, too, who frequent the Public Library or the Municipal Baths or the Playing Fields have their pleasures paid for, in whole or in part, out of the rates. The devotees of the Third Programme depend largely on the enforced bounty of the millions who listen only to the Light. There are abundant precedents to justify the public patronage of the arts for the benefit of the considerable minority who have cultivated a taste for serious pleasures.

This philosophy of elite cultures was an extraordinary conversion in Williams from the tribune of the people to the emperor of national taste. He declared as much in the annual reports which he drafted:

> The Arts Council regards itself not merely as the paymaster of the arts but in some sense the national trustee for the arts. While respecting the rights of self-government of all the bodies it supports, the Council devotes much time and attention to the policy of these bodies. It gives guidance, at one end of the scale, in advising an obscure Music Society on a programme of work suitable for its means and its membership. And at the other end of the scale, it conducts a patient and independent scrutiny of the artistic and economic condition of Grand Opera. Its duties, as laid down in its Royal Charter, are not only those of administering whatever funds Parliament may approve for nourishing the arts, but also the more anxious ones of devising the ways and means whereby the arts may elevate their standards and diffuse their influence.

There was no question that William Emrys Williams now saw himself as the guardian of the various British cultures. Historically, he was correct. Private patrons were a dying breed: there were few Glyndebournes still in existence. The Arts Council was now the chief national giver. But the certainty of the members of his generation, who believed that they had run and won the world war almost without the help of the armed forces, never made him question himself. Were these efforts to influence the cultures of Britain actually effective? Did they not rumble on without investigation? Would these meagre resources well applied make for a good change?

To Williams, who did not doubt himself, the fact was that things were stirring and the principle of collective patronage had, to paraphrase Lord Keynes, become accepted 'in a piece-meal, almost absent-minded, fashion ... The notion of public responsibility for the arts has been growing a long time in this country, like the grain of mustard seed.' Already in several nations, the problem had been entrusted to a Ministry of Fine Arts or Culture. But in Britain, a national lack of logic was balanced by a native good sense, so an empirical solution was sought. The principle of free trade in the arts was fostered by the numerous voluntary bodies which had been created to diffuse and improve the practice of music or dance in the professional or amateur fields: the National Federation of Music Societies, the British Drama League, the English Folk Dance and Song Society, the National Eisteddfod of Wales, the Rural Music Schools Association, the various Philharmonic Societies – to name but a few. By the modest subscriptions of their members, aided sometimes by grants from the Arts Council, such bodies as these had built up a substantial patronage for the arts at many levels.

Yet valuable and essential as such bodies were, they were 'pigmies compared with that Colossus of collective consumption, the BBC, which represented yet another kind of modern patronage ...' Although unique in function and management, the BBC did accept 'free trade' in the arts. It was obviously the major consumer of music and drama in contemporary Britain, as well as the widest diffuser. 'And when television can match the technical resources of sound radio it may, similarly, become the biggest consumer of the visual arts ... There is a new Aesop's Fable to be written on the unthriftiness which permits the wireless to devour the arts without replenishing the supply!'

This marvellous prescience as to the great diffusers of the age, the media which could best carry out the job of spreading the arts to the masses, did not lead the Arts Council to a coalition with the broadcasters. Perhaps these were the shackles of Lord Keynes's limited vision, perhaps there was too much parochialism at the BBC, which wanted to run its own show and preach its own mission. Williams could recognize the revolution in communications, but he could not get the Arts Council to participate. He was conscious, indeed, that the very existence of the Council was open to the criticism that it put too much power into too few hands. 'If State patronage were dominated by a small permanent Sanhedrin the dangers of officialdom would, indeed, be acute.' But the number of persons who had joined in moulding the Arts Council's policies since its creation was several hundred, while currently one hundred and fifteen advisers or staff worked under the guidance of the Secretary-General. There was also, as in ancient Athens, a system of retirement by rotation, which sought to widen counsel and experience. 'It is doubtful whether any of the illustrious private patrons of the past sought such a volume and variety of advice in planning their benefactions!' Even so, safety from a cultural oligarchy did not lie in numbers. The fundamental check was the Council's own conscious determination not to dictate policies or impose fashions in the arts it tried to assist:

> This respect for self-government in the arts is the main bulwark against *L'Art Officiel*. Under this kind of State patronage no restrictions are put upon the individual artist. If Sir John Barbirolli were for any reason dissatisfied with working with the Hallé Orchestra – which he is not – he could transfer himself to Covent Garden, despite the fact that the Arts Council is, so to speak, the principal 'shareholder' in both bodies. He could do it, in fact, just as easily as one of his forebears, dissatisfied with Lorenzo in Florence, might move to Ludovico in Milan. If, on the other hand, he were employed by a Ministry of Fine Arts he would be 'directed' to his post. This policy of artistic freedom is, and must remain, paramount. The health of the arts depends on their being governed by numerous different groups which, in turn, are free to select the individual composers, conductors, soloists, dramatists and actors of their own choice. It is not the business of the State, working through the Arts Council, to furnish a matrix of artistic performances for a receptive and captive audience. The arts flourish best when they are self-governing, and self-government is not incompatible with the acceptance of State subsidies. Our entire educational system is a major vindication of that principle, and the administration of the Arts Council is a lesser instance of the same democratic axiom.

Here Williams was referring to a parallel system, by which the University Grants Committee gave state aid to the various universities without any interference in their administration. Because of his own preferences, however, he had retained *L'Art Officiel* in the Art Department with its arbitrage of national exhibitions and purchases for the collection of the Council. Yet even in the heyday of private patronage, there could hardly have been a wider range or more catholic choice of artists and exhibitions, such as:

> Turner, Ravenna Mosaics, Hogarth, British Watercolours, French Drawings, Gainsborough, 19th-century French Paintings, Blake, Rembrandt Etchings, Chinese Ceramics, Degas, Epstein, Fernand Léger, British Paintings, Edvard Munch, Henry Moore, Toulouse Lautrec, Ethel Walker, Gwen John, Frances Hodgkins, Sculpture by Matisse, Picasso in Provence, Graham Sutherland, Mexican Art, Fuseli, Rowlandson, Hiroshige, William Dobson, Berthe Morisot, 20th-century Masterpieces, Modern Italian Art, and selections from the Royal Academy Summer Exhibitions.

The policy of the Arts Council was emerging from its empirical stage. It had already learned much by the salutary processes of trial and error and still had much to learn about fostering the arts. An instrument of patronage must identify needs 'rather than passively accept their reputed existence. It can spend a fortune dishing out small subsidies to supplicants and yet not build anything of enduring value. If it surrenders the initiative, as some of the great American charitable trusts did early in this century, it becomes a mere debt-paying indulgent maiden aunt.' Yet the Arts Council had the double duty of diffusing the arts as well as stimulating new expressions in them; but if an emphasis must be placed somewhere in the motto of 'Raise and Spread', it seemed 'wiser and more realistic to concentrate on Raise'.

So Williams articulated a policy for the Arts Council with considerable success, supported by the prestige of the members of the Panels, who now included under the principle of rotation such luminaries in art as Sir Jacob Epstein and John Piper, and in drama Peggy Ashcroft, John Gielgud, Michael Redgrave and Flora Robson. They supported another important policy suggested by Williams – Housing the Arts – and the foundation of a network of repertory companies. A Theatre Grid for the provinces was planned in the annual report of 1953–4. It was less than fifty years since Miss Horniman had created at Manchester the first repertory theatre in Britain. Nearly a hundred of them still survived, varying widely in quality and purpose, and beginning to wither along with the music halls and the touring theatres as cinemas, wireless and television ate into their audiences. 'They are not strictly "repertory" at all,' Williams stressed, 'for they have no anthology of productions on which to ring the changes throughout the season.' The way out was to form a pattern of association among eight to a dozen theatres in the larger towns with mobile productions. For there was a limited audience for any given opera, ballet or classical play; and the programme had to be frequently altered if attendances were to be maintained. 'Morton's Fork is a familiar phenomenon in administering the arts.'

Outstanding guest producers and actors might be willing to work on such a countrywide circuit, which would also be an incentive to playwrights. It would also be a nursery and proving-ground for the talent upon which a South Bank National Theatre would have to depend. 'The English theatre today is, nearly everywhere, run on a lottery basis, and most of the men and women who work in it have no sort of security. A circuit of this kind would provide a unity of purpose, and a system of association, on the basis of which stability and morale might be recovered.' A plan of this kind had to begin on the ground and not in the air. Therefore, it had to be based on existing repertory companies of quality, not on buildings, which should include the Bristol Old Vic, the Birmingham Repertory Theatre, the Liverpool Playhouse, the Sheffield Playhouse, the Midland Theatre Company at Coventry, the Nottingham Playhouse and the Glasgow Citizens Theatre. These could provide the elements for a mobile embryo National Theatre in the provinces in a Theatre Grid.

By the following year, the emphasis of the annual report switched to Housing the Arts rather than rotating repertory theatre productions. It had been twenty-five years since a new theatre had been put up in London. During that time, only two new small ones were built in England, while at least one hundred and twenty of them had closed. While London had acquired the Royal Festival Hall for instance, it had lost the Queen's Hall and the smaller Aeolian and Grotrian Halls. Williams wrote that:

> The years of combat and recovery account for much of our backlog in rehousing the arts, and now that such building priorities as houses, schools, offices and factories are being so rapidly diminished the time need not be far distant when, following the example of Vienna and

Hamburg and Berlin, we could begin building homes for the arts. But war, and the economic consequences of war, do not alone account for Britain's present dearth of theatres, concert halls and opera houses; nor is that condition to be ascribed to any failure in our people to appreciate music and drama and ballet.

Although the audience for the arts had been multiplied a hundred times during this period of standstill in the provision of theatres and concert halls, the agencies of diffusion of the arts had chiefly been wirelesses and cinemas, hundreds of which had been built. 'For the thousands who listen to a concert in the Royal Festival Hall, or see a play in a theatre, there are millions who enjoy a comparable experience by switching on Beethoven at their firesides; and even though nine films out of ten may be artistically and morally expendable, the tenth may be the only *Henry V* or *Richard III* which most of our population will ever see.'

Yet the audience for live performances of music and drama was also increasing. And both the cinema and television depended on the prosperity of the theatre for their new material and their trained actors. Moreover, without denigrating the social and artistic potency of wireless and film, the mystique of communication could only be realized on a live stage. 'In the French language the audience is invited *to assist at* a performance, and that verb *assister à* is an excellent shorthand definition of the role of the spectators, and the two-way flow between them and the performers ... In an Old Vic or Stratford Memorial Theatre or Sadler's Wells or Birmingham Repertory Theatre there is developed, in the course of a season, a sense of kinship and continuity which leaves its mark upon every performance.' For these reasons, at the very least, in this time of changing social habits, the living arts had to be properly housed and maintained to fulfil their contemporary mission. And if they were to hold their own in the face of competition, 'their strategy must be to concentrate, not to diffuse'.

This was the nub of Williams's argument, a coherent social and practical philosophy for state patronage of the arts with limited resources. The total expenditure from public funds in maintaining music, opera and drama, amounted in the mid-nineteen-fifties only to fourpence a head, threepence from the Treasury through the Arts Council and a penny from the rates levied by the fifteen hundred local authorities. So the policy must be 'few but roses', 'raise' rather than 'spread'. And the victim would have to be the legacy of CEMA, the Regional Offices based on the civil defence structure of the Second World War. With the decline of direct provision of touring drama and music groups, three of these offices were closed in 1952, and three years later, all the remaining English offices were eliminated. A trio of peripatetic officers, specialists in music and familiar with the provinces, now took care of the Arts Council's relationships with its associated orchestras and choral societies. Three others, one posted in Manchester, were solely concerned with Williams's pet scheme, the direct provision of the visual arts; they maintained a liaison with local art galleries and societies. And the one region which really made a fuss about its dissolution was rewarded with a lesser recreation as the South-West Arts Association of Arts Clubs. Peter Cox remembered travelling up to London on the night train to plead with Williams and being kept waiting in the old ballroom at 4 St James's Square before being ushered into the magnificent presence of the massive and voluble Secretary-General in his office in the converted dining-room of the mansion. For once Williams was not allowed to speak as the forthright Colonel Perry Morgan rapped the table and declared, 'We've come to do the talking', and walked away with enough of a grant to employ somebody to organize the cooperation of the societies and clubs in the south-west of England.

There was some criticism of the Arts Council for pursuing a policy of centralization and destroying the Regional Offices. 'We had a very good one', Peter Cox declared. 'They wanted reorganizing, not demolishing.' Williams responded to such carping by pointing out that their elimination had saved £20,000 annually on administration. The Council had been governed from the start by its committees in London, Edinburgh and Cardiff, for Scotland and Wales had independent and increasing budgets and were responsible to their Secretaries of State as well as finally to the Department of Education and Science. The English regional staff had never been designers or arbiters of policy. The Arts Council did not diminish its aid to associated bodies in the provinces: in fact, this would be increased because of the savings from the reconstruction. The Further Education staff on the Local Education Authorities should fill the gap and assist neighbourhood arts clubs. The priority of the Arts Council was to maintain the standards of excellence at national institutions.

Such a policy made the Council open to a barrage of attacks for showing a bias in favour of funding Covent Garden, Sadler's Wells and the Old Vic. Yet if touring by the major companies based in London was taken into account, the split of funds with the provinces was fifty-fifty. If Covent Garden was considered a national institution like the National Gallery or the British Museum, the split was forty-sixty in favour of the countryside. As Williams justified the central solution:

> The first answer is that a capital city is also the metropolis of the nation's arts. Secondly, it was not the Arts Council which established these three central institutions. The Arts Council did not decide to give half its money to London; it resolved to act as patron to certain institutions already established, and of these the most meritorious and representative were situated in London. If any provincial city had assumed the responsibility for creating and maintaining, say, Sadler's Wells, the Arts Council would gladly have become its patron.

If Williams was vulnerable on this issue, it was because he had been responsible for scrapping the provincial administrations. He had not found them value for money on a shoe-string budget. One of those regional officers, Dick Linklater, who was recalled to become the Assistant Drama Director in London, believed that Williams had found the Regional Offices 'inefficient and a bit of an extravagance'. Although there was an extraordinary amount of trust between the clients and the regional officers, there was duplication. 'The clients liked the seal of approval from the Head Office. The problem was – London had to come up and say the same thing.' His own transfer to the centre of decision was only made possible by Williams shunting aside another relic of the wartime tradition of direct touring, Charles Landstone, 'a strange Rumpole-like figure' who was offended at not being made Drama Director, a post that had gone to John Moody, an opera producer from Sadler's Wells, who was more attuned to Williams's philosophy of concentrating rather than touring. 'I will expect in future the Drama Department', Williams said significantly to the young Linklater upon his arrival at headquarters, 'to speak with one voice.'

Lenin had said 'All power to the Soviets' and then he had destroyed these local powerhouses in favour of a Central Committee. And where Lenin led, Williams was not far behind. He believed in preserving the authority of the focal body founded by Keynes, who was himself no friend of regional controls. Local authorities should look after indigenous arts and crafts, while the metropolis should maintain national standards on its tight budget. This coherent strategy and firm grip on the levers of power was to set the stage for the decade of miracles of the Arts Council in the nineteen-sixties. Ironically, thirty-five years on, when devolution would become a principle of the government and of the administration of state patronage of the arts, the loss of London's authority to regional bodies would put the very future of the metropolitan base of the Arts Council in question. The centre would not hold.

Such was the ruling strategy of William Emrys Williams. He summed up his attitude in an invaluable booklet on the Arts Council, named *The First Ten Years*. Even if the organization had more money to spend it would need to consider several questions before deciding upon extended diffusion:

There are many towns which have consistently failed to reveal an interest in 'live' plays or concerts, and which have allowed their local repertory theatre to collapse. Is public money to be used in the long and expensive business of coaxing the cultural appetites of such places? Are seats to be subsidized whether they are full or empty? The Arts Council lacks the means to pursue diffusion on a massive scale and, since there exist methods more apt for diffusion than those it can command or afford, it seems wiser that the Arts Council should now concentrate its limited resources primarily, but not exclusively, on the maintenance and enhancement of standards. Standards can best be raised in permanent centres: music and drama must have fixed abodes where resident companies can develop their skill and *esprit* and sense of purpose. There is no reason to conclude that the Arts Council will diminish its present scale of diffusion, but, faced with the problem of choice, and a limited budget, the Arts Council must seek to consolidate rather than enlarge its own particular responsibilities to the arts in Britain. It can do so, moreover, in the solid confidence that municipal patronage is taking a large and increasing share of the cost of providing the arts to those communities which express an articulate desire to enjoy them. If Local Authorities will continue at the present rate to carry some of the load of diffusion there will still be an inevitable dearth of the 'living' arts, but there will be no famine. But unless high standards can be maintained in selected strongholds diffusion will be a fruitless and improvident effort.

FOUR

THE STRUGGLE FOR SURVIVAL

The essence of Arts Council policy nowadays is to sustain the best possible standards of performance at a limited number of institutions ... Even if its income were larger it would still prefer to consolidate these priorities than to dissipate its resources upon an extensive provision of the second-rate. If the power-houses were to fail there would be a black-out of the living arts in Britain.

Sir William Emrys Williams, writing in the annual report of the Arts Council of Great Britain, 1961–2.

Dame Ninette de Valois had defined the state of ballet in England as 'Before Keynes' and 'After Keynes'. British culture would now be defined as 'Before Suez' and 'After Suez'. The crisis of 1956 in the Middle East, which was to signal the convulsion of the nineteen-sixties, hardly affected the Arts Council at all, even though it would proceed to subsidize the dramatic reaction to this debacle of Empire. The inept scuttle from the Egyptian Canal marked the end of British global influence and a retreat from an imperial vision into insular perspectives. To the Arts Council, rather appropriately, it was merely a question of falling theatre attendances, which dropped by a quarter and did not pick up until petrol rationing was over. Such blinkered vision was matched by that of a government bent on keeping in office after the disaster to British prestige brought about by Sir Anthony Eden's last effort to wave the flag and send in the gunboats. In such an international crisis, there could be little more spending for the arts. The preoccupation was now the struggle for survival.

When William Emrys Williams, who had by now been given a knighthood, wrote the introduction to the Arts Council report of 1956–7, he called it *Art in the Red*. On a budget of less than a million pounds a year – a sum only to be exceeded at the end of the decade – it was assisting about 125 bodies engaged in opera, ballet, music and drama on a professional basis. All the bodies had survived the year, but most were harassed by economic difficulties. 'A Credit Squeeze is no respecter of moral purpose, and the manager of a non-profit repertory theatre is on no better a footing than a bookmaker when he seeks more accommodation from the bank.'

The trouble in the performing arts was caused by almost a universal lack of working capital among the producing companies. The two leading London organizations, the Royal Ballet and the Old Vic, had to undertake prolonged dollar drives in America to make ends meet at home. Several provincial repertory companies, which were trying to support new drama, were being forced back 'in the servitude and squalor of weekly rep' without proper time for the rehearsal of fewer plays. No national funds existed for capital expenditure on the arts. Since the end of the Second World War, the only new building for the arts provided by public funds was the Royal Festival Hall, although the enlightened Corporation of Coventry was completing the handsome new Belgrade Theatre, unique in the regions.

Such parsimony was derisory. Scores of arts buildings had been built abroad in countries worse off than Britain, such as Austria, Italy, Holland and defeated Germany, which had constructed no less than fifteen opera houses and concert halls in bombed cities. The Turks were having such hard times that they could not afford to import their national drink, coffee; yet a magnificent new opera house was rising in Istanbul. All the Arts Council could do was to set up a Committee of Enquiry under the Vice-Chairman of the Council, Dr Wyn Griffith, into the problems of 'Housing the Arts'. At the same time, the members of the Committee were told that they could not assume any more funds would be made available in the future to accommodate the arts than in the past. 'The hardships of the Briton must almost reconcile the Turk to going without his coffee.'

A National Theatre Company was still a dream, and it still had no home, only a site on the South Bank and a moveable foundation stone. Many theatres had lately been shut down or demolished or had declined into 'a common lodging-house for the less reputable kind of variety show ... The casualty-rate is an alarming symptom of a malady which threatens to extinguish the provincial theatre.' If the rate of closure continued, it would become impossible to maintain the framework of a touring circuit in the provinces. 'Except for what the score of resident repertory companies can produce, the London successes will not be seen outside the boundaries of the metropolis.'

Of the repertory theatres which still survived, the Arts Council could afford to aid some thirty managements from eight per cent of its budget – over fifty per cent went to opera and ballet, a dribble to poetry and nothing to prose, held to be the province of public libraries and publishers. The great glory of the English language was left to fend for itself in commerce. New dramatists, however, were being subsidized – and the English Stage Company under George Devine at the Royal Court Theatre. He was committed to establish 'a writer's theatre rather than a producer's or actor's theatre'. From that small seedbed, the renaissance of the English theatre would grow. The Arts Council expected nothing tangible for at least three years; but John Osborne with *Look Back in Anger* and *The Entertainer* – that lamentation for the old British values sunk at Suez – would produce successes at once.

Three years later, the drama critic Richard Findlater could write a eulogy in the annual report of the Arts Council:

> 'Where are the new dramatists?' has been a familiar poser in the press. Now, in a bevy, they are here ... The prime, neglected cause lies in the policies of the Arts Council. This new efflorescence of the drama springs from seeds carefully disseminated from St James's Square, as a deliberate act of policy and perhaps of faith. When the Council toyed at first with the intention of giving practical encouragement to young dramatists, it met knowing warnings from the worldly that the real reason for the dearth of new plays was the dearth of new talent, which no amount of pump-priming could create. Subsidies will never make a Shakespeare, said the standard-bearers of *laissez-faire*; we must trust to luck – and the fortunes of the

trade – for a twentieth-century drama fit for adults. But such perennial opposition to state aid for the arts has already been exploded by the direct and indirect results of the Arts Council's measures in recent years. Although its doles may or may not have delivered a genius, they have kept many talents and many theatres alive, and have helped to change the social context of the contemporary stage.

The methods for encouraging the dramatist were threefold: direct subsidies to theatres which promoted new work, such as Joan Littlewood's Theatre Workshop in the East End of London and Devine's Royal Court in Sloane Square; guarantees against loss to repertory theatres putting on new plays; and direct grants to young playwrights of promise. The roll-call of honour was the history of the new British theatre: John Arden, Brendan Behan, Samuel Beckett, Robert Bolt, Shelagh Delaney, Nigel Dennis, Bernard Kops, John Osborne, James Saunders, N. F. Simpson and Arnold Wesker. The sums involved were pitiful – a few hundred pounds annually for the dramatists, a thousand for Joan Littlewood and five thousand for George Devine with his vision of a theatre company, as declared to a young aspirant: 'You should choose your theatre like you choose a religion. Make sure you don't get into the wrong temple. For the theatre is really a religion or a way of life.' Rarely has so much good come from so little spent on the stage of wordplay.

And yet too many wanted too much from tiny resources. As Sir W. E. Williams was to point out in 1960, when the Arts Council budget would reach one-and-a-half million pounds, this represented seven pennies a head for the population, one of the lowest subsidies in Europe, the cost of four miles of motorway. It was one-twelfth of the Treasury sum for public libraries, which often provided more recreation than education. On this pittance, several national institutions of the arts had been created or developed:

> Without their present subsidies from the Arts Council there would be no Royal Ballet, no Covent Garden Opera, no Sadler's Wells or Old Vic, and it is more than doubtful whether such fruitful experiments as those of the English Stage Company at the Royal Court Theatre or the Mermaid Theatre at Puddle Dock would have been possible ... Outside London none of the five permanent symphony orchestras would have survived without Arts Council grants, nor would the

thirty repertory theatres in England and Scotland which are nowadays the thin red line of defence against the total mechanization of drama. Since the war many annual Festivals of the arts have been initiated or revived, and again, without the co-operation of the Arts Council it is unlikely that Edinburgh, York, Leeds, Norwich, Aldeburgh, Bath, Cheltenham, King's Lynn and Swansea would continue to mount these exemplary and festive demonstrations of the fine arts.

Yet to those who were the spear-carriers of the minor cultural revolution of the late nineteen-fifties, the policies of the Arts Council and the parsimony of the government were an irrelevance. They were both part of an aristocratic and bourgeois Establishment that was out of touch with the needs of the people. In the important and popular collection of essays of the period named *Declaration*, only Kingsley Amis jibbed at writing a piece. His refusal was short and to the point: 'I hate all this pharisaical twittering about the "state of our civilization" and I suspect anyone who wants to buttonhole me about my rôle in society. The book is likely to prove a valuable addition to the cult of the Solemn Young Man.'

Of the Solemn and Angry Young Men and Women who wrote in *Declaration*, John Osborne saw himself as a spectator at the last circus of a civilization that had lost faith in itself, particularly after the recent hydrogen-bomb explosion on Christmas Island. Royalty was the gold filling in the mouth of decay, while all art was merely organized evasion. To the *enfant terrible* of drama criticism, Kenneth Tynan, judgement in the arts and patronage of it was impossible. Semantic philosophy had removed value judgements, so that now the gelded led the drugged and the only solution was self-love. The film-maker Lindsay Anderson was equally sceptical about the possibility of state action. People now lived between Matthew Arnold's two worlds, one dead, the other powerless to be born. Osborne's anti-hero Jimmy Porter was right in *Look Back in Anger*: there weren't any good brave causes left, just 'the Brave New-nothing-very-much-thank-you'.

Only the novelist Doris Lessing withstood the general disillusion because of her past experience. She had been a Communist sympathizer; even after the Russian attack on Hungary at the time of Suez, she believed in Socialism because of the compassion of its faith. Writers should be committed, the responsible interpreters of their age. The times were so dangerous, violent, explosive and precarious that it was a question of life and death for humanity. 'We are all of us made kin with each other and with everything in the world because of the kinship of possible destruction.' She trusted in a great common cause, the abolition of hunger and poverty in the world. Britain had always sent people into crusading movements, especially in education and arts. In spite of Jimmy Porter, there were great causes left, even if a novelist could only talk as an individual to individuals in a small personal voice. 'There was nothing more arrogant than to demand a perfect cause to identify oneself with.' The answer was a commitment to a just cause.

Conviction was the title of another significant collection of essays, which were produced by the same publisher the following year, a plainsong answer to the incoherent wailing and critical dirge of *Declaration*. Its editor Norman Mackenzie explained why the young lacked causes now in what he called the stalemate state, 'that curious interval in our social history, in which there was no way back to the world which had guttered out into war, yet no clear way forward to a really new society'.

He had no trouble in being a committed Socialist. Memory and hope blended into a Socialist conviction, which was why this belief had become unfashionable among those who had grown up during and since the War. They had no memory of mass unemployment or the Spanish Civil War, and no one had given them much reason to hope with the Cold War and the threat of the hydrogen bomb. Something had happened to paralyse both action and passion. Although much of Britain was still a slum and the Establishment was riddled by snobbery and false values, those who complained, like Sir Orlando Drought in Trollope's novel *The Prime Minister*, that 'everything is dead' in politics, lacked the effort of will to liven everything up. They felt restless or cynical or resigned and then retreated into private worlds. It was because Britain had become a marginal power between two great powers. A demonstration in Trafalgar Square did not persuade the British government to quit Suez or abandon the atom bomb. Only pressure from America or Russia could do that. There was a failure of morals and of caring, but not of dreaming. 'We are full of dreams, but they are dreams of a vanished past, because nostalgia is the opium of the people.' The two parties had converged in their policies. The Tories were the reluctant servants of the Welfare Society, while the Socialists had become the pillars of the Establishment. This was the stalemate state, this was a society without convictions.

In the following essays in *Conviction*, most of which suggested limited social tinkering, only the Labour politician Peter Shore correctly defined the practice of the future. He saw a managerial revolution taking control from the old Establishment. The functions of business at the highest level were becoming increasingly political while the politician and the civil servant were more involved in the conduct of industry. Business lent government its outstanding personalities. Industrialists became Ministers and headed State Boards. Senior civil servants and politicians were recruited to serve huge private enterprises. 'The consequential formation of what has been called a "power élite" must be viewed not as a kind of conspiracy, but as a logical consequence of the unification of business with administration and politics.'

Against this true and pessimistic vision, Raymond Williams stressed that culture was ordinary and even tried to define what it was. Every human society had its own shape and purposes and meanings. They were expressed in institutions and arts and learning. A society could only be made by finding common meanings and directions. It could only grow by active debate and amendment, 'under the pressures of experience, contact, and discovery, writing themselves into the land'. Yet a growing society was made and remade in every individual mind. Culture had two meanings – a whole way of life that included the arts and learning, and also the special processes of discovery and creative effect. 'Culture is ordinary, in every society and in every mind.'

Such an unfashionable and sentimental belief in an ordinary culture common to all made Williams view the few scholars and writers known as the 'Angry Young Men' as people making rude noises in a university tea-shop. There was no need to be rude; if that was culture, nobody wanted it. It was, of course, not culture, but merely made culture into a dirty word. If the people shouting in the tea-shop went on insisting that culture was their trivial differences of behaviour of speech or taste, they could not be stopped, but they could be ignored. They were not that important, they could not take culture from where it belonged. They were only self-important. Culture was ordinary, and it was not doomed. There was no Gresham's Law, by which bad culture drove out good. Through education and more state spending on the arts and a redefinition of what the arts were and the spread of them, the apparent division of a common British culture could be remedied, the divide between 'a remote and self-gracious sophistication [and] a doped mass'. Raymond Williams himself would serve with distinction and controversy on the Arts Council, but his dream about what it might achieve with increased expenditure on the arts would never be realized. 'We now spend £20,000,000 annually on all our libraries, museums, galleries, orchestras, on the Arts Council and on all forms of adult education. At the same time we spend £365,000,000 annually on advertising. When these figures are reversed, we can claim some sense of proportion and value. And until they are reversed, let there be no sermons, from the Establishment, about materialism: this is their way of life, let them look at it.'

Even if Raymond Williams had ever seen vastly increased spending on education and the arts, he would have retained some of the same fears as his namesake, Sir William Emrys Williams. Although he wanted a recreation of the regions to provide his ordinary culture – 'you should not have to go to London to find it' – yet a ready-made culture should not be preferred to the benighted masses. Cultural growth was a continual offering for common acceptance:

> We should accept, frankly, that if we extend our culture we shall change it: some that is offered will be rejected, other parts will be radically criticized. And this is as it should be, for our arts, now, are in no condition to go down to eternity unchallenged. There is much fine work; there is also shoddy work, and work based on values that will find no acceptance if they ever come out into the full light of England. To take our arts to new audiences is to be quite certain that in many respects those arts will be changed.

These declarations and convictions of the leading critics and makers of opinion in the late nineteen-fifties showed how irrelevant most of the intelligentsia found the activities of the Arts Council, which seemed to be pouring soothing drops into the rusty bucket full of holes that was now called British culture. They despaired of state action, and what little there might be was deemed inadequate and administered by a metropolitan élite. Some persons who were too privileged gave too little to too few. It was all very well for the Queen to be pleased to grant a Charter of Incorporation which brought together the Sadler's Wells Ballet, the Sadler's Wells Theatre Ballet and the Sadler's Wells School in a Corporation with the general title of the Royal Ballet, but the blessed new body still danced away beside the Opera at Covent Garden with the lion's share of the state grant – and even then they were in financial difficulties because they were under-subsidized by continental standards. In 1957–8, the problems of the opera companies preoccupied the Council and its Music Panel, which spent most of its meetings discussing opera deficits and the failing Carl Rosa Company. The following annual reports, named 'The Struggle for Survival' and 'The Priorities of Patronage' announced additional funds from the Treasury to sustain the Royal Opera House and to reduce its overdraft – more than two-fifths of its expenditure was to be paid by the state. Although Sir W. E. Williams lauded the city council at Coventry and Nottingham for sustaining the building of new theatres, he did not apologize for continuing to back the metropolitan flagships. 'At a time when the National Theatre project is gaining favour it would be ironic if the decision to build that institution were to coincide with the mass burial of provincial theatres. Unless we nerve ourselves to such an approach in the near future the theatre outside London will be beyond recovery and, where it manages to survive, as poignant as a museum piece.'

For the Secretary-General, the simple arithmetic of equal shares – suggested by Sir John Barbirolli for orchestras – was 'a heresy of patronage'. The Arts Council applied a means test to all applicants before determining what grant or guarantee it would make to an orchestra or a theatre company. It also required periodic trading returns from their bodies so as to observe the course of business, and it appointed an Arts Council officer as an assessor at the meetings of the management committees of the assisted bodies. All the figures and the returns were considered before money was doled out, but success was not penalized. 'The Arts Council could not justify its trusteeship of public funds on the basis of such an avuncular gesture as carving up the cake equally; it must continue to allocate its grants and guarantees on the basis of ascertained need.'

The metropolitan gobbling of the available funds, however, and the patronage of the capital city seemed intolerable to many concerned with the arts outside its walls. That condescension was summed up in the report of 1956–7 from the Visual Arts Director, whose assumptions were Olympian. Centralization had increased the usefulness of the representatives of the Arts Council. 'England is a small country, and the whole area south of the Wash regards London as its arts centre. (The north is admittedly more independent, but this has been recognised by the fact that one of the Regional Arts Officers lives in Manchester, spending a few days in London each month.)' Such attitudes produced a revolt in the shires, mirrored in the vehemence of the attack on the mentality of the metropolitan mandarins in John Osborne's *Look Back in Anger* and Kingsley Amis's *Lucky Jim*. Almost as soon as the Regional Offices were abolished, the Arts Council had to recognize and support the first of the self-promoted arts associations in the south-west, later followed by one in the Midlands and another in the north-east. These were not intended to be mirror-images of the Council in London, but smaller in scale, concentrating on crafts and local activities. Even so, the provinces simply would not be ruled entirely from St James's Square. And the general assault on the metropolitan establishment after the debacle at Suez added power to the country guns.

The South-West Association for the Arts had been born on the table-thumping visit to London by Colonel Morgan, when even Sir W. E. Williams had quailed. 'As an Indian would say,' Peter Cox wrote later in an obituary on Morgan, 'that particular morning was an auspicious time for the visit: it was Trelawney's day, entirely appropriate for a Cornish-led rebellion.' In the north-east, the regional rebellion was led by Arthur Blenkinsop, a Labour Member of Parliament, who persuaded local authorities and businesses to come up with more than £40,000 to back the fledgling Association for the Arts. When asked to match this sum, the Arts Council provided £500.

There was to be a change of heart within the Arts Council, however, in spite of the Secretary-General's warning that though it might be wise to increase support for regional associations so that they could develop a stronger local responsibility for promoting the arts, there would be a risk of standards being lowered. He thought 'it would be essential for the Arts Council to retain freedom of choice to select which items in the programme could be supported by the Council.' Williams would not give up central guidance; national taste was still the affair of London. In fact, the Chairman and the officers of the North-Eastern Association for the Arts went behind the back of the Secretary-General and lobbied Lord Hailsham, who had been appointed minister with special responsibility for the region. However much he did or did not twist the arm's length principle, the Arts Council's contribution to the north-east was to rise to £22,000 by 1963–4 and, under future Labour governments, all Regional Arts Associations were to achieve complete freedom in spending the funds that they received from the Arts Council. By then, the Secretary-General would have retired. Unlike Keynes, he did not leave the legacy of his policies behind him.

Although Sir W. E. Williams continually complained about the lack of support for the arts by local authorities, his concern on concentrating resources and staff in London was unlikely to receive much regional support. 'No Local Authority has yet set up a Fine Arts Committee to survey and supply the civic need for drama, opera and music,' he noted severely in 1954. 'No city in Britain has yet addressed itself to the task of securing a balanced and regular provision of all the arts. No municipal committees or voluntary associations exist to represent civic trusteeship for the arts as a whole.' So Williams sought to pass the responsibility of regional arts onto regional bodies supported by regional tax-payers. As from the end of the decade, the annual report began to list the increasing sums allocated by provincial authorities for the performing arts: £30,000 by the Birmingham Council to the city symphony orchestra, more by Liverpool for its Philharmonic Orchestra, £5,000 from Coventry for the Belgrade Theatre, and business sponsorship from Whitbread and Co. and other firms of £50,000, and from independent television of £100,000 for the live theatre and various festivals. In spite of his centralism, Williams was encouraging a drip-feed into the veins of the arts from commerce and the new media and the local authorities, which would become a lifeline of the future.

Except in the areas hardly covered by the growing power of the media, especially in opera and ballet and art films, where small- and large-scale touring continued, the arts were suffering from insupportable competition. Particularly in the counties of the independent Arts Committees of Wales and Scotland, television was emptying the theatres. In 1957–8, the annual report on Wales noted, festivals, opera, concerts and art exhibitions were well attended, but touring companies in theatreless towns were a failure. The arts could not survive on subsidies alone, if they were being killed off by apathy and indifference. If television drama programmes already satisfied so many, were theatrical tours no longer wanted in Wales? The same concern afflicted Scotland, where there was a very serious decline in audiences in the late nineteen-fifties at the four repertory theatres which worked in association with the Arts Council's Scottish Committee:

> This decline in theatre audiences is probably the most serious crisis that has overtaken artistic endeavour in Scotland since the principle of Government subsidy for the Arts was first accepted. What is to be done about it? Should the theatre managements play for safety by putting on more and more popular farces, 'tea-cup' comedies and old war-horses of the London stage? This expedient has been tried by some of them but it has failed to attract enough of the older patrons to stop the rot, and has clearly alienated the new young audiences which might be built up if they were offered new and exciting plays on serious themes.

Yet in the gaps of television coverage, the remarkable mobile unit 'Opera for All' survived, led by Douglas Craig presenting abridged versions of such operas as *Così Fan Tutte* and *Cinderella* with six singers, two handymen and a pianist. Craig reported on a winter expedition in the Scottish Highlands:

> We arrived without serious mishap. The village was silenced by snow. Nothing moved but the inhabitants. The school hall proved to be bare and difficult. The dressing-room was the school shower-bath … Eventually it was time to give the show. We coaxed our frozen limbs into the eighteenth-century gewgaws and wondered if it was worth it. Would there be an audience? Of course there was: a packed house, wet, hotted-up and smelling. Dozens of children, many of them far too young. The hall was difficult acoustically, the piano inferior, and the children (some of them as young as four) talked,

laughed, giggled, ate, scratched, cried, rustled sweet papers, went out and came back again regardless of what went on on the stage. We packed in the snow and ice. The blizzard had stopped, but there were scores of autograph hunters to be pacified.

Such an undertaking was more than nostalgia for the wartime touring of the arts. It was the first education in the nature of opera that these Highlanders had ever experienced, especially the children. A great deal had to do with the astuteness and dedication of George Firth, the Director of the Scottish Committee with special responsibility for music. To the *Manchester Guardian* he seemed like a field marshal plotting the strategy of an extensive and prolonged campaign;

> 'Opera for All' to St. Cuthbert's Church Hall, Kircudbright; the Glasgow Trio to the Old Gala House, Galashiels; 'Two Strolling Players' to Papdale Infant School, Kirkwall; Eli Prins, with his lecture on 'The Self-portrait,' to Brechin, Wigtown and Ardrossan – their movements all meticulously charted on one of his 'wondrous maps', shoulder-high boards studded with busy coloured flags. And where the flag shows, in glen after glen, the message is the same: culture was here.

A similar small and strolling, but widespread, success across the country was repeated by circulating Art Films in co-operation with the British Film Institute by means of a mobile projection unit in more than a hundred towns. The subjects included Piero della Francesca, Fra Angelico, Botticelli, Giotto's frescoes, Le Douanier Rousseau, Stanley Spencer, Alexander Calder and Henry Moore. Unfortunately, this effort to use the new media and work with other state-funded bodies in spreading arts education to the people was minimal compared with funding the performing arts.

With the theatre dying in the regions, the need for a Theatre Grid and Housing the Arts seemed even more urgent. By 1960, only fifty-one repertory theatres survived in Great Britain; just over half of these were successful in their appeals for financial support either to the Arts Council or to their Local Authority or both; they served as 'the beacon light of the living theatre in places where all else seems to be buried under a forest of television aerials'. Twenty-five had been elected by the Arts Council to be the stanchions of its grid plan of repertory theatres. And yet, in a three-year pattern of patronage, the whole operation still had a patchwork nature. There was little enough evidence of intelligent collusion among the benefactors or of consistent policy within any one group of them.

The answer was to upgrade the theatres and gain the support of the government and more local authorities. The report on Housing the Arts was finally published in two parts in 1959 and 1961, the first part covering London and Scotland and Wales, the second the English regions. All inquiries do come to an end, if sometimes to a dead end. The London section was confined mainly to the West End, although it referred to the Barbican Redevelopment Scheme in the City of London and to the South Bank. The Scottish and Welsh sections dealt fully with the needs of their major cities and their rural areas. The second part of the report on *The Needs of the English Provinces* decided that every town with a population of more than two hundred thousand people should have an art gallery, a hall where concerts could be played and one theatre at the very least. Seventeen cities and towns were targeted, because resources would be limited – Birmingham, Bradford, Bristol, Coventry, Croydon, Kingston-upon-Hull, Leeds, Leicester, Liverpool, Manchester, Newcastle, Nottingham, Plymouth, Portsmouth, Sheffield, Southampton and Stoke-on-Trent. Although the report stated that 'in the housing programme of this country the arts are still right at the end of the queue, and have as low a priority as prisons', it did recommend that £150,000 a year should be made available to the Arts Council or to an approved Arts Trust, which could be used on contributions towards the capital expenses of putting up new theatres and concert halls, also for the refurbishment and renovation of existing premises. The Conservative Chancellor of the Exchequer, Selwyn Lloyd, gave the Arts Council permission to publish 'Housing the Arts', while making it clear that this permission did not mean approval. And indeed, until a Labour government would come to power in 1964, nothing much would be done.

In its reports, the Arts Council hoped to influence the shape of future buildings. At the end of the Second World War, it had come out with a plan for an appropriate Arts Centre, something the Council did not wish to encourage in the nineteen-fifties. Later, plans were introduced for a model theatre and an opera house. But these were pipe-dreams, hopes to shape what was not yet possible.

The urge to affect modern architecture was one of the admirable desires of the Council, but this wish was outside its brief. Not until the nineteen-nineties would the art of architecture bypass its Keynesian exclusion.

Until the end of the decade, arts policy remained resolutely centralist and metropolitan. The function of the Council, Sir W. E. Williams insisted, was to nurture the arts, 'not to provide popular amenities in that field [or] attempt a premature and ambitious scale of diffusion. Public patronage of the arts is a long-term obligation: it must grow like the mustard-seed, not like the beanstalk.' And yet this strategy of backing power-houses run by a central élite was becoming untenable, especially as it emanated from a Secretary-General with a background in adult education. Williams began to give ground under pressure. 'The Panels on Art and Drama and Music and Poetry on the Arts Council were important,' the future Chairman Lord Cottesloe was to observe. 'But the Secretary-General still had a very controlling influence.' Even though Williams called the Panel Directors 'the Barons', and the unpaid members were of the quality of Sir Roland Penrose and Nikolaus Pevsner, Peter Hall, Dame Peggy Ashcroft and Sir Laurence Olivier, Dame Ninette de Valois and Cecil Day Lewis, the Secretary-General managed to have his way. He was no King John at Runnymede, giving way to the barons on Magna Carta or to a Royal Charter in the direction of more democracy and the wider spread of British culture.

Grudgingly, £50,000 was found to diffuse among amateur music societies and arts clubs of various kinds. The National Federation of Music Societies distributed the grant to provide 'professional stiffening' and help to improve local standards. With their right to raise up to sixpence on the rates for the arts – although they did not raise one-sixtieth of that entitlement – the local authorities were encouraged in their support of regional work and the reborn arts associations, rising from the ashes of the Regional Offices. More aid was sought from the principal new source of diffusion, the television companies: ten million licences had been issued to households by the end of the nineteen-fifties. Fresh patrons must be tapped, if more provincial expansion was desired. Local industry and business should oblige and could even show caprice in giving – something the

Arts Council could not afford. For all the possible and different sources of finance, Williams declared that art was a potent ambassador.

What enthralled and bedevilled the Arts Council at this time were the problems of the opera. On the heavenly side, there was the shining light of Glyndebourne, which had had no state subsidy since its £25,000 grant for the Festival of Britain programmes. John Christie was as much of a centralist as his opponent Keynes had been. He had written to Sir Kenneth Clark, stating that Glyndebourne was creating a model scheme; its purpose was that the arts in this country should thrive:

> Our view is that the method, which can achieve this purpose, is to light incandescent fires in a few places, the sparks from which will fall far and wide and are likely to set alight whatever material will burn. Then the problem is to reduce the distance from these fires. We regard London as the Capital of the World, not merely of England. Its Art should and could be supreme in the World ...
>
> Art has nothing to do with equality. Art is essentially unequal. Art is balanced. Art is burning, when it is great. The performance of Art, if it is to be scattered everywhere, must be mediocrity. Mediocrity will set nothing on fire – unless it be temper. Mediocrity is like damp sheets.
>
> The way to distribute Art is by creating great Artistic achievement. Light a few fires in the Country and raise these to incandescence. Select several centres: send the best this country can get all the year round to these centres. Arrange that the Mayors and Corporations and Authorities should touch their hats all the time to this work – but deliver the goods – and the whole neighbourhood will rise and go to the fire. Other centres will ask 'Can not we be a bright spot?' Yes! in time. The sparks from these incandescent fires will fall far and wide. They will light any material – if it will burn. Mediocrity will light nothing.

Such an indirect plea for state help fell on deaf ears. Clark would do no more for Glyndebourne than Keynes had done, in spite of the dominating philosophy of its founder. Christie's tragic and early death launched his son George into his role, and this hard inheritance forged the archetype in British opera of a provincial house which could survive through its excellence and its support by foundations and businesses as well as private patrons. Glyndebourne was an anomaly in this period of increasing government patronage, and yet it worked. It put the unspeakable question – was state aid really necessary?

On the hellish side was the condition of all the other assisted opera companies in Britain. The opera crisis arose from two causes: insufficient subsidies and the failure of the opera companies to agree on any plans for fusion or co-operation or amalgamation. Each was a law unto itself, and never a twain might meet. The Arts Council repeatedly pressed for some measure of integration or association between Covent Garden and Sadler's Wells, the Carl Rosa and the Welsh National Opera Company. There were simply not enough funds or audiences to support four opera companies in Britain at that time, although Glyndebourne managed by itself in Sussex. First, the Arts Council tried to broker a marriage between Sadler's Wells and Covent Garden, then an alliance between the Carl Rosa and the Welsh National Opera Company. This fell through when Sadler's Wells approached the Carl Rosa on its own initiative, later endorsed by the Arts Council, which offered £215,000 to finance the new combination for a year. But the consequences of that pot-pourri in reducing forces and programmes proved too much for the Sadler's Wells Trust; three of its officers resigned. More funds were raised from other sources to keep Sadler's Wells independent and the Carl Rosa was abandoned to its eventual fate. The Arts Council was left to insist that it neither imposed nor sought to impose fusion on any of the opera companies. Although some of the newspapers accused the Council of trying 'to bring off a shot-gun marriage between the Wells and the Rosa, it was no such thing. This abortive amalgamation was conceived by two consenting partners; and only when it failed to come off was the Arts Council charged with sinister intentions.'

What the Arts Council could be charged with was spending too much money and time on the opera companies to the detriment of the other arts of Britain. This was certainly true in the exemplary case of the Welsh National Opera Company. There was no National Theatre or National Orchestra in Wales, even though there was a National Museum and Library. The National Opera had grown from the ashes of the statement in 1951 of the Chairman of the Welsh Committee, Dr Wyn Griffith, that there was 'an essential difference between England and Wales. Wales was a country with its own language, and not a region. It was a land of amateur efforts in the Arts, where attempts had been made to introduce professional standards. It was a land of small efforts which wanted nursing, rather than a land of large enterprises.' With autonomy in 1953 and a block grant, however, more and more money had been allocated to the Welsh National Opera Company in order to turn it into a professional training organization. Dr Griffith himself wrote the libretto for a Coronation year production of the new opera *Menna*, which proved to be a flop. Yet aided by the sympathetic Welsh Secretary-General, Sir W. E. Williams, special grants were made for the Welsh National Opera to visit Sadler's Wells and roar with the English in their own den. The failure to merge with the Carl Rosa Opera led to a proposal to replace it, made by Dr Parry Williams to Sir Kenneth Clark, who merely replied that it was impossible to support four opera companies and one would have to go.

It was not to be the Welsh one. When Dr Griffith retired in favour of Professor Gwyn Jones as Chairman of the Welsh Committee, Sir W. E. Williams was present at the board meeting. 'There was a process of organic growth taking place in the Welsh National Opera Company,' Dr Griffith declared in his swansong, 'and the problem was to find the necessary revenues to foster that valuable plant.' The Arts Council was still fostering the Carl Rosa as a touring company, but the Welsh Company needed to tour as well. By 1959, a unanimous decision was made to close the National Opera and appoint a liquidator, unless it were given £100,000 to become professional, rather than the £18,000 under offer. 'The tragedy is this, the greatest project in Wales is doomed,' the new Chairman declared. 'We have fought for this Company long enough. We lived on hope but all our hopes have been dashed.' The reasons for having to become professional were manifold: it was difficult to get paid leave for an amateur chorus: it was impossible to hire good principals in competition with Covent Garden and Sadler's Wells: only three Welsh venues – Cardiff, Swansea and Llandudno – could stage an adequate opera. The National Company needed a professional nucleus of thirty-six in the chorus and twelve principals. Without provision for these, it could not go on.

Sir W. E. Williams replied from London that opera had reached a saturation point in Britain, but that the members of the Welsh Committee were autonomous and could approach the Chancellor of the Exchequer directly. This might lead, however, to an unhappy rift between themselves and the Arts Council in London, where Williams presided. 'Discord between the Welsh Committee and St James's Square was not to be desired and he was anxious that the Committee should see what quicksands there were.' Thanked for his frankness, Williams was informed that the responsibility for the decease of the National Opera Company must not and would not be the due of the Welsh Committee, which should do its best for the arts in Wales. The solution was a direct approach to Henry Brooke, then the Minister for Welsh Affairs, who was bluntly told by Sir Emrys Evans that the Arts Council in London had already prepared its own plan for opera in the provinces and any attempt by the Welsh Opera Company to go into England might be regarded as an encroachment. A compromise had been tabled before the meeting. The National Opera could survive on its £18,000 for the current year, as long as it received £42,000 for the season of 1960 to begin its programme of professionalization: £7,000 would come from local authorities to support a four-week programme in Wales, with one week at Sadler's Wells and one at Bournemouth. And so a sort of salvation was achieved.

As with the Arts Council in London, however, too much time and too high a proportion of the budget was being given by the Welsh Committee to its fledgling National Opera. It admitted that it had several indigenous problems to solve:

> The arts in Wales are lop-sided. There is an abundance of interest in music but relatively little in painting. There is a strong native tradition of drama, but virtually no professional theatre. Communications are sketchy outside the main centres of population, and there is a general shortage of housing accommodation for the display of the arts. In Wales, again, there is an ancient minority culture to be cherished and developed: drama and literature must be nourished in Welsh as well as in English.

Yet the preponderant concentration on opera did not help to correct this lop-sided situation in Wales.

In a curious parallel to the ousting of Mary Glasgow in London and the impending retirement of Sir W. E. Williams under a new

Chairman, the Director for Wales, Myra Owen, was dismissed by the incoming Chairman Gwyn Jones for writing 'grotesque' minutes about committee meetings on the opera and for failing to consult him over her decisions. She was a Welsh-speaking professional musician who had been Director for Training in the Royal Ordnance Factories during and after the war, before taking that commanding experience to serve as Director for the Welsh Committee for eleven years. She believed, as Sir W. E. Williams did, that she ran the records and the office. She had fallen out with the new Deputy Director David Peters, who had been a bank clerk and had no professional experience in theatre or music or the visual arts, 'a man whose ambitions appear to exceed his ability'. Accused of not delegating sufficient responsibility to the staff and of attaching undue importance to her personal position and prestige, she, a last vestige of the war tradition of service, was forced out. Under her successor, the grotesque but revealing minutes of the Welsh committee meetings, particularly on the contentious subject of the National Opera, became as dry and opaque as a sandstorm on a Mumbles beach.

An interesting solution to the organizational and financial problems caused by the 'opera crisis' was put forward by Lord Bridges in a lecture, when he gave an acute analysis of the relationship between the State and the Arts. He proposed a co-ordinated pattern of provision, a kind of arts University Grants Committee with a quinquennial grant, so that its beneficiaries might lay long-term plans. To solve the problem of the Arts Council and the Welsh Committee allocating too much of their budget to opera and ballet, Lord Bridges suggested two separate votes from Parliament: one for the expensive needs of opera and ballet, and one for the rest of its activities in music, drama, the visual arts and poetry. The responsibility for the costly performances would then be transferred from the Arts Council to Parliament, precisely as it was done in France, Italy and Germany. On present levels the proportions of these separate votes would work out at almost two to one, but 'the issue of how much money this country is prepared to spend on opera could then be settled without calling in question the extent and scope of the other activities of the Council'. This wise suggestion was not picked up by the government, which professed to maintain the arm's length principle, by which the Arts Council would continue to incur the odium of the regions by giving too little to them and too much to Covent Garden, where most of the Ministers enjoyed preferential treatment and good seats, often in the Royal Box, and where the Secretary of the Cabinet also served as Secretary of the Board. This tradition had been established by Lord Waverley at the suggestion of Lord Keynes to link the government to the fate of Covent Garden. The minutes of the meetings there became as bland as those in 10 Downing Street. If there was a major disagreement, the Secretary of the Cabinet and the Opera House would merely record, 'The Board took note.' When Robert Armstrong, however, took up the position of Secretary at Covent Garden while a Principal at the Treasury and before becoming the Secretary of the Cabinet, he insisted that his multiple roles did not create a conflict of interest. 'Nobody ever talked to me about opera in the Treasury. They knew I was a lost cause. They put a Chinese Wall around me. My father was a musician. I was a dangerous personality.'

A certain paralysis afflicted the Arts Council at the end of the seven years of office of Sir Kenneth Clark, soon to be ennobled for his many services to the nation. When his successor Lord Cottesloe took over from him as Chairman, he was advised by his predecessor: 'Everybody says we should have double. If we did, it would only be wasted.' Clark was echoing Lord Keynes, who had warned an early employee, 'As long as the Arts Council doesn't get too much money, the Government won't start interfering.' These were the shrewd observations of experienced men, who walked softly in the corridors of power and who wanted the Council to remain at arm's length from the administration of the country, which was anyway not too interested in the arts. When Clark had at last arranged a meeting with the current Prime Minister, Harold Macmillan, he had been kept waiting for hours and then met with the urbane inquiry, 'Good evening, Clark, now what's this trouble with your Arts Society?'. The new Chairman, Lord Cottesloe, had been a good rower and rifleshot and he had a background in business and politics on the London County Council and the Port of London Authority, while also serving as the Chairman of the Trustees of the Tate Gallery. Now that he was head of the Arts Council, he continued the existing relationship with the Secretary-General. He used to say deprecatingly that he 'took over – or rather Williams took me over. He was a man full of sense and activity, and he didn't press a Welsh connection.'

All the same, Lord Cottesloe did not want the long-serving Secretary-General to run the show at his chosen pace for ever. The years were pressing upon Sir W. E. Williams, however indispensable he thought he was. For those young and essential members of the staff who would try to carry on his principles and policies through the decades to come, Williams was still the *eminence rouge*. To Tony Field, who was to begin as an assistant accountant and rise to become Finance Director of the Arts Council during his twenty-seven years of service, Williams was worthy of worship by nearly all the staff. He was a visionary and a mentor, and the underpaid employees would work inordinate hours for him. He opened the offices in St James's Square on Saturdays as in show business and he ruled from his wonderful panelled offices like a king. Sir Kenneth Clark was not a working chairman; he merely ran the agenda, not the policy. Field himself had been a failed actor, also a young theatrical accountant and impresario at the Comedy Theatre and the New Watergate Theatre Club with Peter Hall: they had effectively broken the censorship powers of the Lord Chamberlain by putting on Arthur Miller's *A View from the Bridge* and Tennessee Williams's *Cat on a Hot Tin Roof*. For Field, as for most of the rest of the Council staff, past experience in the performing arts as well as in administration was essential, if state patronage was to be given to the right companies and the right people on the ground and in the seats.

The stagnation at the beginning of the nineteen-sixties was a result of relatively static funding, except for extraordinary grants to bail out one opera company after another. There was no margin for innovation, while the needs of existing clients as well as the diminution of direct provision lessened the opportunities for improvisation. In spite of these inhibitions, the members of the staff of the Council still found the period exciting, particularly in the Drama Department. 'We introduced changes in the repertory theatre,' Dick Linklater has said. 'It became almost a thing of glory.' And this was achieved during a period of lessening freedom of action. 'In those days, what we did wasn't questioned as things are now questioned.' There was still some liberty of manoeuvre.

A slow and significant change was beginning in the membership of the Panels of the Arts Council from the doers to the administrators. A study of the first sixty-eight members discovered that one quarter had earned their living in artistic programmes underwritten by subsidy. Painters and ballet dancers and sculptors had only played a modest role in determining the policy of the Council, but they were a part of it. The sole sculptor was Henry Moore, the only dancer was Lady Keynes or Lydia Lopokova. William Coldstream, who was to become Vice-Chairman of the Council, was a distinguished painter. Two renowned musicians and composers, one of whom was Ralph Vaughan Williams, and several actors, actresses, theatrical producers, dramatists and poets, including Lewis Casson, Cecil Day Lewis and Eric Linklater, were also members of the Council. Thirteen of these members had been university professors, four in music, three in English literature, two in poetry, and two in the fine arts. Four men had specialised in the commercial side of the arts, particularly Bronson Albery and Hugh Beaumont in the theatre. Both businessmen and journalists had served along with eight Members of the House of Commons, although only two of these were in Parliament while also serving on the Arts Council. The Chancellor of the Exchequer generally 'avoided appointing to the Council persons currently active in politics, thus helping to ensure political neutrality'.

Until this time, only a Junior Minister had been given the responsibility for the arts and spoke in Parliament when that subject unfortunately was necessary. This low profile derived from the odd origins of the Arts Council, which was neither a state nor an independent fief. The members of the body were appointed by the Chancellor of the Exchequer. They consisted of a Chairman, a Vice-Chairman and eighteen members, five of whom generally came from Scotland and Wales. They were unpaid, as were the members of the important advisory panels, although their expenses could be reimbursed. This ordinance tended to favour the appointment of those who could afford the time without salary. They were meant to be selected, anyway, for their personal qualities and qualifications, and certainly not as representatives of any faction or group. Such were the dictates of impartiality.

Five years was the usual term of appointment for the Chairman and the Secretary-General and for all members of the Council and the Panels, although not for the staff. This might allow for rotation of office in a balance between experience and the desirability of new blood. The Panels were essential in their role under the Royal Charter, to 'advise and assist', as were the professional assessors from the Treasury. These civil servants and staff members functioned as the watchdogs of their own departments. And between them and the members of the Panels was a healthy rivalry.

This system of appointments and administration was as good as the times would allow. There was a vigorous tension and a contradictory energy between the staff and the Panels, the finance department and the clients, the Secretary-General and the Chairman and the members of the Council. But if there was one sovereign power, as in the reigning decade of Sir W. E. Williams, then this was rather the model of the unitary French patronage and culture of Colbert and of King Louis the Fourteenth than the competitive arts of the Italian cities of the Renaissance. Even during the era of the rule of Williams and after it, there was a feeling of aristocratic decision, which Professor Harold Baldry of the Regional Committee was to call 'democratic', on the model of Athens, where the citizens made some of the choices in a small city-state dependent upon slaves. When Professor Baldry was to join the Arts Council in later years, he would be told by an eminent member: 'Of course, you realize we are all just rubber stamps.' This was not to be his experience nor the experience of the members of the Panels until the nineteen-eighties, when another powerful Secretary-General would try to reduce them to commentators on executive decisions. As Baldry wrote in *The Case for the Arts*, 'The Council and its Panels and committees were faced with highly controversial issues which demanded – and received – genuine debate. But if ever the Council and its advisory bodies do become mere rubber stamps, that also will be a bad day for the arts.'

The long equilibrium kept by Williams between the Chairman and himself and the Directors of the departments, between the Treasury and the finance officers and the staff and the Panels, between London and Scotland and Wales and the regions, this would end in 1963 with his retirement. Before his going, he blew one or two last blasts, trying to determine a future policy for which he would be no longer responsible. These had the biblical overtones of his previous pronouncements about retribution and grains of mustard-seed: one was entitled 'The Sheep and the Goats'. Most importantly, it pointed out that the Arts Council could not continue without more support in its widespread and thin munificence for ever. The burden of patronage had to be shared, or some beneficiaries would have to meet the blade of the axe:

> Assistance should be given, primarily, to those towns which reveal a sturdy sense of self-help; just as there may be a case for withdrawal of aid from certain complacent and sluggish cities which still fail to contribute even a farthing rate to theatres or orchestras which the Arts Council has been supporting for a long time. The Arts Council is not fifteen years old, and may not yet be ready to revise its initial policy of assisting promising enterprises wherever it finds them. But, as it grows older, it may well decide to separate the sheep from the goats, and to make a substantial measure of local responsibility one of the qualifications for a grant from its limited funds. If a pound for a pound were the rule at present, as between the Arts Council and local subsidies, there would be some dramatic transformations of the scene.

There would be some dramatic transformations of the scene, but Sir William Emrys Williams would no longer be the commander. In fact he was to leave with a Parthian shot at his paymasters, piercing them with his arrow of desire for more patronage of the arts in Britain and less for agriculture:

> There is no art in which Britain cannot claim international prestige. In an Olympic contest we could win gold medals galore for sculpture, opera-singing, ballet-dancing, acting, painting, orchestral music and piano-playing, yet we continue to maintain all this outstanding excellence on a meagre scale of subsidy. We endure heavy taxation to keep down the cost of eggs, but to the cost of the arts we are contributing tenpence apiece. (The equivalent subsidy for eggs this year will work out at more than *ten shillings* per head.)

Priorities did seem to be wrong.

FIVE

MORE MONEY, MORE OPPORTUNITIES

An enthusiastic and ambitious Minister wishes to direct the arts. Between him and that direction is a large independent body of people who rate him as a useful animal for finding money, respect him if he finds it in greater abundance than hitherto, but have no real use for his views on artistic matters.

Lord Goodman in his memoirs,
Tell Them I'm On My Way, 1993

'There is an old Welsh saying that three things are needed to bring a man to his reward:' Dr Wyn Griffith wrote of Sir William Emrys Williams on his retirement as Secretary-General of the Arts Council, 'he must be skilled in action, patient in conference and steadfast in purpose.' His replacement by a civil servant in 1963 signalled a sea change in the intentions of government towards the Arts Council. The Conservative Chancellor of the Exchequer, Selwyn Lloyd, had given the Council the largest increase in its history, nearly half a million pounds, and he was thanked for saving Covent Garden and Sadler's Wells and the hard-pressed repertory theatre. Although most arts buildings remained 'obsolete, unsuitable or shabby', the prospect was brighter. There was a growing acceptance of the principle of public patronage among the legislators. The third Secretary-General, Nigel J. Abercrombie, had been a Professor of French and an Under-Secretary in the Admiralty, before moving to the Cabinet Office. He had written scholarly books and approved of amateur and youth arts. But he had no intention of confronting the

Treasury or the government as Williams had over grants or the occasional interference in policy. When Williams had been asked why money was given here and not there, he had always replied, 'Because we chose to.' And that choice had been respected, given the quality of the officers and the Panels of the Arts Council. Yet Abercrombie had been somewhat imposed on the Council to supervise the increased expenditure – a control that Keynes had foreseen if the budget were to develop. Williams 'had ruffled the Treasury's feathers a bit', the long-serving secretary Mary Endacott noted. 'They wanted a civil servant. It's never a good idea to foist a candidate on an organization.'

Equally long-serving was the Finance Director, the imperturbable James McRobert, with his Assistant Tony Field, both of whom worked for the Arts Council for some three decades. McRobert had been the anchorman for Williams as he would be for Abercrombie; he was 'a slow man of great integrity and charm, content to sit at his desk and not be the chap out front'. Field had worshipped, however, the departed Williams and his vision of the arts in Britain. He was uneasy, though, at yielding to civil servants in the Treasury what Williams had never conceded.

> In our discussions with their officials, they wanted public account-ability for money spent. We were vulnerable because Williams based his claim for funds on the Quality of Life argument. I said that we must change the argument to get more funds. We must say that money spent on the Arts was not subsidy but investment. I produced statistics showing that for each one million pounds invested, the Treasury received three million from foreign tours and tourism, royalties and employment taxes. I led the Arts Council into its sad future decline of quantifying the arts in material terms.

Although a civil servant was now the Secretary-General and the Treasury was asking for more accountability on spending on the arts, a major change in direction could be made. Lord Cottesloe was non-committal on regional policy, saying, 'A good idea, if it could be done.' His Secretary-General Abercrombie was for devolution and the creation of autonomous Regional Arts Associations, prompted by the thinking of both Conservative and Labour governments as advised by the civil service. As early as 1959, J. E. S. Simon, the Financial Secretary to the Treasury, had declared in a debate in the House of Commons announcing supplementary grants to the national museums and galleries as well as to the Arts Council: 'We are doing this not only because we feel that the interest of the people of Britain in the arts has greatly increased and that we are thereby reflecting their general wishes, but also because we believe that our action will enhance the richness and variety of our national life.' Following the election, the Conservative Political Centre had released a pamphlet, *The Challenge of Leisure*, summarizing policy proposals dealing with the arts, sports and youth service. Nothing much had come of this, except a vague promise in the Election Manifesto, called *The Next Five Years*, which indeed it proved to be under the leadership of Harold Macmillan. 'We shall do more to support the arts including the living theatre. Improvements will be made in museums and galleries and in public library service. Particular attention will be given to the needs of provincial centres.' Stimulated by a Bow Group pamphlet named *Patronage and the Arts*, Selwyn Lloyd did give major assistance to the arts in 1964 before the Labour victory. The Tory Party Manifesto then stated: 'We shall continue to expand this support and to increase the resources of the Arts Council.' Although the Prime Minister Alec Douglas-Home lost the election, his triumphant successor in 1965, Edward Heath, despite being a most accomplished conductor and pianist, hardly mentioned the arts in his party statement, *Putting Britain Right Ahead*, hedging with the words, 'We want to see much more choice opening out for people in leisure pastimes, in entertainment and in pursuit of the Arts.'

After an indifferent record on support of the Arts, the Labour Party led by Harold Wilson was to revolutionize the funding and the national acceptance of state patronage. In May 1964, a document appeared, *The Quality of Living*, which commented adversely on what had been done in the previous five years under the Conservatives. The recommendations were that a senior Cabinet Minister should have responsibility for an enlarged Arts Council and a new Sports Council. Housing the Arts should become a priority, while a network of Regional Arts Associations should be instituted to bring in local authority and business support allied with government funding through the Arts Council. This was the basis for the most important White Paper of the government since the draft for the

Royal Charter of 1945. A *Policy for the Arts* of February 1965 detailed what was the future policy of a Labour administration. It stated categorically that 'more generous and discriminating help is urgently needed, locally, regionally, and nationally'. The new government promised to move responsibility for the arts from the Treasury to the Department of Education and Science, and this was to be done. The emphasis of the Labour Party was to Spend as well as Raise. Increased appropriations, *A Policy for the Arts* declared, should enable the Arts Council to 'make a larger contribution to regional associations, to increase their assistance to the leading artistic enterprises in Scotland and Wales, to ease the financial burdens of provincial repertory theatres, to give a much needed impetus to the development of arts centres and to provide assistance for first class orchestras.'

Although the new Secretary-General Abercrombie was sympathetic to more regional funding and associations, he was wary of giving away the metropolitan direction of the Arts Council. His first signed statement in his new office in London promised more than the practice: the annual report was subtitled *Ends and Means*. 'There is no longer any reason,' he averred, 'as there was during the War, for a central agency to take out of people's hands the responsibility for initiating and organizing their own cultural activity in their own way, as the utterly democratic processes of local government allow and encourage.' Increases in local effort were now required more than heavy involuntary drafts on the taxpayer. The present constitution and organization of the Arts Council was better adapted for fruitful liaison with local authorities than any argument with the central machinery of government. 'We no longer have any "regional organization", but we appoint "assessors" to the Arts Council, to keep us in touch with local initiatives and developments, and to inform all those concerned "in the field" about our own policy, relevant experience and resources.' The wording of the Royal Charter was judicious: advice and co-operation came before holding and dealing with money. 'We can sometimes enjoy ourselves in the role of sugar-daddy to the arts, but we are at present more often, better and more characteristically employed as match-makers, midwives and nannies.'

Such maternalism was unfortunate in the phrases of the first

Secretary-General who did care about the regions without letting them slip the leash of the capital. He knew that there would be a change of policy, announcing in his introduction to his first annual report that his appointment coincided with the opening of 'a significantly new phase in the progress of the Council's work'. From his point of view, in his five years of service before his replacement by another innovator, he was the influence behind the creation of the network of new Regional Arts Associations, backed by the local authorities and leading to arts centres across the nation. In his second introduction to the Council's annual report of 1963–4, subtitled *State of Play*, he emphasized the minimal expenditure of local authorities on the arts and the House of Lords debate on state patronage. *A Survey of Municipal Entertainment* had showed that local authorities in England and Wales spent just over £2,500,000 on *all* forms of entertainment, a fifth of which would be called 'cultural', while the rest comprised band and jazz concerts, beauty competitions, carnivals, circuses, dances for fairs, pantomimes, variety and professional wrestling; the performances of these might be expected to pay for themselves. Two million pounds of the expenditure was actually recovered at the box office.

In spite of the Local Government Act enabling a sixpenny rate, the town councils were still not providing a major new source of patronage for the arts. The widowed Lady Gaitskell had commented in the House of Lords on 3 June 1964, that on the fifth centenary of Shakespeare's birth 'there is not one farthing on the rates for the Arts in Stratford'. She also commented on a city councillor who opposed a grant to an orchestra because 'there were only a very small number of people who appreciated good music', and the money 'would be better spent on housing for the old people'. The Lords' debate suggested a 'black list' of local authorities which refused to contribute; but Abercrombie did not support this anathema. The idea of paying for Bartok and Brecht out of Bingo might not appeal to the more high-minded Councillors and Aldermen; but the Arts Council always welcomed the Prodigal Son and the Repentant Sinner. 'Experience shows that *il n'y a que le premier pas qui coûte*, and there is joy in the Arts Council over one authority that takes the plunge ... The arguments that have persuaded Birmingham, Bristol and Oxford to subsidize the professional theatre, for example, have still to be accepted in many other places.'

Again, at the end of this stricture and encouragement of local support, Abercrombie put his pen in his mouth by starting the next piece, entitled 'The London Scene', with:

> London – *a per se*, the 'flower of cities all': if there is today a good measure of justification for quoting Dunbar, it is largely due to the splendour of those enterprises which the Arts Council is privileged to support. Critics (not all entirely disinterested) have suggested that we starve the provinces of money in order to squander subsidy on metropolitan activities. This is not true. But it is true that we spend relatively great sums on the Arts in London, and therefore need to be sure that it is well spent.

How such a contradictory declaration could hope to pacify the regions, only Abercrombie knew.

During his stewardship, however, prompted by government policy and increased subsidies as well as his own inclinations, Abercrombie did manage to put some of the money where his mouth and his pen had not been. The allocation of the Arts Council was increased substantially year by year during his five years in office:

£2,730,000 in 1963–4
£3,205,000 in 1964–5
£3,910,000 in 1965–6
£5,700,000 in 1966–7
£7,200,000 in 1967–8

It is worth noting the unprecedented annual increase of 45.8 per cent followed by 26.3 per cent in the last two years of the period.

There could be little innovation in the policy of the Arts Council without a major increase in funding. With more meagre subsidies, only the needs of existing clients could be met. As it was, the pilot of the future was the new North-Eastern Arts Association. Its director, the remarkable Alexander Dunbar, encouraged the local authorities in his area to match the Arts Council contribution on a pound-for-pound basis. As a result, its income for spending on the arts was to increase three times in the middle years of the nineteen-sixties. It was now setting a standard for other nascent regional associations, which were surging in spite of many centralist tendencies still remaining in St James's Square. The Labour government's wish for more devolution found its Angel Gabriel in the north of England. The annunciation arrived. Twelve Regional Arts Associations would develop to replace the original ten Regional Offices in England at the end of the Second World War. These would be considerably different in size and shape because of their origins and characters and areas, although they all subsidized cultural societies along with the local authorities and were recognized as charitable institutions. They would be wonderfully helped by another signal from Parliament in 1968, when the Select Committee advised in its paper, *Grants for the Arts*: 'The Arts Council should decentralize its support and work through regional associations, concentrating itself directly on national issues and organizations. This would imply building up the regional associations, giving them more active help and more immediate priority in the allocation of funds, perhaps with special inducements for special initiatives.'

The Secretary-General, however, did not have the power nor the persuasion of his predecessor, the redoubtable Sir W. E. Williams. He had trained in academia and the civil service, and he deferred to the priorities of his Chairman. To the staff of the Council, such as Sheila Gold, he appeared to be imposed on the Council by the government to carry out its policies in spite of the arm's length principle. She liked him for his cultivated manner but she suspected him of obeying the commandment of the first Labour minister responsible for the arts, Jennie Lee, 'Thou shalt devolve.' Yet she appreciated his diplomacy with the regions and their feeling for what culture really was. 'We must not impose it,' he told her. 'We must stimulate them to want it.' All the same, she saw that the policy of devolution would finally destroy the authority of the Arts Council in St James's Square. 'What you're doing, you realize,' she heard the accountant Tony Field say to Abercrombie, 'will leave us all without jobs.'

Despite the wiles of the government, the regions were not the paramount concern for Lord Cottesloe nor would they be for his successor as Chairman of the Arts Council, Lord Goodman. The end of the nineteen-fifties had been dominated by the troubles of the opera and ballet companies; but Cottesloe made his priority the translation of the National Theatre from a trolley and a fantasy to a reality and a solid base. He lobbied the Chancellor of the Exchequer Selwyn Lloyd to commit a million pounds towards a building to house it under the terms of the National Theatre Act; in point of fact, the completed structure would cost more than seven times that sum. Cottesloe achieved his object by the old ways of the political élite. He was a personal friend of that Conservative power-broker R. A. Butler, who was interested in the arts and never minded a word dropped in his ear. 'If I thought the Treasury was being a bit mean, I could go to Rab and say, "Can you do anything?"' And something then would often be done.

The creation of the National Theatre set its own drama between leading characters who had played and directed Shakespeare's works often enough to relish conflict and intrigue. A body called the Joint Council for the National Theatre, led by Lord Chandos and Lord Esher with Laurence Olivier as the Director, proposed a company sliced into a quartet – one at the new London theatre when it was built, one at the Royal Shakespeare Company at Stratford-upon-Avon, one at the Old Vic and one on permanent tour of the nation. Selwyn Lloyd suddenly refused to spend the million pounds promised for building the National Theatre, but he offered £400,000 annually to subsidize the regional theatres, particularly at Stratford. This proposal would have effectively made the Royal Shakespeare Company, led by Peter Hall, into a national theatre with its royal charter and metropolitan base at the Aldwych Theatre off the Strand.

However, a surprise approach by Lord Cottesloe to the London County Council led by the socialist Isaac Hayward produced an offer of £1,300,000 for a single auditorium in the arts complex rising on the South Bank. This pledge was conditional on the government contributing its million pounds and would mean an extra penny on the rates for Londoners. Selwyn Lloyd now suggested that there should be a larger scheme to construct a national theatre and opera house as a new home for the Sadler's Wells Company, and that the £400,000 subsidy for the regional theatres should be devoted to this purpose. He had executed an about turn in financial policy that gave everything back to the metropolis. Peter Hall took the Royal Shakespeare Company out of the negotiations and refused Laurence Olivier's offer of three months a year at the new National Theatre, when it should open its doors. This was seen as a poisoned chalice, aimed at closing down the Stratford company's rival base in the capital at the Aldwych. There was no way that Hall or his Royal Shakespeare players would be subservient to Olivier and his National Theatre supporters.

Lord Cottesloe cut the Gordian knot. He used his Chairman's sword at arm's length to allocate a first grant of only £47,000 to the Royal Shakespeare Company for the following year, 1963–64. He also warned it not to overspend and compete with the nascent National Theatre on a countryside level, because its rival's subsidy would be the higher. This in fact turned out to be five times higher, with £130,000 coming to the National Theatre from the Arts Council and another £100,000 from the London County Council. Metropolitan politics had clinched the combat of the theatres, although the Stratford company gained the crown in the celebration of Shakespeare's birthplace on Avon with the extraordinary staging of the complete cycle of the bard's history plays from *Richard II* to *Richard III* in an abbreviated trilogy, *The Wars of the Roses*. If Olivier's victory over the National Theatre was Hall's loss at this Bosworth, the artistic director of the Royal Shakespeare won his Agincourt on the bare boards of his provincial stage. And as a result, a direct Treasury grant was arranged through the Arts Council of £170,000 for the next two years exclusive of touring, which allowed the Royal Shakespeare Company to keep its London base.

As chairman of the new South Bank Theatre and Opera House Board, Lord Cottesloe was also responsible for the choice of the architect of the structure to rise beside the Thames. A committee headed by the designer of the Festival Hall, Sir Robert Matthew, interviewed twenty applicants, winnowed from six times that number. Making a theatrical entrance alone, Denys Lasdun declared that he knew nothing about creating theatres. He would have to sit down and learn what the committee wanted – an amphitheatre, another theatre with a proscenium arch and a small experimental playhouse, which would eventually be called the Cottesloe. During the discussion, Lasdun declared that the most important aspect was 'the spiritual one'. Members of the committee liked that, also his pledge to work closely with them until the design stage, when he would be the sole arbiter in his own style, which owed so much to concrete and Le Corbusier. 'We were only concerned with getting a building that would fulfil the requirements,' Lord Cottesloe later recorded. 'We assumed that the government would find the money to build it and maintain it.'

Although it was a secondary matter to him, Cottesloe did not neglect drama touring and Housing the Arts in the provinces. He recognized the potential conflict between the Council's twin obligations: to improve standards of execution and to increase the accessibility of the arts to the public. The amount of touring by the major national companies was actually being increased as well as the number of repertory companies receiving assistance from the local authorities. And steps were being taken towards building a theatre grid, heralded by the opening of the new Playhouse at Nottingham on 11 December 1963, when Lord Snowdon, acting on behalf of his wife Princess Margaret, declared: 'This will not be just a new theatre in the provinces for actors rehearsing before a London debut. With the amount of talent already involved it will immediately become a cultural centre, respected and envied internationally, making London itself look to its laurels ... Nottingham is on the side of the future.' Proposals for other new theatres were also maturing in Birmingham, Chichester, Croydon, Guildford and Manchester. With the creation of a building fund for the Arts Council to use in order to supplement the contributions of the local authorities, a national theatre grid might yet be achieved. And this would, indeed, come to pass at the end of Lord Cottesloe's time as Chairman with the implementation of the Labour government's White Paper of 1961, *A Policy for the Arts*, and its declaration that a quarter of a million pounds was to be allocated. 'For the first time a building fund has been established to encourage local authorities and regional associations to come forward with building plans.' During the succeeding seven years, one and a quarter million pounds in capital housing grants, split among twenty-seven applicants, would be administered by the Arts Council's Finance Department in its assistance towards the regional homes for opera, music, drama and dance.

By 1965, the Arts Council could pat itself on the back with another success, the revival of the theatre in Britain. Less than ten years before, imminent doom had been forecast. 'Steadily and ominously throughout the year more theatres have been closing their doors,' the annual report had declared. 'Must all this mean that, outside London, we are bound to accept the dissolution of the professional theatre within the next few years?' Yet the Arts Council had proceeded with a new pattern of patronage combining national, municipal, industrial and private resources. 'Patronage works best,' the Council had said, 'when it has many centres of initiative.' The very act of faith of the Council in the theatre gave some hope, as did the small sums available for refurbishment before Housing the Arts was implemented by the government. Some training for the best new talents in the field was also subsidized as was support and publicity for the new drama which had begun to flourish after the Suez crisis. 'That sense of hopelessness about our theatre which prevailed in the 'fifties has disappeared today: there is plenty of criticism and dissatisfaction, but it is directed towards a lively, vigorous and much more stabilized theatre than we ever dared to imagine possible only a few years ago; we haven't got a corpse on our hands any longer.'

In another matter, however, Lord Cottesloe did admit slow progress. Although he was to recommend his Secretary-General to his successor Lord Goodman, he did not support his subordinate's expanding regional commitment, which was summed up by Abercrombie in his last year of office at a UNESCO conference in Ottawa, where he praised the achievements in devolution of the system of state subsidies during the nineteen-sixties:

> Within the space of a decade, the whole system of patronage of the arts in England and Wales has been transformed. The Arts Council of Great Britain and the Welsh Arts Council are still the principal agencies of the Government for this purpose; local authorities continue to increase their contribution; trusts and other private sources of funds are more than ever significant. The new thing is Regional Arts Associations, concerned to promote the practice and appreciation of the arts on a decentralized basis. Ten years ago the total income of the Regional Arts Associations was under £100,000. It is now almost £2,000,000 and growing annually. This means that fully autonomous, regionally inspired and directed agencies can and do improve the quality of life of the people in England and Wales as they would have it, with nobody in Whitehall knowing best.

It was a picture of innovation across the nation, which would hardly have passed muster with either Lords Cottesloe or Goodman, who dragged their feet over devolution and remained unrepentant supporters of urban arts in the hands of professional performers. The obvious solution, to devolve the amateur and 'community' arts onto the Regional Arts Associations, was questionable. The annual report of 1963–4 examined the role of 'Local Activities and the Amateur' and asked where should the boundaries be drawn? 'How far should purely amateur activity be subsidized, and how far or how much further should the Arts Council advance into this debatable territory?' It would rather leave the funding of these activities to the Education Authorities or to the Sports Council. A great deal of government prodding would be necessary to shift these two Chairmen of the nineteen-sixties towards a greater say by the provinces. Jennie Lee tried to suggest Manchester as the best site for the new Arts Council headquarters, when Lord Goodman wished to shift to larger premises from St James's Square. A senior civil servant came up with Basingstoke or Woking as a site rather than Piccadilly; such a move was quashed by the genial voice of the Chairman saying that any direction outside London would be followed by his own resignation and several hundred others within hours. He and his staff would not work outside the metropolis, which was the focus of all approaches to the arts.

As Tony Field has pointed out, there was a concentration of creative and performing artists in London. The leading theatres and concert halls and opera houses were sited there, also the main radio, film and television studios. Since in those days the Council and Panel members were largely drawn from professional and creative artists, it was important that meetings should all be held in London because of their professional commitments. As Gregory Peck commented on the differences between the British Isles and the North American continent, where he was a drama assessor for the United States Environment Fund for the Arts: 'It is easy for you in the United Kingdom to assess the work of companies all over your small island. Think of us trying to sit in Washington and consider applications from Chicago, Dallas, San Francisco and Miami!'.

A separate tack would be taken in dealing with the windfall from Housing the Arts and with the flexible relations to the Regional

Associations. In the first annual report of 1964–5 written under Lord Goodman's tutelage, he made the distinction clear:

> Whether in the case of theatres, concert halls, or arts centres, there is a world of difference between the action of the British Government in endorsing the line consistently taken by the Arts Council, and the plans of the French Government for establishing a national network of *Maisons de la Culture*. If there is to be a great new opera house in Manchester with resident opera and ballet companies, that will come about because the people of Manchester and the north have demanded it – not because Manchester was plotted on a map in St James's Square as the right place for 'establishing full-scale permanent opera in the north of England.' Similarly the appearance of arts centres at Boston, St Austell or Birmingham is something that we will encourage, but had no hand in originating. The principles governing expenditure by the Arts Council from the new capital fund reflect this primacy of local considerations.

As for the Regional Associations, there would be few mutual benefits if the Arts Council gave them no say in the disposal of the funds channelled through them. On the other hand, it was 'quite right and proper for them to allocate funds in support of local enterprises which have little or no claim to the Arts Council support within the terms of our Charter'. It was easier to see than to define the principles to be followed. The presence of an Arts Council representative as an assessor when local funds were distributed was the most effective safeguard. There was also the difficulty of giving to a recognized client of the Council – an orchestra or repertory company or touring organization – within the boundaries of a Regional Association:

> Who is to provide the subsidy? The Arts Council alone? But then where is the 'mutual benefit'? The Association? But we have direct obligations to our client, of which we cannot divest ourselves. This is a fine field for the elaboration of case-law; the extremes to be avoided are, first, treating the Regional Associations as mere post-offices, and secondly allowing them the sort of autonomy that constitutionally belongs to the Scottish and Welsh Committees of Council (this is something we are not entitled to devolve upon anyone in England).

This was a leading lawyer's strict construction of the Royal Charter of incorporation, which would soon be altered to meet more regional demands. The widespread annual festivals across the nation had already achieved unceasing support from St James's Square. As the long-serving Eric W. White declared in 1965, summer was the season of arts festivals – at home and abroad – and the word 'festival' had become an accepted part of the jargon of culture. These were not a new phenomenon, although their proliferation was recent. The Three Choirs Festival had been performed for two centuries in Gloucester, Worcester and Hereford Cathedrals, while the attempt to commemorate Shakespeare in his birthplace went back to David Garrick, although the regular seasons of Shakespeare's plays had only begun a century ago. Mendelssohn's close connection with Birmingham was a matter of municipal history, and two of the old triennial music festivals at Leeds and Norwich had survived into present times. And, of course, the Glyndebourne Festival, begun as a rich man's whim by John Christie and called 'Mozart in a Sussex hayfield', had become an exemplar of provincial opera to the nation. 'The Festival of Britain put the seal of official approval on the festival movement as a whole. New festivals were invented to meet government requirements; and these played their part in the national jamboree.' Although many of these festivals proved ephemeral, the survivors found themselves blessed because of this tradition. At Edinburgh and Aldeburgh, at Bath and King's Lynn, at York and Ludlow and Cheltenham and Chichester, fine professional directors and performers were engaged and attracted large audiences. Although local authorities should bear most of the cost, the Arts Council could be trusted to contribute if the festival showed itself to be of sufficiently high standard. Assessment was still all within this promise of generosity.

The innovations allowed by the increased funding of the decade were being applied in other interesting directions. The Muse, forgotten by John Maynard Keynes, of prose as well as poetry was to be admitted within the fold of the state-supported arts of Britain. Lord Goodman's first report excused this omission from the original scope of the Arts Council by stating that in 1945 'there was nothing to suggest that literature as an art form was also in need of subsidy'. Times were changing, however, as the success of the Poetry Panel had proved. Grants had been given to the Poetry Book Society to help it distribute four book choices a year to its members, poetry recitals and tours by poets were being funded, triennial prizes for poetry and bursaries were being awarded to British poets, and above all a National Manuscript Collection of Contemporary Poets had been launched in collaboration with the British Museum in 1963 with the help of a special grant of two thousand pounds from the Pilgrim Trust. Instead of going to avid American universities, notebooks and worksheets by W. H. Auden, Roy Fuller, Philip Larkin, Edwin Muir and Peter Porter were already acquired and would remain over here.

This fledgling hoard would imitate the extraordinary contemporary British art collection of the council initiated by Sir W. E. Williams and carried through by his Director of Art, Philip James, who had previously served as the Keeper of the Library at the Victoria and Albert Museum. Before he retired at the end of the nineteen-fifties, James had put together a collection of more than four hundred prints, three hundred paintings and water-colours and thirty-four pieces of sculpture, some by Henry Moore. For seventeen years, he worked with diligence and devotion to reveal and interpret visual art to a new and sometimes puzzled audience. Much credit was due to him in a greater public acceptance of experiment in art. He had 'achieved this transformation of opinion by the steadfast conviction that art is a many-splendoured thing and not a repetitive pattern of orthodoxy'. His assistant Joanna Drew would eventually inherit his post and try to carry on the wartime tradition of the direct provision of travelling exhibitions, 'Art for the People', as long as this was feasible.

Another departure heralded the beginning of a new era in the arts. Dame Ninette de Valois volunteered to the Board of the Royal Opera House at Covent Garden that she wished to retire as director of the Royal Ballet and let Sir Frederick Ashton take over. With the help of Keynes and the Arts Council, she and Rambert had created ballet in Britain. How she did it, according to Lord Robbins, was a matter which defied a short description:

> She was a dancer of exquisite accomplishment, a choreographer of masterly vision and imagination. But the qualities which went to the creation of her ballet, both as an internal organization and as an artistic force in the land, transcended all those; there was a jewel-like intensity of purpose, an indomitable will and an authority of judgment, born of a marriage of intellect and taste, which without

any affectation or pretentiousness was apt to silence all objections. When Madame spoke, *she was the ballet.*

In this manifold change at the helm, Lord Goodman was responsible for two significant appointments in his first year of office at the Arts Council: John Cruft replaced John Denison as Director of Music and Tony Field rose to become the Finance Director. Denison's experience was significant in the alterations to come. He had played the horn in the City of Birmingham Orchestra before the Second World War and had been in charge of Theatre and Music Control in the British Zone of Occupied Germany after the war, where he had been 'the British gauleiter', importing sheepguts from Blackpool to make violin and cello strings for the orchestra of the Hamburg Opera House. After he was demobilized, he had joined the British Council in arranging world tours for musical artists. Steuart Wilson had wanted him as a successor at the Arts Council, and when he was given the job, he found the organization still full of 'the flotsam of the C.E.M.A. operation, recruited in the darkest days of the war'. He used his professional experience during his seventeen years as Director of Music at St James's Square, 'trying to produce a structure under which grants could be processed in a logical way'. Sir W. E. Williams had run the show through his 'Directorate', which met weekly on Tuesday mornings and settled policy and grants, advised by the Panels. Great care and scrutiny was involved in spending even little sums. Williams was known as 'ABCA Bill' and ordered things in rather a military fashion; 'he wouldn't stand any nonsense from politicians trying to snipe at the Arts Council – or the Beaverbrook press'. He ran meetings, as Lord Cottesloe was to do, in a most professional way and never allowed them to take more than two hours. 'Our decisions were generally respected because of the high calibre of the senior staff and the Panels.' To Denison, this prestige was eroded by Lord Goodman's appointments, which took in hand the little groups of experimentalists. 'Once you open the door to them, you have to have a Panel which knows about New Orleans jazz.'

That is exactly what Lord Goodman hoped to achieve, including on the Panels 'experimentalists, non-conformists and conformists, the unconventional and conventional, fashionable and unfashionable', trying to comprehend every shade of human activity in the world of art to the dismay of many older staff members and civil servants. 'We travelled to the extreme limits', he was to admit in his later memoirs. 'Sometimes we went over the edge of what to me and many others appeared to be sensible, since only by going over the edge could we cover the total area.' This was the fresh policy of the new Chairman, which was inherited by John Cruft as the Director of Music for the next fourteen years. He had also come from the British Council and had a fairly cordial relationship with Goodman and tried to carry out some of his experimentalism. Although Jennie Lee was the Minister, Cruft did not believe that she knew anything of the arts. 'She believed in people being enabled', not instructed or edified. His job was now diffusion and innovation as well as assessing the quality of performances.

For Tony Field, the chairmanship of Lord Cottesloe followed by the early years of Lord Goodman brought a golden decade of harmony between artistic and financial decisions. The Music and Drama and Art and Poetry (soon to be Literature) Panels chose the recipients, while the accountants assessed how much went to each. Panels proposed, finance disposed. Nobody yet questioned the choices of the Panels because the process of making decisions was respected as was the distinction of the various members. Relationships with Clive Smart at the Hallé Orchestra, David Brierley at the Royal Shakespeare Company, Philip Hedley at the Theatre Royal at Stratford East and Thelma Holt at the Roundhouse were sympathetic and productive. There was also a good relationship between the Arts Council and the civil servants at the Treasury, particularly Molly Loughane, Edward Playfair and John Winifreth, who were sympathetic and understanding to the needs of the arts. They did not want direct government grants even to Covent Garden in case they removed from the Minister the ability to wash his or her hands like Pontius Pilate of any blunder made in the spending of state money on creative trash. Even though the power of the Treasury was enormous at that time of increasing subsidy, it kept its distance and pulled no strings, allowing the Arts Council to do what Hugh Gaitskell had once told the rebellious Labour Party that he would do – 'try, try, and try again'.

On taking over, Lord Goodman found Lord Cottesloe a shy and undemonstrative man with a warm heart, immensely courteous and deeply effective. His technique was the opposite of Goodman's. He did not encourage the members of his committee to be vocal; but he handled an agenda with the greatest expedition. He bequeathed only one major problem to his successor – the survival of the Royal Philharmonic Orchestra – and another lesser problem – the personality of the Secretary-General Abercrombie, a man of religion and rectitude, dignity and culture, who seemed to Goodman to prefer abstractions to flesh-and-blood realities. There was also 'a warm reciprocity of dislike' between Abercrombie and his Minister, Jennie Lee. 'The cold water he poured on my plans', Goodman was to declare in his memoirs, 'would have filled the reservoirs of the Water Board ... As time went on he came to recognize that I was too large and weighty an object totally to obstruct and ultimately he accepted defeat.'

The wise Mr Dooley once said of American politics and justice that the Supreme Court followed the election returns. Although state patronage was now meant to be non-partisan, the victory of the Labour Party in 1964 and again in 1966 at the polls showed that the arts in Britain could also follow the votes. In fact, the new Prime Minister Harold Wilson was no more interested in the arts than any of his predecessors had been except in the matter of films, which had concerned him when he had been President of the Board of Trade. He had made, however, two inspired appointments to administer public patronage. As Under-Secretary of the Department of Science and Education with special responsibility for the Arts, he had appointed Jennie Lee, the widow of the firebrand Aneurin Bevan. A coalminer's daughter with a university degree, she was an ikon of the party with direct access to the Prime Minister. Her friend, the actress Constance Cummings, said of her, 'Nye Bevan knew more about the arts than Jennie. She was more in the political world. She was much more concerned with education and jobs and eating properly. Even artists should eat. Jennie's attitudes to all the arts was that she recognized the *value* of them, but was not educated in them.' On one occasion the new Chairman of the Arts Council, Lord Goodman, told her that for a small amount of money, just over a million pounds, she could gain a large amount of popularity. Her response was forthright. 'To descend to your crude level, how many votes?'

Wilson's second inspired appointment was his choice of a successor to Lord Cottesloe: his own lawyer, Arnold Abraham Goodman, who was also given a life peerage. Educated at the universities of London and Cambridge, Goodman was a leading conciliator, who always preferred a judicious compromise to a confrontation in the courts. He believed that government must increase its spending on the arts. Among the Latin tags he was fond of quoting, he would often say *Bis dat qui cito dat*, 'He gives twice who quickly gives'. Even his Secretary-General Abercrombie recognized that there was a new order in the world, 'that the Arts Council was at a turning-point in its affairs. The old Chinese curse was upon us: "May you live in interesting times." In every field of our action there were evident symptoms of abounding vitality.' The first came from the attitude of Lord Goodman, who intended to run the Council as Keynes would have done, had he lived. Diplomatically, he informed the retired Sir W. E. Williams, who had run the Council when he was Secretary-General: 'I do not see myself in a policy-making role. I shall be a chairman and not a generalissimo ... Like any sensible ship's captain, I shall keep out of the engine-room.' But that was not to be. Abercrombie soon found himself shunted to the petty officer's mess. 'I was never conscious of how much power a Chairman could wield', Tony Field has said, 'until Arnold Goodman arrived.'

Faced with the Trinity of Harold Wilson, Jennie Lee and Lord Goodman, the Secretary-General Abercrombie did not have a chance. He had already blotted his copybook, writing in 1963 against the arts being transferred to 'one of the spending departments – perhaps the Ministry of Education or the Ministry of Public Buildings and Works'. Yet that is what the Labour government did, transferring responsibility for the arts from the Treasury to the new Department of Education and Science. Moreover, Abercrombie had seen no reason for a powerful central agency to take out of people's hands the responsibility for organizing their own cultural activity in their own way. Again he was out of step and marching contrary to his superior officers. The trinity then ruling the arts included the Prime Minister, and he fundamentally believed in central control as much as Lord Goodman did, even if Jennie Lee continually spoke up for more power to the people and local cultures. There might be larger grants to the regions and to innovation, but only if these were administered and assessed from London with the increase given by the Department of Education and Science. Under the Labour government, the budget of the Arts Council would rise from more than three million pounds annually to more than seven million pounds within the space of four years, at an average increase of nearly a third a year. It was still too little, although significant now, and yet as nothing compared to the whole national budget for education. If anyone came to Goodman and said he objected to his income tax being allocated to the Arts Council, the Chairman's favourite reply was that he would happily send him a postal order for it.

Yet there was an unprecedented expansion of opportunity, which played into the hands of a dominant, but conciliatory Chairman, who used all his legal finesse to get his own way. 'He reasons', Lord Annan described him. 'He enchants. His courtesy is proverbial. This, too, is how he negotiates.' On one occasion, the Board of the Arts Council dared to vote unanimously against a policy of the Chairman. 'It is an impasse', Lord Goodman decided. When he was told it was no impasse and he was outvoted nineteen to one, he merely deferred the matter to another meeting and did what he intended to do. Seeing himself as a latterday Goodman in a cultural *Pilgrim's Progress*, he was later to write in his memoirs:

> I took the view, unrepentantly, that some wastage of public money was unavoidable to achieve an ecumenical approach that would give confidence to the whole art world. The wastage was trivial in terms of percentages, but it meant that on the whole almost any artistic experience short of dementia had a chance of receiving some encouragement within our walls, and the effect was healthy and buoyant in relation to artists of real quality. They approved immensely because they sensed that the old canons of restrictive censorship and repression were being reduced to a minimum.

This policy had an importance in itself in the libertarian years to come and helped to foment an atmosphere of artistic freedom.

SIX

THE FURNISHINGS
OF A CAPITAL CITY

It is through its literature more than any other feature of
its life that an age is remembered and judged: and, more
urgent still, writers have the duty to preserve our
language, to affirm civilized values, and to enlarge the
imagination of their contemporaries – 'where there is no
vision, the people perishes.' It is essential work, and we
should give our good writers decent conditions in which
to perform it.

Cecil Day Lewis, Chairman of the Literature Panel
of the Arts Council, later Poet Laureate, 1966

Jennie Lee thought that political action was able to bridge the gaps
between the many different cultures of Britain. Presenting her
opening White Paper, *A Policy for the Arts: The First Steps*, she
appeared confident that the various cultures might become one, if
properly guided. There was no question of state patronage directing
taste or restricting the liberty of the experimental artist or imposing
any controls:

> But abuses can be spotted and tackled, high standards encouraged,
> and opportunities given for wider enjoyment. It is partly a question of
> bridging the gap between what have come to be called the 'higher'
> forms of entertainment and the traditional sources – the brass band,
> the amateur concert party, the entertainer, the music hall and pop
> group – and to challenge the fact that a gap exists. In the world of Jazz
> the process has already happened; highbrow and lowbrow have met.

Later in the debate in the House of Commons on the White Paper,

Jennie Lee expanded on her commitment. The arts and associated amenities must occupy a central place in every region. In a phrase reminiscent of the retired Sir W. E. Williams, she said that an immense amount could be done to improve the quality of contemporary life. There was a great longing to be more of a community, not to have élite cultures separated from popular tastes. 'Before we arrogantly say that any group of our citizens are not capable of appreciating the best in the arts, let us make absolutely certain that we have put the best within their reach.'

These admirable intentions did not change the actual practices of the Arts Council. If the new butter was better spread, the knife was still in the hand of the metropolitan establishment and Lord Goodman. He has declared in private, 'It is idiotic that the regions, which are pretty barren of talent, should run the show. You can't find that in Wigan or Warrington. They need a hard centre.' Such an attitude against outsiders affected the playwright Arnold Wesker's attempt to set up a cultural centre, to be called Centre 42, in Chalk Farm in North London in the Roundhouse, an old railway turning-shed. He had previously persuaded the Trades Union Congress in 1960 to pass a resolution recognizing the responsibilities of the unions towards the arts in an age of increased leisure, following the example of the medieval craft guilds which had staged Miracle Plays five hundred years before. Wesker also believed that there was a common culture ranging from keeping racing pigeons to listening to grand opera, in which all could participate according to their fancy. Jennie Lee had agreed to join Centre 42 as its sole Member of Parliament along with writers and artists and trade unionists. They would run people's festivals and be 'a cultural hub which, by its approach and work, will destroy the mystery and snobbery associated with the arts'.

Although local Trades Councils did back a series of provincial festivals, the fund-raising for Centre 42 in the Roundhouse proved a Tower of Babel rather than Wesker's vision of a New Jerusalem in London. By the end of the decade, he had quarrelled with Jennie Lee, who was a changed being when she had responsibility for all the arts in Great Britain. Wesker failed to receive grants from the Arts Council, let alone the trades unions. Lord Goodman resented the fact that Marcia Williams, the private secretary of the Prime

Minister, had Wesker to tea at 10 Downing Street in an effort to put pressure on him to support the playwright, although the scheme had not found favour in Goodman's eyes. 'He had spent in promoting the scheme money that could have been used in establishing it, and I was both impatient and critical of his capacity to launch and support a large new artistic organization.' The collapse of Centre 42 showed that the independence of the Arts Council was real, and that the arm's length principle worked: it also proved the essential role of government funding. If under Murphy's Law only the impossible were to happen and a common culture were to be created and arts opportunities spread to most communities, only state grants could do it. Otherwise, the consumer culture of the young would pullulate in its many contradictions, or the virus of the 'alternative or counter-culture'.

What was interesting was that it was felt necessary to revise the Royal Charter of the Arts Council in 1967 to widen the scope of its grants. Its purpose might still be to develop and improve 'knowledge, understanding and practice', but this was now of 'the arts' rather than what Lord Keynes had defined as 'the fine arts exclusively'. The Council was still bound to increase the accessibility of the arts to the public throughout Great Britain and to advise and co-operate with government departments, local authorities and other bodies. The Committees of Scotland and Wales were now to be known as the Scottish and Welsh Arts Councils. The comment from Edinburgh on this change was wry: 'There is an old saying that you can give a dog a bad name and hang him. Perhaps, too, if you give him a good one you can expect great things of him.' Cardiff merely commented that the change of title introduced in the new Charter reflected the autonomy which Wales had always enjoyed.

In a debate in the House of Lords, Goodman spoke frankly about the reasons why the Charter and the policy of the Arts Council had been altered since the time of his predecessor as Chairman:

> There has been – and I admit it frankly to the noble Lord, Lord Cottesloe – some change of policy and some change of emphasis since his day. I do not say that our policy is any better, but it is different, in the sense that our major emphasis is on cultivating new audiences for the arts. The question of improving the standard and quality of those institutions which are still there is of great importance, but it is not

our paramount consideration ... I believe that there is a crucial state in the country at this moment. I believe that young people lack values, lack certainties, lack guidance; that they need something to turn to; and need it more desperately than they have needed it at any time in our history – certainly, at any time which I can recollect. I do not say that the arts will furnish a total solution, but I believe that the arts will furnish some solution. I believe that once young people are captured for the arts they are redeemed from many of the dangers which confront them at the moment and which have been occupying the attention of the Government in a completely unprofitable and destructive fashion. I believe that here we have constructive work to do which can be of inestimable value.

Yet the unspoken problem was now the meaning of 'the arts' at a time when the impact of pop art and music had led to the belief that artists were untrained people who said they were artists, and 'the arts' were what the artists wanted to perform – and to be paid for it. As *Encounter* declared, the culture of the period was about the self. 'Whether, in radicalism, in literature, in the performing arts, in philosophy, psychology, music and art, not to mention sociology ... the self, the autonomous self, the performing self, the contemplated self, *above all* the contemplated self – triumphed.' And to define the limits of the arts, as the long-serving and astute James McRobert observed, was an impossible task. 'The boundaries shift and the markers get up and walk away like Alice's croquet hoops.' Yet for an organization dealing with public funds, some guide lines were necessary, however often they had to be redrawn. As the Arts Council was a charity, it could only use its money for charitable purposes. By and large, it decided not to subsidize amateurs or direct educational activities or help commercial enterprises, although there were temptations to dabble in these areas. To McRobert, the chief danger for the Arts Council was diffusion of effort. Limited subsidy must mean some limitation of aims. In the words of Hugh Willatt, Abercrombie's successor as Secretary-General: 'We had to draw the line. We drew it at crafts. We drew it at architecture. We drew it on film, except for a few small art films.' And as for McRobert's importance, Willatt declared: 'Chairmen may come and go, and Secretary-Generals may come and go, but McRobert went on running the Council.'

As a pacifier and a believer, Abercrombie was shifted to

representing the provinces, where he became Chief Regional Adviser. This was a sideways rather than upward move. As with Ovid in imperial Rome, his emphasis was rewarded and exiled by his posting. His successor noted that Abercrombie's appointment indicated the Council's positive attitude to the question of regional development, which Jennie Lee had supported in her White Paper. More Regional Arts Associations were springing up of themselves, and their little grants were doubled within two years. But Hugh Willatt was a practising lawyer, as Arnold Goodman was. He had thirteen years' experience on the Arts Council, ending as the Chairman of the Drama Panel, although he was based in Nottingham; he had also been Chairman of the Ballet Rambert. He did not oppose Lord Goodman on metropolitan and regional issues. As for the Royal Charter, Willatt has blithely asked, 'Did we ever look at it? No, we didn't waste much time hammering out new policies. We responded to what was there.' Lord Goodman was officially pledged to place more emphasis on the regions 'until at least something comparable to the London "density" of culture is available in other parts of the country.' But not too much was done. As Willatt himself wrote to his Chairman of their time of service together:

> Abercrombie's appointment was an effort to develop the relationship between the Council and the Associations and give them a spokesman at top Council level. It was not his fault that the relationship was never completely happy in your time or later. The major organizations in each region, the theatres, orchestras and some galleries, wanted, and kept, a direct relationship with the Council, a relationship needed for reasons of professional standing, among others. Many large local authorities preferred to continue subsidy direct to, say, the Hallé Orchestra or the Nottingham Playhouse, in which they took some pride and on whose Boards they were represented. Their contributions to the Associations were often small and grudging.

With the renaissance of English drama, the Arts Council had persuaded the local authorities to invest in their city theatres at last. It was a success, which Lord Goodman inherited and augmented with the small capital sums now made available, which had been demanded by the 'Housing the Arts' inquiry. New theatres at Coventry, Nottingham, Guildford, Leicester, Exeter, Chester, Worcester, Birmingham, Bolton, Ipswich, Colchester, Edinburgh and

Leatherhead; major improvements at Sheffield, Liverpool, York and Greenwich; salvation for repertory at Bromley, Crewe, Malvern, Sunderland, Hull, Bradford and Watford – these were all initiated or achieved. A 'Civic Theatre' was being created 'to present a mixed programme of events to suit the varied interests of the theatre-going folk in the area'. What was also being created was a national grid of first-class theatres, which would allow the major London companies to tour extensively. Independent television companies and powerful private trusts, particularly the Nuffield and Calouste Gulbenkian Foundations, also contributed to the revival of live theatre throughout the nation. And yet the local authorities still only levied a fraction of a penny rate for all forms of entertainment with the theatre often acting as the Cinderella. One Clerk of the Council wrote to the director of the local playhouse that a grant was being made to it, 'and he accordingly enclosed a cheque for one guinea'.

In his opening declaration as Chairman of the Arts Council, Lord Goodman did state that he would evolve a firm policy, yet a protean one. 'We do not exist to plan artistic and cultural projects. Very few are the fruit of direct Arts Council labours. And this is as it should be. The larger the extent of national subsidy, the more vital that it should neither bear nor seem to bear the imprint of a single body. Artistic life in this country must not be dominated by a small, non-elected, appointed caucus in St James's Square.' Much as he liked to direct, the policy of the Arts Council had to remain one of response to the needs of bodies all over the country, which had grown to excellence by local efforts. London must not seem to rule, even if it largely did. Yet Goodman thought that the metropolis served all the nation, 'and to talk as if England was a country where it was necessary to travel for seven days on a camel in order to reach London' was absurd. In the regions actual inspiration and growth should be promoted, but London must have 'the furnishings of a capital city'.

Lord Goodman's assumption that an élite should lead the arts from London would meet opposition from one man, Hugh Jenkins, who had been a Secretary of the Actors' Union, Equity, and who was a Labour Member of Parliament, and who would briefly serve as the minister responsible for the arts. Asked to join the Board of the Arts Council, he soon locked horns with the Chairman:

> Lord Goodman and I disagreed totally about democracy. Relations between the Arts Council and other bodies were by this time much closer than in earlier days ... but the Council as a whole still believed in the curious proposition that to retain its independence *from* government it was necessary to be appointed *by* the government. There was also a more rational objection. Appointment ensured that the Arts Council consisted of persons dedicated to the Arts. When the Arts Council emerged from the Council for the Encouragement of Music and the Arts there was no demand for democratic control ... It was not until the Council had grown into a great influence in the land and government patronage was taken for granted that complaints began to be heard that this enormous power, this decisive influence, was exercised by a small group of appointees answerable to no one but themselves. By that time the Council had become part of the Establishment and tradition had converted defect into virtue.

In answer to that criticism, Lord Goodman was to widen the membership of the Panels and introduce some young members to them. The first person appointed by Goodman, the Director of Music, John Cruft, approved of the arm's length principle and pointed out the risk which members of the Arts Council took. Unpaid as they were, if they built up debts in their grants or made wrong choices, they would have to fall on their swords, as in Japan. He found more sinister the interlocking of politics and grants to the arts within the local authorities and the Regional Arts Associations, on which elected town councillors also served. Hugh Jenkins was, indeed, one of only four serving politicians also to serve on the Arts Council in its history. Better to be thought an élite or an Establishment and retain independence from government than to be accused of making choices that were influenced by politics.

The golden years of increased funds for the arts did allow for help to youth and innovation. Progress developed from more spending. But no new seeds of culture grew from this mulch. As Lord Goodman admitted, 'We never expected a new Art to emerge, and it didn't.' In a speech in the Guildhall soon after his appointment as Chairman, he had put out his programme along with his fears:

> The major purpose for which we must use our money – is to cultivate new audiences for the arts ... but it must not be done by means of a

confidence trick ... You can't appreciate ... good music without hearing it over a long period from relatively early childhood ... there is no easy way ... It must be made quite clear that one can appreciate simple things without effort and complicated things only by effort ... It is very necessary to make it clear to young people that there is something to be attained if they will work for it, because the situation with them is not satisfactory at the moment ... I believe the pop groups on the whole are winning the battle. At best we are holding our own; but it is very necessary, if we are to be a civilized and cultivated nation; if the standards which mean something to you and something to me, are to be maintained, that we do win this battle, and we can only win this battle by teaching people what are the worthwhile things in life ... History will not grant us a moratorium.

There was no moratorium. There was the revolt of youth and the demonstrations of an 'alternative or counter-culture' across the cities of Europe in 1968. They lost the first battle, indeed, to the forces of the Establishment; but the Arts Council did not win in its efforts to include and guide from its fresh and larger premises at 105 Piccadilly, where Lord Goodman had insisted on moving because his excellent staff had previously been incarcerated in linen cupboards, bathrooms, kitchens and spare bedrooms – no contribution to their efficiency. Some younger members were appointed to the Panels, the number and size of which were greatly increased. During the two decades before 1967, the membership of the Music Panel was increased from fifteen to twenty-four, of the Drama Panel from fourteen to twenty-eight, of the Art Panel from eight to twenty-six, and of the Literature (including Poetry) Panel from seven to twenty. A Young People's Theatre Panel was created with eighteen members, also a New Activities Committee led by the dynamic Michael Astor. The roll-call of the younger members was both a herald of the inclusion of the rebels After Suez and of the nascent movers of the performing arts.

Lord Goodman's eye for the main chance of the future was worthy of an astrologer. Appointed to the Panels for the usual three-year term were in Art, Edward Lucie-Smith, Bryan Robertson, Roy Strong and David Sylvester: in Drama, Judi Dench, Michael Elliott, Bamber Gascoigne, Jonathan Miller, John Mortimer, and Peter Shaffer to join Constance Cummings and Sir John Gielgud; in Literature, Melvyn Bragg, Richard Holmes, Karl Miller and Peter

Redgrove under Professor Frank Kermode as Chairman; in Music, Richard Rodney Bennett, Harrison Birtwistle and John Drummond beside Dame Ninette de Valois and the Earl of Harewood as Chairman; and on the Young People's Theatre Panel, such future leading directors, playwrights and actors as Frank Dunlop, Richard Eyre, Terry Hands, Harold Pinter, Joan Plowright and Diana Quick. Their participation on the Panels was a tribute to Lord Goodman's offer of hope and change in the state patronage of the arts. They believed that they could influence this period of innovation and experiment.

Yet as in the parables of the scapegoat and the narrow entrance to heaven, for the one sinner who was included into the heaven of the Establishment, ten thousand had to be excluded. There was no room at the inn for all. While the Young People's Theatre Panel, led by Constance Cummings, did achieve practical things within its limited brief by working with the major companies and training bodies to extend opportunities for adolescents, the New Activities Committee, led by Michael Astor, became the butt of ridicule and ingratitude. Although it included some of the activists of the counter-culture, these did not think as did their older colleagues. Lord Goodman noted, 'Many of the young people clearly did not like the Arts Council and did their business with it only because of the allure of its money and its premises. Of this, with great candour, they made no secret. They produced magazines containing carica-tures of the Arts Council's hapless chairman, depicting him as an octopus, of which his only comment was that the tentacles were too few and too short.'

This effort to reach the young seemed to them patronizing and inadequate. They could only laugh at Goodman's reasons for trying to reach them at all. As he wrote in 1969, 'The very word "young" now strikes a note of terror in all establishment bosoms, and it would be foolish to pretend that we do not share some of the apprehensions. We have tried, at the Arts Council, to remain contemporary and "with it".' But the establishment of the New Activities Committee to be 'with it' seemed to the militant artists to be an old device of the Establishment that was not with them, but withheld power from them. The point was not to serve on the Arts Council, but to replace it. The hand or tentacle which doled out funds to some innovations must be severed. Even Goodman realized that his Committee might not be viable.

> It has discovered that the major myth is the belief that it is employing a common language. It has, to some extent, underrated the resentment arising from the very fact of its intrusion. It has also underrated the self-contained and palisaded character of the 'activities' and the fact that the occupants of the palisades regard themselves as a community developing along their own lines and requiring nothing from the Arts Council, except possibly its premises and its funds.

Up Piccadilly, towards Park Lane, young squatters took over a mansion. On its white stucco facade, they wrote: WE ARE THE WRITING ON YOUR WALL. They were not, further down the street. One artist might complain to Lord Goodman, 'You're all a very old lot.' But she was confounded by his reply, 'No, it's just the light.' And it was not just a light that failed, as the activists were to fail. Their challenge was to be contained and their demands limited to pittances and then extinguished during the static arts budgets of the next decade. And yet, how the renascent Arts Council was trying! As Lord Goodman pointed out, the Council was suddenly bombarded with applications for grants and aid from unfamiliar quarters: arts laboratories, theatre groups and loosely knit bodies of young people operating in halls and basements. The state-funded body was suddenly both a milch cow and an Aunt Sally. It could not win in the prevailing climate of opinion. While its functions could be compared to those of an unusually benevolent banker, they were necessarily selective. 'To spend money on bad work is just as wasteful as spending it on subsidizing empty seats.' The Arts Council had to exercise the prerogative of choice, even in a time of ferment:

> If the Council accepted at face value criticisms occasionally received from the public about the allegedly 'disgusting', 'decadent', 'alien' or 'incomprehensible' productions in literature, drama, music and the visual arts which receive part of our subsidies; and if at the same time we withdrew our help from Covent Garden (because it has been described as a 'museum of musical antiquities'), from orchestras playing obsolete nineteenth-century symphonies, from theatres which present old-fashioned pantomimes at Christmas, from representational painters and traditional poets: in these conditions we

might easily satisfy all our helpful advisers, except the less vocal
majority who care for the achievement of our declared objectives.

The New Activities Committee under Michael Astor distributed
its allocation of £15,000 for 1969–70 among the eight regions
where the co-ordinators were encouraged to promote 'gatherings'.
The hope was that these gatherings would advance communication
and the interchange of ideas between the regions, and the results
would be passed on to the Committee, which needed the information. Unfortunately, the London representatives did not hold a
gathering, but a series of open meetings to decide how to spend their
share of the grant. A recommendation that the Arts Council should
pay ten pounds to one of them who had been fined for firing a cap
pistol at the American Embassy was turned down. Lord Goodman
said that this device was used as much to twist the tail of the Council
as the general public – and was successful.

In point of fact, the New Activities Committee could never satisfy
its multitude of warring clients and would be disbanded after a
minority recommendation that responsibility for performance arts
and arts laboratories and community arts should be decentralized to
the Regional Arts Associations. This proposal was welcomed by
Nigel Abercrombie. It was totally proper in his opinion that 'new
activities' should be dealt with by the regions, which could judge
whether these would benefit the artistic life of the community. When
such benefit might be in doubt, local authorities and Regional Arts
Associations were 'better placed than the Arts Council not only to
understand local circumstances but to finance activities which may
be essentially non-cultural in content and largely amateur in
execution'. Abercrombie suggested that the ambiguous term 'new
activities' be dropped for 'experimental projects'. And indeed, the
Committee was renamed the Experimental Projects Committee: it
would totter for three years towards extinction under the next
Conservative government. Even the young artists complained that
they were neither experimental nor projects.

The legacy of the defeat of the 'new activities' would be a bitter
one. Until then, the Arts Council had been seen as the friend of the
artist. The eminent members of its Panels, some of them chosen by
Goodman, ensured respect for the process of decision that allocated
funds. With people such as Richard Attenborough, Peter Hall and

Henry Moore as Council members along with Lady Antonia Fraser and the Earl of Snowdon, and with all the young stars on the Panels, experience appeared to be mixed with promise and recent acclaim. An element of the old aristocratic arts establishment, however, remained. 'Antonia Fraser and I', the Earl of Harewood said, 'rather felt odd girl, odd boy out.' Yet he had proved himself at the Edinburgh Festival, and she in literature. Sonatas and ink ran in their blue veins. To the activists, on the other hand, this wise *mélange* represented the temptation of inclusion and must be resisted. Those who joined the Arts Council betrayed their causes, whatever these might be.

In this time of confrontation, however, the offices of the Arts Council remained curiously accessible. Peter Hall recalled his service on the Council under Lord Goodman with great affection:

> We were getting such results from such small resources, little subsidies judiciously applied to places where the arts had taken root. They grew prodigiously. But one day the door burst open, and three or four street people came in, one in a yellow jump-suit with yellow tubes emerging from his head. They demanded a grant for their Performance Art of Protest. Until they received it, they would occupy the premises. Lord Goodman was charm itself, thanked them for coming, and ushered them out without a golden handshake.

On another occasion, a young woman appeared in front of the Chairman's desk, demanding a grant to hold an exhibition on the trees of Green Park. The bemused and amused Lord Goodman gave her seventy-five pounds. But when she reappeared a week later to ask for another grant to place particular pictures in the trees, he asked her about her principles of selection. The answer was, 'Random choice. I will exhibit anyone who brings a picture.' Lord Goodman refused the second grant. Even in a time of experimentation, there had to be some standards. But his mistakes did not remove his belief in sustaining the good artist, who did not need forcible feeding, but equally should not feel that it was ignominious or humiliating to receive a subsidy. 'The state today is organized in a fashion where a large element of a man's earnings are taken away from him to provide him with social and public amenities. The arts are a social and public amenity and the artist is simply receiving that share of the public treasury which enables a government to discharge its duties so far as artistic provender is concerned.'

Perhaps the great 'Catfish Controversy' most clearly illustrated the divide between the established arbiters of the arts and the alternative artists as well as Lord Goodman's own genius for compromise. The Arts Council was running the new Hayward Gallery. One of its two current exhibitions was on Tantra, which explored the Indian cult of ecstasy with the importance of copulation as a dominant theme. The other was the work of eleven Los Angeles artists. One of them, Newton Harrison, showed a portable catfish farm to demonstrate a survival system. 'The feast it yields is an institutional event', the artist tried to explain, 'and in that ritual sense it is "art" as we ordinarily think of art.' Unfortunately, the art consisted of ceremonially killing a hundred catfish with a ball-hammer or a lead pipe or electric currents and serving them to the audience with hush puppies, iced tea, wild clover honey and tomato and cucumber salad.

The press was outraged at this cruelty to catfish in the name of subsidized art. Lord Goodman reputedly arrived at the Hayward to find his client Spike Milligan breaking the glass door of the gallery with his hammer. '*I'm* protesting,' he told Goodman and was later presented with the bill for the cost of replacing the glass. Newton Harrison continued to want to cull his catfish farm exhibit, although Goodman told him that he would upset his viewers by killing fish with moustaches which reminded them of their uncles. 'People should learn by example that life is cruel,' Harrison said. To this Goodman replied, 'It is for a catfish which falls into the hands of a demented American artist.'

At an emergency meeting of the Council in his flat, Goodman was confronted by John Pope-Hennessy and others, who insisted that he must not interfere with free artistic expression. To Peter Hall, this was a classic demonstration of the folly of the liberal conscience. But Lady Antonia Fraser saved the day with her practical observation about killing fish. 'Surely, Arnold, nothing is happening which a woman doesn't do all week.' Hall admired the absolute common sense of Goodman in his solution to the controversy. The culling was suspended, while the Royal Society for the Prevention of Cruelty to Animals was put in charge of killing the catfish. It was then discovered that the small electric chair device which Newton Harrison had designed to slaughter his samples would have electrocuted him as well. As it was, three feasts of catfish were eventually served to the public in a bouillabaisse and in Mrs Beeton's celebrated fish stew. Humane killing solved this crisis of conscience.

In the end, the job of the Arts Council was to maintain standards and select. This process involved some censorship. 'One has to be prepared to recognize that dementia lies in many quarters, especially in the arts,' Lord Goodman has said. 'There you need keen sight.' This is what he used in order to give advice to Sir Roland Penrose, who came to him about a woman artist facing obscenity charges for exhibiting her drawings of male penises. Penrose declared that he would go to court and say that she was an artist and must be free. Goodman advised him not to go to court. 'If you say she is an artist, she will certainly be convicted.' The exhibition was withdrawn and the case did not reach court.

Such covert control was the genius and the method of the first Chairman of the Arts Council to rule it with a velvet glove. 'It really was the Arnold Goodman show'. Lady Antonia Fraser said. 'Every now and then, there were challenges. But they never won, even an infinitesimal rebellion.' He could be defeated, however, by the great companies, as when he proposed the merger of the Royal Shakespeare Company with the fledgling National Theatre. But generally, he was the great defuser. He wanted the system to run as it had so successfully for twenty years, but now under his guidance, smoothly without confrontation. To aid in efficiency, he agreed that a statistician should attend Council meetings. At one of them, a puritan Scottish composer produced a subsidized underground magazine and said, 'On page twenty-seven, the word FUCK is printed thirty-eight times and called a poem.' The magazine was passed to the Chairman, who studied the offending page and forestalled any question of censorship with the remark, 'I think this is a matter we should refer to our statistician.'

A master of committee procedures, Goodman tried to avoid any restriction on artistic expression short of public scandal, while maintaining the standards of what he called civilization and culture. These simply could not accommodate the anti-art and anarchy of the alternative cultures of the young, who wanted to destroy the system, as did a few of the members of the Panels whom Goodman had brought in to leaven the lump. 'I was suffocated by boredom and despair,' the director Jonathan Miller recalled of his days on the Drama Panel. 'We sat at an enormous table with people silhouetted against the light of Piccadilly windows. Foolish decisions were made like keeping the Covent Garden Opera alive. It should have been throttled along with the world of old-boy networks, the tattered representatives of the Establishment.' Even though Miller called the Arts Council 'a singing version of the Beefsteak or White's jeopardized by the possibility of effectiveness', he had to admit it was an open and honest business and better than any other arts body in Europe. 'If you swap another organization for this one, it won't be any better.'

That was the point discovered by Lord Bridges, the Permanent Secretary to the Treasury and Head of the Civil Service, when he floated the idea of a Cabinet Minister of Fine Arts or Culture. He had to report that those who were currently responsible for the arts were against his proposal. They feared that such a Minister or Parliament might intervene to reduce the discretion of the Boards of the Arts Council and of the Trustees of the galleries, museums and performing companies. If there was a question in the House of Commons about a subsidy paid to exhibit some obscene painting or to mount some subversive play, the answer would always be the same: that the Council had the discretion to distribute its grant as it wished and had no artistic control over the Company which put on the objectionable work. Responsibility was at two removes from government. On the basis of the arm's length principle and the supposed independence of the Arts Council and the BBC and the trustees of arts boards, no state interference was possible. Errors of taste were their responsibility. It was an attitude endorsed by John Boyd-Carpenter when he was Chief Secretary to the Treasury, responsible for allocating the budget for the arts. 'Few things other than utter neglect could be worse, and more contrary to our tradition, than official artistic patterns laid down by the Governmental machine. In this country we have sought, I think successfully, to avoid these dangers by interposing between the Government, as a supplier of funds, and the arts themselves bodies of instructed and discriminating people, completely independent of the Government.'

One of Lord Goodman's many achievements was to keep the Arts Council free from any political interference at a time of significant increase in the allocation. To him, the Civil Service was 'a mischievous organization' with which he fought prolonged and bloody campaigns, as did Jennie Lee. 'To outmanoeuvre the civil service,' as his memoirs testified, 'which is indispensable if you are to continue in a sensible way of life, is to arouse their bitterest hatred. You can only be loved if you conform and if you conform you must be inefficient. The Civil Service hated the Arts Council because it broke the rule that no money was to be spent except by the Civil Service. We blued it as we wished.' Jennie Lee might ask for more power for the people and the regions, but she did not get it. In fact she backed the independence of the Council. When a mayor on a local authority protested to her about some subsidized and élite opera with the words, 'This is not what we voted socialist for,' her reply was swift. 'You're an old fuddy-duddy. We, like they, believe in freedom.' Goodman himself was an independent radical. The arts were for the arts' sake, not for the benefit of politicians. But he did pay Jennie Lee the most deserved tribute on her retirement, listing her successes:

> To many she is known as the overlord Minister of the Arts Council, but there was much more to her work. Almost single-handed she has brought into being the University of the Air, an experiment, which has aroused interest throughout the educational world. In her regime the National Theatre at long last, too, came to be built. She has contrived the establishment of a National Film School. She saved the Tate Gallery from a demented (but unavoidable) amputation by persuading the Government to make additional land available for sensible expansion. She gave support and wise counsel to the problems of the British Museum. She has been a friend to art galleries throughout the country and done everything within her power to promote important purchases. She was tireless in visiting artistic activities large and small throughout the country. Her handsome face and winning accents became known everywhere, but her shopping list – as she called her unfulfilled programme – was endless except in the sight of eternity.

Of course, Lord Goodman's success in dealing with Jennie Lee depended on their close relationship, which was nurtured by a civil servant from the Cabinet Office, Keith Jeffery, who managed to secure a job that he coveted – to serve as the first Whitehall bureaucrat ever to work full-time on the arts under the Minister. Jeffery became Jennie Lee's escort and guide to the opera and concerts, also to private meetings with Lord Goodman after dinner, for they lived in the same block of flats. Moreover, once a month, the Minister and her private secretary and Jeffery would visit the Arts Council building in Piccadilly, where Goodman and five members of the Council would discuss every problem under the sun without the onus of an agenda. 'These were the strengths of Jennie Lee,' Jeffery recalled. 'As apolitical as anyone could be when it came to the arts. Although she had a hot line to the Prime Minister, she knew when to use it and when not to. And she never let her own left-wing prejudices show – she had to seem to be impartial.'

In a rare gesture, Jeffery was asked by Goodman to cross over from the civil service to the Arts Council, even though Nigel Abercrombie had not been a conspicuous success as Secretary-General. The Chairman needed one person on the staff who knew the many ways through the corridors of power. A post was invented for Jeffery as 'Advisor for External Affairs'. He had to deal with the Council's blind spots, with the British Council and the Commonwealth and UNESCO, with the Tourist Board and festivals and commercial sponsors. The success of the Arts Council, indeed, in attracting almost the first corporate donor in the early nineteen-seventies caused mutterings from the Treasury about lowering the state subsidy; but Goodman was to insist that the Council was wholly dependent on its grant-in-aid. Another body might be created to deal with commercial sponsorship. Oddly enough Jennie Lee herself sat on the advisory body that was to set up the Association for Business Sponsorship of the Arts; she declared that 'we lived in a mixed economy now – so all sections should support the arts'. And Goodman himself, on leaving the Arts Council, was to become the Chairman of this new commercial patron of the Muses.

In summing up his own achievement, Lord Goodman used to say that 'we failed in producing a philosophy for art in this country. But it was a creditable record for the Arts Council, which was highly admired outside this country. Above all, we kept politics out of decisions.' He did not point out another failure: although he was appointed to the board of the British Council, even with the aid of Keith Jeffery, he did little to improve the liaison between the two different and divided organizations responsible for British arts abroad as well as at home. Yet he had achieved significant improvement within the two arts, in which Britain was supreme at the end of the Second World War, yet which Lord Keynes had driven outside the pale of the initial Arts Council, as the angel with the flaming sword had driven Adam and Eve out of the Garden of Eden. Those refugees were literature and the documentary or art film.

Keynes had considered poetry worthy of assistance, but prose was thrown onto the strange mercy of commercial publishers and some private patrons. Goodman generally agreed with this point of view, saying, 'Publishers can be pretty well relied upon to publish any worthwhile book that is sent to them, and certainly, once its merits are recognized, no subsidy is needed to encourage the publication.' As he told Hugh Willatt, 'The important role of publishers is in keeping authors alive. Even third-rate books are published, because there is a demand for them.' Yet Goodman realized that some prose writers might need direct help as much as poets or playwrights, and so the Poetry Panel was changed to a Literature Panel, still under the leadership of Cecil Day Lewis, although he was soon to be succeeded by the novelist Angus Wilson. For Day Lewis, a longtime dream had now come to pass. 'I believe there should be a hard core of whole-time professional writers – men and women who can give their full energy, thought and skill to the practice of their art at the highest creative level of which each is capable. We do not encourage half-time doctors, engineers, architects, managers or foremen. Failing this professional élite, we can at least buy a writer a period of time in which to study and practise his art, undistracted by other commitments.'

This was the élitism of the left, the idea of a vanguard of intellectuals paid to raise the consciousness of the working classes. It could never become the policy of the Arts Council, although spending on literature would rise to one-and-a-half per cent of budget and fifteen bursaries of some thousand pounds each were awarded to prose writers in the first year of the life of the Literature Panel. This strategy was thought to be unsuccessful, so in the second

year of the new Panel, prizes were also given in certain categories
and grants were made to publishers to assist them in bringing out
translations of major European writers. Literary festivals and little
magazines were also assisted along with the Poetry Book Society,
while there was a new emphasis on promotion and book-selling.
Manuscripts of poets were already being acquired including those of
W. H. Auden and Philip Larkin; but now the notebooks and drafts
of novelists began to be bought. The wise advice of W. B. Yeats to
John Masefield was ignored:

> Accurst, who brings to light of day
> The writings I have cast away.
> But blest be he who shows them not
> And lets the kind worm take the lot.

The Literature Panel further campaigned for the Public Lending
Right Scheme, by which authors would be paid for the amount of
their books borrowed from libraries. It was a reform championed by
Lord Goodman himself, who declared to a seminar of librarians in
Wales. 'In a civilized society one doesn't rob people, particularly
those who aren't able to defend themselves. If the authors had been
strongly organized or powerful people they would have had their
rights long ago: there would have been none of their books on your
shelves in the past fifty years.' But this overdue assistance to writers
offered no hope to beginners. Cecil Day Lewis actually believed that
the young writer should not have things made too easy for him. A
period of struggle and discouragement was a good test of his
vocation, his integrity and his stamina – 'early success was a stern
test of integrity too'. The youthful aspirant had little chance of a
grant; he had to be sponsored by a reputable member of the literary
profession. 'The quality of his work no less than the urgency of his
need will be then assessed by the Panel. It is not our business to
subsidize either failure or untalented ambition.'

In his policy of artistic cleansing, Lord Goodman also saw the
back of almost the last hangover from the first days of the Arts
Council – the Director of Poetry and then of Literature, Eric Walter
White. He had a passion for writing, but for pre-war writing. He
loved making or disallowing grants to coterie magazines, and
particularly enjoyed refusing the requests of those he did not like. To
Goodman, he appeared to be an inadequate and retrograde man,

who had no contact with youth or experiment. The literary prizes given by the Arts Council all seemed to go to authors whose ages were never less than seventy years, such as William Gerhardie – and he had not put pen to paper for three decades. This geriatric complex was under continual attack by the editor of the *Times Literary Supplement*, Arthur Crook, who castigated the Council for its antiquarian bias. Yet Eric Walter White was unmoved until he was removed. An award was even suggested for Gerald Hamilton, the infamous confidence trickster who was Christopher Isherwood's inspiration in *Mr Norris Changes Trains*. White's young Australian deputy, Charles Osborne, was given his post as Director of Literature after his departure, and would remain long enough in the job to acquiesce in the destruction of his own Panel. Although Lord Goodman had raised Lord Keynes's ignored art from the ashes, his appointee would consign it back to the embers.

The general policy of experimentation and innovation was also applied to the revival of the documentary on art, inspired by the film of Alain Resnais on Picasso's *Guernica*. The tradition of Grierson and Jennings had been allowed to die with the Crown Film Unit. Although the British Film Institute and the National Film Finance Corporation had revived the art of documentary, the Arts Council had nothing to do with the early work of Lindsay Anderson or Karel Reisz. Under Goodman's leadership, however, it did fund a film on *Francis Bacon*, who would emerge as the supreme British artist of his age. It was followed by films on *Giacometti* and the *Pre-Raphaelite Revolt*, which showed commercially with Buñuel's *Belle du Jour* at the Curzon Cinema. Films on the arts continued to be toured round the country to increase the understanding and enjoyment of paintings. For the Art Department was still the last refuge of the early Council with its direct approach to raising the consciousness of the people.

This hangover of the promotion of the arts straight from Piccadilly seemed an anomaly to Lord Goodman, while it was to other Chairmen 'the jewel in the crown'. But when the Hayward Gallery was opened in London and the new Institute of Contemporary Arts (ICA) was situated in a Nash Terrace off the Mall, Goodman changed his mind. He accepted that the function of running the Hayward Gallery should devolve on the Arts Council, which should have total discretion on what was put on display there. The Council could facilitate the mounting of innovative exhibitions of modern art in the metropolis outside the Tate Gallery and increased funding was made available, with shows on Matisse and Van Gogh at the Hayward, and Henry Moore, Balthus and de Kooning at the Tate. The ICA and the Whitechapel Galleries received the lion's share of the funding in London, but galleries in Bristol and Folkestone, Oxford and Nottingham, the Lake District and Cornwall also received support. The 'Art Department was a *doing* body', its Assistant Director Joanna Drew declared, although so little was done directly any more by the Arts Council. 'It stuck out like a sore thumb.'

Yet in the new Secretary-General's opinion, the Art Department made its choices 'with skill and sensitivity, given the silly or the shocking current manifestations. The principle that the Council must exhibit or purchase the liveliest examples of what was, in fact, going on was the sound – perhaps the only practical – one.' It was a curious position to take for a body spending taxpayers' money to support what it did not appreciate merely because of the temper of the times. Before his departure, Eric W. White told a splendid story of persuading the editors of *Private Eye* to come round to the Arts Council, after they had mocked Jennie Lee's determination to use the arts 'to foster a Britain that was fun-loving and gay'. (It was this remark that also roused both Henry Moore and the Earl of Snowdon from their slumbers at one Council meeting.) Eric White advised the editors of the satirical magazine how to apply for a grant to make Britain still more fun-loving and gay, but then he showed them an art exhibition of droopy exhibits. He explained that these had been created 'by blowing up rubber balloons and contraceptives, and filling them with plaster of Paris'. Faced with such odd patronage, *Private Eye* never applied for its grant to increase the general fun and gaiety.

Still essential to the old tradition was the support of the growing number of festivals throughout Britain, although the independent Scottish Arts Council was responsible for subsidizing from its grant the major festival of all at Edinburgh. Particularly gratifying in the Goodman years was the conversion of the Maltings at Snape into a concert hall for the Aldeburgh Festival, which had been conceived from the home of the composer Benjamin Britten and the opera singer Peter Pears. Continued support for the Covent Garden Opera and the Royal Ballet and major symphony orchestras was hardly surprising from a Chairman whose chief love was music and who would serve for ten years on the board of the Royal Opera House. But what was most satisfactory was the Greater London Council's matching support for the four London orchestras and the Sadler's Wells Opera and the Festival Ballet – these last two were saved from collapse. The crisis at Sadler's Wells was partially caused by the Arts Council insisting that the opera company spend most of its time and grant on touring the provinces. As its general manager complained, the opera and ballet company had 'been sweating out its lifeblood to provide the viper with his venom'. But the Council did save the company by helping it to move from its inadequate quarters in Rosebery Avenue to the Coliseum in St Martin's Lane, which could seat 2,500 people. After nearly thirty years of wandering, Sadler's Wells had been brought by Lord Goodman right to the middle of London.

There is no question that this was the apogee of the Arts Council. Even the music critics appreciated what had been done at Covent Garden. In 1967, *The Times* summed up twenty marvellous years of subsidized opera. 'Patrons of Covent Garden today automatically expect any new production, and indeed every revival, to be as strongly cast as anything at the Met. in New York, and as carefully presented as anything in Milan or Vienna' – that opera house was compared by Jonathan Miller to working in Berchtesgarten. 'The international stars of opera prefer to work at Covent Garden where everybody knows his job and helps you to get on with yours.' Such praise might not justify the fact that forty per cent of the Arts Council's budget was still spent on opera and ballet; but it was true that the proportion spent on drama had tripled to nearly a quarter of the total grant. Without the loss of quality, larger slices of the cake were being cut for some of the arts, although the Council made increasing efforts to keep all its subsidized bodies alive.

The allocation of the annual grant-in-aid between the clients and the arts was not an exercise in deconstruction. Tony Fields has said:

> We did not break it down, instead we built it up. We would commence the operation, once we knew the total funding figure from

the Treasury, by attempting to ensure that all our subsidized organizations could stay alive. Thus, the results of such an exercise, after the enormous one involving detailed examinations of individual budgets, talks with local authorities and negotiations with Boards of Management would be that the totals given to the individual disciplines were whatever was the outcome.

A harbinger was the salvation of Ballet Rambert, another hangover from wartime touring and glory. Originally the cradle of British ballet where every major choreographer had worked, the influence of Marie Rambert on ballet's creative forces on this island had rivalled that of Diaghilev in Europe. Yet the company had been obliged more than Sadler's Wells to tour without stopping, an endless Flying Dutchman with a steady menu of *Giselle*, *Coppelia* and *Don Quixote*. At the end of its rope and stimulated by modern dance from America, Ballet Rambert abandoned the classic repertoire and organized itself as a modern dance company. In its first few years under this guise, it created no fewer than thirty new works. Resisting a forced marriage with the London Festival Ballet, it found an occasional metropolitan home at the new Jeanetta Cochrane Theatre and became the innovator of modern and experimental dance in Britain. At the same time, Robin Howard created his London Contemporary Dance Theatre with a repertoire based on Martha Graham's techniques in its headquarters at The Place. These two companies, with the miniature touring and teaching *Ballet for All*, pioneered the future of the dance in the United Kingdom. At the same time the dance profession made it clear that dance should be recognized as an art independent of music, and the Arts Council was persuaded to create a separate Dance Panel and Director and eventually a Department. Ballet was leaping into the new age.

Many of these changes were inspired by the *Opera and Ballet Report 1966–69*. The designer and editor of *Dance and Dancers*, Peter Williams, was now a member of the Music Panel and responsible for the dance section of the report – Lord Harewood wrote on opera. The consultations, as Williams said, 'seemed to go on for ever – the discussions, the writing, the research. George Harewood, John Cruft and I met frequently at Lord Goodman's flat for breakfast meetings. One of my hardest battles was to persuade the Council to take contemporary dance seriously.' That was the eventual success of Williams's persuasion, 'also the fact that the report encouraged the formation of regional companies'. He advocated one in Wales, another in the North, another in Scotland and one in western England – only the Welsh Company never really began to pirouette. The report also instigated the creation of pensions and a resettlement fund for dancers – so long a concern of Dame Ninette de Valois, who saw them thrown on the scrapheap like athletes at a young age, because their careers necessarily came to an end so early.

Grants to community arts and arts laboratories also saw a new dawn inching up. These provoked the scorn of some of the officers of the Council, particularly Charles Osborne, the new Director of Literature. His unofficial memoirs, *Giving It Away*, claimed that the Council squandered large sums of money on community arts, 'that perversion of the aesthetic urge invented by bored arts administrators yearning to become social workers'. But these initial grants recognized a public need and were the only effective, if inadequate, response to the revolt of youth and the new gaggle of activities and liberties. As Lord Goodman himself said engagingly, 'One of the most precious freedoms of the British people is freedom from culture.' Although he himself was no supporter of community arts, he did recognize that their time had come, but that responsibility for them should be regional. As he would declare with some asperity in the House of Lords at the end of his term of office as Chairman of the Arts Council, the Regional Arts Associations could speak for their areas in some things only. 'We are concerned with the Arts. This business about amateur theatricals, the crafts and the like is something about which one needs to be very sceptical indeed.'

Official support of the mushroom growth of new action centres was sporadic and soon discontinued. The quintessential producer of his generation, Jim Haynes, had established the Traverse Theatre in Edinburgh, and when he moved to London to found the underground newspaper *International Times* and another Traverse at the Jeanetta Cochrane Theatre, he was given a grant by the Arts Council to help him set up stage. 'It was something like a social movement,' Hugh Willatt recognized, 'with the *International Times* as its parish magazine, but the surrounding whiff of drug-taking raised problems for the Council.' No grants were given to Haynes's next proposal of an Arts Laboratory, although it became the prototype of dozens of similar ventures in provincial cities. Lord Goodman's opposition overruled support from several of the more unorthodox members of the Council. Seven grants were made, however, towards communal studio projects and to the Artist Placement Group and to performance artists such as Peter Logan's Mechanical Ballet and John Epstein's Black Box. At the last resort, however, the Arts Council could not and would not approve of the permissiveness of what many now called a youth culture, although support of 'fringe' drama groups would rise by 1972 to fifty-six clients including Incubus, John Bull Puncture Repair Kit, Landscapes and Living Spaces, Low Mean Spectacular, Sal's Meat Market, 7:84 Theatre Company and The Yorkshire Gnomes.

The libertarian atmosphere of the decade had brought some state prohibitions tumbling down. In 1960, the failure of the notorious prosecution of Penguin Books for the mass paperback edition of *Lady Chatterley's Lover* by D. H. Lawrence had announced the broader tolerance of the following ten years. The patronizing question of the prosecution, 'Is it a book that you would ever wish your wife or your servants to read?', helped to lose the government's case. Eight years on, the Lord Chamberlain's powers of censorship over drama were abolished with Lord Goodman's blessing. Although he tried for his usual compromise with a voluntary scheme of censorship operated by theatrical managements, he abandoned it for lack of support, saying, 'It is better to think yourself mad than the rest of the world mistaken.'

A Theatres Act brought the stage onto the same level as literature. Now a production or a publication had to be deemed 'obscene', and a prosecution had to have the consent of the Attorney-General. Although some successful prosecutions for obscenity were made, they had to be in extreme cases, as against Gustav Metzger and John Sharkey, the ICA Gallery Director, for mounting a show on a greater scale than the controversial catfish. In this avant-garde *petit guignol*, the carcass of a lamb was hacked to pieces and passed round the watchers so that the audience could participate as butchers, while the entrails of the little beast were pulled out of people's flies. Jennie Lee may have said, 'My function is merely a permissive one', but permission had its limits.

The revolt of the young could never be satisfied in its infinite varieties within a country proud of its 'freedom from culture'. Television and consumerism would contain and direct the millipede efforts of the next generation to kick out. Constance Cummings happily paid her income-tax 'because I like to pay for civilization', and she was instrumental in funding with the Arts Council a beacon for youth theatre at the Young Vic. Yet she could not satisfy the demand of the activists she met on her extensive trips round Britain:

> There were complaints that we were the new Establishment, as were the pioneer theatres which had benefited from us like the National and the Royal Shakespeare Company. Young people who had not proved themselves weren't being given a chance to prove themselves. But nothing we saw could be recommended to anybody. People who said they were actors got up and did something and thought that was enough. Nothing sprang up from something inner. It was all an attack on something outer. They were just doing nothing. It was a fiasco.

The givers had become the withholders. The friends of the arts now seemed the enemies of most of the artists. The pioneers of state subsidy from the Second World War appeared as the Wackford Squeers and Scrooges of the artistic Oliver Twists and Tiny Tims of the Welfare State. Yet the truth was, there simply was not enough gruel to slop into every open mouth. So there had to be rules about the rations. Sometimes Lord Goodman himself failed over his pet schemes, such as one for building an Opera House in Edinburgh. It remained a hole in the ground for the future. The Department of Education and Science would not grant the money for it. 'You cannot enter into a commitment', he told his Music Director John Cruft. 'If you take my telegram to the bank, you will not be able to cash it like a cheque.' Cruft admired his Chairman's wit and imperturbability. 'It was so difficult to maintain the peace among the grinding of the logs.'

Owing to the extraordinary capability of Lord Goodman to pour frankincense on mouldy mangers, even the affair of the Nottingham Playhouse was resolved, which concerned particularly his Secretary-General, whose initial experience in the arts had largely been there. Its artistic director John Neville initiated a strong campaign, as Peter Hall so often did, to induce the Arts Council and the local authority to raise their subsidies. Unsuccessful, he tendered his resignation. The trustees accepted it; he then withdrew it. This sparring produced a public debate. 'Friction between artistic directors and governing boards is a price the theatre is paying for being run on public money,' *The Times* pointed out. 'And the more support it receives from the Arts Council and local authorities the more that friction is liable to increase.' In an article in the *Sunday Times*, Neville asserted that the inevitable tension between the theatre director and the board usually ended with the former's dismissal. 'What is it in the way we organize our publicly subsidized theatres which decrees that in any dispute, the scales are weighted in favour of the amateur and not the professional; which pre-ordains that in cultural cricket the gentleman always beats the players.' Grants were given to institutions and not to brilliant individuals; professionals employed by boards could not negotiate directly with their patrons; and the Arts Council backed any board against any director 'in an understandable Establishment abhorrence of anarchical tendencies'. Neville's services were terminated and the Nottingham Playhouse continued to appeal to its public in other hands. The organization did survive the talent at its head.

There was no question of censorship or artistic choice in the rare interventions of the Arts Council in the affairs of the repertory theatre. Lord Goodman, however, did try to persuade Sir Bernard Miles not to play a nude Desdemona in his *Othello* of 1971 at the Mermaid Theatre. Miles responded by quoting Iago's lines:

> Or to be naked with her friend in bed
> An hour or more, not meaning any harm.

Goodman replied that he did not believe that Miles was a pornographer; if he played Othello as the original leader of the Black Panthers, all would be well; but undressing a pretty girl 'when the London theatre – bankrupt of other ideas – is stripping them all like plucked hens, is unfortunate and ill-timed'. Desdemona played with her nightdress on, and more importantly, the National Theatre continued to be constructed, after a timely visit by Lord Goodman to the Chancellor of the Exchequer, Roy Jenkins, who required little persuasion to resume the project which had been put on hold. The area was one, as Goodman remarked, where economics needed to be wisely judged. After all, the Colosseum had served the Roman public well with its delectable spectacles, yet no one could remember the name of a single senator who had tried to cut its subsidy.

The innovations under the Chairman were significant in addressing new problems. The *Opera and Ballet Report* had actually demanded what the audience was really made of, sugar and spice and all things nice, or slugs and snails and puppy-dog tails. In a survey carried out in Leeds and Glasgow as well as at Sadler's Wells in London, only five per cent of the average audience turned out to be manual workers. These were arts that appealed to an élite. And yet the report concluded that there was hardly a limit to their expansion across the classes. 'Ballet and dance theatre can draw an audience as large as any other branch of the theatre or cinema.' This would certainly prove true in Wales, where the National Opera would draw a large share of its audience from the remaining coal-miners and manual workers of that musical nation.

In another area, however, Lord Goodman was pressed by Tony Field to provide for the training of professional arts administrators. The staff of the Arts Council, much praised by the Chairman for its dedication and self-denial, had mainly learned on the job, although many of them had professional experience in the arts which they were representing. Their numbers had been cut to just over a hundred by 1967, but these were nearly doubled in the later expansionist programme; because of the need to run the Hayward Gallery, the Art Department's personnel increased more than twice over to forty-nine. Yet how could arts administrators be chosen if there was no training for them? A one year's course was instituted at the Polytechnic of Central London, where lectures were given by the directors of the Royal Opera House and Sadler's Wells and the National Theatre and the Royal Shakespeare Company, and by the staff of the National and Tate Galleries and the Arts Council. And so a new class of *apparatchiks* was born. 'I did not know', Tony Field declared in later years, 'what monster I was creating.' A new breed of organizers, however, was being bred and would take over the administration of the arts in Great Britain, shunting aside the last of the old artists and performers who knew the tricks and circumstances of their ancient trades.

Lord Goodman's appointment for five years as Chairman of the Arts Council was extended for a further two years. It would not be renewed, as the Conservatives would win the next election. Then, more political appointments would be made to Arts Boards. With small but increasing resources, soon to be frozen, Goodman declared that he had presided over the culmination of 'a profound social change in the last thirty years in this country. Within our society there is now a widespread feeling that the provision of drama and music and painting and all culture in its broadest sense is no longer to be regarded as a privilege for a few, but is the democratic right of the entire community. I think that any government – and happily there is no sign of any such government – that attempted to reverse this trend would find very rapidly how strong and deep it ran.' He was correct in his belief. Even though most of the young and many in the provinces thought that state subsidy was administered by a metropolitan élite and an old Establishment, the principle of giving tax money to the arts had taken root, in spite of constant attacks from the tabloid press and the rumblings of a few backwoodsmen in the House of Lords and back-benchers in the House of Commons. Whatever had been available to give to the arts had been given pretty well so far. And it had been given by a very British institution, which sometimes doubted its country had a culture.

SEVEN

YE BEST THINGS
IN YE WORST TIMES

More for one means less for someone else. The choice,
sometimes, is indeed agonizing. It is easy to say that the
Council's butter has been spread too thin – less easy to
agree on who should have been left with bare bread.

· Sir Hugh Willatt

Lord Goodman had some trouble in securing a knighthood for his
chosen Secretary-General, Hugh Willatt, but his finesse outma-
noeuvred the delaying strategy of the civil service. Willatt responded
by an appraisal of the work of the Arts Council over its first twenty-
five years. Especially, he concentrated on the activities of the fifteen
years before 1970 as against the eulogy of the founding decade that
had been penned by his almighty predecessor, Sir W. E. Williams. It
was a contrast in style as well as substance. Where Williams had
been an advocate of adult education with a compliant Chairman,
Lord Clark, both Willatt and his Chairman Lord Goodman were
trained lawyers of another generation without a hangover from the
depression of the nineteen-thirties and the succeeding wartime
years. On one fundamental matter, however, they agreed: holding
central control was better than giving power to the regions,
whatever was said or written on the subject to placate the
government. Their words were not necessarily their actions. As
Willatt himself has declared, 'There was a difference between what
the top people actually said and what the organization did.'

Willatt began by stating that increases to the grants-in-aid over
the previous fifteen years had been given, almost inevitably, in

response to the proliferation and growing strength of independent enterprises, particularly in the regions. By the middle of the nineteen-fifties it had become clear that the future of the Arts Council was to assist, with money, help and encouragement, the two hundred or so 'separate promotions already then in being or planned, rather than in any direct paternalistic and London-based effort to "bring Art to the people"'. This was the dearest project of Sir W. E. Williams. More than two-thirds of the Council's grant-in-aid was spent outside London, and Regional Arts Associations were burgeoning to replace the abolished Regional Offices of the Williams' regime. The British method of encouragement of the arts was 'very much our own invention', although it was spawning imitators in parts of the Commonwealth and in the United States of America. 'In our changing society it has grown naturally and in conformity with our traditions, particularly in its reliance on voluntary service and committees.' The essential features of this British system for paying for the arts were:

(i) continued acceptance of the principle that the Council itself, though a Government instrument, is effectively independent;
(ii) the provision of a substantial, though by continental standards a small, amount of money from central Government to supplement what is provided by the paying customer, local authorities and private sources;
(iii) promotion of the arts, particularly those involving performance, by autonomous and wholly independent enterprises working on a widely varying scale; the counterpart and the necessary complement to promotion by the mass media;
(iv) encouragement of individual creative artists through a multiplicity of schemes;
(v) the continuance of direct provision in one major field, namely the promotion of art exhibitions, and in certain other areas.

The Williams report on the first ten years of the Council had emphasized 'a primary responsibility to provide in the metropolis exemplary performances' by national institutions. The examples cited were Covent Garden, Sadler's Wells and the Old Vic, and between them was shared nearly half of the grant-in-aid. Their present equivalents such as the National Theatre with a fourth added, the Royal Shakespeare Company, now took less than a third of the available money. These four exemplary institutions were renowned throughout the world as well as Britain. Yet the country's achievements in the arts over the past fifteen years could not be measured only by this remarkable quartet, which now contained within their structures seventeen different operations that actually served the regions as well as London.

> These have also been the years of a new theatrical vitality and a new school of playwrights with an impact in many countries, chiefly associated with the work of George Devine, his colleagues and successors at the Royal Court, with powerful reverberations elsewhere; of Joan Littlewood's important creative period; of the World Theatre Seasons and the Chichester Festival; of the emergence of two or three regional theatres with an artistic strength approaching a metropolitan level; of London as a world centre of music; of the English Opera Group's success with chamber opera here and abroad; of the Ballet Rambert and the Contemporary Dance Theatre as new creative forces in modern dance, and a strengthened Festival Ballet with a big popular audience; of arts and music festivals in many towns and cities, of which Edinburgh is still the highest peak, now in a range of a dozen or more; of the emergence of the Welsh National Opera Company and Scottish Opera as major operatic forces.

Sir W. E. Williams had prophesied it would be better that music and drama were promoted by separate individual organizations than that they should be centrally and officially provided. He had proved wise in his foresight, which had led to the special grace of diversity. Nearly all concerts everywhere of serious music, other than BBC ones, as well as opera and ballet and more than half the British theatre, were now promoted by separate and autonomous bodies – twelve hundred self-governing and non-profit-distributing companies, registered as charities and grown mostly from local roots. The key to this flowering was the effort and enthusiasm of public-spirited citizens, who formed the committees of the various companies and contributed their unpaid and voluntary work and time. 'The members of these Boards of Trusts are a mixed bunch: some professional practitioners of the arts; local councillors and officials; businessmen; solicitors; vice-chancellors (invaluable as chairmen); schoolmasters; BBC officials; a few grandees of city and county; and in all these categories many lifelong and knowledgeable devotees of drama, music, the visual arts and literature.'

There were many combinations among the composition of the

Boards, but generally speaking, the more sophisticated the Board, the greater the freedom given to the artistic director of the enterprise. What was right for one part of the country might be wrong for another. London itself showed great variety, with the Board of the National Theatre appointed by the government and a strong element from the Greater London Council serving on other Boards. A few provincial Boards consisted mainly of local authority nominees, while others had no connection with the councillors and appointed themselves. Sometimes a group gathered around an outstanding artist, such as Ninette de Valois or Benjamin Britten, Laurence Olivier or Bernard Miles. 'These founding figures can rely on the support of a Board to give an organizational structure, shoulder the financial burden, receive and administer subsidy and provide continuity when they are no longer there.'

In the United States, the members of bodies of this sort tended to be wealthy men or women, but in Britain, they were not primarily chosen for their qualities as providers of money, or as prominent figures in the establishment. While fund-raising was often necessary, it was only to bridge the gap between subsidy and takings at the box-office. The main job was to operate the enterprise:

> The effort required is considerable, practical, and to a degree, professional. There is a real difference between the Board and Trust members of today and the 'do-gooders' or the rich patrons of a generation or so ago: dedicated enthusiasts like Barry Jackson or John Christie, those splendid ladies, Miss Horniman, Miss Cons and Miss Bayliss, or the pioneers of adult education and social service who worked for the arts in the same spirit in which they worked for charity and other worthy causes.

Such an outlook could still be found and had its value. Yet members of the present Boards were vastly more numerous and more ordinary, more widely drawn socially and certainly more businesslike in their approach. Some thirty thousand people were involved in this unpaid duty. The system might have its defects, but it had produced results.

> The promotion and operation of nine symphony and a growing number of chamber orchestras, of four large-scale and several small-scale opera companies and half a dozen ballet companies, and of seventy or so theatrical companies; the building or conversion of

seventy-five theatres and a dozen other buildings to house the arts, the promotion and operation of festivals: ultimate responsibility for all these achievements, and they are only a part of the whole, has rested with their promoting boards, and their record suggests enterprise and some considerable degree of business and artistic skill and judgement.

Sir Hugh Willatt's view of the importance of the Arts Boards was based on his own experience at the Nottingham Playhouse Trust and his wife's creation of the Midlands Group of Artists. The judgement of people is influenced by what they have done or known. Willatt did not address a complaint that had arisen during the youth revolution of the nineteen-sixties. The fact that the work on the Boards was voluntary and unpaid tended to favour those who could afford to sit on them, the bourgeoisie, the gentry and the rich. It was, of course, similar to the system of justice in the lower courts, where the magistrates also received no salary and were usually recruited from the advantaged. From the Treasury and the taxpayers' point of view, such a cheap system of administering justice and the arts was a wonderful saving to the national purse and the private pocket. And yet, there was necessarily some class bias in interpreting the law and artistic endeavour, also in the process of patronage, particularly on the Boards of the 'exemplary' institutions. Such a criticism of the dedicated and free service of hundreds of thousands of administrators of the culture and the rules of their country has rumbled to this day. Voluntary efforts cannot always heal social divisions.

From the point of view of the artistic directors and company administrators, the Boards generally gave good service. In Willatt's own experience, there were occasional frictions, as in the case of John Neville at the Nottingham Playhouse; but these were rare enough to emphasize the usual smoothness of practice. Self-perpetuation by the members of the Boards could lead to stagnation. There was always need for fresh blood on them. But in turn, they had to be watchful for the time when the professional direction became stale and flagging. The relationship between the paid artists and their Boards was usually productive, with the Boards content in their subsidiary role as providers of the sinews and resources. A professional indeed, 'often young, and brought up in a narrow world, has benefited and gained confidence from his contact with these ordinary representatives of the community in which he is working. They have, he finds, know-how in the world of money and affairs, a familiarity with the corridors of Town Halls and a long-standing relationship with the Arts Council, all of which prove useful at times.'

In this process, the Arts Council was something of a middleman. Before any subsidy was given, budgets and estimates were scrutinized by its specialist and finance officers. Projects were discussed in London and on the spot. The assessors of the Council regularly attended Board meetings and the performances of the enterprise. In most cases, no offer of a subsidy was made until the Council was satisfied that the applicant was budgeting within available resources. The autonomy and independence of the supported organizations had to be preserved; yet this requirement provided a reasonable safeguard in the expenditure of public money. Throughout the year of the subsidy, returns were monitored. Occasionally and exceptionally, a supplementary grant was offered from the Council's limited reserves. It was a myth that the Council discouraged surpluses or rewarded good housekeeping with a reduced grant in the following year. Equally it was a matter of pride that in twenty-five years, only two or three enterprises had to be wound up for purely financial reasons. From a total expenditure by the Council of £64,186,000 during these two and at half decades, more than double that sum had been generated in turnover from the box office and income from other sources. During this long period, the total deficit for which special provision had to be made represented only just over one per cent of the total turnover. 'The Council and its officers can perhaps claim that they have, over the years, achieved some skill in the art of subsidy. The Council itself, of course, has never accumulated a deficit.'

No one was wholly satisfied. It would be wrong if they were. Unless the Council's clients had been ambitious 'to improve and expand and believed passionately in what they were doing, they wouldn't have got far'. There might be a certain stimulus given by the very fact of limited resources, but excellence still cost money. An artistic institution could not remain static. But in the process of necessary expansion, there were other hands able to give, the local authorities and businesses, foundations, trusts and private sources. During the twenty-five years of the operation of the Arts Council, grants from local authorities had increased, although these were patchy and too little. Industry was beginning to play a larger part, yet it was still inconsiderable. The Gulbenkian Foundation and Pilgrim and Carnegie (UK) Trusts had been generous to the arts, while a number of buildings in themselves recalled private and individual munificence: Rosehill, the Northcott Theatre at Exeter, the Gardiner Arts Centre in Sussex, the Lyons Concert Hall at York, the Nuffield Theatre in Southampton. Watching the trend, the Council had recently appointed a senior officer to give advice to business organizations, foundations and individuals who wished to give donations to the arts.

Answering the predilections of the new minister responsible for the arts, Lord Eccles, Sir Hugh Willatt stressed how much more was being done for the regions. He maintained that they had benefited over the years from the increasing effort of the Council in terms of attention and the sheer number of enterprises involved – 915 of them directly or indirectly were supported in England outside London. The regions were now artistically less dominated by the capital than they ever had been. Fears to the contrary were heard more often in London than in the provinces themselves, where there was a real awareness of what the local theatre, art gallery or orchestra was producing and pride in its contribution to the national picture. People who lived in a provincial city, as had Willatt himself for so long, had one great advantage: each artistic event made an impact on the community in a way impossible in the capital, where provision of the arts, indeed, was mainly centred in the West End, leaving the huge population of the outer boroughs as deprived of the arts as the citizens of Leeds or Newcastle upon Tyne. Hundreds of suburban theatres and halls and clubs had closed. To be a Londoner did not mean culture on the doorstep.

However proud of regional achievement, however loud his praise of its support by the Arts Council, Sir Hugh Willatt did not forget to bang the drum for the national importance of the West End. 'London serves the country as a whole, a country geographically small; it is a centre for the artistic professions and the appropriate location for certain great national institutions which set a standard, and for a great deal more activity which permeates the artistic life of the country, and wins us respect and influence overseas.' Although a third of the total grant-in-aid was spent in a small area in the metropolis, the Arts Council believed in diversity of subsidy. In spite of the increasing size of its operation, the Council had remained reasonably flexible, even inventive, and had not chosen to escape criticism by confining help to the solid and the safe. One of the advantages of a system built on voluntary service from Council and Panel members through to the Boards of all the enterprises was independent and varied judgement – the reverse of monolithic. 'Any influence emanating from 105 Piccadilly is hardly monolithic either. The Council itself has at any one time up to two hundred people giving voluntary and independent service round its own table and on its Panels and Committees; a regularly changing number of people, mostly from the artistic professions and of widely differing outlook.'

The Council, however, still kept direct control over expenditure in the regions. Although two-thirds of the total grant-in-aid was spent there, nine-tenths of the subsidies to local activities was by direct grant and only one-tenth through the medium of the Regional Arts Associations, a development that had taken place mostly within the past five years. Only in Scotland and South Wales and south-eastern England were there now no properly constituted associations. Although their funds were meagre, these allocations usually equalled or sometimes substantially exceeded the contribution of the local authorities. The spending of this money was at the discretion of each association. And the Council did admit that regional collaboration was beyond doubt better than small-scale enterprises given tiny grants from the Arts Council in London. A lot of the little could safely be entrusted to the local.

So far the Council had shown itself adaptable enough to cope with its increasing resources and responsibilities, 'to have a nose for what is, or is likely to be, of special vitality or quality in our artistic life'. That was the main reason for keeping a central control on things, even if the Regional Arts Associations were declared to be a growing force in the future. Anyway, the trend was towards greater size and stability, particularly in housing the arts and national touring by the 'exemplary' companies. There was no megalomania here. The trend towards bigness meant no more than the consolidation and natural development of what had so far been created. And

yet its furtherance raised certain problems, particularly the relationship between the impresario needed to run such Frankensteins and
the part-time laymen on the Boards. A new breed of professional
arts administrator, however, was being trained to address the
matter. It might provide a solution to the question of size.

There was also an opposite trend among artists towards the small
scale, particularly in opera and ballet with chamber music and
group productions. Small fringe theatres were springing up in pubs
and warehouses, while a few musicians would make up an ensemble
to perform jazz and folk songs in small venues. Some of the
boundaries were disappearing. Although the Arts Council had only
spent a little on many of the new activities, these efforts seemed to be
winning a public and a new place for the artist. 'This may be one
way of curing his isolation, even if sometimes the cure lies
underground.'

There had been a general artistic renaissance in the past fifteen
years. The way things had looked in 1956 was very different from
the way things looked now. There was no longer the same need to
place a few organizations on a special pedestal. A really significant
growth in public response and public participation had been
matched not entirely by public subsidy, but by official recognition of
a new way that the arts mattered in the community. The appointment in 1965 of a Minister with special responsibility for the arts
was for the first time in British history a clear sign of that
recognition. Jennie, now Lady Lee's period of office saw a really
fruitful development. With the change of government five years
later, there was again the appointment of a Senior Minister, the
Paymaster General, with responsibilities for the arts even wider than
those of his predecessor. Subsidizing culture was removed from
party politics. Lord Eccles had announced his recognition of the
value of the work of the Arts Council, had secured an increase in the
grant-in-aid, and had supplied important encouragement, particularly to the Council's work in the regions. This did not mean the
creation in Britain of 'official art' or even of an arts establishment.
The system as a whole was truly diffuse and fragmented. Public
money only played a part. The rigidity and conformity of a state
operation had been avoided. What had been shown by the decade of
the nineteen-sixties was artistic 'quality, variety and vitality, and

above all an enormous catholicity: art promotion on the large and the small scale ranging from the drawings of Leonardo and Cézanne to kinetics and inflatables; from Shakespeare to arts laboratories; from symphony concerts to modern jazz.'

This appraisal of the first twenty-five years of the history of the Arts Council by its Secretary-General was an excellent brief, but it depended on one factor, which was under threat. For many years, the grant-in-aid had always been increased. Subsidies could be augmented, innovation could be encouraged, new clients piped aboard. There was little need to drown those who were already on the ship. This was one of the many differences between the Lords Eccles and Goodman.

'We had tried to get rid of Arnold Goodman', Lord Eccles has said. He continued:

> He didn't want to do anything outside London. We didn't want a metropolitan organization. The people in the Arts Council misunderstood what they were doing. Their job was to advertise the arts, not just to promote a few people. They wanted to be upstage all the time. They would not do the education. They would not do their job. They were elitist. Half the artists wouldn't go through the door of 105 Piccadilly – it was too grand. Yet all the same, Jennie Lee and Goodman were a remarkable team. But they didn't care about the quality of life of the British people. The Goodman doctrine was fatal. Once you started a subsidy, you had to keep a client on the books.

When he visited Lord Eccles, Lord Goodman found him rigid in opinion and opposed in policy. 'Not only did he lack any particular affection for artists, but he regarded them as members of the community who could be dealt with on a summary basis.' Although their relationship was a perfectly cordial one, Goodman had already had his term as Chairman of the Arts Council renewed by the previous Labour government, but he had to remain with Lord Eccles – and Eccles with him – for over a year. Their only overt quarrel was over the question of censorship associated with the grant of money. In Goodman's opinion, Eccles was convinced that the modern theatre was a cesspool. He exploded at Goodman that neither he nor the Prime Minister, Edward Heath, would be associated with some of the vulgarities and obscenities in subsidized plays. Soon afterwards the Arts Council issued a statement that censorship was not part of its function, although Eccles had stated in the House of Lords that the Council should accept a 'convention' by which it would refuse funds for productions that were filthy or blasphemous. Goodman regretted that the Council and the Minister had not seen eye to eye, but he stood his ground on censorship and the arm's length principle. It was not the Minister's business to interfere directly with any subsidy to the arts.

In the appreciation which Sir Hugh Willatt wrote for his Chairman on the latter's seven years in office, he quoted Lord Goodman as saying that Eccles was a civilized man with a probing mind:

> His intelligence led him to accept the autonomy of the Arts Council, but he was very interested and had ideas, and he itched to initiate and control. In this major element of his empire he knew he ought not to interfere, and as a former Minister he found the situation, and perhaps the Council's formidable Chairman, a little irksome. Furthermore, he was landed from the start with the commitment to museum charges, and you, wisely, refused him total support over a decision for which he had to carry the political can.
>
> He looked for areas in which to operate, and wooed the Regional Arts Associations, offering extra funds for their development. Outside the Council's sphere, he helped to create a new set-up, and provided money for Crafts, in which as a connoisseur and collector he moved with ease; but with artists – particularly performing artists – he had a very uncertain touch. You will remember the party you generously gave for him when he met the cream of the artistic professions. He never grasped its importance, and in an unprepared speech talked about the value of amateurs and the neglect of marquetry as a craft. He slipped away without a thank you. At an *Evening Standard* lunch, some clumsy reference to the smell of the Theatre made actors (at times as silly and touchy as most of us) claim that the Minister for the Arts said that actors smelt!
>
> On the face of it, these are trivial matters, but they throw light on the problem of a Minister for the Arts in relation to the Council and the world of the Arts. The fact remains that although in this year the grant (negotiated by Lord Eccles's predecessor) was a modest one, in the following year in the expanding climate of the Heath/Barber period there was an appreciable rise, and Eccles was able to demonstrate his intention to help the arts and make his tenure a successful one.

And for Sir Denis Forman, then head of the British Film Institute, the duopoly of David Eccles and Edward Heath was as important for the arts as the trinity of Jennie Lee and Harold Wilson and Arnold Goodman had been: 'If you wanted money and needed another half million pounds, you'd ask Eccles, and he would say yes, and he'd get it off Heath.' But to Lady Antonia Fraser, who was Lord Goodman's appointee as a member of the Arts Council, Eccles was merely a figure who said that a lot of money should go to amateur brass bands. For Keith Jeffery, however, his finest hour as 'Director of Festivals' was the windfall of £250,000 spent on an eleven-day celebration in London of ballet and opera and concert to commemorate Edward Heath's piloting of Britain into the European Economic Community.

That was the fundamental conflict between the Tory Minister and the Arts Council. Lord Eccles favoured the people, the crafts, the regions and marketing, while Lord Goodman put his emphasis on cultural leaders, the performing arts, the metropolis and dissemination from the centres of excellence. 'I learnt my lessons from Mortimer Wheeler, the archaeologist', Eccles has said. 'He taught me, if you advertise a work of art in a sensible way, you get a new public. I tried to apply the Wheeler principle – but I couldn't get the Arts Council to do it. Their way of educating was to get the repertory theatres to advertise themselves. They never understood that. Marketing is what the small arts need – from a central marketing organization.'

Lord Eccles even crossed swords with his old friend André Malraux, who was the Minister of Culture in France under General de Gaulle. 'He made a fool of himself,' Eccles has said, 'building his Maisons de la Culture in the provinces. In six months, they were captured by the middle class. I don't want a class society. The French working class never went through their doors.'

His wish for a classless Britain with more power to the people appealed to Sir Denis Forman, who considered him the best Minister for the Arts that there had been, more knowledgeable and less doctrinaire than Lady Lee. Eccles did secure more recognition for the crafts, although he failed in his aim to give more responsibility in the regions, as he was not in office long enough. In Forman's opinion, Lord Goodman did not have a vision or a sense of direction in the arts. He would adjudicate squabbles and raise money for other people's purposes in the Arts Council. He was the Great Enabler rather than the great director.

What the differences between the Minister and the Chairman did do was to make personal the split and contradictory Royal Charters of the Arts Council. Educating the people or maintaining standards of excellence? The roving missionary of culture or the central flagbearer? Spreading or raising? There was and would be no end to this debate. Lord Goodman declared in 1970:

> I would wish that there might be a million Arts Councils in this country, so that there might be a million men who enjoy the benefits of training as their Chairmen. There is no more liberal education available in the whole wide world. In six years of enthralling office I have – unlike the Bourbons – learnt more and forgotten more than in any period of my life. A chairman of the Arts Council finds that every preconception in relation to the administration of the arts is either mistaken or at least calls for massive qualification ... As it is I am satisfied that a Sanhedrin of Arts Council Chairmen would solve every human problem – except the artistic one – with effortless ease.

In his seventh and last year as Chairman, Lord Goodman felt obliged to follow the direction of Lord Eccles, because the grant-in-aid for 1971–2 was greatly augmented to £11,900,000, an increase of more than a quarter on the previous year. In his notes for his appreciation of the Chairman in that final year, Sir Hugh Willatt admitted a certain defensiveness on the whole regional question in the annual report, which emphasized the spread of resources to the Regional Arts Associations, 'resulting, I suspect, from pressure from Eccles and his department on this question ... I think that Eccles had obtained the increase in grant-in-aid on the understanding that a certain proportion would be allocated to these bodies.' Eccles and the Treasury were interfering with the independence of the Arts Council in choosing where to remit its subsidies; but this seemed permissible when the total grant was so increased that none of the other clients had to suffer. With expanding budgets, raising and spreading was possible. Only with static or diminished budgets would the hard edges shine, the decisions whether to cut or eliminate aid to old clients in order to expand help to the countryside at large.

Lord Goodman exonerated his Minister from responsibility for an unprecedented manoeuvre, 'the sad business' of summoning the Arts Council before a parliamentary Public Accounts Committee Inquiry. The Auditor-General accused the Council of allowing the Sadler's Wells Opera Company to run a deficit during the first year of its move to the Coliseum. The Council was also charged with giving prior indications of its attitude to building schemes, so infringing the conditions for giving subsidies to Housing the Arts. Affronted by this assault on the independence of the Council, Lord Goodman insisted on appearing in person before the Public Accounts Committee – that year, its Chairman happened to be his good friend, Harold Lever. 'The ritual proceedings resembled an Asian bazaar', Goodman later wrote, 'rather than a judicial tribunal.' At the end of the day, the Council was wholly vindicated. In fact, if it had not adopted either course, the Committee would have ruled it at fault. The whole imbroglio convinced Goodman that an Arts Council and a civil service could only live in concord if the bureaucratic element 'was a special and unusual one. When it became a characteristic one, it resented the autonomy of an Arts Council which had power to spend money, a willingness to speak its mind, a capacity to make everything that it did known to the public, and a genuine belief that the public should know.'

Within the Council, the waste of time and public money spent in preparing for and attending the meetings were sickening. In the opinion of the Secretary-General, 'it was disturbing to find how incapable the civil service were of adapting their thinking to any appreciation of what is needed when subsidy goes to independent organizations carrying on businesses, or their unwillingness to do so.' A different and valuable financial investigation was instigated by the Chairman, when he instructed the accounting firm Peat Marwick Mitchell to review the operations of the four flagship enterprises, the Royal Opera House, Sadler's Wells at the Coliseum, the National Theatre and the Royal Shakespeare Company. The result of the inquiry should have satisfied even the Treasury. Possible annual cost savings of less than three per cent on turnover were suggested. When Lord Goodman asked whether these artistic companies were as efficient as average commercial companies of the same size, the answer was 'yes'. It was an unwelcome jingle in the ears of cost-conscious mandarins.

At another and later secret meeting with Treasury officials about the costs of the Royal Opera House, Tony Field found that the three civil servants had never visited a theatre, let alone an opera or ballet. 'They were appalled at the need to have so many sopranos and contraltos, tenors and baritones all singing at the same time. Why could not economies be made in the numbers of the chorus? In desperation I flayed around for a counter-argument and pointed out that if the chorus was cut they could not be heard above the orchestra. "Ah", said the three wise men in triumph, turning back a page, "But not if you cut the orchestra correspondingly!"'

In his valedictory statement as Chairman, Lord Goodman praised his Secretary-General's fair and careful picture of what had been achieved during the first twenty-five years of the Arts Council. It had become a national institution of real consequence. Its great failure had been not to improve the living conditions of the creative and performing artist:

> Despite all the things we have not done and all the things we have done but ought not to have done, and all the things that still need to be done, the Arts Council is a good and worthy institution in a wicked world. It has provided a stimulus and a sense of purpose to a great many people and a great many projects. Much that is good would have been lost without it. Much that is hopeful would never have seen the light of day and some things that are purposeless and pointless and positively nasty would have continued to maintain unproved pretensions.

Lord Goodman could only offer to his successor a tattered banner and a dented sword, but they could be accepted with pride. The last year had been an eventful one. The Council had discovered to its dismay that among its friends were a few determined and embittered enemies, whose pent-up rage was suddenly released. 'We found ourselves engaged in positively mortal battle to defend the integrity and wisdom of our administration.' Rather as General Eisenhower ended his presidential term of office in a warning against the power of the American industrial-military complex, Lord Goodman stressed the vital need for the Arts Council to retain its independence of action:

> It is impossible for sensible decisions about the arts to emerge from Governmental offices. The Arts Council, a body of people who

breathe the fresh air of ordinary life in their normal everyday activities, can – whatever mistakes we make – adjudicate on our problems with commonsense and appreciation of the needs of ordinary human beings. We can marshal to our aid the informed judgement of expert panels, uncoerced by rules and regulations of an academic and artificial character. If the administration of subsidy for the arts is left to the tender mercies of full-time bureaucrats, my experience compels the harsh judgement that we would be better to dispense with the system altogether.

Rather than change a system, the better practice in a democracy is first to change the Chairman and then the Secretary-General of the offending organization. In the middle of the night, Lord Eccles had an inspiration for Lord Goodman's successor – Patrick Gibson, a distinguished businessman rather than a solicitor, the Old Etonian director of *The Economist*, on the board and later chairman of the *Financial Times* and the Pearson holding company. Already a trustee of the Glyndebourne Festival Opera, Gibson was interested in architecture as well as music, and he shared in the Minister's concern for the regions. A good administrator, he retained an open mind. 'The job was a tremendous widener for me', he has said. 'It opened all sorts of doors of experience and perception which I hadn't thought of before. I learned a great deal new about this country.'

In his first Chairman's introduction to the annual report of the Arts Council, Patrick Gibson stressed the reason for his appointment. Recent years had seen a distinct shift in the allocation of resources between London and the rest of the United Kingdom. Activities outside the metropolis had claimed a greater share of the income in the grant-in-aid, and this process must accelerate, if the right balance between the capital and the rest of the country were to be established. Yet if the national institutions were maintained at a high standard, the balance could only be redressed with more funds from the taxpayer. Sir Hugh Willatt seconded his new Chairman in that emphasis. The need to reach even wider audiences was the main theme of his report: 'The more effective steering of money in the right directions – publicity, promotion, new administrative structures – these matters are important, indeed essential, if the arts are to have a proper economic base and the right position in society.' Lord Eccles was finally getting from the Arts Council what he advocated.

Four themes were prominent in the Arts Council report; the need to reach more audiences, administration and publicity, touring and the Regional Arts Associations. 'Artistic trends are a matter for artists', the Secretary-General pointed out, eschewing a concern of the previous Chairman, Lord Goodman. 'It is for the Council to help to solve the increasing and always changing problem of the place of the arts in our confusing society.'

The report of the following year, 1972–3, again concentrated on 'devolution and the emergence of something suspiciously like a nationwide pattern'. An increase of two million pounds in the annual grant made more money available to the countryside. Of special interest were the decisions to create a new Department for Regional Development to help in the promotion of the arts there, and to provide services for the Regional Arts Associations and for the Council's work generally in relation to Marketing and Research. This strategy resulted in prototype schemes in Birmingham, Bristol and Sheffield for more intensive marketing of artistic events financed out of special regional development monies provided by the government. Yet the Secretary-General declared, 'To depict Regional Arts Associations as agents for the Council would be highly misleading.' They were autonomous and an important part in the devolution process. Each year's responsibility for subsidizing certain artistic activities in a region was being handed out to the Arts Association concerned. This process would continue as the Associations developed and grew into the lives of their communities. But did the trend towards devolution result in more art and better art? For the benefit of more people and the people most in need of it? Or was it only middle-class culture for the privileged? Coterie art for a new coterie?

The simple answer was that the Arts Council could only respond and support what the artists themselves were producing. There were still gaps and desert areas, both geographical and social. These seemed to demand of the Council a harder effort to find what needed to be done and how to do it. The Council had to be continuously critical of its old traditional methods, as all the arts were in a perpetual state of change and ferment. Hence the setting up of the Department for Regional Development, and the institution of a new Regional Committee under the chairmanship of a member of the Council, Professor Roy Shaw, from a northern working-class background and a leader in the field of adult education. The previous Secretary-General Nigel Abercrombie had now retired from his post as Chief Regional Adviser, a role which he had once said was a nanny to the arts.

The following year saw Ministers for the Arts leaving office faster than revue performers on the stage. Lord Eccles gave way to Norman St John-Stevas, whose brief tenure was cut short by the Labour victory in the election of February 1974, and the ministerial appointment of Hugh Jenkins, an Equity union official and Member of Parliament, who had served on the Drama Panel and Board of the Council. The loss of Eccles was hard for Gibson to take. He had been appointed by that Minister and was carrying out the broad direction of the government's policies, while retaining the Council's independence. 'It would be hard to imagine a more stimulating Minister,' Gibson wrote. 'His vision of the place of the arts in society, and of the unifying role they can and must be made to play, provided a firm basis for our work.' Even with the financial crisis of 1973 and rampant inflation, the grant-in-aid for the year was increased by nearly fifteen per cent, although inflation was about three per cent higher. This ended the long period of growth for the Council, which would now be forced to cut some subsidies and defer an extension of support for community arts and a beginning of aid to amateur activities. Yet Lord Gibson, who was now given a life peerage, quoted a message of quiet confidence rather than despair. At Staunton Harold in Leicestershire, there survived a beautiful chapel built during the sacrilegious times of the Commonwealth. An inscription over the entrance said of its benefactor, that his 'singular praise it is to have done ye best things in ye worst times. And hoped them in the most callimitous.'

The Secretary-General spent his space in the annual report in replying to the criticism that always attacked subsidies to the arts in the worst times. Whatever the funds available, the Council was accused of an apparent lack of logic and fairness in the distribution of them. Yet its role was not to be a great promoter of the arts, it was a dispenser with quality controls:

To some statisticians and other tidy-minded people a system mainly

based on response to other people's promotional activities, haphaz-
ardly occurring, which allows them complete independence, and
tolerates ups-and-downs and bad patches – all this suggests bad
planning and inadequate cost effectiveness.

To many individual creative artists, it seems that the Council
responds too readily to energetic efforts of promoters of expensive
schemes for the arts involving performance, while ignoring the claims
of the writer, the composer and the artist.

Those, on the other hand, responsible for the operation of
hundreds of enterprises in theatre, music, opera and ballet, think that
the Council spreads its resources too thinly by adding others to their
number, or by embarking on a multitude of schemes for the benefit of
artists and writers who can, at any rate, find some market for their
work, however limited and unrewarding that market may be, or
schemes designed to spread interest, train or elicit experiment. The
Council, they say, should concentrate its funds on their own
admittedly expensive operations, which would simply not exist
without Council subsidy, and whose future is in peril because, in spite
of good audiences, that subsidy is too small.

The emergent companies and experimental groups think that too
much goes to the middle-class establishment.

These criticisms ignored the history and basic principles of the
Council. First, there was the doctrine of discriminating response to
other people's initiatives, which did not mean that the Council had
been blown hither and thither by every wind, or rushed in with help
in response to the loudest cries. If the Council had spread its
resources too thinly, this was a deliberate policy with strong
government encouragement, to further the spread of the arts,
particularly in the regions. If the role of the Council's staff was
sometimes questioned in making grants, these choices were only
made after reviews by the Panels, the Committees and the Council,
all of which had distinguished and rotating members. Grants to
individual artists could never be great. 'There is no burking the fact
that the greater part of the Council's funds is tied up because of
accumulated obligations to the performing arts.' The Council could
not help being the prisoner of its existing commitments. Very
occasionally, advised by a Panel, it had to decide whether a grant to
an organization should cease because of artistic flagging or
dwindling public support. But subsidies to artists, direct promotions
and initiatives of many kinds had markedly increased, even if the

balance might not yet be right. Arts centres were being given more aid, and a Community Arts Working Party under the chairmanship of Professor Harold Baldry had produced a report recommending the increase of the future role of the Council in that area. The arts organization was doing all that could reasonably be done.

When Sir Hugh Willatt himself retired in 1975 at the end of his seven years of service as Secretary-General, his Chairman paid tribute to his dedication and skill, his integrity and his gentle lack of self-advertisement. He had presided over the expansion of the activities of the Council during this period and had seen it enter the doldrums of financial standstill. In his final account he showed clearly how the trebling of the grant-in-aid in the previous seven years had done much to redress the balance between London and the regions. Under his stewardship, there had been five main areas of expansion. There had been more for Scotland and Wales, more for Regional Arts Associations, more for opera and dance countrywide, for training, for arts centres and for other regional projects. The last grant-in-aid was £21,335,000, signalling a triple increase in seven years, although tempered by inflation. The 'new' money had been mainly devoted to areas of growth outside London, while the Council's own functional departments in art and drama and music and literature did much more than they had done to meet new artistic trends.

While the Welsh grant had risen more than fourfold in the period, the Scottish grant had more than trebled to nearly two and a half million pounds. This had enabled Scotland to support the move there of the Western Theatre Ballet, which had become the Scottish Theatre Ballet. This shift was engineered by the Arts Council in a contradiction of its usual policy of non-interference. The Enquiry into the State of Opera and Ballet in the United Kingdom, chaired by Lord Harewood and initiated by Lord Goodman, had envisaged a plan in which various forms of ballet and dance theatre could reach out to most areas of Great Britain, a plan which had also provided a blueprint for future development. As a result of it, the Northern Dance Theatre had begun a successful career; its initial funding was equally shared between the Arts Council and the North West Arts Association; and the Western Theatre Ballet under the direction of Peter Darrell had moved from a precarious existence at Bristol up to

Glasgow, when it became associated with the Scottish Opera. Although nationalistic elements in Scotland resented this southern incursion, especially when Darrell could not find a single Scottish dancer of sufficient quality even to serve in his *corps de ballet*, the quality of his work and his slow recruitment of Scottish dancers overcame initial suspicion, especially when he declared and proved his commitment to founding a national Scottish Ballet.

Ironically enough, the only time that the enterprise nearly capsized was when the Arts Council took its policy of management too far. Darrell had asked for an administrative associate and the Assistant Music Director at the Arts Council, a former dancer called David Reynolds, was appointed to serve as the overall Director of the Scottish Company. His wish to fragment the company into small touring groups, basically to educate the people, conflicted with Darrell's policy of large performances and occasional touring. Darrell offered his resignation with most of the company, but it was Reynolds who took his leave. The experience of serving as an officer in the Arts Council did not necessarily provide the qualities to command a professional artistic body. By the end of the nineteen-seventies, the annual turnover of the Scottish Ballet was over a million pounds and its grant-in-aid from the Scottish Arts Council was two-thirds of that sum. The transplanted company was considered a jewel in the crown of its new country.

That decade was a period of 'cultural efflorescence' in Scotland, as the previous decade of the nineteen-sixties had been south of the border. For John Faulkner, newly appointed Assistant Drama Director in 1972, this was the time of Scottish playwrights such as Bill Bryden and small touring companies such as John McGrath's 7:84; its performances to enthusiastic audiences in halls and clubs on the subject of the Highland Clearances and North Sea Oil were 'a living demonstration of the equation: Relevance + Participation = Enjoyment, and a far cry from Mary Queen of Scots and Bonnie Prince Charlie twice nightly'. Edward Heath said that he had four million pounds in his pocket to build a Scottish Opera House, and Edinburgh was ready to match that sum, although the Prime Minister and the project would go down. Yet there was now a national opera and orchestra and ballet, and the experimental and populist works at the Traverse and the Pool Theatres in the Scottish capital and at the Citizens and the Close in Glasgow were internationally renowned.

This transformation was somewhat the work of the extraordinary and energetic Alexander Dunbar, who had moved from the North-Eastern Arts Association and the Gulbenkian Foundation to take over as Director of the Arts Council of Scotland under a new Chairman, Lord Balfour of Burleigh. If new brooms do not always sweep clean, they certainly raise the dust. 'Money doesn't mean a thing', Dunbar wrote of his fresh programme. 'But when you haven't got any, it takes on a peculiar significance.' Although the customers of the Scottish Arts Council often implied that it was only a bank to keep them afloat, it was 'a thinking, planning, policy-making agency'. Several trends in the arts pointed towards new directions in the renaissance in Scotland: an increasing emphasis on work in and for schools and young people; a recognition of the value of the arts in the community that involved aid to over a hundred arts centres, clubs and guilds throughout the nation; a desire for more experimentation and improvisation; an increased emphasis on research, publicity and selling through the arts; the involvement of local government as well as the development of international contacts. Augmented budgets allowed for some expansion, particularly in giving direct help to authors or assisting their work to be published. 'The Government spends £68,000,000 on making books freely available to the public in libraries: massive help for the reader and little for the writer.' In Scotland, the balance was being tipped.

The year of 1975 saw the apogee of assisted culture in Scotland. An increase of twelve per cent was added to the seventeen per cent of the grant-in-aid by the Arts Council of Great Britain. Even the cautious Scottish Chairman, Lord Balfour, admitted, 'If it had not been for inflation the arts in Scotland would have had a good year. (If it had not been for illness, the patient would have been in splendid health.)' It was the same story in the Regional Arts Associations; their increased budgets were eroded by the loss of the value of money. Yet the Arts Council assisted by the Gulbenkian Foundation did promise a new enquiry into the whole question of support for regional arts, conducted by Lord Redcliffe-Maud. Provision for national touring by the Royal Ballet, the English National Opera Company, the London Festival Ballet and other companies had grown by five times in five years, while there was a whole new pattern of ballet and dance provision for the regions. Jane Nicholas, a former dancer for Dame Ninette de Valois, had replaced David Reynolds at the Arts Council, and she with John Cruft had much to do with the second great success of the Arts Council to date, its introduction of opera and dance nationwide after its revival of the British repertory theatre. Cruft himself was sympathetic to the emphasis of Lord Eccles, even though the Minister used to refer to the Arts Council as 'the Marchioness of Piccadilly'. 'In a sense, the Arts Council was always an advertising body. It was always our job to fight for the arts – not to tell them what to do.'

With inflation and static funding, however, the cuts were coming which threatened the nine symphony orchestras which were being supported. John Cruft knew the importance of this slicing. 'Money was important,' he has said, 'but so was our blessing. To remove our backing was a dagger blow, to achieve it was respectability. If it went, there was all sorts of grief and lobbying. It was assumed you were unsound in your judgement, and you would need support from your Panel members.' There was hell in turning dancers down, particularly as they lived so close physically to their art and retired so early without a pension. 'Anything to do with dancers is like touching open wounds. They were devoted people, and we were killing their children.' Yet a refusal sometimes led to a reshaping which was much better. The standard of performance did not always improve with the size of the fee. Being in the black did not mean dancing or singing or performing music well. Mr Micawber's principle did not apply to the arts, nor to the Arts Council, which had to assess quality in the end, not profit. 'In so far as perfection is unattainable, we did what we could do. The centres of excellence always ripple outwards.'

This admirable statement of practice and philosophy by the Director of Music showed something of the quality of the senior staff at the Council in this period of development. It was matched by Joanna Drew's work as Assistant and then Director of the Art Department, almost the last legacy of direct provision in mounting exhibitions, grants to galleries and to individuals, and purchases of works of art. Clearly to her, the Arts Council was already in trouble. 'I set my face against new clients,' she has said, 'unless they had funding from another source. Clearly we could not sustain those we already had.' Some support was now being given to Performance Art and more to the making of arts films; but these were threatened by the new financial stringency. The bad times were changing for the worse.

In the theatre in the nineteen-seventies, two experienced Drama Directors at the Council, Dick Linklater and John Faulkner, backed by a still glittering Panel of professional experts of the calibre of Alan Ayckbourn, Peter Hall and Trevor Nunn, still spread what they had to the best without much challenge. For Peter Hall, who soon left the Panel, the great days of the Arts Council were already over. It was trying to *plan* art into existence, as in dance and opera, more than watching to see where creativity happened and then encouraging the blooms with extra funds. Yet he himself loved the politics of committees, the ebb and flow of chat, and seldom found them anything but fascinating. 'Such gatherings are a basic form of theatre. Everybody is playing a part, and most people are saying less than they mean.' His appointment as the successor to Lord Olivier as Director of the National Theatre would lead him into conflict with the Arts Council and a revision of his opinion of it. In his memoirs, he was to write that he saw the Council 'turn from an independent champion of the arts to an instrument of government, gradually reducing its support all round, progressively weakening the idea of what a National Theatre should be'.

This bleak vision, however, was only the prophecy of a Cassandra of the arts, who praised above all the BBC and the Arts Council as the examples of the two things done right in Britain in the twentieth century, because they were allowed 'organic growth' and had encouraged it with their patronage. In drama in the past seven years, fifteen new or reconstructed theatres had opened in the regions, and there had also been a great extension of the range of activities in the repertory companies, namely 'Theatre in Education, Young People's Theatre, small touring units, shows in pubs, Studio Theatres, Late Night Shows, lunch-time performances of music, poetry readings and film showings'. Grants to experimental and fringe drama would approach half a million pounds, which pointed to the flourishing state of the theatre in spite of the recession.

Even the poor mouse of the arts, the Literature Department, was said to show improvement in its subsidy and performance. During the period, its allocation had tripled to a meagre two hundred thousand pounds for the art with the most achievement in the nation's history. 'This is still a very small amount,' Sir Hugh Willatt admitted in his final statement. 'We are often criticized for this though our critics are less ready to say what else we should do for literature.' The problem, according to Lord Gibson, lay in the lack of internal pressure for him to do more. There was no battle with the Director of Literature, Charles Osborne, or the Panel. 'It didn't come welling up', he has said. 'There was no beating of the drum or need to refuse.' Osborne was concerned with reducing the advisory role of the Panel: he cut the 'tea and rhubarb' occasions of its meetings from six times a year to four and was to end by acquiescing in the running down of his Department. More interested in singing than in writing as was his predecessor Eric White, Osborne found it amusing to quote in his candid *Memoirs of an Uncivil Servant* the lines of Gavin Ewart upon his reign in office – that it was ironical:

> ... that a Literature Director should be
> a man who only cares about music –
> Charles Osborne,
> the phantom of the opera.

The role of Osborne was hardly challenged by his three distinguished Panel Chairmen – Angus Wilson, Frank Kermode and Stuart Hampshire. Hampshire's ironic detachment suited the Director's own temperament, particularly his support of a National Publishing House to rival the Royal Opera House as a large literary loss-making institution, in order to increase the subsidy. The main campaign of the Literature Department was for the Public Lending Right, which eventually came about despite a filibuster in Parliament by Ian Sproat, who was, to the surprise of some, to become a future spokesman for the Arts. Osborne was neither popular with most authors for failing to defend and promote their cause, nor was he praised within the Council. He inherited Eric White's assistant, Sheila Gold, who found him the opposite of the gentlemanly White, under whose eccentric guidance, the Literature Panel had some influence. Under Osborne's calculated policy, it was to be joked out of existence. In the nineteen-sixties, she and the rest of the staff still felt that they were building a new world. By the middle of the

nineteen-seventies, they were losing hope with a Literature Director, whose wit was greater than his commitment, and who could
describe a prominent Council member as 'a closet idiot in imminent
danger of "coming out".'

The departing Secretary-General had been prodded into his last
'growth area – Arts Centres and Regional Projects – new categories',
in Charles Osborne's opinion, 'which should not have been included
in the annual budget at all'. More than half a million pounds,
however, were promised annually for such new activities, including
community arts. Yet until now, the opening of arts centres had been
largely a result of the vision and efforts of voluntary groups. In
future, that initiative would come more from the increasing
involvement of local authorities, encouraged by the Arts Council,
which would undergo a considerable change in the attitude
described by Lord Feversham, the first chairman of the Standing
Conference of Regional Arts Associations. He said in 1974 to a
regional studies conference that, during the past five years, he could
not remember a time when he had the feeling of being received by
the Arts Council mandarins in Piccadilly as a colleague in the same
business. 'Rather one is given the feeling that one is some kind of
orange three-headed Martian with antennae sprouting from the
forehead who has just landed by flying saucer in Green Park.'

When the outgoing Secretary-General had given up his legal
practice and taken the post seven years before at the insistence of
Lord Goodman, who had turned down another civil servant
recommended by his selection committee, Sir Hugh Willatt already
had an intense belief in the Arts Council and the way it worked – 'a
system based on the Council's own independence, the autonomy of
its "clients" and the voluntary co-operation of people all over the
country engaged in the arts'. It responded to what came up from
below. The key figures were not the Lords Goodman and Gibson,
according to Willatt. They were the Directors and staff of the
Departments and the members of the Panels, who supplied the links
between the arts and the artists and so reached decisions over
funding. The Council was in touch with new trends and ideas. 'We
at the top co-ordinated or created an attitude.' The key activity was
the weekly meeting of the Directorate, where the heads of the
Departments talked to the Secretary-General, 'the unruly barons
reporting on their fiefdoms'.

Yet this was a system devised for a smaller and less complex operation of arts subsidy. All the same, Willatt hoped it would be possible to keep the essentials of the system: 'the freedom, the looseness of control, the encouragement and advice, and some of the informality – when the money and the responsibility were becoming so much greater'. Lord Gibson was already warning that this would be impossible. As Lord Goodman had done, he had refused Lord Eccles's effort to force a merger between Covent Garden and the English National Opera at the Coliseum. He resisted the Minister's attempt to earmark money for only one amalgamated opera company. But with the increase in funding, money had been accepted which was already earmarked for publicity and regional development. Independence and freedom of action was being eroded, willy-nilly. With very large budgets in the future, Lord Gibson thought, arts policy would come to be determined by the government.

Yet the Secretary-General still hoped that the fundamentals of past practice might somehow be preserved, 'that the Council, although a government agency, may remain unfettered in its distribution of public money, and permitted to do this in a way which allows its clients the maximum freedom, artistic and financial, including the right from time to time to fail'. His hope was not vain, but it was under threat from static funding and government encroachment. Innovation was penned within a shrinking room. 'You can't change the system at all,' Dick Linklater has said. 'We started each year with wonderful ideas, but we were trapped into maintaining the empire we had built up.' There would now be little expansion without increased taxation for the arts, which was hardly a feasible choice. As was said by Tony Field, the Finance Director of that time, he did not feel that politicians and the Treasury really wanted to subsidize the arts, because questions were asked which others did not ask. 'They try to brush artists aside with just enough money to keep them relatively quiet.' And with the appointment of a new Secretary-General and Minister under a Labour government, the erosion of the Council's independence could hardly be resisted.

EIGHT

DEVOLUTION
AND DEFENCE

For God's sake, don't!

Michael Elliott, on being asked whether he wished the
Arts Council in London to delegate the responsibility
for the funding of the Royal Exchange Theatre
to the regional authorities in Manchester.

The struggle for the post of the next Secretary-General of the Arts Council also marked the forks in the highway ahead. Although Charles Osborne threw his cloak in the ring with other leading Council officers and reached the shortlist, he was not a serious contender. The two rivals were Professor Roy Shaw, already in charge of regional development, and the Deputy Secretary-General, Angus Stirling, a devoted and inspirational figure, whom his Chairman saw as 'a tremendous liberal, who wanted to see good in everything'. In Lord Gibson's opinion, Stirling was not ready yet for the top job, nor was a thoroughly liberal conscience wanted in that role. And like Gibson, Stirling was an Old Etonian, an obstacle in those years of reverse discrimination. The Chairman felt that somebody was needed from a working-class background, even though Roy Shaw might not be better qualified. Certainly, Shaw wanted to be a second W. E. Williams, tipping the balance in favour of adult education, while the Chairman should stay on the bridge as Lord Clark had done, and merely steer.

Although no longer Minister for the Arts, Lord Eccles was a supporter of Shaw's candidacy, saying to Lord Gibson, 'Well, I love him, but who else does?' Shaw, indeed, claimed to have tutored

Eccles on the arts, and to have shown him that 'class is arts' – a message that Eccles believed, as did his High Tory successor Norman St John-Stevas. To them, the middle classes seemed to have established separate privileged cultures, appropriating the subsidies for their purposes instead of promoting brass bands. Lord Eccles liked Shaw's philosophy of spreading without debasing; but in Lord Gibson's later opinion, Shaw was to prove clumsy with the staff or the clients. The Vice-Chairman and former barrister, Lord Hutchinson, was also to agree with their assessments, saying that Shaw's appointment was Lord Gibson's cross, which he had to carry. Shaw could not communicate well with the organization and the customers, but only with the press. He replaced a more balanced system with home rule from his office.

'When Hugh Willatt and Angus Stirling were there,' Lord Hutchinson has said, 'we were on the side of the artist, we had the respect of the clients. They came to see Angus, who could run things on a long elastic. If artists were worried or in debt, they would come and see us and talk it over.' It was all change now, as Dick Linklater thought, with the 'fatal appointment' of the powerful new Secretary-General. 'Angus Stirling had the Keynesian line. He could have persuaded his Chairman to hold that line. But Shaw could not. The Council began to introduce the frills – education and social welfare. The Departments became dispirited and were hardly consulted. The purpose of the Council was dictated. It began to become a sort of Ministry.'

These were the voices of those who revered the independence and organic growth and old policy of response of the Council. Roy Shaw, however, was a reformer and a zealot for mass education. He occupied Piccadilly as the Parliamentarians had occupied London during the Civil War, determined to pull out the old royal and religious traditions, root and branch. Reaching the arts was all. Shaw believed that the task of education, broadcasting and arts organizations, especially the Arts Council and the Regional Arts Associations, was to make excellence accessible. This was based on 'the eminently democratic assumption that people deserve the best and need it'. He was determined to introduce an education unit with travelling officers into the Council and to encourage the clients to include educational activities in their programmes. He refused to listen to his two more senior colleagues, when they counselled him that education was 'a no-go area'. His deputy was still Angus Stirling.

> He warned me that the government would not allow the Council to meddle with education. Moreover, he believed it was the prime duty of the Council to serve artists, rather than the arts audience. I, however, agreed with Jennie Lee's White Paper, that 'by far the most valuable help that can be given to the individual artist is to provide him with a larger and more appreciative audience'. Tony Field, the Council's Finance Director, simply warned me that there was no money for educational development. Determined not to be thwarted, I negotiated a three-year grant from the Gulbenkian Foundation to appoint one person, to be called an education liaison officer, and a secretary ...
>
> In order to placate those who still felt that the Council should not touch education (despite its chartered duty to develop understanding of the arts), I pointed out that I was not seeking to involve the Council directly in education, but invoked another chartered duty, which is to co-operate with 'other bodies' (in this case educational bodies) to achieve its main tasks to develop knowledge and make the arts more accessible. Despite colleagues' forebodings, the arts minister's civil servants found no cause to oppose the appointment of an education liaison officer. Norman St John-Stevas, who was then shadow arts minister, was very supportive, and remarked that it was the first such appointment in the Council's thirty-two-year history. He also commented that it was extraordinary that the Council had for so long neglected the vital area of education.

As the man in charge, Roy Shaw wanted his rivals and opponents to withdraw. He failed to persuade Charles Osborne to resign from the Literature Department; Osborne gracefully declined, as he did similar suggestions from various literary figures and even a minister for the arts. The Employment Protection Act made it almost impossible to sack him, and he saw Shaw retire before he felt that he had had enough; even then, he negotiated a platinum 'handshake'. As for Tony Field and Angus Stirling, they were both initially essential for keeping the organization going. Shaw had to retain Field in London to supervise finance, but he soon sent Stirling out to grass in the regions as Abercrombie had been sent before on his loss of office as Secretary-General – 'a sad figure, really a don', in

Stirling's opinion, 'a failed spectre at the feast, very ineffectual, who would talk about the arts and do nothing'.

That was hardly Stirling's way. When he was Deputy Secretary-General, he really felt that he understood what the Arts Council was meant to do 'from the point of view of our clients, not for a bureaucracy. I was able to form an understanding with people up and down the country looking for that, not for lots of money.' Although Lord Goodman had been too keen on spreading and usually said yes to every client, the Council did try hard to identify quality and maintain it. Very often regional centres of excellence, such as the Hallé Orchestra, had to be supported against the local authorities; Manchester preferred to support drama, while the Liverpool council preferred its Royal Philharmonic Orchestra to the Playhouse and the Everyman theatres. It was often the job of the Council to keep the balance, however much odium was attracted. And now, rather as cabinet ministers out of favour were sent to Northern Ireland, so Angus Stirling was transported to graze in the provinces as the war against London developed.

From Stirling's point of view, the problem with most of the Regional Arts Associations was that they were being infiltrated and taken over by the local authorities and councillors. Unfortunately, the standards and judgement of most of these authorities were deplorable, and they had no stomach for innovation. Stirling failed on his missionary efforts and thought that the greatest mistake of the Council was to give more funding to the Regional Arts Associations, before they were fit to make the right choices. He remembered thinking, 'We are reaping the harvest that Arnold Goodman has sown', although it had been sown unwillingly. By the end of the nineteen-seventies, he saw a Council that had lost its purpose and its way. Not believing that he was doing good, he left to serve again under Lord Gibson at the National Trust.

Lord Hutchinson generally agreed with Stirling, when he was travelling up and down the country while preparing for the Council a report on regionalism, a precursor to *The Glory of the Garden* report of the nineteen-eighties. He consulted particularly with Michael Elliott, who was in charge of the Royal Exchange Theatre at Manchester. He asked Elliott whether he would prefer to be put under the authority of his Regional Arts Association rather than answering to the assessments of the Council in London. 'For God's sake, don't!' Elliott replied. He had no confidence that twelve people could be picked from Manchester who had the breadth of view and appreciation and knowledge of the officers of the Arts Council, people at the cultural centre of the United Kingdom, who reached out their antennae to Europe. He found that kind of understanding in London, never in Manchester. He was not an élitist any more than was Lord Hutchinson, a left-wing radical and a great supporter of community arts. Yet the truth was that 'culture won't be found in the regions or in government departments. Then it was all in London.'

In Lord Hutchinson's opinion, the professional arts workers in the regions liked coming to London, where they felt safe and part of a national plan. The contact gave them confidence, not a feeling of envy that the capital had everything. This authority and expertise was being undermined by the devolutionary policies of Roy Shaw, particularly aided by the report, 'Support for the arts in England and Wales', produced in 1976 by Lord Redcliffe-Maud. Shaw himself had spent over twenty-five years in university adult education and had seen hundreds of people 'turned on' to the arts in their twenties, middle age and beyond, so he was delighted that Redcliffe-Maud believed as he did, that 'we must reject the long-established fallacy that "arts support" and "education" are two separate things. More positively, we must insist that those responsible for them are natural allies and see to it that they collaborate at national, regional and local levels.' Education could do more to increase the public enjoyment of the arts than anything that support alone could do.

'Large areas of Britain constitute a Third World of underdevelopment and deprivation in all the arts and crafts.' This was Lord Redcliffe-Maud's strongest assertion. He went on to argue that 'we must look to local elected councils, at district and county level, to become the chief art patrons of the future'. He also wrote that if the Regional Arts Associations did not exist, they would have to be invented. But the report was also aware of Angus Stirling's and Lord Hutchinson's objections to giving too much power to the regions at this stage, as well as the hostility to devolution among many of the larger provincial clients, who feared lower standards and less money and even political interference from the regional authorities. As the report warned:

> For most locally elected representatives of the public the exercise of arts patronage is something new, but until they learn from experience how to practise this gentle art and, in particular, come to recognize that the public only gets full value from public money spent on the arts if politicians, by a self-denying ordinance, keep themselves at arm's length from the artists and art organizations that they subsidize, there is no future for arts patronage through local government.

The Chairman of the Arts Council felt bound to endorse this fair and astute judgement of the future of regionalism and devolution. He also took on the Council Denys Hodson, who had made a great success of his job as Controller of Arts and Recreation in Swindon, which became almost a prototype for the community arts and the combination of sport and crafts and the Muses. Hodson had been one of Lord Redcliffe-Maud's most useful advisers and now served as a prophet in London. He acknowledged some interference in the arts from local politicians and pundits, but he thought it was occasional and ineffective. He believed that devolution had to come, or there would be hell to pay. Ministers for the Arts would have to keep their nerve and ram it past strong Chairmen of the Council, who might obstruct the inevitable. It was true, however, that the Regional Arts Associations were not yet ready for a larger role because of the low quality of their staffing, although that was rapidly changing with better recruitment of the newly-trained professional administrators. All the same, there was a need to devote more time to what the Regional Arts Associations would do in the Brave New World, when their time came.

What was significant in a rapprochement between the metropolis and the regions was the policy of the Touring Department directed by Jack Phipps. According to him, in the decade after 1972, nine principal regional theatres were saved by the direct action of the Council, which helped to buy them back from the theatre chains. 'I found I could work with the local authorities', Phipps has said. 'We set up the theatres as trusts so that they could not be taken over. Their rehabilitation was hard to achieve, but if you go round the country in the 'nineties, you will find wonderful touring theatres – to the envy of London.' Phipps was later to help in the establishment of Opera North in Leeds and to develop a moveable stage structure that allowed touring by the Royal Shakespeare Company in village halls as well as a season in Newcastle upon Tyne. For once, the centre and the fringes met.

On the questions of democracy and devolution, Lord Gibson was drawn into a series of skirmishes with Hugh Jenkins, the new Minister for the Arts. The Labour Party manifesto of October 1974 had promised 'to bring forward proposals to make the Arts Council more democratic'. Hugh Jenkins wanted local authority representation on the Council, but not its dissolution and replacement. 'The importance of expert authority and integrity cannot be overestimated', he said. 'I also take the view that local government as much as national government needs bodies like the Arts Council to prevent elected philistines from seeking to control art and artists by starving non-conformists into submission.' Jenkins even wanted local authorities to be given obligatory functions in the arts with controls upon them. 'It is no good', he has said, 'if the alderman can put his daughter on the stage.'

The determined opposition of the Lords Goodman and Gibson prevented any change in the composition of the Council. The terms of the two Royal Charters were used against the would-be reformer and Minister. 'I sometimes wonder whether the Charter has any meaning', Jenkins has said. 'It can't be changed, and it stopped me giving the Council a more democratic bias.' When the Minister appointed the social historian Raymond Williams onto the Council without consulting its Chairman, Lord Gibson found it intolerable. He asked Harold Lever to tell the Prime Minister, Harold Wilson, that he would 'be off, if this was done again'. Jenkins was reprimanded and complained to Gibson, 'You went behind my back to Downing Street', to which Gibson replied, 'I am always going behind your back.' It was always an advantage when the Chairman of the Arts Council had direct access to the Prime Minister.

Hugh Jenkins also proposed a wealth tax from which works of art should not be excluded. He failed in this effort, as he did in trying to legalize the Public Lending Right to give authors something from the use of their books in libraries. He also attempted a little empire-building; but again he did not succeed in seizing responsibility for films from the Board of Trade. 'Civil servants resist that kind of change', he has said. 'You affect their power and their property.' He would have preferred to become Minister of Culture, as in France. How could there be a national policy for the arts, when responsibility was split between the Treasury and the Department of Education and Science; the Foreign Office and the British Council; the Ministry of Works and the Office for Museums and Libraries; the War Office with its military bands; the Arts Council and the BBC; the Sports Council and the Crafts Council; Independent Television and a host of smaller independent cultural organizations? As Minister for the Arts, Jenkins himself was not in the Cabinet and did not have the Prime Minister's ear. There was chaos at the top, yet all change was resisted. Things were as they always had been. 'I tried hard to influence from below', he has said. 'Ideas should flow up.'

Once more Hugh Jenkins failed when he suggested to Lord Gibson that there should be quick rotation of the Chairmen on the Panels and Committees of the Council. Yet it was these very Chairmen who had given the Council its distinction until that time – people of the calibre of Viscount Esher and Alan Bowness, J. W. Lambert and Stuart Hampshire, Philip Larkin and Peter Williams, Richard Rodney Bennett and Stuart Hood. The Minister was supported in this fluid recommendation by the Secretary-General of the Council, for Roy Shaw wanted to remove from the Panels their influence over subsidies and to reduce them to a strict advisory role. In this, he would be fiercely resisted by another lawyer, Laurence Harbottle. Harbottle had been appointed to the Drama Panel by the Minister, although the new Chairman of the Panel, the distinguished cultural historian Richard Hoggart, would ally himself with Roy Shaw and act, in Harbottle's opinion, 'as two ends of a dumbbell'. The effect of this double blow and the determination by the Secretary-General to rule the roost in the manner of the redoubtable Sir W. E. Williams was to achieve what the Minister wanted – the departure of most of the senior staff and Chairmen of the Panels and Committees. It was rotation under pressure, although the result was to diminish the distinction of those who were prepared to serve in the future.

Yet this Minister, who cared so much about the arts that he was ready to interfere in their administration, did achieve some progress.

As he wrote, during his two years in office, he was 'continually badgering the Treasury for more money for one reason or another. Almost every month I had secured sums ranging from a few hundred thousands to a couple of million with the result that the total cost of the arts to the Government would soon be not far short of a hundred million, with about half going to the Arts Council and the rest to Museums, Galleries, Libraries and other claimants. Before my time no one had dreamt of such figures.' But Hugh Jenkins knew that the writing was on the final curtain because of the opposition of the arts establishment to his proposals. 'I was beginning to feel that if I did not get the bullet soon it would after all be best to resign. It was not so much the abuse (from the press), its idiot virulence; my real complaint was against the Cabinet and especially against the system which rendered me helpless to do what I wanted to do and knew how to do. It was too frustrating to put up with for much longer.'

Before he was replaced in office in 1976 by the genial and imperturbable Old Etonian Lord Donaldson, a loyal servant who troubled no backwaters, Hugh Jenkins visited the local Fabian Society at Birmingham to talk on 'A Socialist Policy for the Arts'. To subscribe to peaceful evolution rather than violent revolution had great advantages, but it was emotionally unsatisfying. It demanded the mental strife preached by William Blake and a great resistance to unconscious corruption. 'Indeed, the moment we place our hands upon those famous levers of power that Nye Bevan spoke of, they spring to life and as we clasp them so they clasp us and a struggle ensues. If we are not aware of that then we have lost the struggle before we start. So far from grasping power we have become its instrument and we are managed rather than managing.'

Lord Donaldson came to office with the unchangeable wish to change little. He was profoundly antagonistic to the policy of his predecessor, who now was also ennobled. As he said, 'Lord Jenkins believed that you should alter everything, but it was not necessary. Anyway, you can only alter with a lot more money.' The main interest of Lord Donaldson was less in the performing arts than in securing substantial increases in the purchase grants for the national museums and galleries; these had remained static for twelve years. As he was on good terms with his Cabinet Minister, Shirley Williams, he could get her to fight for the allocations which he wanted, although he had to fight harder for his policies with the civil service mandarins. He had been Under-Secretary and Junior Minister in Northern Ireland: 'There, all you had to do was to keep the lid on', he has said in his deprecating way. 'Here, one was always opposed to somebody with a better brain.' The reports he read were so oracular that they left him feeling it 'better to leave the whole thing alone'.

Under his guidance, however, the scheme for the new British Library was initiated, although he was unsure what would happen to 'reading generally' with the rise of television viewing, which could and should be used for education. He wanted to convert public libraries more into family centres; they had been the clubs of the jobless in the depression of the nineteen-thirties. He could not resemble the great Lady Lee, who was 'like Nuffield in a new market' with expanding resources. Yet he worked on establishing the National Heritage Fund and on securing the funding contribution of one million pounds to the Covent Garden development project. His monument and his pride and joy was the report by a working party, which included Professor Sir Ernst Gombrich, on a 'Framework for a System of Museums' for the Standing Commission on Museums and Galleries. This paper made some thirty recommendations for the thousand and more museums in Britain which were under financial pressure. 'They are as much part of our heritage and as precious as the paintings and other objects whose sale or threatened sale causes so much distress.' Until he lost office in 1979, Lord Donaldson toiled on implementing that report, but only in the modest way that he mentioned in the House of Lords: 'As a member, however humble, of this Government, I do not feel that I can quarrel with my leaders, as long as at least they maintain and do not decrease Government support for the arts.'

In the latter part of the nineteen-seventies the Arts Council was crippled by the clamp on its funds. As Lord Gibson stated, the problem was to maintain intact what was so successfully created before runaway inflation took hold, but to do so without denying all response to new ideas and initiatives. While saying a benevolent farewell to Hugh Jenkins, Lord Gibson welcomed Lord Donaldson as the new appointment. 'His love of the arts, especially music, is equalled only by his lifelong concern for the underprivileged. No better combination could be found in a Minister for the Arts.' Lord Gibson insisted, however, that inevitably and rightly, most of the subsidies had gone to the traditional arts. There was no desire on the part of the Council to dam the flood of change, but each generation had the right to enjoy its cultural inheritance. Even so, a new creed was emerging. The Arts Council was totally opposed to it:

> This is the belief that because standards have been set by the traditional arts and because those arts are little enjoyed by the broad mass of people, the concept of quality is 'irrelevant'. The term cultural democracy has been invoked by those who think in this way, to describe a policy which rejects discrimination between good and bad and cherishes the romantic notion that there is a 'cultural dynamism' in the people which will emerge if only they can be liberated from the cultural values hitherto accepted by an élite and from what one European 'cultural expert' has recently called 'the cultural colonialism of the middle classes'.
>
> This demagogic doctrine insults the very people it is supposed to help. On the other hand, what is undoubtedly true is that many people who have had no chance to enjoy the arts can be helped to approach them by being encouraged to participate in creative activity rather than merely to experience it passively. It is this feature of community arts which is of particular interest to the Council ... But here as elsewhere, we must not jettison our concern for standards, and we need to improve, not abandon, our methods of assessing them.

As the new Secretary-General, Roy Shaw concurred rather subtly in his Chairman's statements. It was difficult to take initiatives when all the funds were being called to respond to events; but a coherent policy still was needed, which did not have to be a dogmatic one. He indicated his way to the future. 'As the late Harold Laski once pointed out, policy is concealed in the interstices of administrative decisions. So the only choice is really between a conscious policy and an unconscious one.' He agreed on the need to maintain quality, although he was nostalgic for the days of Sir W. E. Williams, when he could plump for his slogan 'Few but roses'. Now spreading was as important as raising. Yet 'it would be folly to starve the roses and change to a policy of "Many but dandelions". We must preserve, and indeed improve, traditional centres of excellence, but we must also spread the excellence as widely as possible.' The funding, however, was not there. So Roy Shaw had to accept the gold bug in the woodpile, the Association for Business Sponsorship of the Arts, for which Hugh Jenkins had raised the founding money, also persuading Lord Goodman to act as its first Chairman. Although this rival for raising arts subsidy from industry was welcome, it was suspect. It should never become an excuse to cut the state subsidy or a method of businessmen's interference in the content or independence of the arts.

By 1977, Roy Shaw had the annual report of the Council entitled 'Value for Money'. Despite a 'no-growth' grant-in-aid, there had been considerable achievements by artists and art organizations, helped by the work of the special departments of the Council. The present level of arts subsidy was ludicrous: it amounted each week to twopence-halfpenny per head for the British population. Yet there was a general call for more money. The Trades Union Congress wanted an increase to develop the 'popular' arts; but the key to the enjoyment of 'high' arts by a wider public was better education in them at all levels. They were no longer political. 'It would be truer to say that much art tends to be *critical* – critical of the status quo.' The mark of a free society was that, at worst, it tolerated criticism, which at best was welcome:

> Although art *potentially* belongs to all men, it is often complex and demanding and *actually* belongs only to those who have the education and experience which equips them to enjoy it. By all means let us develop arts at a less demanding, popular level; but to dismiss as elitist the subsidizing of the great works of the past or the often 'difficult' works of contemporary artists, is to condemn the lock on the door to enrichment because you have failed to give people a key that fits it.

Where art required higher education to be appreciated, it was absurd to call the art itself 'bourgeois' and middle-class in its appeal only to a minority. It was the access to higher education which had been restricted. The remedy was not to replace complex and difficult art with works of instant attraction to everyone; it was to enhance the facilities for education. That was why Lord Keynes and the drafters of the first Royal Charter of the Council had described its task as the need 'to develop and improve the knowledge, understanding and practice of the arts'. More money was needed for teaching and raising, rather than for spreading and lowering. 'It is easy to talk rhetorically about "Arts for the people", but if you really mean it, you have to vote more money for the arts. Some might argue that the National Theatre should be closed to find this money, but this would simply be robbing Peter Hall to pay Paul. It makes no sense to cripple existing arts achievement to promote new developments.'

So Roy Shaw moved to arguments of quality control from the centre. Although funds to the Regional Art Associations were increased by two-fifths that year, a working party under Professor Baldry recommended a strengthening of the Council's partnership with the Associations rather than the immediate transfer of the responsibility for the grants-in-aid of the many clients still funded from London. Baldry and Shaw had both heeded the cry of Michael Elliott, 'For God's sake, don't!' The new Chairman of the Arts Council, Sir Kenneth Robinson, was a centralist by temperament, the Executive Chairman of London Transport and of the English National Opera – a post he had to relinquish as 'you can't be poacher and gamekeeper'. He did not see any real role for the Council, if devolution occurred. Competent arts administrators were still thin on the ground. How could the Regional Arts Associations find them when the Council itself had difficulty in selecting good ones? 'The quality of local government was very low', in the new Chairman's opinion. He has said he would not 'entrust the development of the arts to people of that blinkered outlook. To go on that road, we had to do it by gradualism. No sweeping change – we saw to that.'

The arm's length principle was Robinson's principle – the government must keep at arm's length from the Council and the Council at arm's length from its clients. The independence of the arts body was important, particularly when funding was limited. This had been understood by the previous Chairman, Lord Gibson, who based his response on his business experience and said, 'When there is too little to go round, the peripheries have to go. When times are tight, you have to centralize to conserve resources.' The division of the spoils should remain entirely within the competence of the Council. In years of tight money, clients must be cut. The National Youth Theatre, given grants-in-aid by Lord Goodman, would have to be axed by Sir Kenneth Robinson because it was not a professional body. He withstood the outcry and even maintained a good relationship with Peter Hall in spite of continued demands for more money to cover the move of the National Theatre to the South Bank. Two Treasury grants were earmarked for the National and were accepted, although Angus Stirling advised his Chairman not to take them – it was 'the slippery slope from independence'. Sir Kenneth Robinson, however, found Trevor Nunn difficult at the Royal Shakespeare Company. 'Every time we gave him enough to move from red to black, he opened another theatre. He was an empire-builder.' When the Company shifted to a new theatre complex at the Barbican Arts Centre, funded by the City of London, its Corporation thought that the Arts Council should pay for the moving costs. Sir Kenneth Robinson preferred the Shakespeare group to run an educational programme, suggesting to the aldermen, 'Why don't you sell Epping Forest?'. This proved unpopular, but a compromise was reached by that astute diplomacy in which the Arts Council excelled from its long experience.

The Chairman agreed with his Secretary-General over central control of the London organization, diminishing the power of the Panels and the Directors of the Departments, although these had maintained the general respect for the decisions of the Council over the past three decades. 'The Panels were too large', Roy Shaw has said. 'They should not have executive powers. They had to be reminded that their role was advisory.' To such members of the Drama Panel as the lawyer Laurence Harbottle, this doctrine was anathema. Roy Shaw seemed to view the arts as an extension of adult education and he wished to downgrade the influence of the Panels in order to augment his power of choice, removing from them their increasing role in assessing which enterprises should receive the available subsidies. 'I cared', Harbottle has said. 'I could not let the Arts Council and its members be used as a rubber stamp.' Unfortunately, his own Panel Chairman, Richard Hoggart, was a close friend and supporter of Roy Shaw. As he was also a member of the Council and Vice-Chairman, Hoggart even informed his Panel, before the annual Council meeting to distribute the grant-in-aid between the different art forms, that he would not fight for the maximum grant for drama. He might have to decide that the needs of music or the visual arts were more pressing. 'The Panel felt he was letting them down,' in Roy Shaw's opinion, 'but he was entirely right and I often wished that other Panel Chairmen were as successful in managing their double role.' The general policy was greater than the particular demand.

Angus Stirling, still the Deputy to the Secretary-General, thought that Roy Shaw did not understand the purpose of the Arts Council or how it worked. He wanted to turn it into the Workers' Educational Association. While Shaw was right in pushing the Council to further more arts education under the terms of the Royal Charter, he did it in 'a tactless way'. Stirling felt that he had to leave, as did many others of the old guard. One of them was John Drummond, Director of the Edinburgh Festival and an influential missionary for good music at the BBC; he had served for a decade on the Music Panel and had helped to set up the separate Dance Panel, which concentrated on modern dance as much as classical ballet. 'When Roy Shaw set his vision on education,' Drummond has said, 'the Council began to lose its central vision. There was always a need to keep concentration on the top end, and to let the local authorities do the local things.' Under Shaw, the Arts Council lost its consensus, the feeling that no Panel was complete without artistic creators, that the members could be non-partisan. Drummond held it to be the fault of his generation not to have stopped Shaw's divergence towards social and educational aims, although the civil service still blocked any capacity for real change, although the split in the Whitehall departments responsible for the arts prevented any national strategy for them. But most damaging for Drummond in Shaw's efforts to change the administration was that 'the Arts Council lost its authority of judgement, and so lost its ability to recruit'.

Responsible for supporting the new policy as Finance Officer, Tony Field debated it often with Roy Shaw. If it meant changing the composition of the audiences and taking the arts into schools or universities, then it was surely:

> a matter for the Department of Education and Science; to take art into prisons was a matter for the Home Office; to take art into hospitals was a matter for the Department of Health – the Arts Council should concentrate on creativity. If this meant increasing

audiences, we should have to build more theatres, opera houses, concert halls and galleries. But many people were reached by the higher standards of the arts and entertainment achieved through films, radio television and records. What was wrong with that?

Certainly without the subsidized arts, there would be few of these improvements in the media.

Other offices, such as Jack Phipps in charge of Touring, disapproved of the new policy of setting aside the advice of the Panels. He relied totally on the advice of his Panel to tell him when he was going up the wrong line. The members had to be concerned with the whole health of the drama as well as the details which concerned him. It was a creative co-operation. 'The Arts Council relationship is a very good one, when it works well.'

The Directors of the Departments also felt contained by the Shaw regime. During the hegemony of Sir W. E. Williams – as the long-serving and influential Mary Endacott remembered – the Directors had been given their head, which they had liked. Now they were being muzzled and reined in. There was also a degree of ministerial interference, which had never characterized the early days. When John Faulkner took over from Dick Linklater, who had served in the Drama Department for twenty-five years, he felt a tension with Shaw who was trying to make the Council '*his* centre'. On the other hand, Angus Stirling had 'held *the* centre'. Both Shaw and Hoggart, the Chairman of the Drama Panel, thought that Faulkner and the Department favoured the large organizations – Faulkner had run theatre companies in his life before the Council. When he arrived, the Panel was in revolt alongside the nineteen members of staff. But their long tradition was to see out the innovators. Faulkner forged an alliance with the Finance Director, Tony Field, whose roots also lay in the professional theatre, and they would adjudge the cuts increasingly imposed by Labour and Conservative governments and yet keep drama in the forefront of the renaissance of the post-war arts in Britain. 'When I went to London,' Faulkner has said, 'the Arts Council was a great teaching hospital, a centre of excellence and advice. When I was working there, it was also like a field dressing-station. We dealt with the casualties, too. It was a bloody business. Sometimes we had to apply triage – who to send back to the front, who to nurse and revive, who to let die.'

Sir Kenneth Robinson admitted that he never got the relationship between the Council and the Panels quite right. He was also worried about criticism over the composition of the Arts Council. In his first statement as Chairman, he stressed that members were appointed by the Secretary of State following consultation with the Minister for the Arts and himself:

> The objective of all three is to have a Council which is broadly based in more than one sense. There should be members who have an understanding of and a love for the arts in general; there should be some who have perhaps a deeper knowledge of one particular art form. The members should come from different parts of the United Kingdom and from a variety of educational, cultural and social backgrounds. The academic, the practitioner and the consumer should figure in the membership. There need to be enthusiasts for both the traditional and the avant-garde. And not least, a sizeable proportion should have had experience of the process of collective decision-making through committee or other groupings, and each should be ready to support a majority view whatever his own.

What was the alternative to the present method of appointment? How would somebody set about making the Council more representative or more democratic – to choose the two favourite objectives and epithets of the critics? Sir Kenneth Robinson was being asked to have representatives of the local authorities, the trades unions and the arts professions sitting on the Council as of right and nominated by their parent bodies. Yet both the Minister for the Arts and the Council doubted the value of such representation:

> If this trades union were represented, why not that one? If this profession, why not the others? And why this particular local authority? Clearly, there would have to be ruthless selection leading to distinctions of the most invidious kind, which would satisfy almost nobody; or one would have so many representatives that the Council would become a parliament, cumbersome in operation, interminable in discussion and almost incapable of speedy action.

And as for a solution by the electoral process, there would be nothing effective done at the ballot box in the hands of the largely indifferent voter.

These proposals of reform were mainly the recommendations

which surfaced in the Labour Party policy document of 1977, 'The Arts and the People'. Even Roy Shaw did not endorse them, thinking that they would not make things better. Of the present system of selection and nomination, he had reluctantly to echo what Sir Winston Churchill had said of parliamentary democracy – that it was the worst system he knew, *except* for all the others that had been tried. Shaw did not quite have the scepticism over the machinery of appointments which was held by Lord Hutchinson, who wanted a system devised which avoided the Minister putting in his own people. 'When I was on the Tate Gallery, I used to go into Ten Downing Street and up the winding staircase', he has said. 'There I met the Appointments Secretary from the civil service. He used to ask me for my suggestions for new trustees and then produce the government list of the great and the good, who usually turned out to be widows or patrons. I never failed on *my* visits, because I used to ask what his people *knew* about modern art, and that was that.' As for choosing Chairmen of the Panels, Sir Kenneth Robinson told a parliamentary Select Committee: 'If I have lost the chairman of the Drama Panel through the normal process of retirement I will feel it is my duty to suggest one or two names to the Minister, but equally he suggests names to me, and the appointment is ultimately a resolution of these different approaches.'

In a contemporary book called *The Politics of the Arts Council*, Robert Hutchison described it as an 'intensely political organization; and a creature of government'. It was not yet so, and despite some efforts at intrusion from the Treasury and the Minister for the Arts, as yet the arm's length principle only had the rare dirty thumb. What was more distressing, in John Cruft's opinion, was the unwillingness of Whitehall to accept the importance of the arts, as well as trying to control them. Particularly notable in all this discussion over selection was that everybody thought that the problem was how to *man* the Council. 'I was the statutory woman', Lady Antonia Fraser has said of her years as a member. 'The only woman.' There were devoted and influential members of staff such as Jean Bullwinkle, Joanna Drew, Mary Endacott and Jane Nicholas, but nobody had risen to the top since the primal Mary Glasgow. For the past eighteen years, there had been no woman Director of any Council Department, although after 1978 three would be appointed. The statutory women on the Council had risen to four of twenty members, the Marchioness of Anglesey, Ann Clwyd, Annette Page and the Lady Vaizey. Equal opportunities had still not taken a curtsey.

Both the Chairman and the Secretary-General continued to press for more funding so that new initiatives could be resumed after three years of standstill, also a plea for policy for the arts to remain bi-partisan, not 'a political football to be kicked to right or left with every change of government'. All three parties in the country agreed that the arts were underfunded, as Roy Shaw noted, but they did little about that:

> Meanwhile, the Arts Council itself will continue to suffer as piggy-in-the-middle, and although we bear most of our occupational hazards gladly, this one we do not feel we should have to bear. Almost daily we face clients who cannot manage on the most we can give them. Illogically, but understandably, many of them blame the Council, feeling (rather than thinking) that if we really tried harder, we could give them more money. The most thundering platitude, which perhaps ought to be emblazoned over the door of 105 Piccadilly, is: 'The Arts Council cannot give more than it gets'.

The arts needed a good lobby, as it had in the United States. Even for politicians, it was no longer true that there were 'no votes in the arts'. The rising role of business sponsorship was welcome, but problematic: the performing arts could not become a 'mobile billboard'. Both education in the arts and a closer partnership with the Regional Arts Associations and the local authorities were being developed, but it was the responsibility of these last two bodies to fund and develop community arts. '"Where there is no vision, the people perish" we were told long ago.' Now more people desired their vision of the meaning of life from the arts than from religion. 'We believe our clients have done well with the money we were able to give them; we also know that most of them could have done even better with a little more.'

The last year before the victory of the Conservative Party in the election of 1979 was seen by Roy Shaw as a period of 'Patronage and Responsibility'. By coincidence, the Chairman found himself writing his introduction to the annual report of the Arts Council 'during the brief period between the departure of Mr Callaghan's government and the first meeting of Mrs Thatcher's team with Parliament'. He remained cautiously optimistic. The new Minister, Norman St John-Stevas, had advocated more spending on the arts and represented Education as well. The last government had come to realize that money invested in the arts produced many returns, not only the social dividend of providing the citizen with richer leisure opportunities and generally enhancing the quality of life, but more tangible assets in stimulating tourism, contributing to the economy and raising the national prestige in the world. These should recommend themselves with no less force to a Tory administration. Just over a pound a year per head of population was not a high price to pay in order to sustain the country's cultural heritage.

Sir Roy Shaw, who now received his knighthood, was on the defensive to his new masters, emphasizing the discrimination and the responsibility of the Council. Its Chairmen and members and advisers were all unpaid. 'As for political bias, Lord Goodman, when he was Chairman of the Council, said he had never heard a political discussion at any Arts Council meeting, and it seemed to him inconceivable that one should take place.' The Council was neither the tool of the ruling class nor did it favour left-wing arts. The decision to set up the Council had been taken by a wartime coalition government endorsed by a brief Conservative administration and finally implemented by a Labour government. The view that the arts should be funded by the state was whole-heartedly supported by both the major political parties. The British way of organizing public subsidy for the arts was admired and envied throughout the world. 'Government pays the piper, but makes no attempt to call the tune.' It was up to the Council to remain both independent and responsible to its clients and to parliament, working on the arm's length principle which Lord Redcliffe-Maud had declared was the basis of 'the gentle art of patronage'.

The Council was not complacent about the fact that access to excellent productions was achieved by only a minority. It was trying to enlarge the audience for the arts. Expenditure on touring major companies now exceeded three-and-a-half million pounds annually. The Royal Shakespeare Company played to packed houses in Newcastle for seven weeks. The Royal Ballet's performances in circus tents were crowded and brought in new audiences. The creation of English National Opera North in Leeds had attracted large numbers of people even at traditional pantomime time. Much of the audience was still middle-class and highly educated; an Arts Council study of young people's theatre discovered that 'only one half of the children in English schools see even one play a year'. Education, and more education, was the way to spread appreciation of the 'high' arts through the whole population. The Conservative party had made that very point in 1978 in its review of arts policy. Recalling that the nineteenth century had seen the transmission of a culture which was aristocratic in origin to the new bourgeoisie, it concluded that 'our century must do the same for the new classes of our time'.

A growing number of people working in the arts rejected traditional culture as irrelevant to the needs of ordinary folk. They wished to replace it with an 'alternative culture'. This was the view of many who worked in the field of community arts – a term used to describe the work done by professional artists in photography, painting, drama, music, performance art and video-making *in* and *with* a local community, which was encouraged to participate in the process as a way of self-expression, often leading to social action. The subsidy for community arts from the Council had increased during the past year to a million pounds, but if the Government wished to see this new work expand, then more money had to be provided. Community artists were the Council's most difficult clients. They consistently bit the hand that fed them and repudiated the purpose of the Council in its Royal Charters.

Sir Roy Shaw fought a battle over community arts as he did over the beginnings of deconstruction in social thinking. A post-war breed of arts administrators and social engineers was challenging the old principles of workers' education. Strangely, it was a working party for the Arts Council, with Lord Hutchinson in the chair, which reported favourably on the community arts. He upheld this profound innovation against the disdain of Sir Roy Shaw, Raymond Williams and Roy Fuller on the Literature Panel – 'people who never rolled their sleeves up, never got their hands dirty ... people who swan in, swan out, and make grand remarks'. Shaw felt that the Hutchinson report misjudged the situation, largely because of the unconscious cultural guilt of the involved members of the Council. Since people in Wigan or rural Devon could not share their pleasure in the established arts, they might feel it churlish to criticize the 'alternative culture' of the community arts. Sir Roy Shaw went on to say that he was reminded of the Tory peeress in the nineteen-thirties who went round telling housewives in depressed areas how to make soap out of cod's heads:

> She was generally well-received, until one housewife asked challeng-
> ingly: 'Who gets the rest of the cod?' I wanted everyone to have some
> of the rest of the cod and was not happy about the provision of a cod's
> head culture for the poor. Moreover, I was not impressed by some of
> the things community artists said about working-class life. Like
> Richard Hoggart in *The Uses of Literacy*, I could make my own
> Chekhov's claim: 'There is peasant blood in my veins and you cannot
> astonish me with peasant virtues'.

Sir Roy Shaw also believed that the community artists wanted to destroy the Arts Council by questioning its reason for existence. He quoted the author of a survey of forty community arts projects:

> It must be understood that the so-called cultural heritage which made
> Europe great – the Bachs and Beethovens, the Shakespeares and
> Dantes, the Constables and Titians – is no longer communicating
> anything to the vast majority of Europe's population ... It is
> bourgeois culture and therefore only immediately meaningful to that
> group ... The great artistic deception of the twentieth century has
> been to insist to *all* people that this was *their* culture. The Arts
> Council of Great Britain was established on this premise.

Those who took this point of view, in the opinion of the Secretary-General, had a paradoxical attitude to the Arts Council and to the democratic government which funded it. Lord Goodman had questioned whether it was the duty of the state to subsidize those who were actually working to overthrow it. Shaw did not think it good. And he was equally opposed to another growing belief that all judgements on the arts were *wholly* subjective, that no opinion was better than another, and that 'nothing is good or bad but thinking makes it so'. Such deconstruction made nonsense of the assessment procedures of the Arts Council and removed its need to be. As he asked, 'How could you plan the content of arts education, if no one had the right to decide that one poet, composer, painter or playwright was *better*, more worth studying, than another?'.

The deconstructionists and subjectivists joined hands with the community artists who practised 'cultural democracy' – a fashionable phrase in the publications of the Council of Europe. They wanted the destruction of the Arts Council, which held onto the belief that it had the duty to judge and maintain standards of excellence. The right way was still to raise and spread, not to have 'many but dandelions'. It was wrong to offer the public a second best in the arts. As Sir Roy declared:

> Surprisingly, Matthew Arnold detected this trend over a century ago when he wrote that: 'Plenty of people will try to give the masses, as they call them, an intellectual food prepared and adjusted in the way they think proper for the actual condition of the masses'. This is sometimes called 'giving the public what it wants', but it really means giving the public what it can most easily be persuaded to accept.
>
> The main present-day practitioners of this policy are the providers of the poorest kind of mass entertainment, whether in the press, on television or in the cinema. The irony is that here the vulgarians of the media join hands with the arts populists; both underestimate people. According to Arnold, the true men of culture would seek to do away with the distinction between the masses and the classes and would seek to make the best of the arts available 'outside the clique of the cultivated and learned'.

Even within the Council, there was opposition from the brightest and the best of its new recruits, Robin Guthrie, who had been for seven years the Social Development Officer for the new town of Peterborough before moving on to the Department of Health. He succeeded Professor Harold Baldry as Chairman of the Regional Advisory Committee of the Council, and he also chaired the sub-committee on Community Arts. He thought that Sir Roy Shaw's slogan of 'Excellence and Access' was condescending. 'Excellence' was a patrician word that translated a subjective judgement into a universal criterion. All values in the arts were personal. 'Access' was again paternal, 'leading the horses to the water *we* had chosen'. The use of the two words was the cover for a set of policies that risked the exclusion of 'people's own passionate experiences' in the area of community arts. His opinions were shared by Professor Lawrence

Gowing, Deputy Chairman of the Art Advisory Panel and Chairman of the innovatory Special Applications Advisory Committee. The great mural of 'Jackson's Wall' in Battersea, which involved hundreds of local residents, was a triumph and told of how people lived there. To appreciate the arts meant personal involvement in them. 'The argument for excellence and access created a false dichotomy,' Robin Guthrie has said. 'It is more important to judge art in its success in expression and communication. This would resolve the conflict between "high" and "low" and community arts.'

The influential Guthrie and Gowing were already inside the belly of the Trojan horse within the walls of 105 Piccadilly. Yet in his role as Hector, Roy Shaw had two formidable allies: the Vice-Chairman Richard Hoggart and Raymond Williams, who shared with him certain beliefs in the worth of adult education and of the spreading of excellence. To Hoggart, giving public money to the arts was based on a particular judgement of value. He declared: 'the arts are to be kept up because they are the most profound expression of our nature and experience. Without the constant and free practice of the arts, without people aware of the arts and free to come to them, however awkward they often are, a society is the poorer.' Yet if the arts were of value, the opportunities for revealing that value were cramped and biased. Access to excellence must be increased because people did not know what they were missing until they could reach it and appreciate it. To discourage access to traditional art because historically it had appealed mainly to the middle classes was 'like refusing a child the opportunity to discover the most nourishing foods, on the ground that that sort of thing is a bourgeois trick ... Let people in today's cities eat fast food and read the *Sun*. Here the Far Left meets the slick entrepreneurs. People have chosen what they want; who are we to judge them?'

Yet Hoggart could also judge the Arts Council. Its biggest weakness appeared to him to be doing 'the intellectual splits'. It had not thought through the claims of the community arts any more than it had those of the 'high' arts. It continued to fund a bewildering variety of activities. The variety might be a source of strength, but it was just as likely a source of strife. A lot of activity was on the fringes of the circus and the music hall, with clowns and inflatables, face-painting and play-schemes. To the Far Left, this was populist rubbish. And so the Council shied even further away:

> It doesn't want to be embroiled in such internecine strife; it smiles and swears interest in all sides. It hopes it is more nearly meeting its commitment to making the arts more available to new audiences by agreeing to fund as much community arts activity as it can possibly squeeze from the budget. As a result – as a result, that is, of neglecting to think about the question of excellence and its relation to access – it does well by neither side. It blurs its relations to grand opera and to community arts alike. It had become confusedly overstretched, without shape or form, expressing not a rich creative disorder in its giving, but a worried darting from side to side, seeking good repute by trying to be all things to all men and letting the questions of both access and excellence remain murky.

Although generally in support of the positions of Shaw and Hoggart, the third distinguished radical social historian and professor, Raymond Williams, twice offered his resignation as a Council member because substantial internal reform was impossible. He recognized the important and original attempt to create in the Council an intermediate or arm's length body like the BBC to subsidize the arts, but it was still 'in the pocket of Ministers and a Department of State, and its marginal independence had as many disadvantages as advantages'. It was administered through 'consensus by co-option'. The names of Members of the Council emerged 'on no discernible representative basis' after consultation between ministers and civil servants in the Department of Education and Science with the Chairman and senior officers of the Council. The same style pervaded the Panels and the committees. With consensus procedures and the rarity of voting, one of the few means of challenge was to offer resignation – in his own case, he was refused. No consistent cultural policy was possible because there was little correlation of the work of the Arts Council and of the broadcasting organizations, which were under the aegis of the Home Office. There could be none until a Ministry of Arts and Communications was established. Until then, the unreformable arts would be run in the habitual style of the British ruling class, an unusually compact and organic group which administered its duties by unpaid out-work and informal consensus. The Council was open to charges of being unrepresentative, undemocratic and irresponsible – and yet

Professor Williams remained on the Council for his full term of three years, satisfied that within the unfortunate terms of its existence, it was doing as well as it could.

The most astonishing assault on the Council, however, came from within its walls. The distinguished poet Roy Fuller had joined Kingsley Amis and others in the movement from left to right. He served as Chairman of the Literature Panel before leaving the Council in a volley of abuse. In the reaction of his beliefs, his particular targets came to be Richard Hoggart and Raymond Williams and their policies; the Council had 'rather more than bad luck' to have both of them as prominent members. Hoggart had called Fuller a 'blimp', and some of his attitudes were blimps; he used to castigate some applicants for authors' grants as 'layabouts'. Referring to the Literature Panel itself, Fuller wrote of the 'Byzantine way' the Council worked, and of patronage going to 'dotty' writers and 'Arts Council pensioners'. He stood for the merit of achievement. The establishment of the committee on Community Arts was the last straw for him, as he held that 'in such activities there were no standards of excellence, no good or bad.' He was concerned particularly over the 'blurring' of arts education and social work in that area. But he did meet Sir Roy Shaw's approval in his belief that the prevailing scepticism about aesthetic and moral judgements was a threat to what politicians liked to call 'The Quality of Life'. Whatever the force of the poet's attack, the Secretary-General's defence shared in a belief in moral choice and excellence.

With friends like these, what was the Council's need of enemies? The organization was having a rough ride, Raymond Williams admitted; rough ground on the Right and just as rough ground on the Left. Roy Shaw regretfully acknowledged an increasing political polarization in the arts that was evident both outside the Council and within its walls. This was a house of culture divided against itself. It seemed to the drama critic of the *Listener* to be a village post office around which a new town had grown: ill-equipped in methods, money and people to service it. Political theatre and the community arts particularly put the future of the old Council at risk. Modern radical drama, as the actor Michael Denison pointed out, sought subsidies from the Establishment that it wanted to over-throw and created tensions between the politically motivated artist and the taxpayer and the Arts Council. The vital thing was 'that we should not dwindle by sins of omission or commission into a propaganda agency'. More extreme were the demands of the community arts directors, who inherited Roy Fuller's indignation because of their lack of artistic 'standards – the word pops up in the Arts Council debate like the black spot in *Treasure Island*'. But who could give a fair share of the cake to such claimants as Greg Wilkinson of the Commonword Workshop? 'It's not just a question of working-class culture or working-class poetry. If it's going to be any good, it's got to take over the lot.'

Regionalism also threatened the very existence of the Arts Council of Great Britain. The second Royal Charter would have to be altered, if devolution came to Scotland and Wales in 1979 through Labour policy. Then a Scottish and Welsh Assembly might take over responsibility for subsidizing the arts in their own countries. In point of fact, however, the Arts Council was to remain the Arts Council of Great Britain for another fifteen years. The policy of national devolution was stopped by the Conservative victory in the general election of that year, although the pressure on the Arts Council to devolve itself out of existence was to increase, caught between the encroaching and clashing rocks, the Scylla of the regions and the Charybdis of the civil service. And yet, at this time of defence against new threats and challenges, the Arts Council had ironically become an inspiration and a model for the New World as much as the Old.

NINE

ARTS ABROAD

The term 'the arts' includes, but is not limited to, music
(instrumental and vocal), dance, drama, folk art, creative
writing, architecture and allied fields, painting, sculpture,
photography, graphic and craft arts, industrial design,
costume and fashion design, motion pictures, television,
radio, tape and sound recording, the arts related to the
presentation, performance, execution, and exhibition of
such major art forms, and the study and application of the
arts to the human environment.

From Public Law 209 of the 89th United States
Congress, used in setting up the American National
Foundation for the Arts and Humanities, later
endorsed as a definition of 'the arts' in 1982 by
the Education, Science and Arts Committee of
the House of Commons

The British Council had been set up by Royal Charter in 1934,
eleven years before the Arts Council. Its concern was political, to
publicize the British way of life overseas. A part of this policy
included promoting British activities in the world of arts. Yet, as the
knighted Peter Hall pointed out, there was in this dichotomy an
absurdity and an abyss. 'The British Council exists to promote
British arts abroad; the Arts Council exists to promote British arts at
home; but nobody exists to promote foreign art in Britain ... Why,
asked the French and the Germans, weren't we, as the National
Theatre, able to get additional funds from the British government
towards the cost of presenting productions from abroad? Their own
governments did, the other way round.' A little was done rather late

in 1976 through the two Councils and the Foreign and Common-wealth Office and the Gulbenkian Foundation: some £60,000 was provided annually towards a small unit to be run by the British Council 'specifically to encourage, co-ordinate, and to a modest extent financially support, visits to the United Kingdom by overseas artists, companies and exhibitions'.

This token co-operation abroad was supplemented by the export of the role model of the Arts Council. Actually, in two areas, Northern Ireland and New South Wales in Australia, the wartime Council for the Encouragement of Music and the Arts (CEMA) was the prototype of the later Arts Council of Northern Ireland and of the Australian Council for the Arts, as it was for the Arts Council of Great Britain. Yet the grant from the Ministry of Finance to the Northern Irish body was less than to the Welsh Arts Council and to some of the English Regional Arts Associations, while in Australia, voluntary effort rather than funds from the various States had to keep the show on the road. Furthermore, a council to encourage, further and promote the practice and appreciation of the arts was also instituted in 1963 in New Zealand with modest provisions. The Republic of Ireland also set up an imitative Chomhairle Ealaíon under the Arts Act of 1951; but twenty years later funding had still only reached £80,000. Tax concessions were needed to halt the drain of artists from Eire across the Irish Sea.

In Canada, a Royal Commission on National Development in the Arts, Letters and Sciences was instituted with Vincent Massey in the chair. In 1951 he had the findings announced; they were met with scepticism by the Prime Minister and most of his Cabinet. However, two wealthy patrons of the Canadian arts died and their death duties provided the funding for a Canada Council, incorporated six years after the Massey Report. This body was largely based on the Arts Council of Great Britain and used a system of Panels to assess grants-in-aid from deserving applicants. The original endowment of fifty million Canadian dollars was intended to ensure complete political independence, but the growing demands of the arts in Canada led, as in Britain, to increased government funding. Two other sources of central, but arm's length funding, were established; the Canadian Film Development Fund with the National Film Board; also the National Arts Centre in Ottawa, designed to provide a centre of excellence for the performing arts in the capital and to assist the Canada Council in developing the performing arts in the various provinces of the nation.

While the local authorities took a long time in Britain to begin to match metropolitan funding, the provincial governments in Canada were spurred into a cultural competition with Ottawa. As federal involvement grew after the war, the provinces reacted by subsidizing large programmes in arts education, almost resenting this federal intrusion on their rights. By 1990, many of the provinces would have their own cultural departments, and four of them, including Ontario, would have set up quasi-independent arts councils on the model of the Canada Council. In Quebec, the Ministère des Affaires Culturelles became responsible for the arts budget there. The establishment in 1980, however, of direct government funding for the Special Programme of Cultural Initiatives through the Ministry of Communications caused much controversy, because it appeared to be central interference in the autonomous rights of the provinces. Yet this creative tension between the core and the countryside led to more money for artists and the arts – enviably supported, in comparison with Great Britain, with nearly twice as much from each member of the population at national and provincial and municipal levels.

The example of the Arts Council of Great Britain was also significant in the United States of America. Livingston Biddle, who did so much with Senator Claiborne Pell of Rhode Island to conceive and draft the legislation for a National Endowment for the Arts, met Sir Roy Shaw in Washington in the District of Columbia. 'I could tell him that his council in earlier years had served as an important model for my early legislative efforts, and he would tell me that the British shared almost identical problems faced by their "American cousins".' In his engaging memoir, *Our Government and the Arts*, Biddle told of the efforts by himself and Senator Pell to create a government endowment. There were precedents, although they were politically dangerous. During the great depression, President Franklin D. Roosevelt had created, through the Works Progress Administration, jobs for forty thousand artists, while the Federal Writers' and the Federal Theatre Projects were also founded. Some of their participants and directors had fallen foul of the House Un-

American Activities Committee during the heyday of Senator McCarthy. One of them had quoted lines from Marlowe's *Dr Faustus*, only to be asked: 'You are quoting from this Marlowe. Is he a Communist?' Republican Senator Barry Goldwater voiced the fears of many when he said that 'the Federal Government eventually will do more harm in this field than good by over-regulating it, by over-controlling it'. Fear of political interference in the arts was countermanded by Biddle's initiatives.

Although the history of the arts funding in the United States had been mainly a private matter, the Smithsonian Institution in Washington had been established by charter in the nineteenth century and had grown to embrace a number of museums – independent in spite of federal support on the model of the British national museums. What Biddle did was to produce necessary statistics in the early nineteen-sixties: European countries and the Soviet Union and Canada were spending up to twenty-five times per head of population the sum wanted for the arts from the United States government – not more than five cents a person each year, the equivalent then of a small glass of cola. Although President John F. Kennedy tried to establish an Advisory Council on the Arts through an executive order, his murder handed on the matter to his successor, President Lyndon B. Johnson. The testimony of John D. Rockefeller the Third before the Senate Subcommittee on Arts and Humanities was significant: he had helped to fund with the Ford Foundation a Business Committee for the Arts, charged with synchronizing the recommendations of the Rockefeller Panel Report on the Performing Arts, which stated:

> Corporate dollars are important dollars, capable of making the difference between life or death for an arts organization. If business corporations have not done so, as most of them have not, the panel urges that they look carefully at the arts and their place in the community. Support for the arts is a part of community responsibility, and a healthy cultural environment is clearly in the self-interest of the business community.

To the Senate Subcommittee, Rockefeller recommended federal aid for arts education:

> I think for so many in the private sector of American life the arts are a relatively new field in terms of having a responsibility to do

something about them. I think many have thought of the arts as a luxury and for the few. And I think there is a long educational process which is needed to encourage these sources ... to accept their responsibility for the arts as an important and significant community responsibility. So my hope would be, with the passage of time and with this new emphasis on the arts in our national life, that these sources would become aware of the needs and their own responsibilities ... As in other fields, where something is so basic to the well-being of our people, the government, along with others, has a very definite responsibility.

Although so much of Rockefeller's prophecy proved true, it went generally unrecorded – except in congressional circles, where Biddle found that the words meant a very great deal. A bill was prepared to legislate into existence a National Council on the Arts. It easily passed the Senate with a ringing endorsement from Senator Hubert Humphrey: 'We only do harm to ourselves by accepting the thesis that art and democratic government are natural enemies. Other nations and freedom-loving peoples know that it is not so ... The arts have been the rock foundation of every great society since the dawn of civilization.' Although the House of Representatives delayed the bill for a year and tried to emasculate it, finally after a conference between the two Houses, a National Council on the Arts was created to advise the President with a budget of fifty thousand dollars. This small step forward was supplemented by Senator Pell's push for a more comprehensive solution. He told the National Society of Arts and Letters in 1965:

Walk through a small European town and you will hear ... the musical instrument or the voice, the sounds of a rich cultural past – sounds which stem from the vigor of the culture which was thriving long before Columbus crossed the seas ... We are in conflict today with the materialism of totalitarian forms of government which by definition stifle creative thought. We must contribute to the world something better than this, something more lofty, something in tune with free men, something to improve them ... We will give to the world a truly meaningful heritage.

His proposals for a National Foundation on the Arts and the Humanities succeeded because they were to provide seed money for crops to be watered by individual donors, by corporations and foundations, and by other large and small government entities at the state and local levels. 'As the federal catalyst grew,' Biddle noted, 'so did the financial support from these other sources.' The new National Foundation became a legislative fact in 1965 with revisions five years later. It was composed of the National Endowment for the Humanities and the National Endowment for the Arts with the charismatic Roger Stevens as chairman and Biddle as his deputy: from it would spring the American Film Institute. These bodies were formed on British models – largely independent of politics with specialist panels of advisers and assessors. The two National Endowments reported to a Federal Council on the Arts and the Humanities, which advised their chairmen on major problems and the co-ordination of operations. There was also a National Council on the Arts, led by the chairman of the National Endowment for the Arts and comprising twenty-five concerned private citizens. These groups provided the basics of public policy for the arts in the United States. Although federal funding was kept low compared with government spending on the arts in Western Europe, business and private donors were encouraged through tax incentives – charitable gifts would be offset against the levy of the state.

If the example of the Arts Council was the British contribution to subsidizing the arts in the United States, the American Business Committee for the Arts was the answer to the Conservative government's prayer for more corporate sponsorship in the United Kingdom rather than a larger Treasury grant-in-aid. In his founding address to the Business Committee, David Rockefeller began by praising bankers and businessmen, from the Medici to the Mellons, who had been enthusiastic patrons of the arts. At one time, Cosimo de' Medici's private contributions to cultural activities were said to have amounted to twice the income of the state of Florence. Americans were now spending some four billion dollars annually on cultural activities, but business had only contributed twenty-two million dollars that year to the arts. The modern corporation was evolving into a social as well as an economic institution. It had developed ideals and responsibilities going far beyond the profit motive. As leisure had increased among the people, corporations concerned about their environment could not evade responsibility for seeing that this leisure was channelled into the rewarding activities afforded by the arts.

In spite of the federal government moving into the field with the National Arts and Humanities Endowments, Rockefeller declared that the funds appropriated by Congress were very modest – the Metropolitan Opera had a larger budget while the Austrian government spent more on the Vienna State Opera than on its entire Foreign Service. Wealthy individuals and foundations should be joined by business patrons to fund the expansion of the arts into national life in order to replace materialism. Then Rockefeller quoted Archibald MacLeish: 'We have more things in our garages and kitchens and cellars than Louis XIV had in the whole of Versailles.' Were these the hallmarks of a truly Great Society? Clearly, they were not.

This influential speech and the founding of the Business Committee for the Arts more than doubled corporate funding by 1970 with another fifty million dollars given in business expenses such as advertising and public relations. The amount of corporate giving would increase to eight cents in each dollar given to philanthropy during the next decade and would reach two hundred million dollars in direct grants to the arts. The argument that direct giving was against the interest of the company shareholders was dismissed by David Rockefeller: 'Actually, companies that are major supporters of culture and the arts have encountered very little objection from this source. The fact is that many stockholders, as individuals, are heavily engaged in cultural activities and understand the urgent need for corporate backing.' His remarks were amplified by the chairman of a public relations firm: 'Just as parents used to tell children about ghosts and bogeymen, corporate executives tell other people about stockholders, and it's the greatest thing in the world to hide behind.'

Federal, state and city administrations followed to a degree the example of Europe in giving to culture. President John F. Kennedy's interest in the arts was continued by Lyndon B. Johnson and his successors. By 1972, the congressional appropriations for subsidies for the arts and humanities had reached nearly sixty million dollars. There were also twenty-six government departments which paid for nearly two hundred programmes in the arts that same year. Most of the states and major cities also had their own committees for the fine arts, although some cultural funding was regarded as a method for attracting companies to relocate factories in the area. Culture could be competition by other means to attract business.

The American example of corporate sponsorship for the arts hardly existed in Britain. By 1973, only a quarter of a million pounds annually derived from industry. Not until the end of the decade was a transatlantic version of the Business Committee for the Arts established, the Association for Business Sponsorship of the Arts. It was interesting that Lord Goodman was its first chairman, as if in recognition of the need for corporate as well as state patronage. He knew that complete state financing for the arts was a Utopian ideal and believed that 'what one could garner from the private sector was as good money as might come from official sources. *Pecunia non olet.*' Certainly, money did not smell. The founding director of the Association for Business Sponsorship, Luke Rittner, was to travel in the reverse direction and become the Secretary-General of the Arts Council, now becoming more conscious of the need to look for funds from industry as well as the state. In return, the sponsors expected advertising from cultural events, offending some purists; but, as Rittner said, obscurity was not an option. 'If a company sponsors anonymously, that will not be a deductible expense.'

The attempted shift from public to business or private patronage would be a deliberate act of the first Conservative administration under Margaret Thatcher, who had been the Minister responsible in the previous Conservative government for introducing charges for visitors to museums. The Arts Council grant-in-aid would be held in real terms below the rate of high inflation. The new Minister for the Arts, Norman St John-Stevas, would be blunt about the policy, saying that there would be no great sums for the arts from the government in the future. 'We must look to the private sector for new sources of money. That's where the possibilities for the future lie.' Only when the economy was flourishing again would the Conservative party increase state spending on the arts. And only when, as in the United States, the arts were presented as something of a commercial commodity and a tourist attraction.

The only country with an organization remotely similar to the

Arts Council in Europe was Sweden with its Kulturradet, or Cultural Council. As John Allen pointed out in his essay on 'The European Perspective':

> The particular nature of such an organization takes its colour from its national context and many historical and social pressures impossible to identify. If it lacks the authority of its British counterpart this is perhaps because its position is less vulnerable. One of the more distinctive features of the Swedish form of government is that legislative measures are usually proposed not in the first instance by ministries but by a group of experts forming a commission of enquiry which takes its brief from the minister concerned with the approval of the government. There follows what the Swedes admit to being a time-consuming and cumbersome administrative procedure, but it permits a very high degree of democratic consultation.
>
> The National Council for Cultural Affairs was created in 1969 as a result of a lively cultural debate among practitioners of the arts in the latter part of the decade. In 1973 the Council produced a detailed study of cultural policy in Sweden together with proposals for the future of Kulturradet which was envisaged as carrying out very much the same kind of responsibilities as those at present carried out by the British Arts Council: advice to the government on long-term planning, sifting of demands for subsidy and regional cultural organizations, and so on.

In his report 'Support for the Arts in England and Wales', Lord Redcliffe-Maud had included an appendix describing a visit to Sweden and an examination of the National Council for Cultural Affairs. He pointed out that the Council there was more an arm of government than the British Arts Council, but that was because the Swedes conceived the arts and culture as more integral to the educational responsibilities of the state than the British did, as there was less of a divergence of interest. It was 'more a question of the government spending its money via the Council than the Council seeking government money to carry out its policies'.

Through tradition and history, the Federal Republic of Germany took decentralization in the arts field to the verge of dissolution. The nation had developed from a patchwork of principalities, duchies and palatinates, eventually unified by Prussia, but retaining their 'state' theatres. After the end of the Second World War, Western Germany was created from a federation of eleven states or *Länder*: these were given the leading role in the areas of culture and education. The responsibilities of the federal government or *Bund* were limited to artistic copyright and other legal matters through the Ministry of the Interior, also external cultural relations through the Ministry of Foreign Affairs. The *Länder* and the municipalities were responsible for the promotion, administration and funding of culture in their areas. The result was a proliferation of subsidized theatres for drama, ballet, opera and concerts – more than three hundred public and private ones. The *Länder* backed a sixth of them, the German cities the rest. This largess provoked both envy and criticism in England. The mulch was well spread and admirably devolved; but the harvest was thin on the wide ground. It appeared to some in England to be too many dandelions and too few roses.

Historically, France had gone to the opposite extreme since the days of royal absolutism and control from Versailles. When Lord Bridges, in his early report on the British arts, had explained the wish that the State should not be 'an awkward and uncomfortable partner in its relationship with the arts', Edgar Wind, the Reith lecturer of 1960, had doubted whether a patronage so self-effacing could be effective, since it practically abrogated any responsibility for artistic decisions:

> That a responsible Minister would have a depressive effect on art is generally regarded as axiomatic, although historical evidence speaks against it: witness Colbert or Antonin Proust. However, to say that an institution works well does not necessarily mean that it works smoothly. Malraux, for example, has shown himself an annoyingly enterprising minister, and artistic life in France has reacted to him with commendable irritation. No doubt, an uncomfortable partnership, but preferable to the comforts of the void. As long as State patronage is so timid as to confine itself to the avoidance of trouble, the State will receive the vacant art that it inadvertently sponsors.

That commendable irritation with the French Minister of Cultural Affairs, the writer and philosopher André Malraux, and with his centralized *Maisons de la Culture* spreading across his country, crystallized in the May Revolution of 1968 against the government of Charles de Gaulle and changed the dialogue about the value of European culture for decades and perhaps for ever. Ripples even crossed the Channel. The accusation was that the 'high' arts and formal culture were gripped in the dead hand of the state. The ideology of art for art's sake was attacked. As the manifesto issued by the Popular Studio of the École des Beaux-Arts declared, the artist must renounce his privileged status and melt into anonymity.

> We are against the ruling force of our day. What is the ruling force of our day? Bourgeois art and bourgeois culture.
>
> What is bourgeois culture? It is the instrument whereby the ruling class's power of oppression accords artists a privileged status so as to separate and isolate them from all other workers. This privilege locks the artist in an invisible prison. The fundamental concepts underlying this isolating action that the culture exerts are:
>
> - The idea that art has achieved autonomy.
> - The defence of 'freedom of creation'. Culture gives the artist an illusion of liberty.
> 1. He makes what he pleases, he believes everything is possible, he is accountable only to himself and to Art.
> 2. He is a 'creator', that is to say he invents totally something unique whose value is permanent and above historical reality. He is not a worker at grips with historical reality. The idea of creation makes his work an unreality.
>
> By allotting the artist a privileged status, culture renders him harmless and functions as a safety valve in the mechanism of bourgeois society.
>
> This is the situation in which we all find ourselves. We are all bourgeois artists. How could it be otherwise? That is why we use the term 'popular studio,' for there is no question of reform but of a *radical change in orientation*.
>
> We have decided to transform what we are in society.

This concept of the effacement of the artist was taken to the extreme by Jean-Louis Barrault, who announced that he was dead. The duty of the artist was to infiltrate the community and use every skill to create activities on a human scale. At the École des Beaux-Arts, the protest was effective: the Minister of Cultural Affairs closed the institution, which had already been closed by the students themselves. A student poster showed a riot policeman with a paintbrush in his teeth under the slogan – THE POLICE STICK TO THE BEAUX ARTS: THE BEAUX ARTS STICK IN THE STREET. The death of official art appeared to restore the power of inspiration to everyone. LONG LIVE THE CREATIVE MASSES ... ART DOESN'T EXIST: ART IS YOU. Yet with liberation came confrontation. The painter faced the dealer and the critic, while all three stood against the State with its cultural powers and artistic policy.

The very suddenness and ferocity of this 'cultural revolution' seemed to silence the authorities. Throughout the whole of the turmoil in Paris, André Malraux said nothing. In the words of one participant, Michel Ragon:

> culture and art no longer seemed to interest anyone. Drawing the unavoidable conclusions, the museum curators closed their cemeteries of culture. Infected by this example, the private galleries locked their doors. A curious autodestruction of art and culture appeared, bringing to mind what Friedrich Hegel had written a hundred and fifty years before: 'Art, seen in relation to its supreme destination, remains a thing of the past. It has hence lost for us what once made it true and vital, its former reality and necessity.'
>
> During the May Revolution, the city once again became a centre of games, it rediscovered its creative quality; there instinctively arose a socialization of art – the great permanent theatre of the Odéon, the poster studio of the ex-École des Beaux-Arts, the bloody ballets of the C.R.S. and students, the open-air demonstrations and meetings, the public poetry of wall slogans, the dramatic reports by Europe No.1 and Radio Luxembourg, the entire nation in a state of tension, intensive participation and, in the highest sense of the word, poetry. All this meant a dismissal of culture and art, doubtless because 'official' culture and art were empty of any forward-looking content, because they had become arts of pleasing ornamentation.

Although the French authorities rapidly re-established control during the summer, the radical genie would not return to its old bottle. The *Maison de la Culture* intended for each *Département* in France was superseded by the less ambitious and more broadly-based *Centres d'action culturelle*, rather on the lines of the arts centres and laboratories developing in the United Kingdom. 'Cultural democratization' was the new slogan. During the nineteen-seventies – and at an accelerated pace in the nineteen-eighties – the Ministry of Culture was seen by the Council of Europe as making 'its main objective to irrigate the whole community with facilities and institutions which would help to correct geographical imbalances'. In spite of these efforts at devolution, however, central funding and construction still remained Parisian and dominant.

France possessed in 1980 five 'national' theatres, nineteen major regional theatres, or *Centres Dramatiques Nationaux*, and some hundred independent companies that received varying amounts of subsidy. This countrywide organization was administered from the Rue Saint-Dominique in Paris by the Ministry of Culture:

> Subsidy is based on a contract made between the Minister or his representatives, and the director of the company or theatre that is being subsidized for a three year period. (In Great Britain the cheque is made to the chairman of the board of the theatre in question.) The French claim that their procedure gives far more security to the recipient of subsidy than the British procedure, while the three year contract provides an easy escape from unsatisfactory appointments.

As in the United Kingdom, artistic administrators and directors preferred to deal with the experts in the Rue Saint-Dominique or Piccadilly rather than the looser and less experienced bureaucracies outside the metropolis.

There were three levels of local government in France – the Regions, the *Départements* and the communes. All of them spent money on culture and the arts. There were over 36,000 communes ranging from hamlets to villages to towns to cities. Since the Middle Ages and the guilds, municipalities had engaged themselves in artistic endeavours and still provided half of the total expenditure on the arts in France, far higher than in the United Kingdom and so more successful in resisting the influence of the capital. The hundred *Départements* had existed only since the French Revolution, and the Regions were established merely in 1972, unelected bodies originally involved in providing culture through the financing of capital facilities rather like the British programme of Housing the Arts. The role of the Regions, however, would be enhanced in the nineteen-eighties as a mechanism to encourage devolution and establish the indigenous differences in the areas of France by spending revenue on artistic activities. As in Britain, there was a slow relaxation of power from the centre to the peripheries; but how long, O Lord, how long?

The Council of Europe tried to exercise pressure on its members to spread culture and make it more accessible. A series of studies was published with titles such as *The Demystification of Culture* and *Towards Cultural Democracy* and *Cultural Policy in Towns*, an analysis of approaches to the arts in fourteen European centres. There was satisfactory cultural activity, but poor organization:

town halls did not have departments to deal with the events; the artist did not know where to go for help. As for devolution, that was urgent. As the authors of *Décentralisation de la Promotion Culturelle* declared: 'In cultural matters organizations should be decentralized, dynamic, independent, flexible, and to a reasonable extent democratic. No organization alone can meet all these criteria but we have shown in connection with the financing of theatres that it is necessary to set up a regional or provincial authority between central government and local administration and to give it real power.'

Similar advice came from UNESCO publications and conferences in the nineteen-seventies. The former Secretary-General of the British Arts Council, Nigel Abercrombie, wrote a study named *Artists and Their Public*, which stressed the gap between the creators and their audience, and also the plight of artists in modern society. The new direction for all countries should lie in an arts education and cultural centres for all. Abercrombie quoted the former French Prime Minister, Edgar Faure, that education had the dual power to cultivate and to stifle creativity. 'Man fulfils himself in and through creation. His creative facilities are those which are most susceptible to culture, the most capable of flourishing and transcending their achievements and also the most vulnerable to repression and frustration.' Since the revolt of May 1968, there had been no lack of internal pressure in France to modify existing educational practice. But an analysis of the French educational system four years later could still ask: 'Is not the child the one who is really left out of school life, since he serves merely as an admiring public to a schoolmaster who occupies the centre of the stage in the classroom and communicates only with pupils who are the faithful reflection of its own idealized image? A new breed of arts teachers and *animateurs* should be trained worldwide to work with local communities in 'cultural centres', which might be a theatre, a school, a museum, an arts laboratory or workshop as well as the new arts centres, the *Maisons de la Culture* or *des Jeunes*, the Institutes of Contemporary Arts or *agora* or arts camps.

These recommended policies had little effect on the members of the Council of Europe or the United Nations. Each country had its own cultures and resisted any foreign intrusion in its fief. And many nations were like the United Kingdom in having no coherent overall policy. In the Netherlands, for instance, Dutch society had long been divided in religious and political groups – Protestants and Roman Catholics, Liberals and Socialists with a long tradition of local autonomy. Although an Arts Council, or *Raad voor de Kunst*, was set up after the end of the Second World War, the government was not obliged until 1979 to take its advice about the co-ordination of arts policy at central, provincial and municipal levels, also about which companies and groups were worthy of subsidy. Three years later, overall policy became the responsibility of the new Ministry of Welfare, Health and Cultural Affairs, put together from other ministries and split into four divisions: on Arts, on Cultural Heritage, on Media, and on Libraries and Literature, each with its own independent advisory body. This solution took power into the government, yet devolved it – an English compromise.

In the United Kingdom, the Arts Council had never accepted unfavourable comparisons to its European counterparts, only an occasional spurt of jealousy over the total amount available for arts subsidy. In 1973 Sir Hugh Willatt noted that recent contact with Europe had revealed:

> particularly in France, a rather more centrally planned approach to regionalism in the arts. We learn of *animateurs* and a number of strategically placed arts centres, embodying theatres, concert halls, art and film facilities. The comparisons can only be stimulating and our Regional Arts Associations have shown particular interest in their way of doing things … Whatever the final assessment of the two methods may be, we can claim that in Bristol, Liverpool, Nottingham and the rest, our British approach with its reliance on a diversity of individual but encouraged local efforts has been very productive. Our system has developed the growth of sixty regional theatres housing professional companies compared with nineteen in France, and, as the Bristol example shows, a great variety of enterprise housed not in one building, but in many, and reaching large audiences.

The next Secretary-General, Sir Roy Shaw, fiercely resisted the European push towards more cultural democracy and the attack on the related notions of quality, excellence and standards. Writing in 1979, he said that these terms had still been used with assurance in Arts Council reports a decade ago:

Now they are provocations to some arts populists, to the extent that, as an experienced arts administrator has remarked, they regard the very notion of quality as 'authoritarian'. Similarly, a recent study of trends in European ideas about arts policy discerned a 'phobic caution about any statement which implies that some forms of activity are culturally preferable to others'. Another European writer has seriously argued that in the arts quantity may now be much more important than quality. Finally, there is a serious as well as a comic side to a recent exchange between the writer and a local government councillor. Faced with the statement that the arts activity he was asking the Council to subsidize was not good enough, he replied with complete seriousness: 'You know the Arts Council is often accused of excellence.'

The last word on what he called 'foreign comparisons' came from Shaw's compatriot and ally, Richard Hoggart. He thought that such comparisons were unembarrassed by the consideration of historic cultural differences:

We know the French and Germans and almost all other Western European countries spend more on the arts than the British. That is part of their traditions, perhaps to be admired but not easily or automatically transferable. Some of them also spend money on water cannon to quell rioters, or more than we do on the secret services; those too are part of their traditions. Some spend less than the British on public libraries, parks, allotments; and their range of voluntary activities within the community is often much less than Britain's. You cannot legitimately yank out one bit of a culture which suits you, as a stick to beat Britain with whilst conveniently ignoring others. Best to make the case for this place, this society, this culture, here, now.

There might well be insular reasons for more subsidy for the arts, but the rest of the world had nothing to do with it.

John Maynard Keynes. Lord Keynes was
Chairman of the Council for the
Encouragement of Music and the Arts
and Founder of the Arts Council of Great
Britain 1942–46

Queen Elizabeth, Queen Mary, the Queen Mother and Princess
Elizabeth at an Arts Council concert at King's Lynn. This was one
of a series of concerts broadcast from historic towns in 1945

Sadler's Wells Ballet at Covent Garden: *Job*, with choreography
by Ninette de Valois and scenery and costumes by John Piper,
1948–49

Sadler's Wells Ballet at Covent Garden: *The Sleeping Beauty*, seen
from the spotlight, 1948–49

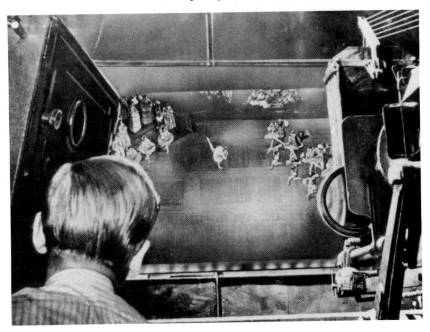

Dr Vaughan Williams, OM,
by Jacob Epstein

Sir William
Emrys Williams

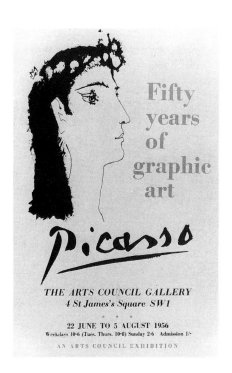

Lord Goodman
by Nicolas Bentley

The Arts Council triennial poetry awards, 1959–62: C. Day Lewis
(centre) and the two prize-winners, Edward Lucie-Smith (left) and
Robert Graves (right)

An Arts Council meeting, 1967: from right to left, Sir Hugh
Willatt, Lord Goodman, Sir John Witt, Lord Gibson, Stuart
Hampshire and Lady Antonia Fraser

The headquarters of the Arts Council, 105 Piccadilly

The seal of the Arts Council, carved above the entrance. Designed by Reynolds Stone and engraved by George Friend

From an Arts Council exhibition in Stevenage town centre, 1969

Brian Rix, later Chairman of the Drama Panel, being given a book by the Chairman of the Arts Council, Kenneth Robinson, at the opening of the new Arts Council shop in Long Acre, London, 1979

Lord Gowrie, Minister for the Arts (left), meets Lord Rees-Mogg, Chairman of the Arts Council, 1984

Sir Roy Shaw, Secretary-General of the Arts Council 1975–83

Anthony Field, Finance Director of the Arts Council 1957–84

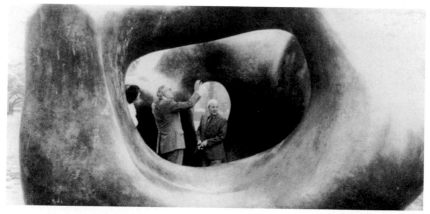

Former Prime Minister James Callaghan (centre) and Henry
Moore at the sculptor's eightieth-birthday exhibition in the
Serpentine Gallery and Kensington Gardens, 1978

Luke Rittner, Secretary-General of
the Arts Council (right), at the press
conference to announce the
appointment of Lord Palumbo (left)
as Chairman of the Arts Council,
September 1988

Anthony Everitt, Secretary-
General of the Arts Council
1990–94. Photograph: Justin
Pumfrey

Mrs Margaret Thatcher was welcomed by Lord Palumbo as the first Prime Minister in history to visit the headquarters of the Arts Council, now moved to 14 Great Peter Street, Westminster

TEN

CUTS AND THE CHANGING OF THE GUARD

The purchase of instruments of amusements for the rich, with money raised by taxes on rich and poor, is depredation.

Jeremy Bentham
the Utilitarian philosopher

'Arts and politics go hand in hand,' Tony Banks said in 1981, when he was the Chairman of the Arts Committee of the Greater London Council. 'Those who say otherwise are total idiots.' The government of Mrs Thatcher was to destroy the Greater London Council, deeming it to be led by radical socialists, and then to re-assign responsibilities for the arts in the metropolis. Other legacies from the Labour government were the holders of the positions of Chairman and Secretary-General of the Arts Council of Great Britain, but these two were permitted to serve out their terms before more suitable appointments, those who might understand the changed temper of the times, would be made. All that the government could do through the Minister for Education and the Arts, Norman St John-Stevas, was to hold the line or diminish arts subsidies, forcing economies on an organization that could only thrive and innovate with increases. The unkindest cut of all of the new Tory government was to compel the Council to trim its clients. Those who were axed in 1981 saw the old ally of artists as their butcher or demon barber, the 'Sweeney Todd of Piccadilly'.

'The arts world must come to terms', the new Minister announced, 'with the fact that Government policy in general has decisively tilted away from the expansion of the public to the private sector. The Government fully intends to honour its pledge to maintain support for the arts as a major feature of policy, but we look to the private sphere to meet any shortfall and to provide immediate means of increase.' This was a hopeful statement, since business sponsorship was then contributing less than two per cent of subsidy for the arts. The only solution for the Arts Council would be to slash its grants equally to everybody or to withdraw some absolutely, a form of the murder of livelihoods. For thirty-five years, the Council had hardly dropped a client. The withdrawal of support from the Carl Rosa Company at the end of the nineteen-fifties, and later from Phoenix Opera, had stirred up a storm of protest. The trouble was that the regular grant had been the kiss of life for many companies: its loss was the throttle of death. For there was no way of raising funds elsewhere. Speaking now for the board of the Prospect Theatre Company, Angus Stirling pointed out in 'Unkindness in the Cut' in the *Observer*, 'what we find hard to understand is that, having decided to withdraw the subsidy, they have done it in such a way as to make it virtually impossible for the company to raise money elsewhere, although it has had a successful season'. The accolade of the Council had almost become a 'Good Housekeeping' seal of approval.

With the whole economic climate rather cloudy worldwide, Sir Kenneth Robinson found himself philosophical in 1981 about the blood-letting. 'The Council's grant-in-aid has by and large survived the major surgery which has had to be applied to many areas of government spending, and certainly the Council does not face the traumatic halving of resources placed on its United States counter-part, the National Endowment for the Arts, by the new administration in Washington.' Yet the nettle had to be grasped. Certain clients, notably the regional orchestras and touring dance compa-nies, were in real difficulties because of long periods of underfund-ing. Their very survival was sometimes in doubt. Therefore, the Council decided that a number of companies must have a significant real increase, which meant the chop for a variety of smaller companies. Unpopularity was inevitable, although the virulence of the attack on the Council dismayed its officers. Many of the forty-one guillotined clients protested vehemently. The bad news was widely reported, the good news was not. It fell to Richard Hoggart as Vice-Chairman to announce the cuts: policemen then had to guard the doors of 105 Piccadilly to keep out protestors carrying banners with the slogans HANGMAN HOGGART and HANG HOGGART HIGH. 'Tory hit lists', which included the National Youth Theatre and National Youth Orchestra, were said to be administered by 'bloodless bureaucrats, bourbons, mandarins, and elitists', who had set themselves up as arbiters of taste. In fact, both Hoggart and Roy Shaw were forced by the money on the table to prefer the professional to the amateur, the excellent to the experimental, and national standards to particular needs. At the necessary hanging ordered by the government, the noose could not have been set by a more exemplary Jack Ketch. The execution, however, also put the Arts Council in the dock of public opinion, from which it could not emerge without cross-examination and vilification.

The Minister for Education had been one of two members of the Shadow Cabinet to have supported Mrs Thatcher's bid for the leadership of the party, but he did not have the ear of the Prime Minister, as Jennie Lee had had of Harold Wilson. When Dr Rhodes Boyson was appointed his assistant at the Ministry, Norman St John-Stevas found this a hindrance as they did not work happily together. Out of sympathy with the general thrust of economic policy and the confrontational tone and approach of the government, St John-Stevas found his defence of the arts budget falling on stony ground. He later wrote:

> Mrs Thatcher regarded the Cabinet very much as her own and Cabinet Ministers as her agents, rather as popes saw bishops in the days before the doctrine of collegiality emerged at the Second Vatican Council. They were there to do her bidding. Mine was the classic view of the role of the Cabinet, with the Prime Minister as *primus inter pares*. The constitutional convention in the nineteenth century was that no Cabinet Minister could be dismissed for a difference of view, only for delinquency or incompetence. This seems no longer to be the case.

When St John-Stevas was expelled from office on a cold and

wintry January day, he found his cutting out a dispiriting, depressing and wounding one. It was the first step in a purge of other
dissenters in the Cabinet. At a stroke, he lost his sense of purpose. In
her memoirs, Mrs Thatcher wrote that she was sorry to see him go,
but that he had turned indiscretion into a political principle. She
offered him the sop of remaining Minister for the Arts alone outside
the Cabinet, but he could not accept that. The independent Office of
Arts and Libraries which he had set up was to be disbanded and
returned to the Department of Education and Science, subject to the
Secretary of State for Education. His empire would be sliced to a
rump. He left for the back benches, unable to carry out his policy in
the arts, which he summarized in his Richmond Lecture at Downing
College, Cambridge. 'We must present the arts in settings where the
barricades set up by opera houses, concert halls and art galleries are
at least scaled down. The arts should not be a fortress but an open
city.' Opera and street theatre need no longer be Dives and Lazarus –
the gap between the two worlds could be bridged. 'If the Minister
for the Arts devoted a substantial part of his time to constructing this
causeway, it would be time well spent.'

The coming of the new economic Conservative philosophy of cuts
in public expenditure turned the Arts Council from Mr Pickwick
into Scrooge. Its old supporters were metamorphosized into its
enemies, although they were really attacking the government rather
than the 'independent' arts body that had to work within a limited
budget. Speaking later, the incumbent Chairman of the Council, Sir
Kenneth Robinson, said that the Thatcher government took 'a
whole lot of institutions admired across the world and mucked them
up – the Arts Council, the National Health Service, and London
Transport'. Sir Peter Hall concurred, saying that the Thatcher years
messed up the two great institutions of organic growth in the
century – the BBC and the Arts Council. The other great betrayal,
which was begun under Norman St John-Stevas, was the limiting of
the government grant-in-aid and the emphasis on business sponsorship; it condemned the national institutions 'to the treadmill of the
Eighties' and stifled new enterprises, 'where you could get extraordinary effects for so little'. In his later memoirs, Sir Peter Hall did
praise Mrs Thatcher for sorting out the corrupt unions, but 'in the
name of free-market dogma she devastated our education system,

our broadcasting system and our performing arts ... We are paying in the Nineties for the excesses of the Eighties when, for the first time in our history, greed was turned into a shining virtue.'

When the Arts Council withdrew its grants from forty-one of its clients, its Draconian action was still its own. As the Minister, Norman St John-Stevas was not extended 'the right to be consulted, the right to encourage, and the right to warn'. He was angered by this display that the arm's length principle still mattered; but Sir Roy Shaw pointedly praised the new Minister, Paul Channon, for stating in public that he did not wish to interfere in the individual decisions made by the Arts Council and certainly would not wish to disagree with its strategy:

> Mr Channon is thereby maintaining the traditional relationship between the Minister and the Arts Council. This has proved crucial to the freedom of the arts in the past; to abandon it now would open the door to political interference in the Arts Council's decisions. Some members of each ruling party have from time to time urged such interference by *their* minister; it is very doubtful whether they would welcome interference by a minister of the opposing party.
>
> The Council welcomes also Mr Channon's statement in the House that the public gets 'good value for money' from public subsidy of the arts, and it welcomes, especially in a 'rough' year, the verdict of Mr Melvyn Bragg, in the *Sunday Times*, that 'The Arts Council of Great Britain is the most effective and successful arts funding organization in the world.'

In point of fact, Paul Channon was to be accused of politicizing the Arts Council. Lord Goodman disapproved of him 'ear-marking' money specifically for the national companies as an erosion of the 'hands-off' approach. The appointment of the new Chairman, Sir William Rees-Mogg, the editor of *The Times*, was seen as further political intervention. (So was the choice of Luke Rittner as the Secretary-General to succeed Sir Roy Shaw, as he came from the Association for Business Sponsorship of the Arts.) Above all, Channon agreed with the Prime Minister on a direct investigation into the economics of the leading national companies by an incisive civil servant from the Management and Personnel Office in Whitehall. 'I invented Clive Priestley', he has said, 'his forays into the arts.' This intrusion of government into the hallowed field of assessment of the Arts Council was to be seen as a mortal blow, although the Council would survive the wound. 'I chose not to make any organizational changes at the Arts Council,' Channon has also said, 'but I started more autonomy for the regions – yet perhaps this would go too far.'

The new broom in 10 Downing Street was already sweeping the corridors of the Arts Council. Richard Hoggart had been appointed internally as Vice-Chairman, but at a routine meeting in 1981 of the Chairman and the Secretary-General with the Minister for the Arts, the latter suddenly declared that Hoggart's time was up. Hoggart wrote later:

> They pointed out that by custom and precedent the Vice-Chairman-ship overrode normal Council terms of service. He insisted; they resisted. Finally, the Minister said something to this effect: 'I have no room for manoeuvre. Number Ten doesn't like him.'
>
> So I went. I wonder now, for the first time since it happened all those years ago, why the two didn't refuse. I doubt if the Minister would then have pursued his shabby little instruction. But they were difficult times, so ... The point of the story is obvious: it confirmed that governmental intervention in the work of such bodies started very early in the Eighties. Fiats from Number Ten and compliance from some of her Ministers. Or, worse, a disposition in some Ministers to be more royal than the Queen, to guess in advance what she might like.

The new Minister for the Arts did not press a reluctant Mrs Thatcher for more subsidy for the arts. He said that they were 'managing to survive' in evidence before the all-party Education, Science and Arts Committee of the House of Commons in 1982, before it finally produced its review of arts policy, 'Public and Private Funding of the Arts'. The Committee found that there was no significant evidence against the principle of public support for the arts, but these were in a precarious state because they were gravely and irresponsibly underfunded. It was surprised at the present degree of dissatisfaction with the Council. Negotiating a grant was held to be a discouraging and demoralizing annual ordeal, where once it had been an exercise in stimulation and encouragement. And the Committee took the view that the double-headed arrangement of a part-time unpaid Chairman and a full-time paid Secretary-General was unsatisfactory. Prospective chairmen could only be drawn from the few people who could afford to serve. And the

Committee did not approve of the growth of 'officer power' at the expense of the Panels – Sir Roy Shaw's reform. While the Council's value lay in avoiding control by a government bureaucracy, it might begin to act as a bureaucracy in its own right.

Sir Roy Shaw robustly defended the status quo. He was all for reducing the size of the Panels and the Committees, because they were so inefficient and time-wasting. The officers knew their art forms well and came to the best conclusions. As for the posts of Chairman and Secretary-General, he had been appointed under the old system by a Chairman, Lord Gibson, 'who said plainly that he wanted me, rather than himself, to be "Mr Arts Council". Lord Gibson's successor, Kenneth Robinson, was less happy with that situation, especially after he retired from his full-time post and was free to spend several days a week at the Council.' In the nineteen-sixties Lord Clark had devoted no more than a few hours a month to his chairmanship. 'Sir William Rees-Mogg was certainly anxious to be an executive chairman. When I retired, he became just that and the role of Secretary-General was quietly diminished. It was perhaps an inevitable development (something similar has happened at the B.B.C.), but it does put more power in the hands of a political appointee.'

Sir Roy Shaw found the new Chairman to be 'a very political animal. He was put in to put the Arts Council right – to put it to the right.' Although Sir William Rees-Mogg always said, 'I'm not really political', causing a colleague of Shaw's to say she would *scream* if she heard the remark again, he did say in his opening statement as Chairman that he had been strongly influenced by his professional experience in the field of communications: he had already been appointed Vice-Chairman of the BBC. That was, indeed, why Mrs Thatcher had picked him, when Paul Channon had brought her a short list of four candidates. 'I know him', she had said. 'He will do.' What she knew was his role as editor of *The Times*. He was the first journalist to run the Arts Council. And while *The Times* took as much pride in its independence as the Council did, it was a wise editor who knew what his proprietor wanted. 'People who get appointed have some knowledge of each other,' Sir William Rees-Mogg has said with his usual understatement, 'the unknown are not appointed. I don't see how you avoid that.'

The new Chairman brought a religious philosophy as well an experience in communications to the arts. 'He believed in obeying a Higher Power,' Sir Denis Forman has said, 'whether the Almighty or Margaret Thatcher. He saw himself as the Great Reconciler of the arts and government.' In his book of 1977, *An Humbler Heaven*, Sir William Rees-Mogg had written of his puritan Catholic beliefs:

> I think that the arts are a part – but only a part – of the total development of man. It seems to me that we still have, in theory at any rate, the Renaissance idea of man as a fully developed person using all his capacities, one of those capacities being artistic appreciation. I don't myself see art as being as important as religion. I think it can contribute to a religious sense in that the highest art can exercise a relationship with a Platonic ideal which has a religious aspect to it ... at its most important art is a way of apprehending God.

Yet as Chairman of the Arts Council, he was most pragmatic. Whatever he believed, his staff could only carry out the functions which were natural to the time. They would not be engaged in Socratic dialogues with him. His emphasis, however, as his philosophy, was a decisive break from the past. As he has declared in *The Times*, arts grants should be primarily:

> a consumer and not a producer subsidy. The aim of arts policy is to provide the public with ample opportunity to benefit from all the major arts forms. This means that the popular arts, in areas where artistic opportunities are limited, need particular support. That includes the regional theatres, and touring. Most dance companies are based in London but depend on touring. Throughout my period, some members of the Council would have preferred a subsidy policy aimed more directly at the artist – and particularly the experimental artist.
>
> This is an important political choice, which applies in all areas of subsidy. Ought the health service to exist for the medical and administrative staff, or for the patients? Ought arts funding to be for the artists or for the audiences? When tax funds are concerned, I think the justification has to be one of access for audiences, although patients need doctors and audiences need artists.

Sir William Rees-Mogg disapproved of the tendency of the post-war arts movement since the time of Keynes. 'The thrust was – arts *instead* of religion.' He was to attend the funeral of Lady Lee; she had insisted that there should be no religious ceremony of any kind.

At the cremation, Michael Foot and Lord Goodman had spoken. Rees-Mogg thought: 'It was a displacement of the religious instinct onto the arts.' For the new Chairman of the Arts Council, his task was to spread the arts, to communicate with the people since 'at its most important art is a way of apprehending God'. Shy himself, he found communication difficult even with his staff; yet his mission was to broadcast the values of the arts to all the land. To one of his critics, he was a mandarin in *The Culture Club* with his rare bookshop and his love for the classical harmony of the eighteenth century. 'His key role is to provide an interruption in the liberal roll of honour. His reign is a hiatus in the intellectual growth of liberal arts funding, but its effects will be largely benign.'

His reign was not held by all to be benign, because of the increase of government intervention, particularly in the case of the forth-coming Priestley Report. Later Rees-Mogg was to claim that the substantial shift of resources away from London was an Arts Council and not a government policy – although it had been a government policy for several years. 'As Prime Minister, Mrs Thatcher was very concerned with support for the great London flagships', the Chairman asserted, 'and would probably herself have preferred a policy which concentrated more on the international impact of the major London companies. Nevertheless, she accepted the arm's length principle, and the government acquiesced in the policy.' She also acquiesced in her Secretary of the Cabinet, Sir Robert Armstrong, remaining as Secretary to the Board of the Royal Opera House, saying to him, 'Of course, you mustn't give up anything which is fun'. Armstrong did not know what to answer. Expecting a verbal slap, he said diplomatically, 'Thank you, Prime Minister', only to hear, 'Take *me* sometimes.' And he did: to *Figaro*, *Fidelio* and *Die Fledermaus*, which she enjoyed, but not *Così Fan Tutte*, which she is said to have found immoral.

The Prime Minister, however, injured the arm's length principle in allowing Clive Priestley to examine the affairs of the Royal Opera House and the Royal Shakespeare Company as the price for an additional five million pounds demanded in 1983–84 to write off accumulated deficits in the arts. A bonus required a scrutiny to see that it was money well spent. Traditionally, the Music and Drama Panels of the Arts Council had not attempted to assess the 'Big Four' metropolitan companies – Sir Roy Shaw noted – particularly as their artistic directors usually held their work above reproach. Attempts to have the 'Big Four' assessed by the Arts Council in the early nineteen-eighties had failed. But now the formation of the Priestley Committee seemed to Shaw to be 'a political act'. Priestley was a civil servant who led the Efficiency Unit under Derek Rayner and who reported directly to the Prime Minister. 'She interested Paul Channon in the scrutiny', Priestley has said, 'as he needed to get more money from her.' His brief was to examine two of the 'Big Four', because of the determined opposition of Lord Goodman, who refused any co-operation from the English National Opera and tried to swing the Board of Directors against the inquiry at the Royal Opera House. 'To have a scrutiny on behalf of the Minister breached the arm's length principle.'

Lord Goodman strenuously objected to Priestley's arrival at a meeting of the Opera Board with two assistants and a long questionnaire. 'We had a rather heated scene', Goodman recalled in his memoirs. 'There were in my view only six people in the world competent to answer it, and I was unhappy to say that those six did not include any of his party of three.' After this confrontation with the other members of the Board who did not support Goodman, his term of office at Covent Garden was not renewed, perhaps because of his frequent use of the phrase 'Back us or sack us'. Priestley continued his investigations with vigilance and zeal, concentrating on the organization of the Arts Council almost as much as on the Royal Opera House and Royal Shakespeare Company. He found its workings unattractive; there was no proper assessment of the major companies even though fourteen criteria were applied before a grant-in-aid was normally given. The officers deplored the 'adventurism' of the Royal Shakespeare Company, which in turn felt that it would never win against the Arts Council or the needs of the National Theatre. 'We always feel we've done something wrong, but no one will tell us what it is.'

Now it was Priestley's job to tell two of the flagship companies what they had done wrong. He began with a series of confidential interviews with senior officers of the Arts Council. The able and young Deputy Secretary-General, Richard Pulford, came from a working-class socialist background, had served in the Department of Education and Science and in the Treasury, and knew the terms of the inquiry:

> He thought that two reasons for the scrutiny were possibly these, first, both the Royal Opera House and the Royal Shakespeare Company had consistently taken the line that, 'it costs what it costs; there is no more to be said; give us what we need or else; our affairs are not subject to scrutiny'. Secondly, both were complex organizationally, which made them impervious to 'casual' inquiry by which he meant, he explained, any inquiry less searching than what we proposed.

The Arts Council was outflanked by the Royal Opera House, anyway, mainly because of its direct contacts with the government through Sir Robert Armstrong. This was not the case of the Royal Shakespeare Company, which had Sir Harold Wilson as its president.

When he gave evidence to Priestley, Tony Field, the Finance Director, defined Arts Council policy as 'to try and maintain in existence its client groups and where possible either add to the list of clients or extend the work of existing clients'. There had been a conscious policy decision to give more money to the regions: the 'national' companies now only received a quarter of the budget, when they had more than half of it twenty-five years before. The Council's case for a budget increase over the rate of inflation was based on the need to strengthen the regions without taking away from the 'national' companies, and on the fact that inflation in the arts was higher than in other sectors of the country. The Council saw expenditure in the arts as an investment which repaid itself many times over: at present, a grant of ninety million pounds would return quarter of a billion pounds to the government. Monitoring and control arrangements had been very efficient: in the thirty-seven years of its existence, the Council had only had to ask for supplementary grants on three occasions, including this last one which had led to the setting up of the Priestley inquiry. As for his own dealings with the Royal Opera House, Field said that he was conscious of facing a board of 'notables' with great political weight. Although he had the power of the purse, any dramatic challenge to his plans for the opera would be met with the riposte, 'I will speak to your Chairman, or the Minister or the Prime Minister'. The only way to change that proud body was constant chipping away at the deficit, 'the drip on the stone'.

When Priestley met with Richard Pulford again and with Sir William Rees-Mogg, it did emerge that the Arts Council had felt bound by a direction from the Treasury in the nineteen-sixties that, if the Royal Shakespeare Company came to London, it should do so at its own peril. Such direction from the civil service had affected the level of Council funding until the latest supplementary grant of five million pounds, from which the Royal Shakespeare Company had received the largest proportion and percentage increase. In future, the company would remain a priority client, recognized as one of two 'national' theatres. As for the Royal Opera House, it had, in the opinion of Sir William Rees-Mogg, been brilliantly run by its chairman, Lord Drogheda. Yet now that its General Director Sir John Tooley also had the job of Chief Executive thrust upon him, it was uncertain about its finances and 'what to do next'. In contrast, the Royal Shakespeare Company was an 'emotional organization ... a skilfully driven team of runaway horses'; it was most difficult for the Council's officers to assess or monitor. 'After all, you are looking at Trevor Nunn and Terry Hands: you as a director, having come out of the middle ranks of the theatre or the B.B.C., are bound to look up ... to have a certain humility.'

Sir William Rees-Mogg largely based his reactions to funding the arts on his experience as editor of *The Times*. He admitted to Priestley that he had no idea what economies might be attempted at the Royal Opera House. 'His experience suggested that there were parallels with the newspaper world. As managers, some editors were naturally extravagant. The Royal Opera House was not in that class. Other editors were quite prudent, but were nevertheless not interested in management.' He himself had been at *The Times* for fourteen years as editor, which 'was four years too long. It was the sort of job where you went through three phases. First you started off not knowing how to handle things. Secondly, when you did know, you enjoyed it. Thirdly, things had become repetitious and it was hard to summon up the necessary energy, one's response lacked freshness and one began to slow down.' After a long time in office, perhaps there should be a change. There had been one at the Arts Council with his appointment as Chairman, a spreading change in its composition and attitudes and 'an ideology which was only partially sympathetic to private funding', while he was very enthusiastic about it. Corporate and individual support was the way to solve the financial problems of the Royal Opera House more than an increase in public subsidy.

On the hornet's nest of the sting of the arm's length principle, the Chairman of the Arts Council tried to apply balm by saying to Priestley that it was essential that there should be a meeting of minds between Council and government and a broad agreement on policy objectives. Neither could be effective without mutual confidence. The Council opposed direct or separate government subsidy to the arts, but he himself was not against extra money being given directly to the 'Big Four'. Yet it should not be done as an isolated thing. The government needed to look at the regional pattern at the same time as it looked at the result of the Priestley scrutiny. Money could not be taken from the regions to give to London. If specific sums were earmarked for the 'Big Four', there would be a rumpus. There had to be more for all, not just the favoured few. Having two sets of clients in the United Kingdom should be avoided; all should be considered within the same strategic view. And 'it was quite important that the arm's length principle should be specifically protected at this stage in a Government's life'.

At this stage in the Priestley inquiry, the Minister for the Arts changed. A poet and artist himself, the Earl of Gowrie did have the ear of the Prime Minister, who would grant him more for the arts as long as he achieved it almost by stealth. Gowrie agreed with the Chairman of the Arts Council that the key to more funding lay in corporate sponsorship. 'My greatest success in office came through cheating', Lord Gowrie has said. 'I kept back from the Arts Council what I was not supposed to do, a bit of money for the Business Sponsorship and Incentive Scheme.' It was to be known as 'the Gowrie Scheme' of matching funds and was to produce tens of millions of pounds for the arts. Yet Gowrie had to be 'street-smart politically' to achieve the result, clawing back funds for special cases against the advice of the civil service, which believed 'in the equality of misery, in taking a bob off everybody here and there'. He had to go behind the back of his Chief Secretary to William Whitelaw and Mrs Thatcher, who would see that Gowrie was all right, on the path that many Ministers had trod with the wise men of the party on the way to 10 Downing Street, built to outflank the Treasury Department.

Coincidental and carefully wrought was the change of the Secretary-General of the Arts Council during the same period. It marked the change of the ideology of arts subsidy, which Sir William Rees-Mogg shared with Lord Gowrie and confessed to Clive Priestley. When Sir Roy Shaw's term of office had been renewed, he had resisted a powerful *putsch* within the organization in favour of Angus Stirling, who had moved to the National Trust. Yet Shaw was unable to resist the new appointment, the personal choice of the Chairman, who wanted a true believer and not an ideological rival, accustomed to playing the role of 'Mr Arts Council'. In the opinion of his Deputy, Richard Pulford, Shaw was obsessively for adult education and against business sponsorship, which would detract from the merit of the Council. 'He had a big sense of what people ought to be like and did not think how they would respond, which was a catastrophic way to manage them.' He certainly mismanaged the question of his successor. If it could not be him, he wanted Tony Field to take over the job with his twenty-five years of experience; Richard Pulford might be too young to be considered.

The Selection Committee, however, unanimously chose somebody even younger: Luke Rittner, the Director of the Association for Business Sponsorship of the Arts, a protégé of Lord Goodman. He had little formal education and had always wanted to be an actor, but he had become Administrative Director of the Bath Festival before moving to London. He was hurt by the opposition of most of the staff of the Arts Council, who wanted one of their own. Sir William Rees-Mogg even found himself opposed by his own Council members in appointing his fellow Catholic Rittner as his Secretary-General; but like Lord Goodman, he was too wise in the ways of committee to be thwarted. He was advised by one member, Sir Hywel Evans, not to put the matter to the vote, but to wait until after Christmas and lobby the other members across the holidays. Another member, Colin Nears, the Chairman of the Advisory Panel on Dance, remembered his Chairman's behaviour at Council meetings. 'I have seen him rarely forced to change his mind, and then he would get angry. Although he was immensely school-masterish, every so often he exploded in laughter and giggled like a schoolboy. But in the end, he was the editor who said, "This is the front page".' And so Luke Rittner received a unanimous vote after his second interview before the Council, although the *Guardian* wrote a leader denouncing his appointment, and Philip Whitehead, then spokesman on the arts for the Labour Party, warned that if the Council was being rebuilt in the image of Mrs Thatcher's government, then it would be dismantled by the next Labour government. If people were now being removed or approved on political grounds, 'then that must invite a measure of retribution'.

Meanwhile, Clive Priestley was proceeding with his scrutiny of the two flagships. Already, he was falling foul of what the Arts Council saw as an intrusion into its private affairs. Sir William Rees-Mogg warned him that the artistic assessments of the Council were confidential. That principle must not be impaired by the Priestley Report. The draft on the Royal Opera House could have a very serious adverse effect internally on that body, where morale was not strong: to make public adverse criticisms from the Arts Council would weaken it further and drive away potential business sponsors. The relationship between the Opera House and the Council would be permanently damaged, and other clients would come to fear that confidential dealings were liable to exposure. The basis of trust which currently existed was essential to the Council's functions; it must not be jeopardized.

The response of Clive Priestley was cogent, although it attacked the privacy of the proceedings of the Arts Council. He said that he would be blasted if he came up with the proposition that artistic assessment was wholly and solely a matter between the Council and the companies involved. 'For one thing the proponents of the general "middle class rip-off" theory would go into overdrive.' Those hostile to the 'national' companies 'would be stimulated to a further and perhaps better sustained attack by a belief that I had produced a whitewash job.' Artistic matters were relevant in terms of value for money, although it would be absurd for himself and his team to pass any artistic judgement on the 'national' companies. That was the function of the Arts Council. As a public body, however, dealing with clients dependent on public funds, the

Council was 'a steward, dealing with other stewards'. As a steward, its assessments should be available to the writers of the report.

Now Sir William Rees-Mogg retreated, suggesting minor amendments to the text of the report; but he did assert again the duty of the Arts Council to assess artistic merit and to keep such assessments confidential in order to maintain the trust of the clients. Priestley disagreed, fearing that if he said nothing about artistic assessment, he would be thought to be working within far too cosy an atmosphere. 'We are here dealing with public money. Your Council itself is a consumer as well as a distributor. The companies are consumers as well as distributors of benefit.' If it was right for the Secretary of State for Education and Science to publish the reports of Her Majesty's Inspectors of Schools on particular institutions, he dared to think it right that the fact that the Council made assessments was known and that the gist of them was 'available to the public which pays for the Council to exist and enables the companies to keep up the good work'.

The assessors in the Council had actually recommended a clean sweep of the Board and the upper echelons of the administration of the Royal Opera House; but Priestley thought that this would not be just or practical. The task of his report was to give the Opera House 'a good shaking, but to stop short of decapitation'. And Sir William Rees-Mogg agreed in that procedure, saying that during difficult negotiations with the members of the Opera House, he had kept throughout the desire to give them his full confidence. Their promise of internal reform in a report by Sir Denis Forman and the recommendations of the Priestley scrutiny would enable the Arts Council to raise the funding of the Opera House in real terms, if the whole grant-in-aid for the arts was also raised.

In his first public statement on the Priestley Report, the Chairman of the Arts Council said that he welcomed the detailed scrutiny of the two flagships. Priestley 'was absolutely right to say that these companies were great national assets which are underfunded, and I am delighted that Mr Priestley concurs in the case we have been making.' But the proposal to nationalize the funding of the Royal Opera House and the Royal Shakespeare Company, making them the responsibility of future governments, was not acceptable. Significantly, Sir William Rees-Mogg now drew on his past experience. 'Direct state funding of an artistic company is as unacceptable as direct state funding of a newspaper. Like the Governors of the B.B.C. the Arts Council exists to protect the independence of creative people.'

Lord Gowrie expressed himself delighted with the report, which had arrived at such comprehensive and valuable conclusions over two of the 'national' companies. In a handwritten postscript to his letter of congratulation to Priestley, the Minister for the Arts declared: 'It's not often that one thanks the parent for leaving the baby on the doorstep – particularly one with this heredity – but I really do so all the same!' In fact, the report was something of a tarbaby. A sharp skirmish broke out between Priestley and the Arts Council, in which the correspondence was referred to the Minister with Lord Gibson acting somewhat as an umpire. If the Arts Council were to be given the responsibility for assessment, in any form and at any interval, Lord Gibson wrote, without the parallel responsibility of funding, it would be to the grave disadvantage of the Royal Opera House. To remove the responsibility for funding the 'national' companies from the Council would force it into the political position of having to be the champion of its remaining regional clients in the battle for public funds. There was a good deal to be said for the direct funding of the flagships, but then the Council should not assess them. Its sympathies should lie with those with whom it was still involved. There could be no fair assessment without the power of the purse.

Before the publication of the report, Luke Rittner wrote to Clive Priestley with a copy to the Minister, stating that the Arts Council would be unable to give his work the support so much of it deserved if the direct funding recommendation remained. Its inclusion would be so controversial that it would overshadow the rest of the report. Other clients of the Council would strongly object to earmarked or direct funding. The report was unclear whether its approach should also apply to the English National Opera and the National Theatre, which had run their affairs with exceptional skill and control over the past three years: their good housekeeping would be seen to be penalized. In his reply to the Secretary-General, Priestley stuck to his guns, stating that his brief was only to scrutinize two of the 'Big Four' and that, as a former official as well as a simple taxpayer, he would find it genuinely astounding if the Arts Council were to 'adopt a dog-in-the-manger attitude on the money issue'.

The Arts Council adopted rather more of a stag-at-bay attitude with its biennial three-day meeting at the Craiglands Hotel at Ilkley, where it was able to give a good deal of time and thought to its response to the Priestley Report. Its tradition, integrity and future appeared to be under threat. With the Chairman abroad, Luke Rittner had to lock horns with Priestley before making the Council's critique public. He sent a list of thirty-seven objections to the Minister and to Priestley, who responded in a reply to Sir William Rees-Mogg. He quoted two of the more offensive suggestions:

> 'There is little doubt that the arts world as a whole – and particularly its less privileged parts will tend to see the Report as something of a whitewash ... There is about the Report as a whole an air which could easily be represented as one giving the companies what they say they need.'
>
> 'Another easy interpretation of the Report ... will say that it represents a charter for the deficit builders ... the Report cannot but lend credence to this view.'
>
> I am disturbed because it seems to me the Council is unwilling to say itself that the Report is a 'whitewash' or 'a charter for the deficit builders' but rather hopes that someone else will. If this interpretation is correct, it looks like another case of willingness to wound, but reluctance to strike!
>
> I am sure I can rely on you to have the courage of your convictions. Do you think that the Report is a 'whitewash' and a 'charter for the deficit builders'? If you do, I am sure that you will wish to say so on your own account; I do not think you would want to wish the accusation into someone else's mouth: that is something Dr Goebbels might have approved of, but not you!

As for the criticism that he had signally failed 'to make any comment about the needs of other parts of the arts world ... we had hoped that this would feature as a significant *obiter dictum*', Priestley stressed that he had stuck to his limited commission from the Minister. And as for the slights about his tenderness towards the Royal Opera House and the Royal Shakespeare Company, Priestley could not understand why the Council also said that they had come to the same assessment as he had. 'This seems to me a case of the Council wanting its cake and eating it.'

With its future independence under question, the Arts Council treated Ilkley as seriously as the Roundheads had treated Marston Moor: they were determined to fight back against the forces of the Queen's government. The Ilkley Letter was sent to two hundred and fifty leading clients of the Council, asking what would happen to them if their subsidy were withdrawn or drastically cut – or substantially increased. In the blood-letting of three years before, only three of the forty-one companies that had lost their subsidy had actually gone to the wall. Bryan Appleyard commented acutely in *The Times* on this strange and oblique approach, which represented perhaps the most important new direction that the Arts Council had taken since it was founded. 'It comes at the end of one difficult year for the Council and marks the beginning of another. The outcome will either be a successful defence of the Council's traditions of welfare-inspired crusading on behalf of the arts and of its belief in the separation of central government from the creativity it supports – or it will be their defeat.'

The Ilkley Letter was related to three major reports and papers that had recently menaced the role of the Arts Council. The Select Committee Report on 'Public and Private Funding of the Arts' of October 1982 had contained serious doubts about the structure of the organization, and had recommended more devolution and earmarking of funds by the government for the arts. The Priestley Report also called for earmarking or direct funding, while the White Paper, 'Streamlining the Cities', outlined the government's plans to abolish the top-tier local authorities such as the Greater London Council, leaving dozens of arts organizations without metropolitan subsidies. Nine performing arts companies and five museums and art galleries were to be designated of national importance and would receive central government aid. As for the rest, they would have to sink or swim on what they could get from the local authorities and commercial sponsorship and the public.

In this context, the Ilkley Letter was an attempt by the Arts Council to win the battle against the assaults from Whitehall. Tony Field recommended a return to the old 'centres of excellence' strategy. Resources would be concentrated in large regional cities, and the client list would be amputated. As Luke Rittner declared in the Ilkley Letter: 'The arts, like seeds, need to grow if they are to blossom. Some of the seeds we have nurtured over the years are now bursting to grow but are held back by lack of space and nourishment. This strategy will help the Council to thin out the seed-bed and to give more room for them to develop, and for new seeds to be planted.' It was an end to the tradition of response in favour of ruthless selection.

'So the Arts Council's will to live is being tested,' Bryan Appleyard wrote. 'The Ilkley Letter is its attempt to respond to the chaos of its inheritance.' The situation made it clear that Rees-Mogg and Rittner were far from being Tory party placemen:

> They are now fighting for the quality of their future lives as much as anybody else. Their primary tactic appears to be to attempt to embarrass Lord Gowrie, the Arts Minister. If all the most dire predictions being made come true then he will find himself being put down in history as the Arts Minister who presided over a drastic contraction of the subsidized arts.
>
> So far as he has indicated he does not wish to see the 'national' companies directly funded, but he could still go for 'earmarking' of cash to be channelled through a necessarily passive council. Meanwhile streamlining of the authorities looms larger, although the more wildly optimistic at 105 Piccadilly are pinning their hopes on the belief that it will never happen.
>
> Infinitely preferable to the Cabinet may well be a large element of direct funding, with a slimmed down Arts Council responsible for general and future planning rather than simply struggling to get the cheque out so the curtain may rise at the Bristol Old Vic. Lord Gowrie's move on his appointment in separating the arts from the Department of Education and Science could eventually be seen as the first step along this road to a Ministry of Culture. Senior civil servants have already been heard to refer to the arts as 'a mini-ministry'. So the trend is towards taking more of the arts into Whitehall. The Ilkley Letter is an indication that the Council has seen the importance of visibly taking charge of its own destiny as a counter to any such moves.

The counter-attack by the Arts Council became a charge. Sir William Rees-Mogg made public the Arts Council's objections to Priestley's recommendation of direct government funding. In a press release, he declared: 'The Council has always attached the utmost importance to the arm's length principle. It suggests that direct funding would create two classes of arts organization by divorcing the national companies from the rest of the profession, which it is one of their purposes to lead and inspire.' He went on to assert that 'Mr Priestley's Scrutiny' had 'accepted' the Arts Council's assessment of the Royal Opera House and the Royal Shakespeare Company, and so 'reinforces the Council's care for all its clients'. This gloss on the Report was not backed by the digest of the Council's objections, which accompanied the press release and strongly stated the traditional case for the primary arts body:

> We have reason to be proud of the history of our dealings with all four national companies over the years. At least some of their present world eminence is attributable to the sustained support, advice and encouragement which they have received from the Arts Council. That they are currently in financial difficulties, arising in turn largely from the constraints on our own budget, should be seen as a poor reason for disturbing that tradition.
>
> The Council therefore regards it as absolutely essential that it should continue to act as the channel for central Government funds for the national companies, as indeed for the hundreds of other arts organizations which it supports ... When political authorities are drawn into funding the arts directly, they cannot by their nature do other than take political factors into account in considering the importance and appropriateness of the activities concerned, however much these questions may seem to be separate from politics. The Report's suggestion that the activities of great national companies would be above political interference flies in the face of experience even in this country.

The counter-charge of the Arts Council at Ilkley was turned into a strategic victory by a rallying-call, most of it written overnight by Richard Pulford. In the further light of day, it emerged under the Chairman's signature as *The Glory of the Garden*. As the Putney Debates may have been to the Commonwealth government, so *The Glory of the Garden* was to the Arts Council. Lord Gowrie found the central concept of the piece to be brilliant. It said to him: 'I am the Minister for those who administer the performing arts. I am not Minister for the Arts.'

The plan was to concentrate on thirteen major British cities with access to the arts provided through subsidized transport for nearly nine people in ten. Lord Gowrie supported the vision of a national grid for the performing arts to be established with local authorities under local management. The problem was that the proposed abolition of the Metropolitan Counties would remove £34,000,000 from arts subsidy. With the backing of Mrs Thatcher and Lord Whitelaw, the Minister for the Arts had the money restored through different channels and the local authorities. One Ministry official, Caroline Morrison, was particularly effective in helping to persuade even such enlightened councils at Birmingham to raise their contribution to its superb Symphony Orchestra led by Simon Rattle. In the new scheme of things, the enhanced support of the local authorities was to become the transfusion needed by the bleeding arts.

'The Glory of the Garden' was the title of a poem by Rudyard Kipling, and a verse was quoted from it:

> Our England is a garden, and such gardens are not made
> By singing: 'Oh how beautiful!' and sitting in the shade,
> While better men than we go out and start their working lives
> At grubbing weeds from gravel-paths with broken dinner-knives.

The report was then subtitled grandly as 'The Development of the Arts in England: A Strategy for a Decade'. It further quoted Maynard Keynes, Thomas Jefferson and John Locke on the principle of liberty to the arts: 'As the highest perfection of intellectual nature lies in a careful and constant pursuit of true and solid happiness, so the care of ourselves, that we mistake not imaginary for real happiness, is the necessary foundation of our liberty ... The variety of pursuits shows, that every one does not place his happiness in the same thing, or choose the same way to it. Men may choose different things and yet all choose right.' The Chairman's introduction continued: 'Care for real excellence, encouragement of variety for the audience, support of freedom for the artist, are the foundation of liberty for the arts. The counterpart of liberty is responsibility. An Arts Council which stands back to respect liberty, puts the responsibility for art on the artists, and the responsibility for practical success on the managers of companies.'

The second aim of Keynes in making London a great artistic metropolis had been achieved, but his first aim, 'to decentralize and disperse the dramatic and musical and artistic life of this country', had not been adequately realized. The quality of London itself as an artistic centre showed up the deficiencies of arts provision in the rest of the country. For this imbalance, the Arts Council had to accept its share of the blame. There was still underfunding throughout the regions, where no theatre company enjoyed a Council subsidy equal to one-tenth of what was given to the National Theatre or the Royal Shakespeare Company, which the Priestley Report agreed was also underfunded. Even so, 'we live as two artistic nations – London and everyone else.'

London was, however, 'a place to visit and to wonder at' for tourists. Any loss of London's arts would cost the balance of trade as much as employment in a major industry. But now was the time to come to grips with Keynes's first priority to decentralize and disperse the artistic life of the country. The measures required to do so were institutional, administrative and financial. Central funding should be added to any place which provided the 'four conditions of success: need, local authority partnership, private partnership, above all talent'. The existing programme of devolution of assessment and funding to the Regional Arts Associations would be accelerated, and even with a static government grant-in-aid, cuts to respected clients would provide more finance for the regions. 'This document announces the largest single programme of devolution in the history of the Arts Council. It is a genuine and major act of administrative decentralization, a step back from centralized bureaucracy as a mode of administering the arts in Great Britain. We are not people who believe that London always knows best.'

Conscious of the government's desire for efficiency and hatred of bad housekeeping, Sir William Rees-Mogg reverted to his past experience. In arts funding, overheads were well contained, productivity was high, waste limited and salaries low:

> Certainly the arts output per pound seems to be a multiple of that in Fleet Street, a less efficient area in the economics of communication. The policy of the Arts Council is to examine expenditure realistically to make sure that the money government provides for the arts is spent as well as possible. That includes setting high financial standards for the Regional Arts Associations.
>
> Obviously the completion of the policy set out in this document will be a long-term matter; the strategy is a reassertion of the original idea, but it is also a decisive change of ambition. It will depend on the support of government, and indeed on the support of future governments down to the end of the century. It will depend on the

Arts Council's continuing its present determination, with changing
membership and changing officers. It will inevitably cost money, and
there is a limit to the funding that can be found out of existing
resources. It is also difficult; perhaps it is more difficult to disperse a
metropolitan quality of art than it is to create an artistic metropolis.

In the summing-up of his appeal to government to support the
new strategy of the Arts Council, the Chairman referred to his own
faith in the link between the arts and the divine. Modern society was
being depersonalized by the scale of its organization, a scale which
was being exploded by information technology. 'The arts, human,
creative, inspiring, individual, warm, alive, provide a natural
healing to this sense of depersonalization, and the appreciation of
beauty can transcend the moon-like chill of an electronic world. For
those of religious faith the human creativity of the arts can be a way
of sensing the beauty of God's creation. Perhaps we demand the arts
more than earlier generations; perhaps we need the arts more than
earlier generations.' A verse from Kipling had prefaced *The Glory of
the Garden*, a familiar metaphor, as in Pope's *Essay on Man*, for the
life of man. 'It is a fair metaphor to describe the work of the Arts
Council; we can dung and we can water, but we cannot create a
single flower. The British garden of the arts has great beauties
throughout, and a magnificent display at the centre, but there are
empty beds and neglected shrubberies. We would like to see the
whole garden in bloom, and all the people walking through it to
enjoy the flowers.'

To accomplish all this, the Arts Council had to undertake a
thorough and fundamentalist review of all its work for the first time
in nearly forty years of existence. The arts had never stood still; but
for some years the Council had been stuck in a groove. Long practice
had committed it to existing clients, leaving little flexibility. Its
resources were being spread too widely and too thinly. A full review
was also necessary because of the important alterations in the nature
of British society. 'The growth of enforced leisure, the severe
economic depression of many of our older city centres, changing
perceptions of the requirements of a multicultural society and the
rapid development of new communications media all have implications for the arts and for those charged with funding the arts.' Hence
the Ilkley Letter and consultation with clients about an increase or

reduction in subsidy, as well as about the possibility of being assessed and funded in future by a Regional Arts Association rather than directly by the Arts Council in London. And hence the policy of support to thirteen major cities or cachement areas, which found favour with the Minister for the Arts and the Thatcher government. Priority in the development programme over the next five years would be given to five main areas of work: Art; Dance; Drama; Music and Education. These must also be subsidized by more corporate sponsorship and the local authorities.

This counter-attack from Ilkley was a Pyrrhic victory. Ever since the time of Jennie Lee and Lord Eccles, both Labour and Conservative governments had been pushing decentralization and devolution on the Arts Council. There were more votes in it. Successive Chairmen had fought a rearguard action about losing power from their headquarters in 105 Piccadilly. Yet after the stout defence of the Lords Goodman and Gibson and Sir Kenneth Robinson, Sir William Rees-Mogg had chosen to save the existence of the Arts Council by acquiescing in its eventual slow demise. For the centre could no longer hold indefinitely while its powers were given to the peripheries. 'A Strategy for a Decade' was a strategy of retreat until, by the end of those ten years, the Arts Council would be holding a severely weakened redoubt, resisting the continuous assaults of the politicians seeking votes, the civil service seeking control and the regions skirmishing with their new arts militia. At Ilkley and in *The Glory of the Garden*, the Arts Council fought off direct funding and preserved the arm's length principle; but it yielded some of its independence to the government's long insistence on the slow sapping of devolution, a policy that would gradually drain the central arts body of its life.

After this major battle, the wounded Arts Council had to go to hospital. It had accepted a prolonged organizational review. Instead of outward confidence, it displayed inner doubts. In terms of the survival of the species, it was no longer hunting for new prey, but spoiling its own nest. The demand for financial scrutinies and management studies was the favoured guerrilla tactic of Whitehall, which compelled a body to decline into self-analysis and haemorrhage through dozens of internal inquiries. There was precious little time left for the officers of the Council to administer the arts countrywide, when most of their days were spent examining their back files to justify their existence. As Secretary-General, Luke Rittner put a brave face on this process in the annual report, saying that his staff had responded very positively to the review and that their contributions were proving invaluable to constructive debate on the many complex issues that had arisen. But then he admitted that *The Glory of the Garden*, the abolition of the Metropolitan Counties and the organizational review had made the year particularly difficult. It was *not* helped by the government offering a below-inflation-rate increase in the grant-in-aid for the following year, which had led to a very public row. 'An unprecedented meeting of theatre directors passed a motion of no confidence in the Arts Council – thus highlighting the Council's problem of balancing the confidence of whatever government is in power with that of the artistic community. I believe the theatre directors would be justified in their fears if the Council were to lose the confidence of government and detrimentally affect the grant.'

Sir Peter Hall had provoked the declaration of no confidence in the Arts Council. He considered that the whole theatre scene, not only the National Theatre, was under attack. Private sponsorship was being used as a means of reducing subsidy. In a letter to Lord Gowrie, Hall said that neither the Minister nor the Arts Council realized what a wasteland was developing, peopled by demoralized directors. At a meeting with the Minister himself, Hall found that Gowrie loathed the new National Theatre building. When the subject of its high running costs came up, the Minister suggested that the National could find it much cheaper to move out to some old, existing theatre such as the Lyceum or Drury Lane. 'The government was at last showing its true attitude towards the arts', Hall was to write in his memoirs, 'and, in William Rees-Mogg, Thatcher had appointed a chairman of the Arts Council who was seemingly content to dismantle the subsidy structure of the previous twenty years and allow the Council to dwindle from an independent agency, fighting the cause of the artist, into a tool of government policy.'

With such beliefs and faced with a huge impending deficit at the National Theatre, Sir Peter Hall persuaded his Board that he should take draconian action. At a press conference in the despised building, he mounted a coffee-table and announced the closure of the small Cottesloe Theatre to save half-a-million pounds annually, also a staff reduction of a hundred people and the end of touring. He then accused Lord Gowrie and Rees-Mogg of betraying the artistic standards of the country. This assault made the rest of the theatre close ranks around Hall, who called a meeting of forty-seven artistic directors of subsidized theatres. They ended by passing a unanimous vote of no confidence in the Arts Council. Ironically, Lord Gowrie counter-attacked Sir Peter Hall in public, and so won more backing in the Cabinet for the Council and arts subsidy.

Such a public declaration of distrust could never have happened if the Panels had still attracted the quality of advisers who had sat on them when Sir Peter Hall himself had served. With their power reduced by Sir Roy Shaw, the long unpaid hours and the uselessness of the proceedings had driven away nearly all of the leading directors and actors, whose eminence had once led to absolute acceptance of their verdicts. When the director Mike Leigh had served on the Drama Panel, a whole day had been spent in discussing the future of a leading repertory theatre going through a bad patch, only to end with the Drama Director saying, 'Most interesting, but I cannot guarantee to pass on your recommendations to the Council.' Leigh left the Panel, finding no point in being on it. 'I feel so impotent', the Vice-Chairman Marghanita Laski told Sir Roy Shaw in 1985; and Donald Sinden said, 'I feel I'm just a rubber stamp.' Half of the Drama Panel resigned that same year in protest against the disregard of their views. For if power corrupts, powerlessness abstains. There was no Lord Olivier or Sir John Gielgud on the Drama Panel to induce respect for the decisions of the Arts Council in the theatre. And the Senior Officers were also leaving under the new regime, because of what they saw as a break with the past and a 'selling out' of old principles. Among those who went was Tony Field and the long-serving Drama Director, John Faulkner, who called the changed quality of the Council: 'Entryism. We matched people to the social task now. We did not want to bring people of national standing back, and also they no longer wanted to serve. It was poor politics.'

Sir Peter Hall found that he had propelled himself into hot politics with a vengeance. Shutting the Cottesloe Theatre proved to be a political act. To enable it to reopen, the Greater London Council provided a special grant of £375,000, one of their last radical acts before being abolished by the Thatcher government. The Prime Minister had become personally incensed with Hall's rhetoric against her policies and she was said to have asked one Minister for the Arts: 'When are you going to be able to stop giving money to awful people like Peter Hall?' The point was that she did not dare to stop giving; she could only freeze the general grant-in-aid to the Arts Council. And yet, by continuing to support the theatre led by the fiercest critic both of itself and the government policy it had to accept, the Arts Council proved the value of the battle of Ilkley, where it had resisted direct government funding for the 'national' theatres, had maintained the arm's length principle and yet had given way to state policy on devolution, even at its own cost.

The medicine that the government was forcing down the throat of the Arts Council was what it had to administer to its clients, who were also becoming its patients because of the cuts in subsidy. Unfortunately, these clients and patients accused the Council of mistreatment, because it declared itself independent and responsible, however much underfunding made it toe the Tory line. 'There is a trap in playing the Treasury game,' the wise new Finance Director Anthony Blackstock has said. 'When you prove you are more efficient, you need less public money.' The internal investigations demanded by the Thatcher government were now being made part of the Council's assessments of its clients, particularly in staff cuts, financial practices and matching funding from business and local authorities. To these criteria, social welfare was being added with an insistence on education policy and 'the employment and other opportunities extended to members of ethnic minority groups'. Such considerations were missing from the two Royal Charters of the Arts Council, but they responded to present political pressure. Thus the clients found themselves faced with an enormous workload of accounting and cost-cutting, along with wheeling and dealing with corporations and town councils and welfare departments, instead of devoting their time to their artistic endeavours. For many directors of the client bodies, the creative process became the treadmill of administration. More businessmen now staffed the boards of the performing arts companies, because they could deal with these matters better than aging practitioners of the trade. The budget now dominated the product, the office was front of stage.

According to Richard Pulford, soon himself to leave the Arts Council to serve as Director-General of the administration of the new South Bank Board that was appointed to flesh out the metropolitan arts on the bones of the Greater London Council, Sir William Rees-Mogg felt that he was let down after his concessions in *The Glory of the Garden*. 'His premise was that if the Arts Council changed its policy, it would get more money. But Mrs Thatcher stopped the funding where it was. He was led up the garden path.' As Lord Goodman pointed out in a trenchant article in the *Observer*, the Council could not have a new strategy for the arts unless the handbag was opened and the purse. 'Even if led by a Napoleon or a Wellington, there is no strategy which enables a platoon to defeat a division.' The present resources were still skilfully used by an admirable organization, but what could it do faced with the dreadful parsimony of the government?

In this most difficult and meagre time, the worst mistake made by the Arts Council was to cut its Literature Department. The axe had been poised in *The Glory of the Garden*. Nearly half of the minimal budget for literature of £800,000 could be saved by ruthless chopping. It was ironical that a Chairman so devoted to old books and eighteenth-century literature should apply the guillotine to modern writing. The reasons given were these:

> There can be no doubt that, without public subsidy, drama provision in this country would be radically different from what it is today: the network of repertory companies would simply cease to exist on anything like its present scale. If there were no public subsidy for opera, it is very unlikely that large-scale opera performance would take place at all outside a limited annual season at the Royal Opera House. English literature, on the other hand, is sustained by a large and profitable commercial publishing industry. It is a basic ingredient in the school curriculum. It is available to the public through the public library system. In these circumstances, the impact of the Arts Council's subsidy for literature other than poetry is highly marginal.

More curious was the fact that the two other most literary members of the Council, the Vice-Chairman Marghanita Laski and the Literature Director himself, Charles Osborne, acquiesced in the decision. In his memoirs, Osborne printed many press comments on his apparent unwillingness to fight for his post. The *Observer* pointed out that he had been sceptical about literary subsidy and seemed to have colluded in his own departure. In his apologia, Osborne stated that there remained a public need for the Arts Council and the Regional Arts Associations to continue to subsidize a few publishers and literary magazines; but there was no popular cry for the subsidy of writers. The voices he heard were those of writers and poets, not of readers. 'It is wrong for the state or one of its agencies to decide which poets should be encouraged, and which should not ... In general, the better the poet, the more private he will wish to keep his art.' In particular, Osborne referred to Philip Larkin, who had resigned from the Literature Panel and had written against subsidies and official support, although he had received bursaries in his time. What Osborne did not know was the contents of the letter Larkin wrote to Kingsley Amis, who also opposed state funding for the arts:

> I am extricating myself from the Arts Council Literature Advisory Panel – not my cup of piss. Just sitting there while lady novelists shoot their mouths off ... and Chas Os sittin and grinnin and fixing it all up afterwards the way he wants it. I agree with you that it should all be scrapped. No subsidies for Gay Sweatshirt or the Runcorn Socialist Workers Peoples Poetry Workshop.

With such members of the Literature Panel and Department, the sight of writers opening their mouths for bread from the state would hardly be heeded. Of the Departments in the Arts Council, that of Literature had always had the least clout and significance. Its own representatives were some of the worst defenders of authors. And yet, the nib could pierce the most delicate skin of the national arts body, which continued to demean it. The pen was mightier than the sword because it wrote the words through which the Arts Council could be praised or blamed, in which the Arts Council dealt and excused itself and promoted its philosophy. Although the Council had long supported the campaign for a Public Lending Right, the final passage into law of that overdue sop to authors owed more to the doughty fighters for the cause than to the assistance of 105 Piccadilly. The only answer to the many critics, who assailed the Council on the diminution of the Literature Department, was the anarchist proposition – the old must be destroyed before the new can be constructed. In truth, as it was being run, there was little worth preserving in the Department, and its redundancy might be the condition of its rebirth. But that particular butchery was the wrong signal to send at the wrong time, for both the government and the Arts Council. They appeared ready, willing and able to sever a limb from the most renowned Muse in the land of Donne and Milton and John Locke.

ELEVEN

CULTURE, COST
AND CITY NEED

Prejudice apart, the game of push-pin is of equal value
with the arts and science of music and poetry. If the game
of push-pin furnish more pleasure, it is more valuable
than either. Everybody can play at push-pin; poetry and
music are relished by only a few.

Jeremy Bentham
the Utilitarian philosopher

By restricting funding, the government had effectively made it a
requirement of the Arts Council to seek money elsewhere if it
wanted to keep its present clients alive, let alone future ones. While
the local authorities were gingerly taking on more, the immediate
answer seemed to lie in business sponsorship particularly with the
appointment of Luke Rittner to become Secretary-General of the
Council. He had been highly effective during his seven years as
director of the Association for Business Sponsorship of the Arts
under the chairmanship of Lord Goodman, a time when he had
watched the policy of arts subsidy shift to the 'market ethic. We
created a perception of sponsorship', he has said, 'in some minds
bad, in some minds good. The left didn't like it, as it seemed a denial
of the welfare state. Those on the right saw it as a way to make the
arts stand on their own two feet. The centre saw it as a good new
support for the arts in difficult times.'

With an administration which believed in the market ethic and
efficiency, the arts were saved by proving that they were an industry.
In 1984, it was believed that the arts had a turnover in Britain of

some billion pounds without broadcasting and publishing. If these trades were added with ancillary economic benefits, the figure could rise as high as four billion pounds. The new perspective was summed up in a booklet called *Partnership: Making arts money work harder*, published by the Arts Council three years later. Its epigraph was written by Lord Rayner, who had been asked by the National Theatre to carry out a scrutiny as Clive Priestley had on two other companies in the 'Big Four' in order to prove that it was also worth its grant: 'Continuing government funding at or above its present level in real terms will be essential in order (for the nation) to obtain effective and full value from its investment.' This sentence implied that Congreve should be cost-efficient and Shakespeare subject to an audit from the revenue.

According to *Partnership*, the past forty years had seen 'a dramatic increase in activity and flowering of enterprise in the arts in Britain'. There had been greater increases in attendance and participation than at any time since the last century. Five new major dance companies and seven new opera companies had arisen, along with thirty new theatre buildings in England alone. There were now over three hundred arts centres, 'a completely new concept that provides a greenhouse for new talent and ideas'. But economics was the cause of this renaissance rather than genius:

> This expansion has led to the development of a vigorous new sector of the economy – the cultural industries – at a time when other, more traditional sectors have declined. At the root of these new industries is the imagination of our artists and the sense of excitement which their work generates. But equally important has been the valuable support for their work and the commitment to developing the arts from an increasingly wide range of organizations. This support has been led by local and national government, but increasingly also comes from business and commerce, education authorities, other national agencies, development corporations and enterprise boards, local and community organizations, trusts and foundations. All recognize the special contribution which the arts make, not only to the quality of life – giving each region, for example, its own sense of identity and boosting morale – but also in stimulating the economy.

The performing arts were now being called the cultural industries. The Muse was termed the machine. The thrust of the Council's policy was to prove that its costs justified the investment. 'Council research has shown that the real economic cost to the Government of financing the arts is substantially less than the actual value of the grant. Direct benefits from investment in the arts arise from the low costs of creating new jobs, from consequent savings in the costs of unemployment and from recycled tax. Indirect benefits result for education, broadcasting and tourism.' There was also a greater benefit to be had from increased government subsidy – social welfare and urban regeneration. 'The arts and associated industries can lead the way in finding a new role for inner cities; they can play a vital role in sustaining rural life and values; they can give a means of expression to many disadvantaged communities and the unemployed. However, for the arts to provide sufficient activities and product, to create those extra jobs and to compete efficiently for that extra free time new investment is needed.'

So the great divide was crossed. The artistic was the economic. The Muse could sit down with Mammon, inspiration was good business. The flaw in the argument was that the Arts Council was reducing itself to another government department. Its merit was that it was uniquely the judge of excellence and quality, while any accountant or civil servant could judge cost-efficiency. By seeming to endorse the drive from 10 Downing Street for 'accountability', the new 'buzzword' of the times, the Council made itself accountable as much as it made its clients. The quality and excellence of the arts could not be submitted to the slide-rule and the calculator. At the last resort, somebody had to have the courage to say what was good and bad for this company and the whole country, accountable or not for that choice which did not depend wholly upon cost. They had to contradict Jeremy Bentham and assert that poetry and music could be relished by the many, when they were made accessible, and that enjoying the arts was better than playing at push-pin – a game of the past.

Examples of partnership were given in the booklet of that name, which particularly stressed Lord Gowrie's Business Sponsorship Incentive Scheme, set up in 1984. An additional £6,300,000 had been given to the arts from corporate funds attracted by incentives of £2,300,000 from the Arts Council. But the aims of the listed partnership projects at Liverpool and Gateshead, Glasgow and Sheffield, Swansea and Nottingham, the South West and the

Medway towns, Stoke-on-Trent and St Andrews and Stirling, Bradford and Barnsley and Leeds, Lincolnshire and Humberside and the Forest of Dean, were not the spread of excellence, but social improvement. The purpose was to:

- bring new life to inner cities
- expand and develop the cultural industries and, consequently, the number of jobs
- improve the quality and quantity of arts provision outside central London
- help develop the skills and talents of ethnic minorities and other specific communities
- enhance the cultural and economic potential of rural areas.

Liverpool's 'Festival of Comedy', Glasgow's 'Mayfest' and Sheffield's 'Big Top' mixed the 'high' arts and street theatre in a carnival atmosphere. The Arts Council wished to help these fresh creative partnerships flourish by contributing to their health and growth in three main areas – marketing, planning and investment. It was setting up a new Marketing and Resources Department to develop projects, systems and networks. The Council was 'committed to redressing Britain's historical imbalance, both geographically and in terms of art form versus art form. The overview offered by the Council can, through careful planning and consultation, help to minimise distortions in the development of new facilities.'

Thus the Arts Council, with its new sociological jargon of 'cultural industries' and 'imbalance' and 'overview' meant to 'minimise distortions in the development of new facilities', appealed for more funding from the government, chiefly as another accountable agency of social welfare and urban regeneration. The packaging was becoming part of the content, the merchandising was the medium and the message. The very language of spreading the arts was declining from the biblical cadences of Sir W. E. Williams or the passionate lectures of Sir Roy Shaw into the vocabulary of graphs and spreadsheets and market surveys. These had been injected by the fresh intake of arts administrators, bred under the initiative of Tony Field in their polytechnic courses and taught the mid-Atlantic mish-mash, feared by Orwell in his novel 1984 and called 'newspeak'. One criticism of the Council at the time, *Saturday Night or Sunday Morning?*, quoted Luke Rittner with relish when he said that he had persuaded corporations to join in creative partnerships as a 'civilized vehicle for business activity'; also Anthony Black-stock's apologia for using the new economic slang, 'You have to talk to this government in a language it understands.'

The Arts Council often accused the purveyors of mass entertainment of setting their sights too low for their audience; but now its appeal for more subsidy on the grounds of cost and social welfare and urban renewal threatened to demean the level of government awareness of the value of the arts. Lord Gowrie had advised the Prime Minister against eliminating the Arts Council and its subsidy; his successor Richard Luce persuaded Mrs Thatcher after two years to increase the grant-in-aid. When he was appointed, he had said that he did not know much about the arts, to which the Prime Minister had replied, 'Jennie Lee didn't know much, but she did very well.' She wanted a Minister who took time and trouble over the job, which he did. It took him two years to make her forgive Sir Peter Hall's opposition to the government: after that, she agreed to increase the static grant-in-aid. 'But you had to see Margaret Thatcher on her own,' Richard Luce has said, 'particularly about the arts. Not in front of other people, or she would show off. Her psychology was all-important. She was very knowing and helpful at the right time in the right place.'

The new Minister was to serve as long as Jennie Lee had and to achieve good working relationships with Sir William Rees-Mogg and Luke Rittner, although he considered that they would not take enough 'harsh, difficult decisions – there had to be some casualties'. He was to give the Arts Council another push on the road to deconstruction and devolution by eventually commissioning the Wilding Report, which would come out strongly for the civil service strategy of regional control and the castration of the power of London. But he was a friend of all the arts, including prose and its concerns: he was the only Minister in this century to address the Royal Society of Literature. He did, however, continue the pressure on the Arts Council, which led to its new policy of creative partnerships with business as well as the local authorities. By 1986, Luce was using figures produced by the Association of Business Sponsorship for the Arts to show that industry was contributing some twenty million pounds annually. Of course, companies were able to set off their expenditure on sponsorship against tax, as Sir Roy Shaw pointed out, precisely because it was money spent in the Inland Revenue's terms 'wholly and exclusively for the purpose of trade'. Thus in sponsoring, most business firms were not acting beyond the call of duty, but were 'simply using a form of publicity and advertising that furthers their commercial interests'. Commercial sponsorship was also fickle and impermanent, usually for a single event; and it tended to play safe, putting its money on the known and the fashionable rather than the new and the experimental. It paid for cheap and good publicity.

And yet, business sponsorship was growing every year, beginning to match some grants from the Arts Council, not serving as the icing on the cake for many companies, but as the necessary bread and butter. To an older generation which had served on the Council, such as John Cruft, sponsorship remained a form of imperialism. 'You can't touch pitch without being defiled,' he has said. 'You can't have a free hand if you shake for the money.' Yet greater freedom for the artist and the artistic director had been exactly what Paul Channon had skilfully suggested in his address in 1982 at the Royal Academy dinner, saying, 'Philosophically and politically, I believe in a mixed economy. In the arts for the foreseeable future the public sector is likely to pay the lion's share. But the private sector has a crucial role to play. How dangerous it would be, how impossible for the rebel, how wrong, if the state were ever to become the sole supporter of the arts.'

Whatever the ideological argument, the Arts Council was being forced by seven years of government pressure down the slippery slope towards furthering regionalism and social welfare, industrial sponsorship and the business ethic in assessing artistic enterprises. Yet every move away from its significant purpose in its original Royal Charter, that of improving the standard of execution of the fine arts, only encouraged its enemies into a blitzkrieg. Nothing had been learned from the Munich Agreement: to appease only invited a more intemperate attack from the far right. The most extreme assault was Professor John Pick's diatribe of 1988 on 'Public Funding and the Arts' for the Adam Smith Institute's pamphlet, *The Art of the State*. Joined by Kingsley Amis, who declared that subsidy as such damaged art directly, Pick took the concessions and language recently employed by the Arts Council to placate the government as another step towards its self-destruction, which he advocated himself:

> One of the most wretched aspects of the arts bureaucracy under the Thatcher government has been the way in which it has sought to worm its way into government favour by adding another slimy layer of bureaucratic self-justification to its activities. It has retained all the old liberal stuff (belief in the 'arm's length' principle and so on) but has grafted on to it an aggregate of gritty 'arts as industry' talk. This comprises the following:
> a) the 'arts' have a 'welfare mentality' and must now move, with Arts Council guidance, into the real commercial world.
> b) The 'arts' must now, with Arts Council guidance, make good the shortfall in 'funding' through state-generated forms of industrial sponsorship.
> c) The 'arts' must think of themselves as a business and must collect business data and must market themselves accordingly.

Even the move of the Council into combating inner-city decay roused the ire of Professor Pick in another of his assaults, *The Arts in a State*. He was particularly incensed by a further document published by the Arts Council, *An Urban Renaissance*, for its jargon and wish to fit the arts into the Tory policy for reviving the inner cities. How could the arts be implanted into depressed areas to attract tourism and jobs? How could slums and closemouths be turned into theme parks? The document was a series of political signals, not a policy of 'developing a greater knowledge, understanding and practice' of the arts, as the Royal Charter had once required:

> A host of cant words (from the same dictionary that gives us 'enterprise' and 'development', 'access' and 'targeted') cascades towards us in a jumble of mixed metaphors:
> The arts create a climate of optimism – the 'can do' attitude essential in developing the 'enterprise culture' this government hopes to bring to deprived areas. Inner city economic stagnation is a downward spiral. Failure breeds on failure, people lose confidence in their ability to succeed and consequently their will to try. The arts provide a means of breaking this spiral and helping people believe in themselves and their community again.

While *The Arts in a State* was right to condemn the slang of sociology and business that was removing its old authority from the publications of the Arts Council, and also correct in discerning more political influence in decisions about the arts, it was wholly wrong in failing to see a future triumph of the Council in helping in the renaissance of the inner cities and the restoration of community pride. In Victorian times, the building of public libraries and museums had rescued the spawning cities of the industrial revolution such as Manchester and Bradford from factory grime and exploitation, from black chimney and low terrace house. Now that the tower block and the council estate were drawing away and deforming the energy of the urban dwellers, while the flight to the suburb was a verdict on the lack of opportunity of the city, the local authorities would find few small industries to replace the crumbling commercial giants which were shedding jobs and lurching towards ruin. The Black Country had flourished in the days of coal and steel: now a depressed area ran from the Humber to the Mersey. To revive civic confidence and to qualify for building grants from the government, the urban councils turned back to Victorian example and sought to establish 'cultural zones' in their cities as well as the 'enterprise zones' favoured by Tory economic policy. Previously the Arts Council had successfully established a national grid of major theatres in the country as well as five new dance and seven new opera companies. Now it would guide and aid in the spectacular flowering of the arts and community pride within the belly of the stranded behemoths of the industrial revolution, until Birmingham could boast the finest concert hall in the land and across the Channel, while Glasgow would become the chosen European City of Culture, following in the wake of Athens, Florence, Amsterdam, Berlin and Paris for one glorious year.

The first major challenge to the Arts Council in using the arts to revive the inner cities was the abolition of the Greater London Council and the five Metropolitan Counties by the Thatcher government. A major catastrophe threatened. In September 1985, the Council published a prospectus for the arts, *A Great British Success Story*, chiefly the work of Luke Rittner, who claimed that 'the arts are to tourism in Britain what the sun is to Spain'. Its managerial and economic language persuaded the government to increase abolition funding by nine million pounds, while the Regional Arts Associations were generally successful in persuading their local authorities to fill the gap in arts subsidy. The Council's annual report was right to praise the success of its staff in coping with this radical situation: 'A major crisis in the arts had been averted by an unprecedented exercise in partnership planning across the country undertaken under intense pressure. Despite highly publicized difficulties of timing over a dozen or so clients, of which Sadler's Wells Theatre was the most prominent, nearly 750 clients' future funding was successfully negotiated in the space of two and a half months.'

In London, the Arts Council was able to delegate responsibility for the South Bank complex, including the Hayward Gallery, to the South Bank Board. The Board was also charged with running the National Touring Exhibition Service and the Arts Council collection on behalf of the Council. Richard Pulford moved to serve as administrator to the Board under the chairmanship of Sir Ronald Grierson. Anthony Everitt became the new Deputy Secretary-General. The fresh policy directives saw to the launch of a 'Code of Practice' on Arts and Disability at the Whitechapel Arts Gallery and a five-point action plan on the ethnic minority arts, pledging a minimum of four per cent of the Council's expenditure to its development of Afro-Caribbean and Asian arts within another two years. The black artist and lecturer, Gavin Jantjes, was appointed to be a member of the Council by Richard Luce. 'I was quite shocked,' he has said. 'I knew it was a level of tokenism, but tokens must carry their weight.' He was made Chairman of a Monitoring Committee charged with writing a report, *Towards Cultural Diversity*. Bursaries were awarded to three young black administrators, who were attached for short periods of practical training to experienced arts managers. But there was to be no policy of giving subsidies to companies only if they employed a quota from the disabled or ethnic minorities. 'We don't need to use a mailed fist,' Jantjes has said. 'We don't need a confrontation. We want radical change by talking it through, company by company, department by department.'

The slow and diplomatic changes in the attitude of the Arts Council under government pressure and under the stewardship of Lord Rees-Mogg, who had now received a life peerage, were

summed up by him in his elegant and valedictory message in the
annual report of 1987–8 after his seven years in office, only equalled
by the long, significant and contrasted tenure of Lord Goodman.
'The Arts Council is in the business of patronage,' he declared, 'and I
hope that in my time it has learnt to avoid the arrogance of one kind
of patron (the aristocrat whose functions the Arts Council has now
in large part assumed) and to court the favour of quite another kind,
the citizen. We are coming to value the consumer's judgement as
highly as that of the official or the expert.' Here the outgoing
Chairman suggested that the Council might adopt as a motto the
lines written by Dr Johnson for the great actor Garrick:

> The drama's laws, the drama's patrons give,
> For we that live to please must please to live.

The Arts Council is proud of its traditional commitment to judgement by peers. Our panels, boards and committees are well stocked
with distinguished representatives from the arts professions. But
their advice, although essential, is not sufficient. The voice of the
public must also be given due weight. This is the fundamental reason
why I support the Council's objective to reduce the art world's
reliance on state subsidy and to lower the proportion (but not of
course the absolute amount) of grant to the overall turnover of arts
organizations; for the way in which the public discriminates is
through its willingness to pay for its pleasure.

Having accepted the consumer philosophy of the government,
Lord Rees-Mogg pointed out that the Arts Council had also
accepted the Tory drive for business efficiency:

The Arts Council as a bureaucracy is now in good shape to face the
challenge of the times. Although there is some streamlining still to do,
the reform of our organizational arrangements – and in particular the
formation of three new departments for Marketing, Film, Video and
Broadcasting and for Planning – has significantly increased our
effectiveness. The outcome has been a great release of energy. We are
moving forward on many fronts; a selection of recent initiatives
include a radical reform of the system of client evaluation; help for
ethnic minority arts; a code of practice on the arts and disability; the
development of incentive funding; the formation of an independent
drama production company, Upstart; the opening of our doors to the
arts of other nations.

Yet at the door of Hades, the threshold of departure, the Chairman of the Arts Council paused to express nostalgia for its founding purpose, at a time when it appeared to have accepted the money-changers' place in the temple. He wrote with regret and warning:

> Finally, those responsible for the distribution of public monies to the arts must never lose sight of the goal of *excellence*. The word fell into desuetude as the Arts Council, in collaboration with the Regional Arts Associations, developed policies which had the central aim of increasing the accessibility of the arts to all sorts and conditions of men and women. The Council was right to adopt this course, but must always take care not to be seen to abandon those on whose daring and skill – the painters, sculptors, actors, composers, film-makers, writers, musicians, dancers – the whole great enterprise of culture depends.

Yet he had been the author of the policy of moving the emphasis of the Arts Council towards the consumer away from the expert, towards the accountant at the cost of the artist. The success of Richard Luce, however, in persuading the Prime Minister to increase the grant-in-aid slightly and to resume three-year funding allowed the Council to rescue some of its direct subsidies to artists and its standards of excellence. As Luke Rittner reported, in addition to increases for the Regional Arts Associations and for Touring, an International Initiatives Fund had been started, largely to encourage the programme for ethnic minority arts, which had also received an improved allocation. Literature had been pulled back from the waste-paper basket and more money given to the new Film, Video and Broadcasting Department. But policy and planning were still the preoccupations of the Council, especially now that artistic enterprises could make projections on a triennial basis. Rittner hoped both the Council and its clients would be able to become more efficient as a result of the important innovation in long-term funding; and yet he conceded that fear was widespread about the commercial approach and appraisals of the officers of the Council:

> All this does mean that there is a lot of talk about measurable objectives, financial management, marketing, consultants and other subjects that are not generally associated with the arts or the Arts

Council. It has aroused worries about increased bureaucracy and less freedom for arts groups. We cannot dispel those fears overnight, but I hope that as long term planning becomes more and more part of our lives so the benefits that undoubtedly follow will become clear. The staff of the Council is watching as closely as anyone else to see that these initiatives help to improve the artistic life of the nation and not to impair it.

The new Marketing and Resources Department was making itself felt within and without the Council as the promoter of enterprise, partnership and efficiency in the arts. Its controller used the inimitable *patois* of his trade to proclaim the results, 'a redirection of energies into pro-active initiatives serving Council priorities, and a radical reorganization of the department into streamlined units covering marketing, communications, press office and information.' With the direct support of the Minister for the Arts, training courses for senior management and board members from visual arts organizations and from touring companies and venues were being developed 'to improve the understanding of the role of marketing, and to increase the support and resources which managers give to their marketing staff'. Internally, the officers of the Council's arts departments had to attend seminars in how to offer their clients marketing advice. A more recent initiative had been the Urban Renaissance campaign. 'This programme of meetings and presentation is already raising awareness among all those involved in inner city regeneration of the contribution which the arts can make – and are already making, thanks to the combined efforts of local authorities, Regional Arts Associations and developers all over the country.' A major boost in March was a speech by the Prime Minister, in which she described the arts as essential to the making of Britain's cities. 'The city was not a real true city, merely by industry and commerce and services. It was only a real true city when it also had libraries, art galleries, music, orchestras, choirs. You needed the whole of the arts to make cities.'

The successful theme of Urban Renaissance appeared to have led to more government funding, and so it was trumpeted in a special report prepared by a journalist from the *Sunday Times*. In the autumn of 1988, there were to be three major conferences on the subject of the arts as an engine for inner city regeneration. It was an idea that had come of age. A recent report from the Policy Studies

Institute had pointed out that the arts were as important to the nation's economy as the motor industry. 'A matching momentum has grown in the numbers of local economies keen to get in on the act, and to use the arts and related 'cultural industries' to boost their own, often ailing prospects.' Glasgow was hosting the largest conference on 'Arts and the Changing City' in preparation for its role as European City of Culture. 'Equally incongruous to outsiders, Bradford is forging ahead – or "Bouncing Back" as its own campaign would have it – with a policy to become a major tourist attraction and "City of Entertainment". Its impetus comes from the success of the National Museum of Photography, Film and Television and the restored Alhambra Theatre.' In Liverpool, the extension of the Tate Gallery in dockland had attracted three hundred thousand visitors in its first three months. 'Birmingham City Council is offering generous terms to have Sadler's Wells Royal Ballet as a permanent resident, and has continued to increase funding to the City of Birmingham Symphony Orchestra on the grounds that it is a standard-bearer for the city.' The Prime Minister herself had recognized the fresh civic feeling, when she had said: 'The spirit of community, the spirit of feeling that life is not whole unless the arts are part of it, is returning.' However, the vital role of local authorities had still to be recognized in this urban renaissance.

> One of the major lessons expected to come from the Glasgow conference, especially from the American experience, is that the 'vision' needed for successful regeneration must come from a local level, and involve an active partnership between the private sector and local government. The C.B.I. in its recent report, *Initiatives Beyond Charity*, also stresses this point ...
>
> Mrs Thatcher is fond of using Pittsburgh as a model for how things should be done here. But while its post-war transformation was originally inspired by local industrialists, it is an article of faith there that it would not have been possible without the involvement of the city authorities at every stage. A spokeswoman for the British American Arts Association said recently: 'People can use the American model. But if they do, then they should use it all.'

There was no question that the decaying industrial cities had now seized the banner of the arts to wave high. They would now compete with the Regional Arts Associations and the Arts Council in providing subsidies for local artistic enterprises. In the first five years of the nineteen-eighties the net revenue expenditure of the local authorities in England and Wales more than doubled to over a hundred million pounds and continued to increase, until it would overtake the static funding of the Arts Council. Economic power was shifting decisively outside London, at a time when the Council itself was trying to allocate more money and control to the Regional Arts Associations, particularly in the areas in which it felt most uneasy. 'Most of the Regional Arts Associations', the Council's report of 1985–86 declared, 'attach a high priority to schemes to develop photography, Black and Asian arts, education, community arts and arts centres and dance. The Council is happy to entrust a large responsibility for such development to the Associations.'

The Regional Director of the Arts Council, David Pratley, who had served on the Merseyside and Greater London Arts Associations, found a 'fascinating sea change' with the arrival of Lord Rees-Mogg and Luke Rittner. 'The agenda altered. We were no longer an advocate for the arts but an agency of government.' Under the stewardship of the new Chairman, however, the Arts Council did survive, while many other quangos did not. In some ways, it was a necessary accommodation, the price to pay for continuing existence. When Pratley had taken up his post in 1981 in Piccadilly, there had been a sense of mission, of expanding the consciousness of the Council in the regions, even of innovation. By the time he left five years later, he found the whole climate had changed. 'Rees-Mogg did want long-term thinking. But at the end of the day, there was a great mish-mash and no overview.' *The Glory of the Garden* was sold as a great regional document, but there was little to fund it. The important Housing the Arts programme was ended in the regions, while the government withdrew from subsidizing many galleries and theatres after the abolition of the Greater London Council and the metropolitan councils. To Pratley, the nineteen-eighties hardly seemed to progress: *The Glory of the Garden* achieved little except introspection and made people within the council think of strategy; the major internal reorganization unsettled the staff. Pratley took redundancy. The agenda of his Department had been set by the Chairman, his powers reduced in favour of the regions. 'Under Rees-Mogg,' Pratley has said, 'the arts community lost faith in the Arts Council itself, as somebody who understood its language.'

That was the issue that most concerned Christopher Gordon, then serving as the County Arts Officer in Hampshire, before taking up the post of Executive Officer of the Council of Regional Arts Associations. 'The corruption of language in the nineteen-eighties in the Rees-Mogg era', he has said, 'is something for which we continue to pay the price.' The emphasis in the arts on market forces rather than quality was lethal, as was the Chairman's refusal to devolve enough responsibility onto his officers, whose morale suffered. And even on regional policy, there was no consistency. Although Lord Rees-Mogg was converted to the devolutionary strategy of *The Glory of the Garden* by acquiescing in his Minister's policy, he did not receive matching funds from the Treasury, and so the change could not properly be implemented. In fact, according to Christopher Gordon, the Chairman ended by opposing the Regional Arts Associations for not being cost-effective and tried to slow the process of devolution, although it was almost too late, as was his coda on the importance of excellence in his final message from Piccadilly.

'Nothing came of *The Glory of the Garden*.' This same opinion was voiced by David Cargill, who joined the Board of the Arts Council as Chairman of the Eastern Arts Board. 'It was total disappointment, it meant nothing.' He had raised consciousness of the arts in East Anglia to seed the association from the grassroots, and he had used Cromwellian tactics to recruit his new model army on an anti-metropolitan platform. All the local artists were still attracted to the great wen. 'London draws off and sustains talent of all kinds,' he has said. 'Our association runs from Scunthorpe to Southend and does not sustain one resident professional author. Things have changed, but the system is still in place. The Arts Council has *not* altered fundamentally, nor seen the error of its ways.' Whatever progress was made seemed to Cargill to be one step forward, two steps back. The alterations in regional policy in the late nineteen-eighties appeared to him to be cosmetic and very much to please Richard Luce. 'We were Levellers, really!' he has said, but he could not achieve the level he wanted, even when he penetrated the walls of the metropolis.

Returning to the struggle, Robin Guthrie became Chairman of the Yorkshire Arts Association before taking up the post in 1987 of

Chairman of CORA, the Council of the Regional Arts Associations. The most formidable of all the advocates of decentralization, he thought that Richard Luce and the civil service 'had got it right. Devolution should be completed after fifteen years.' The quality of the Regional Associations would improve with more money and more power. 'If they only have crumbs from the Arts Council's table,' he has said privately, 'they will behave like dogs.' In his opening and significant speech to the CORA conference at Newcastle, Guthrie stressed that it was an 'embryonic national arts conference'. That year, the theme was 'the form of our support for the arts: the structures we have evolved and their relationship not only to the arts themselves but also to politics, to government, and with regard to resources of every kind.' While the Arts Council of Great Britain had brandished the regional ensign at Ilkley to rout Whitehall, Guthrie was trying to snatch the flag from such metropolitan fingers at Newcastle, where the true representatives of the country outside London were met to plan a national strategy. Richard Luce, reappointed Minister for the Arts after Mrs Thatcher's third election victory, was present to watch this strike for power at the expense of central control, and he was praised for his willingness to travel about the country in pursuit of the arts, which were dynamic and restless, as fleeting as any glimpse of beauty.

Art was said to be about 'the expression of feeling and the transformation of experience. As such it is universal, and inescapable.' Guthrie's aesthetics led to his politics. He quoted Raymond Williams on the dangers of separating art from ordinary life. 'We cannot isolate "reality" and set art in opposition to it; we cannot submit to be divided into "Aesthetic Man" and "Economic Man".' The artistic life of the nation did not lie solely in the 'cultural uplands', but in every aspect of life and at every level. Criteria were basically subjective. 'Whether it be a project in community writing in Taunton, or the Royal Ballet in the Big Top in Sheffield, or Gilbert & George at the Hayward, our judgements are essentially about these three basic elements: perception, interpretation, impact.' If such premises were accepted, the harsh counterpoint was softened of the old debate between excellence and access, 'raise or spread'. 'We have first to make judgements of quality, then of priority.'

None of this made art an easy bedfellow for politics. Artists and politicians were not natural partners. 'It is the temptation for a politician to harness art to the shafts of his own political cart, as it is for an artist to pretend he knows the answers.' The crucial choice in these matters was between the arm's length principle and direct government funding. That principle, anyway, was not universal in Britain. Local government supported the arts directly and now spent more than did central government. The Regional Arts Associations did not spend the local money; their job was to fuse central with local funds, and to promote the arts in every possible way. So they had to work with both systems, the direct and the indirect, at the two levels of operation. They accepted the dangers to any organization or activity where funds come from a single source. They had notable success in applying the principle of multiplication desired by the government, 'whereby every pound is turned into two pounds, three pounds or if possible five'.

Such arithmetic, however, with marketing and sponsorship could not replace basic funding. Priorities still had to be established. The Minister had already put Guthrie himself and two other regional representatives on the Arts Council in London to sit alongside the members from Scotland and Wales, and these appointments helped to resolve the difference in view between the regions and the metropolis. The limits – once the definition of the word 'culture' – still needed to be shifted. 'Local authorities, arts organizations and individuals continue to promote and support the arts in their areas. The boundary between the regional arts associations and the national bodies is where national and local interests meet and are negotiated.' In this single system, the differences between the parts and the whole had to be recognized. It was the view of the regional associations that 'the relationship with the activities and organiza-tions, part of whose support comes through the system with central funds – the "clients", in other words – is best performed at local level: that is where the best deals are struck; and that is where the control can be most effectively exercised.'

The Minister need not worry about 'full accountability'. The danger was rather the other way round. 'Too many developments take place at national level, and particularly in the metropolis, without sufficient regard to what else is happening up and down the country.' All major issues of national importance and significant local impact should receive the attention they needed at appropriate levels. 'Community art, having been promoted and then devolved by the Arts Council, has vanished from the scene of national policy-making and debate, as have arts centres, which are of increasing importance up and down the country.' Now Guthrie delivered the *coup de grâce* of the trained civil servant addressing the politician. 'I would welcome an external review of the system; some of the problems of transition derive from the fact that the last major review was confined, so far as it was in practice possible to do so, to the Arts Council alone: what is needed is a review of the system as a whole, including its relation to funding from other sources such as industry and the local authorities.' Art was too important to be dealt with partially or incompletely: no responsibilities could be neglected for reasons of inconvenience or difficulty or unpopularity.

Death by a thousand reviews was to be the dilatory fate of the Arts Council. The time-bomb commissioned by Richard Luce from the judicious Permanent Secretary Richard Wilding would reveal the long-term strategy of the civil service and the Conservative government for the future of arts subsidy. At the crude value of arts funding which Jennie Lee had demanded from Lord Goodman of 'how many votes?', the ballot boxes would be heavier for every pound spent and every decision made in the regions rather than in London. There was a harvest of Xs on paper to be reaped from nationwide urban renewal rather than a dearth from continuing metropolitan control. In his policy of devolution, Richard Luce was both pulling the shafts of his political cart and appealing to the aspirations of the regions in their historical revolt from London. Politics and arts subsidy for once appeared to saunter along hand in hand.

The attack of Robin Guthrie on the Arts Council for shedding its responsibilities for the growing movement in community arts and arts centres was just. In his time, Sir Roy Shaw had felt that the lobbies for community arts had been too assertive and 'did not care whether they produced a mule'. In *The Case for the Arts*, the Council member Harold Baldry had noticed the burgeoning of community arts and arts centres. While there were less than two hundred in 1981, the impact of increasing leisure would eventually create a thousand. 'The phenomenon is not especially British, but has happened in most developed countries throughout the world.'

The belated decision of the Arts Council, however, to return to maintaining its standards of excellence and to turn community arts and arts centres into local responsibilities was probably wise as a strategy for survival. These matters were best dealt with at the local level, as Robin Guthrie had demanded. But on other policies of social welfare for ethnic minorities and the disabled, the Arts Council could not devolve such problems of national concern. It could only address in a piecemeal way the queries put to the Chairman by the acute Sir Brian Young:

> How much of our concern is
> (a) with funding new work by ethnic artists
> (b) with introducing ethnic audiences to British culture
> (c) with ensuring that ethnic artists get a fair share of work inside existing organizations?

Predictably and tellingly, the new emphasis of the Arts Council on social welfare helped its funding from the government. The appointment of Sir Brian Rix to chair the Drama Panel and to sit on the Board was particularly significant. He had received no benefit from the Council during his many years as an actor manager in the theatre of comedy, but he was for personal reasons committed through the organization called MENCAP to the care of the disabled. His view was that the Arts Council was a charity: it could not take a political position, but it could take a social one. He was to encourage all subsidized drama companies to give access to their theatres to the disabled and to employ them. Of the half a million jobs in the arts, only a handful went to them. He saw his job as 'putting the handicapped into the arts' as much as guaranteeing the quality of performances. He had always thought that laughter from the audience was exactly the same, whether for his own Whitehall farces or for a National Theatre production of *Much Ado about Nothing*. And the appeal of his approach to politicians was obvious. 'With a full disability allowance,' he has said, 'with six to nine million votes, you would always be in government.'

As for ethnic minorities, the Council under Lord Rees-Mogg agreed to make an additional allocation of half a million pounds for 1988–89 to black arts, 'in recognition of the needs of black artists and arts organizations. This financial acknowledgement demonstrated the national significance of the Arts Council's role in providing a platform for black arts and has encouraged other Arts Council departments to identify their priorities and the development needs, for black projects.' Internally, 'racism awareness and cultural awareness training' was given to Arts Council staff and clients, and this educational programme was suggested to other public organizations such as the BBC and the British Film Institute. To Gavin Jantjes, this cause put the arts in front of society, which would only become aware of the need for black people's equality of opportunity, once they had broken through in the arts as they had in sports with Daley Thompson and in pop music, both of which were now called 'cultures'.

Ironically, the effort to adjust the balance in favour of discrimination against black artists nearly put to the torch the renascent Literature Department, which had also risen again from the ashes by espousing an element of current social thinking. Because of its destruction, Luke Rittner has said, 'I received more vitriol on that issue than any other.' With its rebirth, the three available annual bursaries for writers of five thousand pounds each were all given to black authors. The Equal Opportunities Commission supported the case of a white poet Fiona Pitt-Kethley that she had suffered reverse discrimination. The judge, however, unexpectedly found for the Arts Council's decision with a judgement of Solomon. As long as this was a *unique* response to the long exclusion of black writers from government subsidy, the Council was fulfilling its duty to redress that past unfairness, but it must do so only upon this single occasion.

Lord Rees-Mogg had justified the axe falling on the Literature Department because, as he has said, 'literature is so cheap to produce compared with the other arts'. Now his swan-song was to affirm the Council's 'commitment to the equality of literature as an art form within its remit. The Council has looked very searchingly at the role of literature within the arts and now takes a positive and optimistic view of it, aware of its particular value to the Council's educational and multi-cultural policies. Underlying this is a recognition that literature, past and contemporary, is one of the glories of the nation.' It had not been one of the Glories of the Garden. But a belated recognition of the necessity of books and the right words in education and 'multi-cultural policies' had led to a change in awareness. A resolute Literature Director, Dr Alastair Niven, dedicated to the revival of his Department, was appointed; he travelled the country and attended the triennial Conference on Commonwealth Literature. The new emphasis was on internationalism, education and social engineering:

> Plans were laid to establish a multi-cultural policy of support for literary activities, including a fund to assist published translations, backing for projects to extend reading opportunities for children, and a co-ordinating facility for writers' tours. A report on black and multi-cultural publishing was commissioned and steps were taken to introduce a positive policy of support for literature in education ... Much of the year was spent in re-establishing strong links with the Regional Arts Associations. The Director visited many parts of the country to see the range of literary activities – small press publishing, writers' groups, festivals, exhibitions, adult education classes, prison and community attachments, library schemes, etc. – which take place in most parts of Britain.

Although the budget for literature was still minimal, the reason given for its underfunding was the huge amount being spent on the new British Library – over five million pounds to date and still not completed. But the quality of the officers of the Department and the members of the Panel would be revived. Melvyn Bragg has testified to the efficiency and impartiality of the previous Literature Panel: 'It was a decent little system, the Panels, and allowed independence of mind. I never saw a corrupt decision – misguided or stupid, perhaps, but never partial. We felt we were the centre of the arts. We were important.' And under the reign of the new Chairman of the Panel, the writer and civil servant P. D. James, once again the excellence of literature would become paramount in discussion. For she disapproved of the new tendency towards social welfare and so she would create that dynamic tension within the Arts Council that led to its more creative choices. 'We live in a silly age of little enthusiasms', she has said. 'I don't understand why we concern ourselves about women in the arts, a department for this or that, disablement or ethnic minorities. Our concern should be literature.'

The concern for social engineering over the border was accepted by Timothy Mason, the new English Director of the Scottish Arts Council. An Ethnic Minority Arts Panel was created and a broad range of arts and disability projects were supported: all clients seeking funding were asked to submit a statement on what they had done to implement the code of practice on disability. Sponsorship had increased to nearly two million pounds, largely for use on Glasgow for its reign in 1990 as the designated European City of Culture. Yet Scotland was very effectively independent in the arts, although not officially so. There were various discussions on separation from England. The Chairman of the Scottish Arts Council, Sir Gerald Elliot, noted:

> This had been a strong probability at the time of the devolution debate in 1979, but afterwards it receded, though from time to time it was revived either because the civil servants concerned were keen or because we felt increasingly frustrated by our relationship with the Arts Council of Great Britain. This on the whole was good, but we found difficulty sometimes in getting a satisfactory settlement though on the whole we were treated fairly. We also found the management of the Arts Council of Great Britain very unsatisfactory and felt that we could run rather better independently.

The Scottish Chairman did not approve of the reorganization of the Arts Council in London because proper responsibility was still not given to the Committees and Panels, as it was in Scotland. And he would not accept the fatal devolvement of power to the Regional Arts Associations, which drained the parent body dry. Edinburgh remained the centre of the state arts subsidy for all Scotland. Sir Gerald Elliot even wrote to Lord Rees-Mogg, stating that the Regional Arts Associations ought to be abolished or replaced by regional arts councils or offices somewhat similar to the Scottish pattern. But the Associations were there to stay, he supposed, as a matter of practical politics. Yet:

> something clearly must be done to tidy up our relations with them. There is hostility on both sides. They claim that we are keeping from them money to which they have a self-evident right. We do not trust them enough to devolve more clients to them ... I feel that unless we are clear in our minds about a proper relationship and are firm in applying it, we risk giving up a great deal of authority which we are charged to exercise to hybrid bodies, of doubtful constitutional respectability, which were set up for an entirely different purpose.

In Wales, equally independent of London theoretically, three Regional Arts Associations were set up in a developing partnership, which increased the support for the arts of local authorities and universities: theatres or arts centres were provided and subsidized by the colleges in Aberystwyth, Bangor, Cardiff and Swansea. 'Yet despite the unprecedented level of support for the arts in Wales, from all sources,' Thomas Owen, the Director of the Welsh Arts Council, noted, 'we are dropping down the ladder rung by rung.' *Diwedd y gân yw'r geiniog* was a proverb that translated badly into English as 'the end of every song is money'. But worse new words and criteria had appeared. '*Cost-effectiveness* has entered arts jargon as a major disease, to join *de-selection*, the process by which the weakest clients are supposed to give up the ghost, bequeathing their grant to hungry siblings.' Luckily, the Goschen Formula, through which Wales received seven per cent of the budget of the whole Arts Council was being maintained, although the people living there were less than six per cent of the British population: there was also triennial funding, so forward planning could take place. But to keep things going, the Welsh Arts Council had committed all its reserves, so no cash was available for rescue operations, even for the Welsh National Opera. This commitment was based on the dictum of the founder of the Council. When Maynard Keynes had been Bursar of King's College, he had said, 'Cambridge Colleges should not be Savings Banks'. Need must be answered now.

The original generosity of the Arts Council of Great Britain to the two 'independent' regions under the Goschen Formula – twelve per cent of budget to Scotland, seven to Wales – three members out of twenty on the Council to Scotland, two to Wales – was now challenged by the English Regional Arts Associations with grants equivalent to population of far less and only three members on the Council between all ten of them. This inequity was admitted by Richard Pulford in a memorandum on 'The Regional Balance of Provision'. However loosely expressed, there was 'a population element in the grants to Scotland and [Wales] that does not go unnoticed in the English regions, all of which with the exception of London are on the face of it treated much less generously.' To the Finance Director in the headquarters at Piccadilly, the incursion of all the outlying organizations was a curse and a bore. 'The waste of energy in fighting the demands of the Regional Arts Associations was the failure of all concerned,' Anthony Blackstock has said. And as for the two 'independent' bodies, he stated, 'Any time you tried to do anything Scotland and Wales claimed their share of the money. It was galling. They were very good lobbyists, particularly the Welsh. The Scots paid the price for their splendid isolation.'

When the Arts Council finally came round to setting up a Film, Video and Broadcasting Panel and Department, it was forty years too late. The few arts films made and toured had suffered in the cuts of the early nineteen-eighties. As Sir Brian Young noted in a paper for the Council in 1984, there had been a serious loss of momentum in making arts films for the past two years. The preliminary allocation for the next year was 'clearly inadequate, except for a dying area of the Council's work'. A year later, however, there was a change of heart and the new Film, Video and Broadcasting Unit was introduced in the general reorganization, with five new films released and six new co-productions announced. Under a dynamic Department Director, Rodney Wilson, fresh policies were developed. He announced: 'One result, with far-reaching implications for the arts and broadcasting, is the principle now adopted by the Arts Council that grants to clients might be linked to a right of greater access for the public via broadcasting.' The shift towards independent production by the BBC and ITV had also created more opportunities for co-productions, as had connections with Europe. This had particularly applied to the extraordinary film of the artist Richard Long walking in the Sahara and making his sand prints and stone sculptures there.

Yet this initiative was whistling in the dark. Although Lord Rees-Mogg was also Vice-Chairman of the BBC, he could not arrange a coalescence in arts education between the two most important 'independent' bodies in the land. He found that the officers of the Corporation did not want to go 'out of house'. They had their own pride and practices and problems. They filmed the whole of Shakespeare's plays without the help of the National Theatre or the Royal Shakespeare Company. Their reason for being uncooperative was their troubles with the trade unions. However that was, the Chairman could not achieve the vital bonding between the two major state-funded organizations, charged with spreading British values and cultures across the country. Their ways remained apart, while new patrons were growing, who would control the communications that were in most homes and spoke directly to most consumers.

In a remarkable speech at the Barbican arts centre, the international film producer David Puttnam spelled out the nature of the new masters of education and the cultures of the world:

> In most instances they are the media empires and the multinational corporations. Every major film studio, every television network and – increasingly today – many of the major book publishers fall under this financial system. This must be qualified, and in part explained, by a sense of scale. Cinema, television, architecture, newspaper publishing, commercial theatre and much of today's literature are costly undertakings. More and more they fall only within the financial means of global baronies. Minnows can survive at the fringes, but the mainstream of almost any art or communication form today depends for its patronage on these baronies. In such a system, artistic freedom finds itself limited by, and frequently colliding with, primarily economic demands. As a result, its true purpose is diverted or degraded, usually by that corporate discipline uncomfortably known as the bottom line.

The old arts establishment had not opposed the growth of these great new patrons, who controlled the delivery systems. There was now a concentration of media power never before seen or even contemplated. A few multi-national baronies held many of the most popular means of communication. There was a new expansion of media ownership. The baronies of Murdoch and Bertelsmann grew and grew. This concentration of power overlapped into a concentration of the making and distribution of films. In America, even the marketing of books had become reliant on the commercial judgement of two chains of bookstores. One corporation in America, the General Electric Company, had an income in 1987 of forty billion dollars. Nine billion dollars came from defence contracts, three billion from the ownership of NBC, the most successful of America's three leading television channels. Before Ronald Reagan had become President of the United States, he had been a presenter of the General Electric Theatre and had used it as a platform for his political career. This terrible force among the barons of communications threatened to overwhelm the creative artists.

In Britain, there had been ample evidence of the relationship in the past between the quality of patronage and the quality of work, particularly when the BBC commissioned it. As the American critic and professor of jurisprudence, Ronald Dworkin, had written:

> Those who have loved Britain for its sense of community and political culture will love it less now ... artistic achievement has shifted in a direction all too familiar to Americans. Those aspects of high culture that depend on private patrons flourish ... but art of a more public character, much of that which requires direct or indirect government subsidy, has suffered ... and British public television, which made a distinct art form of that medium, has been forced into new economies and a new consciousness of ratings.

The patronage of a culture was no longer in the hands of the state or of people, but in the techniques of diffusion and those who controlled these mechanisms. By print and television and radio waves, by record and disc and tape, by film and photograph and photolithography, by word-processor and computer screen and print-out, sentences and sounds and images flooded the perceptions of the peoples of the world, and these were often called 'the arts' in the debased use of the term. Educational systems, universities and colleges and schools, museums and libraries and arts centres, also preached the signals of many cultures. The apparatus of diffusion was the triumph of the sciences. In Marshall McLuhan's phrase, the medium was the message. A century before, Berlioz had already warned against the overuse of music, which he thought might destroy the whole art by making the listener insensitive to it. As Jacques Barzun protested, there was too much to sort out, let alone assimilate. Technology had multiplied the product, and those who were once choosers and users had become helpless victims of the flood. The music of Vivaldi and Mozart was now piped and inescapable:

> There is also too much to see – type and colour and design – on the periodical page, the wall, the screen, the package, the morning mail. There are too many books, journals and reprints, newsletters, pamphlets and appeals, with graphs, photographs, illustrations, headings, diagrams, poems and prose. The Niagara of words is as inescapable as those other inflictions. Nothing ever gets less by reason of more bursting in another form; all merges together into a single medium with homogenized artistic properties, indistinguishable.

When there had been few patrons and guardians of culture, the old Roman question had been *Quis custodiet ipsos custodes?* Who is to guard those guardians? It was a fair question when there had been a consensual ruling class in Britain: before 1980, all seven Chairmen of the Arts Council had also served, often as chairmen, on the governing bodies of one or both of the national opera companies; nearly half of the trustees of the Tate Gallery had served on the Arts Council; of the first thirteen people who were either Chairman of the Arts Council or Minister for the Arts, eight were at school either at Eton or Winchester, the old royal charitable foundations. Now this ruling elite was losing its influence over national culture to multi-national media barons. In the age of communications, the question was *Quis mediat media?* Who is to mediate the media?

The Conservative government, dedicated to a free market, allowed conglomerates to bid for radio and television franchises, satellite broadcasting and cable television with only a rare reference to the Monopolies Commission. The self-regulating mechanism of the BBC was applied to the independent television companies. Lord Clark himself had served as the first Chairman of the Independent Television Authority at the same time as he was Chairman of the Arts Council. But such efforts to keep the spreading media under the control of the old ruling elite did not hold. The global distribution of films on videos and satellite television defied national means of regulation. The new media recognized no frontiers, and their few owners rarely did. The Australian Rupert Murdoch, who became the arbiter of mass communications in Britain, took up American citizenship to guard his communications empire over there. In film and television, video and the press, the international barons were the masters now.

Powerless to react to this global revolution in communications, the Arts Council recognized its ineffectiveness and dropped nearly all of the traditional areas in which it had intervened. The 'hands-on' principle was unloaded or consigned to the shredder. The Wigmore Hall had been administered by the Arts Council since 1946; but now this treasure of chamber music was transferred to the Westminster City Council. In the Visual Arts, the Serpentine Gallery was hived off to an independent trust, while the experienced Joanna

Drew, who 'accepted the logic of the situation', joined the South Bank centre, to which responsibility for the Council's exhibitions programmes had been transferred together with the management of the Council's collection. 'It was something of a traumatic move for staff', Luke Rittner admitted, '(more than half the Art Department left 105 Piccadilly) both for those making the move to the South Bank and for those left behind.' He then declared hopefully, 'The bonds are too long established and too strong to be broken by a mere change of policy and location and I am sure these bonds will form a strong foundation on which the new arrangements will operate. Future reports will cover the continued withdrawal from directly provided activities.'

Perhaps, in this new way of *not* doing things, the decision was correct. In the opinion of John Faulkner, the Arts Council was as adept at the 'hands-on' policy as Aeneas's helmsman Palinurus. They steered in the night, but look what happened to Palinurus, drowned off Italy. Yet in the opinion of Colin Nears, the Chairman of the Dance Panel throughout the nineteen-eighties, the 'hands-on' principle had been real and important at the beginning of the decade; but it was finished by 1990, when he eventually left the Council. The major internal reorganization had altered the funda-mental assessment process into a procedural policy to put more 'bums on seats'. He could not support the change, feeling himself to be a Keynesian, one of the old guard. He was equally unenthusiastic at the growing power of the local authorities, which insisted on an 'ethnic norm' in all dance companies. While he fought for modern and creative dance at every level, he would not tolerate 'a classical ballet with twenty-three white swans and one black'. He became tired of the endless negotiations about funding, the increased bureaucracy and the greater accountability. And so he departed, feeling that the Arts Council 'was losing its teeth and authority and excellence'.

This was the view of those who could not adapt. Rittner himself thought that he had inherited a disillusioned and frightened organization which felt alienated from the Tory trend of politics. Yet 'by traipsing the building', in the words of Jane Nicholas, 'he made himself acceptable to the staff, who had been wholly against his appointment.' She fought him against the policy of excluding departmental directors such as herself from the meetings of the Council, for then she could not 'fight her own corner' as she had done before. But to her, Rittner had made the best of things. As he said, he 'built a cohesive team and resurrected the family atmosphere', even though real power had been taken by the Chairman from the Secretary-General and the departmental directors, the Panels and the Committees by means of the new centralized administration.

In the same way that the processes of reorganization and education in social welfare and racial awareness put under strain and took up the time of the staff of the Council, so the new methods of the appraisal of client companies proved tiresome and sometimes unproductive. The smaller companies complained about the burden which was placed on a little organization trying to spend its days on artistic endeavour rather than accountability. All was worthwhile only if the grant was increased after the agonizing appraisal. But as the director of the Nottingham Playhouse said: 'I found it a very exciting process and we had a wonderful team but what I reach at the end of the day is – was it all worth it? We have a beautifully typed report containing endless things we want to take up and then we turn round and find we have a standstill grant.'

That was the crux of the crisis of arts subsidy and of confidence in the Arts Council in the nineteen-eighties. Standstill funding or worse had led to cuts and to the failure to support innovation. As the Earl of Harewood has said of arts subsidy in the Thatcher years, 'There were no candle-end savings, they were whole bloody candles.' To the regret of Tony Field, nothing had been done to safeguard clients when the golden days were over. Legally, money could not be withheld for spreading at a later date. 'Our system of cash accounting', Mary Endacott has said, 'meant that there was nothing to put aside for a rainy day.' As a consequence of the inability to keep funds in reserve from the good years, the Arts Council was blamed for the austerities of the lean times. 'For the first twenty-five years,' John Drummond has pointed out, 'the Arts Council largely said "Yes". For the past twenty years, it has been forced largely to say "No".' Thus it had to submit to the fire and wrath of the artistic community for this apparent failure to fight its corner against the Treasury and the various governments. The claim of independence invited the accusation of incompetence, however unjustified that was.

In his acute postscript on his life, *What I Came to Say*, Raymond Williams wrote of his three years of service at the Arts Council. He recognized that it had been formed by and had inherited not only different, but at times incompatible and even contradictory principles:

> With its 'semi-independent' status, with its members nominated by Ministers of the day, with its dependence on tight departmental negotiation and funding, it is not, indeed, in a good position for a fight. Yet because it is there, it is where the argument has to start. The Council are trustees not only for public money but for public policy in the arts. I say 'trustees', but the accent has only to be shifted a little, to 'trusties', to name the most obvious danger. Imprisoned by the most convenient but weakest definitions, locked in by their departmental sponsors and bankers, glancing nervously at the barons of the system who can make their term more comfortable, in any case pressed and hardworked and seeing trees much more often than the wood, they can indeed function as trusties, those other men in the middle, whom neither side respects.

The preservation of the 'semi-independent' status of the Arts Council was the achievement of Lord Rees-Mogg, who fought as Quintus Fabius Maximus had fought Hannibal – *Cunctator*, or the Great Delayer. Yet if he saved 105 Piccadilly as the Roman general had saved his city, he had done so by agreeing to the policies of the government. 'The Arts Council is always a part of social welfare', he has said. 'Like the National Health Service, it must spread, though not through an identical provision.' To him, the customers were more important than the artists. 'We had to concentrate on people who could enjoy the arts rather than on those who could produce it. I was always worried when we were subsidizing something which did not attract a reasonable audience.' These beliefs of the Chairman, however, were so sympathetic to government policy that they attracted the criticism of some members of the Council. 'Lord Rees-Mogg', Sir Brian Young has said, 'performed as a Second Oboe in the orchestra of the Establishment.' He was wholly responsible for the changes in the nature and administration of the Arts Council in the nineteen-eighties. 'He was quite the executive chairman, too dominant. If you were against him, he would move on with a bland remark and get what he wanted later.' In that way and in his time, Lord Rees-Mogg was accountable for what happened to the state arts subsidy. His was the glory of his garden.

A leading opponent of the Council, John Pick, now reckoned that 'accountable' had shifted its meaning. It now meant 'responsible to governments' rather than 'responsible for the allocation of government money'. There was a truth in this accusation; but in point of law and fact, the Council was still 'responsible for the allocation of government money' while only being 'responsible to governments' by listening to their wishes more closely in order to keep arts subsidies flowing towards the policies that Whitehall and the Ministers favoured. Only belatedly had the Thatcher administration discovered that there were votes in urban regeneration, and if the Arts Council jumped on that helter-skelter, it was successful enough to shake out more cash in order to compensate for the jolts of passage.

Professor Pick was more on target when he stated that governments could take over Arts Councils by the simple change of personnel, but the more insidious way was to change the language in which the rulers and the Councils and the clients addressed each other:

> The key shift has been to describe the arts no longer in their traditional language which includes aesthetic judgement, private satisfactions and spiritual benefit, but as a purely commercial entity, to be justified by its economic benefit. Criticism, arts education and cost benefit analysis have in their different realms been replaced by Economic Experts, Management Training and Market Reportage ...

Although Pick himself would become responsible for training the coming generation of arts administrators in a department of the new City University, he was aware of their failings:

> Arts bureaucrats – in this instance those who one way and another administer the public funds which are ostensibly set aside to support the arts, – have, sometimes willingly and sometimes not, come to adopt this kind of managerial language over the last ten years or so on a surprisingly wide scale. Art depends, not on genius, but *marketing* for its effect. Art markets do not depend on people voluntarily paying, but on a much more political notion, getting *funding*. The world of business – stock market speculation, property values,

insurance and so on – is the *real world*. Beethoven, Dante and Shakespeare are unreal. Arts bureaucrats must now set themselves management objectives and be *appraised*, aiming of course always to achieve *efficiency* in their use of physical and financial *resources*, and aiming to achieve *optimum production levels*. Once this kind of language is adopted, then there is little need to agonize over any precise formulation of government intentions towards the arts. For the arts bureaucrats the language *is* the policy.

In its reports and speeches, the Arts Council did appear to be leaving the temple for the market-place. It may have been a necessary strategy for survival in a decade of government emphasis on the commercial rather than the spiritual. Yet the arts were no longer praised for their abiding value to every citizen in the land, but for their effects in reviving the inner cities or attracting tourists, in filling up leisure or stimulating the economy. And in adopting the chosen language of government, as well as in failing to influence the new and dominant communications systems, the Arts Council was condemning itself to appearing to be another arm of Whitehall, which had lost its length and its principle. More and more voices were being raised for the formation of a Ministry of Culture and Communications with the old powers of the central Arts Council devolved to the regions. To these critics, its role appeared archaic and ineffectual.

Yet the Arts Council had evolved from a unique and organic growth. Generally, it had performed splendidly with thousands of staff and Panel members working assiduously to administer the given arts subsidy on low or no wages. Like the Chevalier, it had been almost *sans peur et sans reproche*. It was frightened now, however, as the chorus of reproach sounded more cruelly. Its survival, curiously enough, depended on the divisions of Whitehall, just as its destruction was one of the ambitions of the civil service. Many Ministers of the Arts had tried and failed to take other departments under their wing, particularly the responsibility for broadcasting from the Home Office. Lord Jenkins had tried and been rebuffed; so had Richard Luce, who wanted heritage and art exports. In Paul Channon's opinion, the change to a Ministry of Culture was unlikely. 'Only a determined Prime Minister in his first year of office could change the structure of the arts.' By his judgement, Edward Heath alone had been interested enough in the arts to alter the system; but he had not done it when in Downing Street. Lord Gowrie thought the arts would achieve a bigger subsidy if they were represented by an Assistant Treasury Minister, while Richard Luce joked that they would get the largest grant if they came under the War Office. With so many government departments responsible for administering parts of the arts subsidy for the many cultures in Britain, nobody could foresee at the end of the nineteen-eighties any real change in the way things were.

Thus the Arts Council had made its way forward to an honourable, but choppy mooring. If it had sailed with the tide, it had survived the undertow. It had justified the verdict of Hugh Jenkins, speaking in 1971 in the House of Commons:

> It is not for me to say that the Arts Council is perfect. That would not be true. It can be said, however, that, within limits of human fallibility Britain has evolved a way of supporting the arts which some study has persuaded me has considerable advantages over other systems that I have examined in various parts of the world. Its continued success depends upon the preservation of a series of understandings which have been built up and maintained under successive Governments. Whoever undermines those understandings will not be doing the nation a service.

TWELVE

HOLDING ON

You ask me, what is the purpose of art? I can only reply, what is the purpose of love?

Lord Clark, 1977

To the authors of *Saturday Night or Sunday Morning?*, four different strands combined to inform the thinking of the Arts Council at the end of the nineteen-eighties. There was the 'trickle down theory', enunciated by a civil servant at the beginning of the nineteenth century – 'a drop in the ocean of our expenditure would sufficiently impregnate the powers of taste, in a country nationally prolific in every department of genius'. There was the Council's commitment to professional performances and its bias against amateur activities. An assumption that 'high art' was the moral and spiritual treasury of the nation was complemented by a revulsion against money. The founder of the Council, Lord Keynes, had wanted to protect the arts from the effects of commerce, and he had believed that an increased audience for them would make them self-sufficient. The puritan influence of the followers of the literary critic F. R. Leavis and his disciples had influenced a generation into a Manichean division of culture – mass culture, which was low and commercial and often based on electronics, and minority culture, which was high and unaffected by new technology and set in theatres and concert-halls, galleries and libraries. As John Cruft, the former Music Director of the Arts Council, has said, 'My firm belief is that the downfall of culture in this country comes from the introduction of commercial television, which has debased it ever since.'

Lord Goodman had represented the last of the Keynesian

tradition in the Council, the commitment to professional excellence and spreading that to the masses. When he stepped down from the Chair of the Association for Business Sponsorship of the Arts, he recalled with regret 'the glorious days of my friend Lady Lee, whose impeccable concern for political impartiality in relation to the arts existed in a totally different climate of opinion'. He now accused the Thatcher government of letting politicians influence senior arts appointments. He thought the Arts Council to be:

> one of the more important innovations this country has made. It has succeeded in something which most countries do not even try to do – to put an institution between Government and the arts which until recently was non-political. It would be asking too much of this Government to observe anything like that. Since this Government believes anything remotely progressive in politics has to be stamped out – this is an article of faith with them – it would have been too much to expect them to keep the Arts Council immune from this.

Lord Rees-Mogg, himself due to step down as Chairman of the Council in March 1989, was irritated by this implied criticism. He had had no formal connection with the Conservative party for over twenty years. 'I regarded myself', he said, 'at the time of my initial appointment as at least as politically independent as Arnold Goodman was when he was appointed. He was, after all, solicitor to Hugh Gaitskell, when Leader of the Opposition, and to Harold Wilson at the time of his appointment. He was highly acceptable to the Labour party.' Lord Rees-Mogg did not believe there had been any political bias in appointments or otherwise in his time in office.

To an acute contemporary observer, Bryan Appleyard, writing 'Help yourselves' for *The Times*, the decade of the Thatcher government had opposed government subsidy in general because it was a denial of the new Tory ideal of self-help. The effects on the arts institutions had been obvious:

> As in so many areas, Mrs Thatcher has been shameless about filling key posts with her placemen. As a result, the Arts Council, under Lord Rees-Mogg and Luke Rittner, has changed as radically as the most rabid New Rightist could have wished. Their three-year plan for 1988–91 effectively, and probably finally, overthrows the old Arts Council identity as defined by its founder, Lord Keynes, and perpetuated by its former chairman, Lord Goodman – the posture of

the mandarin dispenser of improving culture to the masses. Rees-Mogg and his successor, Peter Palumbo, see a more functional entrepreneurial role for the Council.

The new Chairman of the Arts Council, however, was of a very different stamp to the former editor of *The Times*. Passionately concerned about architecture in all ages and avant-garde art, Peter Palumbo was a property developer, with a prosperous business which he had inherited from his father. A believer in private patronage as well as state subsidy for the arts, he had made the most appropriate marriage of ancient and modern in the City of London when he commissioned a circular Henry Moore altar for Wren's rotunda church of St Stephen, Walbrook. So perfect was the sculpted stone in its setting under the small dome that Mrs Thatcher herself commented that the Jacobean church seemed to have been built for the round altar. The Moore masterpiece was originally turned down by the Chancellor of the Diocese, but Palumbo had fought it through, summoning an obscure ecclesiastical convocation, the Court of Ecclesiastical Causes Reserved, to win his battle. 'One doesn't achieve anything,' he has said, 'without taking risks.'

The new Chairman praised his predecessor in saying that the job of the Council was to provide the best for the most. Britain's entry into the single European market would open up untold opportunities for cross-fertilization in the arts, in which Britain already excelled in depth of excellence. In purely economic terms, there should be an increase in the annual twelve billion pounds of turnover achieved by the arts in their widest sense, while the arts themselves were crucial in their contribution to the quality of life and to the regeneration of the inner cities. And here Palumbo struck a note which would have touched a chord in Lord Goodman and the old school. 'The Arts Council is not here to be served by the arts', he declared, 'it is here to serve the arts. It is here to speak for artists and art organizations, wherever they may be situated in Great Britain.' The yardstick would be excellence and potential excellence within the resources of a given art form. 'It springs up in many places. It is however essential. I can see no justification in spending taxpayers' money in order to celebrate the second rate.'

The new Chairman believed that the arts in Great Britain were the victim of their own success. 'The explosion of talent, the scale of activity, the craving by the general public for arts of all kinds has led to an increase in demand which the available resources from the public and private sectors are not yet able to satisfy.' Yet there was too little private subsidy in the field. The British had largely abandoned individual giving, although nine-tenths of arts funding came from the private sector in the United States. The mantle of the great patrons of the eighteenth and nineteenth century should be revived to supplement the public sector. Those who could, were artists: those who couldn't, could still be patrons. And here Palumbo sounded the clarion call of his personal crusade. In less than eleven years, there would be the advent of the new millennium, an event of profound symbolic significance. 'I regard it as some great national marker', he wrote, 'towards which we should be directing collectively all our efforts and attention so that when the second hand ticks past midnight into the 21st century our house is in order, socially, economically, culturally and in terms of world stability.'

This trumpet blast for supporting excellence and preparing for the coming of the Year 2000 after the birth of Christ was ensnared by two government investigations. The Minister Richard Luce had commissioned his Permanent Secretary of the Office of Arts and Libraries, Richard Wilding, to go back to the drawing-board to examine the structures of administering arts funding; he found 'great difficulty in dealing with the random list of what the Arts Council kept'. The National Audit Office, which was responsible to the Public Accounts Committee of Parliament, was also examining the Arts Council as well as the four national companies and four representative Regional Arts Associations to see whether the Exchequer was getting value for money. The double threat of devolution into extinction and of direct Treasury funding of excellence in the performing arts once again hung over the Chairman's head. Yet as he knew, the secret of any resistance to change as well as to implementing change was expansion. More money was needed to finance the troops in the trenches as well as the cavalry charge.

While waiting for the new exercises in dissection, Palumbo created his methods of administration, based on his business experience. He had been warned on taking up office by Lord Goodman that his was, 'in some ways, an absolutely horrible job.

Great numbers of people are in quest of sums large and small which would require a bottomless purse to satisfy ... There are few less enviable jobs than confronting virtuous claims with a firm refusal.' Mrs Thatcher was said to have answered Richard Luce's avowal that he was ignorant of the arts with the response, 'Yes, but you say "No" so nicely.' The officers of the Council were practised in exquisite denial as an art form in itself. 'What you have to do in this business is to know how to tell people No –' John Denison has said, 'but they must not realise it until they have walked out of the building.' Giving too little to too many was more delicate than the miracle of the loaves and the fishes.

Disliking controversy and seeking quicker decisions, the new Chairman diminished the number of those attending Council meetings by withdrawing invitations to do so. He was very much an everyday executive Chairman, running the structure developed over forty-five years and still developing with ever more frequent restructuring. A booklet was put out to explain 'How the Arts Council Works'. It was the major channel for public funding of the arts, amounting to £155,000,000 in the first year of this Chairmanship. The Scottish and Welsh Arts Councils, the twelve Regional Arts Associations, and a portfolio of arts organizations and projects functioned independently of the main Council, which was divided into three parts like Caesar's Gaul. Firstly, the Council itself, consisting of the Chairman and nineteen other unpaid members; they were the governing body. Their responsibilities were constitutionally comprehensive; their chief functions were 'to set overall policy, to determine the broad allocation of the Government's Grant-in-Aid, and to guide the operations and activities of its advisory bodies and officers.'

After the members of the Council stood the executive organization, split also into three divisions:

> Firstly, the arts division, with departments for Dance, Drama, Film, Video & Broadcasting, Literature, Music, Touring and Visual Arts. Secondly, the services division, comprising Administration, Incentive Funding, Marketing & Resources, Personnel & Training, and Planning & Development. Thirdly, there is the Finance division ... The chief executive of the Council is the Secretary-General, who is appointed by the Council with the approval of the Minister for the Arts. He is the Accounting Officer to Parliament for all the Council's

expenditure and the Directors of the Scottish and Welsh Arts Councils report to him. He heads the Management Team, which meets as Management Directorate once a fortnight and is responsible for the day-to-day running of the Council's business. In addition there is a small Secretariat.

The Council was also served by advisory Panels of some sixteen members for each specialist arts Department and by advisory Boards for the Touring and Planning and Development Departments:

There are also smaller committees, with more limited functions, attached to the Panels and Boards, and an advisory group for the Photography unit within the Visual Arts Department ... The Panels and Boards have two chief functions: to advise the Council on its overall policy in their fields and to advise on the broad allocation of grants in those fields, especially the grants to revenue and annual clients and the division of the budget between annual client grants and project grants. Panels and Boards advise the Council on the determination of policy and the awarding of client grant.

As for the smaller committees of some eight to twelve members, they advised in detail on the individual applications for project grants and awards made by the Council:

Each of those committees reports to its parent Panel or Board. There are in addition, however, three committees which report directly to the Council. Two are composed of Council members and are, in effect, standing committees of the Council: the Vice-Chairman's Committee considers every nomination that reaches the Council, from whatever source, for appointment to Panels, Boards and committees and makes its recommendations to the Council; the Policy and Finance Committee acts as a steering committee and gives preliminary consideration to appropriate matters on the Council's agenda. The other committee which reports directly to the Council, consisting of members appointed from outside but chaired by Council members, is the Arts and Disability Monitoring Committee, whose function is to monitor the implementation of the Council's action plans in this area.

Such was the structure of the Arts Council, now under scrutiny by Richard Wilding and the National Audit Office. There was little that Palumbo could do to alter things until he knew of the results of these inquiries, except to arrange a change of premises from 105

Piccadilly to 14 Great Peter Street, once the home of The Society for the Propagation of the Gospel in Foreign Parts and much nearer the centres of power in the House of Commons and Whitehall. He travelled to the country to listen to what people in the arts felt, before alterations were made. 'Palumbo actually likes the arts and supports the client,' Peter Jonas, the Director of the English National Opera, said of him. 'He listens. He is an enthusiast. He is an advocate rather than a messenger of government policies. It is a complete contrast to the ascetic and acerbic presence of his predecessor.' Palumbo himself found the translation from running a private business to a highly bureaucratic system 'a culture shock'. But he was becoming rapidly used to it.

The Wilding Report, 'Supporting the Arts', sought to give more power to the regions. And it pre-empted an unflattering report from the National Audit Office, which was prevented from examining the national companies by the Arts Council: because changes were being made, the initial and damning civil service cost analysis was modified. Yet Wilding's own recommendations did not pass the scrutiny of his Minister. He wanted the twelve Regional Arts Associations to be reduced to seven Boards while Luce chose only to bring the number down to ten. Wilding wished the regions to be given a say in the funding of the many distinguished arts companies located in their areas, which had previously looked to London for their grants. A smaller portfolio of strategic clients, perhaps in the twenties, would remain the sole responsibility of the Council. Yet if the new regional Boards might lead in policy, their decisions would still need the approval of the Council, which would retain a fingerhold where it once had a total grasp. Indeed, Wilding had recognized the fault line of the regional arts bodies without seeing the political reality. He suggested that the new Boards should not be appointed by the local authorities, but a third of their members by the Arts Council, which should also approve their Chairmen, who should all sit on the Council. As for the enfeebled centre in London, it would remain an advocate of the arts, a forum for debate and a body for long-term planning. It should also take over responsibility for the Crafts Council and for creative filming and arts programmes on television. Reduced but still somewhat responsible, it should survive.

The Minister, though, could not accept the report in detail. The lobby for the independent Crafts Council was too strong to defy. And as for barring local councillors from the Chairmanship of the Arts Boards, that was impossible. Only five of the Chairmen would be represented on the Council in London, but the local authorities would have a greater representation on the regional Boards, because their funding of the arts was increasing. 'Luce was absolutely right', in the opinion of Jack Phipps, 'and the Wilding Report a disaster. The local authorities were the natural partners of the Arts Council, not the regional associations or Boards.' As for the amount of clients that the Council kept, Luce thought, that was a matter for the new structure which would be created over the next three years, but these might amount to little more than the flagship national companies. The Council appeared to be turned, in Joan Bakewell's words in the *Sunday Times*, 'into little more than an advertising agency with the grandiose-sounding but hollow task of creating an overall national arts strategy, of promoting and marketing the arts, raising sponsorship, holding conferences and, of course, lobbying for the Famous Five'.

She went on to ask.

> Why are arts people not up in arms at the gutting of this national institution? The Arts Council has in recent years alienated many people – including me – by its more tendentious peripheral activities. To others it is already discredited as a stronghold of Tory appointees. Yet it is an institution we love to hate. It was born in the late 'forties at the time of hope in the belief that cultural riches belong to all. It has stood for national standards of excellence, often kept the weak from going to the wall, promoted initiatives in black and avant-garde art and generally been the envy of civilized nations who wished they had the same. Such a legacy is not lightly to be set aside.

As always, the threat to the Arts Council converted many of its critics. Impending destruction clears the air wonderfully. The Council was actually an enviable institution that the arts community hated to love. Its long service for the standards of excellence was to be its salvation. The Minister for the Arts, Richard Luce, had underestimated the quiet tenacity and patient diplomacy of Peter Palumbo. These qualities should have been obvious from his twenty-year struggle to build a modern block designed by Mies van der Rohe and then James Stirling near to the Mansion House and the Bank of England. He would never give up, even though court decisions went against him and the Prince of Wales derided the scheme as a nineteen-thirties' wireless set. 'God bless the Prince of Wales,' Palumbo said, 'but God save us from his architectural opinions'. Now he would have to fight for the future of the Arts Council, trying to claw back so much that was being stripped off.

The first casualty of the campaign was Luke Rittner, the Secretary-General. He felt that if Richard Luce's proposals were adopted, the Arts Council could not survive. If there were to be changes in structure, they must be overseen by him, not by Timothy Mason, the Director of the Scottish Arts Council, who had been selected by the Minister to guide the devolution through. It was an erosion of the arm's length principle. Equally, he could not accept the shedding of more staff in a streamlined organization. He could not implement the required changes. 'We were doing what the government told us', he has said. 'I fundamentally disagreed with the course. I was being ignored in decision-making, yet leaving was the most heart-breaking thing I have ever decided.'

As with the Minister, so with the Secretary-General: they underestimated the staying power of the new Chairman, who for the first time in the Council's history picked the Deputy Secretary-General to succeed to the premier role. Anthony Everitt was an arts journalist for the *Financial Times* before becoming the arts editor of the *Birmingham Post*. He went on to become the Director of the East Midlands Arts Association before progressing to London to become Rittner's administrative second string. He shared in the old belief of Sir W. E. Williams and Sir Roy Shaw in democratic centralism rather than devolution. For him, the Regional Arts Boards might run the community arts, 'a thorn in the foot of the Arts Council', which should still maintain all of its far-flung centres of excellence and apply standards and accountability. All, in the end, was a matter of demarcation. He equally supported the arm's length principle and the old Housing the Arts programme, which the new Chairman wanted to revive on the long march towards the millennium.

This was a fortunate meeting of minds on the part of the new

Secretary-General, who read the quiet determination of his Chairman better than his predecessor had. After all, Palumbo had been appointed for five years, and it was likely that he would see out the present Minister for the Arts and his policies, along with the Prime Minister herself. Actually, Palumbo invited Mrs Thatcher to the headquarters of the Council: it was the first visit of any Prime Minister to that sanctuary. In a debate in the House of Lords, fearful that the arts institution was becoming an obsolete instrument of government, Lord Hutchinson held aloft a photograph of the Prime Minister and the Chairman at Great Peter Street and asked if this demonstrated the arm's length principle. It was excessive of him; they were hardly holding hands. To Lord Gibson, the many stakes were now too high to remain at full arm's length; this reach depended on small budgets to discourage government interference. But the Arts Council was still worth retaining. 'Some independence is better than none.'

The apparent agreement between the government and the Arts Council over devolution and the regeneration of the inner cities produced a windfall for the arts, strapped down to allocations below the rate of inflation by the first of the three-year funding plans. Richard Luce kept on hammering at the door of Norman Lamont, then Chief Secretary to the Treasury, asking to re-open negotiations. Most of the national companies were in deficit, while the state of the museums was parlous. Five meetings with the Treasury took place; Luce described them as 'prolonged and intensive'. At the last two meetings, only Lamont and Luce were present. As one civil servant commented, 'it was clearly a political issue rather than one of financial need that decided the day, and in the end, Luce won.'

His victory meant an additional £40,000,000 for the arts, an increase of nearly thirteen per cent for the next year. Half of that increase was to go to museums for vital repairs and running costs, half to the Arts Council to spend at its discretion. At its conference at Leeds Castle, the Council put aside its hit list of forty bodies. Palumbo recognized the achievement of the Minister with a comparison of the generosity of the British state and that of ancient Egypt. 'One thing is certain: governments are judged by history for the contribution that they have made to civilized life.' The additional £20,000,000 showed the government's eventual determination to support the arts at a time of temporary restraint. 'The sweet smile of reason has prevailed.'

The patient diplomacy of Luce and Palumbo had, in fact, prevailed. As Luce said, 'a quiet revolution' was under way. 'Millions more people are taking to the arts and heritage.' In fact, the quiet revolution in government subsidy had been the work of himself and the Chairman of the Arts Council. He had been warned when he had taken over the office of Minister for the Arts. 'Indeed, one predecessor said each Minister is crucified by the arts world while in the job and promptly becomes a saint and martyr in departure.' Certainly, the perennial critics of arts policy, such as Sir Peter Hall, could see little benefit in the brave new world of Luce and Palumbo. He thought that the Arts Council was in its last years 'because it's been discredited in the arts community, because it has become an instrument of government and because it hasn't had the resources to do the job. Now it's going to have no role at all except perhaps an advisory one after the event.'

As so often happened, Hall's theatrical genius was matched by his political intemperance. Palumbo appeared to accept the policy of the government and the Minister, while keeping the whip hand in the Arts Council and claiming a new empire for it. A devolution to the Regional Arts Boards might be inescapable, but it would depend crucially on the factor of accountability to the central Council, which would assess as well as formulate a national strategy. 'The Arts Council remains the principal champion of the arts in negotiating central government funding, and also remains responsible for the great flagship national companies, and for others outside London as well as touring and innovation.' Yet architecture should now join the province of the Council, which would quantify necessary repair and building projects, in order to construct a policy for the cultural fabric of the nation for completion by the millennium. It was nonsense that architecture was not admitted as an art form, and a department would be established for it within the Council. Finally, the year 2000 should be designated the Year of the Artist, 'as homage to, and official acknowledgement of, the crucial role that artists play in society'.

In the nature of British bureaucracy, no department may poach from another without the blessing of the Prime Minister. English Heritage, which had formerly been the Historic Buildings and Monuments Commission for England, was responsible to the Department of the Environment and took badly to the Palumbo initiative. A spokeswoman declared, 'while we welcome any interest in the state of this country's historic buildings, as the public body responsible for funding the repair of our built heritage, we would, of course, expect the Arts Council to come and consult with us over any ideas they may have.' There had been no consultation. Only a marker buoy had been floated. And yet it was to be a signal for a new kind of Ministry that would combine the arts and the national heritage and many other forms of the disparate cultures of the country in the years to come.

To the lips of the regions, the Luce policy of devolution was milk and honey. The Director of the Council of Regional Arts Associations, Christopher Gordon, declared: 'Our long-term aim has been to get more money to the regions so that decisions can be made by the people on the ground. We welcome the changes. Luce has listened. There will be greater efficiency and cost-effective funding of the arts.' But this would not be the case. Unless the Arts Council were to be abolished, there would only be more expensive bureaucracy across the country. And yet some of the regional executives looked forward to that break-up. It would release many of the metropolitan staff to their bailiwicks. The complaint had long been that the arts in London attracted a better quality of administrator at a higher rate of pay. These people, too, could be devolved to beef up the regions. David Cargill of the Eastern Arts Association even compared the future of arts subsidy in Britain to the collapse of the Soviet Union and the end of central control for the good of all.

The Arts Council, however, would remain true to its word in supporting some devolution and the campaign for the arts to regenerate urban decay. In 1990, the success of Glasgow as the European Capital of Culture of the year seemed to herald the new state artistic policy. The Scottish city declared that it would hold a festival all year round and stage two thousand happenings. It would spend over £30,000,000 mainly on what one London critic called 'using culture creatively as a loss leader for economic rejuvenation. In its post-industrial age, Glasgow was too poor to knock down all its Victorian remnants so that now it is, comparatively, a treasure trove of great buildings and is using them as the main framework for the year's events.'

The occasion, however, was defiantly local rather than international. 'Glasgow writes its own rules', said Pat Lally, the leader of the district council, 'and this is an opportunity for the city and Scotland as a whole. We are not doing what other cultural mandarins in Britain might think obligatory for a cultural city programme. We must be faithful to the city's identity and to artistic integrity.' In spite of such determined parochial nationalism, Anthony Everitt stressed in his opening remarks as Secretary-General of the London Council that Glasgow was leading a renaissance of the arts in Britain, and that the programme of events – for quality, diversity and number – far outclassed its predecessors at Florence, Berlin, Amsterdam and Paris.

The Chairman in London saw Birmingham as the first 'millennium city of culture' out of many. As he prophesied, 'The theme would be music, and with each city for each year there would be a different theme – it might be photography in Bradford one year, dance in Halifax in another, and film rock music and so on at other times. All the arts in Birmingham would take part. There is such a great wealth of talent in our provinces and this would be a wonderful way of giving it the international platform it deserves.' The following year would see the opening of the new concert hall of Birmingham, built at a cost of £27,000,000 to be the best in Europe, while the Sadler's Wells Royal Ballet was already preparing to move from London to the refurbished and extended Hippodrome. The Arts Council expected to contribute a quarter of a million pounds to these millennial preparations, although the leader of the city council, Sir Richard Knowles, displayed the regional and civic pride of his Glaswegian peer, saying, 'If it is to happen, it could hardly be at a better place. Birmingham is becoming the cultural centre in England, with London reduced to being a set of warring Balkan states.'

For Cardiff also, Palumbo launched a 'Strategy for Public Art', announcing the establishment of the Cardiff Bay Arts Trust which would spend some £350,000,000 of public money in the largest dockland development scheme in Europe. The former slum areas of

Butetown, which contained the notorious Tiger Bay, would be transformed as the seafront of Boston had been; they could hold a magnificent hall for the Welsh National Opera to rival the Sydney Opera House. Public art would be incorporated in the scheme from the beginning. It would be basic to the planning, as in Birmingham. And as in Sweden, one per cent of all capital expenditure on construction should be set aside for the commissioning of art work. At the launch of the scheme, Palumbo quoted Lord Keynes, the founder of the Arts Council, when he said that 'the wind which blows the artist moves him in the direction of the spirit'. The wind was now blowing the Council in the direction of the spirit of the regions.

There was also a chord of change struck in the world of music, where the two leading operas survived the scrutiny of the government and its new policies. The outspoken General Director of the English National Opera, Peter Jonas, turned a necessary review by the accountants Price Waterhouse in 1987 to the advantage of the beleaguered company. The scrutiny came out strongly in the organization's favour:

> We have found a company which:
> – attracts just over 40% of the audience for professional opera in the United Kingdom and has an outstanding reputation for innovation which stretches beyond the shores of the United Kingdom.
> – has made determined efforts to stand on its own two feet ...
> – has an urgent need to settle the future of the Coliseum Theatre, on which its lease has just less than 10 years to run.
> – on the basis of past financial trends, faces a widening funding gap ...

According to Peter Jonas, Mrs Thatcher had initially disliked the members of the company, as had Lord Rees-Mogg, who was unlike past Chairmen of the Arts Council and no friend of the opera. She had considered that they were reds under the bed and had not approved of the critical Jonathan Miller's *Rigoletto*. But after the Price Waterhouse report, she had approached Jonas fondly, asking why he could not be more like George Christie at Glyndebourne and run without a subsidy altogether. She was finally converted on her triumphal tour to Russia, when she saw the English National Opera's performance of Handel's *Xerxes* at Kiev. In that piece, the Persian King's Bridge to Europe was destroyed in a storm; but in

Mrs Thatcher's impromptu speech to her Russian hosts, she declared herself present at a moment of history, the reverse of Xerxes's broken bridge to Europe. Her bridge between the new cultures of the East and West would stand for ever.

Her late conversion to an increased subsidy to the arts in Britain seemed to Peter Jonas hardly more valuable than her earlier parsimony and opposition. 'The arts had become more important because they had taken the trouble to resist her,' he has said. 'They were more talked about.' The objects of the wrath of Jonas were more her barons, who seemed to listen to her playing the role of King Henry the Second, when he had asked who would rid him of the contemporary Becket, 'the meddlesome arts'. To Jonas, Lord Rees-Mogg did more damage than the Prime Minister: he was too intelligent to lose a vital argument against his preconceptions. 'He didn't think things through, he had no strategy. He dealt with the day-to-day like an editor.' Endangered by the underfunding of the Rees-Mogg years, although aided by the conversion of the Prime Minister, the English National Opera scraped through to the different climate of the Palumbo succession and to a new lease of life from nowhere, with the Coliseum bought for the company by a special grant of £2,000,000 from the Foundation for Sport and the Arts, instituted by the football pools promoters to head off a national lottery, as well as an unspecified Treasury subsidy of nearly £11,000,000 to procure the building.

Where the English National Opera Company used conversion and waited for succession as their tools of diplomacy, the Royal Opera House used confrontation and summoned the abyss. The new General Director, Jeremy Isaacs, came to the job fresh from his triumphant years as head of Channel Four Television, totally unaware of the quicksands of operatic dissensions. Faced with funding that did not keep up with inflation, he decided not to deal with the annual deficit, but to increase it. He relied on the traditional support of the Treasury mandarins and the Secretary of the Cabinet, in order to gild the gauntlet that he flung down. Peter Palumbo was outraged at the threat to increase the deficit of the Royal Opera House to £5,000,000. 'I must tell you', he said, 'that there are no circumstances whatsoever in which the Arts Council would consider investing tax payers' money in an organization determined as a matter of deliberate policy to spend its way into deficit.' Such a policy destroyed the legacy of forty-five years, during which the Arts Council had run an accounting policy as scrupulous and scant as Mother Hubbard's cupboard. The Arts Council reserved its right to review its funding policy for the Royal Opera House in the year ahead. A compromise was eventually reached with a strategic withdrawal by Isaacs, once Luce had secured the additional funds of £20,000,000 for the Arts Council. The Royal Opera House still received the largest grant, which was raised to over £15,000,000, an increase of one-and-a-half million. This still did not satisfy Isaacs, who complained that it would not be easy to produce a balanced budget for the next year, which now 'we very much want to do'. Yet it did prove that he and his songbirds still had friends in high places.

In the orchestral world, the stringency of the nineteen-eighties had also shaken the complacency and the stuffing out of the established ensembles. Simon Rattle's City of Birmingham Symphony Orchestra had shown what a loyal conductor of genius could do for an urban council which backed him with its political will. Again, the success of the London Symphony Orchestra at the Barbican Centre, funded by the City of London as well as the Arts Council, was an example. At the South Bank, the three London orchestras which used the Festival Hall were underfunded and set against one another in a dangerous rivalry, but their disbanding or amalgamation was not yet an option owing to their intense support. And as for innovation in music and the playing of the work of modern composers, the chairman of the South Bank, Sir Ronald Grierson, did not want to bear such a controversial responsibility. As he wrote:

> the tendency of the major South Bank orchestras has always been to play safe in their programming and to put on music which would attract the public. But our grant from the Arts Council required us to provide for the performance of what is elegantly described as 'challenging music', i.e. music by twentieth-century composers, to which the response of the public is not overwhelming. Half empty (sometimes more than half empty) houses create deficits; and these must be funded from public sources.

Dance had long been a priority of the Arts Council, and it remained so, because it needed large funding as opera did. 'Dance cannot stay in one place and produce a repertoire', the first departmental director, Jane Nicholas, had pointed out. 'It is essentially peripatetic, the opposite of a drama repertory company.' She herself had been a ballet dancer, but the Arts Council no longer wanted a 'hands-on' approach from former professionals in their field. The new director, Susan Hoyle, had been the education officer of the English National Ballet and then the administrator of the Extemporary Dance Theatre. The question now was not to know one's art from the points of one's toes, but of one's brief. A general social and community policy was now being followed, as the annual report for 1989–90 testified, taking 'the first steps in a ten year plan to develop a healthy dance ecology':

> Extra funding was made available for some touring companies; for research and innovation; training for dance artists; administrators and promoters; and regional developments including pilot regional dance agencies. An increasing proportion of project funds are being given to productions which have been created and premiered outside London.
>
> Another objective is to assist the development of culturally diverse dance. New training programmes for Black dance administrators and marketing officers have been set up, and a more secure funding base has been given to South Asian and Afrikan People's Dance.
>
> The diversity of British dance has never been so extensive or so innovative. Major classical and contemporary companies are commissioning stunning new work from choreographers, composers and designers. The cutting edge of the leading independents continues to forge ahead with the dance plays of The KOSH, the highly emotive physical theatre of DV8, the unique British Black dance of Kokuma and Adzido, the fine craft of Siobhan Davies, the humour of Adventures in Motion Pictures, Shobana Jeyasingh's innovative urban Indian dance, and the idiosyncrasy of the Cholmondeleys. Throughout the country, dance animateurs are generating an interest in dance within local communities and young people are creating and performing their own dances.

While this was a plan to develop a healthy dance ecology, whatever that meant, it was hardly a plan to maintain national standards of excellence, another purpose of the Royal Charters of the Arts Council based in London. In drama, however, more of the old standards still prevailed. Although its recent drama director, Dr Ian Brown, toed the current line in stressing new objectives such as assisting the growth of culturally diverse theatre and the development of mime, he was a playwright and his academic background made him recognize the strength and the need of the older theatre companies nationwide. The last brick of the Housing the Arts programme was put in place by Diana Rigg, when she opened in March 1990 the West Yorkshire Playhouse in Leeds. It had cost £13,000,000: the Arts Council had contributed the lees of its capital fund. 'Almost certainly,' Michael Coveney reported in the *Observer*, 'the Playhouse is the final major theatre building project of the century, and perhaps the last and brightest hope of rejuvenating the country's repertory theatre system.' It was also the final wire in the national grid of drama centres that the Council had been bent on establishing over the past thirty years.

For their running costs, the provincial theatres were becoming more dependent on businessmen and local councillors, although the Arts Council tried to maintain the existing level of its subsidies. The problem was the increased effort demanded from the artistic directors to gain the subsidy. That year, five of the top directors of the regional theatres left their posts – in Sheffield, Derby, Nottingham, Leicester and Lancaster – because of a decline in working conditions and new trends in theatre management. One reporter found disagreement between artistic directors and their boards commonplace:

> Boards, usually composed of councillors and businessmen with no direct experience of the arts, fear that sooner or later a theatre will go bankrupt. Artistic directors are under pressure to plan conservatively for big box-office returns and directors who try to insist on bold and controversial programmes find themselves isolated by commercial and administrative restraints. The days when artistic directors were free to pursue creative instincts with the chance of exciting innovation at the end have gone – to be replaced, it seems, by plays seen primarily as product, not art.

One of the artistic directors who was quitting on the grounds of exhaustion, Clare Venables, explained the impossibility of programming the future. 'Planning a season is the most difficult job of all for an artistic director. You are putting your soul down on the stage with the choices you make. But more and more people demand to know why you are doing it and what it will be like when you've finished. Funders, sponsors, administrators, boards, council, your own publicity people ... everyone pushes you into a kind of fruitless endgaming.'

To the older generation which had left the Council, such as Tony Field, the change to concentrating on administration rather than creation was significant. In the trade magazine, *The Stage*, he read of an interview with Anthony Everitt, in which the Secretary-General's phrases about delegating the Council's clients included such criteria as 'geographical locus in the region', 'local authority funding', 'performing base' and 'companies involved with touring' – and nothing about creativity. The Council's criteria were now chosen to rest 'on objective situations rather than subjective value judgements because "we would never stop arguing about them".' Yet personal judgements seemed to Tony Field to have been the merit of the Arts Council for the past forty years:

> From 1945 to 1985 the Arts Council Chairmen and Secretaries-General also did not avoid subjective decisions which led to the greatness of the British arts and entertainment industry as the world now knows it. Lord Keynes's work was taken up as the Arts Council's first Chairman by Sir Ernest Pooley, then Sir Kenneth Clark, Lord Goodman, Lord Cottesloe and Sir Kenneth Robinson. There was a creative line of progression, every step of which could be charted as closely as Lord Clark's Civilization series.
>
> Likewise, the first Secretary-General, Mary Glasgow, handed over to Sir William Emrys Williams, then Nigel Abercrombie, Sir Hugh Willatt, Sir Roy Shaw – another creative line of progression. There has been a similar identifiable contact with creativity in each Deputy Secretary-General, although last time I highlighted the past distinguished personalities on the Arts Council, its Advisory Panels and senior staff, I was referred to by Ian Brown (the Council's Drama Director writing in *The Stage*) as best ignored in kind silence as part of 'golden ageism'.
>
> It is always easy to point out that the great names from the past Advisory Panels are easy to identify in retrospect. However, perhaps we could have identified for us the present individuals on the Council and its Advisory Panels who are as revered by the various arts professions as were, in their time, past members. [Here Field listed the great names of twenty and thirty years ago on the Drama Panel.] Forty years ago it included Sir Bronson Albery, Peggy Ashcroft, Sir John Gielgud, Michael MacOwan, Sir Laurence Olivier, Tyrone Guthrie, Noël Coward, Benn Levy, Sir Ralph Richardson and André

Van Gyseghem. No wonder these tâlents were courageous enough to make subjective value judgements.

What mattered then to the Arts Council was that it was nurturing and fostering a climate in which new drama, music, opera, dance, painting and sculpture could be generated.

All that mattered then was that the work should be created and produced. It was then entirely up to other forces to take up the work, exploit it, tour it, educate audiences, raise sponsorship, disseminate it – to do all the things which the Arts Council now tends to concentrate upon while neglecting the basic need to create the work in the first place.

This just indictment from a former financial officer of the Arts Council of long service and great dedication was to be answered by the success of Luce and Palumbo in securing a sudden increase in funding, which saved most of the leading theatres from deficits and dark stages. The Royal Shakespeare Company had been forced to close its London headquarters at the Barbican for the winter to keep its losses below £4,000,000; but now it was given that sum by the Arts Council from its enhancement fund as well as an increase of eight per cent on its basic subsidy. The Royal Court Theatre could reopen its Theatre Upstairs and prevent partial closure through an increase of seventeen per cent in its grant. Most drama companies were thrown a lifeline of a rise of eight per cent, while the Northern Ballet Theatre was reprieved after a threat to cut its grant entirely. The only victim in these flusher times was Kent Opera because of its high prices and low attendances: the removal of its subsidy led to its liquidation amid fierce controversy. In general, however, because of the munificence of the Minister, the Arts Council now seemed more like a Maecenas than a miser.

Four institutions or events fell between the various departments of the Council that survived or were created by the internal reorganization: these were the Notting Hill Carnival; the Institute of Contemporary Arts; the South Bank; and the Roundhouse in Camden. A Multi-disciplinary and Arts Centres Committee, which included the chairs of the various arts panels, was set up to look after the disparate quartet. It found the Notting Hill Carnival to be a great success with a bad press, an exhilarating cultural event without parallel in Europe, full of artistic and social significance. The older Institute of Contemporary Arts was managing to continue on the proceeds of an art auction, while the South Bank survived a damaging staff dispute and reduced its deficit and chose the London Philharmonic as its resident orchestra. Only in the futile and costly battle over seven years to make the Roundhouse of Arnold Wesker's aspirations into a black arts centre did the Council finally bow out. Two million pounds had been wasted on it: nothing had been achieved. Thelma Holt, who had run the Roundhouse at the end of its first incarnation, was asked to return to the Board; but she found that the best thing she could do was to be 'a mortuary attendant. It was all over when I got there. It was already too late.' One of the few projects ever backed by the Arts Council that failed, the Round-house showed the risk of giving too much backing to some minority arts.

Although most critics foresaw the demise of the Arts Council or its diminution to an advisory board for a Ministry, its former Drama Director John Faulkner did not. He had found it 'more wily and robust than people give it credit for. If it is slated for a sea-change, it will survive like a Whitehall department. It will say, "Yes, yes, Minister" – and wait for the next one.' Its history was the size of its funding. When the threshold was raised, it was more heavily investigated. And yet it would remain the necessary soft belly of state culture. 'You can kick it, but you will not get through to the belly of the beast. It can absorb radical and subversive elements. It can discipline its own dissidents. It can take on board what will be creative, and so it will survive.'

And so it did with the change of the Minister. Within four days of succeeding Richard Luce at the end of September 1990, David Mellor announced that the Arts Council would retain responsibility for four times as many organizations in its devolution plan than had been forecast – eighty-one in all, with ninety-two given to the new Regional Arts Boards. In point of later fact, it would retain responsibility for many more, which refused to leave its sheltering wing, including the Royal Court Theatre and the four major London orchestras. Mellor further announced more central control. He would himself appoint the Chairmen of the new Regional Boards, their membership would be halved to a dozen or so, and these would be selected after consultation between the Arts Council and the Minister. Only a third of the appointees to the Boards would be nominated by local authorities. Such dashing of the hopes of the regions provoked a letter from John Considine, the Chairman of Humberside County Council's committee on leisure services: 'It is a clear signal to us that the Minister intends to take away the autonomy of the Regional Arts Boards and reduce them to regional arms of the Arts Council.'

The Times found some pleasure in viewing the change of policy under the new Minister:

> Considering how loudly the subsidized institutions have savaged the Arts Council in the past, the decision to delegate their funding downwards might have been received with thanks. Instead, the ninety-two have almost all howled with anguish and the list is far shorter than was originally envisaged. However philistine they may think the Arts Council and its comrade-in-arms, the Arts Ministry, they fear they are being pushed out of the frying pan into the fire. Regional committees in the past were characterized by favouritism, artistic interference and log-rolling by party politicians. For all its faults, they say, the Arts Council had an expert staff and understood the need for 'arm's length' handling of artistic freedom ... The Arts Minister, David Mellor, has said that delegation must wait until he has cleaned up the regional boards. The theory is fine, but it raises fears that a new partisanship will replace the old.

A reason for the retreat from devolution was another ill-starred government policy, the poll tax or community charge. The local authorities were presently spending more than the Council on 'the arts' and leisure activities: about £200,000,000 annually. The difficulty of collecting the poll tax, however, and charge-capping cuts on high-spending municipalities, led to arts spending becoming the first victim of local trimming. Derbyshire sliced half off its arts budget, Hammersmith Council took a third off its grant to the Lyric Theatre. Museum collections were being put on the market, which was selling the public's gold. As Joan Bakewell pointed out, subsidy had come round full circle:

> Local authority funding for the arts has for some four years now attracted parity funding from the Arts Council. All goes well as long as local sums of money are increasing. But when local grants fall, the entire obligation to parity funding shudders. Companies that lose local authority grants could, for no other reason, lose their Arts Council grant, too. The poll tax is not only driving local authority

arts funding into a corner with a gun to its head, it's also putting a noose round its neck.

The problem was that the arts were now politics. Because they were seen as an element in urban renaissance and social welfare and the struggle for power between the regions and the metropolis, the Muses now had to lie down with the Ministers. And this would be a year of three different Ministers for the Arts, all with different policies, 'each putting in their twopennyworth', as one Board member of the Council noted, 'one with aggressive rudeness on one occasion'. The votes and the grants were too large now not to put the arm's length principle in a wrist lock. And yet, the Council was still surviving in another guise and remaining an inspiration for arts funding in the United States and across Europe, at least a prophet with honour abroad.

THIRTEEN

FOREIGN EXAMPLES

Talking about funding for anything these days is a very
risky business; I think that one has to follow Cocteau's
advice that 'tact consists in knowing how far to go in
going too far'.

The Prince of Wales at the Awards
Ceremony of the Association for
Business Sponsorship of the Arts, 1992

A little before he left the Arts Council, Luke Rittner inquired, 'as
new technology shrinks the world in which we live, I do not see how
we can continue to ignore what goes on beyond our shores. Are we
to have no say in EEC cultural policies? Is Commonwealth cultural
development of no interest to us? Is there nothing we can learn from
the artistic experience in the USA or Russia? We say we have the best
theatre in the world. Do we know?'

By the end of the nineteen-eighties, there was still no way of
comparing the quality of the arts in Britain, only the quantity of
their subsidy. A most important issue of *Cultural Trends* in 1990
from the Policy Studies Institute compared direct public expenditure
on the arts and museums between seven nations three years before.
The home country did not fare well. Counting payment by heads in a
cultural poll tax, the study found that Sweden spent three times as
much as Britain, the Federal Republic of Germany and France and
The Netherlands over twice as much, while Canada was well ahead
and only the United States lagged far behind, because of its tradition
of private and corporate giving. The first five European countries
contributed a remarkably similar amount of their Gross National

Product in subsidizing the arts and museums: Britain spent far less. The inquiry did admit, however, that the BBC spent some £50,000,000 on arts features and music, including £8,000,000 on its eight orchestras, and more than £100,000,000 on drama; these sums were not included in the figures for direct grants, although they were funded by the taxpayer through broadcasting licence fees.

The study gave ammunition to those who wanted more state grants. In the words of the artistic director of the Royal Shakespeare Company, Terry Hands: 'Britain has never adequately subsidized its arts in comparison with the rest of Europe.' These were the first comparative figures that had appeared with the whiff of truth about them. They also delivered a criticism. 'What comes as a surprise is the lack of spending through local authorities', commented Graham Hitchen of the National Campaign for the Arts. 'We have tended to centralize while the big spenders, Germany and France, have diversified through the regions and made it much more part of the national policy to foster local government patronage.' That was already changing in the United Kingdom, although any devolution did not appear to increase direct funding to match that of other countries in Europe.

Of state expenditure on the arts, the Arts Council and British museums received over a quarter each, the libraries about a fifth, the British Film Institute three per cent, and the Heritage less than two per cent. The share for the Regional Arts Associations had grown rapidly throughout the nineteen-eighties to reach a quarter of the budget of the Arts Council. There was definitely a trend towards decentralization, although dilatory in comparison with the rest of Europe. Yet the real problem was simply the lack of comparable grants to the arts. As the distinguished American playwright Arthur Miller told a group of English theatre writers in May 1989: 'Society has to make a decision. Do we want to have a significant theatre? If we do, we've got to pay for it.' The brinkmanship of arts funding in Britain rather than the steady and annual subsidies of Europe were not helpful. As one theatre critic wrote, reflecting on the past decade: 'The other side of the Smilesian self-help doctrine consists of wars of nerves with the Treasury. Bargaining strategies such as the "managed disaster" (for example, Hall's closing of the Cottesloe); Arts Council power-games like "Please, would you be the Titanic?", and "eating the cabin boy" (for example, threatening to sacrifice assets one by one) are demoralizing for all concerned.'

As long as the government refused significantly to increase direct funding to match the European example, the only way forward was to use overseas patterns to enhance national subsidies. A year before the publication of *Cultural Trends*, a most interesting inquiry had been published by the Arts Council of Finland in Helsinki. *New measures for financing the arts and culture* identified a number of ways in which the governments of Europe could support the arts indirectly:

1. Encouraging individual charitable contributions through tax incentives.
2. Encouraging business sponsorship through forgoing tax on business contributions.
3. Tax measures to benefit the artist, by averaging income tax payable over a number of years.
4. Tax measures to benefit the arts organization. In Great Britain all arts premises benefit from a mandatory fifty per cent reduction in rate relief. The regulations on rate relief for charitable organizations are changing but the principle remains the same.
5. Tax measures to encourage the consumption of cultural goods by exempting certain goods from sales tax or Value Added Tax – in the United Kingdom, all reading material is exempt from Value Added Tax.
6. Tax measures to encourage investment in cultural industries. Some of the strongest evidence for the benevolent influence of tax allowances comes from the tax investments of the film industry, and the consequences of their removal. Both Canada and the United Kingdom had a policy of tax allowances for investment in film production. During the 1980s, both countries altered the rules for taxable allowances in this area – in the UK the capital allowances were scrapped and in Canada, tax relief of one hundred per cent was reduced to thirty per cent in 1987 over a two year period. In each case the changes are considered to have had a serious effect on the flow of funds into the film production industry – they are largely blamed for the fall in investment in UK film production from a high point of £300 million in 1985 to £64.5 million in 1989. In Canada, the effect of the reduction in tax allowances meant that private funds immediately disappeared.
7. The imposition of levies on consumption within a particular

sector to generate funds to service that sector. The use of television licence fee income is an example of this form of indirect funding (or alternatively, the levy on cinema admissions to fund film production – in France, Germany and, until 1985 in the United Kingdom).

The United States had long relied on tax incentives as a method of encouraging private individuals and businesses to subsidize the arts without having to dig into the public purse. In 1986, the administration of Ronald Reagan had abolished the tax benefits on gifts of 'tangible personal property' to charitable institutions. What this had meant was that the donor of a work of art to a museum was able to offset its current market value against that year's tax bill instead of merely its value at the time of purchase. The change in that concession had badly affected the rate and value of gifts to American institutions. The American Association of Museums showed a fall of nearly a half in the value of objects given to them in two years. Many important works of art on loan to museums were withdrawn to appear in sale rooms. One was Van Gogh's *Dr Gachet*, which had been on exhibition at the Metropolitan Museum of Art and was sold to Japan. The argument that the tax situation was not only damaging museums, but was also allowing the United States to lose its masterpieces to foreigners, persuaded the Senate Finance Committee to restore the tax break and keep the national heritage.

It was not so in Britain. There was no tax concession for presenting works of art to museums, although these could be offset against death duties by agreement with the authorities. Purchase grants for the national art museums had been frozen for several years at some £9,000,000 annually, in spite of Mrs Thatcher's declaration at the Tate Gallery: 'It is not good enough to conserve the heritage, we have to enlarge it before we pass it on and that means we have to buy new pictures.' The budget of the National Heritage Memorial Fund, an independent government fund for the acquisition of all kinds of heritage from sculpture to moorland, had its annual budget increased by four times to a total of £12,000,000. Yet even this increase could not cope with the large numbers of important works such as Canova's *The Three Graces* put up for sale and only prevented for a while from going abroad by the temporary refusal of an export licence. Its purchase price would have consumed the annual grant of all the museums. Salvation for the nation needed private donations. As Georgina Naylor of the Heritage Fund declared: 'It is not our function to subsidize museums. We are a safety net.'

Both Italy and Germany, however, pressed forward in an effort to conserve their artistic heritage. The Italian Ministry of Finance took eight years to process a Law 512, recognizing the financial worth of works of art and historic buildings in private hands and permitting their transfer to the state in lieu of taxes. Certain payments could also be offset against taxes for the restoration of historic buildings and sometimes for exhibitions and other cultural initiatives. In Germany, a new law was passed by the parliament and the Federal Council to encourage private and corporate sponsorship of the arts. Donors and sponsors were enabled to offset notable contributions to the arts and sciences at the rate of ten per cent of annual income or profits against tax over a period of eight years. Also no estate duty had to be paid if the accepted masterpiece or bequest were donated within two years to the state or a *Land* or city administration, or to a foundation which served scientific or cultural purposes.

As in political unity, Britain dragged behind Europe in incentives for artistic giving. In the budget of 1986, the miserly concessions on funding the arts proved to be a failure, particularly in payroll-giving. Four years later, with John Major as Chancellor of the Exchequer, tax relief was granted for major and single donations, which ran up to £5,000,000. Payroll-giving was increased to £50 a month, but still proved ineffective. Covenants to charities which ran for more than three years also qualified for income tax relief and this concession was said to be worth £50,000,000 a year. In spite of the recession, company donations to charity and the community were estimated at more than £300,000,000 a year and could have reached one billion pounds, if gifts of equipment and executive time were included. Corporate donations now totalled about half a per cent of pre-tax profits, just half the level of corporate giving in America. But as across the Atlantic, there was a growing trend to shift sponsorship away from sport and the arts towards social and environmental and local issues.

As a *Times* leader pointed out:

> The holy grail of charities tax reform – full personal tax deductibility

for donations on the American model – is thus still held at bay by the Inland Revenue. The latter's aversion to spending public money through tax relief has long been respected by Chancellors of the Exchequer, however eager they may be to help their artistic and charitable friends and for all Mrs Thatcher's enthusiasm to encourage private giving. In a nutshell, the Revenue and its Treasury masters believe that public money is better dispensed to good causes by cash-limited direct subsidies than by the reckless scatter of deductible private generosity. The man in Whitehall not only knows best but 'gives' best. The Arts Council is a far finer conduit of Treasury patronage than Corporate sponsors or private donors.

Commercial sponsorship, however, had become a political issue. Even in a time of recession, the funds raised by the Association for Business Sponsorship of the Arts would exceed £60,000,000 a year by the early nineteen-nineties. Of the ten thousand companies quoted in the London Stock Exchange, nearly one in six made a contribution. But they did not intend to pay for an increase in arts subsidy if the government froze its grant-in-aid to the Arts Council. In the words of the Director of the Association, Colin Tweedy: 'We now have to decide if sponsorship is the icing on the cake or whether sponsors are expected to provide the flour, the sugar and the butter as well.' The most generous sponsor of all, Royal Insurance, had stepped into the breach because its chief executive Ian Rushton averred: 'The merchant princes who used to support the arts have disappeared, so business had to take their place.' Royal Insurance had arranged a package over three years with the Royal Shakespeare Company for more than £1,000,000 at a time when the theatrical group was forced to make stringent cuts in its staff and performances because it claimed underfunding by the Arts Council. Both the Minister for the Arts, Richard Luce, and the new Chairman of the Arts Council, Peter Palumbo, were told by Ian Rushton that business could not pick up the inflation tab for the arts. This warning helped the Minister for the Arts to procure more funding for the Arts Council and for the Royal Shakespeare Company from the next grant-in-aid. It was what Palumbo had requested the administration to do, when he said, 'The private sector is willing to give as a supplement to government funding; but it is not prepared to become a substitute for it. More would be done by the private sector if the right sort of signals were made by the government.'

The reason for the change of heart of the Conservative party over the funding of the arts was that the economy had improved significantly during the nineteen-eighties; business was also beginning to invest significantly in the arts, and the arts themselves were being considered more and more as major leading earners of income as well as standard-bearers of British excellence. In the speeches of the royal family at the annual awards made to those companies which were the best sponsors, the Prince of Wales pointed out that more donations were being made to football in Britain than to the arts – in fact, nearly one in four listed companies gave more than £230,000,000 to sports, nearly eight times the total sponsorship for the arts. The following year, the Duchess of York referred to the arts as 'a commodity which had to be fought for'. A fight had always been necessary but, as Lord Goodman had stressed in his last speech as Chairman of the Association for Business Sponsorship, all donors should be giving more to the arts, the state and industry, the wealthy and the people. 'I have learned to love the rich,' he said, 'but only when they give generously to the arts.'

It was fair enough, the ideal of the Athenian citizen and the Renaissance banker and the American billionaire. As Palumbo put it in his first annual report as Chairman of the Arts Council, 'Many people have made substantial personal fortunes in the past few years and, with encouragement and the lowest rate of income tax for fifty years, I believe that they will be prepared to acknowledge their privileged position and return to the community a portion of their good fortune.' It was necessarily so in terms of architecture. Other than the building of a new British Library, the state still seemed content to leave the housing of its masterpieces to the last of the great private patrons. Rich from a chain of supermarkets, the retiring Sainsbury family donated a museum of contemporary arts and crafts to the University of East Anglia and a new wing to the National Gallery. Proper hanging space for the Turners bequeathed to the nation was finally provided at the Tate Gallery from a foundation set up by the property magnate Charles Clore. The National Portrait Gallery had been housed behind the National Gallery by a gift from another man of property, W. H. Alexander, and was later extended through the munificence of Lord Duveen; but the government did eventually acquire a freehold site from the

Crown Estate for its further extension and gave matching funds for the construction of more galleries, leaving private foundations to pick up nearly half the estimated cost of £10,000,000. Fortunes made from industry, retailing or property were still being channelled into foundations such as the Leverhulme, Nuffield or Wolfson trusts, and these were the perennial targets of the fundraisers for cultural or educational purposes. They were truly in the business of returning to the community some of the riches which their families had derived from it in the past.

There were still donations of great private collections to the people, and curators lived in the hope of them because the soaring prices of works of art on the international dealing market would have beggared Croesus, let alone an impoverished museum. The cultural life of Glasgow was transformed by the bequest of a local shipowner, Sir William Burrell, who once said he made money like slate-stones. Following Pierpont Morgan, he also collected art treasures; they are now displayed in a new museum of outstanding clarity. In all history, Viscount Norwich has written, no municipality has ever received from one of its native sons a gift of such munificence, which even earned money for the community from its visitors. The renowned collection of Baron Thyssen-Bornemisza also seemed to be on offer to England after it was exhibited at the Royal Academy, but it ended up in Spain; as in the days of King Charles the First, heads of state were involved in the negotiations to capture such treasures for their countries.

The problem of corporate sponsorship was its powers of censorship and interference, paying the piper and seeking to call the tune. Yet in his decade as Chairman of the Association for Business Sponsorship of the Arts, Lord Goodman claimed that he had never encountered a single case where a sponsoring body attempted to interfere with the artistic quality of the performance that was being supported. 'The dark fears that the sponsor would wish to substitute Gilbert and Sullivan for Wagner in an opera house, that he would insist on happy endings being substituted for the originals in *Romeo and Juliet* or *Hamlet* have turned out to be wholly baseless.'

On the contemporary American scene, indeed, the state seemed more ready to gag the artist than the corporation. The National Endowment for the Arts came under fire from a group of conservative Senators for subsidizing an exhibition of the homo-erotic photographs of the late Robert Mapplethorpe, and 'Piss Christ', another photograph by Andres Serrano of a plastic crucifix immersed in urine. Congress would not accept the arm's length principle that separated art subsidy with its consequences from politics, as the Arts Council tried to do in Britain. The Chairman of the American agency, John Frohnmayer, said that his job was 'like trying to catch the grenades as they came over the wall and throw them back before they explode'. Congress ended by imposing a form of loyalty oath on recipients of the state subsidy, who had to promise not to use their grants to produce works which 'may be considered obscene, including but not limited to depictions of sadomasochism, homo-eroticism, the sexual exploitation of children or individuals engaged in sex acts ...' This pledge was attacked in the arts world as something similar to the anti-Communist oaths required of federal employees in the era of Senator McCarthy and led to resignations from the staff of the National Endowment for the Arts because few wished to serve as the art police.

In point of fact, federal subsidy for the arts in the United States was minimal. In 1990, the National Endowment for the Arts received $171 million dollars, less than the Arts Council of Great Britain for a population five times the size, and $22 million dollars less than the Pentagon spent on military bands. Corporate and foundation and private money funded the arts in the United States, and these sources exercised an occasional censorship that was the prerogative of the patron. The multi-national companies, indeed, were becoming the leaders in pan-European sponsorship, as they were in communications between the arts. The collapse of the Warsaw Pact and of Communism in Eastern Europe and the slow progress of Western Europe towards unity encouraged what a report by *The Economist* called 'cross-border' sponsorship, chiefly by American multi-national companies with European affiliates.

In the five leading countries of Western Europe, arts sponsorship by corporations had grown by 1990 to some £200,000,000 a year. The word *mécénat – mazene* in German and *mecenazgo* in Spanish – was used in many countries when referring to activities that were designed to promote a company's corporate image. It was derived, *The Economist* report stated:

from the name of Gaius Maecenas, who supported Horace, Virgil and other artists by means of permanent grants; seeking – and obtaining – in return influence in the political circles around the Emperor Augustus. The present day concept of *mécénat* has retained the option of exchanging social and political benefits for money. *Parrinage*, meaning the act of being a godparent, is a more recent arrival in the vocabulary of French communications strategists, and represents an attempt to bridge the gap between the rather oblique self-interest of *mécénat* and the straightforward marketing implied by the European use of the word sponsoring.

Of the other recommendations for helping the artist in *New measures for financing the arts and culture,* Ireland led the way in exempting the income earned from creative work wholly from income tax. As the Irish Finance Minister said at the time, 'the measure was much more important as a gesture than as an act of patronage'. Its purpose was both to acknowledge the value of the Irish artist and to reverse the flow of talent and earnings back to Dublin from the Mecca across the sea, London, where no such tax relief was contemplated. And the policy worked, for three hundred artists returned to live tax-free and sing of the wearing of the green. Yet in the United Kingdom, Value Added Tax was not yet put on the sale of books and magazines, although many a Chancellor was tempted to add even that burden to the underfunding of literature.

As for a tax levy to help specific arts, there was one on cinema admissions to fund film production in France and Germany and, until 1985, in the United Kingdom. Yet the most successful method for arts subsidy in wide use abroad was gambling on a national lottery. In the United States, million dollar wins in thirty-three local lotteries were commonplace, while in Australia, the proceeds from a special lottery had built the Sydney Opera House. In Europe, these devices raised some eleven billion pounds annually, ranging from El Gordo, 'The Fat One', in Spain to the five national games in France. Every European country except for Albania and Britain ran a national lottery to provide funds for charity and culture; Britain was only accustomed to privately-owned football pools and book-makers. Peter Palumbo was an early supporter of a lottery scheme, saying, 'It works well, in general, in Europe, Ireland, Australia and other countries, and there is no reason why it shouldn't work well here. If this is sinful money, let us put it to virtuous uses.'

Government reluctance to take up the idea was ascribed to Mrs Thatcher, whose Methodist upbringing may have inculcated in her a distaste for paying for the arts through wagers. Yet her administration was already satisfying the British liking for a flutter through Premium Bonds, while some billion pounds a year was raised in betting taxes. In these circumstances, the moral argument against a national lottery appeared to be hypocrisy.

The expected coming of the Common Market in 1992 also gave ammunition to the lottery lobby, for if Britain did not have its own, its people would only be able to buy tickets in foreign ones, and the cash for good causes would be exported. Moreover, the additional money was desperately needed by the arts for capital projects and for the preparations for the millennium. 'Look around you', said Lord Birkett of the new Lottery Promotions Company, 'at what the arts in particular need and what resources there are to provide it. There are none. There is no alternative and that's why I think it will happen sooner rather than later.' But there was a catch in the proposal: lottery funds should not simply replace public money for the arts, they should top it up and expand the potential.

The parting shot of Richard Luce had been to charge the Arts Council with producing a national strategy for the arts. The Chairman of the Council also had a vision of restoring the national heritage and commissioning new architecture for the millennium. The increased funding from a national lottery, which might be allocated through the Arts Council and through a Millennium Fund, would provide the large capital sums needed to enhance the structure of the arts across the nation. There were many early applications for this cornucopia of the future, most readily from London. The largest claim was based on the vision of Queen Victoria's husband and the Great Exhibition of 1851. It could create after a hundred and fifty years an Albertopolis in South Kensington: a scheme designed by Sir Norman Foster would link the Royal Albert Hall, the Royal College of Art, the Imperial College of Science, the Royal College of Music, the Science Museum and most of the other institutions already within the precinct of a hundred acres off Hyde Park. Another scheme proposed to build an opera house on the South Bank and unify that arts centre with the Festival Hall and Royal National Theatre, using covered gardens and walkways. The Tate Gallery wanted £60,000,000 to expand, while the Royal Opera House needed £45,000,000 from the National Lottery to complete its ambitious rebuilding plan, which was costed at two-and-a-half times that sum. The British Museum desired to fill in the space left by the removal of the British Library to Euston, also to increase its own galleries at the cost of £80,000,000. Moreover, the Scots and the Welsh were demanding their fair share of the lottery for their opera houses in Edinburgh and Cardiff. And all this at a time when the government was berated by a former Minister for the Arts, Lord St John of Fawsley, now Chairman of the Royal Fine Art Commission, for the poor quality of its planned buildings. *Medicis and the Millennium?* demanded that the opportunity to rebuild the heritage should not be wasted.

The Lottery Bill could not pass the Houses of Parliament until there was a new Prime Minister and a new Ministry of National Heritage that would combine the functions of many of the old Whitehall departments, which had split the responsibility for funding the arts between them, and had made the giving of allocations to large building schemes almost impossible. Until then, the fabric of the nation would continue to deteriorate, particularly the older museums. Some new museums were being born on private and local government generosity: the Museum of the Moving Image on the South Bank, largely due to the munificence of the American billionaire John Paul Getty the Third; a new children's museum called Eureka! in Halifax; a museum of animation in York; a museum of mousetraps in Glamorgan. Some seventy-five million visitors from home and overseas attended them; but their very name and purpose were in question, as in the rest of the subsidized arts, because of the jargon of their new administrators.

The Director of Glasgow's nine museums and art galleries, Julian Spalding, noted that life was unfortunately not something that the public associated with museums. It was death, however bright and lively they might become. The leisure industry preferred any other word for them – 'heritage centres', 'theme parks' or some sorts of 'experience'. He personally liked the word 'museum' with its evocation of the Muses or nine daughters of Zeus and Mnemosyne, who had for so long inspired study and the arts:

Britain in its nineteenth century heyday established throughout the country a chain of museums and galleries, most of them looking like Greek temples. These museums were the repositories of our heritage, and of learning. There was nothing uncertain about them. Now our museums' confidence has gone. They are riven with internal disputes between those who want to go out into the market place to entertain and earn income and those who want them to preserve their traditional role as educators.

These were the rivalries forced upon the Arts Council by the Minister for the Arts, who was also responsible for museums and libraries. To entertain or to educate, to aid community arts or grand opera, to attract sponsors or to support excellence. The French example, of course, resolved these conflicts by lavishing money on every concept, however contrapuntal. There had long been a historical tension between the authoritarian patronage of Colbert and Louis Quatorze and the *égalité* and *fraternité* of the French Revolution. But the socialist government under President Mitter-and, with Jack Lang as his Minister of Culture, both sought to decentralize the arts and even to fund pop music, and yet build monuments to *La Gloire* such as the I. M. Pei glass pyramid entrance to the Louvre and the immense concrete elephant of the new Opéra de la Bastille. With enough funding, arts subsidy could resemble Stephen Leacock's hero, who galloped off in several directions simultaneously.

Peter Palumbo, however, had used the French example to put together an ambitious plan, aiming at restoring and renewing British architecture. He revealed it to the Prime Minister when she visited the headquarters of the Arts Council. He wanted a new Domesday Book to be written, which would list all the national monuments in need of refurbishing and repair. He told Mrs Thatcher that a billion pounds would be needed to be spent, but that the bill for the millennium could be split between the public and the private sector. At a private lunch, the Prime Minister listened to Sir Geoffrey Cass, the Chairman of the Royal Shakespeare Company, who made a compelling case for subsidizing the arts; to Lord Gowrie, who had been Minister for the Arts and would be chosen as the next Chairman of the Council; to Lord Sainsbury of Preston Candover, the former Chairman of the Royal Opera House; and to Lord McAlpine of West Green, who was also serving as the Treasurer of the Conservative Party. They argued for more money for capital spending on the arts, although the main topic was the underfunding of the Famous Five flagship companies. Mrs Thatcher was enthusiastic but cautious. She was not certain that spending on the arts merited more than health or education. But she reckoned on the appeal of the millennium and the national heritage, even in political terms, and she was aware of the value of Palumbo's call:

> This is a chance for Britain to go into the next century with a visionary ideal. It could be a partnership between the government and the nation which will bring a permanence to our cultural fabric as well as create jobs ... Why do we always have to do things piecemeal in this country? It takes us twenty-five years to build a new British Library, while the French are able to build their Bibliothèque Nationale in just three years. We need to have vision, some urgency and to make sure that our heritage, which is one of the finest in the world, is preserved and maintained.

The problem with any comparison between the arts and cultures of Britain and Europe was a difference of languages as much as performances or forms. The French language, for instance, was only a third of the size of the English one and desperate to prevent its colonization by this sprawling and alien vocabulary. Based chiefly on Latin, the smaller French language held itself to be rational: its fewer words meant more. *La Gloire* was a significant term, for which monuments could be built and millions could sacrifice themselves, charging *en masse*; whereas the English would only sing 'Land of Hope and Glory' and die as a matter of fact. It was the same for the word 'culture'. In France *la culture* had a resonance, as did *kultur* in Germany; in England 'culture' signified everything from a farming practice to a bacterial growth to an ill-defined area of performances and games – the concept of a 'national culture' was viewed with aversion. It was not that the British were general philistines, but that their robust sense of democracy often made them view their arts and cultures with scepticism as well as some suspicion.

There was little pride in British cities to match the intense feeling held by every Italian citizen for the treasures of the Renaissance and the Baroque, left in the *piazzas* and *campaniles* of thousands of ancient urban centres. The industrial revolution in Britain appeared almost to have destroyed a sense of continuity in the uprooted farmworkers who came to labour in the factories and mills, a tradition never to be regained after their transfer to brick and grime. Historically, the Reformation and the Civil War had led to the destruction of the medieval legacy of the Catholic Church and a reaction against pomp and ceremony, treasure and ornament – the civic glue of most Italian communes over the centuries. Oliver Cromwell and the Puritans still induced a mass distrust of the lavish arts as the property of a minority, a court of the élite. The passion behind the burning of idols of the Virgin Mary and the smashing of stained glass persisted in the perennial attacks of the regions on the subsidies for the Royal Opera House or the Royal Shakespeare Company. While Italy had long ignored Savanarola, the United Kingdom could not forget the iconoclasm of the New Model Army and the Covenanters.

And yet, the revolution in communications was denying all frontiers and borders in the spread of the various arts and cultures. 'Television is the key to modern culture', the film-maker Jean-Luc Godard was quoted as saying. He continued 'but culture has nothing to do with art. Culture is simply a product, such as when we speak of a "culture of fish".' It was a rare use of the word 'culture' from a Frenchman, but he was correct in saying that television was the dominant influence in spreading cultures, and that television spoke of a product rather than of an art or of excellence. The language and demands of television and video debased cultures and arts even more than the jargon and priorities of the new breed of administrators, who were already setting up in Brussels and Strasbourg a terminology to administer European arts subsidy that was as dense as Godard's 'culture of fish', millions of minnows darting about in incomprehensible shoals of sociological cant. Paradoxically, as the means of spreading the rich and diverse arts and cultures of Europe were discovered, so the priorities and slang of the new technology packaged and made trivial the important and the variant in the name of the international. The medium was the Mercury of the arts, but the sweetmeats it carried were turned into slurry.

With budgets larger than national subsidies for the arts, the international communications companies and Hollywood film studios spread their versions of what came to be called arts and cultures over the five continents of the Americas, Europe, Africa, Asia and Australasia. No Marxist interference could keep out the signals and the images: in fact, these destroyed repressive ideologies by depicting other affluent styles. And the word 'art' became applied to scrawls with spray-cans on urban walls, to tin toys, or china dolls. As for 'culture', it was used to describe not only the animated films of Walt Disney as a form of 'cultural imperialism', but also the world of drug dealers in mean streets. After a policeman was shot and killed in London by 'crack' dealers, the police superintendent talked of coping with 'a very violent culture. They do not respect life.' Such a use of the word showed how debased a term it had become, analogous to its medical meaning as the 'culture' from which one breeds a drug such as penicillin, although hardly cooked cocaine. What had demeaned the word 'culture' was deconstruction – the idea that any way of life might be called 'a culture' – and that one 'culture' was as good as another, as any art form was as good as another. This doctrine equated violent criminal activity with the playing of Beethoven. Street 'culture' in a slum was merely different from 'high' culture in Versailles, neither better nor worse. There was no distinction between an act of murder, the art of using a gun, and the wielding of a brush on a wall or a canvas, *graffiti* or Titians, be that as it may. One of the myriad 'cultures' in this world might produce mayhem or Francis Bacon, but they should not be judged for that. Just as a rose is a rose is a rose, a culture is a culture is a culture, until it becomes a stink.

The problem with the doctrine of many and equal 'cultures', of social and ethnic relative values, was that it left a national arts body with no reason to exercise choice, to give or to withhold. The only possible policy was to spread thin and wide and grow 'many, but dandelions'. In its far-flung conferences and consultations and committee meetings for its 'National Strategy for the Arts', the Arts Council took French deconstruction on board as well as social welfare. Thus it would shoot itself in both feet. By allowing that the viewer made the picture and the reader made the book, it would remove from itself the power of discrimination, and thus the reason for its existence. If it could not choose, why should it be chosen to choose at all? If the arts were whatever the consumer called the arts and everybody chose their own, how could the Council select which should have a subsidy? The forty-five years of battle for standards of excellence and quality for the whole nation were being lost by yielding to fashionable and international fears of acting as an élite, condemned because it claimed to know what was better for all as well as good for some.

FOURTEEN

ART IS POLITICAL

On the whole I do not think culture will have much
influence. For most people it is something that happens in
London and costs a lot of money.

> Professor Laurie Taylor,
> speaking on voting choices
> in the 1992 General Election

The stabbing of the Caesar of her party, Margaret Thatcher, by her
cabinet colleagues had a dramatic effect on arts policy. A fresh
Minister for the Arts had just taken office: he would hold the job for
a couple of months. David Mellor had sung in the choir at
Cambridge, where he became close to a rising group of Conservative
politicians. Abrasive and active, he was a centralist and had little
time for his predecessor's quest for devolution. 'I do not believe in
the movement to the regions', he has said. 'There would be excessive
bureaucracy, too many committees in the way. There ought to be
leading lights running the arts, top performers with records of
achievement. That has led to the fall of the Arts Council itself – too
many people without distinction on it – too much power given to
arts administrators.' With such principles, Mellor set off at speed on
a reform programme, bursting into a Council meeting flanked by
photographers to disprove the arm's length principle by direct
action, rather as Cromwell had invaded the Rump Parliament.
Mellor's great success when he was still Chief Secretary to the
Treasury was going 'on his knees' to procure the unspecified grant
that bought the Coliseum for the English National Opera: as he has
said, 'You have to be more than a time-server to achieve.'

What he also achieved was the selection of John Major to succeed Margaret Thatcher as leader of the Conservative Party. He was an adviser to the new Prime Minister on his strategy, as was another Cambridge politician, Richard Ryder. Both were instantly promoted: Mellor became Chief Secretary to the Treasury and Ryder was given the job of Chief Whip. The previous Chief Whip, Timothy Renton, was demoted from the Cabinet into Mellor's old position as Minister for the Arts. An urbane and cultured Old Etonian with an interest in opera and the visual arts, Renton wanted to revert to Luce's tactics. 'It's in my nature to be a devolutionist,' he said, 'providing it does not lead to extra bureaucracy.' He was not 'the fanatic for the arts', which Mellor had called himself. In fact, Renton saw his new job as 'a cross to bear. You get used to the Oliver Twist argument – can I have more, please? It's always there.' What displeased him was brinkmanship and political theatre – the Royal Shakespeare Company putting on *Moscow Gold* to poor houses and then closing the Barbican for four months to attract a larger grant. Doing that did not keep the show on the road. Every theatre 'must provide a good menu for the customers'.

The new Minister moved to distance himself from the previous one, although Mellor now held the whip over arts subsidy at the Treasury: he had once joked in his former role after the annual spending negotiation, 'What does the Arts Minister do for the rest of the year?' Mellor had objected to the inclusion in a European summit meeting at Rome of a discussion on the scope of cultural union; but his successor welcomed the prospect of such talks, which resulted in a £6,000,000 grant for a European Arts Festival 'to celebrate', in the Minister's words, 'the richness of British artistic achievement within a European context and to underline the strength of our commitment to the Community'. What he could not prevent was the Chairman of the Arts Council, who was now given a peerage, from approaching Mellor directly at the Treasury to gain an increased grant-in-aid without going through himself as Minister. And when Lord Palumbo publicly thanked Mellor first and fully for the increased grant before he thanked Renton, the Minister was most put out. The incident almost led to the end of the Arts Council.

Lord Palumbo had gone even higher when Mrs Thatcher had been Prime Minister:

You could go and see her, her door was always open. Though the arts were not the epicentre of her interest, she made you think they were the most important of all. She had read the briefs, she had a thorough understanding of them, her questions were penetrating. 'Tell me what they cost,' she said. 'What do they generate?' Give me examples. What is your evidence for this statement?' She was absolutely dazzling. If I asked her for thirty million, I would get twenty-five or twenty-seven. She knew the arts were important. 'Don't talk to me about government money,' she would say. 'There is none. It is taxpayer's money.' She wanted every pound put into the arts to return two pounds to the Treasury.

Lord Palumbo's approach to the 'art fanatic' Mellor when he had been Minister for the Arts had resulted in the special Enhancement Fund, which saved so many of the larger companies from bank-ruptcy. When the money had been granted, Mellor had indicated where he wanted the bulk of it to go. But now there was a new Minister for the Arts and the priorities were being changed. The Welsh National Opera hardly benefited, while the Royal Shake-speare Company and the London Symphony Orchestra at the Barbican profited at the expense of the South Bank Centre and the London Philharmonic Orchestra. Yet when Lord Palumbo directly approached Mellor at the Treasury for another increased grant for 1992 and received a 13.9 per cent funding for the Arts Council, many of Mellor's priorities were re-established. The London Philharmonic Orchestra received an increase in its grant of an unprecedented 130 per cent to put it on a par with the London Symphony Orchestra, while the Welsh National Opera had an increase of 120 per cent. Yet Renton also insisted on a substantial shift towards regional and touring companies at the expense of the large London-based clients, including the troubled Royal Opera House. The third largest increase of 61 per cent went for touring to Glyndebourne, the Sussex opera house that the Minister actively supported. There was no question now that both the Chief Secretary to the Treasury and the Minister for the Arts were 'earmarking' funds for their favoured policies and clients. As Mellor once told Lord Gowrie, 'I won't accept the brickbats without giving the laurels. The ministers are there to do what ministers do.'

As for the arm's length principle, Mellor supported it officially, although he wanted it to be rigorous, 'not an excuse for lazy people not to do things'. But when it came to the crunch, the funding of the clients must be dealt with by the Arts Council and not by the government. And yet there were directions to be given. 'I asked Palumbo', Mellor has said, 'to tell me in what areas the needs were, both as Minister for the Arts and Chief Secretary to the Treasury. And if reasons were given the money had to go to where the needs were. The Arts Council was in the driving seat, but I had to know the needs to battle the Treasury. This was consistent with the arm's length principle, if the *final* decision was with the Council.' What Mellor wanted to do was 'to get rid of sloppy procedures at the Council – to get the biggest possible bang for your buck.' The Council had let the Welsh National Opera slip through the net, and it had only been bailed out exceptionally by the Welsh Office.

'Some people's arms are longer than others', Timothy Renton has said cryptically. He also talked to Lord Palumbo before any settlement of the annual grant-in-aid to ensure, as he has said, that it reached 'more tiddlers round the country in need of seed-bed money'. And certainly, he floated the idea of wrenching off the arm completely. In its continuing deliberations in a National Strategy for the Arts, the Council was asked by the Minister to examine the possibility of direct Treasury funding. This initiative unleashed a letter to *The Times* from the five previous Chairmen of the Council defending the political independence of the arts body. 'He really is a novice as a minister', Lord Goodman said of Renton, 'and out of the blue he decides to violate what is almost a hallowed principle without talking to any of us or anybody else as far as I know, and it makes me very cross. Where does he think he's going to get the expertise to decide on how to allocate arts money? Certainly not from the civil service, and it's taken the Arts Council almost fifty years to recruit such experts.'

Yet Renton insisted on leaving the matter on the agenda in his apparent push to ease the Council out of its central role for the benefit of the regions:

> My remark was a debating point rather than an action point, made in the context of the setting up of regional arts boards and their imminent success and the delegation of the majority of regional clients to them. When you've got delegation of regional clients you've got to address what happens to the major clients, and this should also

be seen in the context of the national arts strategy in which Lord Palumbo remarked that even the unthinkable should be considered.

He continued to press the Council to delegate more and more to the ten new regional Boards for their direct funding and to tear up its proposals to retain more clients. 'Devolution does pose the question', Renton said. 'What *is* the role of one hundred and fifty people living in very expensive quarters in London?' Was the Arts Council really 'a centre of artistic excellence? Who's *on* it who's really artistically excellent? It's got a very difficult role balancing nationals and the regions, and balancing the art forms; but it's become too concerned with socio-economic matters, a cross between the social services and the Department of the Environment. It's lost its artistic genius.' As for the dismay caused in the venerable institution by his review of it, the Minister merely smiled and said, 'I don't think chickens ever vote for chicken pie.'

The assault by the Minister provoked thunder in a leader in *The Times*:

> The national companies have seen their work rewarded with lower subsidies. Exciting ventures have been undertaken and failure risked. An arm's length principle that once meant little more than a licence to moan has led to a new rigour. Lord Keynes's ideal is coming good, of independent minds deciding matters of taste in disbursing public money, of patronage kept distant from policies.
>
> The new pragmatism may be simpler, a minister ticking off grants each year to his friends and letting the rest go to the poorhouse. But it is a recipe for an ever narrower and more expensive status quo. The Arts Council concept was a good one, a pluralism to which Mr Major's government is alarmingly hostile. A single non-government filter for arts spending should not be abandoned just because big arts institutions and star-struck ministers want it so.

A general election was approaching. And indeed, the arts had become of much more political and social significance. Another contributor to the debate, Sir John Burgh, the President of Trinity College at Oxford, accepted that the arm's length principle had been eroded during the last decade, but 'fortunately, while the withered arm has been increasingly twisted, public interest in the arts has been greatly increased.' The next government should devise an acceptable national strategy for the arts which would stand the test of time. The current strategic review by the Arts Council might be useful, but it was not sufficiently wide-ranging. In fact, David Mellor did not even think that Richard Luce should have given the Council the task at all. It was the job of the government to provide a national strategy – and he was already planning in secret a coherent Ministry which might achieve it.

Lord Palumbo stressed that arts funding was too precious to be a political drama. The recent removal by President George Bush of John Frohnmayer, the Chairman of the National Endowment for the Arts, illustrated what damage could be done by meddlesome politicians. His tenure of office had demonstrated what the Arts Council had long known, 'namely that artists need freedom to experiment, and that freedom can be costly and controversial'. In an election year, there were always siren calls for the direct funding of the arts, but the political fall-out would be too great for any Minister who tried it. The present system had public support and produced more revenue than the motor industry. In 1990, seventeen million adults regularly attended more than one type of arts event, while one hundred million people visited art galleries and museums, far more than attended football matches. According to the Treasury itself, the arts contributed six billion pounds to the balance of payments in the United Kingdom, the trade in cars and trucks only four billion. In changing the structure of the arts, the Conservatives were promising 'an expanding partnership between the state and the private sector', while both the Labour Party and the Liberal Democrats looked for a new Ministry of Arts and Media. The Labour Party also proposed statutory responsibilities for local authorities to subsidize the arts, while the Liberal Democrats undertook to raise the level of funding up to the average of the nations in the European Community. These ambitious designs proved that the political parties were now taking the arts more seriously than at previous elections.

There were influential voices, however, who believed that the time for direct government grants had come with Europe as the example. With his usual trenchancy, Sir Denis Forman observed:

> The funding demands of the arts have so far outstripped the resources that the government makes available, that the Arts Council has become not so much a grant-giving body as broker between the arts institutions, many of them struggling for survival, and their paymaster, who must surely share the responsibility if not for their welfare,

at least for their continuing existence. The arts have so greatly gained in national importance since the arm's length principle was formulated that the time must come sooner or later when we accept that they must take their place in the direct line of government responsibility either nationally, as in France, or as the responsibility mainly of regional government, as in Germany.

As a principle, too, the arm's length one had been working for many years on Saki's observation about cooks: 'It was a good principle as good principles go, but as good principles go, it went.'

Such was the public debate that informed political choices before the general election. 'As a government, "by their works ye shall know them"', declared Timothy Renton, 'and I am happy to be known by mine.' But whether cultural considerations influenced voters at all was in question. Polls did show, however, that seven out of ten British people now approved of subsidy for the arts, and over half of them agreed that public money should go to innovation and experiments. 'The vote is there,' Renton asserted, 'and it wasn't there ten years ago. You see how much people care about their local theatre or museum. It's part of the feel-good, quality-of-life factor.' In more staid language, Robert Maclennan, who spoke for the arts for the Liberal Democrats, said, 'There are many people more interested in the arts than anything else – even than in what they do for a living.' The very scourge of the class system and the Tory party in the House of Commons, Denis Skinner, the Member for Bolsover, stated that the arts should be an issue in the election: 'Art is political: look at the underfunding of the Arts Council, particularly regionally.'

Curiously, the three leading figures in the world of politics and the arts were Old Etonians – Timothy Renton, the Conservative Minister for the Arts; Mark Fisher, the Labour Shadow Minister; and Lord Palumbo, the Chairman of the Arts Council. There was a certain political consensus that national cultures did exist and could be managed by new structures. Mark Fisher mocked the Conservatives for producing no specific paper on arts policy, as he had. 'When they have such a poor story to tell,' he said, 'any document would be a cross between a suicide note and a public apology.' Renton's riposte to Labour's plans for a Ministry of the Arts and Media, based on the French Ministry of Culture of the flamboyant Jack Lang, was alliterative. Fisher's plan would produce 'a bevy of bureaucrats, an assembly of administrators, a concert of clerks, a symphony of secretaries – and they all cost money. What is going to happen to the artists?' Renton had rather forgotten that the institution of the ten new Regional Arts Boards before the Arts Council was allowed to wither away had added to the assemblies and bevies and concerts and symphonies of arts executives. He also had no answer for Fisher's correct view of a future, which had to comprehend the communications revolution. 'The Tories don't see any relation between the cultural industries –' the Labour shadow minister said, 'publishing, film, video – and the arts at all. Theirs is just an arts-funding industry.'

It was not to be so. More surprising even than the narrow victory of John Major in the general election was his creation of a kind of Ministry of Culture for his friend and supporter, David Mellor. A fundamental change in policy had always been considered impossible. Since the formation of the Arts Council, responsibility for sectors of the arts had been divided between most of the ministries, each with its defensive civil servants, and different Treasury departments. Efforts by Ministers for the Arts, such as Richard Luce, to poach another portion from another ministry had been blocked by the delaying tactics of the civil servants, even though the transfer might have been approved by their political chiefs. 'No, Minister', had always ruled the funding and control of the various cultures of Britain.

Yet now the impossible happened. The commissioning of a National Strategy for the Arts by Luce and his successors, the prospect of a national lottery releasing large sums to implement that strategy; the promise by the two opposition parties to set up a minor version of the French Ministry of Culture – these were the stimuli which prodded the Conservatives into a radical change. When he had been Minister, Paul Channon had never thought that a revolution in financing or organizing the arts was feasible. 'It would have to happen in the first term of a new Prime Minister,' he had said. 'That is the only time the civil service will accept reorganization. After a year in office, it is too late. The civil servants already control the agenda. And the Prime Minister must make the arts a priority, as Mitterand did in France. And frankly, the only Prime Minister really concerned about the arts in this century was Edward

Heath, and he wasn't in for long – and he had other pressures on him.'

Yet Major had a radical solution in place *before* he won his first mandate. Its main architect was David Mellor, who had only served briefly as Minister for the Arts before being translated to the Treasury, from where he effectively still controlled spending on the arts, and learned to know of the divisions and the jealousies of Whitehall. The manifesto did talk of a ministry which could be a pathfinder for the millennium. His appointment to cabinet rank – with responsibility for Museums and Libraries as well as the BBC and television, the British Film Institute and film industry, English Heritage and the Arts Council, the Craft Council and the Sports Council, tourism and aspects of the art trade as well as the responsibility for running the proposed national lottery – gave him the power and the means to create a kind of Ministry of Culture, although it would never bear that dread name.

Mellor was given the chance to be the Cromwell of an Arts Revolution. Its perennial battles within its civil war – national strategy against regional strategy, maintaining centres of excellence or educating the people, large capital projects or community arts – these struggles and skirmishes now had an authoritarian commander. Since John Maynard Keynes with his restricted Bloomsbury vision of what the nation could afford for some performing arts, and since the blessed trinity of Wilson, Goodman and Jennie Lee raising and spreading initiative and endeavour, nobody had such a challenge or an opportunity. His first act was to draft some of the brightest and the best of the civil servants to staff his new hodge-podge of the Department of National Heritage. The previous Office of Arts and Libraries had been understaffed by six civil servants brought from other departments, such as energy and agriculture: the Principal rode to hounds and was a connoisseur of wine. Now Mellor brought Hayden Phillips and other brilliant lesser lights from the Treasury to run his new ministry. 'When we set up the department,' he has said, 'I was expected to take the livestock on the premises. I took the high-fliers, and Hayden was a great catch. I knew how to do it because of my experience in the Treasury.' The full staff would number 350 people, but, as its Permanent Secretary Phillips said, it was a collective enterprise with no regard for 'the classic bureaucratic practice of shoving material up tunnels towards ministers. We don't have to fall into the existing pattern of Whitehall management. We can design our own systems ... We have a series of small regiments in perfect order for the battles.' According to the former Secretary of the Cabinet, now Lord Armstrong, Hayden Phillips was 'almost knocked over by the rush of people wanting to get out of other departments and join his one'.

In Mellor's vision, the department would be about the promotion of artistic and sporting excellence, and about improving facilities for all. 'The focus is to upgrade the level of government involvement', the Minister declared, 'without a Stalinist mission. We are not in the business of creating white elephants and we are also not in the business of whipping people into line and sending them down for nightly exercise.' His first job in what others were calling 'The Ministry of Fun' was to promote the six hundred events planned for the Festival of Europe by its director John Drummond in order to celebrate Britain's presidency of the Community. The purpose, in Mellor's words, was 'to bring Europe, its heritage and our place in it to young people on an unprecedented scale'. He intended to renovate the structure of the arts to an astonishing degree. 'I can't think of a single area', he said, 'where there is an existing policy that doesn't have to be taken down, inspected, scrutinized and at the very least polished up and probably frankly dismantled and put together again.'

That was the bad news for the Arts Council. More internal reviews were threatened. The good news, however, was that Mellor was a centralist and a believer in rebuilding the fabric of the national heritage for the millennium, just as Lord Palumbo was. Initially, Mellor had been something of a devolutionist prompted by the civil service; but Lord Palumbo made him see the economic futility of building up a new class of bureaucrats on the ten Regional Arts Boards, which had expected half of the grant of the Arts Council, but ended with only a sixth in direct funding, while the Council continued to spend a quarter of its grant in subsidizing its remaining major clients in regional areas. Mellor secured another increment in arts funding, which increased by nearly thirty per cent during his three brief stints as Minister for the Arts, Chief Treasury Secretary and now Minister of National Heritage. He was certainly one of the most effective advocates for the arts that Britain had seen since the Second World War, particularly because he also worked, as Lord Keynes had, at the Treasury and knew how to get the money. His resignation over a sexual scandal was tragic for his cause and for the future of a metropolitan Arts Council. 'Had Mellor stayed on,' Lord Palumbo has said, 'the regions would have got nothing.' Mellor had wanted 'a quantum leap forward in arts funding – "just like that", as Tommy Cooper used to say.' If he had not achieved it, he did reach an expenditure 'three time as much in real terms as in the days of Jennie Lee.'

Mellor had wished to preserve the Arts Council, mainly because it was there and served well. 'It is not self-evident Whitehall can do better', he has said, even though he set up the Whitehall Department that could have replaced it. The very history of the Council made the case for its existence, although when asked whether it should ever have been set up, Mellor would respond with the Irish answer, 'If I were you, sorr, I wouldn't start from here.' Yet because it had started in the past and succeeded in getting as far as it had, it was a fine instrument. 'Mellor wanted to use the Arts Council as a tool,' the Secretary-General Anthony Everitt has said, 'not to break it up. We would have remained theoretically independent.'

The regions were naturally disappointed by the Mellor regime. Under Renton or a Labour government, much would have gone their way. What they ignored, however, were dichotomies very similar to those which split the Arts Council; some of these divisions, indeed, led to the preservation of the London organization. Firstly, many of the local authorities in the foremost cities did not want to work through their Regional Arts Boards, which might be biased in favour of rural and folk arts. Secondly, the diamonds in the tiaras of the regions, the performing companies with an excellent international reputation, often desired to deal as little as possible with the local authorities because of likely political pressure, and not at all with their regional Boards because London was where the European contacts and influence lay. In the words of the artistic director of Manchester's Royal Exchange Theatre, Braham Murray, protesting against devolvement: 'My fear is that the natural bias of local arts associations is towards community-based arts. They will see big companies as establishment, boring leeches and we will become less potent. The danger is we will become marginalized, which is the opposite of why we came to the regions: to bring national standing here in the north.'

Other than Glasgow, Birmingham had put more money into a cultural renaissance than any other city. Its council did not want its major arts institutions to be devolved to the West Midlands Arts Association or Board because of a perennial rural bias. It wanted them connected to a national and European network with a higher level of status and financing. Actually, Birmingham had qualified as an 'assisted area' and had won nearly £200,000,000 in regional development grants from the European Community over the past decade. The emphasis on assistance was changing, however, away from northern industrial cities in Europe towards southern agricultural areas, and it was becoming difficult to maintain that level of arts subsidy. Yet the chairman of the council's leisure services committee, Bryan Bird, remained confident as long as the central connection was kept. 'This is a city', he said, 'which has never been constrained by tradition. Birmingham has always had a frontier mentality. It's a place where if you want something, you work for it nine days a week. There's a lot of envy at what we've achieved, and sometimes I feel that the Government would like to hammer us into the ground. But Brummies can ignore that sort of thing. We've always made our own way.'

The miraculous year of 1990, when Glasgow was the European City of Culture, might have been the Armageddon of the arts with over-expansion leading to huge deficits and empty seats through later indifference. Yet the leading arts analyst, John Myerscough, whose report on *The Economic Importance of the Arts* had done so much to persuade the government that public money was more than recouped by tourist spending and Value Added Tax and invisible earnings, now showed that the £33,000,000 invested in the Year of Culture generated twelve times that sum in returns, created six thousand full-time jobs, increased tourism by seventy per cent to three million visitors, and attendances at arts events by a half. What Glasgow needed was to continue to invest in its cultural institutions and not to rely on single and spectacular events such as the visit of the Bolshoi Opera. And that it would do, now that the city council had established international links and prestige.

The cultural renaissance of some of the provincial cities was drawing leading curators and arts administrators from the metropolis. One of them was Helen Rees, who left her post as director of the London Design Museum for the Eureka Children's Museum in Halifax. She found that the new local authority orthodoxy was the argument that the arts were a means to an end rather than an end in themselves, as the Arts Council used to preach. 'Art *pays*', as John Myerscough had pointed out. It created trade and employment for a town, and by improving the quality of life there, it made the place a magnet for tourists and for companies wanting to cut costs by moving from the capital. New jobs then helped the local economy, and these released more money to spend on the arts. It was 'a virtuous circle'. Outside the renovation of Birmingham and Glasgow, old theatres had been refurbished in the north as arts centres, the Alhambra in Bradford, the Theatre Royal and Opera House in Wakefield, and the Lyceum in Sheffield. Manchester proposed to build a concert hall for the Hallé Orchestra in its new convention centre complex that would cost £100,000,000; Leeds was adding to the West Yorkshire Playhouse with the Henry Moore Sculpture Institute built by the Henry Moore Foundation; and Halifax had attracted the Northern Ballet from Manchester and the touring company Compass Theatre. Halifax was successful because of the Dean Clough development by Sir Ernest Hall, the Chairman of the Yorkshire and Humberside Arts Board and later Vice-Chairman of the Arts Council – an imaginative metamorphosis of Blake's dark, satanic mills into light, celestial studios which attracted excellent performers. 'I wanted to create a practical utopia from a rundown factory area,' Hall has said, 'a new democracy of culture.' And he did so. For as Jack Phipps, the head of the Arts Council's Touring Department for twenty-two years, clearly perceived: 'Local authorities are realizing that there are votes in the arts. If you give people the right arts facilities, they just don't think it's elitist any more.'

However the excellent companies in the regions were to be funded, directly by the local authorities or the Regional Arts Boards or the Council in London, there would never be an end to the demands of the areas outside the capital. Every year, the members of the Council had to go through the gruelling exercise of withstanding the demands of Scotland and Wales and the regional boards for more at the expense of the flagship and metropolitan companies. This had been a developing clash for nearly fifty years. There was only one solution to the struggle, and it would be adopted to all intents and purposes by the next Minister of National Heritage. Lord Armstrong, who had been the Secretary of the Cabinet, pronounced that the share of arts subsidy between the national companies and the regions was a political decision, 'since even if it is taken outside government, it has strong political implications'. He suggested that, while the arm's length principle should be maintained on:

> the distribution of slices – or crumbs – from the Arts Council's cake to individual clients, decisions not only as to the size of the cake but also as to its division between the nationals and the regions should be taken where political decisions are best taken: in government. The government's grant to the Arts Council should be divided into two parts, or two separate grants, one for the nationals as a whole and the other for the regions as a whole; the Arts Council should be responsible for decisions on the allocation of funds to clients out of each of the two grants, but should have no power to transfer them between the two grants except with the agreement of the Minister for the Arts.

Paradoxically, the creation of the powerful new Department of National Heritage promised more central government control for the arts, although devolution was being preached. In a sense, Whitehall had obtained what it had always wanted. While Ministers might come and go along with their governments, the Permanent Secretary Hayden Phillips would remain with an immense power over shaping the National Arts and Media Strategy for the Arts in the nineteen-nineties, a document that the Arts Council was signally failing to produce. More cost analysis and reorganization was being forced on that institution, so that it would have to brood upon itself and cut its fat to a state of anorexia. In spite of hopeful statements from the Chairman about the millennium, the annual reports of the Council reiterated the bulimia which now had to take place after gorging on each grant-in-aid.

In 1991, Anthony Everitt admitted that the last year had been heavily burdened by the process of structural reform on the instructions of three different Ministers. 'We are sometimes', he confessed, 'infuriatingly accused of being a kind of Social Engineering Council or a Business Marketing Council – at the expense of creativity. The implication is that questions of equal opportunity or of administrative competence are somehow irrelevant to the life of art. How can that be true?' Yet the criticism did have a grain of truth. The time spent on institutional changes was necessarily taken from time used for extending artistic excellence. And when in the following year, the Secretary-General was able to report on a twenty-six per cent increase in government funding in the past two years because of David Mellor's efforts, he also had to acknowledge that 'the new money was handed over on strict conditions. Recipients were asked to demonstrate the return on increased public investment, both in terms of earnings and of artistic production.' Meanwhile, most of those working for the arts funding system were being directed to be busy changing it:

> Twelve Regional Arts Associations have given way to ten Regional Arts Boards. A unified planning process has been devised. The Arts Council has restructured and reduced its staff. Further delegation of funding responsibilities to the regions is planned.
> At the same time a far-reaching consultation exercise has taken place and has led to the setting of new priorities for the arts in the National Arts and Media Strategy, to be published shortly. Consonant with these priorities, a Charter for Arts in Scotland has been produced and the Welsh Arts Council has established its own blueprint for the development of the arts in the Principality. Throughout we have collaborated closely with the Regional Arts Boards, the British Film Institute and the Crafts Council ...
> The organizational reforms have been expensive both in time and money. How are we to judge whether or not they have been successful? The Arts Council is the servant, not the master, of the arts and, indeed, of the taxpayer.

In addition, the point was that the Arts Council was the servant of standards of excellence in the arts. It was not being given the time to perform that cultural arbitrage. It was, indeed, throwing away its right to exercise the judgement of Solomon because of the methods and the premises used for drawing up what was now called the National Arts and Media Strategy under the instructions of a succession of past Ministers. In Everitt's words, it was 'the largest consultation exercise ever undertaken in the arts' and the product of forty-four discussion papers and more than sixty seminars. In the consultative document issued in the spring of 1992, an introduction proved the futility of the whole expensive exercise, which cost more than £300,000 to produce a *reductio ad delendum*. There was no attempt to define the cultures of Britain, let alone the arts, which were 'both individual and communal; spiritual and earthy; celebratory and subversive; special and everyday'. The authors of *Saturday Night or Sunday Morning?* were quoted in a banal rephrasing of T. S. Eliot's effort in 1948 to define some aspects of British culture:

> Who is doing most to shape British culture in the late 1980s? Next Shops, Virgin, W. H. Smith, News International, Benetton, Channel 4, Saatchi & Saatchi, the Notting Hill Carnival and Virago, or the Wigmore Hall, Arts Council, National Theatre, Tate Gallery and Royal Opera House? Most people know the answer, and live it every day in the clothes they wear, the newspapers they read, the music they listen to and the television they watch. The emergence (and disappearance) of new pursuits, technologies, techniques and styles ... represent changes which bear little relation to traditional notions of arts and culture and the subsidized institutions that embody them.

A fashionable deconstruction permeated the whole paper, which had the intellectual clarity of a blancmange and was the worst pudding that could be offered to the rigorous spoons of the new Department of National Heritage. In an effort at an appeal both to popular tastes and the fresh ministry, the arts were also defined as 'a way that people use their leisure time, as participants and consumers, alongside sport, tourism and hobbies ... The creation of the new Department of National Heritage, encompassing the arts, heritage, sport, tourism and broadcasting, is a welcome and exciting recognition of the shared interests of their fields.' This diminishing of the arts to the level of the football pitch and the pinball machine, a mere way of passing the time of day for players and consumers, removed any cause for the existence of the Arts Council or for its ability to adjudicate on who should receive what portion of its grants. The conclusion of the section called 'The Arts in Context' was still more of a reduction of any argument for cultural standards:

> What does this prove?
> First, it demonstrates that the arts are a major series of industries. Even what the pundits like to call the 'pre-electronic arts' involve

many millions of people doing, watching, listening and reading. Second, we – the Arts Council, British Film Institute, Crafts Council and Regional Arts Boards – are significant but relatively small players in a big game. Third, we are responsible for only a minority of central government expenditure on the arts and cultural activities – and a relatively small minority of *total* government expenditure, central and local, in this area.

If the Arts Council had such a limited responsibility, its main reason for survival lay in its role as the keeper of the holy flame of excellence and the preserver of those moths which fluttered about that fire. Yet in a debate on 'Quantity or quality?', the writers of the document sacrificed the particular to the general. 'Centres of excellence can stay excellent in the long term only if they are part of a broad and various range of arts provision.' That was not the case: centres of excellence could be funded apart from any national or community strategy. And in their discussion of an 'hierarchy of the arts', the authors threw away the Council's ability to choose for the cant and claptrap of relative values. While the concept of quality was necessary in making judgements about allocating money, it was not 'associated solely with particular art forms, and we entirely repudiate the idea that some forms are of themselves superior or inferior to others'. *Vive la différence*, indeed, but how then choose among the million hands reaching for the minute portions? 'We shall seek to encourage variety of arts provision and activity by every means we can ... Innovation, quality, need and competing priorities are relevant factors; the art form label is not.'

These were hopeful words, but meaningless in the actual provision of scarce revenues to longstanding clients of international renown in the traditional performing arts. The authors even questioned the very basis of the Council's ability to make any choice among its clients, although it had done so with such conspicuous respect for nearly fifty years, shedding few and responding to many. 'If one accepts that judgements can and must be made, then the minimum consensus arising from consultation is that *there is more than one scale, and indeed more than one type, of critical judgement*.' Seven different 'types of quality' were then listed: 'creator or producer quality' which was called 'essentially subjective' – and yet was the main criterion for the Council's choices; 'expert assessor/critic quality', again called 'subjective' – yet essential for any acceptance of the decisions of the Council; 'consumer quality', which merely turned out to be a numbers game or 'full theatre'; 'quality in community', a kind of 'shared vision'; 'quality in variety' to reflect social diversity; 'quality in longevity' of works that had 'passed the test of time'; and quality as 'fitness for purpose' – 'in certain places, at certain times, opera is more appropriate than rock music; at others, vice versa'.

When these seven 'qualities' were totted up, only two reflected the role of the Arts Council in spreading excellence, and both were called 'subjective'. And worse was to come from *Towards a National Arts and Media Strategy*, which seemed to be writing *Restat In Pace* on the tomb of the arts body, which had carried out the lengthy exercise, and was already sick unto death from the influenza of innumerable reviews and policy documents. 'The funding bodies' were recommended to move to a 'more contractual relationship' with their clients. Reams of paperwork would be involved, three to five year plans demanded along with detailed and costed assessments. Not only would innovation be required, but education and equal opportunities agreed. In this nightmare of performing additional office work rather than Shakespeare, the authors had the grace to back away from yet another bureaucratic attempt to erode artistic control. 'It will generally be far more effective to use funding as a carrot than as a stick.'

'Whose culture is it?' the next question asked. The answer was fair, that the United Kingdom was made up of a multiplicity of cultures, cultural groups and interests. But then the plea emerged for funding every form of diversity of age or sexual preference or ethnic minority, a gargantuan catchall of social welfare programmes in the name of subsidizing the arts. 'There are many artists and art organizations where work springs from and pays tribute to specific communities, whether Black, gay or disabled ...' To these 'communities', the document added a whole gender, 'women and the arts' as well as 'young people' and 'old people and the arts'. The only people not included in this majority of the population who were held to be culturally deprived and in need of special treatment were adult white straight males, a minority presumably thought to receive its improper share of arts subsidy, although the document did stress that those who already worked in the field were underpaid and Britain got its arts on the cheap.

Such a document was as specific as a seaweed bed. It represented the arts as services in social engineering and welfare. Not only did it make any national strategy for the arts and media impossible to fund or to direct, but it severed the hand which fed it, the Arts Council itself. The folly of the exercise was seen by some of those unpaid and excellent advisers on the Panels of the Council. To Baroness P. D. James, then in the Chair of the Literature Panel, the whole thing was 'a bureaucratic conceit'. While the Council itself was being forced into a process of reorganization, how could it produce a national strategy from its own turmoil? And how could there be an overall plan which excluded museums and libraries, cathedrals and private art collections? Her successor in the Chair, the distinguished biographer Michael Holroyd, was asked to help in the final draft of the strategy entitled *A Creative Future: The way forward for the arts, crafts and media in England.* He considered the work too incoherent to review. To its arrangers and authors, Howard Webber of the Council and Tim Challans of the East Midlands Arts Board, the process had been a success. A digest of it was presented to the new Secretary of State for National Heritage in October 1992, although its effect was doubtful. As a spokesman for the National Campaign for the Arts said: 'There seems to be no safeguard that it has any more commitment from government than a large number of other reports produced over the last twelve years. Ministers will do as they've done before: pick out the bits they fancy and avoid anything they don't like. Unless the government makes proper financial provision for the arts, one gets the idea that all of this process is rather a whitewash.'

That was the fact of the matter. An arts journalist was asked to write a summary of the forty-four discussion documents and millions of words from the seminars and the submissions. Oddly enough, no paper had been commissioned directly on funding, in case that seemed to be an effort to dictate government policy. Yet the size of the grant-in-aid was the stark reality of any national strategy; no army could march without a war chest. The strategy 'must face the fact that the theatre is now playing safe to survive its seemingly permanent cash crisis; that the film industry is moribund;

the library service is buckling under the demands made on it; the subsidy system is unstable and often chaotic; that British companies are increasingly unable to compete economically with their European counterparts; that performers are glaringly underpaid (when paid at all).' Sponsorship had largely done all it could, and new alliances between the public and private sectors could not hope to bridge growing deficits. There were pressing needs for a national dance theatre, a national arts archive, the inclusion of the disabled in arts projects, support for amateur arts and 'a less insulting wage for performers and creators. The proposed new project, coupled with the fact that many essential institutions are in need of rescue, lead to one inescapable conclusion: substantially more public money must be found for the arts.'

In spite of its forced reorganization and its commitment to producing a national strategy for the arts, the Council had enabled the national companies and the touring groups to survive because of the increased funding provided by David Mellor. With his fall, this was to cease. Yet there had been progress. Writing in the annual reports between 1990 and 1992, the Chairman Lord Palumbo was struck by the insistent

> theme of the celebration of the arts: as a precious national asset, as the means by which we are perceived as a nation in the eyes of the rest of the world, as a means of transforming inner city blight or reviving the economic fortunes of towns and cities throughout the country which have lost their traditional industries, as an earner of hard and soft currency, and as a civilizing influence that enhances the quality of life. All this is evident in the insatiable demand for the arts.
>
> London stands at a world crossroads and it is vital that our capital retains its position as the financial and cultural hub of Europe. We face stiff opposition from friends and rivals in the Single Market. Our leading edge will only be maintained and honed by an act of political will and crucially by harnessing our artistic resources to take up the challenge of making London *the* capital city in Europe, in which people most want to live and work and invest.

This was more like a language which might persuade a government obsessed by arguments about costs and efficiency to recognize there still were British cultures and arts that attracted worldwide attention. The signals sent by the Arts Council had been scrambled for a decade, particularly in the most important document in its history, its national strategy. It had adopted the terms of the exchange and of sociological obscurity instead of blowing blasts on brazen trumpets for the virtues of the arts. It was ceding to Whitehall the high bench where the king of taste had once sat, as if Solomon had lost the power to judge between rival claimants in different cultures. It was acquiescing in political direction rather than guiding artistic intention. Its vocabulary was the mutant of its message. Welfare was replacing the good. Social engineering answered for performing excellence. Political imperatives were becoming the arbiters of the arts. If in the beginning was the word, the ending of the Arts Council might lie in the misuse of the word.

FIFTEEN

HISTORICALLY CORRECT

Oh, you artists, we give you money and you go on. We cut
your money and you still go on.

Margaret Thatcher
on proposed cuts to the Arts Council,
as reported by Timothy West

The new Minister of National Heritage, Peter Brooke, had tried
previously to solve the problems of Northern Ireland. It was a moot
point which job would prove the more intractable. Although only a
collector of old books and watercolours at a low price, Brooke was a
Tory patrician and conciliator in the manner of Lord Whitelaw. He
was deeply concerned about the values of the past: his family trust
owned Dove Cottage, the most popular of the poet Wordsworth's
homes in Lakeland. His chief interests were churches and conserva-
tion, and he always travelled with *Parish Churches of England &
Wales*, the work of the former Poet Laureate, John Betjeman. He
loved the eight hundred years of their evolving architecture and their
ecclesiastical eccentricities, as Betjeman had done. Church-watch-
ing was his favourite spectator sport and belief. As Lord Palumbo
said of him when he took office, he was a very decent man. 'It'll be
up to him to make up his own mind about the Arts Council. I don't
fear that, because I think that we actually do a good job.'

There should have been more fear, for the new Minister behaved
like most previous Tory Ministers in their first year of office: he
stuck out for savings and devolution. The Department of National
Heritage itself lost a greater proportion of its funds in 1992 in the
debate about the annual spending round than any other department

of state. Five million pounds were taken away by the Treasury to contribute to the regional European fund, while administration costs for the new Department rose by £7,000,000 with its move to its new headquarters in Cockspur Street off Trafalgar Square. Every sector which it funded had its grant frozen or cut in real terms. Under the next three-year plan, the Arts Council was due to lose £5,000,000 in 1994, which reneged on a previous pledge to increase its grant in line with inflation, although £800,000 would later be restored. David Mellor's replacement as Chief Secretary to the Treasury, Michael Portillo, had undone all the good work for the arts of his predecessor. And the new Minister appeared not to have fought hard enough for his Department against the axe of the Treasury, so that the Arts Council, now starved of its life-blood, would have to execute some of its own victims.

Lord Palumbo wrote a dignified protest, using economic arguments against Portillo:

> These cuts would create unavoidable job losses, reduce productivity and quality standards; deplete audience attendance and, therefore, box office receipts, with a consequent loss to the Exchequer of value-added tax and invisible earnings. This is the stark reality of the situation. Moreover, the arts represent one of the few areas in this nation's affairs which can be counted an unqualified success during the last few years; one of the few areas which generate a two-fold return for every pound of taxpayers' money invested in them. Can it really be the intention of the government to penalize such success?

The new Minister was determined that the Arts Council also would be cut to the bone. Soon after being presented with the cultural bran-tub of *A Creative Future*, he commissioned another cost analysis of the Council's administration from the leading firm of accountants, Price Waterhouse. Economy would begin at home. In a speech to the Royal Fine Art Commission, however, he denied that the trim in the Council's funding in real terms reflected future priorities. 'I must emphatically reject', he said, 'the idea that the health of an area, or the esteem in which we hold it, is measurable either by the aggregate of direct government funding or by trends in that aggregate.' He stated that the arm's length principle would continue. 'We are not about to enter the era of Ludwig of Bavaria, or Louis XIV, and there will be no state-approved artists or styles of artistic endeavour.' Other areas of the Department's responsibility, however, were important to him. He hoped that the main spending events could be shared as 'national pageants'; and as for an alternative method of subsidy for sports and the arts, the national lottery, it 'has provoked an excitement, which I cannot help but share.'

Yet the proceeds of the lottery would not arrive for some years. Presently, the lessening of the annual grant and the audit would compel harsh decisions on the Arts Council. The review by Price Waterhouse supported the arm's length principle and 'the future of the Arts Council operating under it to discharge its overall responsibility for the health and contribution of the arts'. The auditors shared the views expressed to them by members and officials and clients of the Council, namely:

- Arts Council members and officers serve the arts with energy and commitment
- frequent changes in structure, funding and delegation arrangements have imposed considerable burdens on all concerned
- there is uncertainty about whether the Arts Council should become a creature of government or a robust and independent voice for the arts
- the Arts Council does not prioritize its activities clearly
- the integrated planning system is not yet working well ...
- the structure of the Arts Council organization should reflect its core functions of:
  * making artistic judgements and overseeing the state of the arts in England
  * managing the grant-in-aid
  * conducting appraisals of artistic bodies and artists
  * advocacy on behalf of the arts.

This shrewd appraisal was accompanied by severe recommendations for a smaller organization. The present Council was 'cumbersome and costly'. It had too many bureaucrats producing irrelevant documents about causes that were 'politically correct', such as *Introductory Guide to Travel Opportunities for Black Arts Practitioners* and *Women in Arts: Networking Internationally*. Half or more of the staff of 160 people could be dismissed to make it more efficient before it handed more direct funding over to the Regional

Arts Boards. Departments should be merged or eliminated, committees be reduced and accountability be increased. Functions such as information technology, cultural diversity, publication and touring operations could be put out to tender. One Council member was reported as saying of the Minister's visit to Great Peter Street to discuss the review: 'He thinks we have spent too much time faffing about and waste time having too many meetings about everything.'

In point of fact, there were too many meetings about planning and reconstruction as well as social engineering for the staff to concentrate on the auditor's goal of 'making artistic judgements and overseeing the state of the arts in England'. As one arts correspondent noted, "The increasing amount of paperwork sent by the Council to its clients has become the subject of innumerable jokes at theatres and art galleries. One has a theatre's artistic director appearing on stage before a performance and telling the audience that the advertized play has been cancelled, but there will be a reading of the company's corporate plan instead.' Robert Gordon Clark, of the London Arts Board, said that 'our overriding impression is that we seem to have become fixated by the idea of planning and it is distracting us from the artist and the public. Accountability is important, but there should be a balance between accountability and the artist. At the moment that balance is tipped too far.'

It had been tipped too far. The Council was becoming inoperable, not through its own shortcomings, but through the demands of government. And the shortage of funds was the hand on the throat of the Council. It could either spread the misery or select the lambs for the slaughter. Initially, it chose sacrifice rather than shared pain. At a strategic Council meeting in May 1993 at The Bear Hotel at Woodstock, Beverly Anderson and Christopher Frayling presented the findings of the Artistic Review Working Group, which had been established to propose how best to implement the priorities put forward in *A Creative Future* against the background of the threatened reduction of £5 million in the Council's grant-in-aid for the next year. These key principles were endorsed:

> support for quality is paramount;
> increased support for new work;
> education to become a higher priority;

no client organizations to be accorded protected funding status; redistribution of existing expenditure allocations to be considered; fewer organizations to receive subsidy, but at more realistic levels.

It was also decided that drama should get less so that contemporary dance and the visual arts should receive more funding.

This recipe for artistic cleansing was put in motion, particularly in the theatre and in music. Yet the furore which was struck up proved how difficult any change would prove to be. After a series of meetings to discuss the withdrawal of grants from some leading theatres, the Chairman of the Drama Panel, Lord Rix, resigned with the threat that most of the rest of the members would walk out with him. Targeted with destruction among others were the Bristol Old Vic, which Keynes himself had saved, and the Greenwich Theatre, the Watford Palace, the Belgrade at Coventry, the Oldham Coliseum, the Plymouth Theatre Royal and the Lyric in Hammersmith in London. Lord Rix spoke of the Council 'devising fatuous so-called policies' and 'the contents of the chamber pot being poured on our heads'. 'The idea that the drama department is there to serve its clients seems to have gone,' the artistic director at Greenwich said. 'Now we are just a nuisance. But they simply have to grasp the nettle and understand the way out is not to close theatres.' Benedict Nightingale in *The Times* argued for the misery-for-all strategy rather than the noose for some. The Arts Council was no longer believed in the way it reached its decisions. 'Something is wrong when it has not merely lost the trust of many of its clients, but is regarded by them as eagerly playing Jack Ketch to the government's Judge Jeffreys ... It is as if the heroine of *Sophie's Chorus* were to seek out her enemy and say, "Hallo, I think you may want to kill one of my children, so please remember that I love the girl less".'

The very procedures of the Council were now being questioned. As Nightingale asked:

What is the purpose of its advisory Panels, if not to be heard when key issues are at stake? Should the Council itself really be making life-or-death decisions in as quickfire a way as men potting birds on a grouse moor? If theatres must endure cuts, this should surely be part of an overall plan. For instance, it is absurd that Plymouth and Bristol should both be victims, leaving the West of England with just one subsidized theatre, the tiny Northcott in Exeter ... The resignation of

Lord Rix has, shockingly, left the Council with no member whose primary interest was in the theatre.

This damning comment on those who were now staffing the Council – arts administrators rather than practitioners – was followed by a riposte from the Minister. He announced a building grant for the Belgrade Theatre at Coventry to increase its backstage facilities along with another £2,000,000 to repair other provincial theatre buildings. He was reputed to be angry at the Council's decisions to give contemporary dance priority over regional drama. Other paladins sprang into the breach. The director of the National Theatre, Richard Eyre, discerned a threat to 'the whole of British theatre, which I see as a living organism, a body which has limbs, digits, arteries and – Arts Council willing – blood coursing through its veins. Start carrying out random amputations, and the whole body will begin to atrophy. The life will literally go out of it.' What the Woodstock meeting appeared to have done was to set one art against another in a cockfight, where there was no victory, only flying feathers and dead birds.

At the end of the day, Lord Palumbo personally took the responsibility from his staff for the threat to withdraw the subsidy from some of the leading provincial theatres. He put the blame where it truly lay, on the Treasury. The Drama Panel had leaked the list of victims, and the protest was too great to resist. The cuts would now wound all the clients: there would be no blood on any particular stage. As he stated in his final address as Chairman:

> Funding for the arts has steadily increased over the past five years but it is now threatened by an attack of traditional Treasury pecksniffery which affects understanding of the arts but ignores the crucial fact that artistic talent is a resource so precious that it is not easily subject to the regulation by parsimony ... There is more than a whiff of a suggestion that the arts have done so well that they must be put in their financial place. The point was eloquently put by a correspondent to *The Times* recently: 'When, oh when, are we going to learn that cultural matters transcend balanced books?'

The amalgamation of some of the four London orchestras, excluding the fifth one supported by the BBC, had been attempted sporadically over the past thirty years. Lord Palumbo rightly called the question of the survival of each and every member of the grand quartet of metropolitan symphony orchestras 'an old chestnut'. In 1965, a committee chaired by Lord Goodman had recommended the withdrawal of the arts subsidy from the Royal Philharmonic, but the Chairman had himself frustrated the attempt. Helped by a young barrister, Leonard Hoffman, Goodman had instituted the London Orchestral Concert Board with Hoffman as its secretary: it was charged with sharing out fairly the Arts Council and Greater London Council subsidies between the four orchestras. This system had continued until the abolition of the Greater London Council in the nineteen-eighties, despite an inquiry in 1970 into the provision of funding to orchestras nationwide, which recommended that London should have only two grant-aided orchestras. 'Goodman did not like the report', its author Sir Alan Peacock has said, 'but it was people's money spent on a patrician principle. Why not have consumer choice? Goodman told me, "Either amend the report or I will issue a disclaimer". And so he did: his preface denounced my report.'

In 1990, the London Philharmonic had won the coveted residency at the Festival Hall in the South Bank centre in a competition with the Philharmonia and the Royal Philharmonic, while the London Symphony occupied the Barbican with a successful programme that was both popular and adventurous. The grants from the Arts Council for the year 1992–3 were:

London Symphony	£1,110,880
London Philharmonic	£1,062,000
The Philharmonia	£ 700,000
The Royal Philharmonic	£ 400,000

Thus there had already been discrimination in funding before Sir Leonard Hoffman, now knighted and a Lord Justice of Appeal, was recalled to head a special committee and to judge which two of the three orchestras, the London Philharmonic, the Philharmonia and the Royal Philharmonic, should lose their subsidies from the Council and perhaps dissolve, while the third should receive enhanced funding. The Lord Justice did not seem to relish the job, writing to the general secretary of the Musicians' Union that he would prefer no action to be taken on his recommendations: he felt he had been 'handed a poisoned chalice'. Indeed, protests were powerful and vociferous: they came from the Berlin Philharmonic,

which received four times the subsidy of all four London orchestras
put together, as well as the most distinguished of musicians such as
Lord Menuhin, Sir Colin Davis and Sir Peter Maxwell Davies, who
even threatened to return his knighthood, if the Royal Philharmonic
was axed. Along with other commentators he particularly objected
to the method of destruction, by which the Council sloughed off its
responsibility onto a form of review by a Justice that appeared
impartial.

Sir Peter Maxwell Davies thundered:

> The Arts Council is supposed to encourage the arts. Instead it is doing
> the Government's dirty work for it. And it is doing it divisively and
> incompetently. It has appointed a non-musical legal judge to decide
> which two (orchestras) are to die. Nastier still, it has appointed
> anonymous spies, slinking into concerts to report back on their
> fellows, thus setting musician against musician and orchestra against
> orchestra, as each struggles for life.
>
> The Arts Council appears not only determined to cut music as
> much as possible out of our lives; but worse, it is wantonly sowing
> despair, disillusion and enmity in a profession where hitherto there
> were only friendly rivalries. Its dogmas are as demeaning and
> disrespectful of human values as anything dreamt up by the
> Communists. Officials and accountants should not be allowed to
> destroy the very fabric of our culture for the flimsiest and most short-
> sighted of reasons.

This philippic from a leading British living composer was unfair.
The Council had been forced to cut somewhere, and wherever the
blade would descend, there would be a chorus of pain. The passing
of the decision onto the Hoffman Committee was unusual, but not
unprecedented. Execution in England is normally preceded by a
review or a committee. Moreover, the lack of distinction of most of
the members of the advisory Panels had lost in the nineteen-eighties
the respect of the arts community for their choices. The Music Panel
itself had in the Chair Bryan Magee, a journalist and a philosopher
who had become a Labour Member of Parliament: he certainly did
not have the prestige of a Sir Thomas Beecham, who had founded
two of the threatened London orchestras, nor of the leading
composers engaged in denouncing the Council. Other members of
the Panel included a producer from Radio 3, a percussionist, an
electro-acoustic specialist, the founders of Jane's Minstrels and of

Music Works, and the head of promotions at Boosey and Hawkes. The Music Director, the Chairman and half the members of this divided Panel were to resign: one because she thought none of the orchestras should be cut, while another left when the Council was to renege on giving the money saved to jazz and ethnic music. The surviving members of the Music Panel wrote an open letter of complaint to the Secretary-General, disassociating themselves from the process of a pointless exercise, leading to nowhere but ill fame.

Yet the real cause of the controversy was not the Arts Council, but the government and the new Ministry which were compelling the Council to wield the knife, even if at second hand. As the Executive Director of The Lottery Promotion Company pointed out:

> John Major and David Mellor must be heartbroken to realize that their creation, the Department of National Heritage, is becoming the worst engine of destruction the British arts world has known. Ballet and theatre companies, and now orchestras, are being stamped out whilst the expenditure on bureaucrats in the arts increases. The Department itself will cost £30 million this year and arts administration £16 million, whereas a mere £5 million cut in subsidy to the Arts Council has caused havoc.

That havoc was, indeed, hardly the fault of the Council, which was still doing its best to administer its diminished resources. The ferocious assaults on it by supporters of its few victims seemed to its Chairman to be part of a general vilification of the great and the good by the petty and the press. He stated:

> I am not surprised at the attacks upon the Arts Council of Great Britain and we are and should always be, ready to repel them because we live in times of wholesale denigration of the great formal institutions of State, the Crown, the Church, Parliament and the Law, exacerbated by the rigorous cutbacks in public expenditure. The Arts Council of Great Britain, for all its frailties, is still a national centre of excellence. Its *raison d'être* is the artist and the dissemination of knowledge and understanding of the artistic impulse and its creations.

He himself came under criticism for saying nothing on the issue of the orchestras. He was held to favour the creation of a London orchestra of global renown such as the Berlin Philharmonic on the broken bowstrings of the others; but he did not speak out. 'From him, a magnificent silence:' a critic wrote in *The Times*, 'John Cage would have been envious.' Lord Palumbo was wise to be mute, for the Council would take two meetings to resolve the fate of the London orchestras as Lord Goodman had done, denying the advice he was given and keeping all four of them going. What this deleterious process and delay in decision did achieve was to flush out the latent enemies of the Council. In an astonishing open letter to Peter Brooke, the former Minister for the Arts, Timothy Renton, demanded its abolition. Direct financing of the flagships by the Department of National Heritage and direct funding of the rest by the ten Regional Arts Boards would make the Minister into a Jack Lang and the London Council superfluous. 'Axe the Arts Council, and you will save eight million pounds a year in administration.' One million could go on a larger staff for the Department, £4,000,000 to bind the wounds of the cuts, £3,000,000 of new money to help theatre, galleries, dance and music throughout England. Even David Mellor thought the Council rudderless and incapable of making sensible decisions, while the Department of National Heritage sat back in a state of inertia. 'All those who willed this dog's breakfast upon London should be embarrassed at what has happened. There is a real sickness at the heart of arts policy-making in this country. It is time it was sorted out.' That final solution over the orchestras, indeed, was no sorting out, but a round dance. All the three London orchestras were to retain their subsidies with the London Philharmonic grant cut to the level of the Philharmonia, and the Royal Philharmonic remaining under review.

So the ruffled feathers settled in place, until the Chairman of the Arts Council was to leave office and feel that he could reply openly to his detractors. 'Nobody should shrink from constructive criticism', he wrote in the *Sunday Times*, 'but I found it difficult to take seriously that levelled against us by Tweedledum and Tweedledee, alias the comedy duo of Tim Renton and David Mellor, who called for the abolition of the Council, or at the very least, its deconstruction, while having done nothing to further those objectives when they themselves were Ministers for the Arts.'

The cockfights extended to the streets, where members of the union Equity protested against the lesser drama subsidy. Luke Rittner, now the Chairman of the English Shakespeare Company, announced that it would have to cease its many successful years of touring, while the riposte of the Minister Peter Brooke was to stress that he had allocated more funds to finish the refurbishment of the Albert Memorial and the British Library as well as to aid museums. This policy appeared to be robbing performers to pay for monuments. To Lord Palumbo, the cuts to the arts were a bitter disappointment and 'of enormous significance, and the implications will do irreparable damage to a precious national asset.'

To the Ministry, it was merely a question of tightening more belts. Rigour and savings were recommended by the Department of National Heritage to the artistic companies. Yet what was the point of drawing up yet another three-year plan, which allowed for these rations rather than the increased spending in line with inflation that had previously been promised? As the executive director of the Nottingham Playhouse declared, 'God knows if our budgets are worth the acres of Amazonian forests that were felled to print them … I don't believe I can cut the staff. I can only reduce the quality of our work and that's a vicious circle because you earn less at the box offices when audiences see you're not so good as you used to be …'

Opera and ballet were equally under threat. After severe financial criticism in the Warnock Report and a Price Waterhouse scrutiny, the management of the Royal Opera House cancelled its new production of Halévy's opera *La Juive* along with a revival of Kenneth MacMillan's full-length ballet *The Prince of the Pagodas*, which was replaced by the safer attraction, *The Sleeping Beauty*. There was a pay freeze and forced redundancies in staff. 'We can't make further cuts without actually compromising our ability to generate income', the Director of Public Affairs said in Covent Garden. 'One could do more revivals, but you can only revive *The Magic Flute* a certain number of times before the audience runs out.' No successful or sacred cow was too holy to be spared the inquisition. After twenty-five years of taking Glyndebourne's excellent productions to Oxford, Manchester, Norwich and Plymouth, the Glyndebourne Touring Opera was warned that in the years to come, its subsidy of £630,000 would no longer be guaranteed. Like the menaced London orchestras it would have to 'tender' for grants to perform in places chosen by the Council.

To Glyndebourne's supporters, 'the Arts Council's capacity for losing friends and turning itself into a laughing stock has entered a new phase'. As in the case of the London orchestras, the future of the Glyndebourne Touring Opera would be reprieved. But what was under attack was the review process by which the Arts Council reached its current decisions, now that it was forced to make cuts. By March 1994, British orchestral life seemed to *The Times* to be at its worst and its best with five regional orchestras and the Royal Philharmonic asking for more funding from the Council. 'They will feel like beggars scrabbling for crumbs. The available money is pitifully limited. But since nearly everybody involved in cooking up the Arts Council's disastrous orchestral policy has resigned in the past two months, one hopes that the mood at the meeting will be as chastened as in a nunnery on Ash Wednesday.'

There was trouble even in the world of dance. The modern and innovative small groups that had proliferated to number two hundred across the country were being allocated larger subsidies in proportion to the more traditional older organizations, and certainly to the regional theatres. The Rambert Dance Company and the London Contemporary Dance Theatre received standstill grants, while the English National Ballet managed an increase of two per cent compared with more than three times that increase for Adventures in Motion Pictures and the Siobhan Davies Dance Company. What money there was went to a network of national dance agencies, centres in Swindon, Newcastle, the East Midlands, Suffolk, Birmingham and Leeds, where professional and amateur dancers could gather for training, classes and performances. All the ten Regional Arts Boards had an agency in place or had received a development grant for one. The London City Ballet, however, announced that it would close – and then was resuscitated. Brinkmanship was the name of survival.

The success of the Council lay now in continuing its policies of innovation and education rather than its long struggle to maintain standards of excellence. A legacy of more than £1,000,000 left to the Council was channelled into The Arts Foundation, which was meant to attract private patrons and encourage new work by young people. It was run by Stephen Bayley, who had been in charge of the Boilerhouse Project at the Victoria & Albert Museum, then of the Design Museum at Butler's Wharf. Lord Palumbo wanted the new

Foundation to be 'audacious, even irreverent, energetic, uninhibited and questioning'. As Bayley himself had said of the traditional arts, 'opera, ballet, orchestral music, literature, they are all bankrupt, finished, empty', and great changes were expected. Bayley announced an awards scheme, a *salon des refusés* art gallery and an international television lecture on patronage. 'I want what we do', he said, 'to be Promethean, dangerous, subversive, erotic, radical, exalted.' Unfortunately Bayley soon resigned, to be succeeded by Russell Willis Taylor, who announced a more practical initiative to help experimental artists. 'There is continuing concern about money for innovation,' she said. 'In the 1980s money was moved away from risk-taking art and towards having business skills. We have to help to change that.'

Before he took office, indeed, the Chairman of the Arts Council had declared, 'Experimental art must be encouraged. This involves nothing less than giving the artist the right to fail.' Thus the last annual report of his term announced the highlights of the year of 1992–93 mostly as innovations in the arts:

MUSIC
'Sounds like Birmingham' successfully launched the Arts Council's Arts 2000 initiative, which celebrates a different city or region each year. Nearly 3,000 events were attended by more than one million people. The year left a rich legacy in Birmingham, including a clear policy of support adopted by the city council, for non-western music and early music.

DANCE
Matthew Bourne's contemporary dance version of *The Nutcracker* performed by Adventures in Motion Pictures, attracted full houses in a 1,500 capacity theatre over three nights at the Edinburgh Festival. As part of a double bill commissioned by Opera North, it helped to introduce opera audiences to contemporary dance.

DRAMA
Co-productions between innovative companies such as Tara Arts, and building-based theatre companies like the Theatre Royal, Stratford East, have increased the audience for innovative work. The Royal National Theatre/Théâtre de Complicité co-production of *The Street of Crocodiles* achieved international acclaim as one of the most exciting achievements of the decade.

COMBINED ARTS
Heatwave 1993 – Station House Opera presented one of four specially commissioned pieces, funded under the Arts Council's Live Arts Commissions scheme. This was the fifth consecutive year that the Serpentine Gallery showed its commitment to live art. This popular event attracted 2,000–3,000 participating audience members.

VISUAL ARTS
The Arts Council's Architecture Unit was founded in 1992/93, the first time that architecture has featured in the arts funding system. The first architectural grants scheme, which offered £150,000, generated a further £350,000 secured from different sources. The unit will work to enhance public understanding and appreciation of architecture.

FILM, VIDEO AND BROADCASTING
Several festival awards were won during the year, by productions supported through the Arts Council. They include Kinoki: *We Jive Like This*, awarded the UNESCO Prize at Video Danse 1992; and two productions funded under the Animation Award Scheme, namely Oliver Harrison: *Spirit of Place*, awarded the Certificate of Merit and Best Cinematography at the Cork Film Festival; and Phil Mulloy: *Cowboys*, which won the Best Short Film Award at the Melbourne Film Festival.

LITERATURE
V. S. Naipaul became the first winner of the newly established David Cohen British Literature Prize, presented by the Arts Council, sponsored by Coutts & Co. He was awarded £30,000 provided by the David Cohen Family Charitable Trust. The Arts Council contributed an additional £10,000 to enable the winner to commission new work. This is the most valuable literature prize at present, and is awarded in recognition of a lifetime's achievement in writing.

Innovations in the two areas where the Arts Council had historically always failed to succeed, in film and literature, could have little effect at this late date. To the director of the British Film Institute, Wilf Stevenson, Lord Keynes had been correct to exclude film from the performing arts, as it was an industrial process, something which the Arts Council could not manage. The few art films which the Council supported were a drop in the ocean of television programmes, while its attempts to liaise with the other longstanding disseminator of the arts, the BBC, had always ended in tears. To Michael Grade, who had left the BBC to run the independent Channel Four, the Arts Council should only have given grants to those groups which guaranteed cheap access to television companies for filming their major productions. The flagship companies rarely made their work available to mass access through the airwaves because they looked on television 'as the gravy train, not as the great educator. The Arts Council failed to grasp the nettle of using broadcasting as the best means of mass access to its clients. We remained a milch cow.' Grade found great similarities between the Council and the Broadcasting Corporation; both had too many vested interests within their structure and were almost impervious to change. And like the Council, the Corporation was 'a cultural institution, which had adopted the language of the market-place, not held the high ground. It will cost them dear when the renewal of their Charter comes up.'

Even the new Department of National Heritage appeared not to have a strategy for the arts or broadcasting. There was no long-term thinking. 'You cannot keep on restructuring the arts every year', Grade has said. 'All is a giant pending tray – the same in education and the health service. All in the name of cutting costs. Yet what costs you money is changing your mind.' All the organizations closely tied to government had spent the last ten years trying to convince their masters how efficient they were. 'But at the end of the day, if the programmes are no good, who cares?' The Arts Council and radio and television had been the great teachers of social democracy in Britain; but now the interminable revisions imposed upon them threatened the quality of what they did. By never engaging fully in the opportunities for access to the best offered by the communications revolution, the Arts Council now found itself a spectre at a moveable feast like the last one given by Timon of Athens, with the bowls all bare.

In literature, too, the Arts Council's innovations were tardy and took place after the funding stopped. The major literary award given to V. S. Naipaul was mostly the gift of a private foundation. Schemes of sending writers to teach in prisons and civic centres and libraries were overdue, although they were now promulgated, and some annual bursaries were awarded to authors. At a lunch to express solidarity with the condemned writer Salman Rushdie, Lord Palumbo announced another £1 million for literature despite the stringency of the times. It was not enough, but it was the first step in what the Literature Panel had been demanding, 'a radical revaluation of priorities'. As a leading publisher has said, the time had already come economically when few publishers would now support young novelists through their first three or four books. But as the new Chairman of the Literature Panel, Michael Holroyd, also recognized of the decisions of the Arts Council, 'There is no level paying-field. Choices are weighted by the past. It is almost impossible to break out of the original exclusion or present underfunding of literature.' Yet the number of awards to writers was increased to sixteen a year, a translation fund of £100,000 annually was instituted, and authors were sent to gaols to teach the inmates how to use words and so not see their prison bars as a cage.

Moreover, there was innovation in the Department of the Visual Arts, which was trying to educate new audiences. It was operating 'in a stereophonic way' in the opinion of its retiring Panel Chairman, Professor Christopher Frayling. 'On the one hand, the revenue clients and partnerships', such as aiding the Lucien Freud show at the Whitechapel Gallery and the Jack Yeats show at the Arnolfini; 'on the other, raising the temperature of public understanding and awareness, and improving the infrastructure'. In particular, the founding with the London Arts Board of the Institute of New International Visual Arts in order to promote and create a space for diverse English cultures attracted an extraordinary amount of regional, national and international interest. As Frayling pointed out, forty per cent of the inhabitants of Westminster did not have English as their first language. 'It is the first new gallery or institutional development with which the Arts Council has been involved for over a quarter of a century – and a world leader.' Frayling left the championship of the Panel to the leading architect Sir Richard Rogers, who might be expected to pursue the policy of vigorous experimentation of the preceding seven years.

Yet in general the remorseless process of chopping off the arms and legs of the Council was continuing. It was government policy. The environment minister announced a new era in relations between central government and the regions with a £1.4 billion budget to improve job prospects and housing, also to encourage greater economic development, including more funding from the European Community. As for the Arts Council, the Minister of National Heritage announced that it was to keep no more than twenty-five organizations of national importance as its clients: the rest would be directly funded by the Regional Arts Boards after April 1994, when yet another evaluation of the role of the Council would be completed. This devolution would not take place, but the threat was there. Riding between the Department and the regions put the Council in the role of King Lear, going from daughter to daughter for shelter, only to have more of his knights eliminated as the condition for taking him inside. And there would be a second revision of the Royal Charter, by which Wales and Scotland would receive their formal independence, and the Arts Council become that of England alone. There would no longer be a Great Britain of the arts.

Both of these separate countries had nearly been devolved fifteen years before, and they were in fact responsible for their own countries, answering to their Secretaries of State. In Wales, curiously enough, the arts were already in better shape than anywhere outside London. 'A bit of serendipity, really', the Director of the Welsh Arts Council, Tom Owen, has said. 'It was not really planned.' He ascribed the general feeling for the arts among the Welsh to a homogeneous social situation with very few class distinctions. The arts were, anyway, 'what we choose to support'. And outside the Welsh National Opera, the choice was very much in those areas where the London Council was weakest, in films and literature. In 1992–93, the film grant was trebled, not only to initiate a national film archive, but to aid the renaissance of animated films in Cardiff. As for literature written both in the Welsh and English languages, who would save it unless the Council did? Although Tom Owen refused to attempt to define the arts, there were two of them which he did say 'were more arts than others'. And modern Welsh poets were grateful for this munificence. As Harri Webb wrote:

> White Jesus bach, let no ill
> Befall Big Heads Art Coucil.
> Pounds they have, many thousand,

Like full till shop draper grand.
Good is the work they are at,
Soaped they shall be in Seiat,
Reserved shall be for them
A place in Big Seat Salem.
Praised let them be for this thing,
Money they are distributing
Like Beibil Moses his manna,
Tongue we all, bards Welsh, Ta!

Uniquely from Edinburgh, there emerged a coherent Charter for the Arts in Scotland subtitled *Arts for a new century*. It had one experienced author, Joyce McMillan, to distil the seminars and discussion papers into a smooth malt. It concluded that central government together with national funding bodies should take a 'holistic' view of cultural funding and development in Scotland. Although barriers between 'high' art and popular cultures should be removed, particularly in the music industry, the Scottish Arts Council must strengthen its commitment to traditional arts as well as 'applied arts' and the formal and informal education system. Films were a 'cultural industry' and should be supported as should broadcasting organizations. Although the distinction between amateurs and professionals should be reviewed and community arts be encouraged, the Scottish Arts Council should 'act as an advocate for artistic quality' as well as consulting the appropriate language for artistic assessment. While taking aboard the new criteria, there was no throwing of the old standards over the guard rail.

That had long been the case in Scotland. The former Director of the Council, Timothy Mason, had been sceptical of welfare attempts south of the Tweed. He had called Sir Roy Shaw's offices in London the 'Headmaster's study (where) social engineering meant more than the arts. It was like little boys playing football in the 'eighties, with twenty little boys rushing after the ball and two in the goalmouth, all shouting, "Tourism, Access, Accountability, and the Economy!" They all rushed after the ball and forgot they were playing the arts.' Although Lord Goodman had thought that the Scots 'loaded their gold on the mules and carried the loot north of the border', Mason personally had found in the English regions that he was talking to social workers and not people in arts administration. That was why he was a devolutionist. Scotland had maintained its standards in the quality of its education and the arts. 'The culture speaks for the nation. If it doesn't speak, it won't have nationhood.'

The previous Chairman of the Scottish Arts Council, Sir Alan Peacock, was a self-confessed gadfly. Although he admitted that making any changes in the giving of arts subsidies was very difficult, he was proud of the excellence of the membership of his Panels because they had power. 'In England, Panels advise officials, who spend subsidies', he has said. 'In Scotland, the reverse. Officials advise Panels, who decide.' A man who questioned the value of the arts funding itself, Sir Alan Peacock thought that the Arts Council in England misused economic arguments to prove the *material* need for the arts. He would prefer consumer choice through vouchers rather than direct grants to producers; but he could not break the system, merely change what he could in Scotland. And there, formal independence was welcomed by the new Director, Seona Reid. Aid to the national cultures had long been determined in point of fact in Edinburgh, but this had to be seen to be so. It was always difficult to disentangle emotion from argument about Scottish independence; but there was no question that there had been a renaissance in the arts, which were now 'unapologetically Scottish in the sense of a national identity'. The new Charter would confirm the past happenings.

In England, the interminable alterations imposed upon the Arts Council had demoralized its staff, who no longer knew what they should do and questioned the very future of the organization. 'This disenchantment is certainly not due to personality problems', one regional representative on the Board has written. 'The last three years have been obsessed by the restructurings – the Council and its staff are still not fully in agreement with or even aware of the roles they are to play – money is short – demands are increasing. The road to a potential *better* future has been made almost criminally difficult, obtuse and tortuous.' What had come into question was the very basis of the Council with its unpaid freelance advisors on the Panels and committees and Boards, and with its salaried and diminishing number of officers.

In an agony of self-criticism, the Council commissioned an internal report, which it decided not to publish. The report condemned the profound misjudgement of policy over the *annus horribilis* of the past year – also suffered by the Queen and the Royal Family. It called for much greater openness, criticizing 'the secrecy and opacity of our decision-making processes'. Any decisions that were made were unsustainable 'on the basis of inadequate paper-work and in particular lack of briefing'. The Woodstock conference had bred the greatest mistakes, because the aborted London orchestra policy and the list of threatened regional theatres had emerged from that meeting. Blame for the resulting fiascos was widely spread, but the Secretary-General, Anthony Everitt, chose to announce his resignation as head of the executive of the Council. He saw his achievement in the hidden agenda of delaying devolution and the dissolution of the Council under pressure from one Minister after another.

Still under question was the matter of paying the members of the Council. The powerful Beverly Anderson was a teacher, who had decided that she could afford her advisory roles for some years, which included the leadership of the Book Trust, but all the same, 'the citizens must be paid for their time'. The system of unpaid members of Arts Boards left them in the hands of those who could afford the time: 'it was the weapon of the élite'. Another member of the Council, Anthony Smith, once the Director of the British Film Institute and now the President of an Oxford college, was in agreement. 'The Arts Council has retained the flavour of great and good people doing good works, visiting their predilections on society. Their view of service was to contribute their opinions, they were not managers. We now want efficiency and experts, not just holders of aesthetic and social ideas.' There was even talk of paying the Chairman of the Council, something in which the former Vice-Chairman Lord Hutchinson agreed. He had lost a third of his income when he had held the job, and he has said, 'You don't want rich people, necessarily.' Certainly, there was now a lobby for choosing the Chairman from the regions and even locating the headquarters of the Council in the Midlands or further to the north.

That was not to be. When the next Chairman of the Council was selected, he would be unpaid and taken from the metropolitan establishment. He was the Earl of Gowrie, the only Minister for the Arts ever to become the Chairman of the Arts Council. However much he had to do with that choice, the Minister of National

Heritage still had not got on with the new at the sacrifice of the old. The paradox of proliferating bureaucracies at the same time as cutting costs had left the Council in a straddle and a muddle. As Luke Rittner declared in the *Sunday Times*, the Council was a small organization distributing a large amount of money:

> The government, not the Arts Council, has set up the ten regional arts boards, the costs of which are greatly in excess of their predecessors, the regional arts associations. Why? For political expediency – nothing to do with the well-being of the arts. If the government had been honestly concerned about reducing the cost of delivering its money to the arts, it should have abolished the regional arts associations and invited the Arts Council to undertake their role, or abolished the Arts Council and let the regional arts boards do its work. Either way, there would have been savings. Under the guise of economy, the government has created a far more costly structure than existed before.
>
> Arts organizations lurch from funding crisis to funding crisis, trying to respond to the rising tide of paperwork demanded by an Arts Council itself relentlessly pestered by a powerful ministry for justification for every penny spent. There is no clear government policy for the arts, and no public debate. If the government wants to kill off the Arts Council, it should say so and there should be a debate. If it does not, it should also say so and prove it by getting off the Council's back.
>
> Of one thing I am sure, for all its shortcomings, the Arts Council will be sorely missed if, or when, the last breath is finally squeezed from its exhausted lungs.

The Council soldiered on. Its longevity was the argument for its survival in whatever form was finally decided by the procession of tinkering or destructive ministers. Admired across the world for its low costs and high record of success, the Council appeared to attract at home only critics and mechanics. It had done well for nearly fifty years. Although it was now annually directed to do better, it was assigned the distribution of the funds for the arts which would derive from the national lottery – some five per cent of the proceeds estimated at £70,000,000 a year. This additional subsidy would enable it to play a role in the millennium, which had long been the dream and the concern of Lord Palumbo, who did not wish to create for future ages 'a string of white elephants'.

If the end of the Second World War had created the Arts Council, the coming of the millennium might save it. The Council's first success had been the Festival of Britain of 1951, itself a celebration of the Great Exhibition a century ago. The Minister of National Heritage announced the official date of the millennium for Britain as 2001, as much to prophesy a third national festival after intervals of one-hundred-and-fifty and of fifty years as to assign the right date to the two thousandth year after the birth of Christ. One of the older institutions of Britain, the Royal Society for the Encouragement of the Arts, Manufactures and Commerce, had devised the Great Exhibition and suggested the Festival of Britain. Now it was planning a 'Festival 2000 & 1', dedicated to the technology of living and learning rather than to monuments. Yet enough of these were already tendering for a billion pounds to be spent by the forthcoming Millennium Commission of nine members, with the Minister in the Chair. Half of that sum would be demanded by English Heritage projects alone.

The Chairman of the Arts Council had done much himself to provoke the planning for the national approach to the turn of the century, having launched his crusade a decade before the event. By involving the Council in the preparations, not least with its new architectural unit, he had done much to keep the ark afloat. The government now seemed to him to be:

> Seriously interested in encouraging various cultural agencies – English Heritage, the National Trust, The Museums and Galleries Commission, the Arts Council of Great Britain – to draw up a survey of need for the refurbishment of the buildings for which they are responsible, category by category; as well as to identify the need for new buildings. By this means cathedrals and parish churches would qualify, as would industrial architecture and even the piers which personify the English seaside.
>
> Country houses and listed landscapes could also qualify, as well as theatres, opera houses, arts centres, concert halls and cinemas – anything in fact that could properly be defined as forming a part of the cultural fabric of the nation. Once these agencies have completed their surveys there would emerge the Millennium Map of Need.

With that map, a planned programme of the reconstruction of the fabric of the country might begin. Over the next twenty-five years, it could use the skill of modern British architects and revive the medieval crafts and trades. 'The current abysmally low level of public awareness in the visual arts in this country could be transformed. It is hardly surprising that those who are surrounded by a sea of mediocrity have no yardstick by which to judge what is good and excellent, or even sublime, and *that* is what art, and in particular the great art of architecture, at its best can achieve.' This call for the appreciation of excellence did not forget the economic and social benefits of navigating the Millennium Map of Need. 'My proposal', Lord Palumbo declared, 'puts the arts to work, creates jobs, invites tourism, generates spending on travel in hotels and the retail industry; regenerates inner cities, lifts the spirit, boosts morale, increases confidence, heightens civic pride and creates hope for the future. Art offers certainty, order, abiding value and a spiritual dimension to a tormented world which at the present time has lost direction or certainty.'

During his five years as Chairman of the Arts Council, Lord Palumbo had seen out many Ministers for the Arts and now had inherited a Secretary of State for National Heritage. In that period, there had been more contradictions of policy than continuity of principle in dealing with the structure and role of the Council. Yet Palumbo had been the durable preserver, a Chairman of quiet purpose and shrewd resistance to Whitehall as well as a strategist and visionary of the future of the arts in Britain. His last message in the annual report quoted the concluding lines of John Donne's *A Valediction Forbidding Mourning*:

> Thy firmness makes my circle just,
> And makes me end where I beganne.

The couplet provided for him an injunction and a reflection as he prepared to leave 'this most British, splendid and necessary national institution. Whatever the present difficulties, whatever the criticisms that have been made of the Arts Council and its decisions, nothing shakes my conviction that the arts in this country are best served in the dispensation of Government funding by a body independent of Government, ready to fight for the one individual upon whom our artistic life depends – the artist.'

ENVOI

The two words 'Arts' and 'Culture' in England do make people reach for their blackjack.

Clive Priestley,
Chairman of the London Arts Board

The Arts Council of Great Britain was slipped in by stealth. It was a sleight-of-hand, said its founder, John Maynard Keynes, fifty years ago. Yet if there was going to be state money for the arts, it was not going to be for a Ministry of Culture. Look what had happened in Germany under Hitler: the burning of the books and Lord Haw-Haw. Having defeated the Third Reich at the cost of fifty million dead in all, propaganda became a dirty post-war word. And so the principles of the Arts Council of Great Britain were established. Although funded by taxes, it was to be independent. The government disposed, the Council proposed. And it was at arm's length. If the Council doled out money to a catastrophic company that put on pornography or backed anti-Semitism, the Minister could wash his hands in the House of Commons like Pontius Pilate. 'It was the Council did it, not I.'

Yet Keynes left the Council a dual role by Royal Charter, and ever since, 10 Downing Street and Whitehall have struck at it with a forked tongue. The Council was meant to develop knowledge and access to the fine arts – later the arts – but also to improve the standard of their execution. The purpose was to educate everybody to appreciate the arts, but also to maintain their excellence. Various slogans came out of this double duty, chiefly 'Raise and spread', then 'Few, but roses' rather than 'Many, and dandelions'.

Although the Council grew more by responding to the needs of artists and companies, there were always too many Oliver Twists stretching out their bowls for too few slops of gruel. The Council was criticized for spending too much on opera, too little on brass bands; a fortune on London, a pittance in the regions; and a pottage for innovation, ethnic minorities and the disabled. For its last fifteen years, under intense pressure from successive cabinets and the civil service, the Council had to swing towards more devolution and social welfare programmes and business practices. It had always been a dedicated and careful organization. The changes, however, made it appear to the young artistic community to be acting more like Mr Gradgrind and Scrooge than Mr Pickwick and Tiny Tim.

The arm was no longer at full length: it was being twisted. Grants were being earmarked for government policy. The more the Arts Council in London gave power to the new Regional Arts Boards, the less its appraisals and direct subsidies seemed necessary. Like the serpent swallowing its own tail, it was devolving itself out of existence. And its usually admirable Panels of experts in the various arts and its officers of the various Departments were being given little time to stoke the engines of the multiple cultures of Great Britain. They were being bled to death by a thousand internal reviews and lessons in fashionable social thinking.

There was hardly an hour left to arrange for excellence or to provide access to it. Cost-conscious Ministers made the Council cut itself and its clients to the bone marrow. It had only survived, really, because the arts had played a major part in the 'Urban Renaissance' of recent times. Halifax and Bradford, Birmingham and Liverpool, Bristol and Glasgow, all these cities had seen a growth of civic pride, often through the revival of the arts in them. In a sense, the terminal throes of the industrial revolution had led to the arts being viewed as some of the building-bricks against inner-city decay, as the Victorians had done with their libraries and museums. All the recent Ministers for the Arts had agreed on their major achievement, the boost to urban regeneration. A policy of devolution to the regions had long been on the political agenda as a way to fill the ballot-box as much as the theatres.

Yet if jumping on the urban trolley saved the metropolitan Arts Council, it also missed the bus. Local authorities were spending more on what they called the arts than the Council was given, while business sponsorship had risen to a quarter of the central government subsidy – and a larger proportion of that was allocated to the regions every year. Local Boards, heavily staffed by councillors and executives from industry as well as trained arts administrators, gave most of the available funds more to win votes and to entertain than to hold events of high quality. With the current shibboleth that art was in the eye of the beholder, and so standards and values were personal, the duty of the Council to keep up excellence made it appear to be the stranded whale of a London élite.

This was totally untrue. From nurturing George Devine's Royal Court Theatre in the nineteen-fifties to establishing a national network of opera and dance companies in the nineteen-eighties, the Council had helped to make England a global magnet of the performing arts. Other than the monuments of Britain, the excellence of its performing arts brought tourists into the country. For every pound spent on subsidizing that excellence, three were returned in employment and tourism, another concern of the new Department of National Heritage, an odd hybrid which the parliamentary National Heritage Committee found had taken over responsibility for managing forty-eight different bodies which had previously been the responsibility of six other Departments. 'These included the National Lottery, museums and galleries, the heritage, tourism, live arts, sport, broadcasting and the press.' Yet compared with the rest of Europe, arts subsidy remained minimal in Britain, while it was envied for the quality of its work. Of course, the performers achieved that, while all artistic directors in the land admitted that, but for the grace of the Arts Council, there went they.

Almost to a man or woman, these directors wanted to keep the Arts Council and the central system. They did not want the *political* influence of the local authorities set against their productions. They were also reaching out towards Europe. Touring was now essential to balance the books. They felt that only London could deal with Paris or Rome or Berlin on their behalf. National excellence might well demand a central group of appraisers and advisers, who should be regularly selected from the brightest and the best in their professions rather than from the older tradition of the great and the good, and certainly not from the politically correct.

The Arts Council had been ground between the two millstones, the wish of Whitehall directly to fund the 'flagships' such as the Royal Opera House, and the desire of the regions to have the power of the purse over their own cultures. It had been wounded by switching its language from maintaining quality to seeking for efficiency. After fifty years of distinguished service, the Arts Council of Great Britain was divided, like Caesar in Gaul, into three parts. In a sense, Scotland and Wales had always run their own arts affairs through their Committees, but their disproportionate membership on the Council in London and their incessant demands for larger slices of the cake had made their independence quite a relief for the truncated Arts Council of England. There was little loss of power in sending independence to Scotland and Wales, only a greater peace.

The perennial squabble with the regions over the share of funding and how independent the Regional Arts Boards should be was hardly resolved. Lord Armstrong was probably right in his recommendation that the government should fix the proportion of the grant-in-aid given to London and the provinces, while respecting the arm's length principle. This unresolved matter was handed on to the Earl of Gowrie, with the battle focused on control of the Research and Development Fund, which administered Projects and Schemes, the vital share which supported innovation in the Arts. Were that to be taken from metropolitan control, many of the staff thought that the Arts Council might as well shut up shop.

Already the Chairman of the Arts Council of England was inheriting in 1995 an easier task. There was more of an emphasis on maintaining standards of excellence and on giving the people access to the best, while considerations of social welfare were declining with the lesser subsidy. The Council's Departments concerned with cultural diversity and disability and women's affairs were being wound down. Assessment of quality was being given priority over binding the sores of society. From the arts was dropped the art of healing.

What lay ahead was the approach to the millennium with increasing funding for the arts from the National Lottery. Hopefully, the agonizing and debilitating decade of reorganization and self-appraisal was over. Under an experienced and dynamic new Chairman, the Arts Council of England could seize the opportunity, if it could retain its power and was allowed to share its resources fairly with the regions. It had done well on the whole for half a century. It had become the role model for many of the state arts organizations of the world. Its failures had been more induced by its political masters than its own shortcomings. Only when the arm's length principle was cut to a short stump, had the Council begun to bleed to death.

But it had survived by its tenacity and its competence – 'a very British institution', as Lord Keynes had said. And it had survived in a country that never rated its arts and its cultures too highly, unless they were threatened by foreign influences or invasions. As Lord McAlpine wrote in his wise and incisive examination of political power, *The Servant*, certain areas of public life were small but vital like the arts, but they were hardly important. They were 'a perfect distraction for a political enemy'. Those involved in the arts, however, were extremely dangerous, but luckily self-seeking in calling for money to promote their own interests and enthusiasms. So they alienated themselves 'from the citizens, who by contrast are interested first in finding work and then in entertainment, usually of a sort that these men would have only contempt for.'

True enough. The words 'arts' and 'cultures' remained suspect to much of the British people and secondary to the considerations of its politicians. And yet, in the fifty years of its existence, the Arts Council of Great Britain, along with the BBC, had been one of the two semi-autonomous bodies which had truly spread and nurtured the arts and cultures of their country. They had fulfilled their Royal Charters, they had done their duty with foresight and economy. Without their guidance, Britain would not enjoy its present excellence in music and opera, dance and drama. The arts left outside their influence, particularly the cinema and prose, were puny in their survival. All arts and cultures did better under the sprinklers of national subsidies.

Given the post-war desolation of Britain fifty years ago, the Arts Council of Great Britain was to serve as the Sower and the Enabler of the last half of this century. Without its being, there would have been a wasteland of bland pap, the commercial reign of Alexander Pope's Dullness:

Thus at her felt approach, and secret might,
Art after art gives out, and all is night.

At the felt approach of the next century, the Arts Council of England and of Scotland and of Wales still continue:

With the millennium and its outlay,
Art after art ignites, and all is day.

Dr Andrew Sinclair, FRSL
London, March, 1995

APPENDIX A

The Texts of the
Two Charters of Incorporation

I

GEORGE THE SIXTH, by the Grace of God of Great Britain, Ireland and the British Dominions beyond the Seas King, Defender of the Faith, Emperor of India:

To all to whom these Presents shall come, Greeting:

WHEREAS is has been represented to Us by Our Chancellor of the Exchequer that for the purpose of developing a greater knowledge, understanding and practice of the fine arts exclusively, and in particular to increase the accessibility of the fine arts to the public throughout Our Realm, to improve the standard of execution of the fine arts and to advise and co-operate with Our Government Departments, local authorities and other bodies on any matters concerned directly or indirectly with those objects, and with a view to facilitating the holding of and dealing with any money provided by Parliament and any other property, real or personal, otherwise available for those objects, it is expedient that the unincorporated Institution formerly known as the Council for the Encouragement of Music and the Arts and now known as the Arts Council of Great Britain should be created a Body Corporate under the name of the Arts Council of Great Britain with the powers and subject to the provisions hereinafter contained:

NOW KNOW YE that We, by virtue of Our Royal Prerogative and of all other powers enabling Us in that behalf, do, of Our special grace, certain knowledge and mere motion given and granted by this Our Charter for Us, Our Heirs and Successors, hereby grant, will, direct and ordain that the following persons (being members of the said unincorporated Institution) that is to say:

1. Sir Ernest Henry Pooley, KCVO, MA, LLB
   Ivor John Carnegie Brown, FRSL
   Sir Lewis Casson, MC
   Sir Kenneth McKenzie Clark, KCB
   Oliver Sylvain Baliol, Viscount Esher, MBE
   Benjamin Ifor Evans, MA, D Litt
   Barbara Ayrton Gould, JP
   The Right Honourable William George Arthur, Baron Harlech, GCMG, DCL, FSA

Thelma Cazalet Keir
Professor Sir Stanley Marchant, CVO, D Mus, FSA, FRAM, FRCM, FRCO
Ralph Vaughan Williams, OM, Mus D, D Mus
William Emrys Williams, CBE

and all the other persons who shall for the time being in pursuance of and in accordance with this Our Charter be members of the Arts Council of Great Britain, shall be one Body Corporate under the name of 'The Arts Council of Great Britain' (hereinafter referred to as 'the Council'), having a perpetual succession and a Common Seal, with full power by and in such name –
(a) to sue and be sued;
(b) to enter into contracts or agreements in furtherance of the said objects of the Council;
(c) to accept, hold and dispose of money or other personal property in furtherance of the said objects, including sums voted by Parliament to that end;
(d) to accept any trusts, whether subject to special conditions or not, in furtherance of the said objects;
(e) to invest any moneys and funds of the Council which are not immediately required to be expended in furtherance of the said objects in or upon any investments for the time being authorized by law for the investment of trust funds and to vary, or transpose, any investments held, or made, by the Council into investments of a nature so authorized;
(f) generally to do all other lawful acts whatsoever that may be conducive or incidental to the attainment of the objects for which the Council is hereby established.

POWER TO ACQUIRE LAND

2. We do for Us, Our Heirs and Successors license, authorize and for ever hereafter enable the Council or any person or persons on its behalf to purchase, take on lease or otherwise acquire any lands, tenements or hereditaments now held by or in trust for or for the use of or belonging to the said unincorporated Institution, and also to purchase, take on lease or otherwise acquire any additional lands, tenements or hereditaments, and to hold all or any lands, tenements or hereditaments, or interest therein, in perpetuity or on lease or otherwise and from time to time grant, demise, alienate or otherwise dispose of the same or any part thereof.

And We do for Us, Our Heirs and Successors give and grant Our licence to any person or persons and any body politic or corporate to assure in perpetuity or otherwise, or to demise to or for the benefit of the Council any lands, tenements or hereditaments whatsoever within Our United Kingdom of Great Britain and Northern Ireland.

APPLICATION OF INCOME

3. (1) The income and property of the Council wheresoever derived shall be applied solely towards the promotion of the objects of the Council as set forth in this Our Charter.

(2) Subject to the provisions of Article 8(1) in the case of a member of the Executive Committee, no member of the Council shall receive any remuneration

for his services, but nothing in this paragraph shall prevent reimbursement to any member of the Council of actual expenses incurred by him in the performance of his duties.

ORGANIZATION
I. *The Council*

4. (1) The persons whose names are set out in Article 1 of this Our Charter shall be the first members of the Council and shall continue in office until they respectively retire or vacate such office as is hereinafter provided and the first Chairman thereof shall be the said Sir Ernest Henry Pooley who shall retire on the 31 December, 1948.

(2) The following members of the Council, being persons whose names are set out in the said Article 1, shall retire from such membership on the dates set out opposite their names respectively, that is to say:

Ivor John Carnegie Brown, FRSL	31 December, 1947
Sir Lewis Casson, MC	31 December, 1947
Sir Kenneth McKenzie Clark, KCB	31 December, 1947
Oliver Sylvain Baliol, Viscount Esher, MBE	31 December, 1947
Benjamin Ifor Evans, MA, D Litt	31 December, 1948
Barbara Ayrton Gould, JP	31 December, 1948
The Right Honourable William George Arthur, Baron Harlech, GCMG, DCL, FSA	31 December, 1948
Thelma Cazalet Keir	31 December, 1948
Professor Sir Stanley Marchant, CVO, D Mus, FSA, FRAM, FRCM, FRCO	31 December, 1949
Ralph Vaughan Williams, OM, Mus D, D Mus	31 December, 1949
William Emrys Williams, CBE	31 December, 1949

5. (1) The Members of the Council shall, from time to time be respectively appointed by Our Chancellor of the Exchequer after consultation with Our Minister of Education and Our Secretary of State for Scotland and shall not exceed sixteen in number.

(2) The Chairman of the Council shall be such one of the members thereof as Our Chancellor of the Exchequer, after such consultation as aforesaid, shall appoint to such office and shall, subject as provided in paragraph (5) of this Article, hold office for a period of five years and on the expiration of any such period shall be eligible for re-appointment.

(3) The members of the Council, other than the Chairman, subject as provided in paragraph (5) of this Article, shall hold office for such period not exceeding five years as may be determined at the time of their appointment.

(4) On the expiration of his period of office a member of the Council, other than the Chairman, shall not be eligible for re-appointment until the expiration of a period of one year Provided that a member who, immediately before his ceasing to hold office, was also a member of the Executive Committee hereinafter referred to, may be immediately re-appointed, if, in the opinion of Our Chancellor of the Exchequer, such immediate re-appointment is especially desirable.

(5) A member of the Council shall *ipso facto* cease to be a member thereof

(*a*) if his membership be terminated by Our Chancellor of the Exchequer, or

(*b*) if he accept or hold the office of Auditor of the Council, or

(*c*) if he becomes of unsound mind or bankrupt or compounds with his creditors, or

(*d*) if he sends in a written resignation of his membership to the Council.

6. The Council shall, with the approval of the Lords Commissioners of Our Treasury, appoint one of their members to be the Vice-Chairman thereof for such period not exceeding five years as may be determined by the Council.

7. (1) The Council shall meet at least four times in every year.

(2) The Chairman, or in his absence, the Vice-Chairman, shall preside at every meeting of the Council and may, with the consent of any meeting whether or not a quorum is present, adjourn the meeting from time to time and from place to place.

(3) Questions arising at any meeting shall be decided by a majority of votes of those personally present and in case of an equality of votes the Chairman, or, if the Vice-Chairman is presiding, the Vice-Chairman, shall have a second or casting vote.

(4) The Chairman or Vice-Chairman may at any time, and shall at the request in writing of the Executive Committee hereinafter referred to or of any three members of the Council, summon a meeting of the Council.

(5) The quorum necessary for the transaction of the business of the Council shall be seven members of the Council personally present.

(6) Subject to the foregoing provisions of this Article, the Council may regulate its own procedure.

II. *The Executive Committee*

8. (1) The Council shall appoint an Executive Committee consisting of the Chairman, the Vice-Chairman and such other members of the Council as the Council and the Lords Commissioners of Our Treasury shall agree and the Council may pay to the members of the Executive Committee such reasonable remuneration as the Council think fit.

(2) A member of the Executive Committee shall *ipso facto* cease to be a member thereof

(*a*) if his membership be terminated by the Council after consultation with the Lords Commissioners of Our Treasury, or

(*b*) if for any cause he ceases to be a member of the Council.

9. The Executive Committee shall exercise all the powers of the Council except those powers which the Council may specifically reserve to itself.

10. (1) The Executive Committee shall meet at least once in every month for the despatch of business and may with the consent of any meeting whether or not a quorum is present adjourn the meeting from time to time and from place to place.

(2) The Chairman or in his absence the Vice-Chairman or in the absence of both of them some other member of the Committee elected to the Chair by the other members of the Committee present shall preside at all meetings of the Committee.

(3) Questions arising at any meeting shall be decided by a majority of votes of those personally present and in the case of an equality of votes the person presiding shall have a second or casting vote.

(4) The Chairman or Vice-Chairman may at any time, and at the request in writing of any member of the Committee shall, summon a meeting of the Committee.

(5) The quorum necessary for the transaction of the business of the Committee shall be three members of the Committee personally present.

(6) Subject to the foregoing provisions of this Article, the Council may make regulations governing the procedure of the Executive Committee.

11. The person presiding at any meeting of the Executive Committee shall, in any case where any matter before the Committee in his opinion

(a) is of exceptional novelty or importance or is likely to lead to considerable expense, or

(b) gives rise to or is likely to give rise to a serious difference of opinion in the Committee or among its advisers and officials and he considers that the Council should be so informed, or

(c) gives rise or is likely to give rise to criticism or opposition on the part of a responsible section of public opinion,

refer the matter to the Council with a view to obtaining further instructions thereon.

III. Committees and Panels

12. (1) The Council shall appoint,

(a) with the consent of Our Secretary of State for Scotland, a Committee for Scotland,

(b) with the consent of Our Minister of Education, a Committee for Wales,

to advise and assist the Council in the promotion of the objects of the Council in Scotland and Wales respectively.

(2) The members of any such Committee shall consist of such member or members of the Council and such other persons as the Council may from time to time appoint after consultation with Our Secretary of State for Scotland or Our Minister of Education according as to whether such Committee is to be appointed for Scotland or Wales respectively and the Council shall, after such consultation as aforesaid, appoint one of the members of any such Committee, being also a member of the Council, to be Chairman thereof.

(3) The Council may at any time revoke the appointment of any such Committee or member thereof after such consultation as aforesaid.

(4) The Council may, from time to time, make such regulations as to quorum and procedure of any such Committee as it thinks fit and any such Committee shall conform to such regulations.

13. (1) The Council may appoint panels (consisting of such member or members of the Council and such other persons as the Council think fit) to advise upon the general promotion of all or any one or more of the objects of the Council and may, at any time, revoke the appointment of any such advisory panel or member thereof.

(2) The Council may, from time to time, make such regulations as to quorum and procedure of any such panel as it thinks fit; any such panel shall conform to any regulations so made.

14. The members of any Committee or panel appointed under Article 12 or 13 shall be entitled to be reimbursed expenses actually incurred in the course of their duties as such members but shall not be entitled to any payment for their services as such members.

IV. *Assessors*

15. Each of them, Our Chancellor of the Exchequer, Our Secretary of State for Scotland and Our Minister of Education may, at any time and from time to time, appoint, in writing, an officer of his to be an assessor to the Council and any such officer so appointed shall be entitled to attend meetings of the Council, the Executive Committee and any Committee and panel appointed under Articles 12 and 13.

V. *Officers*

16. (1) The Council shall with the approval of Our Chancellor of the Exchequer appoint a Secretary General who shall be the Principal Executive Officer of the Council.

(2) The Council may appoint such other officers and servants as it may consider necessary for carrying out its objects.

17. The terms as to remuneration, pension and otherwise upon which appointments are made under Article 16 shall conform with any directions that may be given by the Lords Commissioners of Our Treasury.

ACCOUNTS AND MINUTES

18. The accounts of the Council shall be made up for each financial year ending on the 31st day of March and shall be prepared audited and submitted to the Lords Commissioners of Our Treasury in such manner and at such times as the Lords Commissioners may direct.

19. The Council shall cause true accounts to be kept of the sums of money received and expended by the Council, and the matters in respect of which such receipts and expenditure take place, and of the assets and liabilities of the Council.

20. The Council and the Executive Committee shall cause Minutes to be made in books provided for the purpose
(a) of all appointments of officers or servants made by the Council or the Committee,
(b) of the names of the members and other persons present at each meeting of the Council or the Committee,
(c) of all resolutions and proceedings at all meetings of the Council or the Committee.

21. The books of account and minutes of the Council and of the Executive Committee shall be kept at the headquarters for the time being of the Council, or at such other place or places as the Council may think fit, and shall always be open to the inspection of the members of the Council.

ANNUAL REPORT

22. (1) The Council shall, as soon after the month of March as may be possible, prepare a General Report of its proceedings for the year preceding.

(2) The Chairman shall, on the completion of every such annual General Report, forthwith submit the same to the Lords Commissioners of Our Treasury.

GENERAL

23. No act or proceeding of the Council or of the Executive Committee or of any Committee or panel appointed by the Council under Articles 12 or 13 shall be invalidated or questioned by reason of the existence of any vacancy or vacancies in its membership or the disqualification of, or any irregularity in the appointment of, any member or members or by reason of any accidental omission to give to any member or members or the non-receipt by any member or members of notice of the meeting.

24. (1) Any instrument which, if made by a private person, would be required to be under seal, shall be under the seal of the Council. Any notice, appointment, contract, order or other document made by or proceeding from the Council or the Executive Committee which is not required to be under seal shall be signed by such members or officers as the Council may direct.

(2) The Council shall provide for the safe custody of the Seal of the Council which shall not be affixed to any instrument except by the authority of a resolution of the Council, and in the presence of at least one member of the Council and the Secretary-General, or such other person as the Council may appoint for the purpose, and such member of the Council and the said Secretary-General or such other person as aforesaid shall sign every instrument to which the seal of the Council is affixed in their presence.

GENERAL DECLARATION

25. Lastly We do by these Presents for Us, Our Heirs and Successors grant and declare that this Our Charter or the enrolment thereof shall in all things be valid and effectual in law according to the true intent and meaning of the same and shall be recognized as valid and effectual by all Our Courts and Judges and by other officers, persons and bodies politic and corporate whom it may concern, and that the same shall be construed in the most favourable and beneficial sense for, and for the best advantage of, the Council as well in all Our Several Courts of Record as elsewhere, notwithstanding any non-recital, mis-recital, uncertainty or imperfection in this Our Charter.

In witness whereof We have caused these Our Letters to be made Patent.

Witness Ourself at Westminster, the ninth day of August in the tenth year of Our Reign.

By warrant under the King's Sign Manual

(*Signed*) NAPIER

II

ELIZABETH THE SECOND, by the Grace of God of the United Kingdom of Great Britain and Northern Ireland and of Our other Realms and Territories Queen, Head of the Commonwealth, Defender of the Faith:

To all to whom these Presents shall come, Greeting!

WHEREAS His Majesty King George the Sixth in the year of our Lord One thousand nine hundred and forty-six by Royal Charter (hereinafter called 'the Original Charter') dated the ninth day of August in the tenth year of His Reign constituted a Body Corporate by the name of 'The Arts Council of Great Britain' (hereinafter referred to as 'the Council') with perpetual succession and with power to sue and be sued by the said name and to use a Common Seal:

AND WHEREAS the Original Charter was amended by the Secretary of State for Education and Science Order 1964 and the Transfer of Functions (Cultural Institutions) Order 1965:

AND WHEREAS it has been represented unto Us that it is expedient for the better execution of the purposes thereof that the provisions of the Original Charter as so amended should be further amended and that this may best be done by the grant of a new Charter replacing the original Charter:

NOW THEREFORE KNOW YE that We, by virtue of Our Prerogative Royal and of all other powers enabling Us so to do have of Our especial grace, certain knowledge and mere motion granted and declared and do by these Presents for Us, Our Heirs and Successors, grant and declare as follows:

1. The provisions of the Original Charter, except insofar as they incorporate the Arts Council of Great Britain and confer upon it perpetual succession, are hereby revoked, but nothing in this revocation shall affect the legality or validity of any act, deed or thing lawfully done or executed under the provisions of the Original Charter.

2. The Council shall have a Common Seal, with power to break, alter and make anew the said Seal from time to time at their will and pleasure and by their name shall and may sue and be sued in all courts and in all manner of actions and suits, and shall have power to enter into contracts, to acquire, hold and dispose of property of any kind, to accept trusts and generally to do all matters and things incidental or appertaining to a Body Corporate.

3. The objects for which the Council are established and incorporated are as follows:

(a) to develop and improve the knowledge, understanding and practice of the arts;

(b) to increase the accessibility of the arts to the public throughout Great Britain; and

(c) to advise and co-operate with Departments of Our Government, local authorities and other bodies on any matters concerned whether directly or indirectly with the foregoing objects.

4. All moneys and property howsoever received by the Council, including any moneys voted by Parliament, shall be applied solely towards the promotion of the objects of the Council and no portion thereof (except as otherwise provided in this Our Charter) shall be paid or transferred directly or indirectly to the members of the Council.

5. (1) The Council shall consist of a Chairman, a Vice-Chairman and not more than eighteen other members.

(2) The Chairman and the other members shall be appointed by Our Secretary of State after consultation with Our Secretaries of State for Scotland and Wales and the terms of their appointment shall be determined by Our Secretary of State.

(3) The Vice-Chairman shall be appointed by the Council, with the approval of Our Secretary of State, from among the members of the Council and the terms of his appointment as such shall be determined by the Council.

(4) Every member shall hold and vacate his office in accordance with the terms of his appointment but

(a) a member shall not be appointed for a term of more than five years;

(b) a member other than the Chairman and the Vice-Chairman of the Council, of the Scottish Arts Council and of the Welsh Arts Council and the Chairman of a panel shall not be eligible for re-appointment on ceasing to be a member until the expiration of one year; and

(c) a member may at any time by notice in writing to Our Secretary of State resign his office.

(5) The Council shall not make to any member of the Council any payment by way of remuneration for his services as such, but may reimburse to any such member expenses reasonably incurred by him in the performance of his duties.

6. (1) The Council may act notwithstanding a vacancy among the members and the validity of any proceedings of the Council shall not be affected by any defect in the appointment of a member.

(2) The quorum of the Council shall be seven members personally present or such greater number as the Council may from time to time determine.

7. Subject to the provisions of this Our Charter, the Council may regulate their own procedure.

8. (1) The Council shall, with the approval respectively of Our Secretary of State for Scotland and Our Secretary of State for Wales, appoint committees, to be called the Scottish Arts Council and the Welsh Arts Council, to exercise, or advise them on the exercise of, their functions in Scotland and Wales.

(2) Subject to such approval, the Council shall appoint as chairman of each committee a member of the committee who is a member of the Council.

(3) The Council may appoint to either committee persons who are not members of the Council and, subject in the case of the chairman of each committee to such approval as aforesaid, may at any time revoke the appointment of any member of either committee.

9. (1) The Council may appoint other committees and panels to advise and assist them in the exercise of such of their functions as may be determined by the Council.

(2) The Council shall appoint as chairman of any such committee or panel a member of the committee or panel who is a member of the Council.

(3) The Council may appoint to any such committee or panel members who are not members of the Council and may at any time revoke the appointment of any member of such committee or panel.

10. (1) The Council may regulate the procedure of any committee or panel appointed by them in pursuance of Articles 8 and 9 of this Our Charter.

(2) Article 5(5) of this Our Charter shall apply to members of such committees and panels as it applies to members of the Council.

11. Any officer of the Departments of Our Secretaries of State for Education and Science, for Scotland or for Wales who is appointed by the relevant Secretary of State to be an assessor to the Council, or to any committee or panel of the Council, shall be entitled to attend any meeting of the Council or as the case may be of any committee or panel to which he is so appointed.

12. (1) The Council shall, with the approval of Our Secretary of State, appoint a Secretary General who shall be the principal executive officer of the Council and may appoint such other officers and take into their employment such other persons as the Council may determine.

(2) The Council may

(a) pay to their Secretary General and to their other officers and to other persons employed by them such remuneration as the Council may, with the approval of Our Secretary of State and the Lords Commissioners of Our Treasury, from time to time determine; and

(b) as regards any officers or other persons employed in whose case it may be determined by the Council, with the approval of Our Secretary of State and the Lords Commissioners of Our Treasury, so to do, pay to or in respect of them such pensions (including gratuities), or provide and maintain for them such pension schemes (whether contributory or not), as may be so determined.

13. The Council shall keep proper accounts and other records, and shall prepare for each financial year statements of account in such form as Our Secretary of State with the approval of the Lords Commissioners of Our Treasury may direct and submit those statements of account to Our Secretary of State at such time as he may direct.

14. The Council shall as soon as possible after the end of each financial year make to Our Secretary of State a report on the exercise and performance by them of their functions during that year.

15. The application of the Seal of the Council shall be authenticated by the signatures of the Chairman or of some other member of the Council authorized generally or especially by the Council to act for that purpose, and of one of such officers of the Council as may be so authorized by the Council so to act.

16. The Council may by resolution in that behalf passed at a meeting of the Council by a majority of not less than three-quarters of the members present and voting (being an absolute majority of the whole number of the members of the Council) and confirmed at a further meeting of the Council held not less than one month nor

more than four months afterwards by a like majority, add to or amend this Our Charter, and such addition or amendment, when allowed by Us, Our Heirs or Successors in Council, shall become effectual, so that this Our Charter shall thenceforward continue and operate as though it had been originally granted and made accordingly: and this provision shall apply to this Our Charter as added to or amended in manner aforesaid.

17. In this Our Charter references to Our Secretary of State are to Our Secretary of State for Education and Science.

In witness whereof We have caused these Our Letters to be made Patent.

Witness Ourself at Westminster the Seventh day of February in the Sixteenth year of Our Reign.

By warrant under the Queen's Sign Manual

(Signed) COLDSTREAM

APPENDIX B

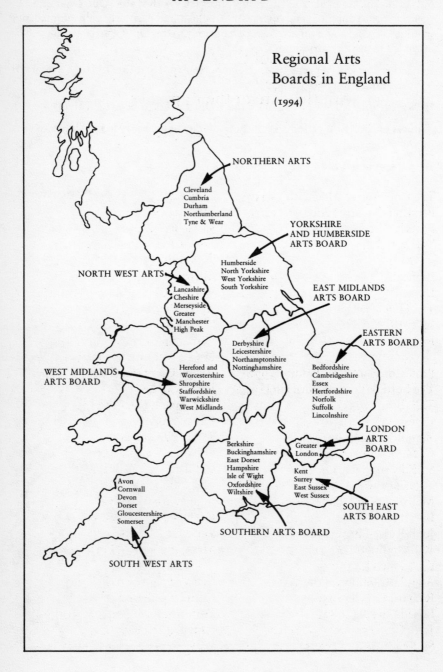

Regional Arts
Boards in England

(1994)

NORTHERN ARTS

Cleveland
Cumbria
Durham
Northumberland
Tyne & Wear

YORKSHIRE
AND HUMBERSIDE
ARTS BOARD

Humberside
North Yorkshire
West Yorkshire
South Yorkshire

NORTH WEST ARTS

Lancashire
Cheshire
Merseyside
Greater
Manchester
High Peak

EAST MIDLANDS
ARTS BOARD

Derbyshire
Leicestershire
Northamptonshire
Nottinghamshire

EASTERN
ARTS BOARD

Bedfordshire
Cambridgeshire
Essex
Hertfordshire
Norfolk
Suffolk
Lincolnshire

WEST MIDLANDS
ARTS BOARD

Hereford and
Worcestershire
Shropshire
Staffordshire
Warwickshire
West Midlands

LONDON
ARTS
BOARD

Greater
London

Berkshire
Buckinghamshire
East Dorset
Hampshire
Isle of Wight
Oxfordshire
Wiltshire

Kent
Surrey
East Sussex
West Sussex

SOUTH EAST
ARTS BOARD

Avon
Cornwall
Devon
Dorset
Gloucestershire
Somerset

SOUTHERN ARTS BOARD

SOUTH WEST ARTS

Members of the Arts Council of Great Britain from 1946 to 1994 with the date of their appointment

The Countess of Albemarle (1950)
Bronson (later Sir) Albery (1947)
Beverly Anderson (1990)
The Marchioness of Anglesey (1971)
Professor James F. Arnott (1976)
Dame Peggy Ashcroft (1961)
The Hon Michael Astor (1967)
Bernard Atha (1978–81)
Richard (later Lord) Attenborough (1969)
Professor Harold C. Baldry (1972)
The Lord Balfour of Burleigh (1970)
T. E. Bean (1957)
Ernest Boden (1956)
Alan Bowness (1972)
C. M. Bowra (1947)
Sir Edward (later Lord) Boyle (1966)
Melvyn Bragg (1977)
Ivor Brown (1945)
John Russell Brown (1979)
William Brown (1991)
David Buckle (1977)
Alan L. C. Bullock (1960)
Richard Capell (1950)
David Cargill (1987)
John Carter (1950)
Sir Lewis Casson (1945)

Lady Casson (1971)
Mrs Cazalet-Keir (1945)
Sir George Christie (1987)
Tony Church (1982–85)
Sir Kenneth Clark (1945)
Michael Clarke (1985)
William Cleaver (1979)
Ann Clwyd (1974)
Professor (later Sir) William Coldstream (1952)
Lt Col. Vere Cotton (1953)
Joseph Compton (1948)
James Cooke (1987)
Sir Kenneth Cork (1984)
John Cornwell (1985)
The Lord Cottesloe (1959)
Frederic R. Cox (1967)
Col (later Sir) William Crawshay (1962)
John Culshaw (1974)
Constance Cummings (1964)
Edric Cundell (1950)
Mrs (later Lady) Hugh Dalton (1948)
Cedric Thorpe Davie (1967)
Cecil Day-Lewis (1965)
Professor Basil Deane (1977)
Lady Digby (1981–85)
Professor T. A. Dunn (1970)

Gerald H. Elliott (1979)
Michael Elliott (1972)
Buchi Emecheta (1981)
The Lord Esher (1945)
Martin Esslin (1975)
Sir Emrys Evans (1957)
Sir Hywel Evans (1980)
Dr B. Ifor Evans (1945)
Lord Feather (1973)
Ruth, The Lady Fermoy (1952)
Lady Antonia Fraser (1969)
Professor Christopher Frayling
   (1987)
Albert E. Frost (1981)
Roy Fuller (1975)
Patrick (later Lord) Gibson (1971)
Sir William Glock (1971)
Lord Goodman (1964)
Noel Goodwin (1978–81)
Mrs B. Ayrton Gould (1945)
Professor Lawrence Gowing (1961)
The Earl of Gowrie (1994)
Sir Cecil Graves (1949)
Ronald (later Sir) Grierson (1984)
Wyn Griffith (1948)
Maggie Guillebaud (1993)
Peter Gummer (1990)
Robin Guthrie (1978)
Ernest (later Sir) Hall (1989)
Peter (later Sir) Hall (1968)
Stuart Hampshire (1971)
G. Laurence Harbottle (1975)
Jeremy Hardie (1983)
The Earl of Harewood (1965)
The Lord Harlech (1945)
Pamela, Lady Harlech (1985)
Gavin Henderson (1994)
Dr Ronald Henson (1980)
The Lady Hesketh (1961)
Denys Hodson (1987)
Dr Richard Hoggart (1975)
Michael Holroyd (1992)
Thelma Holt (1993)

Jeremy (later Lord) Hutchinson QC
   (1979)
Brian Ivory (1982–86)
P. D. James (later Baroness James of
   Holland Park) (1988)
Gavin Jantjes (1985)
Professor A. N. Jeffares (1979)
Hugh (later Lord) Jenkins MP
   (1967)
Professor Gwyn Jones (1956)
Philip Jones (1983)
Councillor J. D. Kelly (1959)
Robert Kemp (1954)
Professor Frank Kermode (1967)
The Lady Keynes (1946)
Gavin Laird (1983)
J. W. Lambert (1968)
Marghanita Laski (1978–85)
John Last (1979)
Benn W. Levy (1952)
Sir Anthony Lewis (1952)
David Lewis (1990)
Eric Linklater (1947)
Sir Joseph Lockwood (1966)
James Logan (1983)
Alistair (later Lord) McAlpine
   (1980)
Bryan Magee (1992)
Capt J. H. F. (later Sir John)
   McEwen (1951)
George (later Sir) McGlashan
   (1950)
Colin Mackenzie (1962)
The Viscount Mackintosh of
   Halifax (1958)
John Manduell (1975)
Sir Stanley Marchant (1945)
Dr A. H. Marshall (1972)
Hugh Marshall (1966)
Professor Denis Mathews (1971)
Dr H. O. Mavor (1945)
Dr Jonathan Miller (1974)
Henry Moore (1963)

James Morris (1977)
Clare Mulholland (1985)
Colin Nears (1981)
Sir John Newson (1952)
Trevor Nunn (1964)
Lady Ogilvie (1952)
Dr Alun Oldfield-Davies (1967)
Annette Page (1975)
Peter (later Lord) Palumbo (1989)
Neil Paterson (1973)
Professor Alan Peacock (1985)
Stephen Phillips (1994)
Mrs Myfanwy Piper (1964)
Sir Ernest Pooley (1945)
Sir John Pope-Hennessy (1967)
Usha Prashar (1978 and 1994)
Mathew Prichard (1982)
Clive Priestley (1991)
Anthony Quinton (1978)
Sir William (later Lord) Rees-Mogg
   (1981)
Professor D. Talbot Rice (1963)
The Hon. Sir Jasper Ridley (1954)
Dame Jean Roberts (1964)
Lewis Robertson (1969)
Duncan Robinson (1980)
Sir Kenneth Robinson (1976)
Stella Robinson (1992)
Sir Richard Rogers (1994)
The Countess of Rosebery (1947)
Robert Rowe (1981)
Sir Brian (later Lord) Rix (1985)

Rt Hon. Sir Leslie Scarman (1967)
Colin Shaw (1977)
Sir Roy Shaw (1971)
Councillor Sally Shaw (1988)
Donald Sinden (1981)
George Singleton (1967)
Prudence Skene (1992)
Anthony Smith (1990)
The Lord Snow (1970)
Robert Southgate (1992)
The Earl of Snowdon (1963)
Sir Roy Strong (1982)
David Sylvester (1979)
Mrs Elizabeth Thomas (1974)
The Lady Vaizey (1975)
Adrian Ward-Jackson (1988)
Dame Veronica Wedgwood (1957)
Dr James Welsh (1946)
Sir Wyn Wheldon (1954)
Hugh Willatt (1957)
Peter Williams (1972)
Professor Raymond Williams
   (1973)
Sir W. E. Williams (1945)
Dr R. Vaughan Williams (1945)
Angus Wilson (1966)
Professor Colin St John Wilson
   (1990)
John (later Sir John) Witt (1961)
Dr Robert Woof (1982)
Dr Thomas Wood (1948)
Sir Brian Young (1982)

APPENDIX D

Senior Posts at
the Arts Council, 1946–94

Secretary-General
Mary Glasgow (1946–1951)
Sir W. E. Williams (1951–1963)
N. J. Abercrombie (1963–1968)
Sir Hugh Willatt (1968–1978)
Sir Roy Shaw (1978–1983)
Luke Rittner (1983–1990)
Anthony Everitt (1990–1994)
Mary Allen (1994–)

Deputy Secretary-General
M. J. McRobert (1950–1971)
Angus Stirling (1971–1979)
Richard Pulford (1979–1985)
Anthony Everitt (1985–1990)
Margaret Hyde (1991–1992)
Mary Allen (1992–1994)
Sue Hoyle (1994–)

Assistant Secretary-General
Eric Walter White (1946–1972)

Director of Finance and Resources (since 1989, various titles before then)
E. L. Horn (1946–1951)
D. P. Lund (1951–56)
M. J. McRobert (1956–71)
Anthony Field (1971–84)
Anthony Blackstock (1984–89)
Lew Hodges (1989–)

Director of Arts Development (since 1989, previously Director of Arts Coordination)
Graham Marchant (1986–89)
Iain Reid (1989–94)

Visual Arts Director (since 1986, previously Art Director)
Philip James (1946–59)
Gabriel White (1959–72)
Robin Campbell (1972–75)
Joanna Drew (1975–1986)
Sandy Nairne (1987–1992)
Marjorie Allthorpe-Guyton (1993–)

Combined Arts Director
Iain Reid (1994–)

Dance Director
Jane Nicholas (1980–89)
Sue Hoyle (1989–94)
Hilary Carty (1994–)

Drama Director
Michael MacOwan (1946–47)
Llewellyn Rees (1947–50)
John Moody (1950–55)
J. L. Hodgkinson (1955–73)
N. V. Linklater (1973–79)
John Faulkner (1979–83)
Dickon Reed (1983–85)
Ian Brown (1986–94)

Film, Video & Broadcasting Director
Rodney Wilson (1986–)

Literature Director
Eric Walter White (1968–71)
Charles Osborne (1971–85)
Alastair Niven (1987–)

Music Director
Steuart Wilson (1946–1948)
John Denison (1948–67)

John Cruft (1967–80)
Basil Deane (1980–83)
Richard Lawrence (1983–88)
Ken Baird (1988–94)
Kathryn McDowell (1994–)

Regional Director
Jack Phipps (1973–81)
David Pratley (1981–86)

Touring Director
Jack Phipps (1986–92)
Andrew Kyle (1992–94)
Kate Devey (1994–)

APPENDIX E

Drama 1948–77

A personal comment by N. V. Linklater, Drama Director,
who retired at the end of the year [1977]

This does not attempt to be a record of the Arts Council's drama activities during the last 25 years or so: the Council's Reports provide this and, especially for the period of Sir William Emrys Williams' secretary-generalship, present the picture vividly.

It is firstly worth remembering that the Council's drama policy is activated, guided or modified by the Drama Panel – which means, over the years, about 175 distinguished professional theatre people, and also by a succession of Committees of Enquiry, Working Parties, and Reports, on individual companies, or specialised subjects like Entertainment Tax, Theatre Censorship, Computer Bookings, Seat Prices, as well as those more wide ranging like the Theatre Enquiry of 1968–1970. Thus the Council's policy is not dreamed up simply by the officers, or a remote group of faceless people who might or might not know much about the theatre, but it grows from, and reflects the wishes of, the profession itself.

The 29 years I have been with the Arts Council – 25 of them in the Drama Department – have of course been a period of great change in the theatre. The Council has always kept up with events, indeed has often successfully kept a move or two ahead of changing ideas and has initiated development; but being a part of these changes has meant little time for looking back.

When making a final report to the Drama Panel in March I wondered how much had been achieved. In the previous ten months I had visited more than sixty companies (mostly, and most of, the regional theatres), and had found the standard of work on the whole very acceptable: I had enjoyed my evenings in their theatres and felt that the public was getting good value for the prices they paid, and, generally, the Arts Council and Local Authorities had a fair return for their subsidy. The acting, direction and settings were good, the front of house seemed friendly, efficient and in most cases clean; and the range of plays was a marvellous cross section of world drama. This surely was real improvement, I felt.

419

For comparison I looked through my file of programmes of the plays I'd seen in 1952 when I came from the Council's Regional Office in Nottingham to the Drama Department, and was amazed to be reminded of the variety and quality of what I had seen then in far fewer theatres.

Has there been progress and improvement to justify the expenditure of so much money and effort? Yes, of course; especially in the conditions of work for the artists and staff, and in the comfort and service given to the public.

In the 1950s there were about 100 repertory theatres; many were commercial companies, and a good number were non-profit-distributing, but getting along quite well without subsidy from the Arts Council or any public source: the Arts Council supported about 30 companies. The trouble was that the majority had to have a weekly change of play: fortnightly was managed by a few, and the luxury of three-weekly or longer by hardly a handful. Weekly rep. meant finding say 45 plays a year – perhaps 22 for a fortnightly company – and thus the range of plays was often wider than it need be today: in one way, therefore, the public might seem to have been perhaps better served. At the same time the pressure and working conditions of weekly rep. were killing. In the Arts Council's first Annual Report, and regularly throughout the Fifties, the Council expressed its determination to abolish the 'pernicious treadmill of weekly repertory' and encouraged any attempt to get away from it. Special grants were given to enable companies to engage extra actors and producers so that they could give some shows two weeks' rehearsal even though new productions still had to be put on every week. Subsidy was given to help companies exchange productions occasionally with similar theatres, and so find extra rehearsal time for the next show. There was the idea of a Theatre Grid, or network of theatres doing fewer productions themselves but touring them between other theatres in the circuit: a number of exchanges were made and a committee considered the practicalities, but there were too many difficulties and the plan could not be realised. At last weekly repertory in Arts Council-supported theatres was finally gone by the mid-Sixties. Now few companies play for less than three weeks, often not opening a new production until the Wednesday. The conditions are much better; the standards should be. Although the public in town X will see only 15 plays instead of 45, perhaps they are happy with television for the other weeks.

In the 1950s most repertory companies needed to keep one eye, if not both, on the West End, and the latest release, and the crumbs from the then rich men's tables sometimes seemed grudgingly given. This dependence on what London had finished with has largely gone, and most companies now pursue a far more individual policy. In fact the roles have been rather reversed, and commercial managers nowadays have to keep a sharp eye on, and compete for, what the regional theatres and independent theatre companies are doing. Transfers of shows from repertory theatres to London were almost unknown before the war (Sir Barry Jackson being the notable exception), and were extremely rare in the years immediately after it. Apart from two Repertory Festivals in London arranged by the Arts Council, Bristol Old Vic and Birmingham Repertory Theatre were about the only companies to play occasionally in London in the early Fifties; it was almost as unusual for a new play to start its life in repertory and be re-cast and mounted for the West End. But during 1976/77 companies from eight regional theatres played in London, and many of the shows in the West End had originated in subsidised out-of-town companies. All this is healthier, surely.

The overall quality has been improved by a number of schemes which have been developed and modified to meet the changing situation over the years – particularly, and starting in 1952, the schemes for encouraging the production of new, and later, neglected plays, and for giving bursaries or commissions to dramatists as well as 'topping up' their royalties to slightly more realistic figures: these schemes have positively encouraged new writing for the theatre. Then came training schemes for administrators and theatre managers; designers; directors; technicians; actors; and modest sums to maintain the standards of some Drama Schools. The value of all these schemes to the theatre as a whole has been quite disproportionate to the relatively tiny sums spent on them. Even smaller amounts given to help some of the organisations that support the theatre – Council of Regional Theatre, Theatres Advisory Council, and Association of British Theatre Technicians for example – have enabled them to continue giving a service over the years which, had it ceased, would have reduced the efficiency of the whole industry.

The new, or re-built theatres – 28 so far – have given the people working in them better conditions, where in the past they were often disgracefully bad, and audiences a more comfortable night out; they have also enabled the companies to give a far wider and better public service than ever was possible in the old places which opened their doors half an hour before curtain up. With food before and after the show – bookstalls – lunchtime and late night shows – studio theatres – poetry readings – concerts, and so on, and with their audiences younger and from a broader cross-section of the community. Unfortunately we have all learnt that these fine new buildings cost far more to run than had been bargained on, and it is depressing and absurd that most of them can only afford to provide an artistic output that is a fraction of the building's capability. Because so much unavoidable expenditure must go on the overheads, and inflation has for some years outstripped takings plus subsidy, it is only the artistic work that can be watered down.

Naturally the theatre is sharing the country's economic crisis, and most companies are in a precarious financial position. But there was a different, more dispiriting feeling in the Fifties, when the imminent death of the provincial theatre was not only talked about but was a real fear. Business generally seemed disappointing; buildings were deteriorating; and there was the endless struggle to make ends meet. Countless theatres closed, often because their sites were more valuable for re-development – mostly, to be sure, variety theatres, but many fine playhouses too. Any sense of hopelessness in the Fifties largely disappeared during the Sixties. Public subsidy had become respectable and accepted as essential, and there was a changing attitude to patronage. Local Authorities were more inclined to help their theatres, although nothing like adequately. Trusts, foundations, industry, private patrons, supporters' clubs were all more willing and able to find money. The building or refurbishment of theatres became possible and plans for many new theatres got under way. The bondage of weekly repertory was a thing of the past. Entertainment tax was abolished. Attendances were higher. At long last the National Theatre Company was formed and the theatre itself was going to be built. The Arts Council was to operate on a financial triennium and sensible planning seemed possible. It would indeed be tragic if the high hopes which were then built up – the growth which was then stimulated – were to be drained away now.

A change during the early years was away from direct management by the Arts Council of companies or theatre buildings, and from the one-night-stand tours of Wales, the North East and Midlands, which had been started by CEMA during the war and often achieved a remarkably high standard of direction, design and acting. One interesting statistic from the period of direct management: the Midland Theatre Company, based in Coventry, performed one week in the Technical College there, then toured the same play for a further fortnight to (at various times) Nuneaton, Netherton, Dudley, Loughborough or Cheltenham, and kept drama alive in Coventry with a high standard until the Belgrade Theatre was built in 1967. In its 11 years' existence it played to 1,000,000 people and cost in subsidy £104,000 – that is 10p per head. If this was the average per capita subsidy these days the Arts Council would be in clover.

Two important developments during the Sixties and Seventies were the Arts Council's decision to provide subsidy for Young People's Theatre, and the consequent burgeoning of this together with Theatre in Education: and the slow-to-start-with emergence of a genuine alternative theatre, which has expanded enormously and rapidly in the last few years. It is impossible or unwise to categorise the latter by a single designation: the groups began with a variety of motivation – lunch time, experimental, new writing, ethnic, fringe, political, social, community, children's, or anti-establishment companies. Perhaps the only policy all have in common is the intention to seek out new audiences in new places, and perform for people who would not otherwise see a live show. Their quality is as varied as their impulse, and there are far more than the forty or so at present supported by the Arts Council. Unfortunately, some of the regional theatres' young people's theatre sections, and some independent theatre groups, are of a bad and boring standard. As they are the only live theatre seen by some of their audiences they possibly do as much harm as good.

All sorts of people, and increasingly within the last few years, have told me that they find the London, the regional and the 'experimental' theatre less enjoyable than they did a few years ago, because so many shows seem increasingly boring and drab, if not downright unattractive or repellent. These people are not Aunt Edna or her niece, but still-addicted theatregoers. The West End, once a kind of Mecca to which the provincial theatre manager or director bowed, or emulated, seems to me now, alas, a shadow of its former self, hardly to be looked up to as a pace- or taste-setter for the British Theatre, and most worryingly in serious financial difficulty, with soaring costs, narrow margins and the burden of VAT. Throughout half my lifetime with the Arts Council, the theatre has always been having a bad time. But we were not simply crying 'wolf': every theatre has gone through innumerable very real and frightening crises and some haven't survived. It is amazing, and a tribute to the courage, resilience and professionalism of those who work in them (as well as some Arts Council money!) that so few companies have in fact gone bankrupt over the last 25 years. Those that closed are losses that still sadden me.

For those like me who love the theatre in spite of everything, and who have had so much pleasure from it, no praise or thanks can be too extravagant for the countless artists and staff who work in it today under all kinds of difficulty, but especially those who put up with bad pay, bad conditions, the 'pernicious treadmill of weekly repertory', and yet did good work throughout the bad years, and kept the theatre alive and capable, as it is now, of being beyond compare.

APPENDIX F

Memorandum Submitted by the Arts Council of Great Britain to the House of Commons Select Committee on Education, Science and the Arts, 13 May 1981

ORIGINS

1. The Arts Council grew out of the Council for the Encouragement of Music and the Arts (CEMA), set up following the outbreak of the Second World War in 1939. On 12 June 1945 it was announced in the House of Commons that CEMA would continue as a peacetime organisation under the name The Arts Council of Great Britain, and the Council was granted a Royal Charter of Incorporation on 9 August 1946.

THE PRESENT CHARTER

2. In February 1967 the Council was granted a new Charter which provides that the Council is established and incorporated: 'To develop and improve the knowledge, understanding and practice of the arts; to increase the accessibility of the arts to the public throughout Great Britain; and to advise and co-operate with Departments of Government, local authorities and other bodies on any matters concerned whether directly or indirectly with the foregoing objects.'

SOURCE OF INCOME

3. The Council receives an annual grant-in-aid from the Government, and the grant for the year ending 31 March 1982 was announced in December 1980 as £80,000,000, of which £2.5m is for capital and £77.5m for revenue purposes and on this basis the Council will enter into revenue commitments totalling £77,750,000. ... The Council's annual reports contain full details of the expenditure of the grant-in-aid.

MINISTERIAL AND DEPARTMENTAL RESPONSIBILITY

4. For the first twenty years of its life the Arts Council received its grant direct from the Treasury and was responsible to the Chancellor of the Exchequer. However, in 1965 it was decided in future to route the grant through the

Department of Education and Science and a Minister of State in the DES was given special responsibility for the Arts. The Secretary of State for Education and Science became responsible in Cabinet for the arts vote, and for the appointment of Council members and an assessor to the Council.

CHAIRMEN

5. The following have served as Chairmen of the Council:

1945–1946: Lord Keynes
1946–1953: Sir Ernest Pooley
1953–1960: Lord Clark
1960–1965: Lord Cottesloe
1965–1972: Lord Goodman
1972–1977: Lord Gibson
1977–   : The Rt Hon. Kenneth Robinson

SECRETARIES-GENERAL

6. The following have served as Secretaries-General:

1945–1951: Miss Mary Glasgow
1951–1963: Sir William Emrys Williams
1963–1968: Mr Nigel Abercrombie
1968–1975: Sir Hugh Willatt
1975–   : Sir Roy Shaw

MEMBERSHIP OF THE COUNCIL

7. The Charter provides for a Council consisting of 'a Chairman, a Vice-Chairman and not more than eighteen other members' all to be appointed by the Secretary of State for Education and Science after consultation with the Secretaries of State for Scotland and Wales.

8. Appointments are made for periods not exceeding five years. Members are not eligible for immediate reappointment at the end of their term unless they hold office as Chairman or Vice-Chairman of the Council, of the Scottish Arts Council or the Welsh Arts Council, Chairman of a panel.

9. Although it is not laid down in the Charter, the present practice is that two members of the Council should be from Scotland and two from Wales.

10. Members of the Council (and its committees and panels) are not paid for their services as such but may claim reimbursement of expenses incurred in the performance of their duties. They are chosen as individuals, not as representatives of particular interests or organisations.

SCOTTISH AND WELSH ARTS COUNCILS

11. The Council is enjoined by the Charter to appoint, with approval respectively of the Secretary of State for Scotland and the Secretary of State for

Wales, 'committees, to be called the Scottish Arts Council and the Welsh Arts Council,' to exercise, or advise on the exercise of, its functions in Scotland and Wales. The Chairmen of these two committees must be members of the Arts Council of Great Britain.

12. The Scottish and Welsh Arts Councils are virtually autonomous, although their allocations form part of the Arts Council of Great Britain's total grant-in-aid.

OTHER COMMITTEES AND PANELS

13. In the words of the Charter, 'the Council may appoint other committees and panels to advise and assist them in the exercise of such of their functions as may be determined by the Council ... The Council shall appoint as Chairman of any such committee or panel a member of the committee or panel who is a member of the Council ... The Council may appoint to any such committee or panel members who are not members of the Council ...'

14. There are two committees of the Council which concern themselves with matters affecting Great Britain as a whole. They are the Finance and Policy Committee and the Housing the Arts Committee, and both have Scottish and Welsh representation. The Chairman of the Council chairs the Finance and Policy Committee and a member of the Council chairs the Housing the Arts Committee. All members of the Finance and Policy Committee are also members of the Council; the Housing the Arts Committee includes members with specialist qualifications who are not serving Council members. The principal functions of the Finance and Policy Committee are to recommend the allocation of the annual grant and the apportionment between England, Scotland and Wales and to give initial consideration to matters of policy and forward planning. The Housing the Arts Committee advises the Council on the spending of a special allocation, for Great Britain as a whole, from which contributions are made towards the cost of building new concert halls, theatres, arts centres and galleries, or adapting and improving existing buildings.

15. Five panels have been appointed to advise the Council and the officers on the formulation and implementation of policy on Art, Dance, Drama, Literature and Music. Each panel has as its Chairman a member of the Council. The Scottish and Welsh Arts Councils have similar advisory structures. The Council's structure of Advisory Panels, Committees and Sub-Committees is shown later.

The membership of these advisory groups totalling about 170 enables the Council to draw on a wide range and rich variety of experience in each area of activity. For example the Drama Advisory Panel comprises directors, performers, playwrights, a designer, the Chairman of a repertory company, two Council members and members with academic and broadcasting experience. This membership is able to cover the range of artistic, administrative and budgetary experience necessary to fulfil the Panel's advisory function. In addition a further 40 independent ad hoc advisers based in the regions attend performances and report on them to the Council.

HOW THE ARTS ARE SUPPORTED

16. The Council's financial support for the arts is advanced principally through assistance to the professional arts. The arts are defined in practice as widely as possible, and are supported chiefly under the following heads: dance, drama, literature, music, visual arts, including arts films and photography, community arts, and multimedia experimental projects that often combine two or more of the disciplines mentioned above.

17. The Council responds with subsidy, advice and encouragement to initiatives being taken to promote the arts, subject to its assessment of their quality and value and to the availability of resources. At the same time, however, it is ready to take or promote initiatives of its own where it identifies substantial gaps in existing provision. It also lays particular emphasis on co-operation between arts providers and education providers of all kinds.

18. In accordance with its chartered duty 'to develop and improve the knowledge, understanding and practice of the arts,' the Council encourages its clients to engage in broadly-based educational work without duplicating the work of education providers. The Council has a small Education Unit where staff encourage exemplary forms of co-operation. The Unit's role is an advisory and co-ordinating one. It has no specific funds to provide financial assistance; grant applications are considered by the appropriate art form department.

19. One of the perennial problems of the Council in pursuing its chartered aims had been the rival claims of maintaining standards on the one hand, and bringing the arts to as many people as possible on the other. This has often been summarised as a dilemma between whether to 'raise' or 'spread'. In its early years the Council decided unequivocally to raise. The present climate of opinion puts greater emphasis on the need to spread – reflected in the subsidising of small-scale touring theatre and community arts. Some would argue that the need to spread is now greater than the need to raise, but the policy of the Council is still to attempt to do both. To do both adequately would, however, call for much larger resources, and difficult choices often have to be made. Hence the Council cannot please everyone.

20. In making choices it is salutary to remember that the room for innovation by panels and committees, and the Council itself, is limited by past decisions and commitments – just as succeeding panels and committees will be limited by the consequences of decisions being made now.

21. Most of the Council's funds are made available as subsidies. Among the organisations receiving financial assistance on an annual basis are the national opera, dance and drama companies: the Royal Opera, the Royal Ballet, the English National Opera, the National Theatre, and the Royal Shakespeare Company at Stratford and London. The Council's subsidies cover visits to regional centres by those companies and others such as London Festival Ballet, Cambridge and Oxford Theatre Companies, Kent Opera, Scottish Opera and Welsh National Opera. Annual subsidy is also made available to the 9 principal orchestras, 6 major regional theatre companies (in Birmingham, Bristol, Leicester, Manchester, Nottingham and Sheffield) and 34 other building-based theatre companies in the regions as well as smaller touring and community theatre companies and children's/young people's companies, 4 dance companies, music and arts festivals and art galleries. All of these – and most of the Council's other clients – are established on a non-profit-distributing basis and registered as charities.

22. Among other organisations to which help is given, often for specific programmes or projects, are community arts groups, arts centres, small dance, mime and drama companies, music and opera groups, organisations concerned with literature and magazine-publishing, and groups and galleries engaged in visual arts activities.

23. The Welsh and Scottish Arts Council support a similar range of arts organisations in those countries. Organisations supported by the Scottish Arts Council include Scottish Opera, Scottish Ballet, Scottish National Orchestra, Scottish Philharmonic Society, the Edinburgh Festival, the Third Eye Centre, Glasgow, and 7 repertory companies including Glasgow Citizens and Edinburgh Lyceum theatres.

24. Organisations supported by the Welsh Arts Council include, Welsh National Opera, BBC Welsh Symphony Orchestra, Moving Being, Chapter Arts Centre, Cardiff, Theatr Clwyd, Theatr Bara Caws, Mostyn Gallery, Llandudno and the Welsh Books Council. In Wales support for literature and drama relates to work in both English and Welsh. The Welsh Arts Council also supports film and craft activities in Wales with the help of funds from the British Film Institute and the Crafts Council.

25. All subsidies are agreed by the Council after careful scrutiny of estimates prepared by clients. In many cases the amount of subsidy to be provided is agreed in negotiation with local authorities, who are frequently expected to contribute to the total subsidy required.

26. Once an organisation is in receipt of continuing subsidy the Council appoints an assessor to evaluate its work. Continuity of support is dependent

on the annual re-assessment by the Council of client organisations' programmes and policies.

27. A proportion of the grant is also spent on the Council's own promotions, mainly exhibitions at the Hayward Gallery and the Serpentine Gallery; the circulation of art exhibitions throughout the country; the production and distribution of films on the arts and films by artists; tours of modern music through the Contemporary Music Network; the administration of the Wigmore Hall; and the Arts Council Shop in Long Acre, London.

28. The Scottish Arts Council operates the Fruit Market Gallery in Edinburgh as well as a Travelling Gallery which tours throughout Scotland, visiting communities which have no gallery of their own.

29. The Welsh Arts Council operates Oriel, a gallery and bookshop in Cardiff; creates and tours art and craft exhibitions; promotes some 50 orchestral and chamber concerts throughout Wales each year; promotes recordings of contemporary music; and publishes series of volumes on the literature of Wales.

30. Local authority expenditure on a range of leisure and recreational activities throughout the country is substantial but in the sectors in which they and the Arts Council act jointly there are variations which make generalisation impossible. Some authorities are approaching parity with Arts Council subsidies to organisations in their areas, a very few exceed Arts Council subsidies but most are markedly the minor contributors. Present restrictions on local government expenditure and the fact that arts spending is discretionary seem likely to lead to some deterioration.

AID FOR CREATIVE ARTISTS

31. The Council gives aid to individual artists as well as to organisations, through a great variety of bursary and award schemes – an area in which the guidance of the Council's advisers has a special importance. Details are provided in a periodically updated *Guide to Awards and Schemes*, published by the Council. The Councils also maintain a Slide Index of the work of contemporary British artists. Details are also available of grant schemes through the Scottish and Welsh Arts Councils.

REGIONAL ARTS ASSOCIATIONS

32. A network of 12 regional arts associations now covers England (except Buckinghamshire). For some years the Council has gradually decentralised support for activities in England which are wholly regional in scope and character, by transferring responsibility for such activities to the regional arts associations. Grant-aiding the associations is a central feature of the Council's

policy for regional development of the arts. On average the associations receive over 70 per cent of their income from the Arts Council.

33. Regional arts associations are concerned with all the arts. They are independent and autonomous, being neither regional branches of the Arts Council, nor purely local authority associations, but they are funded by, and work in partnership with, both. Many also receive funds from the British Film Institute and the Crafts Council. There are no regional arts associations in Scotland where the Scottish Arts Council has developed a working relationship with district and regional local authorities. In Wales 3 regional arts associations are funded by the Welsh Arts Council to promote and market the arts in their regions and offer grant-aid to arts organisations serving local communities.

STAFF AND DEPARTMENTS

34. The Council's chief executive officer, appointed by the Council with the approval of the Secretary of State for Education and Science, is the Secretary-General. He is supported in the central administration of the Council's work and policies by his deputy. There are separate departments for Art, Dance, Drama, Finance, Literature, Music and Regional matters, each headed by a director. In addition, the Personnel and Administration Department has specialist staff dealing with central services such as information, personnel, marketing and publications and there are separate sections dealing with press and education. The Scottish and Welsh Arts Councils have similar departmental staffing structures headed by a director in each case.

35. Most of the Council's staff in England are based at 105 Piccadilly, London, in Scotland at 17 Charlotte Square, Edinburgh and in Wales at Holst House, Museum Place, Cardiff.

36. In mid-1980 there were 266 staff in England; 52 at the Scottish Arts Council and 66 at the Welsh Arts Council. The Council's departmental and staffing structure in England is shown in the following diagrams:

THE COUNCIL'S GUIDELINES TO THE SECRETARY-GENERAL

1. The Council delegates to the Secretary-General, supported by his senior officers, the responsibility for the day-to-day administration and management of the Council's business within the framework of policy advised by panels and committees and agreed by the Council. He is, however, expected to report to the Council on matters of current interest, and Council bears the ultimate responsibility for decisions taken on its behalf, and for the allocation of grant.

2. The Council itself expects to take decisions in respect of the following matters in particular.

THE COUNCIL'S DEPARTMENTAL AND STAFFING STRUCTURE IN ENGLAND

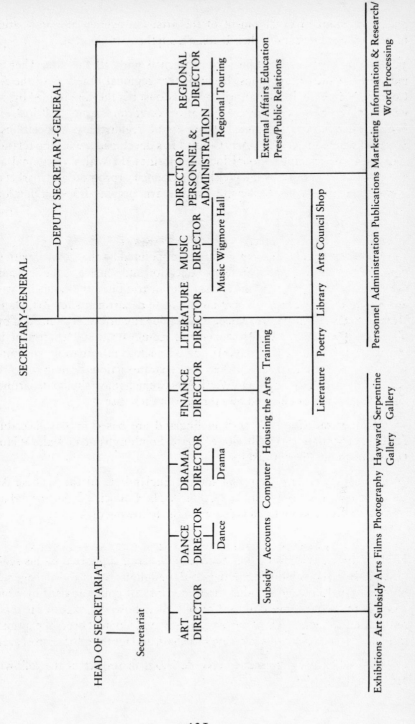

ARTS COUNCIL ADVISORY PANELS AND COMMITTEES FROM 1 APRIL 1980

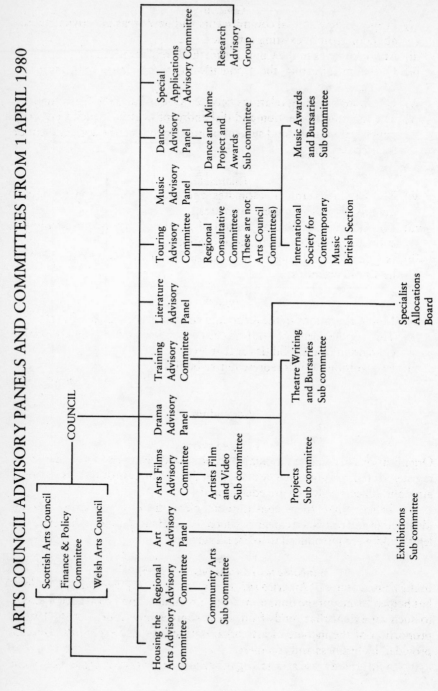

General

i) Proposed new annual commitments and new areas of activity and the abandonment of existing activities.
ii) Major changes in the Council's methods of operation.
iii) Questions affecting the Council's rights or obligations under its Charter.
iv) Questions affecting relations between Council and the Government.
v) The function, formation and disbandment of the Council's advisory panels, committees and sub-committees including the appointment of their chairmen.

Financial

vi) The Council's annual estimates and any major alterations subsequently proposed in these estimates.
vii) The Council's annual allocation of grant and any major alterations subsequently proposed in the allocation.
viii) Negotiations relating to the acquisition or disposal of freehold or leasehold premises.

Staff

ix) Major alterations in the terms and conditions of service of staff.
x) The appointment of staff at Director level and above and major changes in responsibilities at that level.
xi) Recognition of staff representative bodies.

March 1980

Addendum

1. *TAXATION*

Organisations in receipt of annual revenue subsidy from the Arts Council are registered charities governed by non-profit distributing constitutions the main aims and objects of which are educational.

We believe that their constitutions place these organisations in an identifiable and restricted category which would limit the area of benefit if tax legislation were introduced to assist this group.

i) *Income tax concessions for individuals*

In the United States of America substantial tax relief for charitable donations has helped to encourage donations from individuals and private foundations to such an extent that funds from these sources now represent the largest proportion of the income of arts organisations and far exceed the amount provided by business and commerce.

It would greatly assist arts organisations in Britain if legislation were

433

introduced allowing individuals donating funds to arts educational charities to offset such donations against their assessments to income tax.

ii) *Value added tax*

The charitable status referred to above has enabled successive governments to relieve from corporate and various other taxation organisations in receipt of subsidy from the Arts Council. However no such relief has been granted from value added tax.

The imposition of VAT at the full rate of 15 per cent distorts the natural elasticity of the market in which arts organisations operate and deprives them of the full benefit of maximising box office revenues. In effect, the Government gives public subsidy with one hand, and takes a large slice of it back with the other.

In most countries of the EEC the arts are more favourably treated for VAT purposes than in this country. In West Germany subsidised theatre is totally relieved of this tax.

The Council believes that arts organisations registered as charities should be granted zero-rated status for the purposes of value added tax.

2. NOTIFICATION OF GRANT-IN-AID

The greatest single impediment to sensible planning in the Arts Council's operations is the lack of early notification of the annual grant-in-aid.

The reason why early notification is of crucial importance to us is that unlike most other items of government expenditure, by far the greatest proportion of the Council's grant-in-aid is allocated in turn as subsidy to other organisations. The grant for the current financial year was announced on 9 December 1980, which was appreciably earlier than in previous years (when it was once as late as the middle of February). Even so, the period of notice which this enabled the Council to give its clients in relation to their 1981/82 subsidies was quite inadequate: all the organisations the Council supports have themselves to plan ahead on a far longer timescale than such a period permits.

Following the recommendations of the Estimates Committee session 1967/68, the Council's grant-in-aid was put on a rolling triennial footing on a 'not-less-than' basis. Regrettably as a result of general economic pressures this system lapsed within its initial triennium.

Present economic circumstances perhaps make it unrealistic to hope for a return to advance notification of grant-in-aid on the rolling triennial basis recommended by the 1967/68 Estimates Committee. Nevertheless, the earlier the grant-in-aid can be announced, the more efficient will be the use of the funds available. In this connexion the Government's published forecasts of expenditure offer very little guidance because the Arts Council's figure is bound up with other arts expenditure figures and because of the inevitable uncertainty about the allowance to be made for inflation from one year to the next.

The problems generated by the lack of advance notification of grant-in-aid were highlighted by the events of last December when in the light of the total funds available for 1981/82 the Council decided that it could not continue to provide subsidy for all its existing clients. The Council readily acknowledges and is keen to repond to the general view that there should have been a longer period of notice of withdrawal. However, under present arrangements, the Council could only do this by indicating which companies might lose their subsidy on the basis of a series of quite hypothetical alternative figures for its own total grant. Apart from its inherent absurdity, such a procedure would be highly disruptive and disturbing to all the organisations supported by the Council and by implying that their futures were at risk could destroy their trading positions unnecessarily.

This is not to say that the Council is in any doubt about the need to warn clients when, irrespective of the level of its own grant, their subsidy is at risk as a result of inadequate performance: the Chairman has already publicly undertaken to the Minister that the Council will ensure this is done.

3. PROBLEMS CAUSED BY A STATIC GRANT IN REAL TERMS

By the measure of the retail price index, the Council's grant-in-aid in 1981/82 was almost at the same level in real terms as for 1980/81. This has led some commentators to ask why it was necessary for the Council to terminate the grants referred to above.

In recent years, the Council has come under increasing criticism from its clients, the unions and the public generally for spreading available finance too thinly leaving companies with insufficient funds to mount their work. Thus new theatre buildings have sometimes been closed for as much as a third of the year; new performing groups have often been unable to perform for more than a few weeks at a time; orchestras have been denied the opportunity to develop a wider repertoire; and established opera and dance companies have had to restrict touring and cancel projected new productions.

The Council set out these problems clearly in its submissions to the Government on its financial needs for 1981/82. It explained that its clients were experiencing growing financial difficulties; and that without an increase in its grant which provided real growth over and above the expected level of inflation, the situation would inevitably deteriorate in 1981/82 precipitating the uncontrolled collapse of some companies.

The arts almost by definition represent development and it is difficult to sustain the arts on the basis of static resources. Arts organisations depend on the capacity to improve and develop in terms of output and standards. An artistically successful organisation cannot stand still. If the total available resources remain at the existing level the result would inevitably be the erosion of standards and further diminution of the numbers of organisations we can sustain.

In addition to the need for a controlled and planned progression of development in established companies, the Council also has to recognise the needs of those new or less established organisations supported for the first time in quite recent years when there seemed good reason to expect continued growth in the resources available.

Finally, the retail price index does not represent inflation in the arts. First the arts are highly labour-intensive by their nature and do not benefit from the general improvements in labour productivity which help to keep the overall index down. Secondly, they are highly dependent on such things as hotel, transport and utility prices, which are normally well ahead of the overall index and on specific materials such as wood, which are soaring in price even today. A research study is in progress which is designed to quantify these problems as far as possible.

4. THE ARTS COUNCIL AND THE REGIONAL ARTS ASSOCIATIONS

As a result of almost simultaneous suggestions made independently by CORAA and the Council's Organisation Working Party in 1979, the Council invited an informal working group of Regional Arts Associations and Arts Council officers to examine working relationships between the Arts Council and the RAAs and to make recommendations.

The group's report *Towards a New Relationship* (a copy of which was enclosed to the Committee) was received by the Council at its meeting in May 1980 when it was agreed that it should be widely distributed as a public discussion paper. Council returned to a substantive discussion of the report at its meeting in January 1981 in the light of comments made by interested organisations and individuals.

Throughout their discussion of the report, members of the Council were warmly supportive of the Regional Arts Associations (RAAs). From the Council's point of view the RAAs perform four vital functions:

   i) given that the impetus for establishing RAAs began with local authorities, they provide a common focus for the interest and involvement in the arts of individual local authorities from District to County Council levels;

  ii) they provide at regional level a body of specialist expertise and advice which is more extensive than any individual local authority could normally hope to provide and which is also directly available to arts organisations of all kinds;

 iii) they provide a means of assessing local artistic needs and demands on the basis of a degree of day-to-day familiarity with the regions which the national body like the Arts Council could never develop for itself;

  iv) as a result of (i) to (iii), they constitute an invaluable resource to which the Arts Council itself can turn for advice, consultation and discussion in developing those of its own policies which have a regional dimension.

The Council recognises that, for a variety of reasons explored in the report, the RAA system itself and the pattern of relationships between central funding bodies, local authorities and RAAs have had their imperfections. However, it firmly believes that the advantages of the system very substantially outweigh any such imperfections, and that the right course for the foreseeable future is to work with the RAAs themselves and with other central and local funders to improve the system rather than to embark on any fundamental changes.

As with any system – and perhaps particularly one which depends on regional bodies within a wider national framework of government which lacks a regional tier – many of the imperfections of the past can be attributed to inadequate communications between the various parties involved. The recommendations in the report on working links between the Council and the RAAs should contribute to a major improvement, and the Council has broadly endorsed them.

Some of the problems have, however, been seated in constitutional matters, affecting both the RAAs and the Arts Council, and in uncertainty about certain aspects of RAA funding. Here too, the Council has generally endorsed the relevant recommendations of the report.

The question of devolving to the RAAs responsibility for assessing Arts Council clients and activities has been a major source of friction for some time, and continues to attract controversy, particularly among the clients themselves and their representative bodies. However, the Council believes that the report's reformulation of the devolution issue in terms of the need to determine the most appropriate assessment base for individual clients and activities is both sensible in itself and likely to offer a constructive basis for future progress. The precise details of such progress will nevertheless require a good deal of thought, not least in relation to the highly contentious question of whether clients should ever be devolved against their own wishes. Council has asked that the matter be examined on a client-by-client basis, initially by its own and RAA officers working informally together, with a view to a further discussion by the Council of the complex issues of practice and of principle involved. The Council will be returning to the whole question of devolution at its next meeting.

One important area on which the report touched at several points (though comprehensive detailed discussions would have been outside the working group's terms of reference) is relationships between the RAAs and local authorities. Following a meeting with the local authority associations convened by the Minister for the Arts, the Chairman of the Council has agreed to chair a small group of members and officers representing the Council, the local authority associations and the Council of Regional Arts Associations to explore the report's implications for those relationships.

One issue which will no doubt arise during discussions by such a group will be the level of local authority finance for the RAAs, which currently averages only about 20 per cent of total RAA incomes and is in the case of one RAA as low as 8 per cent.

May 1981

APPENDIX G

The Glory of the Garden:
The Development of the Arts in England

PREFACE

Our England is a garden, and such gardens are not made
By singing: "Oh, how beautiful!" and sitting in the shade,
While better men than we go out and start their working lives
At grubbing weeds from gravel-paths with broken dinner-knives.
The Glory of the Garden Rudyard Kipling

In July 1945, on the occasion of the formation of the Arts Council, Maynard Keynes, who was our first Chairman, gave a BBC talk in which he outlined the new Council's purpose and priorities. The decision to create the Arts Council was one of the last acts of the wartime coalition – as Keynes noted – and he went on to say:

> At last the public exchequer has recognised the support and encouragement of the civilising arts of life as a part of their duty. But ... everyone, I fancy, recognises that the work of the artist in all its aspects is, of its nature, individual and free, undisciplined, unregimented, uncontrolled. The artist walks where the breath of the spirit blows him ... The task of an official body is not to teach or to censor, but to give courage, confidence and opportunity ...
>
> We of the Arts Council are greatly concerned to decentralise and disperse the dramatic and musical and artistic life of this country, to build up provincial centres and to promote corporate life in these matters in every town and county. It is not our intention to act on our own where we can avoid it. We want to collaborate with local authorities and to encourage local institutions and societies and local enterprise to take the lead ... We look forward to the time when the theatre and concert hall and the gallery will be a living element in everyone's upbringing ...
>
> But it is also our business to make London a great artistic metropolis, a place to visit and to wonder at. For this purpose London today is half a ruin. With the loss of the Queen's Hall there is no proper place for concerts. The Royal Opera House at Covent Garden has been diverted to other purposes throughout the war ... We hope that Covent Garden will be re-opened early next year as the home of opera and ballet. The London City Council has already allotted a site for a National Theatre.

439

Whatever may be the controversies in economics I remain an avowed Keynesian in the arts. When one reads his remarkably far-sighted talk, it is clear that the Arts Council has in nearly forty years kept faith with his ideal of giving support and opportunity rather than trying to teach or censor the artist.

We might indeed follow Jefferson's example in framing the Declaration of Independence and apply John Locke's celebrated principles of liberty to the arts: 'As the highest perfection of intellectual nature lies in a careful and constant pursuit of true and solid happiness, so the care of ourselves, that we mistake not imaginary for real happiness, is the necessary foundation of our liberty … The variety of pursuits shows, that every one does not place his happiness in the same thing, or choose the same way to it. Men may choose different things and yet all choose right.' Care for real excellence, encouragement of variety for the audience, support of freedom for the artist, are the foundation of liberty for the arts. The counterpart of liberty is responsibility. An Arts Council which stands back to respect liberty, puts the responsibility for art on the artists, and the responsibility for practical success on the managers of companies.

It is clear also that Keynes' second aim of making London 'a great artistic metropolis' has been achieved, to a degree even beyond what he envisaged. With the four national companies, the London orchestras, the post-war development of galleries and exhibitions, London is probably the greatest artistic metropolis of the modern world, challenged only by New York and more than bearing comparison with any continental European city. Considering the part Arts Council funding has played in this development, and the fact that London was indeed 'half a ruin' when it began, this is an achievement which alone would justify the comparatively modest public expenditure on the work of the Arts Council in the period.

It is, however, also clear that his first aim, 'to decentralise and disperse the dramatic and musical and artistic life of this country', has not been adequately realised. Despite the excellent work that has been done in Scotland, Wales and the English regions, the Arts Council has fallen short in its first priority, just as it has surpassed expectations in its second. The quality of London itself as an artistic metropolis shows up the deficiencies of the arts provision in the rest of the country. For this the Arts Council must accept its share of the blame. The decision in 1956 to abolish the regional offices which Keynes had created was an almost unbelievably retrogressive step. Fortunately, they were replaced by the Regional Arts Associations, and fortunately also the Regional Arts Associations were a partnership between the Arts Council and the local authorities just as Keynes envisaged. But time was lost and the Regional Arts Associations were funded only on a modest scale.

The same underfunding occurs throughout regional provision. Neither in drama, music, art nor opera is the regional provision other than badly funded by comparison either with London or with what is demonstrably needed. One comparison will show how wide the gap is. No theatre company based entirely in the regions enjoys an Arts Council subsidy equal to one-tenth of that given to either of the two national theatre companies, the National Theatre or the Royal Shakespeare Company. Most receive less than a fiftieth. That does not mean that these two theatre companies receive too much. Indeed the Priestley Report found to the contrary. But it is a clear indication that some provincial theatres receive too little. There are many good drama companies, orchestras, exhibitions, and opera and dance companies throughout Great Britain that would not exist without the Arts Council. But we live as two artistic nations – London and everyone else.

No fair examination would therefore conclude that Keynes' first priority had been adequately achieved. Yet it would be a great mistake to try to strengthen the regions by destroying the metropolis, to achieve Keynes' first priority by losing the achievement of the second. London is 'a place to visit and to wonder at' and that achievement – one of the most important of the postwar achievements of British culture – must not be put at risk.

On the whole I prefer to argue the case for funding the Arts Council on the contribution of the arts to British civilisation. But it is obvious that the attraction of London as an artistic metropolis is essential to Great Britain's appeal to tourists. The loss of London's arts would cost the balance of trade as much as the loss of a major industry. The economic argument is quite clear-cut and it applies most strongly to London, though it also applies to the regional arts.

Nevertheless, after forty years it is time to come to grips with Keynes' first priority, to decentralise and disperse the dramatic and musical and artistic life of this country. The measures required to do so include the institutional, the administrative and the financial.

The Arts Council wants to encourage and respond to local initiative in helping to create new institutions or strengthening old ones. The ideal possibility is this: an area with a large potential audience, still under-served in the provision of a particular art; a local authority or local authorities keen to work with the Arts Council or the Regional Arts Associations on developing the arts to the highest possible standard; local private initiatives through administration and sponsorship to help finance the development; a core of talent of high quality wanting to carry the work forward. These are ideal conditions, not always realisable, but they illustrate four conditions of success: need, local authority partnership, private partnership, above all talent. To these Arts Council funding should be added.

In administration the Arts Council wants to carry forward the existing programme of devolution of assessment and funding to the Regional Arts Associations. This document announces the largest single programme of devolution in the history of the Arts Council. It is a genuine and major act of administrative decentralisation, a step back from centralised bureaucracy as a mode of administering the arts in Great Britain.

We are not people who believe that London always knows best.

The financial steps are the most difficult. The Arts Council recognises the financial constraints inside which government is working. We have therefore decided to make a start even if it has to be a relatively small one out of our own existing level of funding. That does mean painful choices, including transfers inside existing provision. Yet it has one great advantage: it demonstrates the determination of the Arts Council to carry out this strategy even though it involves decisions of great difficulty and hardship for respected clients.

In general the Arts Council has to set criteria for public funding which are at least as strict as those which apply in other areas of public expenditure, and preferably more efficiently monitored. Arts funding is harder to measure in terms of productivity than some other public funding, and quality cannot be measured in financial terms at all; such evidence as I have seen suggests that overheads are well contained, productivity is high, waste limited and salaries low. Certainly the arts output per pound seems to be a multiple of that in Fleet Street, a less efficient area in the economics of communication. The policy of the Arts Council is to examine expenditure realistically to make sure that the money government provides for the arts is spent as well as possible. That includes setting high financial standards for the Regional Arts Associations.

Obviously the completion of the policy set out in this document will be a long-term matter; the strategy is a reassertion of the original idea, but it is also a decisive change of ambition. It will depend on the support of government, and indeed on the support of future governments down to the end of the century. It will depend on the Arts Council's continuing its present determination, with changing membership and changing officers. It will inevitably cost money, and there is a limit to the funding that can be found out of existing resources. It is also difficult; perhaps it is more difficult to disperse a metropolitan quality of art than it is to create an artistic metropolis.

Yet we believe that it is necessary. The arguments for the arts are either universal or they are untrue. If the support we give to the arts in London is justified – and I believe that it is abundantly justified – then so is comparable support for the arts in the other great areas of population. Of course London will always be favoured – there is a strong historic case for an artistic metropolis – but the present gap is much too wide.

The strongest argument of need is the existence of a demand for art which springs up in response to supply. The levels of box office demand for quite exacting forms of art are to me always surprising as well as delightful. The audience for live theatre as opposed to electronic entertainment, the new young audiences for dance, the exaltation of opera, the crowds at art exhibitions prove the genuine social demands which justify a significant, if thrifty, public expenditure.

One does not have to paint the modern world black to see one reason for that demand. Modern society – even in democracies and much more so in totalitarian states – is depersonalised by the scale of its organisation, a scale which is being exploded by information technology. The arts, human, creative, inspiring, individual, warm, alive, provide a natural healing to this sense of depersonalisation, and the appreciation of beauty can transcend the moon-like chill of an electronic world. For those of religious faith the human creativity of the arts can be a way of sensing the beauty of God's creation. Perhaps we demand the arts more than earlier generations; perhaps we need the arts more than earlier generations.

Whatever the reasons, the demand is a fact, and so is the emotion behind it. The depth of the emotion, particularly in the regions, can be measured by public anxiety about the future of the Metropolitan Counties. The arts represent less than one hundredth of those Councils' expenditure; an observer might well have supposed recently that the arts were their only function. We should welcome this profound emotional concern – it represents a real and broad public love of the arts as a necessary part of civilised life.

We have taken a stanza from Kipling as an epigraph for this report. The garden is a familiar metaphor, as in Pope's *Essay on Man*, for the life of man. It is a fair metaphor to describe the work of the Arts Council; we can dung and we can water, but we cannot create a single flower. The British garden of the arts has great beauties throughout, and a magnificent display at the centre, but there are empty beds and neglected shrubberies. We would like to see the whole garden in bloom, and all the people walking through it to enjoy the flowers.

William Rees-Mogg

Sir William Rees-Mogg
Chairman, Arts Council of Great Britain
30 March 1984

I. THE NEED FOR CHANGE

1. The Arts Council has been in existence for nearly forty years, but not until now has it undertaken a thorough and fundamental review of all its work. Forty years is too long a period for an organisation like the Arts Council, which needs to be lively and flexible in adapting to changing circumstances, to operate without undergoing such a review. The arts never stands still, and the Council needs to move with them. The need for a review has increased in recent years, since the resources made available to the Council by the government have remained virtually static in real terms, making it very

difficult for the Council to respond to changes in the arts and in the expectations of society.

2. For some years the Council has been stuck in a groove. It has committed itself to a long list of revenue clients (that is, companies and organisations funded annually for their complete year's work) and it has given itself little flexibility even in its list of non-revenue or project clients (that is, companies given grants for specific projects or other short-term purposes). The Council has also been wedded by long practice even to the categories of grant available to its clients. Quite apart from financial pressures, it is therefore desirable that the Council should consider other ways of doing its work.

3. Since the Council was established in 1945, its list of clients has grown longer and longer: the number of its revenue clients in drama, for example, has grown from thirty in 1950 to more than eighty in recent years. The scope of the Council's work has also broadened over the years to include areas such as the production of documentary films on the arts and the support of artists' films and video, community arts, education, photography, support for literature and training in the arts. This expansion took place without the Council's withdrawing from existing areas of work in order to make room for new ones. Not until 1981/82 did the Council withdraw its support from a significant number of organisations, and even in that year the average size of those organisations was very small, so that the withdrawals permitted only marginal adjustments in favour of the clients who were retained.

4. Against this background, it is understandable that the Council should ask itself whether it has been spreading its resources too widely and hence too thinly, at the expense of the vital, primary aspects of its work. The Council's anxiety about this matter has been reinforced in recent years by increasingly vociferous expressions of the same concern by a large number of its clients and by other commentators on the arts.

5. Moreover, the present climate within which the arts are administered is undergoing significant change. The report of the House of Commons Select Committee on Education, Science and the Arts, *Public and Private Funding of the Arts*, provided a comprehensive account of the difficulties faced by the arts and made a number of major recommendations for the Arts Council's consideration, including in particular the question of the imbalance in arts provision between London and the regions. The pattern of distribution of Arts Council funding was examined in a Policy Studies Institute working paper, *A Hard Fact to Swallow*, which also underlined the dominance of the capital at the expense of the regions. The report on the financial affairs and needs of the Royal Opera House and the Royal Shakespeare Company conducted by Mr Clive Priestley provided firm evidence of the difficulties experienced by those organisations in attempting to operate within the funds which the Council

444

had been able to make available to them, funds which, as the Council had continually made clear to the government, were inadequate for the needs of those two companies, as were those for the Council's other revenue clients. Another major development was the publication of the government's proposals for funding the arts following its intended abolition of the Greater London Council and Metropolitan County Councils. The Arts Council responded to those proposals at the end of January 1984 in a published document, *The Arts in Metropolitan Areas*.

6. There have also been important changes in the nature of the society which the Council seeks to serve through its spending on the arts. The growth of enforced leisure, the severe economic depression of many of our older city centres, changing perceptions of the requirements of a multicultural society and the rapid development of new communications media all have implications for the arts and for those charged with funding the arts.

7. Given these pressures, the Arts Council is unwilling to continue year after year simply to apportion among its clients small increases in resources which barely keep pace with inflation. But a strategic review does not mean that the Council will cease to press vigorously for the increases in funding which it believes the arts to require. The Select Committee report has already described the arts in Great Britain as 'irresponsibly underfunded', a judgment which the Council heartily endorses. In developing its strategy the Council has necessarily to begin from the resources currently available. If the strategy is to develop in the longer term in the ways which the Council considers essential, that development will require additional resources. The Council believes that the changes outlined in this document, taken together, will strengthen the case for additional resources for the arts, a case which it will continue to urge with all the persuasiveness at its command.

II. THE PROCESS OF THE REVIEW

8. It was against this general background that the Council decided, at its two day meeting at Ilkley in October 1983, to undertake a thorough review of its policies and the allocation of its grant-in-aid in order to determine its priorities and develop a strategy of development for the arts during the remainder of this decade and beyond. At that meeting the Council decided that the review should be conducted in the fullest possible collaboration with its clients, its advisory panels and committees, the Regional Arts Associations and local authorities. The time-scale for the review has been tight, putting maximum pressure on all those involved in the consultative process, particularly on the Council's own staff. The Council gratefully acknowledges the immense amount of work which has been done on its behalf with so little complaint.

9. In November the Secretary-General wrote to all the Council's annual clients

445

(that is, all revenue clients and many regular project clients). His letter said that, in seeking to establish a more flexible mode of operation better suited to the circumstances of the next five years and beyond, the Council wished to pay regard to three basic principles: the maintenance of the highest standards in all the arts; adequate provision of, and financial support for, the new and developmental as well as the established; and a reasonable geographical spread of provision across the country. Each client was asked to answer three questions:

i. how it would respond, structurally and artistically, to a substantial increase in subsidy (say, 25 per cent) from all sources;
ii. how it would respond to a similarly substantial decrease in subsidy;
iii. how it would view the possibility of being assessed and funded in future by its Regional Arts Association rather than directly by the Arts Council.

10. The Secretary-General's letter was also sent to the Directors of Regional Arts Associations, who were invited to apply the first two questions to their own operations. In addition, the Council of Regional Arts Associations was invited to submit a general statement presenting its overall view of what shape the Council's new strategy for the arts should take.

11. The letters to clients and the Regional Arts Associations invited them to send copies of their replies to the local authorities with responsibility for their areas. The Council also wrote to the Chief Executives of every local authority in England (including District Councils and London Boroughs), inviting their comments both on the exercise as a whole and on the specific responses made by clients. The Council has received replies directly (as opposed to indirectly through the Regional Arts Associations) from about half the local authorities, including all those with a substantial arts budget. Representatives of the Council have also had some discussion of the exercise with representatives of the Arts and Recreation Committees of the Association of District Councils, the Association of County Councils and the Association of Metropolitan Authorities. The local authorities have welcomed the exercise in general; on points of detail they have normally aligned themselves with the responses from the Arts Council's clients in their areas.

12. Throughout December, while the Council was awaiting replies from clients and local authorities, a series of consultative meetings took place between officers of the Council and representatives of each Regional Arts Association in order to discuss specific issues in relation to the individual areas of the Council's work. Those meetings proved invaluable in helping to establish common ground and in cementing further the good relationships which had already existed between the Council and the Associations.

13. The Council wishes to thank all those who responded to the consultative

process for the time and care which they devoted to their replies. Those replies have been of great service to the Council and its officers and advisers in the course of the strategy review.

14. Assisted by the evidence collected from the consultative process, each department of the Arts Council, together with its advisory panel or committee, prepared for consideration by the Council recommendations on three broad fronts:

    i.   proposals for making, if required, a 10 per cent saving from its current allocation of grant in order to provide a pool of monies from which the Council could finance new developments or alter the proportions in which it allocated its grant-in-aid to its various areas of activity;
    ii. proposals for the future development of the art form concerned;
    iii. proposals for the devolution of clients to Regional Arts Associations.

15. Thus it is in the light of the evidence gathered during the past four months, in addition to its own accumulated knowledge and experience, that the Council has deliberated upon a future strategy for the arts and determined a framework for their future funding from within the resources made available by central government.

16. The review was conducted in a short space of time. But the Council believes it to be fair that clients should be given twelve months' notice of withdrawal of subsidy; therefore the development strategy cannot be put into its initial operation until 1 April 1985. To have delayed longer would have put at severe risk companies which are in great financial difficulty.

III. THE LIMITS OF THE REVIEW

17. The decisions which are announced in this document represent the first, and the most important, stage in the Council's strategy review. It is proper that the Council's attention should be directed in the first place to the provision of the arts across the country, that it should seek to help to rectify gaps in that provision and to improve the standards of existing provision, before turning to the implications of such changes for its own functions and internal methods of operation. The Council acknowledges, nevertheless that the structure of its organisation requires review, all the more so in the wake of the new development strategy. During the next twelve months, the Council will be considering its internal organisation, as the second stage of its review, at the same time as it is preparing, in further consultation with its clients, the Regional Arts Associations and local authorities, to launch its new strategy in 1985/86.

18. In the course of the internal review, the Council will be considering whether it is beneficial to retain its traditional departmental structure. It will also be reviewing the structure of its advisory panels and committees. And it

will be asking itself whether the streamlining of its function entailed by the devolution of a significant number of clients to the Regional Arts Associations, the withdrawal of subsidy from some others, and retrenchment in certain areas of its work, should lead it to take on a more explicit and extended role in the promoting and marketing of the arts, in research and in the gathering, processing and dissemination of information and statistics.

19. A further major task for the Council in the coming twelve months will be to investigate whether in future its aims may be better fostered by a change in its traditional methods of funding. Hitherto, Arts Council clients have either enjoyed the benefits of revenue funding, with the implication that (except at times of fundamental review) their tenure of grant is freehold in nature, or they have had to rely on short-term grants which provide no basis for continuity or forward planning. Many of those involved in the consultation process described in the preceding section have suggested that the Council should introduce a system of limited franchise-funding, whereby subsidy would be effectively guaranteed for a short period of years on the understanding that it would then (or perhaps after a single extension) come to an end. In principle, the Council finds such an approach attractive, but franchise-funding, in however limited a way, raises a number of practical difficulties (both for the Council and its clients) which require detailed examination before a decision can be taken to adopt it. There is also the question of how extensively a franchise approach, were it to be adopted, would be suitable for the two present categories of Arts Council clients, revenue-funded and project-funded.

20. The present review has involved careful consideration of the work of all the Council's current clients. In this process the Council has continued to rely on the list of criteria previously announced as those by which it assesses the work of its clients. For the foreseeable future the criteria remain as follows:

a. quality of artistic product, including, as appropriate, standards of presentation, performance, design and direction, and their relationship to the conception of the company's overall programme;

b. actual and potential creative strength in relation to both new and established work;

c. the extent to which stated aims and objects are realised;

d. the fullest practicable use of facilities and the widest provision of the arts to the community;

e. education policy in relation to the artistic programme;

f. the employment and other opportunities extended to members of ethnic minority groups;

g. overall value for money, including any success in extending audiences through other media;

h. box office and attendance returns;

i.   the company's success in raising local authority support and other income;

j.   the efficiency shown in using available resources and the accuracy and control of budgeting;

k.   the urgency and nature of any fundamental financial problems;

l.   the adequacy and security of tenure of premises;

m. the balance of provision between London and other regions;

n.   the Council's existing declared policies, particularly the emphasis which it places on full-time professional work.

21. These criteria are not set out in order of priority. Individual criteria may become of paramount importance in the assessment of any particular client. The Council would be deeply concerned about a client which was failing artistically, even if it were performing comparatively well by reference to other criteria. It would be similarly concerned about a client which demonstrated an inability to control its financial affairs, even if its work were of a high standard. So far as regional balance is concerned, the Council has for some time declined to take on new revenue clients in Greater London, whatever their artistic, financial or administrative strengths. But none of these observations detracts from the importance which the Council continues to attach to the place of an arts organisation within the community as a whole, including its relationships with local authorities, the strength of its educational work in broadening knowledge and understanding of the arts and its recognition of the implications for the arts of a developing multi-cultural society.

22. The Council wishes to emphasise that it subsidises many companies to do work of a specifically small-scale or middle-scale nature. It is a natural tendency for companies to grow bigger. But the Council will not come to the financial aid of a company whose size outgrows the purpose for which the Council funds it.

23. Finally, the review which is the subject of this document has been essentially concerned with the Council's responsibilities in England. Some of the details may have implications for the Scottish and Welsh Arts Councils. But that is not their main focus. Although they are technically sub-committees of the Arts Council of Great Britain, the Scottish and Welsh Arts Councils are largely autonomous in their decision-making, reflecting the fact that artistic priorities in Scotland and Wales may be substantially different from those in England. The Scottish and Welsh Arts Councils are conducting their own reviews, the results of which will be announced later this year. Where appropriate and necessary, those reviews will take account of this document, but both Councils will retain the flexibility to take a strategic view of their own requirements.

24. In seeking to adapt its policy to emerging needs, the Council has formulated four broad principles to serve as the foundations of future development. They are:

    i. raising the quality and increasing the quantity of arts provision in the regions to bring it nearer the standards of provision in London;

    ii. in identifying new developments in the regions for direct support from the Arts Council itself, focussing on the dozen or so areas within England where the population is most densely concentrated;

    iii. making a start towards redressing certain historical imbalances in funding which favour some art forms at the expense of others;

    iv. in appropriate cases, basing the Council's own subsidy decisions more consistently and deliberately than in the past on the availability of matching funds raised locally.

Arts Provision in the Regions

25. It has for some time been the Council's policy to develop the arts in the regions. The large subsidies for the major repertory theatre companies in the regions and for the regional symphony orchestras, the support for Northern Ballet Theatre and the establishment of Opera North are all manifestations of that policy, as is the encouragement which the Council has given to the growth of the Regional Arts Associations. The policy has been matched by the Council's refusal in recent years to fund new developments in London. Nevertheless, the arts in London still attract almost half of the Council's expenditure in England. The Policy Studies Institute working paper, *A Hard Fact to Swallow*, suggested that the Council's expenditure per head of the population in Greater London in 1980/81 was three-and-a-half times as much as in the next-best-provided region (Merseyside Arts) and nine times as much as in the least-well-provided region (Eastern Arts). The Council has some reservations about the way in which those figures were put together, but the picture which they paint is broadly accurate.

26. In the past, the Council has tended to argue that its function is to respond to artistic initiative wherever it arises, that artists are inevitably drawn to London for reasons beyond the Council's control (the size of the capital and its potential audience, the concentration of film and television opportunities in and around London, the commercial gallery network and so on), and that the distribution of the Council's subsidy therefore reflects an inevitable, if perhaps regrettable, fact of artistic life. Yet several of the Council's policies have tended in a contrary direction. The rejection of applications for subsidy from new companies in London has not been on artistic grounds, but simply on the ground that London's needs are already well supplied; the establishment of Opera North was deliberately aimed at helping to satisfy a growing opera audience outside London; and the whole of the Council's touring policy is

predicated on the needs of the major regional areas of population. In the past year, however, London has received additional favour from the government's decision, in the light of the Priestley Report on the Royal Shakespeare Company and the Royal Opera House, to award a substantial uplift in subsidy to those companies and the English National Opera, an increase to London which was only partially offset by smaller increases provided by the government for Opera North, Scottish Opera and Welsh National Opera and by the fact that part of the Royal Shakespeare Company's operation is based in Stratford-on-Avon.

27. Although London's present predominance in the arts reflects to some extent an imbalance in London's favour across a wide range of many aspects of national life, the Council considers it inequitable that London, which holds about one-fifth of the population in England, should attract about half the Council's spending. To allocate subsidies on the basis of population alone would ignore the special role which any large capital city necessarily plays in a country's artistic life. Nevertheless, the Council's grant-in-aid is provided by taxpayers throughout the country and those taxpayers who live outside London have a legitimate claim to a fairer proportion of the Council's funds.

28. The Council therefore believes it right to make increased and improved provision in the regions the central objective of its development strategy. Its development programme lays great emphasis, for example, on strengthening the major resources in drama which already exist in the regions, on the needs of the eastern part of the country for a better provision of orchestral music, on improving dance provision in the regions, and on greater cooperation between the Council and the municipal art galleries. For those purposes, the Council has determined to increase the grants available to a number of its own clients working in the regions. It has also decided substantially to increase the responsibilities of the Regional Arts Associations, both by devolving to them responsibility for some clients and areas of work which it now funds directly and by providing them with a significant amount of development money in order to sustain and enhance their existing work, especially in areas of the arts for which funding responsibility has already passed largely to them.

The Major Areas of Population

29. The great bulk of the English population lives in, or within comparatively easy reach of, eleven major cities: Birmingham, Bristol, Leeds, Leicester, Liverpool, London, Manchester, Newcastle, Nottingham, Sheffield and Southampton. A map of these cities shows the areas lying within an approximate 30-mile radius of these centres and in London's case within a 50-mile radius. By concentrating new development on the eleven areas, it is possible to reach a population of about 40 million people (out of a total English population of some 47 million). The eleven areas, however, leave out

of account two parts of the country which, although much less densely populated, are very large in area – the south-west and most of the eastern seaboard. On grounds of geography, therefore, if not of population, the areas around Plymouth in the south-west and Ipswich/Norwich in the east have been included as strategic areas.

30. The Council already has a significant interest in all these strategic areas, and in a period of limited economic growth, it believes that the best way to deploy its resources is to make maximum use of existing regional assets. Each area already has a building-based repertory company funded by the Council or (in Southampton's case) by a Regional Arts Association. The areas include the home bases of all the regional orchestras. Most of them are reasonably well supplied with art galleries and museums. They include the home bases of the only large-scale regional dance and opera companies. And all the areas except Leicester and Sheffield have major receiving houses for large-scale productions toured with Arts Council funds.

31. The spread of provision is, however, more patchy than this account may imply. No less important, even the largest regionally-based organisations are seriously underfunded, both in absolute terms and by comparison with the largest companies based in London. To bring provision in the main areas of population nearer to that enjoyed by London and also to move towards a greater measure of equality between the regions will require more money than the Council currently has to spend. Nor can these things be done over a mere five-year period. The Council's strategy is to make a significant start towards these objectives, and, by demonstrating thereby the potential benefit of its regional development programme, to make a powerful argument for increased funding in the future from the government, local authorities and private sponsors of the arts.

The Balance Between the Art Forms

32. The Arts Council has never attempted to devise any kind of formula for the apportionment of its grant-in-aid among the various art forms. It does not believe it to be desirable, nor possible, to determine on *a priori* grounds precisely what percentage of its money should be devoted to each of them. An arithmetical analysis of the monies which might be regarded as due to each art form would, for example, probably fail to register the high place which the theatre has occupied in the history of modern English civilisation, a consideration which has led the Council to include in the development programme set out below radical proposals for enhancing regional drama provision. The Council's spending on opera has necessarily been high by comparison with its spending both on other art forms and on other kinds of music. The government's recent decisions, consequent on the recommendations of the Priestley Report, have led to the earmarking for the benefit of

opera companies of a substantial proportion of the increase in the Council's grant-in-aid for 1984/85. In 1983/84, opera was allocated £17,312,500 from the Arts Council directly, 23 per cent of its total revenue support for the arts in England (excluding Housing the Arts). In 1984/85, opera will receive £19,467,250, or 24 per cent of total spending. By comparison, spending on other forms of music in 1984/85 will total only £5,830,500; and dance whose total audience throughout the country slightly exceeds in number the audience for opera, will receive only £8,005,250. The report of the Council's working party on Opera and Dance, published in February 1983, strongly recommended that the funding of dance should be raised and that the proportion of total spending devoted to opera should not increase. At a time when so many of the Council's clients are underfunded the Council has concluded that the proportion of its funds spent on opera is too high. Thus the development programme set out below seeks to go some way towards redressing the imbalance between spending on opera on the one hand and spending on other music and dance on the other.

Challenge Funding

33. The Council's development programme represents, to some degree, a shift away from its more habitual practice of responding to the initiatives of others and towards a policy of identifying needs and seeking to help supply them. The Council does not believe, however, that it is possible to establish successful artistic enterprise by decree. Nor does it believe that, were it possible, such a course of action would be desirable. It hopes, rather, that, by setting forth its plans, it will engage the enthusiasm of all those people – artists, administrators, local authorities, business sponsors and the public – on whom the success of any new development in the arts depends. To finance many of its proposals, therefore, the Council will issue challenges to local communities to match its funding, at least in part, whether from local authority resources or other locally-raised funds. This principle lies at the heart, for example, of the Council's hopes for the future development of its major drama clients in the regions. It also underlies the future development it would like to see in the contemporary visual arts, whether in existing arts centres or in a new creative partnership between the Arts Council and the network of municipal art galleries across the country. Where talent exists, and where it is supported by local financial resources, the Arts Council will be ready to play its part in creating conditions in which that talent can have the optimum opportunity to express itself.

34. The Council appreciates that many local authorities are experiencing severe pressures to reduce their overall levels of expenditure; even with the best will towards the arts, some of them will find it impossible to give priority to increases in their arts spending. But the position varies from authority to authority. The Council hopes that some at least will be able to respond

positively to its proposals in 1985/86 and that others will be ready to do so in subsequent years. The tradition of joint support for the arts by local authorities on the one hand and the Arts Councils on the other is by now sufficiently widely established to give reason for optimism.

35. The Council also wishes to encourage greater support for the arts from business and industry. In recent years, the contribution that business makes to the arts in the United Kingdom has increased considerably. It is still very small by comparison with public expenditure on the arts, but it is nevertheless a much-needed contribution. The Council endorses the view of the Association for Business Sponsorship of the Arts about the importance of further tax concessions as a means of encouraging the growth in business sponsorship. But in any event it will do all it can to develop business and other private sponsorship and to encourage its clients to attract increasing support from that source. In assessing the level of finance raised locally in response to its own proposals for development, the Council will be ready to take additional sponsorship into account, despite the fact that sponsorship income from any one particular source may not be guaranteed for more than a comparatively short period.

V. THE DEVELOPMENT PROGRAMME

36. The Council's development programme over the next five years will give priority to five main areas of work. Those areas are Art, Dance, Drama, Music and Education. To help it in its work, the Council will also increase the responsibilities of the Regional Arts Associations and its funding of them. Neither the Council's present resources, nor the prospects of the national economy in the foreseeable future, enable the Council to move forward on all fronts. Although the Council will always be ready to consider new individual applications in any field, it is necessary in the development programme to focus attention on the areas where its clients have been most severely handicapped financially in recent years and where the artistic return on investment can be most confidently predicted . . .

APPENDIX H

Digest of *Towards a National Arts & Media Strategy*, as reproduced in *A Creative Future*, both works cited. This was submitted to the Secretary of State for National Heritage in October, 1992.

THE CONCEPT

In the half century since the Second World War, the arts, crafts and media in Britain have been transformed. Theatre, opera and dance companies have been established throughout Great Britain. There is a rich orchestral life. Poets and novelists maintain the country's long literary tradition. Television and radio reach into almost every home, creating new art forms and transmitting existing forms. There is an extensive network for the distribution and exhibition, if not the production, of film. Britain remains one of the leading international centres for the crafts and visual arts. Hundreds of thousands of amateurs make music, present plays, write poetry, paint pictures and take photographs, so helping the arts to flourish in local communities and neighbourhoods.

As the working week shortens, as the population ages, people have more time than ever before to participate in the arts, whether as receivers or makers. Research shows that a majority of the population values the arts for the quality they add to life.

Many of our themes for the future arise from the strengths and weaknesses of the present:

> The funding system has long been committed to the support of new work and of education and outreach activity. Apart from the crafts, the emphasis has been on the provision of assistance to organisations rather than to individuals. But in the funding of institutions, we must keep clearly in view the product – the art itself – which will generally be the work of individuals. Their artistic and economic welfare must be our concern too.
>
> One example of the focus on institutions is the great post-war theatre building programme, largely financed by local government. But many of these theatres are

455

now in a poor state of repair. Outside London there are too few high-quality spaces for temporary art exhibitions or for dance. In some parts of the country, important gaps remain to be filled (for example, there is no purpose-built concert hall in the North-East).

Although the Arts Council of Great Britain's predecessor, the Council for the Encouragement of Music and the Arts, saw the arts as an integrated whole, the public funding system has mainly focused on the professional rather than the amateur. There is a growing acknowledgement of the creative contribution from those whose artistic practice is voluntary and is not their main profession or vocation.

The major cities, particularly London, receive the majority of public funding. We must ensure that this artistic investment benefits the country as a whole – and that high quality touring work and the organic development of the arts are properly supported outside the big cities.

Great Britain is a diverse society. Funding tends to be directed towards the long-established and to those whose concerns reflect the dominant culture. But there is a great deal more on offer. Artists in the African, Caribbean and Asian communities are a major influence on the arts in Britain. Disability culture is a source of original and exciting work. The arts of the indigenous linguistic minorities in Scotland and Wales flourish.

Just as Great Britain is politically and economically part of wider international networks and interests, so its arts are an aspect of world culture. There is evidence of a growing enthusiasm among both public and promoters for a more comprehensive diet. Likewise, through the British Council much of the best of British arts is presented abroad – but more organisations and individuals could benefit from the experience than have the opportunity to do so at present.

In recent decades, local authorities have made a huge contribution to the development of the arts. Without their work, the artistic life of the country would be decimated. But the record is still uneven. Moreover, there have been many recent changes to local government and to the education system, and more are in the pipeline. Many believe that support for the arts in both areas is at threat.

This country possesses artistic talent in abundance; money is in shorter supply. Much of this strategy can be achieved within existing resources, requiring no more than partnership between the many bodies which share a concern for the arts, or improvements in the funding system's own ways of working. Other aspects, inevitably, need more money. There are, finally, matters which must be dealt with at the political level – for example, the reviewing of certain aspects of the national curriculum in England and Wales and of local government finance. With the creation of the Department of National Heritage, the prospects are bright for such issues to be given the consideration they require and deserve.

We live in a society which is pre-eminent in many art-forms and well-endowed in virtually all of them. This must be sustained and enhanced. The arts fulfil needs which are personal as much as social, and success cannot be judged exclusively in utilitarian terms. All those who have been working over the course of many months on the strategy process have realised that Great

Britain is poised for a leap forward in the arts, one which could transform the position of the arts in the minds of all the people in this country.

PRINCIPLES AND AIMS

The national debate of the past months has led to the identification of the ten following principles, which are consistent with the broad objectives of the arts and media funding bodies but develop and refine them. Each is accompanied by an aim which relates to it. We begin with the most general principles.

(1) The arts, crafts and media are central to the lives of individuals and the well-being of communities. They offer inspiration, pleasure and comfort; and help people to criticise and celebrate society and understand their relationship to it.
Our aim is to persuade both the general public and the government of this centrality and to ensure that audiences, artists, producers and participants are moved and challenged by the arts.

(2) Everyone should have the opportunity to enjoy the arts both as participant and as audience member.
Our aim is to make this opportunity effective, by increasing the availability of the arts, crafts and media, and by breaking down the barriers – social, physical, economic and others – to their active enjoyment.

(3) Education is at the heart of enjoying and understanding the arts and media. It is fundamental to a vital, varied culture.
Our aim is to ensure that education becomes more central to our work and that of arts and media practitioners; and that the arts and media become more central to the work of the education sector, formal and informal.

(4) Quality is the pre-eminent criterion for public funding of the arts. Quality is a broad term, encompassing such concepts as fitness for purpose. Work of high quality and originality may be produced in any form, at any scale and from any cultural aesthetic or community.
Our aim is to support high quality arts and media work in whatever form it is to be found and from whatever cultural aesthetic or community it springs, and to support particularly the creation, production, exhibition and publication of original work in all forms and media.

(5) Diversity and variety in the arts and media are valuable in themselves and as a reflection of contemporary life.
Our aim (as the complement to (4) above) is to support the widest possible range of arts and media, in order to promote choice, understanding and respect for all cultures.

(6) It is imperative that the arts of the past be renewed and kept alive.
Our aim is to ensure that artists, producers, curators and audiences,

now and in the future, are able to benefit from the arts of the past, whether in performance, audio and visual recording, publication, collections or archives.

(7) The arts and media should be viewed in an international as well as a local, regional and national context.

Our aim is to facilitate and support an international dimension to the work of artists and arts organisations in Great Britain, and to assist audiences and communities in Great Britain better to enjoy and understand artistic forms and activities from all over the world.

(8) Public funding of the arts and media, in people, buildings and equipment, is an investment. Its dividends are creativity, inspiration, civic pride and personal pleasure and confidence, as well as economic benefit.

Our aim is to act as effective advocates for increased funding of the arts and to promote the greatest benefit from such funding, through partnerships with the public and private sectors and other means.

(9) The arts should be generally available throughout the country.

Our aim is to encourage artistic development nationwide, continually to reassess the geographical and art form distribution of our resources and to alter the distribution nationally, regionally or locally in support of the principle.

(10) The arts and media funding system is accountable to the public through Parliament. It should seek to represent, be advised by and deserve the trust of the arts community.

Our aim is always to operate fair, simple and open procedures, with decisions taken at the most 'local' level appropriate; and to act as constructive and creative agencies in the support and development of the arts and media.

THE FUNDING SYSTEM'S PLEDGES

This section is complementary to the principles and aims above and to the policies below: our ability to make progress is dependent not merely on adequate resourcing but also on our ensuring effective, efficient and fair working methods. As with the rest of this paper, detailed targets and methods of review and assessment will be included in individual corporate plans.

These are our pledges to the public, the arts community and the government.

1 We shall become more effective advocates for the arts, crafts and media and their development, backing this up by co-ordinated research and effective dissemination of information.

2 We shall ensure that our application procedures are marked by simplicity, openness and fairness, with reasons provided for our decisions.

3   We shall ensure that there is a clear and consistent division of responsibility, function and duty between the national and regional elements of the system, with decisions taken at the most local practicable level (which will mean, where appropriate, delegation of decisions and funding from the national to the regional level and in some cases the 'franchising' of funding responsibility from the regional to the local level).

4   We shall maintain and improve our partnership with local authorities, which has been an essential feature of the post-war development of the arts.

5   We shall ensure that our decision-making is informed by a comprehensive range of sources of advice, including external advisers from a wide variety of backgrounds and cultural interests, self-assessment, funding body assessment and audience review. This range will enable us to realise the ideals of Principles 4 and 5; and it presupposes the retention of an 'arm's length' relationship between government and the funding system.

6   We shall work towards a relationship with funded arts and media organisations based on contracts negotiated and agreed with them in advance, which will define the purpose and conditions of funding and the process of assessment. Where practicable, such funding contracts will be jointly negotiated with other funding agencies such as local authorities.

7   We shall work with arts and media practitioners to identify and provide, subject to financial and staffing constraints, support services in such areas as marketing, training, board development and management advice.

8   We shall place a high priority on effectiveness, efficiency and value for money, both for ourselves and for those we fund, in order to ensure that our investment and other activities achieve the greatest possible benefit.

9   We shall create or strengthen practical working partnerships with other bodies which have an interest in heritage and cultural issues. These partners or potential partners include museums support bodies; the commercial and industrial arts and media sectors; the formal and informal education sectors; the public library service; the private sector and the Association for Business Sponsorship of the Arts; tourism and economic development agencies; national organisations with a cultural role (such as English Heritage, the British Council and the broadcasting companies); and the Department of National Heritage and other government departments.

POLICIES

This section sets out key policies for the funding system, each of them deriving from one or more of the principles and aims above. Under each heading, the policies are put in a rough order of priority, and the most relevant principles and aims are listed. The headings themselves are also in order of priority, but in practice they are interdependent and of broadly equal status. It is necessary to renew the building stock in order to house a wide range of high quality arts activity; participation and diversity are the other side of the coin to 'the artistic imperative'; and, in different ways, education and money underpin all other areas of development.

The following programme is an integrated whole. All of it is necessary if we are to provide a comprehensive service to the public and to the arts, crafts and media; though obviously it will be implemented in various ways, according to the art forms, regions and organisations concerned. Where examples are used in what follows, they are for illustration only: many others could have been chosen.

Some but not all of the programme will require a significant increase in resources. In current economic circumstances, this is unlikely in the short term. But our programme looks forward to the year 2000. It is right that, over this longer period, the funding system should be planning the use of increased resources.

In the meantime there are, inevitably, choices to be made. The detail of these choices is a matter for individual funding body corporate plans. We are, nonetheless, already taking action on some of the policies below. Others, particularly in the area of advocacy, can be implemented at little cost. Still others, which represent a change of direction or emphasis, are so important that we have determined to make a start on their implementation pending a real increase in grant-in-aid from the government. This need not require a significant re-allocation of funds away from current uses. In our funding role, we work *with* and *through* artists and arts organisations (though, as noted above, the BFI and Crafts Council are primarily direct providers rather than funders). This will continue to be the case. But our client list and our relationship with clients will evolve and develop. One of the most important developments will be contractual funding. This will enable us to ensure that, by mutual agreement, clients are funded specifically for work in some of the policy areas below.

The policies marked with an asterisk – which constitute the majority of those listed – are those on which we shall begin or continue action in the short or medium term. We can make no such commitment about those not marked with an asterisk, though individual funding bodies may well begin or continue action on some of these also. Resources permitting, we expect to be able to report progress in all these policy areas within three years.

I *The artistic imperative*

These policies re-affirm our support for the 'originating artist' in all forms and media. We wish to encourage an increase in the amount of original work created and presented by artists and to improve the economic status and, indirectly, the public standing of the artist in society.

*1   Support for the creation of original, and where appropriate innovative, work by artists and groups of artists through means which match the needs of the art forms and artists concerned – such as funds for commissioning; for affordable rehearsal or studio space; for facilities for artists with disabilities; for setting-up crafts businesses; and for increased investment in film and video production. (Principle 4)

*2 Support for the distribution, exhibition and presentation of original work in all media to existing and new audiences – for example, through funds for recording subsidies, for new means of presenting the visual arts and crafts, for assisting Black and other culturally diverse companies to run their own buildings and for permitting more dance and theatre companies to move to a fuller 'producing year'. (Principles 2 and 4)

*3 Support for a network of arts and media organisations to preserve and renew the arts of the past, to encourage new work and new means of presentation, to serve the communities in which they are based and to act as a resource for artists and other arts organisations – for instance, through investment in programming and the promotion of conductor/ choreographer/playwright (etc)-in-residence schemes. (Principles 2, 4, 6)

*4 Support for both initial training and re-training of arts practitioners in all forms, and others in the arts and media industries, through improved links with training providers (such as industry training organisations, TECs and LECs), training bursaries and so on; making available training to meet the needs of disabled artists; working to ensure that training is not dependent on economic status; and assisting artists to bridge the period between training and establishment in the professional world. (Principles 1 and 4)

*5 Support for the use of new technologies in the arts, crafts and media. (Principles 4 and 5)

*6 Support for art as an integral part of the environment – for instance, through funds for the development of public art, lobbying for percent for art and promoting public debate on architecture and planning. (Principles 1, 2 and 8)

*7 Support and advocacy for archives – for the preservation in appropriate institutions and collections of records of the arts and media, in sound, vision and print – for the benefit of posterity and the national heritage. (Principles 2 and 6)

II *Participation and diversity*

We intend to encourage an improvement of artistic standards in the amateur and community-based arts; and to increase the stability and influence of culturally diverse arts organisations.

Our programmes and practices should take into account the demographic changes occurring in Great Britain. Furthermore, opportunities to participate in the arts should be provided in ways which suit the individuals and communities to which they apply – rural or urban, young or old, male or female, deaf or hearing, Black or White: cultural diversity must become a practical reality, and one not restricted to the arts of particular communities or cultural aesthetics.

*1   Support for the full range of the arts – which includes amateur and community-based arts activity, as well as professional performance (these are merely terms of convenience, not watertight categories). We shall provide funds for advisory, training, membership and support organisations, and for professional input in participatory arts. Our aim will be to encourage new work, to increase local participation and diversity and to assist those who are seeking to raise standards. (Principle 2)

*2   Support for the arts of the diverse cultures of Great Britain. Significant artistic movements are more likely to realise their potential if provided with structural support and funding (including funding for 'umbrella' support organisations) rather than with short-term project grants alone. Culturally diverse art has too seldom received such structural support. We shall alter this emphasis in the future. (Principles 4, 5 and 9)

*3   Support for the indigenous contemporary, folk and traditional arts of Scotland, Wales and England. (Principles 4, 5 and 6)

III *Education*

Our ambitions in the field of education and the arts go well beyond the quantifiable. We propose initiatives which will enrich the lives of children and others in the education system; and encourage a new generation of active and adventurous readers, viewers, listeners and participants – an important pre-condition of development of the arts and of audiences.

Many arts organisations have pioneered inspiring educational programmes, which have helped thousands of people to understand and share in the arts. These programmes must be maintained and enhanced. Many of those in both the education and arts sectors fear that insufficient funding and the recent reforms of the education system (including local management of schools and opting out), whatever their other effects or benefits, may put this work at risk.

*1   Advocacy of the value of the arts, crafts and media in education (including special education) and advice on best practice to providers of education, including central government education departments, local education authorities, teacher education institutions, providers of further, higher and adult education, school and college governing bodies and broadcasters. (Principles 1, 2 and 3)

*2   Advocacy and lobbying particularly in two areas: the provision of mandatory grants at full cost for all arts courses in further and higher

462

education; and inclusion of an arts subject, of the pupil's choice, as a mandatory part of the national curriculum for the 14–16 age group in England and Wales. (Principles 1, 2 and 3)

*3 Forging links between pre-professional education and professional arts and media practice, with particular emphasis on the development of new creative talent. (Principles 3 and 4)

4 Increasing the training and funding available for high quality education work by funded arts and media organisations, particularly for programmes that introduce artists and media practitioners into formal and informal education; and the careful evaluation of such programmes. (Principles 2, 3, 4 and 5)

5 Partnership with the public library, museum and gallery and broadcasting services, which are vital resources in arts and media education. (Principles 2, 3 and 6)

6 Advocacy to the public at large of the value of education as a means of increasing enjoyment and understanding of the arts. (Principles 1, 2 and 3)

IV *Audience development*

Our aim is to increase both the number and the social range of audiences. Effective access for disabled audience members is an important element of this. Further, we are as much concerned with the quality of experience as with numbers; the public has high expectations of the arts, and attention to its wishes will benefit the quality of art as well as the arts economy.

'Audience development' has at least three aspects: heightening the experience of viewing, reading, listening to the arts, crafts and media; increasing the numbers of people throughout society who have the opportunity to do so; and assisting the process of mutual understanding between maker or performer and receiver.

*1 Support for touring and distribution, including assistance to those who work in arts buildings (including arts centres, community facilities, and other performing arts venues, film theatres and cinemas, museums, galleries and libraries) to create a range of imaginative programmes; an increase in performing arts touring, particularly to reach new audiences; an increase in visual arts touring, arising particularly from improved links with museums, galleries, arts centres, collections and archives; initiatives in publishing; and 'electronic touring' – video, CD-I and so on. (Principles 2 and 4)

*2 Support for marketing as a means of developing existing and new audiences for the arts. (Principle 2)

*3 Reaffirming commitment to the principle of public service broadcasting by both the BBC and the commercial companies, to provide an environment within which broadcasting as an art form can flourish and arts programming is supported. (Principles 1, 2 and 4)

4   Support for arts festivals presenting original work or reaching new audiences, and for local, regional, national and international artistic celebrations; where necessary through 'major events' funds to assist such initiatives as Arts 2000, the Cinema Centenary in 1996 and the possible Festival of Britain in 2001. (Principles 2, 4, 7 and 8)

5   Research to improve our understanding of audiences and participants in the arts and their needs – including the barriers (psychological, educational, geographical, social, economic and physical) to full enjoyment of the arts. (Principle 2)

6   Support for outreach work by arts organisations to develop new audiences and participants, where necessary linked to programmes of research and evaluation. (Principle 2)

V *Renewal of the building stock*

By the end of this century, we hope that the stock of arts buildings will have been refurbished and where necessary new buildings constructed – so enabling people in every part of the country to enjoy the arts, crafts and media in settings which are welcoming, exciting and beautiful.

A large part of our building stock is in urgent need of refurbishment. The last boom in arts buildings – roughly, the fifteen years from 1955 – created its own problems in terms of running costs, maintenance and repair. Furthermore, certain art forms, such as dance, were left short of properly equipped spaces.

A key need is to ensure that arts buildings are accessible to disabled people. 'Accessible' must be seen as a broad term, covering physical access for both audiences and practitioners, signing, audio description and disability equality training.

Local authorities play the leading role in the provision of arts buildings, but the arts and media funding system has a broad strategic responsibility as well. The priorities which follow call for significant and bold investment by government.

*1   Drawing up a 'millennium map' based on a national audit of existing arts buildings (eg. theatres, concert halls, galleries, film theatres, arts centres and other multi-use buildings) and of the need for new buildings (such as a dance house and a deaf theatre). The question of access for disabled people will be addressed. (Principles 2 and 8)

*2   Initiating a ten year programme, taking full account of value for money, and identifying resources from central and local government, charitable foundations and private sources, to meet the needs identified in the millennium map and validated by feasibility studies (see below, 3). This should include a more visionary look to the future – including the need for arts buildings equipped for work using new technology. It is hoped that the central government contribution to this may be met from the proceeds of the National Lottery. (Principles 2 and 8)

3   Establishing funds to go towards feasibility studies and for commissioning investment appraisals of arts and media building improvements – particularly to assist in establishing priority uses for National Lottery funds. (Principles 2 and 8)

4   Encouraging the flexible, imaginative and cost-effective use for the arts, crafts and media of multi-purpose and redundant buildings (such as schools, churches and mills) and of 'non-traditional' venues (such as sports arenas). (Principles 2, 5, 8 and 9)

5   Raising public awareness of the architecture of arts buildings, to underpin the above priorities: positively or negatively, the artistic quality of arts buildings affects the status and perception of the work that takes place in them. (Principles 2 and 8)

VI *Internationalism*

In collaboration with the British Council, Visiting Arts and other agencies, we wish to increase the quality and quantity of international arts activity enjoyed by the public and to broaden the understanding and appreciation of world cultures within this country.

We shall concentrate on supporting international contacts between creators, producers, promoters, venue managers and others, the exchange of information, co-productions and other forms of co-operation. Our strategy does not address cultural diplomacy, which is the British Council's responsibility. This programme represents no radical break with the past, but hitherto our approach has been unsystematic. We shall develop clear, principled and consistent practice.

*1   Providing grants for artists, producers and promoters to train, work and undertake research outside Great Britain. (Principles 4 and 7)

*2   Increasing funds for promoters, distributors and exhibitors to bring in the best work from all parts of the world, in all forms and media. (Principles 2, 4 and 7)

*3   Seeking development of the European Commission's programmes in support of the audiovisual sector through enhanced funding of MEDIA, and UK entry to the Council of Europe production and distribution support scheme EURIMAGES. (Principles 7 and 8)

*4   Providing up-to-date information on cultural trends, programmes and funds within and beyond the European Community, good practice, international cultural issues, and sales and marketing opportunities. (Principles 7, 8 and 10)

*5   Backing international networks, as services provided *by*, not *for*, artists and arts organisations. Support of cultural diversity networks will be a high priority: the enhanced profile of disability arts, for instance, owes much to the growth of international networks of disabled artists. (Principles 5, 7 and 10)

6　Facilitating cultural exchange and the development of British artists and arts organisations by relaxing restrictions on the use of domestic funding agencies' resources for work outside Great Britain. (Principles 4 and 7)

7　Encouraging a cultural dimension to such areas of international exchange as town twinning. (Principles 1 and 8)

VII *Money*

A fully effective and efficient system of plural funding is required: the arts, crafts and media should receive a level of investment reflecting their needs and their importance to society.

We need to help the market to function effectively and to intervene where it does not. This section differs from most of the others, since a number of priorities are matters where the primary responsibility rests with government or other agencies. Our key role will be advocacy.

*1　Ensuring as far as possible that subsidy from funding bodies to artists and arts organisations is enhanced by their own earned income; helping them to earn more; and enabling them to use public funding in an effective, efficient, flexible and entrepreneurial way. (Principles 8 and 10)

*2　Encouraging – in collaboration with the Association for Business Sponsorship of the Arts where appropriate – individual donations, sponsorship, corporate giving and investment in the arts and media through greater use of recently introduced tax incentives and concessions. (Principle 8)

*3　Exploring more flexible and innovative ways of using some of the money within the public funding system, such as low-interest loans and art purchase schemes. (Principle 8)

*4　Making the case for support of the arts to be a statutory responsibility of local authorities in England and Wales, eligible for revenue support grant from central government. The government has long endorsed arts provision by local authorities. The creation of a statutory responsibility would ensure that people are not denied arts opportunities merely because of where they live. (Principles 2 and 8)

*5　Building on welcome new arrangements by seeking further fiscal and other incentives to stimulate investment in UK film production, distribution and exhibition. (Principle 8)

*6　Making the case that a significant proportion of receipts from the National Lottery should go to the arts, crafts and media, particularly for capital investment; these funds to be distributed through the existing agencies, but not at the expense of their existing grants. (Principles 2, 8, and 10) . . .

NOTES

PROLOGUE

While the prologue is chiefly based on a previous book by this author, *The Need to Give: The Patrons and the Arts* (London, 1990), the essential source on the growth of state patronage remains Janet Minihan's important *The Nationalization of Culture: The Development of State Subsidies to the Arts in Great Britain* (London, 1977). *The Waning of the Middle Ages* was published in London in 1924; Vasari's *Lives of the Artists* was published in six volumes in Florence, 1878–82; John Pye's *Patronage of British Art* was published in London in 1845; Matthew Arnold's *Culture and Anarchy* was published in London in 1869, and T. S. Eliot's seminal *Notes towards the Definition of Culture* was published in London in 1948.

CHAPTER ONE

The outbreak of the Second World War has been treated by this author in *War Like a Wasp: The Lost Decade of the Forties* (London, 1989). Dame Ninette de Valois spoke to this author about Before Keynes and After Keynes. William Emrys Williams, who edited and mostly wrote *The First Ten Years: The Arts Council of Great Britain: 1946–56* (London, 1957), is the expert on adult education in the 1930s, and the quotations came from his pamphlet. Those of the civilization 'this country is supposed to be fighting for' came from 'Memorandum for Informal Conference', 18 December 1939, Public Records Office (PRO) ED 136/188B and M. G. Holmes to Sir Alan Barlow, 22 December 1939, PRO ED 136/188B and 'Committee for the Encouragement of Music and the Arts', December 1939, PRO EL 1/2.

H. G. Wells's *The Shape of Things to Come* was published in London in 1938. John Strachey's quotation from *The Author* was published in 1940 and Cyril Connolly's opening editorial of *Horizon* was vol. 1, no. 1, January 1940.

Mary Glasgow's opinion of Dr Thomas Jones and of the founding of CEMA came from her unpublished *The Nineteen Hundreds: A Diary in Retrospect* (Oxford, 1986). Dr Jones's account of the founding of the wartime arts organization is in his 'The Origins of CEMA', *CEMA Bulletin*, May 1942. Earl De La Warr wrote to Thomas Jones about the 'pathetic hunger' for the arts on 13

December 1939, PRO ED 136/188D. William Emrys Williams further stated his version of the founding of CEMA in 'The Pre-History of the Arts Council', *Aims and Action in Adult Education* (E. M. Hutchinson ed., London, 1971) as well as in *The First Ten Years*, work cited. The aims of CEMA are listed in 'Memorandum in support of an Application to the Treasury for Financial Assistance', 6 March 1940, PRO EL 1/2.

Eric W. White, an officer in the Literature Department of the later Arts Council, is invaluable on the early days in his book, *The Arts Council of Great Britain* (London, 1975), as is the article by F. M. Leventhal, '"The Best for the Most"; CEMA and State Sponsorship of the Arts in Wartime, 1939–1945', *Twentieth Century British History* (Vol. 1, No. 3, Oxford, 1990), which tells of the enthusiasm for the travelling players and musicians. This is also told in H. C. Dent, *Education in Transition* (New York, 1946) and in Ivor Brown, 'Paying for the Arts', *Old and Young* (London, 1971). Dr Jones wrote to Violet Markham about the need to play in the 'dreary Dagenhams' on 21 January 1940, in the Jones papers, Class T, Vol. 7–12, National Library of Wales. Dame Sibyl Thorndike's letter to her son about enthusiastic wartime audiences is quoted in John Casson, *Lewis and Sibyl: A Memoir* (London, 1972). Charles Landstone, who worked in drama for both CEMA and the Arts Council, tells of the Old Vic at war in his two illuminating memoirs, *Off-Stage: A Personal Record of the First Twelve Years of State Sponsored Drama in Great Britain* (London, 1953) and in *I Gate-Crashed* (London, 1976). Constance Cummings spoke to this author about her touring experiences in wartime. Sir Stephen Spender wrote on the significance of the arts in the war in *World Within World* (London, 1951). B. Ifor Evans and Mary Glasgow wrote a book that was important for this period, *The Arts in England* (London, 1949).

John Christie's view of CEMA lagging in mediocrity was written to Mary Glasgow, 25 July 1940, PRO EL 2/9. Dr Jones wrote of the vision of the Music Travellers in his bulletin, 'The Origins of CEMA.', already cited. J. M. Keynes wrote to Mary Glasgow about Donald Wolfit on 3 July 1940, PRO EL 2/36, and she wrote about meeting him in her unpublished diary in retrospect, and in 'The Concept of the Arts Council', *Essays on John Maynard Keynes* (Milo Keynes ed., Cambridge, 1975). The achievement of CEMA in its first two years was summarized in the *Pilgrim Trust Annual Report*, 1941. In her unpublished diary, Mary Glasgow tells of Thomas Jones's watchword of 'Action' and of Lord Macmillan's refusal of committees and of her lack of surprise that Keynes became the CEMA Chairman. Keynes wrote to Jones of his appreciation on 22 January 1942, King's College, Cambridge (KCC), Keynes Papers. Roy Harrod wrote of Keynes's thoughts in *The Life of John Maynard Keynes* (London, 1951). Keynes wrote to John Christie about not being a musician on 30 September 1940, Glyndebourne Archives (GA), Keynes Papers. John Christie's accusation that Keynes was copying his ideas was written to Lord Esher, president of the British Drama League, in early February, 1943, GA, Christie Papers. There is no reply preserved.

W. E. Williams accused Keynes of 'donnish superiority' in his cited article, 'The Pre-History of the Arts Council'. Keynes wrote to R. A. Butler about his incompetent advisory Panels on 25 January 1945, PRO ED 136/196A, and about their conflicting views to Mary Glasgow on 11 August 1943, PRO EL 2/38. He wrote on 'respectable deadheads' on the panels to R. A. Butler on 2 March 1943, PRO ED 136/196B. Again Mary Glasgow wrote of Keynes's thoroughness in her unpublished diary in retrospect, while Charles Landstone wrote of reviving ballet and Marie Rambert in his cited works: both of them praised Keynes in their memoirs. Keynes wrote in *The Times* of saving the Theatre Royal, Bristol, in May 1943, while Vaughan Williams's objection to a string of subsidized local theatres were recorded in the CEMA Minutes of 20 July 1943, PRO ED 136/192. Charles Landstone in his memoirs reported on Tyrone Guthrie's antipathy to Keynes, despite his efforts to bring the two men together. I am indebted to Peter Cox, as a Dartington instructor and founder member of the South-West Arts Association, for the information on Christopher Martin and the Political and Economic Planning Initiatives supported by the Nuffield College Social Reconstruction Survey, and also for his opinions on the fate of the surveys. Sir Alan Peacock spoke to this author about Lord Keynes and the arts in Scotland.

Keynes wrote of his inability to go on to Mary Glasgow on 31 March 1944, PRO EL 2/39, and to Samuel Courtauld on 20 April 1944, also on PRO EL 2/39, while he told R. A. Butler that there was no one else on 19 May 1944, PRO ED 136/188B. Kenneth Clark gave his opinion of Keynes in his autobiography, *The Other Half: A Self-Portrait* (London, 1977). Keynes's broadcast on the creation of 'The Arts Council: Its Policy and Hopes', later quoted at length, was printed in *The Listener*, 12 July 1945. John Christie cabled from the United States of America to his wife Audrey about England as the world cultural centre on 20 January 1944, and drafted his letter to Sir John Anderson in the early part of 1944, and extended his olive branch to Keynes early in 1945, GA, Christie Papers. The estimation of the intention of Lord Keynes is that of F. M. Leventhal in his cited article, ' "The Best for the Most" ...' while W. E. Williams explained the practical importance of CEMA to the Arts Council in his cited bulletin, 'The First Ten Years ...'

In his final broadcast on the Arts Council, Keynes also stressed the importance of the BBC as the great educator and the creator of public demand for the arts, as well as a contradictory wish to decentralize and yet make London a great artistic metropolis. Further extracts from his speech show how influential his founding and guiding ideas were to be.

> But we do not think of the Arts Council as a schoolmaster. Your enjoyment will be our first aim. We have but little money to spill, and it will be you yourselves who will by your patronage decide in the long run what you get. In so far as we instruct, it is a new game we are teaching you to play – and to watch. Our wartime experience has led us already to one clear discovery: the unsatisfied demand and the enormous public for serious and fine entertainment. This certainly did not exist a few years ago. I do not believe that it is merely a war-time phenomenon. I fancy that the BBC has played a big part, the predominant part, in creating this public demand, by bringing to everybody in the country the possibility of learning these new games which only the few used to play, and by forming new tastes and habits and thus enlarging the desires of the listener and his capacity for enjoyment. I am told that today when a good symphony concert is broadcast as many as five million people may listen to it. Their ears become trained. With what anticipation many of them look forward if a chance comes their way to hear a living orchestra and to experience the enhanced excitement

and concentration of attention and emotion, which flows from being one of a great audience all moved together by the surge and glory of an orchestra in being, beating in on the sensibilities of every organ of the body and of the apprehension. The result is that half the world is being taught to approach with a livelier appetite the living performance and the work of the artist as it comes from his own hand and body, with the added subtlety of actual flesh and blood ...

We of the Arts Council are greatly concerned to decentralise and disperse the dramatic and musical and artistic life of the country, to build up provincial centres and to promote corporate life in these matters in every town and county. It is not our intention to act on our own where we can avoid it. We want to collaborate with local authorities and to encourage local institutions and societies and local enterprise to take the lead. We already have regional offices in Birmingham, Cambridge, Manchester, Nottingham, Bristol, Leeds, Newcastle-on-Tyne, Cardiff and Edinburgh. For Scotland and for Wales special committees have been established ... Certainly in every blitzed town in this country one hopes that the local authority will make provision for a central group of buildings for drama and music and art. There could be no better memorial of a war to save the freedom of the spirit of the individual. We look forward to the time when the theatre and the concert-hall and the gallery will be a living element in everyone's upbringing, and regular attendance at the theatre and at concerts a part of organized education ...

But it is also our business to make London a great artistic metropolis, a place to visit and to wonder at. For this purpose London today is half a ruin. With the loss of the Queen's Hall there is no proper place for concerts. The Royal Opera House at Covent Garden has been diverted for other purposes throughout the war. The Crystal Palace has been burnt to the ground. We hope that Covent Garden will be re-opened early next year as the home of opera and ballet. The London County Council has already allotted a site for a National Theatre. The Arts Council has joined with the Trustees of the Crystal Palace in the preparation of plans to make that once again a great People's Palace.

CHAPTER TWO

The full text of the Royal Charter of 1946 can be found in Appendix A. Alan Ross wrote on the decade in *The Forties: A Period Piece* (London, 1950). G. S. Fraser commented on post-war London in his *The Modern Writer and his World* (London, 1953). Gilbert Frankau expressed his views in Donald Brook, *Writers' Gallery: Biographical Sketches of Britain's Greatest Writers and their Views on Reconstruction* (London, 1944). J. B. Priestley wrote on the disappearance of class in favour of the people in *Out of the People* (London, 1941); it was the unique herald of a planned series of Vigilant Books which would deal with the problems of reconstruction after the war. John Pick wrote a critique of the Arts Council in his introduction to essays on it, which he edited under the title, *The State and The Arts* (London, 1980).

The reports on the Arts Council were published annually after 1945–6 for the following fifty years. Dame Ninette de Valois kindly gave an interview to this author. John Lehmann wrote dismissively of post-war ballet in *New Writing and Daylight*, 1946. Eric Blom was the critic who wrote on 'The Future of Music' in *The Prospect Before Us* (London, 1948). Sir Kenneth Clark commented on Sir Ernest Pooley's appointment as Chairman in his memoirs, already cited. Mary

Endacott informed this author about the early days of the Arts Council. Mary Glasgow's unpublished memoirs have already been cited. Rudi Bing's comment on John Christie is quoted in Wilfred Blunt, *John Christie of Glyndebourne* (London, 1968). The acrimonious correspondence between Steuart Wilson and John Christie is preserved in the Glyndebourne Archives: Wilson challenged Christie to a duel on 6 April 1946. Robert Speaight, *Drama Since 1939* (London, 1947) made the remark about the absence of war plays in the English theatre. T. S. Eliot, *The Cocktail Party*, was published in London in 1950. And Christopher Hassall, 'Notes on the Verse Drama', filled the whole issue of *The Masque*, No. 6, 1948.

Charles Landstone wrote of his time at the Arts Council in *Off-Stage: A Personal Record of the First Twelve Years of State Sponsored Drama in Great Britain* (London, 1953). Sir Alan Peacock gave an interview to this author. Eliot's *Notes towards the Definition of Culture* has already been cited. Keidrych Rhys wrote on Welsh culture in *Wales*, 1947, also the year of publication of *Scottish Arts and Letters*. Patrick Kavanagh wrote on 'The Parish and the Universe' in his *Collected Prose* (London, 1967), while Norman Nicholson wrote 'On Being Provincial' for *The Listener*, 12 August 1954. For the attacks of F. R. Leavis on the metropolitan establishment, see his 'Mr Pryce-Jones, The British Council and British Culture (1951)', collected in *A Selection from Scrutiny Compiled by F. R. Leavis* (Vol. I, Cambridge, 1968). V. S. Pritchett's comments on the influence of the war and post-war period on writers come from his *Midnight Oil* (London, 1971). Peter Cox told this author about the Regional Arts Associations and supplied early archival material.

Paul Ferris quoted Huw Wheldon's opinion of a job for the Arts Council in his absorbing biography, *Sir Huge: The Life of Huw Wheldon* (London, 1990). The minutes of the early meetings of the Welsh Committee are preserved in Cardiff and were made available to this author. Mary Glasgow wrote her advice to local authorities in the *Municipal Review*, April, 1948. M. J. McRobert, 'Some Notes on the History of No. 4 St. James's Square' was published by the Arts Council in May 1951, while he wrote on 'The Mechanism of the Arts Council and Some Problems of Policy' for John Pick in his cited *The State of the Arts*. Osbert Sitwell and Henry Green made their comments on post-war literature in the pamphlet, *The Battle of the Books* (London, June 1947). The two volumes of *Since 1939* were published in book form in London in 1948 and 1949. Michael Balcon, 'A Glance Backwards, With No Lament', appeared in *Soho Centenary 1844–1944* (London, 1945). Sir Denis Forman kindly talked to this author, as did Dame Ninette de Valois. Eric Walter White, *The Arts Council of Great Britain*, was published in 1975 in London. Sir Ernest Pooley's address to the representatives of the local authorities on 9 June 1949, was published as an appendix to the Annual Report of the Arts Council, 1949–50. Matthew Arnold, *Culture and Anarchy* (London, 1869) has already been cited.

CHAPTER THREE

Gerald Barry was also editor of the *News Chronicle* and declared in that newspaper that the Festival of Britain was a way of showing 'what the Land had made of the People, and what the People have made of themselves'. Harold

Nicolson, 'Visit to the South Bank', appeared in the *Spectator* and was reprinted in *Spectator Harvest* (London, 1952) along with Gerald Hodgkins, 'Festival Preview', which compared the Skylon to the Quangle-Wangle. The final novel of Evelyn Waugh's war trilogy, *Unconditional Surrender*, was published in London in 1961. Michael Frayn has written the definitive article 'Festival' on the event of 1951 for *Age of Austerity* (ed. M. Sissons and P. French, London, 1963). Vanessa Redgrave, playing the part of Joe Orton's agent Peggy Ramsey, spoke the lines about the Festival of Britain in Alan Bennett's screenplay for *Prick Up Your Ears*. Stephen Spender condemned the festival and the post-war social revolution in *The Thirties and After: Poetry, Politics, People (1933–75)* (London, 1978).

Herbert Morrison was Lord President of the Council and the Labour Minister ultimately responsible for the festival. Valuable descriptions of the achievements of the festival appear in Michael Yorke's *Spirit of Place: Neo-Romantic Artists and Their Times* (London, 1988) and in Robert Hewison's, *In Anger: Culture and the Cold War* 1945–60 (London, 1981). Roger Berthoud's *Life of Henry Moore* was published in London in 1987. The excellent guidebook, *The South Bank Exhibition* by Ian Cox (London, 1951), tells of cinematic and art contributions to the festival. John Hayward voiced his complaint in his introduction to the Penguin collection of the festival verse entrants, *Poems, 1951* (London, 1951). The extract from Christopher Fry's *A Sleep of Prisoners* comes from its text, published in 1951 in Oxford. And the Arts Council report of 1950–51 compliments itself on its activities: it was drafted by William Emrys Williams.

Mary Glasgow's unpublished memoirs, *The Nineteen Hundreds: A Diary in Retrospect* (Oxford, 1986) remain significant. Sir Denis Forman told this author of his opinion of W. E. Williams, as did John Curtis, then a junior editor at Penguin Books. Michael Frayn's opinion of the period of the Festival of Britain has been cited. Sir Kenneth Clark's memoirs, *The Other Half: A Self Portrait*, have also been cited. Mary Endacott remembered W. E. Williams's behaviour as he reigned over 4 St James's Square. Sir Kenneth, later Lord Clark, wrote of the incomprehensibility of the new cosmos in *Civilization* (London, 1971). Joanna Drew spoke to this author about Lord Clark. The quotations from W. E. Williams are from his brilliant and measured accounts of the policy of the Arts Council in the Annual Reports from 1950–51 to 1954–55. Both Peter Cox and N. V. Linklater enlightened this author in long interviews and provided him with relevant papers dealing with the Regional Arts Associations.

CHAPTER FOUR

Sir W. E. Williams's writing of the introductions to the Annual Reports of the Arts Council between 1956 and 1962 remain polemics and analyses of high order. Richard Findlater wrote in the Council Report of 1959–60. George Devine's homily to a young aspirant to join the theatre was printed in the English Stage Company's *Ten Years at the Royal Court 1965–66* (London, 1966). *Declaration* was published in London in 1957 by MacGibbon and Kee, as was *Conviction* in 1958. Peter Cox has already been cited for giving this author all information on the south-west. Douglas Craig's reportage on the tour of 'Opera for All' in the Highlands comes from the Council Report of 1954–5. The *Manchester Guardian* reported on George Firth on 2 January 1964. John Christie wrote to Sir Kenneth Clark on 26 October 1953, including a paper called 'The Future', Glyndebourne Archives, already cited.

Dr Wyn Griffith spoke at the 16th Meeting of the Welsh Committee on 2 February 1951. Dr Parry Williams spoke to Sir Kenneth Clark on 24 October 1956, at 4 St James's Square in London. Dr Griffith spoke at the time of his retirement at the 37th Meeting of the Welsh Committee on 25 January 1957. The new Chairman Gwyn Jones spoke at the Meeting of the Welsh Committee of 17 July 1959, of appointing a liquidator for the Welsh National Opera Company, and Sir W. E. Williams's reply to him was quoted at the meeting. The rendezvous with Henry Brooke, Minister for Welsh Affairs, was announced on 25 November 1959. Miss Myra Owen, the Director for Wales, submitted her Statement on the circumstances of her forced resignation to be attached to the copy Minutes of the Meeting of the Welsh Committee held on 22 April 1960. I am indebted to Dr T. A. Owen for access to all this particular material on the Welsh Committee, and to Lord Armstrong for telling me about Covent Garden, and to Keith Jeffery for his memories of Jennie Lee.

Lord Bridges delivered his important Romanes Lecture in April 1957. John Denison, who served for seventeen years as Director of Music for the Arts Council, kindly informed this author of the Secretary of the Cabinet's minutes at Covent Garden. Lord Cottesloe graciously gave an interview to this author dealing with his service on the Arts Council, as did Professor Anthony (Tony) Field and N. V. Linklater. An important analysis of *Government Patronage of the Arts in Great Britain* was written by John S. Harris and published in Chicago and London in 1970, and the quotation is taken from his book. Professor Harold S. Baldry wrote *The Case for the Arts*, which was published in 1981 in London. And Sir W. E. Williams signed off in his mannual Reports for the Arts Council between 1960 and 1963.

CHAPTER FIVE

For information on this chapter, I am deeply grateful for interviews with and papers from Lord Cottesloe, John Cruft, Constance Cummings, John Denison, Mary Endacott, Tony Field, Sheila Gold, Lord Goodman and Denys Lasdun. I am also indebted to the Annual Reports of the Arts Council from 1960–61 to 1965–66: the praise of Sir W. E. Williams by Dr Wyn Griffith appeared in the report 1962–63. J. E. S. Simon, Financial Secretary for the Treasury, spoke on 23 January, 1959, *House of Commons Debates*. Vol. 598, Cols 650–1. *The Next Five Years* was printed in London by the Conservative and Unionist Party in 1959, and *Patronage and the Arts* by the Conservative Political Centre on behalf of the Bow Group in the same year. The Conservative Party manifesto of 1964 was called *Prosperity with a Purpose*; it preceded the next year's *Putting Britain Right Ahead: A Statement of Conservative Aims*. The Labour document, *A Policy for the Arts: The First Steps* was published in London (Cmnd. 2601, HMSO, 1965).

A Survey of Municipal Entertainment in England and Wales for the two years 1947/48 and 1961/62 was published by the Institute of Municipal Entertainment in April, 1964. Lady Gaitskell spoke on local authority grants to the arts in the

House of Lords on 3 June 1964 in a general debate. *Grants for the Arts* emerged from the House of Commons Estimate Committee, Eighth Report, 1967–68. Peter Lewis wrote a useful book on the founding and the early years of the National Theatre, *The National: A Dream Made Concrete* (London, 1990). Lord Snowdon's words on dedicating the new Nottingham Playhouse were recorded in the Annual Report of the Arts Council, 1963–64. Nigel Abercrombie quoted his own statement in 1967 on the success of the Regional Arts Associations in *Artists and their Public* (Unesco Press, Paris, 1975). Lord Goodman's ineffable and illuminating memoirs, *Tell Them I'm On My Way* were published in 1993 in London. Eric W. White's article on 'Festivals' was first published by *New Society*, 19 August 1965. Joanna Drew spoke to this author of the value of Philip James in the Visual Arts and meticulously corrected this manuscript, while Lord Robbins's appreciation of Dame Ninette de Valois was printed in the Annual Report of the Arts Council of 1962–63. Lord Annan wrote an appreciation of Lord Goodman's character in the latter's *Not for the Record: Selected Speeches and Writings* (London, 1972).

CHAPTER SIX

For information on this chapter, I am deeply grateful for interviews and papers from John Cruft, Constance Cummings, Joanna Drew, Tony Field, Lady Antonia Fraser, Lord Goodman, Sir Peter Hall, the Earl of Harewood, Lord Jenkins, N.V. Linklater, Jonathan Miller, the Earl of Snowdon, Charles Osborne and Peter Williams.

I am also indebted to the memoirs of Lord Goodman, already cited; to Robert Nisbet writing in *Encounter*, March 1972; to James McRobert writing in *The State of the Arts* (John Pick ed., London, 1980); to the *Sunday Telegraph*, 4 April 1965, for Lord Goodman's remarks to Sir W. E. Williams; to Hugh Jenkins, *The Culture Gap* (London, 1979); to Lord Goodman's speech to a conference organized by the Institute of Municipal Entertainment of March, 1969; to H. M. Treasury, *Government and the Arts*, 1958–64 (HMSO, 1964); and to Lord Goodman's eulogy of Jennie Lee in the *Evening Standard*, 25 June 1970, which also contained these words:

> Jennie Lee is not a great intellectual and she claimed no profound knowledge of the arts. But she secured the confidence of artists, great and small, talented and less talented. They instinctively felt the profundity of her belief that the artist was the most important member of the community; of her other belief that the first essential of a civilized country was to promote the interests of the artists and to make art in every sense available to the greatest number.
>
> She met, of course, the élitist argument that art was decreed by the Almighty for the few; and that an increasing size of audience would necessarily imperil the quality. She treated this as the poppycock it was; and she is a woman who speaks her mind firmly. But for all that, she made no enemies and countless friends, and she was an inspiration for youth who for her could do little wrong.

I am further obliged to the remarks of Cecil Day Lewis in *Socialist Commentary*, May, 1966; to *Libraries and the Arts* (David E. Gerard ed., London, 1970); to Eric W. White, *The Arts Council of Great Britain* (London, 1975); to *The Times*, 15

October 1967; to Charles Osborne, *Giving It Away: The Memoirs of an Uncivil Servant* (London, 1986); to this author's *The Need to Give: The Patrons and the Arts* (London, 1990); and to Jan Murray's profile of 'Peter Williams, O.B.E.: A Cornerstone in the Advancement of Dance'. Lord Goodman spoke in the Regional Arts Associations in the House of Lords on 22 March 1972, *Hansard*, Col. 728. *The Times* commented on the affair of the Nottingham Playhouse on 30 August 1967, and John Neville wrote in the *Sunday Times* on 3 September 1967.

CHAPTER SEVEN

Above all, I am indebted for material in this chapter to long interviews with John Cruft, Joanna Drew, Lord Eccles, John Faulkner, Tony Field, Sir Denis Forman, Lady Antonia Fraser, Sheila Gold, Lord Gibson, Lord Goodman, Noël Goodwin, Sir Peter Hall, The Earl of Harewood, N. V. Linklater, Jane Nicholas, Charles Osborne, Jack Phipps, Sir Hugh Willatt and Peter Williams. I am also dependent on Sir Hugh Willatt's 'The First 25 Years' (The Arts Council of Great Britain, London, 1971–2) and the Annual Reports of the Council between 1970 and 1975, including the separate sections on the Arts Council in Scotland.

Lord Goodman's memoirs have already been cited and are a goldmine of information on his differences with Lord Eccles and the civil service. Sir Hugh Willatt wrote an unpublished appreciation of Lord Goodman's years as Chairman for his later memoirs and kindly made these available to this author. Noël Goodwin wrote informatively on *A Ballet for Scotland: The First Ten Years of the Scottish Ballet* (London, 1980) and Peter Williams wrote on the plan for nationwide dance in 'Arts Bulletin – Ballet', published by the Arts Council of Great Britain, No. 4, Spring, 1971. Sir Peter Hall has written his engaging memoirs, *Making an Exhibition of Myself* (London, 1993), while Charles Osborne's indiscreet memoirs have already been cited – he quoted Gavin Ewart's poem on himself. Lord Feversham spoke on 'The Role of Regional Arts Associations' at a conference on 'The Arts and the Regions' in June 1974 at the University of Sussex. And Tony Field wrote on the relationship between the Treasury and the Royal Opera House in *The Stage and Television Today*, 19 March 1992.

CHAPTER EIGHT

Again, my chief source of material for this chapter has derived from the long interviews granted to me by John Cruft, Lord Donaldson, John Drummond, Lord Eccles, Mary Endacott, John Faulkner, Lady Antonia Fraser, Lord Gibson, Robin Guthrie, Laurence Harbottle, Denys Hodson, Lord Hutchinson, Lord Jenkins, N. V. Linklater, Jack Phipps, Sir Kenneth Robinson, Sir Roy Shaw and Angus Stirling. I am also indebted to the Introduction of the Chairman and the analyses of the Secretary-General in the Annual Reports of the Arts Council, 1975–79. Lord Redcliffe-Maud's Report on the arts was published by the Gulbenkian Foundation in 1976. Lord Jenkins gave an invaluable and informed account of his experience in office in *The Cultural Gap: An Experience of Government and the Arts*

(London, 1979). The Report on a 'Framework for a System of Museums' for the Standing Commission on Museums and Galleries was published in 1979 (HMSO, London). Lord Donaldson spoke in the House of Lords on 10 February 1977 (*Hansard*, cols 1275–6). Professor Harold Baldry's *The Case for the Arts* (London, 1981) is always illuminating. And Tony Field wrote to this author an illuminating letter on 30 November 1993 on his protracted debates with Sir Roy Shaw, from which the quotation is taken.

Sir Kenneth Robinson spoke on the process of selection to the House of Commons Education, Science and Arts Committee on 'Public and Private Funding of the Arts' on 13 May 1981. Robert Hutchison, who worked as a research officer for the Council, wrote *The Politics of the Arts Council* (London, 1982), and with Susan Forrester, *Arts Centres in the United Kingdom* (London, 1983); a valuable book on its subject is John Lane, *Arts Centres: Every Town Should Have One* (London, 1978). Sir Roy Shaw's significant book, *The Arts and the People*, was published in London in 1987. The author of the survey of the community arts projects was Su Braden, *Artists and People* (London, 1978). Lord Hutchinson's report on 'Community Arts' was prepared for the Arts Council in, February 1977. Richard Hoggart kindly sent me his draft of a chapter for a future book, 'Culture, Communications, Censorship Revisited: 1976–90', from which his quotations were taken. He also delivered an important paper to the Gulbenkian Conference of Commonwealth Arts Councils at the University of Kent, 6–8 April 1979; it was entitled 'Excellence and access: and the Arts Council'. Raymond Williams wrote a significant essay, 'The Arts Council', for the *Political Quarterly*, Spring, 1979, and commented further on the subject in *Resources of Hope: Culture, Democracy, Socialism* (London, 1989). Roy Fuller's outburst against the Arts Council, 'Taxpayers, the Arts and Big Balloonz', appeared in *Encounter*, October, 1977. It was answered by Sir Roy Shaw at length in the November issue of the magazine and by Lord Hutchinson in a letter in the December issue, which said that Fuller saw himself as the Council's jester, replying to the question of supporting Ethnic Arts with the contribution, 'a lot of wogs cavorting about in the street', and to the question of keeping the great National Companies afloat with the contribution, 'prestige houses run by megalomaniacs for foreign tourists'. Fuller found Hutchinson's reply inaccurate, abusive and probably defamatory, but was much more temperate about his reasons for resigning as Chairman of the Literature Panel in his autobiography, *Spanner and Pen: Post-War Memoirs* (London, 1991). The drama critic of the *Listener* was John Elsam, and Janet Watts fully reported the political polarisation of the Arts Council in the *Guardian*, 30 November 1977.

CHAPTER NINE

Sir Peter Hall's autobiography has already been cited: he comments on the gap between the British Council and the Arts Council. I am grateful to the Arts Council Annual Reports of 1972–73, 1975–76, 1978–79 for the remarks of Sir Hugh Willatt and Sir Roy Shaw. Eric W. White's *The Arts Council of Great Britain*, work cited, has a useful section in 'New Lines of Policy'. Invaluable in general on the Arts Abroad is *Cultural Trends*, Issue 5: March, 1990 (A. Feist and R. Hutchison eds, Policy Studies Institute, London). Livingston Biddle, *Our Government and The Arts: A Perspective from the Inside* (American Council for the Arts, New York, 1988) is unique in its examination of the relationship between politics and arts subsidy in the United States of America: the quotations from Senators Claiborne Pell, Hubert Humphrey and John D. Rockefeller the Third derive from this book. William J. Baumol and William G. Bowers, *Performing Arts – The Economic Dilemma* (Cambridge, Mass., 1965) also dealt with American politics and the arts for The Twentieth Century Fund. This author's cited work, *The Need to Give: The Patrons and the Arts*, examined the rise of the American Business Committee for the Arts; it quoted David Rockefeller and William Ruder, the chairman of the corporation public relations firm. Alan H. Reiss, *Culture & Company* (New York, 1980) also deals with business sponsorship in the United States. Luke Rittner's comment on sponsorship is contained in *The Case for the Arts*, work cited, as is Norman St John-Stevas's remark on future government funding.

John Allen's excellent 'The European Perspective' was included in *The State of the Arts* (John Pick ed., 1980): the quotations on arts subsidy in Sweden and in France come from his work. Edgar Wind's Reith lectures of 1960 were published in London in 1963 in a revised and enlarged edition. The Manifesto issued by the Popular Studio of the École des Beaux-Arts in May, 1968, was reprinted in André Fermigier, 'No More Claudels' in *Art and Confrontation: France and the Arts in an Age of Change* (London, 1970), as was Michel Ragon's 'The artist and society: Rejection or integration'. The authors for the Council of Europe were Finn Jor, *The Demystification of Culture*; J. A. Simpson, *Towards Cultural Democracy*; and Stephen Mennell, *Cultural Policy in Towns*. J. Goldberg and P. Booth, *Décentralisation de la Promotion Culturelle* was published in 1976 in Strasbourg. Nigel Abercrombie, *Artists and their Public*, was published by the Unesco Press in Paris in 1975: he quoted Edgar Faure from *Cultural Policy and Arts Administration* (Cambridge, Mass., 1973) and Joffre Dumazedier from *The School and Continuing Education* (Unesco Press, Paris, 1972). The remarks of the Secretaries-General of the British Arts Council come from the Annual Reports cited, while Richard Hoggart's opinions are contained in his paper cited in the previous chapter.

John Pick in his *The Arts in a State* (Bristol, 1988) showed how diverse arts subsidy was in the United States:

> The publication by the Washington International Newsletter in 1972 of the Senate report on Federal and State Cultural Programmes, *Millions for the Arts*, raised many eyebrows both inside and out of the country. The document for the first time listed 43 government agencies concerned with state funding of the arts (4 in the Legislative branch, 16 in the Executive branch, 12 independent agencies and 11 Boards, Committees and Commissions), listed 50 State Arts Councils and in each case listed their policies, programmes, budgets and attendances at their various venues and promotions.
>
> It thus became clear how comparatively minor the 'official' state funding body, the National Endowment for the Arts, was in the overall picture. In 1970,

for example, the total spent on grants by the NEA was $4,250,000. In that year the Army Entertainment Programme, itself responsible for more than 400 venues, spent $5,020,016, the Army Crafts programme spent $9,750,000 and the Army Service Club Programme (which operates the army library service) spent $11,189,053. In the same year the NEA was able to spend $2,000,000 on state-assistance in the arts, but the states themselves spent many times that sum. In 1970, New York State spent $2,300,000 on the arts on its own account, Pennsylvania $600,000, and Puerto Rico an amazing $1,450,000. Throughout the report, it is the emphasis on the arts allied with education which is striking, with schools, universities and youth programmes much more integrated with the overall programme than would be the case in most European countries.

CHAPTER TEN

Tony Banks is quoted in Sir Roy Shaw, *The Arts and the People*, work cited. Norman St John-Stevas made his announcement in the *Observer*, 14 October 1979. Laurence Marks quoted Angus Stirling in his article, 'Unkindness in the Cut', the *Observer*, 10 May 1981, while *Time Out* called the Arts Council the 'Sweeney Todd of Piccadilly'. I am indebted as always to the Annual Reports of the Arts Council between 1980 and 1984, as I am to the personal interviews for material on this chapter with Anthony Blackstock, Paul Channon, John Faulkner, Tony Field, Sir Denis Forman, the Earl of Gowrie, Sir Peter Hall, Mike Leigh, Colin Nears, Charles Osborne, Clive Priestley, Richard Pulford, Lord Rees-Mogg, Luke Rittner, Sir Kenneth Robinson and Sir Roy Shaw. Richard Hoggart's paper and working chapter has already been cited, as has Norman St John-Stevas's memoirs about his dismissal. Margaret Thatcher in *The Downing Street Years* (London, 1993) gave her reasons for dismissing her Minister for Education and the Arts. Sir Peter Hall's memoirs have previously been cited.

'Public and Private Funding of the Arts', the Report of the Education, Science and Arts Committee of the House of Commons was published in October 1982. Lord Rees-Mogg's book, *An Humbler Heaven*, was published in 1977 in London, while he wrote 'Affording art for all' in *The Times*, 7 July 1993. Bryan Appleyard's important *The Culture Club: Crisis in the Arts* was published in 1984 in London. Lord Goodman's memoirs have already been mentioned. I have seen papers bearing on the Arts Council's input to Clive Priestley's scrutiny of the Royal Opera House and the Royal Shakespeare Company in 1983. Ironically, after his tussle with the Arts Council, Clive Priestley would be appointed to the Board of the Royal Shakespeare Company and serve as a member of the Arts Council from 1991 to 1995, and eventually become Chairman of the London Arts Board. To the scrutineer, the spoils.

Bryan Appleyard commented on the Ilkley Letter, the reasons for it and the consequences in *The Times*, 11 November 1983. The Chairman of the Arts Council gave his press release after Ilkley on 23 November 1983. *The Glory of the Garden* was published by the Arts Council, 30 March 1984. Lord Goodman wrote on the arts in the *Observer*, 25 March 1984. Charles Osborne's memoirs have already been cited, while Philip Larkin's letter to Kingsley Amis of 23 February

1982, appeared in *Selected Letters of Philip Larkin; 1940–1985* (Anthony Thwaite ed., London, 1992).

CHAPTER ELEVEN

For material in this chapter, I am indebted to the Annual Reports of the Arts Council between 1984 and 1988, and also to interviews with Anthony Blackstock, Melvyn Bragg, David Cargill, Paul Channon, John Cruft, Joanna Drew, John Drummond, Sir Gerald Elliot, Mary Endacott, John Faulkner, Tony Field, Christopher Gordon, the Earl of Gowrie, Robin Guthrie, the Earl of Harewood, Baroness P. D. James, Gavin Jantjes, Lord Jenkins, Sir Richard Luce, Colin Nears, Jane Nicholas, Dr Alistair Niven, Thomas Owen, David Pratley, Richard Pulford, Lord Rees-Mogg, Luke Rittner and Lord Rix. *Partnership: Making Arts Money Work Harder* was published by the Arts Council in 1987. *Saturday Night or Sunday Morning? From Arts to Industry – New Forms of Cultural Policy* by Geoff Mulgan and Ken Worpole was published in 1988 in London. Sir Roy Shaw's book on the arts has already been cited. John Pick wrote on 'Public Funding and the Arts' for *The Art of the State*, published in 1989 by the Adam Smith Institute (Research) Limited, P. O. Box 316, London SW1. His book, *The Arts in a State*, has been cited.

A *Great British Success Story* was published by the Arts Council in September 1985. The controller of the Marketing and Resources Department was Dylan Hammond, who had worked for Saatchi and Saatchi. The journalist from the *Sunday Times* who wrote the special report on Urban Renaissance was John Davison. Robin Guthrie kindly made his papers available to me, as did Sir Brian Young and Sir Gerald Elliot. Richard Pulford told this author of Sir Roy Shaw's attitude on the community arts. Harold Baldry, *The Case for the Arts*, has already been cited. Sir Brian Young wrote to Lord Rees-Mogg about film funding on 23 December 1986. Richard Pulford wrote his memorandum on 'The Regional Balance of Provision' in 1984. David Puttnam delivered his Financial Times Arts Lecture at the Barbican Centre on 30 November 1988: an edited version was later published in *Sight and Sound*. Jacques Barzun, *The Use and Abuse of Art* was published in 1974 in New York. I am indebted to Robert Hutchison's cited work, *The Politics of the Arts Council*, for the analysis of the interlocking elite in metropolitan cultural life, while I have also used material from my own book, *The Need to Give: The Patrons and the Arts*. Raymond Williams, *What I Came to Say*, was published in 1989 in London. John Pick's last assault on the Council was published in his cited *The Arts in a State*, while Hugh Jenkins, *The Culture Gap*, has also been quoted.

CHAPTER TWELVE

The book *Saturday Night or Sunday Morning?* has already been cited. I am most grateful for material in this chapter to personal interviews with David Cargill, John Cruft, John Dennison, Anthony Everitt, John Faulkner, Lord Gibson, Sheila Gold, Christopher Gordon, Sir Ronald Grierson, Lord Hutchinson, Peter Jonas,

Sir Richard Luce, David Mellor, Jane Nicholas, Lord Palumbo and Luke Rittner. I am also indebted to the Annual Reports of the Arts Council between 1988 and 1990. Lord Goodman wrote 'This Tragedy for the Arts' in *The Times*, 10 December 1988: he also had spoken further on political appointments in the *Daily Telegraph*, 30 November 1988, to which Lord Rees-Mogg had replied. Bryan Appleyard wrote 'Help yourselves' in *The Times*, 1 May 1989. Lord Goodman gave the new Chairman of the Arts Council the benefit of his advice in the *Observer*, 1 April 1989. Sheila Gold reported John Dennison's remark on the way to say 'No'.

'How the Arts Council works' was published by the Council in 1990. The Wilding Report, 'Supporting the Arts', was published by HMSO in London in 1989. Joan Bakewell wrote in the *Sunday Times* on 25 March 1990. Geordie Grieg reported on the Luce and Lamont negotiations for the *Sunday Times* on 19 November 1989. Lord Palumbo wrote on 'Recognition of the Artistic Imperative' for *The Times*, 17 November 1989, while Sir Richard Luce wrote on 'The Arts of the quiet revolution' for the *Mail on Sunday*, 12 February 1989. Sir Peter Hall's criticism of the Arts Council was quoted by Bryan Appleyard in the *Sunday Times*, 20 May 1990. Again in *The Times*, 30 March 1990, Lord Palumbo wrote on architecture and the millennium.

The spokesman for English Heritage rejecting the Palumbo initiative was quoted in *The Times*, 30 March 1990. Glasgow as the European Capital of Culture was described by Marina Vaizey in 'Showcase in the balance' in the *Sunday Times*, 4 February 1990: it also quoted Pat Lally on 28 January 1990. Lord Palumbo was quoted on Birmingham in *The Times*, 7 March 1990, as was Sir Richard Knowles. Lord Palumbo was again quoted on Cardiff in *The Times*, 28 June 1990. The Price Waterhouse report on the English National Opera was completed in 1987. *The Times* reported Lord Palumbo's opposition to Jeremy Isaacs over the Royal Opera House on 28 April 1990.

Michael Coveney reported on the West Yorkshire Playhouse for the *Observer*, 4 March 1990. Judy Meweezen was the reporter for the *Sunday Times* on 1 April 1990, and Clare Venables spoke to her. Tony Field wrote 'Use your imagination' for the *Stage*, 13 December 1990. Thelma Holt spoke on the end of the Roundhouse to the *Evening Standard*, 9 August 1990. *The Times*, 29 September 1990, quoted John Considine's letter to the new Minister for the Arts, and wrote its leader comments that same day, while Joan Bakewell wrote in the *Sunday Times*, 23 September 1990, on the effects of the poll tax on arts subsidy. Sally Shaw was the member of the Arts Council: the quotation about the changing Ministers comes from a letter of 20 October 1991 to this author.

CHAPTER THIRTEEN

Luke Rittner asked about other countries in the Annual Report of the Arts Council, 1987–88. The most significant issue of *Cultural Trends* for the Policy Studies Institute of 1990 has already been cited. Its summary table of direct public expenditure on the arts and museums in 1987 stated:

	Canada	Federal Republic of Germany	France	The Netherlands	Sweden	United Kingdom	United States
Central government revenue expenditure (£ billions)	55.7	⎫ 184.9	121.5	44.3	32.5	98.8	651.0
Local government revenue expenditure (£ billions)	76.4	⎭	34.3	21.9	23.4	37.2	370.4
Gross Domestic Product (£ billions)	250.7	681.9	536.8	130.0	96.7	408.6	2,728.7
Arts expenditure (£ millions)	445	1,466	1,192	300	233	557	485
Arts expenditure as percentage of public expenditure	0.34	0.79	0.77	0.45	0.42	0.41	0.05
Arts expenditure as percentage of GDP	0.18	0.21	0.22	0.23	0.24	0.14	0.02
Local/regional government arts expenditure per head (£s)	9.9	23.7	17.0	10.5	9.8	4.5	0.9
Central government arts expenditure per head (£s)	7.4	0.2	4.4	10.0	17.9	5.3	1.0
Arts expenditure per head (£s)	17.4	24.0	21.4	20.5	27.8	9.8	2.0

Terry Hands and Graham Hitchen were reported in *The Times*, 8 December 1990. Arthur Miller was reported by Irving Wardle in his piece on 'Subsidy and subsistence' in *The Times*, 8 November 1989. *New measures for financing the arts and culture* by Ritva Mitchell was published in Helsinki in 1989 and has been cited. For a full discussion of the tax status of artists in Europe, see *Tax and the artist: Survey of European Tax Codes as they affect Creative and Interpretative Artists* (Arts Council of Ireland, Dublin, 1986). *The Art Newspaper*, Vol. 1, No. 3, December 1990, reported on tax incentives in the United States and Europe. Mrs Thatcher's declaration at the Tate Gallery was reported in *The Times*, 25 January 1990, as were the remarks of Georgina Naylor. *The Times* estimated corporate donations to charity and the community on 18 February 1991, as did Ian Christie in *Companies and Communities* (PSI, London, 1991). The leader in *The Times* on charities tax reform was printed on 7 April 1990, while Colin Tweedy was quoted on 11 December 1989, in the *Daily Telegraph*, and Ian Rushton of Royal Insurance on 10 October 1989 in *The Times*.

Lord Goodman wrote well of the Association for Business Sponsorship of the Arts on 10 December 1988 in *The Times*. John Frohnmayer was quoted by Charles Bremner in 'Art as political ping-pong' in *The Times*, 12 April 1990, while Tom Mathews summed up the cultural debate in the United States in 'Fine Art or Foul?' for *Newsweek*, 2 July 1990. The important report for The Economist Intelligence Unit by Mary Allen, No. 2069, was entitled *Sponsoring the Arts: New Business Strategies for the 1990s*. Peter Palumbo and Lord Birkett were quoted in *The Times*, which also wrote a leader on the National Lottery on 7 July 1991, while

Lord St John of Fawsley produced his pamphlet, *Medicis and the Millennium?* for the Royal Fine Art Commission that same year.

Julian Spalding wrote his pamphlet *Is There Life in Museums?* for W. H. Smith Contemporary Papers, ed. Philip Ziegler, in 1993. The *Sunday Times* on 1 and 8 July 1990 reported on Palumbo's visionary plans for the millennium and the national heritage. Jean-Luc Godard gave an interview and talked of culture on 17 June 1991 to *Newsweek*. And the *Sunday Times* printed on 8 July 1990 a selected list of what some museums, galleries, theatres and cathedrals thought they would need for refurbishment by the year 2000:

> National Theatre, London £20m
> Portsmouth Theatre Royal £13m
> St George's Hall, Liverpool £13m
> Brighton Pavilion Theatre, Dome and Corn Exchange £12m
> Worcester Cathedral £10m
> The Coliseum, London £7–8m
> Hackney Empire £7m
> Hereford Cathedral £7m
> Salisbury Cathedral £6.5m
> Ely Cathedral £6m
> Hull Museum £5m
> Gloucester Cathedral £4m
> York Minster £4m
> Cambridge Arts Theatre £3–4m
> Grand Theatre, Clapham £3m
> Manchester City Art Gallery £3m
> Festival Theatre, Cambridge £2m
> Birmingham Science Museum £2m
> Oxford Playhouse £2m
> Margate Theatre Royal £2m
> Norwich Theatre Royal £1.75m
> Wilton Music Hall, London £1.7m
> Hull and East Riding Museum £1m
> Norwich Castle Museum £750,000
> York Theatre Royal £650,000
> Buxton Opera House £450,000
> Harrogate Theatre £250,000
> Thorndyke Theatre, Leatherhead £250,000

CHAPTER FOURTEEN

In this chapter, I am most grateful to the Annual Reports of the Arts Council between 1990 and 1992, and to personal interviews with Beverly Anderson, Paul Channon, John Drummond, Anthony Everitt, the Earl of Gowrie, Sir Ernest Hall, Sir Richard Luce, David Mellor, Lord Palumbo, Hayden Phillips and Sir Timothy Renton. Barry Baker wrote 'Renton puts his art where his heart is' in the *Daily*

Mail, 28 December 1990, while the *Art Newspaper*, No. 4, January 1991, interviewed the Minister for the Arts in 'The art of understatement'. The five previous Chairmen of the Arts Council and Sir John Burgh wrote to *The Times* on 26 February 1992 and its leader thundered on that day. Michael Church reported the opinions of the Minister on the Arts Council in the *Observer*, 4 December 1992. And Lord Palumbo wrote in the *Financial Times* on 20 March, 1992, that art was too precious to become a political drama.

Sir Denis Forman wrote on arts and politics in *The Times*, 4 March 1992. And Robert Hewison contributed his important article, 'Culture's poll position', to the *Sunday Times*, 15 March 1992. Hayden Phillips spoke to *The Times*, 30 April 1992. David Mellor spoke about restructuring everything to the *Sunday Times*, 10 May 1992. Braham Murray protested against devolvement in the *Sunday Times*, 6 July 1990, while Bryan Bird spoke about Birmingham in the *Observer*, 22 November 1992. The important evaluation by John Myerscough, *The Economic Importance of the Arts*, was published by the P.S.I. in 1988. The *Sunday Times* reported on the urban renaissance in Glasgow on 9 February 1992, and on the nationwide upsurge in Hugh Pearman's 'Regional Arts ring the changes' on 22 March 1992. Lord Armstrong of Ilminster wrote to *The Times* on 9 March 1992. *Saturday Night or Sunday Morning?* has already been cited. *A Creative Future: The way forward for the arts, crafts and media in England* was published by the HMSO in 1993. In this final arrangement of the forty-four discussion papers and more than sixty seminars, the authors did try to define the arts as follows:

> It is notoriously difficult to say what art is or what it is for. One possible definition runs: art is a form of symbolic communication by which an artist represents and arranges objects, signs, sounds or events in a manner likely to imply meanings or arouse emotions. But that definition does not conjure up a sense of what art *does*.
>
> Once the term implied a skilful activity carried out according to firmly prescribed rules; in modern times it has come more often to be applied to a non-pragmatic product which is free from constraints as to its utility, but whose creator possesses extraordinary qualities. These notions are often mixed up, but great differences exist between cultures as to who is thought to be and who is thought not to be an artist. In Chinese art great emphasis is placed upon continuity of knowledge and skill over centuries, upon the achievement of perfect realizations of the conventional; in modern Western art originality tends to be treated as a prerequisite of artistic identity.

A Creative Future also printed a digest of *Towards a National Arts and Media Strategy*, published by the Arts Council in the spring of 1992, prepared by Howard Webber and Tim Challans in consultation with the National Arts and Media Strategy Group with Beverly Anderson in the Chair. This digest was submitted to the Secretary of State for National Heritage in October 1992; it formed the 'strategic framework within which the funding bodies would produce their individual corporate plans'. It is reproduced in Appendix H. Charles Morgan was the spokesman for the National Campaign for the Arts on 10 September 1991 and Michael Church was commissioned by the Arts Council to write his review of the national strategy documents.

CHAPTER FIFTEEN

I am grateful for material in this chapter to the Annual Reports of the Arts Council between 1991 and 1993, and to interviews with Beverly Anderson, Anthony Everitt, Professor Christopher Frayling, Michael Grade, Michael Holroyd, Baroness James, Timothy Mason, Dr Alastair Niven, Tom Owen, Lord Palumbo, Sir Alan Peacock, Hayden Phillips, Seona Reid, Christopher Sinclair-Stevenson, Anthony Smith and Wilf Stevenson. Peter Brooke was interviewed by Valerie Grove in 'Our patrician priest of pleasure', *The Times*, 24 October 1992; Lord Palumbo was also quoted in the *Sunday Times*, 27 September 1992. *The Times* reported the result of the annual spending round on 13 November 1992, while Lord Palumbo wrote a public letter to Peter Brooke in *The Times*, 10 June 1993. *Review of the Arts Council: Working Papers* was made available by Price Waterhouse in May 1993. Caroline Lees reported on the Minister's opinion on the Price Waterhouse Review on 18 July 1993 in the *Sunday Times*; in the same newspaper on 30 May 1993 she reported on the increasing amount of paperwork sent out by the Arts Council.

Minutes of the Council Meeting on 12/13 May 1993 at The Bear Hotel, Woodstock, C 93 m 4, were made available to this author. Lord Rix was reported after his resignation by the *Evening Standard*, 4 August 1993, as was Matthew Francis, the Artistic Director at the Greenwich Theatre. Benedict Nightingale wrote on the cuts in the subsidies in *The Times*, 3 August 1993. Richard Eyre was quoted in *The Times*, 31 July 1993, and the *Observer*, 20 March 1994, while Robert Hewison wrote on the cuts in 'Darkness at Noon', in the *Sunday Times*, 19 September 1993. Lord Palumbo took responsibility for mismanaging the cuts to the drama companies in *The Times*, 16 November 1993, while that same newspaper printed Sir Leonard Hoffman's letter about the choice between the three London symphony orchestras, a matter fully discussed by Hugh Canning in the *Sunday Times*, 28 November 1993, in an article, 'Made to sing for their supper'. Sir Peter Maxwell Davies thundered on 12 November 1993 in the *Daily Mail*.

Denis Vaughan was the Executive Director of The Lottery Promotion Company who wrote to that newspaper on 13 July 1993. Luke Rittner announced the touring demise of the English Shakespeare Company on television on 1 December 1993, while the following day, Lord Palumbo reported his bitter disappointment to *The Times*, which also printed on 25 November 1993 the opinion on the cuts of Ruth Mackenzie, the executive director of the Nottingham Playhouse, and of Keith Cooper, the Director of Public Affairs at the Royal Opera House. Richard Morrison compared Lord Palumbo to John Cage in *The Times*, 6 December 1993, while the *Evening Standard* reported Timothy Renton on 9 December 1993 and David Mellor on 6 December 1993. Lord Palumbo's counter-assault on the two former Ministers for the Arts appeared in the *Sunday Times*, 3 April 1994. Hugh Canning attacked the Arts Council over the Glyndebourne Touring Opera in the *Sunday Times* on 10 October 1993; that newspaper also reported on The Arts Foundation on 19 May and 8 September 1991. *The Times* reported on the worst and the best in British orchestral life on 2 March 1994, while Russell Willis Taylor was quoted in *The Times* on 9 May 1992. The Discussion Document, No. 29, on 'Literature' was edited by Dr Alastair Niven.

John Gummer was the environment minister who announced the massive shift to the regions in *The Times*, 5 November 1993, while the same newspaper on 12 December 1992 announced Peter Brooke's move towards the Regional Arts Boards. *Charter for the Arts in Scotland: Arts for a New Century* (ed. Joyce McMillan) was published by the Scottish Arts Council in 1993. Sally Shaw was the regional representative on the Board of the Arts Council and wrote to this author on 20 October 1991. Anthony Everitt announced his resignation as Secretary-General in *The Times*, 19 February 1994; the same newspaper reported on the internal Arts Council report four days later. Luke Rittner wrote on the Arts Council in the *Sunday Times*, 15 August 1993. Lord Palumbo wrote on his view of the future in 'Countdown to the millennium', The Culture Special, the *Sunday Times*, 24 October 1993; he quoted John Donne in the Council's Annual Report of 1992–93.

ENVOI

Some of this material was published in the *Evening Standard*, 11 November 1993 under the title of 'The Future of the Arts Council'. The National Heritage Committee of the House of Commons, Session 1993–4 (HMSO, 139–I) specified what was taken from the six Whitehall Departments to be collected within the new Department of National Heritage. 'The arts, museums and galleries, libraries, and some aspects of film were dealt with by the Office of Arts and Libraries; heritage by the Department of the Environment; film and export licensing of art, antiques and collectors' items by the Department of Trade and Industry; tourism by the Department of Employment; broadcasting, press and the safety of sports grounds by the Home Office; and sport by the Department of Education and Science (now Department for Education).'

I am also grateful for final interviews with Lord Armstrong, Anthony Everitt, the Earl of Gowrie, Dr Alastair Niven, and Lord Palumbo. Alistair McAlpine, *The Servant*, was published in 1992 in London.

INDEX

Abercrombie, Nigel J. (Secretary-General)
128–9, 133, 134, 145, 158; and regions 129,
131–2, 138, 151–2, 206–7; Chief Regional
Adviser 151–2; and Lord Goodman 138, 145,
146, 164; retirement 194; *Artists and Their
Public* 244
academies of arts 10, 11
'accountability' 280, 294–5, 308, 321, 374
Adam Smith Institute 283
Adam style 11
advisory boards of AC 316; *see mainly under*
panels
Advisory Council on the Arts (USA) 234
Albert Memorial 382
'Albertopolis', South Kensington 344
Albery, Bronson 58, 125
Alcuin 7
Aldeburgh Festival 56, 68, 141, 168
Aldwych Theatre, London 135, 136
Alexander, W.H., patron 340
Alexandrian Library 3
Allen, John, on Sweden 239
'alternative culture' 155, 161, 224
amateurs, and subsidies 117, 139, 249
American Association of Museums 337
American Business Committee for the Arts 234,
236–7
American Film Institute 236
American National Foundation for the Arts and
Humanities 231, 235–6
Amis, (Sir) Kingsley 107, 112, 229, 276, 283
Anderson, Beverly 375, 391
Anderson, Sir John 45, 46
Anderson, Lindsay 107, 167
Angerstein, Sir John Julius 15
Anglesey, Shirley Paget, Marchioness of 222
'Angry Young Men' 109
animateurs 244, 245

Annan, Noël, Lord, on Lord Goodman 147
Appleyard, Bryan 265, 266, 312–13
architecture: and Arts Council 321; and
Millenium Fund 344
Architecture Unit (AC) 321, 385
Arden, John 106
Armstrong, Sir Robert (later Lord Armstrong)
364, 398; and Royal Opera House 123, 255,
257
Arnold, Matthew 18–19, 76, 226
art, nature 1
Art Department (AC) 86, 95–6, 167–8,
199–200; staffing 175, 305
art exhibitions 34, 37, 70, 96, 142, 305
art films 115, 167, 200, 301
'Art for the People' (CEMA) 34, 37–8, 142
art galleries, and AC shows 167–8
'L'Art Officiel' 95–6
Art Panel (CEMA/AC) 38, 58, 144, 155, 387
artist, role vis-à-vis patron 14
Artist Placement Group 172
Artistic Review Working Group 375
arts: as defined by Arts Council 51, 150–1;
comparative figures 1987 334; financial
aspects 222–3; Government responsibility for
125; and market ethic 278–9, 284; and
politics 221, 247, 293–4, 333, 357; public
popularity 356, 357; United States 231
arts, visual: and CEMA 34, 37–8; and Arts
Council 90, 92, 95–6, 142, 167–8, 376, 385,
387; and Festival of Britain 79–80; funding 39
arts administrators 175, 185, 308; and 'cultural
industries' 281
Arts Boards *see* Boards of Trustees
arts centres 202, 294, 295
Arts Council: advisory staff 95; art collection 90,
142, 286, 305; arts centres 116–17; Arts
Foundation 383–4; and Boards of Trustees

182; and Peter Brooke 374; and business efficiency 287; business sponsorship 282–3; rises from CEMA 42–9; and centralization 99–100, 177; and Centre 42, 149; changes in 1980s 291, 308–9; and Civil Service 163, 190; Code of Practice on Arts and Disability 286; commissioned work for Festival of Britain 79; community arts *see separate heading:* community arts competitions for verse and plays 81–2; *A Creative Future* 373, 375; digest of strategy 455–66; criticism 65, 110–11, 225–6, 227–9, 272, 283–5, 312–13, 380–1; and deconstructionism 225–6; defended 392; demoralized 390–1; direct funding issue 267; Directorate meetings 202–3; educational role emphasised 205–6; employees *see subheading:* staff ethnic concerns 274; and Europe 245; and Festival of Britain 67–8, 70, 74, 79–80, 81, 83–5; Film, Video and Broadcasting Department 287; finance 42, 149, 157, 196, 257; budget 1956–57 104; grant 1945 54; under Labour Government 74, 128–9, 133; subsidies increased 186; grant increases 189, 196, 282, 320–1; long-lasting commitments 195; cuts 248–9, 250–1, 373; *The First Ten Years* 101–2; funding policy 157, 257, 267; and Lord Gibson 192–3; *The Glory of the Garden* 267–71, 291, 292; text, 439–54; Lord Goodman's policy 154–5; Lord Goodman's view of 189, 191–2, 312; as 'Government arm' 309; *A Great British Success Story* 285–6; headquarters buildings 70, 155, 316–17; and Richard Hoggart 227–8; House of Commons Select Committee, memo to, 1981 424–38; Ilkley meeting and letter 264, 265–6, 271; independence 203, 216, 307; influence abroad 232–46; and Keynes 51–2; Literature Department cut 275; and local authorities 267–71, 285; long-lasting commitments 195; and Richard Luce 320–1; machinery 74–5; Marketing and Resources Department 281, 287, 289; and David Mellor 360–1, 381; membership 125–6, 154, 210, 220–1, 304–5; lists 1946–94 413–15; Monitoring Committee: *Towards Cultural Diversity* 286; National Audit Office examination 314; and national lottery 344; 'National Strategy for the Arts' 344, 349, 354, 358, 364, 365–71; digest 455–66; and opera 119; and orchestras 378–9; and Lord Palumbo 313–19; *Partnership: making arts money work harder* 279; patronage 90, 91–6; Planning Department 287; policy c.1970 178; policies compared by Tony Field 329–30; and politics 154, 162–3, 223, 229–30; Price Waterhouse review 373, 374; Priestley enquiry 256, 261, 264; priorities set by

Keynes 51–2; and Public Accounts Committee Inquiry 190; purposes 45–6, 50–1; and Lord Rees-Mogg 307; reform suggested 252–3; and regions 63–70, 103, 152–3, 178, 192–4, 196, 202, 230; regional offices closed 99; and Regional Arts Associations 140, 152, 271; Regional Arts Boards 388; and Tim Renton 352–4, 354–5, 381; review 270–1, 274; role 194–6, 218, 354–5; Royal Charters (1946 and 1967) 50, 150–1, 388; texts 401–11; scope in 1960s 150–1; under Roy Shaw 205–6, 218; social welfare concern 274; staffing 75, 95, 175, 291, 305–6; lists of senior posts 1946–94 416–18; structure 315–16; theatre building 137–8; theatre directors' censure 272; *Towards Cultural Diversity* 286; and Treasury 126, 129, 144, 191; *An Urban Renaissance* 284; Wilding report 317–18; Willatt's appraisal of first 25 years 177–86; and Raymond Williams 228–9; Working Party on Community Arts (Hutchinson) 224–5; and young people 151, 155, 156
Arts Council Collection 90, 142, 286, 305
Arts Council of Northern Ireland 232
The Arts Foundation 383–4
arts funding 334–50; possibilities seen in Finland 336–7
arts laboratories 157, 158, 171–2
Ashcroft, Dame Peggy 96, 117
Ashton, Sir Frederick 55, 56, 142
Association for Business Sponsorship of the Arts 164, 215, 238, 251, 278, 282, 312, 339, 340, 341
Astor, Michael 155, 156, 157–8
Attalus, King of Pergamon 4
Attenborough, Sir Richard 158
Auden, W.H., manuscripts 166
Australia, lottery 343
Australian Council for the Arts 232
authors 26, 71, 198, 275–6; *see also* literature
Authors' Planning Committee 26
Ayckbourn, Alan 200
Ayrton, Michael 56, 79

Bacon, Francis, film on 167
Bakewell, Joan 318, 332–3
Balcon, Sir Michael 72
Baldry, Professor Harold 126, 216, 226, 295
Balfour of Burleigh, G.J.G. Bruce, Lord 198
ballet *see mainly under* dance
Ballet for All 170
Ballet Rambert (Rambert Dance Company) 40, 170, 179, 383
Ballets Jooss 40
Banham, Rayner 79
Banks, Tony 247
Barbican Arts Centre, London 217, 326

Barbirolli, Sir John 111
Barrault, Jean-Louis 241
Barry, Sir Gerald 77
Barzun, Jacques 303
Bath Festival 141
Bax, Sir Arnold 82
Bayley, Stephen 383-4
Baylis, Lilian 21
Beaumont, Hugh 'Binkie' 58, 60, 63, 125
Beckett, Samuel 106
Beecham, Sir Thomas 21
Behan, Brendan 106
Belgrade Theatre see Coventry
Bennett, Alan 78
Bennett, Richard Rodney 155, 211
Bentham, Jeremy, quoted 247, 278
Berlin Philharmonic Orchestra 378
Bertelsmann 302
Bevan, Aneurin 145
Beveridge Report 52
Biddle, Livingston 233, 234, 235, 236
Bing, Rudi 59
Bird, Bryan 362
Birkett, William Norman, Lord 344
Birmingham 323; concert hall 285, 323;
    marketing of art 193; Mendelssohn Festival
    141; millenium 323; orchestra 113, 268, 290,
    326; repertory theatre 97; theatre 137, 152;
    and West Midlands Arts Association 362
Birtwistle, (Sir) Harrison 155
black arts see ethnic arts
Black Box 172
Blackstock, Anthony (Director of Finance) 274,
    282, 301
Blake, William 12
Blenkinsop, Arthur, MP 112
Bliss, Sir Arthur 82
Board of Education, and CEMA 26-8, 35; loses
    Arts Council 46
Boards of Trustees 179-82
Bolt, Robert 106
Bolton (Lancs), theatre 152
books, and AC 165-6; see also authors;
    literature
Boosey and Hawkes, and Covent Garden 44
Bourgeois, Sir Francis 15
bourgeois art, attack on 241
Bow Group, Patronage and the Arts 130
Bowness, Sir Alan 211
Bowra, Sir Maurice 81
Boyd-Carpenter, John (Lord) 162
Boyson, Dr (later Sir) Rhodes 249
Bradford (Yorkshire) 153, 290, 363
Bragg, Melvyn 155, 251, 298
Bridges, Edward, Lord 122, 162, 240
Brierley, David 144
Bristol 193; theatres 40-1, 97, 376; Britain: and

culture 347-8; expenditure on arts 334-5;
    postwar problems 51-4; tax incentives 338
British Broadcasting Corporation (BBC): and
    Arts Council 301, 386; creation and functions
    22, 24; expenditure on arts and music 335;
    patron of music 56, 94; radio drama 62
British Council 65, 232; and Arts Council
    164-5; foundation 1934 20, 231; and
    literature 71-2
British Drama League 23
British Film Institute 73; art films 115, 385-6;
    documentary film 42, 167; foundation 1933
    22; share of state expenditure 334
British Library 213, 298, 340, 345, 382
British Museum 13, 15, 25; and Arts Council, re
    verse manuscripts 141-2; and national lottery
    345
British National Opera Company 21
British Restaurants 34
Britten, Benjamin (Lord Britten) 55, 58, 61, 82,
    168, 180; see also Aldeburgh Festival
broadcasting, and AC 228, 301, 386
Bromley (Kent), theatre 153
Brooke, Henry 120
Brooke, Peter (Secretary of State for National
    Heritage) 372, 373-4
Brown, Dr Fan (Drama Director) 327-8
Brown, Ivor 30, 32, 57
Bryden, Bill 197
Bullwinkle, Jean 221
Bulwer-Lytton, Edward 16
Burgh, Sir John, on arts funding 355
Burgundy, art 8-9
Burnley (Lancs), headquarters of Old Vic 31-2
Burrell, Sir William, sponsor 341
Bush, President George 356
business sponsorship of arts 113, 117, 164, 183,
    248, 259, 278, 338-43; amount 282-3; of
    sports 340; in USA 234, 236-8; see also
    Association for Business Sponsorship of the
    Arts
Business Sponsorship Incentive Scheme 259,
    280-1
Butler, R.A. 35, 36, 46, 135
Butler, Reg 80

Calouste Gulbenkian Foundation 153, 183, 198,
    232
Camargo Ballet Society 36
Cambridge: Arts Theatre 34, 36; Fitzwilliam
    Museum 15
Canada, and the arts 232-3, 334
Canada Council 232
Canada Film Development Fund 232
Canova, Antonio, Three Graces 337-8
Canterbury, Festival of Music and Drama 68
Cardiff 323

Cargill, David 292, 322
Carl Rosa Opera 45, 111, 119, 120, 248
Carlyle, Thomas 19
Carnegie United Kingdom Trust 23, 35, 183
Carolingian art 7–8
Cass, Sir Geoffrey 346
Casson, Sir Lewis 30, 31, 34, 57, 125
'Catfish Controversy' 159–61
cave painting 1
Cecil, Lord David 81
CEMA see Council for the Encouragement of
    Music and the Arts
censorship 172 and AC 161, 186–7; USA 341–2
Centre 42, 149–50
Centres d'action culturelle 242, 244
Chadwick, Lynn 80
Challans, Tim 369
Chancellor of the Exchequer, appointment of
    AC members 125
Chandos, Oliver Lyttelton, Lord 135
Channel Four 386
Channon, Paul (Minister for the Arts) 251, 252,
    256, 309, 358; on business sponsorship 283
Charlemagne, and art 7–8
Charles, Prince of Wales 334, 340
Cheltenham Festival of Contemporary Music 68,
    141
Chester, theatre 152
Chichester, theatre 137
Chichester Festival 141, 179
China, ancient 2
Christianity, early, and art 7
Christie, Sir George 118
Christie, John 34, 37, 45, 118, 141; and Arts
    Council 59, 74
Church, Richard 81
Churchill, Sir Winston 78
cinema 22, 72, 80; see also film
Citizens Theatre see Glasgow
City of London, funding of Barbican 217, 326
City University, arts administration courses 308
Civic theatre movement 153
Civil Service, and AC 163, 190
Clark, Sir Kenneth (later Lord Clark) 28, 81,
    118; and CEMA 30, 38, 42; and Arts Council
    43–4, 57; Chairman, Arts Council 88–90, 91,
    123, 124; Chairman Independent TV
    Authority 90, 304; and Mary Glasgow 63;
    quoted on art 311
Clark, Robert Gordon 375
class, influence on arts 205
Clemo, Jack 81
Clore, Sir Charles, patron 340
Clunes, Alec 58
Clwyd, Ann 222
Cobbett, William 14
Cocteau, Jean, quoted 334

Colchester (Essex), theatre 152
Coldstream, Sir William 125
Coleridge, Samuel Taylor 16
Coliseum theatre, London 169, 203, 324–5, 351
combined arts 385
Committee on Community Arts 229
committees, of Arts Council 316
community arts 295; and AC 139, 158, 171–2,
    202, 214, 222, 228, 295; Hutchinson
    Working Party report 224–5; Scotland 198
concerts, classical music 56
Confederation of British Industry (CBI) 290
Congress, US, and censorship 342
Connolly, Cyril 26, 65
Conquest, Robert 81
Conservative Government, and patronage 238
Conservative Political Centre, The Challenge of
    Leisure 130
Considine, John 332
consumers, AC working for 286–8, 307
Conviction 108–9
Cornish culture 64
corporate donors see business sponsorship; local
    authorities
Cottesloe, John Fremantle, Lord 117, 123; and
    Lord Goodman 144–5; and National Theatre
    134–5, 136–7; and regions 129, 137, 138
Cottesloe Theatre, London 136, 273–4
Council for the Encouragement of Music and the
    Arts (CEMA): foundation 27–30; objectives
    30; under Keynes 36–9; directors and advisory
    panels 38; financial policy 38–9; change to
    Arts Council 42–9; achievements 48; influence
    overseas 232
Council of Europe 226, 242, 243–4
Council of Regional Arts Associations (CORA)
    292, 293, 322
counter-culture 155, 161
court patronage 8, 12
Courtauld, Samuel 38, 44, 58
Courtauld bequest 21
Coveney, Michael 328
Covent Garden: development 213; and Arts
    Council 45, 54–5, 82, 89–90, 119, 162, 168,
    178; Ministry of Works lease 74
Covent Garden Committee 44–5
Covent Garden Opera 21, 203
Coventry: Belgrade Theatre 104, 113, 152, 377;
    Midland Theatre Company 97; cuts 376
Cox, Peter 66, 99, 112
crafts 187, 188
Crafts Council 317, 318
Craig, Douglas 114–15
Crewe (Cheshire), repertory theatre 153
Cripps, Sir Stafford 73
Crook, Arthur 167
Crown Film Unit 73, 167

Croydon (Surrey), theatre 137
Cruft, John (Director of Music) 143, 144, 154, 170, 199, 221; on culture 311; on Lord Goodman 173; on sponsorship 283
cultural democracy 226
cultural industries 279
cultural revolution, France 241-2
Cultural Trends 1990 334
'cultural zones', in cities 285
culture 18-19, 347-9; and Britain 347-8; changing 302-4; TS Eliot on 1, 19-20, 25, 50, 63-4; and Europe 242-4; France 347, 348; freedom from 172-3; Government responsibilities split 211; redefined in National Arts and Media Strategy 366; variety of 19-20; and Raymond Williams 109-10
Cummings, Constance 32, 145, 156; and youth culture 172-3
customers *see* consumers

dance: and CEMA 32, 39-40; and Arts Council 54-5, 82, 111, 122, 142, 169-70, 196, 326-7, 376, 384; financial cuts 383; regional companies, 170-1; and Sadler's Wells 21
Dance Department (AC) 170
Dance Panel 170, 305
dancers, a vulnerable profession 199
Darrell, Peter 196-7
Dartington Hall Arts Centre, Devon 42, 66
Davies, Sir Henry Walford 28-9, 30, 34
Davies, Sir Peter Maxwell 379
Davis, Sir Colin 379
De La Warr, Herbrand Sackville, Lord 27-8, 29
De Valois, Dame Ninette 32, 40, 55, 58, 117, 142, 171, 180
Dean, Basil 33
Declaration 107-8
deconstruction 224, 225-6; and culture 349, 366
Delaney, Shelagh 106
Dench, Dame Judi 155
Denison, John (Music Director) 142, 315
Denison, Michael 229-30
Dennis, Nigel 106
Department for Regional Development (AC) 193
Department of Education and Science: and Arts Council 131, 146; and Edinburgh Opera House 173
Department of National Heritage 359-60, 364, 373; cuts in finance 372-3, 380, 382; lack of strategy alleged 386
Derbyshire County Council 332
Devine, George 105, 106, 179
devolution 230; and Arts Council 101, 134, 138, 193, 216, 269, 321, 322, 331, 335; and Keynes 46-7; *see also* regions
direct funding 203, 262-3, 264-7, 271, 314, 354, 356

directors, constrained by Roy Shaw 219
disabled, and AC 286, 296
Dobson, Frank 80
documentary films 22, 42, 73, 80; and AC 72, 167
Dolin, Anton 82
Donaldson, John, Lord (Minister for the Arts) 212-14
Donat, Robert 32
drama: short account 1948-77 by N.V. Linklater 419-23; and CEMA 31, 35, 39; and Arts Council 54, 60-2, 87, 100, 105-6, 169, 179, 200, 218-19, 327-9, 376-7, 384; censorship abolished 172; Festival of Britain 81-2; *see also* theatre
Drama advisers 31, 37
Drama Department (AC) 124-5
Drama Panel 58, 144, 155, 200, 219, 273; threat from 376, 377
Drew, Jane 79
Drew, Joanna (Art Director) 142, 168, 199-200, 221; on Kenneth Clark 91; to South Bank Centre 304-5
Drogheda, Charles Moore, Lord 258
drug culture 171
Drummond, John 155, 218, 306, 360
Dulwich College 15
Dunbar, Alexander 133-4, 198
Duncan, Ronald 61, 81
Dunlop, Frank 156
Duveen, Joseph, Lord, patron 21, 340
Dworkin, Ronald 303
Dyson, Sir George 30

Eccles, David, Lord Eccles 183, 185, 199, 204-5; critical of Arts Council 187, 188; and censorship 186-7; chooses Patrick Gibson as Arts Council Chairman 192; on Lord Goodman 186; and opera 203; and regions 183, 187, 189; assessment by Hugh Willatt 187; leaves office 194
Ecole des Beaux-Arts 241
Edinburgh: proposed Opera House 173; Pool Theatre 197; theatre 152; Traverse Theatre 171, 197
Edinburgh Festival 56, 68, 141, 168, 179
education 16, 23; an Arts Council role 86, 205-6, 227; for culture 18-19, 215-16
Education Liaison Officer 206
Egypt, ancient 1-2
Elgin Marbles 15, 21
Eliot, T.S. 61, 71; on culture 1, 19, 25, 50, 63-4
elite 92-3, 149, 175
Elliot, Sir Gerald 299
Elliott, Michael 155, 204, 207-8
Embassy Theatre, London 62
Encounter, on culture 151

Endacott, Mary (Secretary, AC) 58, 129, 221, 306
England, early patronage of art 11
English Folk Dance and Song Society 23
English Heritage 322, 393
English National Ballet 383
English National Opera Company 198, 203, 263, 324–5, 351; see also Opera North
English Opera Group 179
English Shakespeare Company 381–2
English Stage Company 105
Enhancement Fund 353
Entertainments National Service Association (ENSA) 26, 33
Epstein, Sir Jacob 80, 96
Epstein, John 172
Equal Opportunities Commission 297
Equity, versus AC 381
Esher, O.S.B. Brett, Lord 26, 57, 135, 210
ethnic arts 286, 288, 296–7, 327
Eureka! children's museum, Halifax 345, 363
Europe: devolution 335, 343–4; example to Britain 245–6, 356–7; little imitation of Britain 239–46; lotteries 343–4
European Arts Festival see Festival of Europe
European City of Culture (Glasgow) 285, 290, 299, 322–3, 362
European Community 360
European Economic Community, celebrations of UK entry 188
Evans, Dr B.Ifor 33–4, 57
Evans, Sir Emrys 121
Evans, Sir Hywel 260
Everitt, Anthony (Secretary-General) 286, 319, 323, 329, 361, 364–5; resignation 391
Ewart, Gavin, verse quoted 201
excellence, a buzz-word 226–7
Exeter, theatre 152
exhibitions, art 34, 37, 70, 96, 142, 305
experimental art, and Arts Foundation 384
Experimental Projects Committee 158
experimentalists, on Panels 143–4
export of works of art 337–8
Eyre, Richard 156, 376

Fascism, rise 23–4
Faulkner, John (Drama Director) 197, 200, 219, 273, 305, 331
Faure, Edgar 244
Federal Council on the Arts and the Humanities 236
Federal Writers' and Theatre Projects 233
Festival Ballet, London 82, 169, 198
Festival Hall see Royal Festival Hall
Festival of Britain 67–8, 70, 74, 77–85, 141; planning for 75–6; dismantling 83; assessment 82–3

Festival of Europe 352, 360
Festival 2000 + 1 393
festivals, supported by AC 140–1, 168–9
Feversham, Charles Duncombe, Lord 202
Field, Anthony (Finance Director, AC) 129, 134, 139, 143, 144; on the allocation of funds 169–70; and arts administrators 175; and Civil Service 191; and the education role 206; on finance policy 306; on government lack of interest 203; and Lord Goodman 146; and local authorities 265; on past policy 329–30; and the Priestley enquiry 257; under Roy Shaw 206, 218–19, 260; on W.E. Williams 124; resignation 273, 329
film: and AC 72–3; and Festival of Britain 80; and Welsh Arts Council 388; see also art films; cinema; documentary film; film industry finance 22, 343
Film, Video and Broadcasting Department (AC) 287, 288, 301, 385
Findlater, Richard, on drama 105
Finland, Arts Council of, on arts funding 336–7
Firth, George 115
Fisher, Mark 357–8
Florence, Uffizi galleries 16
Fonteyn, Dame Margot 55
Foot, Michael 255
football pools, Foundation for Sport and the Arts 325
Ford Foundation 234
Foreign and Commonwealth Office 232; foreign art, and Britain 231, 2362
Forman, Sir Denis 73, 86, 188, 254, 262, 356–7
Foster, Sir Norman, and Albertopolis 344
Foundation for Sport and the Arts 325
France: and arts 240–3, 244; culture 347, 348; lottery 343; Maisons de la Culture 140, 188, 240–1, 242; spending on the arts 334, 346
Frankau, Gilbert 53
Fraser, Lady Antonia: and the Arts Council 158, 159, 221; catfish controversy 160; on Lord Eccles 188; on Lord Goodman 161
Fraser, G.S. 52
Frayling, Professor Christopher 375, 387
Frayn, Michael, on Festival of Britain 78, 86
free market 304
French language 347
Freud, Lucian 80
fringe drama 172, 185
Frohnmayer, John 342, 356
Fry, Christopher 61, 81–2
Fry, Maxwell 79
Fuller, Sir Roy 224, 229
funding see Arts Council: finance; direct funding

Gaelic culture 64
Gaitskell, Lady 132

Gascoigne, Bamber 155
'Gatherings' on new activities 158
General Electric Company 302
George III, patron 12–13
George VI, death 82
Gerhardie, William 166
Germany, export of works of art 338
Germany, Federal Republic: decentralization of
    arts 239–40; expenditure on arts 334
Getty, John Paul III, patron 345
Gibson, Patrick, Lord, (Chairman, AC) 192;
    view of AC 203, 320; and Lord Donaldson
    213–14; and Lord Eccles 194; and Hugh
    Jenkins 210; and Literature Department 201;
    and regions 192; and Roy Shaw 204, 253
Gielgud, Sir John 41, 61, 96
Gielgud, Val 58
Gilmour, Sally 39–40
Glasgow, Mary (Secretary-General) 27, 28, 29,
    31, 42, 58, 221; quoted 33–4; attacked 57; on
    Kenneth Clark 88; and Keynes 35, 39, 40; and
    local education authorities 68–9; and theatre
    63; contract not renewed 88
Glasgow: Burrell Collection 341; Citizens
    Theatre 197, 198; Close Theatre 198;
    European City of Culture 285, 290, 299,
    322–3, 362; Mayfest 281
Glyndebourne Opera 34, 45, 118–19, 141; and
    AC 59, 353, 382–3
Godard, Jean-Luc 348
Goering, Hermann, and culture 24
Gold, Sheila 134, 201
Goldwater, Senator Barry 234
Gombrich, Sir Ernst 213
Goodman, Arnold, Lord Goodman (Chairman,
    Arts Council) 145–6, 143–4, 146, 147, 173;
    and Nigel Abercrombie 138, 145; appoint-
    ments by 142–3, 155–6; and the Arts Council
    143–4, 147, 153, 154–5, 175, 210; own view
    of the AC 189, 191–2, 312; and new AC
    headquarters 139; and business sponsorship
    215, 238, 340, 341; 'catfish controversy'
    160–1; and censorship 172, 186–7; on chan-
    ges after 1967 150–1; and community arts
    171; and Lord Cottesloe 144; criticised 154,
    186, 188; and Government finance 275; and
    Jennie Lee's funeral 255; membership of AC
    widened 154; and orchestras 378; and Lord
    Palumbo 314–15; and the Panels 155–6; and
    the Peat Marwick review 190; against politics
    and bureaucracy 162–3, 223; and Priestley
    enquiry 256; and Public Lending Right 166;
    and the quality issue 311–12; quoted 128; and
    regions 139–40, 148, 152; and Tim Renton
    354; and Luke Rittner 260; and Wesker
    149–50; and young people 151, 156–7, 159
Gordon, Christopher (CORA) 292, 322

Goschen formula, and Wales 300
Gothic art 8
Gould, Mrs B.Ayrton 57
Government: and arts grants 47, 122–3; aid for
    CEMA 30; direct finance issue 203, 264–7,
    271, 314, 354, 356; expenditure 106–7; and
    World War II 26–7; see also state patronage
Gowing, Professor Lawrence 226–7
Gowrie, A.P.G. Hore-Ruthven, Earl of: Minister
    for the Arts 259, 282, 310, 398; and the
    Priestley report 263, 266; and The Glory of
    the Garden 267; and 'national grid' 267–8;
    and the National Theatre 272; criticised by
    Peter Hall 272, 273; and Mrs Thatcher 346;
    Chairman, Arts Council 391–2
Grade, Michael 386
Graham, Martha 170
Grant, Duncan 38, 58
Grants for the Arts (1968) 134
Greater London Council, financial support 169,
    274, 378; on Boards of Trustees 180; des-
    troyed by Thatcher Government 247, 265,
    274, 285, 378
Greece, ancient 2–4
Green, Henry 71
Greenwich, theatre 153, 376
Grierson, John 73
Grierson, Sir Ronald 326
Griffith, Dr Wyn (Vice-Chairman AC) 67,
    119–20; 'Housing the Arts' report 104; on
    WE Williams 128
Guildford, theatre 137, 152
Guinness, Sir Alec 61
Gulbenkian Foundation see Calouste Gul-
    benkian Foundation
Guthrie, Robin 226–7, 292–3, 294, 295
Guthrie, Tyrone 32, 41, 58

Hailsham, Quintin Hogg, Lord 113
Haley, Sir William 91
Halifax, arts and museum developments 363
Hall, Sir Ernest 363
Hall, Sir Peter 117; and the AC 158, 159, 200,
    272–4, 321; catfish controversy 160; closes
    Cottesloe Theatre 273–4; on foreign art in
    Britain 231; and National Theatre 200; and
    Royal Shakespeare Company 135–6; and
    Thatcher Government 250–1, 321
Hallé Orchestra 39, 56, 144, 207, 363
Hammersmith Borough Council 332
Hammersmith, Lyric Theatre 41, 84, 376
Hampshire, (Sir) Stuart 201, 211
Hands, Terry 156, 335
Harbottle, Laurence 211, 217
Harewood, George Lascelles, Earl of 156, 159,
    170; Enquiry into the State of Opera and
    Ballet in the UK 196; on Thatcher era 306

Harkness, Edward J. 27
Harlech, W.G.A. Ormsby-Gore, Lord 57
Harrison, Newton 160
Hassall, Christopher 61–2, 81
Haynes, Jim 171
Hayward, Isaac 135
Hayward, John 81
Hayward Gallery, London: and AC 167–8, 175; catfish controversy 160; and South Bank Board 286
Heath, Sir Edward 188; and the arts 130, 358–9; and Ministry of Culture 309–10; and obscenity 186; Scottish Opera House 197
Hedley, Philip 144
Hegel, Friedrich, quoted 242
Helpmann, Sir Robert 55
Henry Moore Foundation 363
Hepworth, Dame Barbara 80
Herbert, A.P.(Sir Alan) 26
heritage 20; funding 335, 393
heritage industry 345
Hess, Dame Myra 25, 28, 58
Hitchen, Graham 335
Hobbes, Thomas, on culture 18
Hobhouse, John 14
Hodson, Denys 209
Hoffman, Sir Leonard 378
Hoggart, Richard (Vice-Chairman, AC) 211, 217, 219; critical of AC 227–8; and AC cuts 1981 249; and Europe 246; and quality 227; axed as Vice-Chairman 252
Hollywood 47, 72
Holmes, Richard 155
Holroyd, Michael 369, 387
Holt, Thelma 144, 331
Hood, Stuart 211
Horizon 65
Housing the Arts policy 40, 96–7, 115, 116, 291; and Everitt 319, 328; and Government 138, 139; Griffith Committee 104–5
Howard, Robin 170
Hoyle, Susan (Dance Director) 327
Hull, repertory theatre 153
Humphrey, Senator Hubert 235
Hutchinson, Jeremy, Lord 320; and AC appointments, 221, 391; Community Arts working party 224–5; and regions 207, 208; on Roy Shaw 205
Hutchison, Robert, The Politics of the Arts Council 221
Huxley, Dr Julian 42

Incubus 172
Independent Television 113, 117, 153, 304; and Kenneth Clark 90, 304
industry, and the arts, 18th century 11–12
inflation, eroding grants 198

inner cities see urban regeneration
innovation 398; see also experimental art
Institute of Contemporary Arts (ICA), London 167, 168, 330–1; obscenity prosecution against 172
Institute of New International Visual Arts 387
International Initiatives Fund 288
International Times 171
Inverness, and Festival of Britain 84
Ipswich, theatre 152
Irish Republic, Chomhairle Ealaíon 232, 343
Isaacs, Jeremy, and Royal Opera House 325–6
Italy 347–8; against export of art 338

Jackson, Barry 65
Jackson's Wall, Battersea 227
Jacques, Dr Reginald 29, 30
James, P.D. (Baroness James) 298, 369
James, Philip (Art Director) 142
Jantjes, Gavin 286, 297
Jeanetta Cochrane Theatre, London 170, 171
Jeffery, Keith 163–4, 188
Jenkins, Hugh (Lord Jenkins of Putney) 153–4, 212; and the AC 210–11, 310; and business sponsorship 215; and Lord Goodman 154; Minister for the Arts 194, 210–12, 309; replacement 212
Jenkins, Roy (Lord Jenkins of Hillhead), and National Theatre 174
Jennings, Humphrey 73
John Bull Puncture Repair Kit 172
Johnson, President Lyndon B. 234, 237
Johnson, Dr Samuel, quoted 287
Johst, Hans 24
Joint Council for the National Theatre 135
Jonas, Peter 317, 324–5
Jones, Professor Gwyn 120, 122
Jones, Dr Thomas, and CEMA 27–8, 29, 30, 31, 36, 48; withdrawal 35

Kavanagh, Patrick 64
Keir, Mrs Thelma Cazalet 57
Kennedy, President John F. 234, 237
Kent Opera 330
Kermode, Professor (later Sir) Frank 155, 201
Keynes, John Maynard, Lord Keynes: and arts and commerce 311; and arts subsidies 22; and ballet 55; and Bristol Theatre Royal 40–1; and BBC 23; attack on CEMA 34–5; chairman, CEMA 36–7; advocate of centralization 37–8; creates Arts Council 42–9, 268; sets AC priorities 43, 51–2, 54; on finance 123; quoted 77, 300, 324; death 47
King's Lynn (Norfolk) 84, 141
Knowles, Sir Richard 323
Kops, Bernard 106

Labour Government 78; 'The Arts and the

People' 221; and Arts Council 74, 146–7; and film industry 72–3; *A Policy for the Arts* 131, 137, 148

Labour Party 130–1, 210, 356

Lallans 64

Lally, Pat 323

Lambert, Constant 55, 56, 82

Lambert, J.W. 211

Lamont, Norman 320

Lancaster, Sir Osbert 79

Länder (German Federal Republic) 239–40

Landscapes and Living Spaces 172

Landstone, Charles 39–40, 58, 62, 63, 100

Lane bequest 20–1

Lang, Jack 346, 357

language *see* Orwell, George

Larkin, Philip 166; and AC 211, 276

Lasdun, Sir Denys 136

Laski, Marghanita 273, 275

Lawrence, D.H. *Lady Chatterley's Lover* 172

Leatherhead (Surrey), theatre 152

Leavis, Dr F.R. 65, 311

Lee, Jennie (Lady Lee), Minister for the Arts 134, 139, 144, 145, 163–4, 185, 188; and the Civil Service 163; Goodman's tribute to 163; *A Policy for the Arts: The First Steps* 148–9; and regions 152; funeral 254–5

Lee, Laurie 81

Leeds: Henry Moore Sculpture Institute 363; Music Festival 141; Opera North 210, 224

Lehmann, Beatrix 58

Lehmann, John 26, 65

Leicester, theatre 152

Leigh, Mike 273

Leigh, Vivien 81

Leighton, Margaret 61

Lenin, V.I. 101

Leonardo da Vinci 9

Lessing, Doris 107–8

Lever, Harold (Lord Lever of Manchester) 190, 210

Leverhulme Trust 341

Lewis, Cecil Day 81, 117, 125, 148, 165, 166

liberal arts 8, 9

Liberal Democrats 356

libraries, public 17

Linklater, Eric 125

Linklater, N.V. 'Dick' (Drama Director) 100, 124–5, 200, 203, 205, 219; account of drama 1948–77 419–23

literary festivals 165

literature: not at first an AC concern 71, 105; and AC 81, 141, 165, 297–8, 385, 386–7; and Scottish arts Council 198

Literature Department (AC) 200–1, 275–7, 297

Literature Panel 144, 155, 165, 200–2, 387; and community arts 224; and Public Lending

Right 166; curtailment 167, 201, 229, 275–7

little magazines 165, 166

Littler, Prince 60

Littlewood, Joan 106, 179

Liverpool 84; Festival of Comedy 281; Liverpool Philharmonic 56, 113, 207; Playhouse 40, 97; Tate Gallery 290; theatre 152, 207

Lloyd, Selwyn 116, 128, 130, 135

local authorities: and Arts Council 267–71, 285; and culture 17, 20; evening institutes 23; expenditure on arts postwar 56, 66, 68–9, 98–9, 113, 117, 183, 278, 286, 294, 335, 363; France 243 new initiatives 290–1; and poll tax 332; and possible national grid 267–71; and Regional Arts Associations 132, 207; and Regional Arts Boards 318; and theatres 152–3, 209, 328; under threat 265; *see also* urban regeneration

Logan, Peter 172

London: Arts Council centre 139; and AC funding 112, 113; centre of national culture 64, 133, 153, 208, 268–9

London Artist's Association 36

London Arts Board 387

London City Ballet 383

London Contemporary Dance Theatre 170, 179, 383

London County Council 17, 23, 135, 136

London Orchestral Concert Board 378

London Philharmonic Orchestra (Royal Festival Hall) 31, 353, 378, 381

London Symphony Orchestra (Barbican) 31, 326, 353, 378

Long, Richard 301

Lopokova, Lydia, Lady Keynes 125

Lord Chamberlain 172

Lottery Promotion Company 380

Loughane, Molly 144

Low Mean Spectacular 172

Luce, Richard (Minister for the Arts) 282, 309, 310, 315; and Arts Council 318, 344, 356; increased funding 286, 288, 320, 326; and devolution 292, 293, 294, 322; national strategy demanded 344, 356; and regions 317; and Wilding report 295, 314, 317, 318; replacement 331

Lucie-Smith, Edward 155

Ludlow Festival 141

McAlpine, Robert, Lord 346, 399

McCarthyism 233–4, 342

MacDiarmid, Hugh 64

McGrath, John 197

Mackenzie, Norman 108

MacLeish, Archibald 237

Maclennan, Robert, on the arts 357

McLuhan, Marshall 303

Macmillan, Harold 123
Macmillan, Hugh Pattison, Lord, and CEMA 27–8, 29, 35–6; withdrawal 35
McMillan, Joyce 389
MacOwan, Michael (Drama Director) 58
McRobert, James (Finance Director) 70–1, 129, 151
Maecenas, Gaius 6, 343
Magee, Brian 379
The Magic Box (film) 80
Major, John 338, 352, 358
Malleson, Miles 58
Malraux, André 188, 240, 242
The Maltings, Snape 168
Malvern, repertory theatre 153
Manchester: possible AC headquarters 139; Hallé Orchestra 363; Royal Exchange Theatre 204, 207–8, 361; theatre 137, 207
Marchant, Sir Stanley 44, 57
market ethic 278–9, 284, 304
Market Theatre 31
marketing, and AC 193
Marketing and Resources Department 281, 287, 289
Markova, Dame Alicia 82
Martin, Christopher 42, 66
Mason, Timothy 298, 319, 389–90
mass culture 226
Mass-Observation, and World War II 26
Massey, Vincent 232
Matthew, Sir Robert 136
Mavor, Dr O.H. (James Bridie) 57–8
Mécénat 342–3
Mechanical Ballet 172
media, and culture 348–9
media empires 302–4
Medici, Cosimo de' 9–10
Melbourne, William Lamb, Lord 14
Mellor, David: Arts Minister 331–2, 351; continued concern with the arts 352, 353, 354, 356, 360–1; 'Ministry of Culture' 358, 359–60; resignation 361, 370; on the Arts Council 381
Mendelssohn, Felix 141
Menuhin, Yehudi, Lord Menuhin 379
Mermaid Theatre, London 174
metropolitan authorities 265, 268, 285
Metropolitan Opera, New York 237
Metzger, Gustav 172
Michelangelo 10
Middle Ages, and art 8–9
Midland Group of Artists 181
Midland Theatre Company, Coventry 97
Midlands Arts Association 112
Miles, Sir Bernard 174, 180
Millenium, significance 314
Millenium Commission 393

Millenium Fund 344, 346–7, 392–3
Millenium 2000 321, 323; funds 392–3
Miller, Arthur 335
Miller, Dr Jonathan 155, 161–2, 169, 324
Miller, Karl 155
Milligan, Spike 160
Ministry of Arts and Media, wanted by Labour and Liberal Democrats 356
Ministry of Culture, France 242, 243, 357
Ministry of Culture, idea 266, 309–10, 357, 358; under David Mellor 358, 359; see also Department of National Heritage
Ministry of Information, and documentary film 42–3
Ministry of Supply, hostels 33–4
Mitterrrand, François, and arts 346, 358
Mond bequest 21
Moody, John (Drama Director) 100
Moore, Henry 34, 38, 79, 80, 125, 142, 158
Morgan, Colonel Perry 99, 112
Morgan, Pierpont, collector 341
Morrison, Caroline 268
Morrison, Herbert 33, 79
Mortimer, John 155
Multi-Disciplinary and Arts Centres Committee 330
multi-national companies, sponsorship 342
Murdoch, Rupert 302, 304
Murray, Graham 361
muses, Greek 8
museum charges 187, 238
Museum of the Moving Image, London 345
museums 3, 17, 20, 345–6; deterioration 344; and Lord Donaldson 213; international comparison of expenditures 334–5; sale of objects from 332, 337
music 303; and AC funding 54, 56, 99, 179, 199, 326, 376, 377–8, 384; and BBC 23; and CEMA 31, 32–3, 3–4; Festival of Britain 82; funding 17, 39; see also opera; orchestras
Music Department (AC) 86–7
Music Panel 58, 111, 144, 155, 379–80
Music Travellers 31, 37
Musicians' Union, and orchestras 378
Myerscough, John 362, 363
Mythos 2

Naipaul, V.S. 385, 386
National Arts Centre, Ottawa 232–3
National Audit Office, arts and AC 314, 316, 317
National Campaign for the Arts 335
National Council of Music, rival to AC 34, 37
National Council of Social Service 23, 35
National Council on the Arts (USA) 235, 236
National Endowment for the Arts (US) 233, 236, 237, 248, 341–2, 356

National Endowment for the Humanities 236, 237

National Federation of Music Societies 23, 117

National Film Finance Corporation 73, 167

National Foundation on the Arts and the Humanities *see* American Foundation

National Gallery, London 15–16; private patronage 20–1; and World War II 25, 28; Sainsbury Wing 340

National Heritage Memorial Fund 213, 337

national lotteries 325, 343–4, 345, 358; funds distributed by AC 392

National Manuscript Collection of Contemporary Poets 141–2

National Opera 44–5; Wales 175; *see also* English National Opera; Welsh National Opera

National Portrait Gallery, London 340–1

National Publishing House, idea 201

National Theatre, London; slow progress towards 21, 105; National Theatre Committee 60; foundation stone laid 82; and AC 92, 178, 200; regional support 97; Lord Cottesloe pushes 134–5, 136; not merged with RSC 161; resumed 174; Board 180; Peat Marwick review 190; Peter Hall 200; Treasury grants 217; funding issue 263; scrutinised by Lord Rayner 279

National Touring Exhibition Service, South Bank Board 286

National Trust 20

National Youth Orchestra 249

National Youth Theatre 216–17, 249

Naylor, Georgina 338

Nears, Colin 260–1, 305

Nero, Emperor 5–6

Netherlands 245, 334

Netherton Arts Centre, Dudley 69

Neville, John 173–4, 181

New Activities Committee 155, 156, 157–8

New South Wales, influence of AC 232

New Theatre, London 60

New Writing 65

New Zealand, arts council 232

Nicholas, Jane (Dance Director) 199, 221, 305–6, 327

Nicholas, Norman 61, 65

Nicolson, Sir Harold 77–8

Nightingale, Benedict 376–7

Niven, Dr Alastair (Director of Literature) 298

North of England, culture 64, 65

North-Eastern Association for the Arts 112, 113, 133–4

North West Arts Association 196

Northern Ballet Theatre 330

Northern Dance Theatre 196

Northern Ireland 64, 232

Norwich, John Julius Cooper, Earl of 341

Norwich 84; Music Festival 141

Notting Hill Carnival, London 330

Nottingham Playhouse 97, 137, 152, 173–4, 181, 306, 382

novelists' manuscripts 166

Nuffield College social reconstruction survey 42

Nuffield Foundation 153, 341

Nunn, Trevor 200, 217

obscenity 172

Office of Arts and Libraries 250, 359

Old Vic theatre: and CEMA 31, 34, 41; and AC 60–1, 178; Festival of Britain 81; and National Theatre 135; tours for cash 104

Oldham Coliseum 376

Olivier, Laurence (Lord Olivier) 41, 60–1, 81, 117, 180; and National Theatre 135–6, 200

Ontario, arts provision 233

opera 21; and AC 74, 82, 83–4, 92, 114–15, 118–22, 169, 324–6; and BBC 22; national, and Keynes 44–5; wartime stagnancy 55

Opera and Ballet Panel 73, 83

Opera & Ballet Report 1966–69 170, 175

'Opera for All' unit 114–15

Opera North, Leeds 210, 224

orchestras: and AC 56, 82, 111, 168, 199, 326, 331; amalgamation discussed 377–8; grants 1992/93 378; and cuts 383

Orwell, George: Newspeak 281, 292, 308–9; on regional culture 64

Osborne, Charles (Literature Director) 167, 171, 201–2, 204, 206; and Literature Department cuts 275–6

Osborne, John 105, 106, 107, 112

Owen, Myra (Director for Wales) 122

Owen, Thomas 300, 388

Oxford, Ashmolean Museum 13

Page, Annette 222

Palumbo, Peter, Lord Palumbo (Chairman, Arts Council) 313–17, 318–19, 357, 370; and architecture 321–2; Arts Foundation 383–4; on Birmingham 323; and Peter Brooke 372; and Cardiff 323; corporate sponsorship 339, 340; criticised 381; and Anthony Everitt 319–20; and experimental art 384; and funding cuts 373, 382; and Richard Luce 320–1; and David Mellor 361; and national lottery 343, 344, 346–7, 394; and National Opera House debacle 325; and orchestra cuts 380–1; and Tim Renton 352; and Mrs Thatcher 320; and theatre cuts 377; retirement, and last annual report 384–5, 394

Panels: appointments to 126; change from doers to administrators 125; 1960s enlargement 155; and Roy Shaw 211, 217–20; weak in the

1980s 273; 1990s 316; *see also under the names of individual panels*
Paris, new projects 346, 347
parochialism 64–5
Pasmore, Victor 79
patronage, state *see* state patronage
patrons: classical 5; renaissance 9–10; private 340–1; USA private 314
Peach, Dr L.du Garde 29, 30
Peacock, Sir Alan 43, 378, 390
Pears, (Sir) Peter 168
Peat Marwick Mitchell, review of enterprises 190
Peck, Gregory 139
Pell, Senator Claiborne 233, 235
Penguin Books, and *Lady Chatterley's Lover* 172
Penrose, Sir Roland 117, 161
performance arts 158, 200
Pergamon 4
permissiveness 172
Peters, David 122
Pevsner, Sir Nikolaus 117
Philharmonic Orchestra 378, 381
Phillips, Hayden 359, 364
Phipps, Jack (Touring Director) 209–109, 219, 318, 363
Phoenix Opera 248
Pick, Professor John 283–4, 308; *The Arts in a State* 284–5
Pilgrim Players 31, 61
Pilgrim Trust 27, 29, 30, 35, 142, 183
Pinakotheke 4
Pinter, Harold 156
Pipe, John 34, 55, 79, 96
Pitt-Kethley, Fiona 297
The Place, London 170
Planning Department (AC) 287
Playfair, Edward 144
Plowright, Joan, Lady Olivier 156
Plymouth, Theatre Royal 376
poetry 81
Poetry Book Society 141, 165
Poetry Panel 81, 141, 144, 155
A Policy for the Arts (1961) 137
Policy Studies Institute 289–90, 334
politics, and arts 221, 247, 293–4, 333, 357; Greek 3
poll tax (community charge) 332
Polytechnic of Central London, arts adminis-tration courses 175
Pooley, Sir Ernest (Chairman, Arts Council) 57, 73; and Festival of Britain 75–6, 83; increased funds 75; and theatre 63
Pope, Alexander, quoted 399–400
Pope-Hennessy, Sir John 160
popular arts 215

Portillo, Michael 373
Post Office Film Units 22
Powys, John Cowper 53
Pratley, David (Regional Director) 291
Price Waterhouse: examination of AC 373, 374; review of English National Opera 324; and Royal Opera House 382
Priestley, Clive: Chairman, London Arts Board 395; and Royal Opera House/RSC 251, 255–9, 261–4, 266–7, 269
Priestley, J.B., on postwar period 53–4
Pritchett, (Sir) V.S. 66
private collectors 341
Private Eye, criticism of Jennie Lee 168
private funding of arts, USA 314
prizes, literary 165, 166
promenade concerts 23, 56
Prospect Theatre Company 248
provinces 116
provincialism 64–5, 84–5
public, and payment for all arts 92–4
public funding *see* state patronage
Public Lending Right 166, 201, 210, 276
public libraries 106, 213, 335
publishers, and literature 165
Pulford, Richard (Deputy Secretary-General) 256, 258; on allocations 300; *The Glory of the Garden* 267–71. 291, 292, 439–54; on Roy Shaw 260; leaves AC to become Director-General, South Bank Board 275, 286
Puttnam, David, on media empires 302

quality issues 103, 214, 230, 311–12, 367–8; *see also* elites; excellence
Quayle, Anthony 65
Quebec, arts provision 233
Quick, Diana 156

racism, and AC 297
radical drama 229–30
radio 22–3, 24
Ragon, Michel 242
Rambert, Marie 40
Rambert Dance Company *see* Ballet Rambert
Rank, J.Arthur 72
Rattle, Sir Simon 268, 326
Rayner, Derek, Lord Rayner 256, 279
Reagan Administration, cuts in tax benefits 337
Redcliffe-Maud, John, Lord 239; enquiry into support for regional arts 198, 208–9
Redgrave, Sir Michael 96
Redgrave, Peter 155
Rees, Helen 363
Rees, Llewellyn (Director of Drama) 58
Rees-Mogg, Sir William (Lord Rees-Mogg) 258–9; Chairman of AC 251, 253–5, 271, 272, 291, 307–8; Vice-Chairman BBC 253;

belief in consumer not producer subsidies 254;
and Priestley enquiry 258–9, 261–2, 264;
appointment of Luke Rittner 260–1; versus
direct funding 266; on future funding 269–70;
criticism of 272, 291–2, 325; ethnic art 296;
and quality issue 288; and Literature Department 297; and politics 312; not an opera buff
374; end of term of office 286–7
Regional Advisory Committee 193–4, 226–7
Regional Arts Associations 113, 117, 134,
138–9, 184, 209; and Abercrombie 129, 132;
not agents 193; and Arts Council 140, 152,
271; and community/experimental arts 158,
171; devolvement to 298; and Lord Eccles
187, 189, 193; funding 216, 269, 288, 291,
335; and Labour Party 130, 131; and
Literature Department 298; and local
authorities 286, 290, 294; Scotland 299; Standing Conference of 202; and Angus Stirling
207; Wales 299–300; and Wilding Report 317
Regional Arts Boards 317, 321, 331, 392; and
ballet 383; funding 388; map of 412; and
David Mellor 331–2, 360, 361
Regional Offices (CEMA/AC) 37, 66; closed
99–100
regions and regionalism 63, 112; and AC 63–70,
103, 129, 152–3, 178, 192–4, 196, 202, 230;
and ballet 170–1; Festival of Britain 84–5; and
Government 387–8; and Lord Keynes 63; and
Lord Palumbo 323–4; Redcliffe-Maud
enquiry 198, 208–9; Wilding Report 317
Reid, Seona 390
Reisz, Karel 167
Reith, John, Lord Reith 22
Renaissance, and arts 9–10
Renton, Timothy (Minister for the Arts) 352,
353, 354, 357; demands abolition of AC 381;
and regions 354–5
repertory theatres 62; and AC 96–7, 174; fun-
ding 104, 105, 115–16; and local authorities
137
Research and Development Fund 398
Resnais, Jean 167
revolutions, 1968 240–2
Reynolds, David 197
Reynolds, Sir Joshua 13
Rhys, Keidrych 64
Richardson, Sir Ralph 41, 60–1
Ridler, Anne 61
Rigg, Diana 328
Rittner, Luke (Secretary-General AC) 251, 260,
281–2; on loss of art exhibitions 305; and AC
288–9, 305–6, 394; AC review 272; and
Association for Business Sponsorship 238,
278; criticised 297; direct funding issue 263; A
Great British Success Story 285–6; and the
Ilkley letter 265–6; and the international scene

334; and Literature Department 297; and the
Priestley report 264; resignation 319; and
theatre cuts 381–2
Rix, Sir Brian 296, 376
Robbins, Lionel, Lord, on Ninette de Valois 142
Robertson, Bryan 155
Robinson, Sir Kenneth (Chairman, AC) 216,
217, 253; and appointments to AC 220;
criticism of Thatcher government 250; on
1981 cuts 248; and panels 220
Robson, Dame Flora 96
Rockefeller, David 236, 237
Rockefeller, John D.III 234–5
Rogers, Sir Richard 387
Romans, and art 4–7
Roosevelt, President Franklin D. 233
Ross, Alan 52, 66
Rotha, Paul 42
Rothenstein, Sir John 38, 58
The Roundhouse, Camden 144, 330, 331
Royal Academy, London 12, 13
Royal Ballet: and AC 168; and Birmingham 323;
origins 55, 111; regional tours 198, 223–4;
tours for cash 104
Royal College of Art, London 16–17
Royal College of Music, London 17
Royal Court Theatre, London 105, 106, 179,
331; Theatre Upstairs 330
Royal Exchange Theatre, Manchester 204,
207–8, 361
Royal Festival Hall, London 79, 84, 97; orches-
tras at 326
Royal Fine Art Commission 345
Royal Insurance, sponsor 339
Royal Opera House: and CEMA 44; and AC
111, 168–9, 353; Peat Marwick review
190–1; Priestley examination 255, 256–8,
261, 262, 263; direct funding issue 262–3;
under Jeremy Isaacs 325; and national lottery
345; and cuts 382
Royal Philharmonic Orchestra 145, 378, 379,
381
Royal Shakespeare Company (RSC) 65, 135–6;
and AC 144, 178, 217, 353; not merged with
National Theatre 161; Peat Marwick review
190; touring 210, 223; Priestley examination
255, 256–7, 258, 263; direct funding issue
262–3; closed at Barbican 330, 352; sponsored 339
Royal Society of Arts 11, 393
Rural Music Schools 23
Rushton, Ian 339
Ruskin, John 2, 24
Ryder, Richard 352
Rylands, George 'Dadie' 81

Sadler's Wells: and AC 89–90, 178; review by

Peat Marwick 190

Sadler's Wells Ballet Company 21, 44–5, 82; AC grant 54–5; into Royal Ballet 111; possible move to Birmingham 323

Sadler's Wells Opera 45, 119; AC grant 54–5; and Greater London Council 169; deficit challenged by Auditor-General 190

Sadler's Wells Theatre 21, 32, 286

Sainsbury family, sponsors 340

Sainsbury, John, Lord Sainsbury of Preston Candover 346

St James's Theatre, London 61, 62

St John-Stevas, Norman (Lord St John of Fawsley): Minister for the Arts 194, 205, 223; and AC 206; and State patronage 238, 247–8; and the financial cuts 249, 251; loses office 249–50; criticism of architecture 345

Sal's Meat Market 172

Saunders, James 106

Sayers, Dorothy L. 26

School of Design, Somerset House 16

Scotland: authors aided 198; some autonomy from CEMA 43; and Arts Council 63; in 1970s 197, 198; Scottish Assembly 230; and national lottery 345; Charter for the Arts 365; see also Edinburgh Festival

Scottish (Art) Committee 114, 115

Scottish Arts Council 150, 389–90; subsidizes Edinburgh Festival 168; 1970s grant 196; under Alexander Dunbar 198; Ethnic Minority Arts Panel 298–9; allocation to 300, 301; independence 388; Arts for a New Century 389

Scottish Ballet 197

Scottish Opera 179, 197

Scottish Opera House, abortive project 197

Scottish Theatre Ballet 196

Scrutiny 65, 81

sculpture, Festival of Britain 80; see also Moore, Henry

Serpentine Gallery, London, independent trust 304; 7:84 Theatre Company 172, 197

Seyler, Athene 58

Shaffer, Peter 155

Shakespeare, William 136, 141, 301; productions 41, 174

Sharkey, John 172

Shaw, Glen Byam 65

Shaw, Professor (later Sir) Roy (Secretary-General): Chairman, Regional Committee 194; Secretary-General AC 204–5; criticised 205; belief in educational role 205–6, 208; social concerns 389; devolutionary views 208; and Panels 211, 217–19; and quality 214–15, 216, 225–6, 227; and AC composition 221; late 1970s 223; and community arts 224–5, 295; sees politics come in 229; help to USA

233; and Europe 244–5; under Thatcher Government 253; resignation 260

Sheffield 193, 281; Lyceum 363; Playhouse 97, 152

Shelley, P.B., quoted 24

Shore, Peter 109

Sim, Alistair 58

Simon, J.E.S. 129–30

Simpson, N.F. 106

Sinden, Donald 273

Single European Market, Britain and the arts 313

Sitwell, Sir Osbert 26, 71

Skinner, Denis, MP 357

Sloane, Sir Hans 13, 15

Smart, Clive 144

Smith, Anthony 391

Smithsonian Institution, Washington 234

Snowden, Anthony Armstrong-Jones, Lord 137, 158

Soane, Sir John 11

social welfare see welfare

Soutar, William 64

South Bank Board 275, 286, 304–5

South Bank complex 83, 326, 330–1, 344, 353

South Kensington 16–17

South-West Arts Association of Art Clubs 99, 112

Spain, lottery 343

Spalding, Julian, on museums 345–6

Spence, Sir Basil 79

Spender, Sir Stephen 33, 65, 79

sponsorship, cross-border 342; see also business sponsorship

sports, and business sponsorship 340

Sports Council 139

Sproat, Ian 201

'standards' see quality issues

Standing Commission on Museums and Galleries 213

Standing Conference of Regional Arts Associatons 202

State and the arts 122, 334–5, 340

state art, Christian 7

State patronage 90–102, 176; too little 107; reduction by Conservative Government 238, 247; House of Commons report 'Public and Private Funding of the Arts' (1982) 252, 265

Stevens, Roger 236

Stevenson, Wilf 385–6

Stirling, Sir Angus (Deputy Secretary-General) 204, 205, 206; and AC cuts 248; and National Theatre direct grants 217; and regions 206, 207–8; critical of Roy Shaw 218; leaves for National Trust 207, 218; possible return to AC 260

Strachey, John 26

Stratford-upon-Avon 84; theatre 65, 135, 136
'Streamlining the Cities' (White Paper) 265
Strong, Sir Roy 155
subsidies, state, to opera 21–2
Suez 103
Sumeria 1
Summerson, Sir John 78
Sunderland, repertory theatre 153
Sutherland, Graham 34
Sweden, and the arts 239, 334
Swindon (Wilts), community arts 209
Sylvester, David 155
symphony orchestras see orchestras

Tate, Sir Henry, bequest 21
Tate Gallery, London 21, 167–8, 340, 345
tax, levies for the arts 343
tax incentives 337, 338
Taylor, Professor Laurie 351
Taylor, Russell Willis 384
technology, and media 303
television 114, 311, 348–9; and AC 386; Festival
    of Britain 79, 80
Tennent (HM) Ltd (Tennent Productions) 41,
    60, 62, 63, 86
Thatcher, Margaret: and AC 255, 312, 320;
    quoted on arts funding 372; and English
    National Opera 324–5; and Lord Gowrie 259,
    268; and Peter Hall 274, 282; on heritage 337;
    and Richard Hoggart 252; and Richard Luce
    282, 315; and national lottery 344; and Lord
    Palumbo 346–7, 352–3; and N.St John-Stevas
    249–50; on urban values 289, 290; fall 351
Thatcher Government 238, 247, 250, 312, 339
theatre: and CEMA 31, 34–5, 40–1; and AC
    59–62, 96–8, 105, 115–16, 137–8, 173–4,
    200, 327–9; directors' censure of AC 272–3;
    France 243; and local authorities 152–3, 209,
    328; local funding 328; loss of top directors
    328; see also drama
Theatre Grid policy 96–7, 115, 137, 285
Theatre Royal, Stratford 144
Theatre Workshop 106
theatres, and AC 209–10, 376–7; see also reper-
    tory theatres
Theatres Act 172
Thomas, Dylan 81
Thorndike, Dame Sybil 31
Three Choirs Festival 141
Thyssen-Bornemisza, Baron, sponsor 341
The Times: on Arts Council 332, 355; letter
    from Chairmen of AC 354; on tax concessions
    338–9
Tippett, Sir Michael 58
Tooley, Sir John 258
Topolski, Feliks 79
Touring Department (AC) 209, 219, 288

Townswomen's Guilds 23
trades councils, and festivals 149
Trades Union Congress (TUC), and arts 149,
    215
training: arts administrators 175, 185, 308; and
    theatre 138
Treasury: and AC 126, 129, 144, 191; grants to
    National Theatre 217; loses Arts 131
trusts: music and drama 179–80; and theatre
    153
Tweedy, Colin 339
Tynan, Kenneth 107

Ulster 64, 232
UNESCO, and culture 244
United States of America: AC influence 233–8;
    arts expenditure 334; federal subsidies 342;
    lotteries 343; state patronage 341–2; tax
    incentives 337
university extra-mural departments 23
University Grants Committee 95
Upstart (company) 287
urban regeneration, and the arts 280, 281,
    284–5, 289–90

Vaizey, Marina, Lady 222
Valois, Ninette de see De Valois, Ninette
value added tax, UK 343
Vaughan, Keith 79
Venables, Clare 328–9
verse manuscripts 141–2, 166
Victoria and Albert Museum, London 16,
    17–18, 25
Victorian age, and art 14–15
Vienna, National Gallery 16
Virgil, patronised 6
visual arts see arts, visual

Wakefield (Yorkshire), theatre 363
Wales: and CEMA 43; and AC 64, 66–7, 69;
    Arts Committee 114, 120–2; independence for
    arts 388; national lottery 345; opera 119–20,
    175; and Regional Arts Associations 299–300;
    possible Welsh Assembly 230; see also Welsh
    Arts Council
Walpole, Sir Robert, collection 14–15
Walton, Sir William 44
war, influence on art 2, 24
war artists, World War II 26, 34
War Artists' Advisory Committee 28
Warnock report 382
Watford, theatre 153, 376
Watt, Harry 42
Waugh, Evelyn 78
Waverley, John Anderson, Lord 123
wealth tax, proposed 210
Webb, Harri, poem 388–9

Webber, Howard 369
Wedgwood, Josiah 11–12
welfare, and AC 274, 280, 281, 284–5, 296, 298–9, 307, 389
welfare state 52
Welsh Arts Committee see Wales: Arts Committee
Welsh Arts Council 150, 196, 232, 388; allocation to 300, 301; blueprint for 1990s 365
Welsh language and literature 388
Welsh National Opera Company 67, 119–22, 179, 300, 324, 353, 388
Welsh National Symphony Orchestra, proposed 66
Welsh Office, and opera 354
Wesker, Arnold 106, 149–50, 331
West End of London, dominance 183–4
West Midlands Arts Association 362
West Yorkshire Playhouse 328, 363
Western Theatre Ballet 196–7
Westminster City Council, and Wigmore Hall 304
Wheldon, (Sir) Huw 67–8, 79; and Arts Council in Wales 66–7
Wheldon, Sir Wynn 66
Whitbread & Co, sponsor 113
White, Eric Walter (Deputy Secretary-General) 74–5, 140–1, 168; retirement 166–7
Whitechapel Gallery, London 168
Whitehead, Philip, MP 261
Whitelaw, William (Lord Whitelaw), and Lord Gowrie 259, 268
Whiting, John 82
Wigmore Hall, London 304
Wilding report ('Supporting the Arts') 282, 295, 314, 316, 317
Wilkinson, Greg 230
Willatt, Sir Hugh (Secretary-General): and alternative culture 171; and arts centres 202; appraisal of AC's first 25 years 177–86; and the AC 152, 194–5, 196, 202–3; on the scope of 'arts' 151; and Europe 245; on financial allocations 177; on Lord Goodman 187; Literature Department 201; and regions 183, 192, 193, 202; retirement 196
Willey, Basil 81
Williams, Emlyn 31
Williams, Marcia, and Wesker 149–50
Williams, Dr Parry 120
Williams, Peter 170, 211

Williams, Sir Ralph Vaughan 34, 41, 57, 125
Williams, Professor Raymond 109–10, 224; and AC 110, 210, 228, 307; quality issue 227; quoted 293
Williams, Shirley (Lady Williams) 212
Williams, Sir William Emrys (Secretary-General): and CEMA 29, 30, 48; and AC 29, 57, 70, 103; Secretary-General of AC 85–9, 126; The First Ten Years 101–2, 177, 178; arts exhibitions 34, 37, 70, 142; Art Panel 38; centralizing policy 99–101, 117; and Lord Cottesloe 124; 'Directorate' 143; financial aspects 106–7, 111, 127; and patronage 91–100; the quality issue 103; and regions 112–13; staff attitude towards 124; and Tennent 63; at War Office 37–8; and Welsh National Opera 120–1; retirement 127, 128
Wilson, (Sir) Angus 165, 201
Wilson, Harold 73, 130, 145, 257; and AC 210
Wilson, Rodney (Director Film Video and Broadcasting Department) 301
Wilson, Steuart (Music Director) 44, 58–9, 143
Wind, Edgar 240
Winifreth, John 144
wireless 22–3, 24
Wolfit, (Sir) Donald 34–5
Wolfson Trust 341
women, and AC 221
women's institutes 73
Wood, Cyril 66
Wood, Sir Henry 23, 56
Worcester, theatre 152
Workers' Educational Association 23
Works Progress Administration (USA) 233
World Theatre Seasons 179
World War II, and arts 25–49
Wright, Basil 42
Wright, Joseph 11, 12
writers see authors

Yeats, W.B., quoted 166
York, Sarah, Duchess of 340
York: Festival 141; Festival of Britain 84; theatre 152
The Yorkshire Gnomes 172
Young, Sir Brian 246, 301, 307
young people: and the arts 151, 156–7, 159; revolts in 1968 155
Young People's Theatre Panel 155, 156
youth culture 172–3